T0140200

# Lecture Notes in Computer Science 13772

Founding Editors

Gerhard Goos
Juris Hartmanis

## Editorial Board Members

The series Lecture Notes in Computer Science (LNCS), including its subseries Lecture Notes in Artificial Intelligence (LNAI) and Lecture Notes in Bioinformatics (LNBI), has established itself as a medium for the publication of new developments in computer science and information technology research, teaching, and education.

LNCS enjoys close cooperation with the computer science R & D community, the series counts many renowned academics among its volume editors and paper authors, and collaborates with prestigious societies. Its mission is to serve this international community by providing an invaluable service, mainly focused on the publication of conference and workshop proceedings and postproceedings. LNCS commenced publication in 1973.

Yevgeni Koucheryavy · Ahmed Aziz
Editors

# Internet of Things, Smart Spaces, and Next Generation Networks and Systems

22nd International Conference, NEW2AN 2022
Tashkent, Uzbekistan, December 15–16, 2022
Proceedings

Springer

*Editors*
Yevgeni Koucheryavy 🄳
Tampere University
Tampere, Finland

Ahmed Aziz 🄳
Tashkent State University of Economics
Tashkent, Uzbekistan

ISSN 0302-9743                    ISSN 1611-3349 (electronic)
Lecture Notes in Computer Science
ISBN 978-3-031-30257-2           ISBN 978-3-031-30258-9 (eBook)
https://doi.org/10.1007/978-3-031-30258-9

This Springer imprint is published by the registered company Springer Nature Switzerland AG
The registered company address is: Gewerbestrasse 11, 6330 Cham, Switzerland

# Preface

We welcome you to the proceedings of the 22nd International Conference on Next Generation Teletraffic and Wired/Wireless Advanced Networks and Systems (NEW2AN 2022) held in Tashkent State University of Economics, Tashkent, Uzbekistan, December 15–16, 2022.

Originally, the NEW2AN conference was launched by the International Teletraffic Congress (ITC) in St. Petersburg in June 1993 as an ITC-Sponsored Regional International Teletraffic Seminar. The first edition was entitled "Traffic Management and Routing in SDH Networks" and held by the R&D Institute (LONIIS). In 2002, the event received its current name, NEW2AN. In 2008, NEW2AN acquired a new companion in Smart Spaces, ruSMART, hence boosting interaction between researchers, practitioners, and engineers across different areas of ICT. From 2012, the scope of ruSMART conferences has been extended to cover the Internet of the Things and related aspects.

Presently, NEW2AN is a well-established conference with a unique cross-disciplinary mixture of telecommunications-related research and science. NEW2AN is accompanied by outstanding keynotes from universities and companies across Europe, USA, and Asia.

The NEW2AN 2022 technical program addresses various aspects of next- generation data networks, while special attention is given to advanced wireless networking and applications. In particular, the authors have demonstrated novel and innovative approaches to performance and efficiency analysis of 5G and beyond systems, employed game-theoretical formulations, advanced queuing theory, and machine learning. It is also worth mentioning the rich coverage of the Internet of Things, optics, signal processing, as well as digital Economy and business aspects.

We would like to thank the Technical Program Committee members of the conference, as well as the invited reviewers, for their hard work and important contributions to the conference. This year, the conference program met the highest quality criteria with an acceptance ratio of around 21%. The number of submissions sent for peer review was 282, while the number of full papers accepted was 58. A single-blind peer-review type was used for the at least three reviews per accepted paper.

The current edition of the conference was organized in cooperation with Tampere University and Tashkent State University of Economics.

We believe that the NEW2AN 2022 conference delivered an informative, high-quality, and up-to-date scientific program. We also hope that participants enjoyed both the technical and social conference components, the Uzbekistan ways of hospitality, and the beautiful city of Tashkent.

December 2022                                                                 Yevgeni Koucheryavy

# Organization

## International Advisory Committee

Sergei Balandin      FRUCT, Finland
Yevgeni Koucheryavy      Tampere University, Finland
Kongratbay Sharipov      Tashkent State University of Economics, Uzbekistan

## Organizing Committee

Mansur Eshov      Tashkent State University of Economics, Uzbekistan
Gulnora Abdurakhmanova      Tashkent State University of Economics, Uzbekistan
Dilshodjon Rakhmonov      Tashkent State University of Economics, Uzbekistan
Maqsudjon Yuldashev      Tashkent State University of Economics, Uzbekistan
Ahmed Mohamed      Tashkent State University of Economics, Uzbekistan
Abbos Rakhmonaliev      Tashkent State University of Economics, Uzbekistan
Sanjar Mirzaliev      Tashkent State University of Economics, Uzbekistan
Mohammad Hammoudeh      King Fahd University of Petroleum & Minerals, Saudi Arabia

## Technical Program Committee

Torsten Braun      University of Bern, Switzerland
Paulo Carvalho      Centro ALGORITMI, Universidade do Minho, Portugal
Chrysostomos Chrysostomou      Frederick University, Cyprus
Roman Dunaytsev      The Bonch-Bruevich Saint-Petersburg State University of Telecommunications, Russia
Dieter Fiems      Ghent University, Belgium

| | |
|---|---|
| Alexey Frolov | Skolkovo Institute of Science and Technology, Russia |
| Ivan Ganchev | University of Limerick, Ireland |
| Jiri Hosek | Brno University of Technology, Czech Republic |
| Alexey Kashevnik | SPIIRAS, Russia |
| Joaquim Macedo | Universidade do Minho, Portugal |
| Ninoslav Marina | UIST, North Macedonia |
| Aleksandr Ometov | Tampere University, Finland |
| Pavel Masek | Brno University of Technology, Czech Republic |
| Edison Pignaton de Freitas | Federal University of Rio Grande do Sul, Brazil |

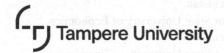

# Contents

# Tangential Shear Stress in an Oscillatory Flow of a Viscoelastic Fluid in a Flat Channel

Kuralbay Navruzov[1], Rabim Alikulovich Fayziev[2(✉)], Akmal Ahadovich Mirzoev[3], and Shoista Bekbergan kizi Sharipova[1]

[1] "Mathematical Engineering" Department, Urganch State University, Urgench, Uzbekistan
[2] "Mathematical Methods of Economics" Department, Tashkent State University of Economics, Tashkent, Uzbekistan
r.fayziyev@tsue.uz
[3] "Mechanics of Fluids and Hydraulic Drive Systems" Laboratory, Institute of Mechanics and Seismic Stability of Structures, Tashkent, Uzbekistan

**Abstract.** The problems of the oscillatory flow of a viscoelastic incompressible fluid in a flat channel are solved for a given harmonic oscillation of the fluid flow rate. The transfer function of the amplitude-phase frequency response is determined. This function is used to determine the influence of the oscillation frequency, acceleration, and relaxation properties of the liquid on the ratio of shear stress on the channel wall to the average velocity over the channel section. Changes in the amplitude and phase of the shear stress on the channel wall in an unsteady flow are also determined depending on the dimensionless oscillation frequency and the relaxation properties of the liquid. It is shown that the viscoelastic properties of the fluid, as well as its acceleration, are the limiting factors for using the quasi-stationary approach. The found formulas for determining the transfer function during the flow of a viscoelastic fluid in a non-stationary flow allow, to determine the dissipation of mechanical energy in a non-stationary flow of the medium, which are of no small importance when calculating the regulation of hydraulic and pneumatic systems.

**Keywords:** Viscoelastic fluid · unsteady flow · transfer function · oscillatory flow · amplitude · phase

## 1 Introduction

The study of the oscillatory flow of a viscous and viscoelastic fluid in a flat and rectangular channel under the action of harmonic oscillations of the fluid flow rate can be used in biological mechanics, in particular, for the operation of a microchip system [1]. These systems are designed to diagnose the functioning of various human organs, as well as targeted delivery of drugs to them. In addition, in order to ensure a constant flow of liquid, pneumatic micro pumps with periodic displacement of liquid from free volumes are often used in biomedical installations [2]. In such systems, it can be economical to install with a pulsating flow. In addition, when transporting high-viscosity and heavy oil and oil products over long distances and circulating drilling fluids in a well, one of

© The Author(s), under exclusive license to Springer Nature Switzerland AG 2023
Y. Koucheryavy and A. Aziz (Eds.): NEW2AN 2022, LNCS 13772, pp. 1–14, 2023.
https://doi.org/10.1007/978-3-031-30258-9_1

the important tasks is to develop an effective method for reducing the hydraulic flow resistance [3–5]. In all the industries listed above, the liquid used, both drugs and oil products or drilling fluids, treated with high-molecular polymers can be classified as viscoelastic liquids [3–5]. As the authors know, at present there is no information on the effect of flow rate pulsations on fluctuations in the coefficients of hydraulic resistance and friction resistance. However, these studies are very important for calculating the pressure gradient and other hydrodynamic characteristics, which have a special place in some biomedical and other technological studies [1, 2]. Thus, the study of shear stress on the wall during oscillatory flow of a viscous and viscoelastic fluid, together with other flow parameters, is of great importance.

The most simplified approach to the theoretical study of the oscillatory flow of a viscous fluid is based on the assumption that a viscous fluid, incompressible, moves laminar in an infinitely long cylindrical tube of circular cross section under the action of a pressure gradient that changes harmonically in time. Investigated in the works of B.C. Gromeka [6, 7], pulsating flows of viscous incompressible fluids in rigid and elastic pipes. In them, he determined the propagation velocities of the pressure pulse wave and their attenuation. Then the oscillatory flow of a viscous fluid in a pipe was studied in the work of I.B. Krendala [8].

Solving the problems of the oscillatory flow of a viscous fluid in a round endless pipe, derived formulas for the velocity profile, fluid flow and impedance during the propagation of a sinusoidal pressure wave. A few years later, P. Lambosia published his findings of the same velocity profile in [9] and, in addition, calculated the viscous drag. J.R. Womersley in [10] re-deduced P. Lambosia's solution. His distinctive qualitative results were that it was found: firstly, a phase shift between the pressure fluctuations and the cross-sectional average velocity and, secondly, the formation of a non-monotonic distribution of velocity profiles. For the first time, the effect of superimposed oscillations of the cross-sectional average velocity in a laminar flow in a pipe was published in an experimental work [11]. The so-called "annular effect" of Richardson was obtained at relatively high oscillation frequencies, which appears as a maximum on the profile of the oscillating component of the longitudinal velocity in a narrow near-wall layer, the thickness of which decreases with increasing oscillation frequency. In the rest of the pipe, the liquid oscillates as a whole in accordance with the fluctuation of the average velocity over the section. In [12], experiments were also carried out on pipes with an internal diameter of 40 mm, in which the piston creates harmonic changes in the fluid flow rate near zero. The graph shows points obtained from oscillograms, on which local velocities were recorded using an electrothermoanimometer at various points in the pipe section. It can be seen from the graphs that the local velocities have the maximum values near the wall. These experimental results are in good agreement with the results of [11]. Theoretically, the problem of a laminar pulsating fluid flow in a pipe was solved in [12]. In [13], the solution of this problem was carried out similarly to [12], but under the condition that not the harmonic oscillation of the average velocity over the cross section, but the oscillation of the pressure gradient was specified. From the analytical solution of the equation of motion for a pulsating flow, it follows that at certain Reynolds numbers of the time-averaged flow and relatively high frequencies and amplitudes of oscillations, there is a zone of return (reverse) flows near the wall, when the local velocity is directed against the average flow. The presence of these zones was confirmed experimentally in [14] with very good agreement between theory and experiment. In [15], I will carry out a similar solution to the problem of a pulsating flow in a flat channel and in a cylindrical pipe. It is noted that the patterns of fluctuations of hydrodynamic quantities for the flow in a flat channel and in a round cylindrical pipe qualitatively coincide.

Unsteady pulsating flows of a viscous fluid in a round cylindrical pipe of infinite length under the action of a harmonic changing pressure gradient were studied in [16]. By solving the problem, calculation formulas for the distribution of velocity and fluid flow are obtained. Numerical calculations have shown that in a pulsating flow at lower values of the dimensionless oscillation frequency, the velocity, flow rate, and other hydrodynamic parameters from the zero initial state are established slowly, relatively at high oscillation frequencies, and are close to the parameters of a non-pulsating flow. In an oscillating flow at high oscillation frequencies, these parameters are set almost instantly. Pulsating flows of a viscous incompressible fluid were studied in [17] in a rectangular channel.

The problem is solved by the finite difference method. The optimal parameters of the difference scheme are determined, and data are obtained on the amplitude and phase of oscillations of the longitudinal velocity, the coefficient of hydraulic resistance, and other flow parameters. At low vibration frequencies, it is shown that all hydrodynamic parameters fluctuate according to the laws of the average velocity over the cross section. For rectangular channels with different cross-sectional shapes (flat, rectangular, and round cylindrical) in high-frequency oscillations, the dependences of the hydrodynamic quantities on the dimensionless oscillation frequency are of the same nature. The authors also obtained an analytical solution for a developed oscillating flow in triangular [18] and toroidal [19] channels.

Of interest is the study of the pulsating flow of a viscoelastic fluid in a flat channel and in a cylindrical pipe under the influence of harmonic oscillations of the pressure gradient or when harmonic oscillations of the flow rate are superimposed on the flow. In [20], the motion of a viscoelastic fluid along a long pipe under the action of an oscillatory pressure gradient was studied. Laminar oscillatory flows of Maxwell and Oldroyd-B viscoelastic fluids were studied in [21]. Where many interesting features are demonstrated that are absent in Newtonian fluid flows. The results of the study [24] show that in the inertialess mode, when Re $\ll$ 1 the properties of the flow depend on three characteristic lengths.

Wavelength $\lambda_0$ and attenuation length of viscoelastic shear waves $x_0 = (\frac{2\nu}{\omega_0})^{1/2}$, Where is the $\nu$ -kinematic viscosity; $\omega_0$-oscillation frequency, as well as the characteristic transverse size of the system $a$. In this regard, according to the length, they are divided into three scales and three independent dimensionless groups: $\frac{t_\vartheta}{\lambda}$ (viscosity to relaxation time), $De$ (relaxation time to oscillation period) and (viscosity factor). At the same time, the oscillatory flow regions are divided into two systems corresponding to the "wide" ($\frac{a}{x_0} > 1$) и«narrow» ($\frac{a}{x_0} < 1$) system. In wide systems, oscillations are limited by near-wall flows, and in the central core by a no viscous one. In narrow systems, transverse waves cross the entire system and cross its center too, which ultimately leads to constructive resonances that lead to a sharp increase in the amplitude of the velocity profile. In [22], unsteady flows of a viscoelastic fluid were analyzed using the Oldroyd-B model in a round infinite cylindrical tube under the action of a time-dependent pressure gradient in the following cases: (a) the pressure gradient changes with time in accordance with exponential laws; b) the pressure gradient changes according to harmonic laws; c) the pressure gradient is constant. In all cases, formulas have been obtained for the distribution of velocity, fluid flow, and other hydrodynamic quantities in a pulsating flow. Based on the Maxwell model, the problem of unsteady oscillatory flow of a viscoelastic fluid in a round cylindrical pipe was considered in [23]. Formulas for determining dynamic and frequency characteristics are obtained. With the help of numerical experiments, the influence of the oscillation frequency and the relaxation properties of the liquid on the tangential shear stress on the wall is studied. It is shown that the viscoelastic properties of the fluid, as well as its acceleration, are the limiting factors for using the quasi-stationary approach.

In recent decades, electro kinetic phenomena, including electro osmosis, flow potential, electrophoresis, and sedimentation potential, have attracted much attention and provided many applications in micro and Nano channels. In this connection, the authors of [24] studied the electro kinetic flow of viscoelastic fluids in a flat channel under the influence of an oscillatory pressure gradient. It is assumed that the movement of the fluid occurs laminar and unidirectional, in this regard, the movement of the fluid is in a linear mode. Surface potentials are considered small, so the Poisson-Boltzmann equation is linearized. Resonant behavior appears in the flow when the elastic property of the Maxwell fluid dominates. The resonant phenomenon enhances the electro kinetic effect, and at the same time, the efficiency of electro kinetic energy conversion is enhanced.

In the works listed above, the field of fluid velocities is mainly studied for various modes of change in the pressure gradient. The change in shear and normal stress that occurs during motion has been studied relatively little. In most cases, in hydrodynamic models of unsteady flows, liquids were replaced by a sequence of flows with a quasi-stationary distribution of hydrodynamic quantities. However, the structure of unsteady flows differs from the structure of stationary flows, and in such cases such a replacement should be justified in each particular case. At present, the question of the legitimacy of studying quasi-stationary characteristics for determining the field of shear stresses in non-stationary flows of viscous and viscoelastic fluids is far from being resolved. Naturally, under such conditions, it becomes necessary to use hydrodynamic models of non-stationary processes that take into account the change in the hydrodynamic characteristics of the flow depending on time. It should be noted that in the general case, the hydrodynamic characteristic in pipeline transport cannot be determined from the characteristics that correspond to stationary flow conditions.

In this paper, we study the oscillatory flow of a viscoelastic fluid using the Maxwell model in a flat channel when harmonic oscillations of the fluid flow rate are superimposed on the flow. The transfer function of the amplitude-phase frequency characteristics (APFC) is determined. This function is used to study the dependence of the nonstationary shear shear stress on the wall on the dimensionless oscillation frequency, acceleration, and relaxation properties of the fluid.

## 2   Statement of the Problem and Solution Method

Let us consider the problems of a slow oscillatory flow of a viscoelastic incompressible fluid between two fixed parallel planes extending in both directions to infinity Let us denote the distance between the walls through $2h$. Axis $0x$ runs horizontally in the middle of the channel along the flow. Axis $0y$ directed perpendicular to the axis $0x$. The flow of a viscoelastic fluid occurs symmetrically along the channel axis. The differential equation of motion of a viscoelastic incompressible fluid in stress has the following form [25].

$$\rho \frac{\partial u}{\partial t} = -\frac{\partial p}{\partial x} - \frac{\partial \tau}{\partial y}. \tag{1}$$

where $u$ - longitudinal speed; $p$ -pressure; $\rho$ -density; $\mu$ -dynamic viscosity; $\tau$ -tangential stress; $t$ -time. The rheological equation of the state of the liquid is taken in the form of the Maxwell equation

$$\left(1 + \lambda \frac{\partial}{\partial t}\right) \tau(y, t) = -\mu \frac{\partial u}{\partial y}. \tag{2}$$

where $\lambda$ -relaxation time. In (2) at $\lambda = 0$ we obtain Newton's law of viscous friction. Substituting (2) into the equation of motion for the fluid velocity (1), we obtain

$$\rho\left(1 + \lambda \frac{\partial}{\partial t}\right) \frac{\partial u}{\partial t} = -\left(1 + \lambda \frac{\partial}{\partial t}\right) \frac{\partial p}{\partial x} + \mu \frac{\partial^2 u}{\partial y^2}. \tag{3}$$

We consider that the oscillatory flow of a viscoelastic fluid occurs due to a given harmonic oscillation of the fluid flow rate or the longitudinal velocity averaged over the channel section.

$$Q = a_Q cos\omega t = Re(a_Q e^{i\omega t}). \tag{4}$$

$$<u> \; = a_u cos\omega t = Re(a_u e^{i\omega t})$$

where $a_Q$ and $a_u$- the amplitude of the liquid flow rate and the amplitude of the longitudinal velocity averaged over the channel section. In this case, the flow occurs symmetrically along the channel axis, and the no-slip conditions are satisfied for the channel wall, i.e. the longitudinal velocity on the channel wall is zero. Then the boundary conditions will be:

$$u = 0 \, \text{at} \, y = h$$

$$\frac{\partial u}{\partial y} = 0 \, \text{at} \, y = 0 \tag{4a}$$

The linearity of Eq. (3) and the given harmonic fluctuation of the fluid flow or the longitudinal velocity averaged over the channel section in the form (4), it is possible to write the longitudinal velocity, pressure, shear stress on the wall in the following way

$$u(y, t) = Re(u_1(y)e^{i\omega t})$$

$$p(x, t) = Re(p_1(x)e^{i\omega t}) \tag{5}$$

$$\tau(t) = Re(\tau_1 e^{i\omega t})$$

Substituting expressions (5) into Eq. (3), we obtain

$$\frac{\partial^2 u_1(y)}{\partial y^2} - \frac{\rho i \omega \eta^2(i\omega)}{\mu} u_1(y) = \frac{\eta^2(i\omega)}{\mu} \frac{\partial p_1(x)}{\partial x}. \tag{6}$$

Here $\eta^2(i\omega) = (1 + i\omega\lambda)$.

The fundamental solutions of Eq. (6), without the right side are the functions $cos(\frac{i^{3/2}\alpha_0}{h}\eta(i\omega)y)$ and $sin(\frac{i^{3/2}\alpha_0}{h}\eta(i\omega)y)$.

and the solutions of the inhomogeneous part have constants

$$\frac{1}{\rho i \omega}\left(-\frac{\partial p_1(x)}{\partial x}\right)$$

Thus, the general solution of Eq. (6) has the form.

$$u_1(y) = C_1 cos\left(i^{\frac{3}{2}}\alpha_0\eta(i\omega)\frac{y}{h}\right) + C_2 sin\left(i^{\frac{3}{2}}\alpha_0\eta(i\omega)\frac{y}{h}\right) + \frac{1}{\rho i \omega}\left(-\frac{\partial p_1(x)}{\partial x}\right). \tag{7}$$

To determine constant coefficients $C_1$ and $C_2$ we use boundary conditions (4a)

$$\frac{\partial u_1(y)}{\partial y} = -C_1\frac{i^{3/2}\alpha_0}{h}\eta(i\omega)sin(i^{3/2}\alpha_0\eta(i\omega)\frac{y}{h})$$
$$+ C_2\frac{i^{3/2}\alpha_0}{h}\eta(i\omega)cos(i^{3/2}\alpha_0\eta(i\omega)\frac{y}{h}) \tag{8}$$

for has $y = 0$ (8) the form

$$0 = C_2\frac{i^{3/2}\alpha_0}{h}\eta(i\omega)$$

From here it's easy to find

$$C_2 = 0$$

from (7) we determine $C_1$ on condition, what $u_1 = 0$ at

$$C_1 = -\frac{1}{\rho i \omega}\left(-\frac{\partial p_1(x)}{\partial x}\right)\frac{1}{cos\left(i^{\frac{3}{2}}\alpha_0\eta(i\omega)\right)}$$

As a result of this, to determine the speed, we will have:

$$u_1(y) = \frac{1}{\rho i \omega}\left(-\frac{\partial p_1(x)}{\partial x}\right)\left(1 - \frac{cos\left(i^{\frac{3}{2}}\alpha_0\eta(i\omega)\frac{y}{h}\right)}{cos\left(i^{\frac{3}{2}}\alpha_0\eta(i\omega)\right)}\right) \tag{9}$$

where $\alpha_0 - \sqrt{\frac{\omega}{\nu}}h$ -vibration Womersley number (dimensionless oscillation frequency).

Using the equation

$$\tau_1 = -\frac{\mu}{\eta^2(i\omega)}\frac{\partial u_1(y)}{\partial y}|y = h. \tag{10}$$

find the tangential shear stress on the wall

$$\tau_1 = -h\left(-\frac{\partial P}{\partial x}\right)\frac{1}{i\alpha_0^2}\left(\frac{i^{\frac{3}{2}}\alpha_0 sin\left(i^{\frac{3}{2}}\alpha_0\eta(i\omega)\right)}{\eta(i\omega)cos\left(i^{\frac{3}{2}}\alpha_0\eta(i\omega)\right)}\right) \tag{11}$$

Now we will integrate both parts of formula (9) over a variable ranging from $-h$ to $h$, find formulas for fluid flow.

$$Q_1 = 2h\left[\frac{1}{\rho i\omega}\left(-\frac{\partial p_1(x)}{\partial x}\right)\left(1 - \frac{sin\left(i^{\frac{3}{2}}\alpha_0\eta(i\omega)\right)}{\left(i^{\frac{3}{2}}\alpha_0\eta(i\omega)\right)cos\left(i^{\frac{3}{2}}\alpha_0\eta(i\omega)\right)}\right)\right]. \tag{12}$$

Given the formula (12) $Q_1 = 2h < u_1 >$, we find the longitudinal velocity averaged over the channel section.

$$<u_1> = \frac{h^2}{\mu i\alpha_0^2}\left(-\frac{\partial p_1(x)}{\partial x}\right)\left(1 - \frac{sin\left(i^{\frac{3}{2}}\alpha_0\eta(i\omega)\right)}{\left(i^{\frac{3}{2}}\alpha_0\eta(i\omega)\right)cos\left(i^{\frac{3}{2}}\alpha_0\eta(i\omega)\right)}\right). \tag{13}$$

Here $\rho i\omega$ can be written in the form

$$\rho i\omega = i\frac{\omega}{\nu}h^2 \cdot \frac{\mu}{h^2} = i\alpha_0^2\frac{\mu}{h^2}$$

Then formula (13) takes the form:

$$<u_1> = -\frac{h}{3\mu}\tau_1 \cdot \frac{3\left(i^{\frac{3}{2}}\alpha_0\eta(i\omega)cos(i^{\frac{3}{2}}\alpha_0\eta(i\omega)\right) - sin(i^{\frac{3}{2}}\alpha_0\eta(i\omega)))}{\left(i^{\frac{3}{2}}\alpha_0\right)^2 sin(i^{\frac{3}{2}}\alpha_0\eta(i\omega))}. \tag{14}$$

Using formula (14) we determine the transfer function $W_{\tau,u}(i\omega)$ for shear stress on the walls, as

$$W_{\tau_1,u_1}(i\omega) = \frac{\tau_1(i\omega)}{u_1(i\omega)} \tag{15}$$

from Eq. (14) we obtain

$$W_{\tau_1,u_1}(i\omega) = \frac{h}{3\mu}\frac{\tau_1(i\omega)}{<u_1(i\omega)>} = -\frac{\left(i^{\frac{3}{2}}\alpha_0\right)^2 sin(i^{\frac{3}{2}}\alpha_0\eta(i\omega))}{3\left(i^{\frac{3}{2}}\alpha_0\eta(i\omega)cos(i^{\frac{3}{2}}\alpha_0\eta(i\omega)\right) - sin(i^{\frac{3}{2}}\alpha_0\eta(i\omega)))}. \tag{16}$$

The transfer function (16) is sometimes called the amplitude-phase frequency response (APFR). This function allows you to determine the dependence of the shear stress on the channel wall on time for a given law of change in the longitudinal velocity averaged over the channel section. As is known, in most cases, when solving non-stationary problems, shear stress on the wall is used, obtained in the quasi-stationary regime of fluid flow. In real cases, such assumptions are valid when the distribution of local velocities over the flow section has a parabolic distribution law. In this case, the tangential shear stress on the channel wall fluctuates in one phase with the fluctuation of the average longitudinal velocity over the channel section.

In this case, the value $\tau_{0,kc}$ can be calculated using the formula

$$\tau_{0,kc} = \frac{3\mu}{h} < u_1 > \tag{17}$$

And instead of a quasi-stationary flow of tangential shear stress on the wall $\tau_{o,kc}$, can be accepted

$$\tau_{0,kc} = \tau_{HC} \tag{18}$$

Thus, relation (18) makes it possible to replace the quantity $\tau_{HC}$ on the value $\tau_{0,kc}$, only under the condition that the actual distribution of local velocities over the flow cross section differs little from the quasi-stationary one. However, in many cases, in a non-stationary flow, the law of distribution of local velocities differs significantly from the quasi-stationary one. In most works [9–12, 17, 21] it was shown that in the case of oscillatory laminar flow in a cylindrical pipe, the change in local velocities in the adjacent layers is ahead of the change in local velocities in time than in the central layers. The oscillatory flow due to a change in the law of distribution of local velocities over the channel cross section of the value $\tau_{HC}$ actually differs significantly from $\tau_{0kC}$. The linear model of unsteady flow is the most complete representation of the dependence $\tau_{HC}$ OT $<u_1>$ can be obtained using the transfer function (16).

## 3   Calculation Results and Analysis

In an unsteady flow, to determine the dependence of the shear stress on the channel wall between the longitudinal velocity averaged over the channel section, we use the transfer function (16). In this regard, we take into account the law of change of the longitudinal velocity averaged over the channel section

$$< u_1 > = a_{u_1} cos\omega t. \tag{19}$$

where $a_{u_1}$-amplitude of the longitudinal velocity averaged over the channel section. Using formulas (19), it is possible to determine the dependence of the shear stress on the wall between the longitudinal velocity averaged over the channel section. Due to the Eqs. (19) used to find the shear stress on the channel wall, its value will also be harmonic, but in the general case, shifted in phase with respect to $< u_1 >$.

Thus, the change in shear stress on the wall is determined as follows:

$$\tau_1 = a_{\tau_1} cos(\omega t + \phi_{\tau_1}). \tag{20}$$

where $a_{\tau_1}$ - shear stress amplitude on the channel wall; $\phi_{\tau_1}$ - phase between magnitude $\tau_1$ and $<u_1>$

Using the relation

$$cos(\omega t + \phi_{\tau_1}) = cos\omega t cos\phi_{\tau_1} - \sin\omega t \sin\phi_{\tau_1}$$

And given that

$$\frac{\partial < u_1 >}{\partial t} = -a_{u_1}\omega\sin\omega t$$

we reduce Eq. (19) to the form

$$\tau_1 = \left(\frac{a_{\tau_1}}{a_{u_1}}\cos\phi_{\tau_1}\right) < u_1 > + \left(\frac{a_{\tau_1}}{a_{u_1}}\sin\phi_{\tau_1}\right)\frac{1}{\omega}\frac{\partial < u_1 >}{\partial t}. \tag{21}$$

Quantities $\left(\frac{a_{\tau_1}}{a_{u_1}}\cos\phi_{\tau_1}\right)$ and $\frac{a_{\tau_1}}{a_{u_1}}\sin\phi_{\tau_1}$ are respectively the real and imaginary parts of the transfer function (16), so from (16) we obtain

$$W_{\tau_1,u_1} = -\frac{1}{3}\left(\frac{-i\alpha_0^2\sin(i^{3/2}\alpha_0\left(1 + iDe\alpha_0^2\right)^{1/2})}{i^{3/2}\alpha_0(1 + iDe\alpha_0^2)^{1/2}cos(i^{3/2}\alpha_0\left(1 + iDe\alpha_0^2\right)^{1/2}) - sin(i^{3/2}\alpha_0\left(1 + iDe\alpha_0^2\right)^{1/2})}\right) \tag{22}$$

$$= \chi + \beta i$$

Here $De = \frac{\nu\lambda}{h^2}$ - elastic Debory number characterizes the elastic properties of a fluid,

$$\chi = \left(\frac{a_{\tau_1}}{a_{u_1}}cos\phi_{\tau_1}\right), \quad \beta = \frac{a_{\tau_1}}{a_{u_1}}\sin\phi_{\tau_1}$$

Then (21) the formula takes the form.

$$\frac{h}{3\mu}\frac{\tau_1}{< u_1 >} = W\tau_1, u_1 = \chi + \beta\frac{1}{\omega}K_H \tag{23}$$

Here $K_H = \frac{\partial < u_1 >}{< u_1 > \partial_t}$ - parameter characterizes the fluid acceleration, $\chi$ and $\beta$- dimensionless quantities, $t$ dimensional values, so it needs to be converted to a dimensionless form, using the transformation

$$t = \frac{h^2\rho}{3\mu}t^*$$

Taking into account (17) and (23) on (22) we obtain the calculation formulas

$$\frac{\tau_{HC}}{\tau_{0\kappa C}} = \chi + \frac{3\beta}{\alpha_0^2}K_H \tag{24}$$

Here $\tau_{0\kappa C} = \frac{3\mu}{h} < u_1 >$ and $\tau_1 = \tau_{HC}$.

Using formula (24), graphs in Fig. 1 are constructed showing the change in the relative shear stress on the wall in an unsteady flow depending on the dimensionless oscillation frequency when the Debory number is equal to zero.

The constructed graph in Fig. 1 shows that when $K_H = 0$ relations $\frac{\tau_{HC}}{\tau_{0\kappa C}}$ close to unity while $\alpha_0^2$ less than units. If a $\alpha_0^2$ takes on values greater than unity, then even if

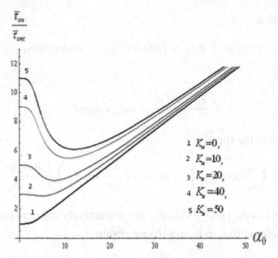

**Fig. 1.** Change in the ratio of the non-stationary shear stress on the wall to the quasi-stationary shear stress depending on the dimensionless oscillation frequency, for different values of the liquid acceleration parameter $K_H$

$K_H = 0$ relations $\frac{\tau_{HC}}{\tau_{0\kappa C}}$ becomes greater than unity and increases with an increase in the dimensionless oscillation frequency. This suggests that shear stresses on the channel wall during unsteady fluid flow can exceed their quasi-stationary values even at those times when the fluid acceleration is zero. Attitude $\frac{\tau_{HC}}{\tau_{0\kappa C}}$ increases with increasing parameter $K_H$ which is explained by a change in the shear stress on the wall, occurs with a phase advance compared to the average speed over the cross section.

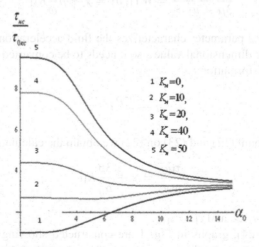

**Fig. 2.** Change in the ratio of the non-stationary shear stress on the wall to the quasi-stationary shear stress depending on the oscillation frequency, for different values of the liquid acceleration parameter $K_H$ and the elastic Debory number 0.01

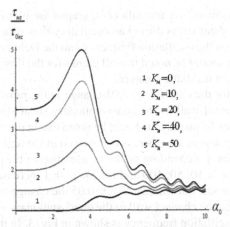

**Fig. 3.** Change in the ratio of the non-stationary shear stress on the wall to the quasi-stationary shear stress depending on the oscillation frequency, for different values of the liquid acceleration parameter $K_H$ and the elastic Debory number 0.05.

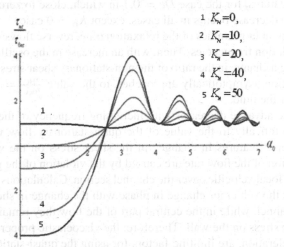

**Fig. 4.** Change in the ratio of the non-stationary shear stress on the wall to the quasi-stationary shear stress depending on the oscillation frequency, for different values of the liquid acceleration parameter $K_H$ and the elastic Debory number 0.1

The flow of a viscoelastic fluid in a flat channel shows a significant change in the shear stress on the wall at low vibration frequencies depending on the elastic Debory number. In [21], an oscillatory flow of a viscoelastic fluid in a flat channel and in a cylindrical pipe was studied, where the flow region is divided into two classes, of which $\alpha_0 > 1$ belongs to the "broad" class, and the other $\alpha_0 < 1$ to "narrow". In the "wide" classes, the oscillatory fluid flows are limited near the wall flows, and in the central part of the inviscid. In "narrow" systems, shear waves cross the entire flow area, which ultimately leads to a sharp increase in the amplitude of the velocity profile and other hydrodynamic parameters, such as shear stress on the wall, fluid flow, depending on the elastic Debory number. Based on formula (24), graphs are plotted in Figs. 2, 3 and 4 showing the change in shear stress during an oscillatory flow of a viscoelastic fluid in a flat channel depending on the oscillation frequency and the Debory number, respectively $De = 0.01; 0.05; 0.1$ It should be noted that all graphs for the flow of a viscoelastic fluid in a flat channel are of an oscillatory nature.

Figure 2 presents, for the case $De = 0.01$ change in the ratio of the non-stationary shear stress on the channel wall to the quasi-stationary shear stress depending on the dimensionless oscillation frequency. It should be noted that in this case, in contrast to the Newtonian flow, an increase in shear stress is observed in the region near the zero value of the oscillation frequency, depending on the acceleration of the liquid. Then there is a gradual decrease for $K_H = 10; 50; 100$ and for $K_H = 0; 1$ increase to value $\frac{\tau_{HC}}{\tau_{0\kappa C}} = 3$ at high oscillation frequencies. For the case $De = 0.05$ the change in the ratio of the non-stationary shear stress on the channel wall to the quasi-stationary shear stress depending on the dimensionless oscillation frequency is shown in Fig. 3. In this case, near the zero value of the oscillation frequency, a decrease in shear stress is observed depending on the acceleration of the liquid, and then there is an increase to a maximum in the region $2 < \alpha_0 < 4$, then gradually asymptotically decreasing to the value $\frac{\tau_{HC}}{\tau_{0\kappa C}} = 1.5$.

We note the features, for the case $De = 0.1$ in which, close to zero, the oscillation frequency, a sharp decrease occurs in all cases, except $K_H = 0$ case.

This means that at large values of the relaxation time, reverse flows of the liquid can occur at low oscillation frequencies. Then, with an increase in the oscillation frequency, all curves showing a change in the ratio of the non-stationary shear stress on the channel wall, with oscillation asymptotically approaches, to the value $\frac{\tau_{HC}}{\tau_{0\kappa C}} = 1$ depending on the acceleration of the fluid.

Then the phase advance decreases with increasing frequency of the oscillation and approaches asymptotically to the value of the quasi-stationary flow with oscillation. Thus, the considered features in changes in the shear stress on the wall for a given harmonic fluctuation of the flow rate are caused by the violation of the parabolic law of the distribution of local velocities over the channel section. Calculations show that in the near-surface layer the velocities change in phase with the change in shear stress on the wall along the channel, while in the central part of the flow they remain in phase with the phase of shear stress on the wall. Therefore, the viscoelastic properties of the fluid, as well as its acceleration, are limiting factors for using the quasi-stationary approach. In addition, the found formulas (21) and (22) for determining the transfer function during the flow of a viscoelastic fluid in a non-stationary flow allow, to determine the dissipation of mechanical energy in a non-stationary flow of the medium, which are of greater importance when calculating the regulation of hydraulic and pneumatic systems.

# 4 Conclusion

The problems of the oscillatory flow of a viscoelastic incompressible fluid in a flat channel are solved for a given harmonic oscillation of the fluid flow rate. The transfer function of the amplitude-phase frequency response is determined. Using this function, the influence of the oscillation frequency, acceleration, and relaxation properties of the liquid on the ratio of the tangential shear stress on the channel wall to the average velocity over the channel section is determined. Calculations show that the non-stationary shear stress on the channel wall during the flow of a viscoelastic fluid increases no monotonically with the acceleration of the fluid particle, at low oscillation frequencies.

Reaching the maximum value, then decreasing with increasing dimensionless oscillation frequency and asymptotically approaching the values without accelerated flow with oscillation. Then the phase advance decreases with increasing frequency of the oscillation and approaches asymptotically to the value of the quasi-stationary flow with oscillation. It is shown that the viscoelastic properties of the fluid, as well as its acceleration, are the limiting factors for using the quasi-stationary approach.

Formulas are found for determining the transfer function for a viscoelastic fluid flow in an unsteady flow, which are of no small importance in calculating the regulation of hydraulic and pneumatic systems.

# References

1. Marx, U., et al.: Homan-on-a-Chip developments: a translational cutting- edge alternative to systemic safety assessment and effecting evacuation in laboratory animals and man? ATLA **40**, 235–257 (2012)
2. Inman, W., Domanskiy, K., Serdy, J., Ovens, B., Trimper, D., Griffith, L.G.: Dishing modeling and fabrication of a constant flow pneumatic micropump. J. Micromech. Microeng. **17**, 891–899 (2007)
3. Akilov, Z.H.A.: Non-stationary motions of viscoelastic fluids. Tashkent: Fan (1982)
4. Khuzhaerov, B.K.H.: Rheological properties of mixtures. Samarkand: Sogdiana (2000)
5. Mirzajanzade, A.K.H., Karaev, A.K., Shirinzade, S.A.: Hydraulics in drilling and cementing oil and gas wells. M. Nedra (1977)
6. Gromeki, I.S.: On the theory of fluid motion in narrow cylindrical tubes, pp. 149–171 (1952)
7. Gromeki, I.S.: On the propagation velocity of the undulating motion of a fluid in elastic pipes.Sobr.op. - M, pp. 172–183 1952
8. Crandall, I.B.: Theory of vibrating systems and sounds D. Van. Nostrand Co., New York (1926)
9. Lambossy, P.: Oscillations foresees dun liquids incompressible et visqulux dans un tube rigide et horizontal calculi de IA force de frottement . Helv. Physiol. Acta. **25**, 371–386 (1952)
10. Womersly, J.R.: Method for the calculation of velocity rate of flow and viscous drag in arteries when the pressure gradient is known. J. Physiol, **127**(3), 553–563 1955,
11. Richardson, E.G., Tyler, E.: The transverse Velocity gradient neat the mothe of pipes in which an alternating or continuous flow of air is established. Pros. Phys. Soc. London, v. 42 (1929)
12. Popov, D.N., Mokhov, I.G.: Experimental study of the profiles of local velocities in a pipe with fluctuations in the flow rate of a viscous liquid. Izv. Univ. Eng. No. 7, pp. 91–95 (1971)
13. Uchida, S.: The pulsating viscous flow superposed on the stead laminar motion of incompressible fluid in a circular pipe. ZAMP. **7**(5). 403–422 (1956)
14. Ünsal, B., Ray, S., Durst, F., Ertunç, Ö.: Pulsating laminar pipe flows with sinusoidal mass flux variations. Fluid Dyn. Res. 37, 317–333 (2005)
15. Siegel, R., Perlmutter, M.: Heat transfer with pulsating flow in a channel, pp. 18–32
16. Fayzullaev, D.F., Navruzov, K.: Hydrodynamics of pulsating flows, Tashkent, Fan, p. 192 (1986)
17. Valueva, E.P., Purdin, M.S.: Hydrodynamics and heat transfer of pulsating laminar flow in channels. Teploenergetika, no. 9, pp. 24–33

18. Tsangaris, S., Vlachakis, N.W.: Exact solution of the Navier-Stokes equations for the oscillating flow in a duct of a cross-section of right-angled isosceles triangle. ZAMP, **54**, 1094–1100 (2003)

19. Tsangaris, S., Vlachakis, N.W.: Exact solution for the pulsating finite gap Dean flow. Appl. Math. Model, **31**, 1899–1906 (2007)

20. Jons, J.R., Walters, T.S.: Flow of elastic-viscous liquids in channels under the influence of a periodic pressure gradient. Part 1. Rheol. Acta, **6**, 240–245 (1967)

21. Casanellas, L., Ortin, J.: Laminar oscillatory flow of Maxwell and Oldroyd-B fluids. J. Non-Newtonian Fluid. Mech. **166**, 1315–1326 (2011)

22. Abu-El Hassan, A., El-Maghawry, E. M.: Unsteady axial viscoelastic pipe flows of anOldroyd-B fluid in // Rheology-New concepic. Appl. Methods Ed by Durairaj R. Published by In Tech. ch. 6, pp. 91–106 (2013)

23. Akilov, Z.A., Dzhabbarov, M.S., Khuzhayorov, B.K.: Tangential shear stress under the periodic flow of a viscoelastic fluid in a cylindrical tube. Fluid Dyn.**56**(2), 189–199 (2021). SSN 0015–4628,

24. Ding, Z, Jian, Y.: Electrokinetic oscillatory flow and energy microchannelis: a linear analysis. J. Fluid. Mech. **919**, 1–31 (2021). A20. https://doi.org/10.1017/jfm. 380A20

25. Astarita, G., Marrucci, G.: Principles of non-Newtonian fluid mechanics. McGraw-HILL, p. 309 (1974)

# Comparison of Finite Difference Schemes of Different Orders of Accuracy for the Burgers Wave Equation Problem

Murodil Erkinjon Ugli Madaliev[1] [iD], Rabim Alikulovich Fayziev[2]([✉]),
Eshmurod Sattarovich Buriev[3], and Akmal Ahadovich Mirzoev[2]

[1] Fergana Polytechnic Institute, Fergana, Uzbekistan
m.e.madaliyev@ferpi.uz
[2] Tashkent State University of Economics, Tashkent, Uzbekistan
r.fayziyev@tsue.uz
[3] Tashkent Institute of Architecture and Civil Engineering, Tashkent, Uzbekistan

**Abstract.** A large number of problems in physics and technology lead to boundary value or initial boundary value problems for linear and nonlinear partial differential equations. Moreover, the number of problems that have an analytical solution is limited. These are problems in canonical domains such as, for example, a rectangle, circle, or ball, and usually for equations with constant coefficients. In practice, it is often necessary to solve problems in very complex areas and for equations with variable coefficients, often nonlinear. This leads to the need to look for approximate solutions using various numerical methods. A fairly effective method for the numerical solution of problems in mathematical physics is the finite difference method or the grid method, which makes it possible to reduce the approximate solution of partial differential equations to the solution of systems of algebraic equations. The article studied the most popular numerical methods of the first, second, third and fourth order of accuracy. All of these circuits have been compared with exact solutions.

**Keywords:** Mathematical model · Wave Equation · finite-difference schemes · computational algorithms · nonstationary · high order · Gas movement · mathematical physics

## 1 Introduction

Mathematical modeling, as one of the ways to obtain new knowledge, today is one of the main research methods in various fields of natural science. Gas movement in a wind tunnel, tsunami wave propagation, plasma scattering in a trap, weather changes and other numerous phenomena in science and technology are described by various mathematical models represented in the form of integral and partial differential equations. Modern computational algorithms make it possible with sufficient accuracy to solve these systems of equations in two-dimensional and three-dimensional approximations when solving various classes of problems, taking into account real geometries and nonstationarity of

Y. Koucheryavy and A. Aziz (Eds.): NEW2AN 2022, LNCS 13772, pp. 15–25, 2023.
https://doi.org/10.1007/978-3-031-30258-9_2

the process. Further progress in the development of numerical methods is associated with the development of new numerical algorithms and an increase in the speed and power of modern computing technology [1].

Modern problems of mathematical physics impose different requirements on the applied numerical algorithms, the main ones of which are:

- high order of approximation (provides a more accurate solution on sufficiently coarse grids);
- stability of algorithms (allowing calculations with large time steps);
- conservativeness (correct resolution of discontinuous solutions);
- monotonicity (no oscillations in areas of high gradients);
- efficiency (as minimizing the number of arithmetic operations per grid point);
- the universality of algorithms (the possibility of their extension to multidimensional 2D, 3D problems);
- adaptation of algorithms to irregular or unstructured meshes;
- the ability to parallelize computations (when using multiple computing processors - cores).

In this article, various finite-difference schemes are described and studied in detail, with the help of which one can solve the simplest model equations. We will restrict ourselves to consideration - the first order wave equation. These equations are called model equations because they are used to study the properties of solutions to more complex partial differential equations. Thus, the heat conduction equation can be considered as a model for other parabolic partial differential equations, for example, boundary layer equations. All considered model equations have analytical solutions for some boundary and initial conditions. Knowing these solutions, it is easy to evaluate and compare the various finite difference methods used to solve more complex partial differential equations. Of the many existing finite-difference methods for solving partial differential equations, this article mainly describes methods that have properties characteristic of a whole class of similar methods. Some finite-difference methods useful for solving equations are not presented, since they are similar to those described [2, 3].

For comparison, the most popular finite difference schemes were used, such as: explicit Euler scheme, upstream scheme, Lax scheme, implicit Euler scheme, leapfrog method, Lax - Wendroff method, McCormack method, Warming - Cutler - Lomax method, Abarbanel–Gottlieb–Turkel method.

In this article, as a model equation, we will choose Eq. (1), which we will call the one-dimensional wave equation of the first order, or simply the wave equation. The one-dimensional wave equation is a linear hyperbolic equation describing the propagation of a wave with a velocity $u$ along the $x$-axis. It simulates in an elementary form nonlinear equations describing gas-dynamic flows:

$$\frac{\partial u}{\partial t} + \frac{\partial F}{\partial x} = 0. \tag{1}$$

In the general case, both the unknown $u$ and $F(u)$ the function are vectors.

For the stability of the numerical schemes, the CFL criterion was used.

The Courant-Friedrichs-Levy criterion (CFL criterion) is a necessary condition for the stability of an explicit numerical solution of partial differential equations. As a consequence, in many computer simulations the time step must be less than a certain value or the results will be incorrect. The physical criterion of CFL means that a liquid particle in one time step should not move more than one spatial step. Or, in other words, the computational scheme cannot correctly calculate the propagation of a physical disturbance, which in reality moves faster than the computational scheme allows "tracking", that is, one step in space for one step in time.

$$|u| \frac{\Delta t}{\Delta x} \leq C$$

Here the constant $C = 1$ depends on the equation, but does not depend on $\Delta t$ and $\Delta x$.

## 2 Description of Schemes

### 2.1 Explicit Euler Method

This method leads to two simple explicit one-step difference schemes but only one scheme was presented in the article:

$$\frac{u_i^{n+1} - u_i^n}{\Delta t} + \frac{F_{i+1}^n - F_{i-1}^n}{2\Delta x} = 0,$$

$$u_i^{n+1} = u_i^n - \frac{\Delta t}{2\Delta x}(F_{i+1}^n - F_{i-1}^n). \tag{2}$$

with an approximation error $O(\Delta t, (\Delta x)^2)$, respectively. Both of these schemes have the first order of approximation, since the leading term in the expression for the error is of the first order $(\Delta t)$. Difference schemes (2) are explicit, since each difference equation contains only one unknown $u_i^{n+1}$. Unfortunately, the analysis of the stability of difference schemes (2) by the Neumann method leads to the fact that both of them are absolutely unstable and, therefore, are unsuitable for the numerical solution of the wave equation.

### 2.2 Differences Upstream

A simple explicit scheme (2) (Euler's method) can be made stable if, when approximating the spatial derivative, one uses not forward differences, but backward differences in cases where the wave velocity c is positive. If the wave velocity is negative, then the stability of the scheme is ensured by using forward differences. This issue will be considered in more detail in the book [3] when describing the method of splitting the matrix coefficients. When using backward differences, difference equations take the form [4]:

$$\frac{u_i^{n+1} - u_i^n}{\Delta t} + \frac{F_{i+1}^n - F_{i-1}^n}{2\Delta x} = 0,$$

$$u_i^{n+1} = u_i^n - c\frac{\Delta t}{2\Delta x}(F_i^n - F_{i-1}^n). \tag{3}$$

This difference scheme has the first order of accuracy with an approximation error $O(\Delta t, \Delta x)$. It follows from the Neumann stability condition that the scheme is stable for $\frac{\Delta t}{\Delta x} \leq 1$.

## 2.3  Lax's Scheme

Difference scheme (2) (Euler's method) can be made stable by replacing it with the spatial average $\frac{u_{i+1}^n - u_{i-1}^n}{2}$. As a result, we obtain the well-known Lax scheme [5]:

$$\frac{u_i^{n+1} - \left(\frac{u_{i+1}^n - u_{i-1}^n}{2}\right)}{\Delta t} + \frac{F_{i+1}^n - F_{i-1}^n}{2\Delta x} = 0,$$

$$u_i^{n+1} = \left(\frac{u_{i+1}^n - u_{i-1}^n}{2}\right) - \frac{\Delta t}{2\Delta x}\left(F_{i+1}^n - F_{i-1}^n\right). \tag{4}$$

This is an explicit one-step scheme of the first order of accuracy with an $O\left(\Delta t, (\Delta x)^2 / \Delta t\right)$ approximation error. She's stable with $\frac{\Delta t}{\Delta x} \leq 1$.

## 2.4  Implicit Euler Method

All three methods of Euler, versus Stream and Lax are explicit methods. Consider an implicit difference scheme [6–9].

$$\frac{u_i^{n+1} - u_i^n}{\Delta t} + \frac{F_{i+1}^{n+1} - F_{i-1}^{n+1}}{2\Delta x} = 0, \tag{5}$$

This is a first-order scheme with an approximation error $O\left(\Delta t, (\Delta x)^2\right)$. Analysis of the Neumann stability (Fourier analysis) shows that it is stable at any time step, that is, it is absolutely stable. However, when using this scheme, at each time step, you have to solve the sweep.

$$u_i^{n+1} = u_i^n - \frac{\Delta t}{2\Delta x}\left(F_{i+1}^{n+1} - F_{i-1}^{n+1}\right). \tag{6}$$

## 2.5  Leapfrog Method (Leapfrog Method)

Until now, only schemes of the first order of accuracy for solving a linear wave equation have been considered. The simplest second-order accurate method is the step-over method. Applying it to the first-order wave equation, we obtain an explicit one-step three-layer time difference scheme:

$$\frac{u_i^{n+1} - u_i^{n-1}}{2\Delta t} + \frac{F_{i+1}^n - F_{i-1}^n}{2\Delta x} = 0. \tag{7}$$

The step-by-step method is called three-layer in time, since in order to determine the value of and at the $n + 1$-th time step, it is necessary to know the values at the $n - 1$-th and n-th time steps.

The method has an approximation error of $O\left((\Delta t)^2, (\Delta x)^2\right)$ and is stable for $\frac{\Delta t}{\Delta x} \leq 1$.

## 2.6  Lax-Wendroff Method

The Lax - Wendroff scheme [10] can be constructed based on the Taylor series expansion:

$$\frac{u_i^{n+1} - u_i^n}{\Delta t} + \frac{F_{i+1}^n - F_{i-1}^n}{2\Delta x} = \frac{F_{i+1}^n - 2F_i^n + F_{i-1}^n}{2\Delta x},$$

$$u_i^{n+1} = u_i^n - \frac{\Delta t}{2\Delta x}\left(F_{i+1}^n - F_{i-1}^n\right) + \frac{(\Delta t)^2}{2(\Delta x)^2}\left(F_{i+1}^n - 2F_i^n + F_{i-1}^n\right). \tag{8}$$

This is an explicit one-step scheme of the second order of accuracy with an approximation error of $O\left((\Delta t)^2, (\Delta x)^2\right)$, stable at $\frac{\Delta t}{\Delta x} \leq 0.01$.

## 2.7  McCormack Method

McCormack's method [11] is widely used to solve the equations of gas dynamics. McCormack is especially handy for solving nonlinear partial differential equations. Applying the explicit predictor-corrector method to the linear wave equation, we obtain the following difference scheme:
Predictor

$$\frac{\overline{u_i^{n+1}} - u_i^n}{\Delta t} + \frac{F_{i+1}^n - F_i^n}{2\Delta x} = 0,$$

$$\overline{u_i^{n+1}} = u_i^n - \frac{\Delta t}{\Delta x}\left(F_{i+1}^n - F_i^n\right). \tag{9}$$

Corrector

$$\frac{u_i^{n+1} - \left(u_i^n + \overline{u_i^{n+1}}\right)/2}{\Delta t/2} + \frac{F_i^n - F_{i-1}^n}{\Delta x} = 0,$$

$$u_i^{n+1} = \left(u_i^n + \overline{u_i^{n+1}} - \frac{\Delta t}{\Delta x}\left(\overline{F_i^{n+1}} - \overline{F_{i-1}^{n+1}}\right)\right), \tag{10}$$

$$O\left((\Delta t)^2, (\Delta x)^2\right).$$

Initially (the predictor) the estimate of the $\overline{u_i^{n+1}}$ value and at the $n + 1$-th time step is found, and then (the corrector) the final value of $u_i^n$ is determined at the $n + 1$-th time step. Note that in the predictor pro and input $\frac{\partial u}{\partial x}$ is approximated by forward differences, and in the corrector - by backward differences. You can do the opposite, which is useful in solving some problems. Such problems include, in particular, problems with moving discontinuities.

## 2.8  Warming - Cutler - Lomax Method

Warming et al. [12] proposed a method of the third order of accuracy, which at the first two time steps coincides with the McCormack method and at the third with Rusanov's method:

Step 1

$$\overline{u_i^{n+1}} = u_i^n - c\frac{2\Delta t}{3\Delta x}(F_{i+1}^n - F_i^n),\tag{11}$$

Step 2

$$\overline{\overline{u_i^{n+1}}} = \left(u_i^n + \overline{u_i^{n+1}} - c\frac{2}{3}\frac{\Delta t}{\Delta x}\left(\overline{F_i^{n+1}} - \overline{F_{i-1}^{n+1}}\right)\right).\tag{12}$$

Step 3

$$u_i^{n+1} = u_i^n - 1/24c\frac{\Delta t}{\Delta x}(-2F_{i+2}^n + 7F_{i+1}^n - 7F_{i-1}^n + 2F_{i-2}^n)$$
$$-3/8c\frac{\Delta t}{\Delta x}\left(\overline{\overline{F_{i+1}^{n+1}}} - \overline{\overline{F_{i-1}^{n+1}}}\right) - \omega/24(u_{i+2}^n - 4u_{i+1}^n + 6u_i^n - 4u_{i-1}^n + u_{i-2}^n).\tag{13}$$

This is an explicit three-step scheme of the third order of accuracy with an approximation error $O((\Delta t)^3, (\Delta x)^3)$, stable at $\frac{\Delta t}{\Delta x} \leq 0.01$.

## 2.9 The Abarbanel–Gottlieb–Turkel Method

The article [13] presents a scheme of four step schemes of the fourth order of accuracy. This scheme has the following form:
Step 1

$$u_{j+\frac{1}{2}}^{(1)} = \frac{1}{2}\left(u_{j+1}^n + u_j^n\right) - \frac{\Delta t}{2\Delta x}\left(F_{j+1}^n - F_j^n\right),\tag{14}$$

Step 2

$$u_j^{(2)} = \frac{1}{8}\left\{10u_j^n - \left(u_{j+1}^n + u_{j-1}^n\right)\right\} - \frac{\Delta t}{2\Delta x}\left(F_{j+\frac{1}{2}}^{(1)} - F_{j-\frac{1}{2}}^{(1)}\right),\tag{15}$$

Step 3

$$u_{j+\frac{1}{2}}^{(3)} = \frac{1}{16}\left\{9\left(u_{j+1}^n + u_j^n\right) - \left(u_{j+2}^n + u_{j-1}^n\right)\right\}$$
$$-\frac{\Delta t}{8\Delta x}\left(8\left(F_{j+1}^{(2)} - F_j^{(2)}\right) + 3\left(F_{j+1}^n - F_j^n\right) - \left(F_{j+2}^n - F_{j-1}^n\right)\right),\tag{16}$$

Step 4

$$u_j^{n+1} = u_j^n - \frac{1}{96}\frac{\Delta t}{\Delta x}\left(\begin{array}{l}16\left(F_{j+\frac{1}{2}}^{(3)} - F_{j-\frac{1}{2}}^{(3)}\right) + 16\left(F_{j+1}^{(2)} - F_{j-1}^{(2)}\right)\\ +56\left(F_{j+\frac{1}{2}}^{(1)} - F_{j-\frac{1}{2}}^{(1)}\right) - 8\left(F_{j+\frac{3}{2}}^{(1)} - F_{j-\frac{3}{2}}^{(1)}\right)\end{array}\right)$$
$$+\frac{1}{96}\frac{\Delta t}{\Delta x}\left(10\left(F_{j+1}^n - F_{j-1}^n\right) - \left(F_{j+2}^n - F_{j-2}^n\right)\right).\tag{17}$$

This is an explicit four-step scheme of the fourth order of accuracy with an approximation error $O((\Delta t)^4, (\Delta x)^4)$ stable at $\Delta t / \Delta x \leq 1$.

When use methods of the third and fourth order of accuracy, the increase in the accuracy of the algorithm has to be paid for by an increase in the computation time and the complexity of the difference scheme. This must be carefully considered when choose a method for solving a partial differential equation. Usually, for most applications, methods of the second order of accuracy can be obtained with sufficient accuracy.

## 3   The Discussion of the Results

In Fig. 1 shows graphs comparing the results of various schemes with experimental data.

Figure 1 shows the explicit Euler scheme, the implicit Euler scheme, the leapfrog method, the Lax - Wendroff method, the McCormack method gives the same results. The upstream schemes, the Warming - Cutler – Lomax and Abarbanel–Gottlieb–Turkel methods give results close to experimental data.

Now let's consider how changing the grids affects the results of the first-order versus-flow, second-order McCormack, third-order Warming-Cutler-Lomax and fourth-order Abarbanel–Gottlieb–Turkel methods.

In Fig. 2 shows the effect of meshes in the resultant upstream circuit.

Figure 2 shows the upstream diagram when the computational grids change, approximates the experimental data, but the upstream diagram is not stable when time changes because this diagram is explicit and gives the first order of accuracy.

In Fig. 3 shows the effect of grids in the resulting McCormack scheme.

Figure 3 you can see McCormack's method describes the process more accurately, but due to the second order of accuracy, the result oscillates.

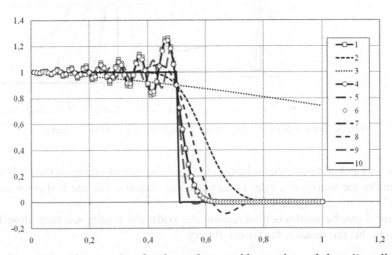

**Fig. 1.** Comparison of the results of various schemes with experimental data: 1) explicit Euler scheme, 2) upstream scheme, 3) Lax scheme, 4) implicit Euler scheme, 5) leapfrog method, 6) Lax - Wendroff method, 7) McCormack method, 8) Warming - Cutler - Lomax method, 9) Abarbanel–Gottlieb–Turkel method, 10) exact solutions.

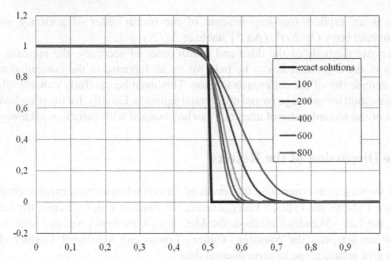

**Fig. 2.** Influence of computational grids in the upstream method.

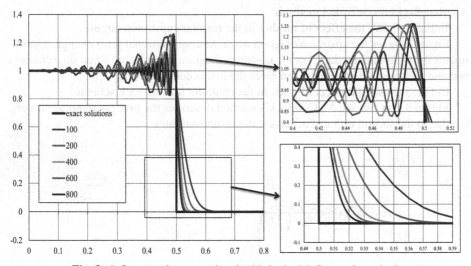

**Fig. 3.** Influence of computational grids in the McCormack method.

Now let's look at third-order schemes. In Fig. 4 shows how changing the grids affects the results of the Warming-Cutler-Lomax method. Because this method gives a closer result.

Figure 4 can be seen when increasing the grids, the results are very close to the experiment, but the result is highly oscillatory.

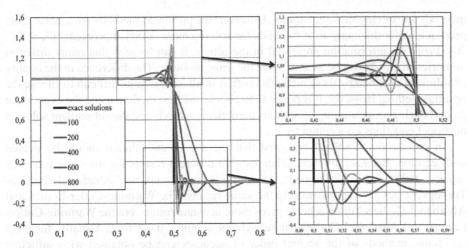

**Fig. 4.** Influence of computational grids in the Warming - Cutler - Lomax method.

In Fig. 5 shows how mesh changes affect the results of the Abarbanel–Gottlieb–Turkel method.

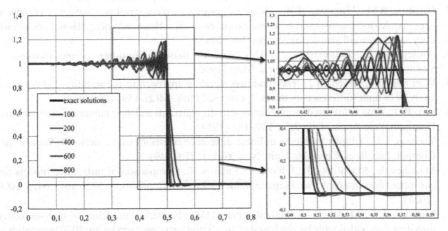

**Fig. 5.** Influence of computational grids in the Abarbanel–Gottlieb–Turkel method.

When using Abarbanel–Gottlieb–Turkel methods, the position of the fracture is determined more accurately. The calculation results differ from those obtained by the first to third order method.

## 4  Conclusion

In this article, the basic finite-difference solution methods for simple model equations have been studied. At the same time, the task was not set to describe all the known methods for solving these equations. However, the presented methods are a reasonable prerequisite for the analysis of methods for solving more complex problems [7, 8, 14–20]. From the information presented in the article, it can be seen that many different numerical methods can be used to solve the same problem. The difference in the quality of solutions obtained by these methods is often small, so it is quite difficult to choose the optimal method. However, it is possible to choose the best method using the experience gained during programming by various numerical methods and the subsequent solution of model equations on a computer.

In conclusion, it should be noted that the use of the scheme should be treated with caution. Because different schemes give different results for the same task. For separated flows, the McCormack, Warming-Cutler-Lomax and Abarbanel-Gottlieb-Turkel schemes give approximately the same results. The Warming-Cutler-Lomax and Abarbanel-Gotlieb-Turkel scheme gives more accurate results, but the Warming-Cutler-Lomax and Abarbanel-Gotlieb-Turkel scheme requires more time. Usually, for most problems, methods of the second order of accuracy can be obtained with sufficient accuracy.

# References

1. Ковеня, В.М.: Разностные методы решения многомерных задач (2004)
2. Ковеня, В.М., Чирков, Д.В.: Методы конечных разностей и конечных объемов для решения задач математической физики. Новосибирск: Новосибирский государственный университет, pp. 7–8 (2013)
3. Андерсон, Д., Таннехилл, Д., Плетчер, Р.: Вычислительная гидромеханика и теплообмен: В 2-х т.: Пер. с англ. Мир (1990)
4. Warming, R.F., Hyett, B.J.: The modified equation approach to the stability and accuracy analysis of finite-difference methods. J. Comput. Phys. **14**(2), 159–179 (1974)
5. Lax, P.D.: Weak solutions of nonlinear hyperbolic equations and their numerical computation. Commun. Pure Appl. Math. **7**(1), 159–193 (1954)
6. Thomas, L.H.: Elliptic problems in linear difference equations over a network. Watson Sci. Comput. Lab. Rept. Columbia Univ. New York **1**, 71 (1949)
7. Madaliev, E., Madaliev, M., Adilov, K., Pulatov, T.: Comparison of turbulence models for two-phase flow in a centrifugal separator. In: E3S Web of Conferences 2021, vol. 264, p. 1009 (2021)
8. Mirzoev, A.A., Madaliev, M., Sultanbayevich, D.Y.: Numerical modeling of non-stationary turbulent flow with double barrier based on two liquid turbulence model. In: 2020 International Conference on Information Science and Communications Technologies (ICISCT), pp. 1–7 (2020)
9. Abdulkhaev, Z.E., Abdurazaqov, A.M., Sattorov, A.M.: Calculation of the transition processes in the pressurized water pipes at the start of the pump unit. JournalNX **7**(05), 285–291 (2021). https://doi.org/10.17605/OSF.IO/9USPT
10. Lax, P.: Systems of conservation laws. Los Alamos National Lab NM (1959)
11. MacCormack, R.W.: The effect of viscosity in hypervelocity impact cratering. J. Spacecr. Rockets **40**(5), 757–763 (2003)
12. Warming, R.F., Kutler, P., Lomax, H.: Second-and third-order noncentered difference schemes for nonlinear hyperbolic equations. AIAA J. **11**(2), 189–196 (1973)
13. Abarbanel, S., Gottlieb, D., Turkelm, E.: Difference schemes with fourth order accuracy for hyperbolic equations. SIAM J. Appl. Math. **29**, 329–351 (1975)

14. Malikov, Z.M., Madaliev, M.E.: Numerical simulation of two-phase flow in a centrifugal separator. Fluid. Dyn. **55**, 1012–1028 (2020). https://doi.org/10.1134/S0015462820080066
15. Nazarov, F.K., Malikov, Z.M., Rakhmanov, N.M.: Simulation and numerical study of two-phase flow in a centrifugal dust catcher. J. Phys. Conf. Ser. **1441**(1), 12155 (2020)
16. Malikov, Z.M., Madaliev, M.E.: New two-fluid turbulence model-based numerical simulation of flow in a flat suddenly expanding channel. Her. Bauman Mosc. State Tech. Univ. Ser. Nat. Sci. **4**(97), 24–39 (2021). (In Russian). https://doi.org/10.18698/1812-3368-2021-4-24-39
17. Abdukarimov, B., O'tbosarov, S., Abdurazakov, A.: Investigation of the use of new solar air heaters for drying agricultural products. In: E3S Web of Conferences, vol. 264, p. 1031 (2021)
18. Erkinjonson, M.M.: Numerical calculation of an air centrifugal separator based on the SARC turbulence model. J. Appl. Comput. Mech. **7**(2) (2021). https://doi.org/10.22055/JACM.2020.31423.1871
19. Hamdamov, M.M., Mirzoyev, A.A., Buriev, E.S., Tashpulatov, N.: Simulation of non-isothermal free turbulent gas jets in the process of energy exchange. In: E3S Web of Conferences, vol. 264, p. 01017 (2021)
20. Fayziev, R.A., Hamdamov, M.M.: Model and program of the effect of incomplete combustion gas on the economy. In: ACM International Conference Proceeding Series, pp. 401–406 (2021)

# Numerical Solution of the Combustion Process Using the Computer Package Ansys Fluent

Ismatulla Ko'shaevich Khujaev[1]([⊠]), Rabim Alikulovich Fayziev[2],
and Muzaffar Muhiddinovich Hamdamov[1]

[1] Institute of Mechanics and Seismic Stability of Structures of the Academy of Sciences of the
Republic of Uzbekistan, Tashkent, Uzbekistan
i_k_hujaev@mail.ru

[2] Department Mathematical Methods in Economics, Tashkent State University of Economics,
Tashkent, Uzbekistan
r.fayziyev@tsue.uz

**Abstract.** The results of numerical studies of the processes of mixing, ignition and combustion during the expiration of jets of methane-air mixture in an axisymmetric channel. Numerical modeling of a turbulent subsonic nonequilibrium flow was performed within the framework of two-dimensional stationary equations of a "narrow channel" taking into account final rates of chemical kinetics within the framework of the global mechanism. The purpose of this work is to develop a numerical method for calculating the mixing, combustion, and propagation of various compositions of combustible mixtures in a cylindrical chamber, which makes it possible to conduct a computational experiment to study the processes of heat and mass transfer. The main problem of mathematical modeling of gas fuel combustion processes within the framework of the ANSYS Fluent software package is the choice of a turbulence model. In this work, the Patankar-Spaulding finite-difference method is used. The application of this method makes it possible to move from a rectilinear finite-difference grid to a modified curvilinear grid, which automatically "adjusts" to the flow area. Such a grid is especially convenient when calculating expanding free flows, since it does not require the addition of additional finite-difference grid nodes associated with the expansion of jet particles during the calculation process.

**Keywords:** turbulent jet · components · chemical reaction rate · total enthalpy · Arrhenius law · finite differences · computational experiment

## 1   A Subsection Sample

In the world, jet streams of reacting media are widely used in bits, in the generation of thermal and electrical energy, in internal combustion chambers, in chemical lasers, in the production of mercury and building materials, in power plants of rocket engines and many other equipment and production. Depending on the purpose of the organization and design of gas combustion devices, various problems of facility management arise. In particular, the gas component in the global energy balance is about 70%. Despite the

© The Author(s), under exclusive license to Springer Nature Switzerland AG 2023
Y. Koucheryavy and A. Aziz (Eds.): NEW2AN 2022, LNCS 13772, pp. 26–37, 2023.
https://doi.org/10.1007/978-3-031-30258-9_3

constant improvement in the performance of gas combustion devices, their efficiency is still very low.

In the world, due to the expansion of directions and scales of implementation, large-scale studies of the flows of reacting systems continue. An indispensable tool in the study of various ways of organizing the process of fuel combustion and their control are mathematical modeling and computational experiment. Adequately constructed mathematical model and numerical algorithms are integral components of today's development of methods for cognition of objects and their control. Mathematical modeling of the flows of reacting systems is developing dynamically due to the emergence of new models of turbulence and chemical reactions, effective numerical methods and high-speed, powerful computer technology. The implementation of these possibilities in solving the multidimensional full Navier-Stokes equations and their simplified analogs contributes to the successful solution of problems of complex heat and mass transfer, in particular, in relation to the problems of gas combustion in jet streams.

Today it is impossible to imagine the development and design of various technical devices without preliminary numerical simulation of the physical processes underlying their operation. No exception is the simulation of liquid and gas flows, which is of crucial importance for design in the aerospace industry, in turbomachinery and in many other industries. Most of the flows important for practice are turbulent, so the ability to calculate turbulent flows is extremely important for training a wide range of specialists.

In recent years, an increasing volume of calculations is carried out using general-purpose computational codes that allow solving a wide range of problems. One of the most common codes of this type is the ANSYS FLUENT package [1], which provides the user with a rich set of methods for calculating turbulent flows. The knowledge of this package and the ability to calculate various turbulent flows with its help becomes a very important skill for specialists who solve problems in the field of continuum mechanics.

Combustion modeling is a complex task that requires a harmonious and correct combination of heterogeneous physical and mathematical models that reflect such aspects of the combustion process as turbulent heat and mass transfer, chemical reaction kinetics, flame front propagation, radiation and heat transfer with the walls of the vortex chamber. ANSYS CFX has 13 turbulence models, 7 chemical kinetics models, 4 radiation models, and 6 combustion models. Obviously, the number of possible combinations of these models is very large, even if we discard their incompatible combinations. Therefore, it is necessary to apply a method that will lead to a set of physical and mathematical models that make it possible to correctly reflect the occurrence of a flow according to the law of a free vortex in a vortex chamber and the formation of a flame front limited by a peripheral flow of unreacting air. This method is based on the principle of separate testing of elements of a physical and mathematical model on simple model problems with their subsequent integration when solving a complex industrial problem. The final complex model is compiled according to the principle of selecting the best models in its class [1].

The following model tasks were chosen for verification calculations:

Air flow in the vortex chamber I.I. Smulsky [2] - choice of turbulence model;

Air flow in a vortex countercurrent burner module [3] - assessment of the influence of turbulence anisotropy when air moves without combustion in a vortex chamber of complex geometry;

Calculation of the adiabatic combustion temperature of a perfectly mixed mixture, partially mixed combustion Sandia Flame D [Sandia National Laboratories, Turbulent Diffusion Flame Laboratory Web Site, [4] – choice of combustion model and kinetic mechanism;

Combustion of a homogeneous mixture of air and methane in a vortex countercurrent combustion chamber [5] - a comprehensive check of the joint operation of turbulence and combustion models, the choice of a radiation model and a method for modeling heat transfer with walls.

In [6] an analysis of the working process and the conditions of self-ignition of the fuel-air mixture in a vortex countercurrent igniter was carried out, where the flame front was stabilized in a chamber with a perforated wall. Numerical simulation was carried out in the CFX-TaskFlow package in a full 3d statement on the SST model of turbulence without combustion. The calculations determined areas where, due to the action of the vortex effect, the maximum temperature of the air flow exceeds its value at the inlet. The precession of the vortex core and large-scale vortex shear structures are found.

Numerical modeling was used to create an oxygen-hydrogen superheater to study the conditions for stabilizing the flame and assess the thermal state of the elements of the burner module [7]. The calculations were carried out in full 3d formulation, turbulence model, EDM combustion model. Analysis of the temperature distribution of the combustion products at the exit, that the calculations qualitatively correspond to the experimental data obtained for vortex flame stabilizers.

Authors of the study [8] note that the calculation result can be improved by using more complex turbulence models, and the question of the existence of a set of flame front solutions should be investigated experimentally.

Also in ANSYS CFX are models based on the equation of specific energy dissipation rate $\omega$ - RSM and RSM BSL. These models use the concept of specific energy dissipation rate $\omega$, first proposed by Kolmogorov (1942) [9]. This parameter has the dimension of frequency (1/s) and characterizes the dissipation rate per unit of kinetic energy of turbulent fluctuations.

The advantage of model $\omega$ - RSM is that it provides more accurate results in the boundary layer, and the most versatile model is RSM BSL. The RSM BSL model is essentially a two-layer model, where a set of constants for the model including $\omega$ is used near the wall, and a set of model constants is used in the main flow. Cross-linking and regions is carried out similar to Menter's $k - \omega$ SST model [10].

Comparison of the results of calculations and experiment was carried out for the temperature profile at the outlet of the vortex chamber [11]. For calculations, the isotropic turbulence models $k - \varepsilon$, $k - \varepsilon$ RNG and the anisotropic turbulence model RSM in combination with the combustion model EDM and the two-step mechanism of methane oxidation were used. An analysis of the calculation results showed that the $k - \varepsilon$ RNG and RSM models show a flow structure close to the experiment. In particular, the coincidence of the flow structure and temperature for the $k - \varepsilon$ RNG and RSM models may mean that the turbulence in the chamber volume is isotropic.

In [12], the effect of oxygen enrichment of a pre-mixed ethane-air mixture on the rate of heat release was numerically investigated. The obtained results showed that the enrichment of the mixture with oxygen reduces the thickness of the flame by 10% and increases the rate of heat release.

The study of diffusion combustion, where the oxidizer and fuel are fed towards each other, is given in [13]. The effect of preheating the air on the structure of the flame and on the quantitative ratio of the emission of harmful substances is shown. The relevance of this study lies in the fact that preheating of air is used in many heat exchangers. Combustion chambers, where the air temperature is higher than the atmospheric temperature, include gas turbines and diesel engines. During operation, the air temperature varied from 300 to 560 K.

The presence of well-studied mechanisms of combustion reactions of some types of gas makes it possible to obtain a detailed description of a large number of ongoing processes and a wide range of chemically reacting components.

Among the numerous combustion modeling techniques, an approach based on the proportion of mixing of fuel and oxidizer, the flamelet model, stands out separately. To date, the flamelet model has been seriously modified compared to the original version.

## 2  Problem Statement

Let us consider a reacting cocurrent jet of methane propagating in a stationary environment, the flow diagram of which is shown in Fig. 1. The most common gaseous fuel is natural gas, which has a high calorific value. The basis of natural gases is methane, the content of which in the gas is 76–98%. Other gaseous hydrocarbon compounds are included in the composition of the gas from 0.1 to 4%.

A horizontal jet of methane flows out of a round nozzle of radius $r_1$ with initial velocity u1, initial temperature $T_1$, and initial concentration $c_1$. An oxidizer jet with initial parameters $u_2$, $T_2$, $c_2$ also flows coaxially to it from a round nozzle with radius $r_2$. In the region of mixing of these two jets, a combustion front arises, forming a diffusion flame.

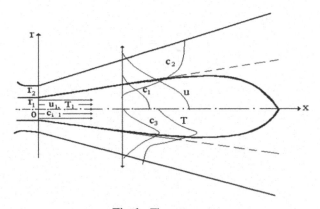

**Fig. 1.** Flow pattern

Air is used as an oxidizing agent, and it is considered that it consists only of oxygen (23.2%) and nitrogen (76.8%). Nitrogen is present as a diluent and does not participate in the reaction. The generalized methane combustion reaction can be written as the following equation [12–18]:

$$CH_4 + 2O_2 + N_2 = CO_2 + 2H_2O + N_2.$$

Here methane $(CH_4)$ is fuel, oxygen $(O_2)$ is an oxidizing agent, carbon dioxide $(CO_2)$ and water $(H_2O)$ are reaction products, nitrogen $(N_2)$ is an inert diluent;

The specific heat capacities of all components of the mixture are equal and do not depend on temperature;

The effect of heat loss on radiation is negligible;

The diffusion coefficients of all components are equal to each other and equal to the thermal diffusivity, i.e. $Le = 1$;

## 3  Mathematical Model

The presence of a tangential discontinuity in the flow indices at their common boundary and a high-temperature flame in the region of intense heat and mass transfer causes the flow turbulence in the region under consideration. Since there is a predominant direction of movement of gases, then at describing the process, one can use the equations of the turbulent boundary layer.

The flow is compressible, i.e. $\rho \neq$ const. It is assumed that the equation of state for an ideal gas can be used to determine the density:

$$\rho = \frac{PM}{RT}, \ M = \frac{1}{\sum\limits_{i=1}^{n} \frac{c_i}{M_i}}, \ c_i = \frac{m_i}{m}.$$

here $m_i$ is the mass of the $i$-th component, $M_i$ is the molar mass of the $i$-th component;

В соответствии с законом сохранения вещества справедливо следующее равенство:

$$\sum_{i=1}^{n} c_i = 1$$

Taking into account the assumptions and assumptions made, the system of equations for describing an axisymmetric jet turbulent reacting flow has the following form [1]:

$$
\begin{cases}
\dfrac{\partial}{\partial x}(\rho u r) + \dfrac{\partial}{\partial r}(\rho v r) = 0, \\[2mm]
\rho u \dfrac{\partial u}{\partial x} + \rho v \dfrac{\partial v}{\partial r} = -\dfrac{\partial P}{\partial x} + \dfrac{1}{r}\dfrac{\partial}{\partial r}\left(\rho r \mu_{eff}\dfrac{\partial u}{\partial r}\right) + (\rho - \rho^{*})g_{x}, \\[2mm]
\rho u \dfrac{\partial c_{1}}{\partial x} + \rho v \dfrac{\partial c_{1}}{\partial r} = \dfrac{1}{Sc}\dfrac{1}{r}\dfrac{\partial}{\partial r}\left(\rho r \mu_{eff}\dfrac{\partial c_{1}}{\partial r}\right) - \omega_{1}, \\[2mm]
\rho u \dfrac{\partial c_{2}}{\partial x} + \rho v \dfrac{\partial c_{2}}{\partial r} = \dfrac{1}{Sc}\dfrac{1}{r}\dfrac{\partial}{\partial r}\left(\rho r \mu_{eff}\dfrac{\partial c_{2}}{\partial r}\right) - \omega_{2}, \\[2mm]
\rho u \dfrac{\partial c_{3}}{\partial x} + \rho v \dfrac{\partial c_{3}}{\partial r} = \dfrac{1}{Sc}\dfrac{1}{r}\dfrac{\partial}{\partial r}\left(\rho r \mu_{eff}\dfrac{\partial c_{3}}{\partial r}\right) + \omega_{3}, \\[2mm]
\rho u \dfrac{\partial c_{4}}{\partial x} + \rho v \dfrac{\partial c_{4}}{\partial r} = \dfrac{1}{Sc}\dfrac{1}{r}\dfrac{\partial}{\partial r}\left(\rho r \mu_{eff}\dfrac{\partial c_{4}}{\partial r}\right) + \omega_{4}, \\[2mm]
\rho u c_{p}\dfrac{\partial T}{\partial x} + \rho v c_{p}\dfrac{\partial T}{\partial r} = \dfrac{1}{Pr}\dfrac{1}{r}\dfrac{\partial}{\partial r}\left(\rho r c_{p}\mu_{eff}\dfrac{\partial T}{\partial r}\right) + Q\omega_{1}.
\end{cases}
$$

Here $\mu_{eff}$ are the effective viscosity coefficients, respectively, $Q$ is the thermal effect of the reaction, determined per unit mass of fuel; $i$ is the number of the mixture component, $\omega_{i}$ is the rate of chemical reactions.

Here and further $u$, $v$ – average longitudinal and transverse (radial) components of the velocity vector $(m\ s^{-1})$ in cylindrical coordinates; $\rho$, $T$ – density $(kg\ m^{-3})$ and absolute temperature (K) of the gas mixture; $p$ – hydrostatic pressure $(Pa)$; Pr, Sc – turbulent analogues of the Prandtl and Schmidt numbers; $c_{p} = \sum\limits_{n=1}^{N} c_{pn}c_{n}$ and $c_{pn}$ – heat capacity of the gas mixture and $n$- th component at constant pressure $(Dj\ kg^{-1}\ K^{-1})$.

Pressure gradient $\frac{\partial p}{\partial x}$, which is non-zero in internal flows (combustion chamber) and equal to zero in external flows.

Lifting force $(\rho - \rho^{*})g_{x}$, arising due to the difference in densities. In accordance with the law of conservation of matter, the following equality is true:

$$
\sum_{i=1}^{5} c_{i} = 1, \quad C_{5} = 1 - \sum_{i=1}^{4} c_{i}
$$

Model $k - \varepsilon$ is used to simulate a wide range of problems, its strengths are simplicity, good convergence of calculations, universality while maintaining good accuracy. Known shortcomings of this model are manifested in insufficiently accurate modeling: flow separation points from smooth surfaces, flows in the boundary layer, strongly swirling flows and flows with large curvature of streamlines. The model consists of two transfer equations for the kinetic energy of turbulent fluctuations k and its dissipation ε, as well as an equation for calculating the turbulent viscosity:

$$
\begin{cases}
\rho u \dfrac{\partial k}{\partial x} + \rho v \dfrac{\partial k}{\partial r} = \dfrac{1}{\delta_k} \dfrac{1}{r} \dfrac{\partial}{\partial r}\left( \rho r \mu_{eff} \dfrac{\partial k}{\partial r} \right) + \mu_t \left( \dfrac{\partial u}{\partial r} \right)^2 - \rho \varepsilon, \\[4mm]
\rho u \dfrac{\partial \varepsilon}{\partial x} + \rho v \dfrac{\partial \varepsilon}{\partial r} = \dfrac{1}{\delta_\varepsilon} \dfrac{1}{r} \dfrac{\partial}{\partial r}\left( \rho r \mu_{eff} \dfrac{\partial \varepsilon}{\partial r} \right) + c_{\varepsilon 1} \dfrac{\varepsilon}{k} \mu_t \left( \dfrac{\partial u}{\partial r} \right)^2 - c_{\varepsilon 2} \rho \dfrac{\varepsilon^2}{k}
\end{cases}
$$

Here $\mu_{eff} = (\nu + \nu_t)$, $\nu_t = \dfrac{c_\mu k^2}{\varepsilon}$, $c_{\varepsilon 1} = 1.44$, $c_{\varepsilon 2} = 1.92$, $c_\mu = 0.09$, $\delta_k = 1$, $\delta_k = 1.3$.

This turbulence model was used to solve the task under consideration. For the rates of a chemical reaction, the following dependencies take place

$$
\omega_2 = \frac{m_2}{m_1}\omega_1, \quad \omega_3 = \frac{m_3}{m_1}\omega_1, \quad \omega_4 = \frac{m_4}{m_1}\omega_1, \quad \omega_5 = 0.
$$

Then the equations take the form

$$
\begin{cases}
\dfrac{\partial}{\partial x}(\rho u r) + \dfrac{\partial}{\partial r}(\rho v r) = 0, \\[4mm]
\rho u \dfrac{\partial u}{\partial x} + \rho v \dfrac{\partial v}{\partial r} = -\dfrac{\partial P}{\partial x} + \dfrac{1}{r} \dfrac{\partial}{\partial r}\left( \rho r \mu_{eff} \dfrac{\partial u}{\partial r} \right) + (\rho - \rho^*)g_x, \\[4mm]
\rho u \dfrac{\partial c_1}{\partial x} + \rho v \dfrac{\partial c_1}{\partial r} = \dfrac{1}{Sc} \dfrac{1}{r} \dfrac{\partial}{\partial r}\left( \rho r \mu_{eff} \dfrac{\partial c_1}{\partial r} \right) - \omega_1, \\[4mm]
\rho u \dfrac{\partial c_2}{\partial x} + \rho v \dfrac{\partial c_2}{\partial r} = \dfrac{1}{Sc} \dfrac{1}{r} \dfrac{\partial}{\partial r}\left( \rho r \mu_{eff} \dfrac{\partial c_2}{\partial r} \right) - \dfrac{m_2}{m_1}\omega_1, \\[4mm]
\rho u \dfrac{\partial c_3}{\partial x} + \rho v \dfrac{\partial c_3}{\partial r} = \dfrac{1}{Sc} \dfrac{1}{r} \dfrac{\partial}{\partial r}\left( \rho r \mu_{eff} \dfrac{\partial c_3}{\partial r} \right) + \dfrac{m_3}{m_1}\omega_1, \\[4mm]
\rho u \dfrac{\partial c_4}{\partial x} + \rho v \dfrac{\partial c_4}{\partial r} = \dfrac{1}{Sc} \dfrac{1}{r} \dfrac{\partial}{\partial r}\left( \rho r \mu_{eff} \dfrac{\partial c_4}{\partial r} \right) + \dfrac{m_4}{m_1}\omega_1, \\[4mm]
\rho u \dfrac{\partial H}{\partial x} + \rho v \dfrac{\partial H}{\partial r} = \dfrac{1}{Pr} \dfrac{1}{r} \dfrac{\partial}{\partial r}\left( \rho r \mu_{eff} \dfrac{\partial H}{\partial r} \right), \\[4mm]
\rho u \dfrac{\partial k}{\partial x} + \rho v \dfrac{\partial k}{\partial r} = \dfrac{1}{\delta_k} \dfrac{1}{r} \dfrac{\partial}{\partial r}\left( \rho r \mu_{eff} \dfrac{\partial k}{\partial r} \right) + \mu_t \left( \dfrac{\partial u}{\partial r} \right)^2 - \rho \varepsilon, \\[4mm]
\rho u \dfrac{\partial \varepsilon}{\partial x} + \rho v \dfrac{\partial \varepsilon}{\partial r} = \dfrac{1}{\delta_\varepsilon} \dfrac{1}{r} \dfrac{\partial}{\partial r}\left( \rho r \mu_{eff} \dfrac{\partial \varepsilon}{\partial r} \right) + c_{\varepsilon 1} \dfrac{\varepsilon}{k} \mu_t \left( \dfrac{\partial u}{\partial r} \right)^2 - c_{\varepsilon 2} \rho \dfrac{\varepsilon^2}{k}.
\end{cases}
$$

Here $H = c_p T + Q c_1$ - Enthalpy.

# 4  Combustion Models

Currently, several models of chemical reactions have been developed, differing in approaches to modeling combustion processes. In addition, each model has its own scope. To eliminate this shortcoming, some models are combined into groups through a special function, the role of which is to select one or another combustion model depending on the reaction conditions. The issue of modeling sources in the equations of energy and concentration transfer associated with chemical reactions occurring in the combustion process deserves special attention. In the general case, sources are defined as follows [1].

Variable $\omega_1$ - the rate of decrease in fuel as a result of a chemical reaction of combustion is determined using the Arrhenius law [20]:

$$\omega_1 = k_0 \rho^2 c_1 c_2 \, e^{-\frac{E}{RT}}$$

where $A-$ is the pre-exponential factor; $E-$ activation energy.

# 5  Calculation Algorithm

The equations described above are integrated by the finite volume method in the Ansys Fluent package. Convective and diffusion flows are calculated with the second order of approximation. Due to the fact that all the problems modeled below are quasi-stationary, the first order of approximation in time is used. The velocity and pressure fields are linked by the PISO algorithm. Solution algorithms, depending on the selected combustion model, have distinctive features.

# 6  Calculation Results

The problem is solved in a two-dimensional formulation, the cylindricity is taken into account due to the computational grid built in the form of a sector. To simplify the presentation, in the section describing the boundary conditions, hereinafter, the parameters are given immediately both for the flamelet model and for models of the kinetic reaction rate.

Boundary conditions for the system of equations. At $x = 0$ (at the exit from the nozzle), the initial values of all the desired functions are set [19–21]:

$$0 < r < r_1: \quad u = u_1, \ c = c_1, \ H_0 = c_p T_0 + Q c_1,$$

$$r_1 < r < r_2: \quad u = u_2, \ c = 0, \ H_0 = c_p T_0,$$

$$0 < r < r_2: k = \alpha_1 u_0^2, \ \varepsilon = \alpha_2 \frac{k_0^{3/2}}{r_2}.$$

We set the symmetry conditions on the jet axis:

$$x \geq 0, \ r = 0:$$

$$\frac{\partial u}{\partial r} = \frac{\partial H}{\partial r} = \frac{\partial c_1}{\partial r} = \frac{\partial c_2}{\partial r} = \frac{\partial c_3}{\partial r} = \frac{\partial c_4}{\partial r} = \frac{\partial k}{\partial r} = \frac{\partial \varepsilon}{\partial r} = 0$$

At the free boundary, the values of the functions tend to their values in the environment (air at rest): $x \geq 0$, $r \to \infty$:

$$u \to \infty, \ H \to c_p T_\infty, \ c_1 \to 0, \ k \to 0, \ \varepsilon \to 0.$$

Let us consider the problem of the flow around a horizontal solid surface by a turbulent jet of water flowing from a nozzle, the radius of which is $R = 0.02$ m, with a speed $U = 82$ m/s, at $T = 293$ K, $\rho = 1000 \frac{\text{kg}}{\text{m}^3}$. The problem will be considered isothermal, and the physical properties of the liquid are constant.

Grid convergence was studied on various finite-volume meshes with non-uniform steps: $40 \times 100 \times 1$ (№1), $60 \times 160 \times 1$ (№2), $70 \times 200 \times 1$ (№3). Significant quantitative differences in the results are observed when calculating on grids №1 and №2. However, when calculating on grids № 2 and № 3, the differences in the distribution of parameters are small. Therefore, the main calculations are carried out on a $60 \times 160 \times 1$ grid (Fig. 2).

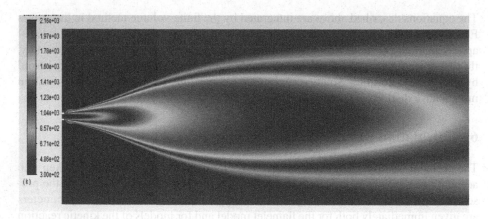

**Fig. 2.** Static temperature

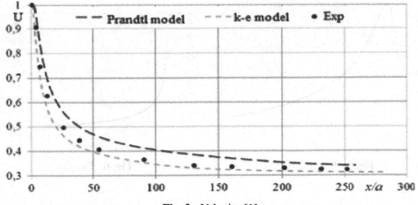

**Fig. 3.** Velocity [1]

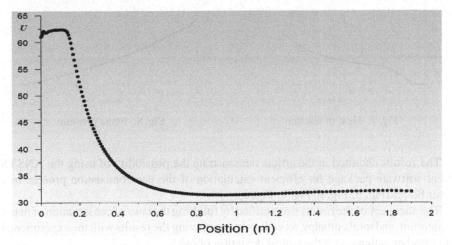

**Fig. 4.** Velocity Magnitude

Comparison of the calculation results for the change in the axial flow velocity according to two turbulence models and experimental data from is made in Fig. 3.

For a certain set of initial data, a calculation of a jet with combustion of a pure methane-air mixture was carried out and the parameters of the jet and torch were studied. In particular, it was found that in the initial zone of intense heat and mass transfer, the highest temperature in the jet cross section is formed at the fuel nozzle exit, then its coordinate moves away from the flow axis. Having reached its maximum value, this coordinate gradually tends to the jet axis and subsequently coincides with the coordinate axis (Fig. 4).

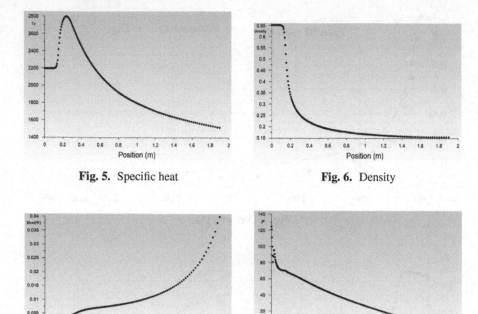

**Fig. 5.** Specific heat                    **Fig. 6.** Density

**Fig. 7.** Heat of reaction                 **Fig. 8.** Static pressure

The results obtained in the article demonstrate the possibility of using the ANSYS Fluent software package for efficient calculation of the gas combustion process in a power boiler (Fig. 5, Fig. 6, Fig. 7, Fig. 8).

The adequacy of the results was verified by fulfilling the laws of conservation of mass, momentum, and total enthalpy, as well as by comparing the results with the experimental data of other authors with the largest deviation of 6%.

# References

1. ANSYS Fluent Theory Guide. SAS IP, Inc. All rights reserved. Unauthorized use, distribution or duplication is prohibited. ANSYS, Inc. is certified to ISO 9001:2008 (2013)
2. Smulsky, I.I.: Aerodynamics and processes in vortex chambers, VO "Nauka". Siberian Publishing Company, Novosibirsk, p. 301 (1992)
3. Guryanov, A.I.: Experimental and theoretical refinement of the methodology for designing vortex countercurrent low-drop burners: discand. tech. Sciences. RGATA, Rybinsk, p. 138 (2007)
4. Electronic resource. http://www.sandia.gov/TNF/DataArch/FlameD.html
5. Najim, S.E.: Flame movement mechanisms and characteristics of gas fired cyclone combustors. In: 18th Symposium (International) on Combustion, vol. 18, no. 1, pp. 1949–1957 (1981)
6. Guryanov, A.I.: Vortex burners. Eng. J. (5), 8-15 (2005)
7. Guryanov, A.I., Piralishvili, S.H., Vereshchagin, I.M.: Vestnik SSAU, (3–2), 137–144 (2011)

8. Kumar, A.: Computational study of premixed gas fired cyclone combustor. In: Proceedings of the 15th National Conference on Internal Combustion engines and Combustion. Allied Publishers, pp. 701–711 (1997)
9. Kolmogorov, A.N.: Equations of turbulent motion of an incompressible fluid. In: Izv. Academy of Sciences of the USSR, Teor. fiz. vol. 6, no. 1–2 (1942)
10. Menter, F.R.: Two-equation eddy-viscosity turbulence models for engineering applications. AIAA-J. **32**(8), 1598–1605 (1994)
11. Matveev, I.: Experimental and numerical definition of the reverse vortex combustor parameters. In: 44th AIAA Aerospace Sciences Meeting and Exhibit. AIAA Paper 2006–0551, p. 12 (2006)
12. Kangping, Z., Ge, H., Shiyong, L.: Numerical study on the effects of oxygen enrichment on methane/air flames. Fuel **176**, 93–101 (2016)
13. Jongmook, L.: A study of the effects of air preheat on the structure of methane/air counterflow diffusion flames. Combust. Flame **121**(1–2), 262–274 (2000)
14. Zeldovich, Y.B.: To the theory of reaction on porous or powdery material. J. Phys. Chem. **13**(2), 161–168 (1939)
15. Galenko, Y.A., Sypin E.V., Pavlov A.N.: Statement of the problem of modeling the process of non-stationary combustion of a methane-air mixture in coal mines. Bull. Biysk Technol. Inst. (branch) FGBOU VO "AltGTU", (1), 20–33 (2018)
16. Zambon, A.C., Chelliah, H.K.: Self-sustained acoustic-wave interactions with counterflow flames. J. Fluid Mech. **560**, 249–278 (2006)
17. Hamdamov, M., Khujaev, I., Bazarov, O., Isabaev, K.: Axisymmetric turbulent methane jet propagation in a wake air flow under combustion at a finite velocity. In: IOP Conference Series: Materials Science and Engineering this link is disabled, vol. 1030, no. 1, p. 012163 (2021)
18. Hamdamov, M., Mirzoyev, A., Buriev, E., Tashpulatov, N.: Simulation of non-isothermal free turbulent gas jets in the process of energy exchange. In: E3S Web of Conferences, vol. 264, p. 01017 (2021)
19. Fayziev, R.A., Hamdamov, M.M.: Model and program of the effect of incomplete combustion gas on the economy. In: ACM International Conference Proceeding Series, pp. 401–406 (2021)
20. Khujaev, I.K., Hamdamov, M.M.: Axisymmetric turbulent methane jet Propagation in a co-current air flow under combustion at a finite velocity. Herald of the Bauman Moscow State Technical University, Series Natural Sciences, (5), 89–108 (2021)
21. Akhmedov, D.M., Shadimetov, K.M., Hayotov, A.R.: Optimal quadrature formulas with derivatives for Cauchy type singular integrals. Appl. Math. Comput. **317**, 150–159 (2018)

# Simulation Modeling of Reliability of Packet Switching Unit

Abdujabbar Abdukhamidovich Abidov[✉]

Tashkent State University of Economics, Tashkent, Uzbekistan
Abidov53@bk.ru

**Abstract.** Reliability analysis has been a hot research topic since the early 1960s. However, most of the methods were applied at the stage of software implementation. Reliability assessment at an early stage of system design is a faster formal method. It creates a probabilistic real-time system model and time property analysis based on schedule analysis. It proactively identifies potential security threats so costly changes are made during the system design phase. There is a lot of literature that mainly deals with the relationship between task priority and worst-case response time under a fault-tolerant state. Due to the growing security requirements of embedded software, many studies have emerged in the field of fault tolerance and reliability assessment. The traditional approach mainly relies on software testing bug data to predict future bug behavior. The issues of formalization of the problem of a complex hierarchical structure of real-time systems under conditions of a perturbing effect on the control object are considered, the parameters of the object under study are identified, and its simulation model is built.

**Keywords:** Adaptive switching node · packet switch unit (PSU) · rate monotonic (RM) simulation modeling · earliest deadline first (EDF) · real-time systems · parameter identification · reliability theory · failures · poisson distributions · elementary event flow

## 1 Introduction

Embedded electronic devices may operate in an undefined environment. Electromagnetic interference, voltage fluctuations, and high or low temperatures can easily cause intermittent or permanent failures in semiconductor devices, potentially leading to operational errors in a real-time system. To deal with such a situation, real-time systems usually have a fail-safe mechanism. although the existing fault-tolerant mechanism allows for some kinds of errors, there are limitations. It cannot handle some fatal errors or situations with a huge number of errors.

Currently [1], embedded software operating in safety-critical systems such as avionics, mission recalculation, and vehicle control is mainly used to collect information from external stimuli and respond to various interferences in a timely manner in an environment around. To meet the requirements for its critical properties, especially reliability,

© The Author(s), under exclusive license to Springer Nature Switzerland AG 2023
Y. Koucheryavy and A. Aziz (Eds.): NEW2AN 2022, LNCS 13772, pp. 38–45, 2023.
https://doi.org/10.1007/978-3-031-30258-9_4

it is necessary to accurately assess the fault tolerance capability of the real-time system, otherwise failure to meet the time requirements can lead to system failures, which can lead to catastrophic consequences. For example, IEC61508 [2] offers a set of risk assessment methods.

## 2  Methodology

Fault tolerance can be provided either by hardware or software, or temporary redundancy. Security-critical applications have strict time and cost constraints, which means that you must not only make mistakes, but also respect the limits. The scheduling deadline means that the task with the earliest required response time is processed. The most common scheduling algorithms are: rate monotonic (RM) and earliest deadline first (EDF). Fault tolerance is the ability to continue operating despite the failure of a limited subset of hardware or software.

Real-time systems can be divided into hard real-time systems, in which the consequences of timing violations can be catastrophic, and soft real-time systems, in which the consequences are relatively tolerable. In hard real-time systems, it is important that tasks are completed on time even in the event of a failure [3]. Examples of hard real time systems are space station control systems, autopilot systems, and critical care patient monitoring systems. In soft real-time systems, it is more important to detect a fault as soon as possible than to mask it. Examples of soft real-time systems are all kinds of applications for booking airline tickets, banking and e-commerce.

In the case of watchdog timers [4], the program flow or transmitted data is periodically checked for errors. The simplest watchdog scheme, the watchdog timer, keeps track of how long processes are running to see if it exceeds a certain limit.

There are two ways to make the system more resilient to failures [4, 5]. Hardware: this method relies on adding additional redundant hardware to the system to make it fault-tolerant. Software: this method relies on duplication of code, process, or even messages, depending on the context.

A typical example of the application of the above methods can be an autopilot system on board a large passenger aircraft [6].

## 3  Results

In the theory of reliability, when the occurrence of a certain number of identical events is of interest (such events are failures), the poisson distribution is used [7]. The occurrence of each event number corresponds to some point on the timeline.

According to the study of the structure of the simplest flow of events [7], the probability of occurrence of n events in a given period of time corresponds to the poisson distribution, and the probability that the time intervals between events will be less than some predetermined number m corresponds to the exponential distribution.

$$P(t) = e^{-vt} \tag{1}$$

The distribution function of T is defined as

$$F(t) = 1 - e^{-vt} \tag{2}$$

Differentiating expression (2) we find the distribution density of the quantity

$$f(t) = \lambda e^{-vt} \tag{3}$$

Numerical characteristics of the value T - the mathematical expectation (average value) $m_t$, dispersion $\eth_t$ and standard deviation $\sigma_t$ are determined by the formulas

$$m_t = \frac{1}{v} \tag{4}$$

$$\eth_t = \frac{1}{vx^2} \tag{5}$$

$$\sigma_t = \sqrt{(\eth_t)} \tag{6}$$

The developed simulation model, based on the application of (1)–(6), serves to assess the performance of the block of the adaptive switching node (AS) in the computer network (CN) both with and without the use of control and recovery tools.

The simulation model takes into account:

1. The operation of the AS Node block in queuing systems (QS) of the M/M/1 type with the intensity of arrival ($\lambda$) and service ($\mu$) of packets for a load factor $\beta < 1, \beta = \lambda/\mu$

2. Failures that make up a simple poisson flow, the probability of hitting a given interval of failures is

$$P_m = \frac{(vt)^m}{m!} e^{-vt} \tag{7}$$

where $v$ - is the failure rate.

3. Time intervals for the occurrence of faults, distributed according to the exponential law and determined by the formula

$$\psi_i = -\frac{1}{v} ln \xi_i \tag{8}$$

where $i = 1, m$; $\xi_i$ - pseudo-random numbers in the Interval [0,1].

4. The moments of time of occurrence of faults, determined by the formula:

$$t_k = t_{k-1} + \psi_k \tag{9}$$

for $k = 1, t_0 = 0$

5. Intervals of periods for launching periodic control programs, calculated by formula (10)

$$n = \frac{Tnk}{\frac{\beta z - \beta p}{\lambda} - Tok} \tag{10}$$

where $n$ is the minimum number of processed packets, after which it is advisable to start periodic control.

6. **Criteria:**

    a) time to failure

$$T = \frac{1}{v} \tag{11}$$

    b) tecovery time $t_z$
    c) the probability of failure-free operation

$$R(t) = exp(-vt) \tag{12}$$

    d) readiness of the as node block

$$K_{rq} = \frac{T}{T + \tau} \tag{13}$$

    e) efficiency ratio

$$K_{ef} = \frac{Co}{Cn} \tag{14}$$

    where $C_o$, $C_n$ are the number of processed and received software's.
    f) The probability of detecting and eliminating errors $P_o$, $P_b$.

7. When compressing the period of passage of failure (T) in $k_c$ time, you can get

$$T_c = T/\kappa_c \tag{15}$$

for the intensity of failure passage in the period

$$v_c = 1/T_c \quad and \quad v_c = \kappa_c/T \quad and \quad v_c = \kappa_c v \tag{16}$$

Then the failure passage periods for the time between failures are determined by

$$T_c = \frac{-1}{vc \, ln \, \xi i} = \frac{-1}{(\kappa_c v) \, ln \, \xi i} = \frac{t\prime}{\kappa_c} \tag{17}$$

The total time of the experiment ($T_{eks}$) will be the sum

$$T_{eks} = \sum_{k=1}^{N} t(k) \tag{18}$$

and after compression it can be defined as

$$T\prime_{eks} = \frac{Teks}{\kappa_c} = \frac{\sum_{k=1}^{N} t(k)}{\kappa_c} \tag{19}$$

On the basis of the above mentioned material, a simulation model of the process of functioning of the PSU block of the adaptive switching node in the aircraft with malfunctions was developed. The main purpose of this model is as follows:

– study of the operation of the PSU block, to the input queues of which packets, both long and short, are fed from the outside (alternately);
– analysis of the operation of the block after processing each packet;
– maintaining statistics of received and processed packets;
– generation of faults in the data area with which the PSU unit operates;
– evaluation of the effectiveness of the means of control and restoration used.

The developed simulation model consists of the following components:

– PSU block simulator for joint operation of this block with and without operational control procedures;
– simulator of the assembly-dismantling unit (ADU);
– error models (fault generator);
– a monitor to manage all the processes of the simulation model.

Let's move on to the description of the functions of the constituent parts.
The PSU block simulator performs the following actions:

– extracts the packet from the queue of input paths, or the queue of the input line to the block PSU;
– performs packet routing;
– inserts packets one by one into the input queues of paths or lines;
– connects operational control procedures to the operation of the PSU unit.

The functions of the ADU block simulator include:

– inserting packets one by one into the input queue of paths or packet lines; at the same time, both long and short packages are inserted;
– maintenance of the count of packets submitted to the input queues of the PSU block;
– analysis of the output queues of paths and lines in order to establish the fact of processing or operating time of the PSU block of the submitted software's;
– maintenance of the count of processed packets from the output queues of the path and Line.

The error model is designed to generate:

– fault occurrence time $t_k$;
– addresses of the memory cell of the data field of the AS node;
– disturbance.

The choice of the exponentiality of the distribution law for the occurrence of faults is explained by the lack of experimental data that would allow us to make more complex assumptions about the flow of failure situations in the aircraft during the execution of programs in real time [1, 8]. In this case, for the selection, the assumption of the occurrence of a failure on average one failure per hour was used.

The monitor controls the sequence of execution of all components of the simulation model.

# 4  Analysis of Experimental Results

The duty on simulation modeling was carried out in 2 stages.

At the first stage, the following works were carried out:

a) Shortening the duration of the experiment. to do this, at $k_c = 120$, according to formulas (15) – (19), the intensities of the passage of a failure (error) $\lambda c = 0.0333$ and the time between failures $T_c = 30$ s were obtained. Then, choosing $N_0 = 100$, the modeling accuracy $\varepsilon$ is determined for a confidence estimate $\lambda = 0.95$ from the normal distribution table, the value of $T_\lambda$, choosing $p = m/N_0$, the number of realizations N is obtained. $\varepsilon$ and N are, respectively, 0.005599 and 3931, and m = 116.

b) Analysis of the deviation of the experimental error intensity ($v_i$) from the theoretical one ($v$) depending on the number of generated errors (m) at the chosen simulation error ($\varepsilon$). The analysis results show for a given confidence estimate ($\varepsilon = 0.95$) out of 100 cases in 95 the difference | $v - v_i$ | does not exceed the specified error;

At the second stage, work was carried out related to the simulation of the process of functioning of the PSU block in a computer system with malfunctions.

For this, the following was done:

a) the run of the block of the PSU during the time T'eks, determined on the assumption that the 1 packet arrives in 1 s;

b) on-line input of errors into the relative addresses of the components of the adaptive switching node located in the common memory area;

c) periodic launch of monitoring and recovery tools. the start period is determined by (10) for $n$ at $\beta z = 0.8$, $\mu = 50$, $t_{pk} = 0.003$ s, $t_{ok} = 0.0078$ s for $\lambda = 30$ and $\beta_p = 0.6$ amounted to 5;

d) maintaining statistics of submitted ($C_p$) and processed ($C_o$) packets;

e) fixing the number of failures ($N_{otk}$).

The results of the experiment make it possible to compare the main indicators of the reliability of the operation of the psu with malfunctions for the case of using control and recovery tools and without them. Efficiency ratio $K_{ef}$ improved at the expense of controls and recovery from 0.679 to 0.962.

$K_{rq}$ from 0.991 to 0.993, and the number of failures has been reduced by an order of magnitude. A significant decrease in the $K_{ef}$ coefficient occurs for the case of operation of the PSU, when the means of control and restoration were not used. For example, for the origin of the 4th failure, when errors did not immediately lead to failure, $K_{ef}$ was reduced to 0.14 and the loss reached more than 80%, by the end of a 10-h experiment with ten errors. In another experiment, the failure-free operation of the PSU block lasted about 67 h.

the accumulation of about 67 errors in the software data area of the adaptive switching node led to a decrease in $K_{ef}$ by 0.32.

Dependences of $K_{ef}$ on the time of the experiment for the operation of the PSU block with control and recovery tools shows that the proposed means of control and recovery by timely localization and elimination of errors allow maintaining the coefficient $K_{ef}$ within 0.95–0.96.

In general, it follows from the obtained results that the accumulation of critical errors leads to a sharp decrease in throughput. In some cases, the accumulation of critical errors leads to a failure (within 1–4 h); in some cases, the accumulation of critical errors will not significantly affect the uptime (67 h). However, the average time to failure was 11.43 h for the case of operation of the PSU unit without means of control and recovery. Whereas with the means of control and restoration, this number is 105 h.

The time between failures established by the experiment made it possible to construct the reliability function R(t) of the operation of the PSU unit of the AS node.

In the proposed time between failures ($T_n = 3600$ s), the reliability of the software with a duration of operation without means of control and recovery of more than 10 h is significantly reduced, and with a duration of operation ($T_d$) of more than 50 h, the probability of failure-free operation is almost zero. When as the use of monitoring and recovery tools allows at $T_d = 10$ h to maintain the reliability of the software of the adaptive switching node close to 0.95–0.97, and at $T_d = 50$ h R(t) is more than 0.6.

In the case of the assumed ($T_n = 50$ h), the reliability decreases slightly, and for a very long duration $T_d$, more than 230 h, it is 0.62. for the case with control and recovery, this number is close to one.

In general, with long time between failures $T_n >> 50$ h, a significant decrease in reliability does not occur, and in this case, control and recovery tools are not used. However, when $T_n < 50$ h, the need to use controls and recovery increases.

During the experiment, it was confirmed that the distortion in pointers leads to failure: out of 20 failures, 14 were errors in the tables.

For the experiment, 1 tract with a queue and 2 lines with queues were selected.

In general, out of a set of 223 critical errors in 208 cases, critical errors did not cause a failure, however, $K_{ef}$ was significantly reduced and amounted to 0.69 and the use of control and recovery tools made it possible to improve the $K_{ef}$ to 0.962, while the number of failures was reduced by an order of magnitude.

## 5 Discussions and Conclusions

The process of destruction of design faults differs from the process of ("hardware") natural flaws. Obviously copies of (regular) software will fail together if run with the same parameters. This shows that the independence assumption is not satisfied. And the probability of failure of software copies depends entirely on the original text. This renders many principles of hardware fault tolerance ineffective for software. Instead of using redundant copies, the reliability of software can be improved through design diversity. A common approach for this is the so-called n-version programming (discussed in Avižienis, introduced by Chen and Avižienis [9]). However, research by knight and Leveson indicates that design diversity is likely to be less effective for software than n-module redundancy in hardware reliability design.

Some studies have shown that for complex systems, most failures are usually caused by software failures (see, for example, gray). While software bugs are design bugs, their behavior in reliable systems is similar to non-fixed hardware bugs. This is due to the stochastic conditions of their activation.

# References

1. Chen, X., Hou, W., Zhang, Y.: Reliability evaluation of embedded real-time system based on error scenario. In: From the book Current Trends in Computer Science and Mechanical Automation, vol. 2. Published by De Gruyter Open Poland (2022). https://doi.org/10.1515/978 3110584998-056
2. IEEE (1990) 610.12–1990 - IEEE Standard Glossary of Software Engineering Terminology, pp. 1–84
3. Dobiáš, P.: Online fault tolerant task scheduling for real-time multiprocessor embedded systems. Embedded Systems. Université Rennes 1, 2020. English. NNT: 2020REN1S024. https://hal.archives-ouvertes.fr/
4. Izosimov, V.: Scheduling and optimization of fault-tolerant embedded systems, Ph.D. Thesis, Linkopings University, November (2006)
5. Persya, C., Gopalakrishnan, T.R.: Fault tolerant real time systems. In: International Conference on Managing Next Generation Software Application (MNGSA-08), Coimbatore (2008)
6. Autopilot (2017). http://en.wikipedia.org/wiki/Autopilot
7. Guide to solving problems in probability theory and mathematical statistics: Proceedings of the allowance for university students/V. E. Gmurman. - 9th ed., erased. - M .: Higher. shk., 2004. - 404 p., ill
8. Malika, B., Kalla, H.: A fault tolerant scheduling heuristics for distributed real time embedded systems. Bul. Acad. Sci. Cybern. Inf. Technol. 18(3), 48–61 (2018)
9. Avizienis, A., Chen, L.: On the implementation of IV-version programming for software fault-tolerance during program execution. In: Proceedings of the 1977 COMPSAC, International Computer Software and Applications Conference, Chicago, pp. 149–155 (1977)

# Analytical Model for Assessing the Reliability of the Functioning of the Adaptive Switching Node

Abdujabbor Abidov, Dilmurod Mirzaaxmedov[(✉)], and Dilmurod Rasulev

Tashkent State University of Economics, Islam Karimov Street, 49, Tashkent, Uzbekistan
mirzaakhmedovdilmurod@gmail.com

**Abstract.** This paper proposes an analytical model for the functioning of the software of the switching node of a computing system in which failures and failures occur. The fault-tolerant mechanism allows some kinds of errors, limitations. It can't handle some fatal crashes or situations with a huge number of errors. When developing the model, assumptions are made about the Poisson flow of all events occurring in the node. The work of the node is considered with the method of adaptive switching. In switching nodes, which are one of the main elements of transmission, storage and processing of information in computer networks, ensuring reliability is of particular importance. In the theory of reliable software, in contrast to the theory of reliability, failure and failure are classified according to the duration of recovery. A corruption is considered a failure if it recovers in less than the threshold time, otherwise it is considered a failure. The choice of the threshold time generally depends on the maximum required time to eliminate one failure. Each system under study has its own threshold time. For example, for control on board an aircraft, the threshold time is chosen to be less than 1 s, then for control of information and reference systems in the range it is much longer.

**Keywords:** Computer network · adaptive switching · fault-tolerant systems · Poisson event flow · Markov chain · software reliability

## 1 Introduction

Currently, one of the main tasks in identifying computer networks is to ensure high noise immunity, reliability, survivability as a network as a whole, so that its elements are often exposed to failures in the transmission and processing of information.

In switching nodes (SN), which are one of the main elements of transmission, storage and processing of information in computer networks, ensuring reliability is of particular importance.

The adaptive switching (AC) node, which provides operation in the circuit switching (CS) and packet switching (PS) modes, consists of complex software that operates in a real-time (online) system in the conditions of failures of individual blocks. In this regard, the issues of monitoring and restoring the normal state of the node are vital.

Y. Koucheryavy and A. Aziz (Eds.): NEW2AN 2022, LNCS 13772, pp. 46–56, 2023.
https://doi.org/10.1007/978-3-031-30258-9_5

Based on the foregoing, the relevance of this work lies in solving a practically important problem: creating an analytical model of fault-tolerant systems. The development of an analytical model is caused by the need to study the impact of failures on the throughput and availability of the adaptive switching node software; control of the interval for switching on periodic control at various load factors; determination of the average loss of efficiency due to operational and periodic control and recovery.

## 2 Methodology

The methodological basis of the work constitutes the methods of the theory of software reliability, the theory of computer networks, and the theory of adaptive control. The work also uses the methods of probability theory, simulation modeling, queuing theory and system programming.

Reliability analysis has been a hot research topic since the early 1960s. However, most of the methods were applied at the stage of software implementation. Reliability assessment at an early stage of system design is a faster formal method. It creates a probabilistic real-time system model and time property analysis based on data synthesis. It identifies potential security threats early, so costly changes are made during the system design phase.

Due to the growing security requirements of embedded software, many studies are being carried out in the field of fault tolerance and reliability assessment. The traditional approach mainly relies on software testing fault data to predict future error behavior.

A statistical based method such as Monte Carlo simulation [1] has been used to deal with transient faults dependent on a simulation experiment with large copy numbers.

The structure of real-time software fault tolerance of the system and the method of checkpoint and temporary redundancy [2, 3] provide the main models for predicting software reliability. A. Burns [4] introduced a probabilistic model in the analysis of the order of execution in the framework of the probabilistic guarantee that all tasks are always completed by their deadlines. I. Broster [5] extended this method in the CAN network to calculate accurate predictions of the probability of failure from the probability distribution of the response time. However, these approaches [4, 5] have certain limitations and lead to extremely pessimistic results.

Security-critical applications must work correctly and within the time constraints, even in the presence of faults. G. Lima [6] proposed the worst case: analysis of response time planning for fault-tolerant hard real-time systems, taking into account the recovery of tasks started with a higher priority, and then introduced a priority assignment algorithm [7] to improve the fault tolerance of the system. They discussed the relationship between CPU usage and fault tolerance. Lee [8] proposes a new fault-tolerant prioritization algorithm based on a worst-case response-time scheduling analysis for fault-tolerant hard real-time problems with limited priority levels and arbitrarily long deadlines [9, 10]. In the scientific work [11] the worst-case response time for tasks within group proactive scheduling and checking the time property early in system design has been discussed.

M. Sebastian et al. presented a reliability assessment method [12], which calculated the reliability of a system over a certain period of time. In the study [13], a reliability model is written to analyze the possibility of scheduling in the event of failures and calculate the probability that tasks can still be scheduled in the worst-case execution scenario, but the time factor in reliability was not taken into account. References [14, 15] propose several optimization algorithms for real-time display. It identifies security-critical applications on distributed embedded systems by handling re-execution and replication for tolerable transient failures.

Another reliability method [16] focuses on transient faults such as temperature variation and electromagnetic interference rather than dealing with permanent faults.

## 3  Results

Markov's random processes are called a Markov chain when the state and time in them are discrete, and a continuous Markov chain when time is continuous [17].

In practice, random processes with continuous time are much more often encountered. For example, failure of any piece of equipment can occur at any time; the completion of the repair (recovery) of this element also cannot be fixed in advance, etc.

In such a chain, the transition of the system (S) from state to state appears to occur under the influence of some flows of events with intensity $\lambda ij$. If all these flows are Poisson (that is, ordinary and without consequences, with a constant or time-dependent intensity), then the process occurring in the system S will be Markovian [18]. In addition, if all flows of events that transfer the system from state to state are the simplest (i.e., stationary Poisson with constant intensities $\lambda ij$), then in some cases there are final (or limiting) state probabilities that do not depend on which state of the system S was at the initial moment.

For the existence of final probabilities of states, one condition $\lambda ij = \text{const}$ is not enough. The following condition must also be satisfied: if the system S has a finite number of states $S1, S2, \cdots, Sn$, then for the existence of final probabilities, it is sufficient that from any state of the system it is possible (in a certain number of steps) to go to any other.

To obtain the final state probabilities (FSP), the following mnemonic rule is used: for each state, the total value of the outgoing probability stream is equal to the total incoming one. Another way to obtain FSP is to solve algebraic equations obtained from Kolmogorov's differential equations when the left side (derivatives) is equal to zero [19, 20].

By virtue of the statement [20], if all flows of events are the simplest, then the process occurring in the QS is a Markov's random a process with discrete states and continuous time (a continuous Markov chain) for which the final state probabilities exist under the above conditions.

It is known [21, 22] that in data transmission networks the assumption of the Poisson distribution of the flows of receipt and servicing of requests is the only assumption close to reality. In [22], the admissibility of Markov chains for the analysis of the work of aircraft nodes is substantiated.

In this regard, and by virtue of the above statement, an analytical model is built on the assumption that all events occurring in the AC node constitute a simple Poisson flow.

The process of functioning of the software of the adaptive switching node in a computer system with faults without the use of control and recovery procedures (process A) and with them (process B) can be represented as a labeled graph (Fig. 1).

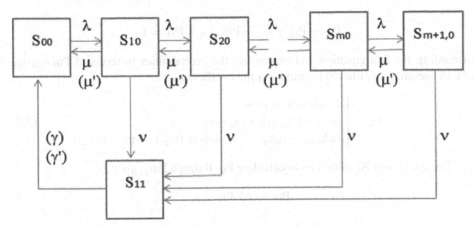

**Fig. 1.** Analytical model of the process of functioning of the software.

Of the adaptive switching node in a computer system with faults, where:

$S_{i0}$ $(i = 0, m + 1)$, $S_{11}$ in condition QS:
$S_{00}$ - QS is free and serviceable;
$S_{10}$ - the channel is busy and good, there is no queue;
$S_{20}$ - the channel is busy and in good condition, there is one request in the queue;
$S_{m0}$ - the channel is busy and in good condition, there is one request in queue $m - 1$;
$S_{m+1,0}$ - the channel is busy and good, there are m plus one request in the queue;
$S_{11}$ - the channel is faulty, is being restored;
$\lambda$ - intensity of receipt of applications;
$\mu$ - intensity of servicing applications without the use of operational control;
$\mu'$ - the intensity of servicing applications using operational control;
$\nu$ - intensity of transition to the failure state;
$\gamma$ - intensity of restoration by the operator;
$\gamma'$ - intensity of (program) recovery;
$P_{ij}$ is the probability of transition to states $S_{ij}$, where $i = 0, m + 1, j = 0,1$.

The algebraic equation for the FBS of process A is as follows:

$$\left. \begin{array}{l} \lambda P_{00} = \mu P_{10} + \gamma P_{11} \\ z P_{10} = \lambda P_{00} + \mu P_{20} \\ \quad \cdots \\ z P m_0 = \lambda P m_{1,0} + \mu P m_{+1,0} \\ (\mu + \nu) P m_{+1,0} = \lambda P m_0 \\ \gamma P_{11} = \sum_{m+1}^{i=1} Pio \end{array} \right\} \tag{3.1}$$

Taking into account the normalization condition.
where

$$z = \lambda + \mu + v$$

$$P_{00} + P_{10} + \cdots + P_{m+1,0} + P_{11} = 1$$

discarding the first equation and expressing the probabilities in terms of $P_{m+1,0}$ we obtain recurrent calculation formulas for the coefficients

$$A_K = \begin{cases} 1, \text{ where } k = m+1 \\ (\mu + v)/\lambda, \text{ where } k = m \\ (zA_{k+1} - \mu A_{k+2})/\lambda, \text{ where } 0 \le k \le m - 1 \end{cases} \tag{3.2}$$

The coefficient $A_k$ allows us to calculate $P_{k0}$ through $P_{m+1,0}$ т.е.

$$P_{k0} = Ak\,P_{m+1,0} \tag{3.3}$$

$$P_{11} = A_{11}\,P_{m+1,0} \tag{3.4}$$

where

$$A_{11} = \frac{v \sum_{i=1}^{m+1} Ai}{\gamma} \tag{3.5}$$

Taking into account the normalization condition, we have

$$P_{m+1,0} = \frac{1}{A_{11} + \sum_{i=1}^{m+1} Ai + A_0} \tag{3.6}$$

or

$$P_{m+1,0} = \frac{1}{\frac{v}{\gamma}\left(1 + \frac{\gamma}{v}\right) \sum_{i=1}^{m+1} Ai + A_0} \tag{3.7}$$

The calculation of the coefficients should be carried out in the following sequence $A_{m+1,0}, \cdots, A_0, A_{11}$.

Substituting Ak в (3.7) or Ak, $A_{11}$ в (3.6) we find $P_{m+1,0}$. The probability of Pk (k = 1, m) and $P_{11}$ are found according to the formulas (3.3), (3.4).

According to [17], the relative throughput is calculated by the formula

$$Q = (1 - \text{Potk})(1 - P_{11})\text{pp} \tag{3.8}$$

where: Potk - the probability of denial of service, $(1 - P_{11})$ - the probability of being in a working state, p - the probability that the channel will not fail during the service of requests $(p = \mu/(\mu + v))$, p is the probability of error-free service in case of a malfunction, when both for the council does not entail aircraft failure (or p is the ratio of the number of correctly processed applications to the total number of accepted applications).

This scheme allows you to determine the coefficient of loss of efficiency Knom, which is characterized by the probability of being in a state of recovery after errors – $P_{11}$. Then it is possible to calculate the readiness of the CS of process A by the formula

$$Krq = 1 - Knom \qquad (3.9)$$

For the process of functioning of the software of the adaptive switching node in the aircraft with faults using control and recovery procedures (process B), the analytical model is similar to the model of process A. The only difference is that instead of the parameters $\mu$ and $\gamma$, $\mu'$ and $\gamma'$ are used. The parameter $\sigma'$ takes into account the temporary redundancy introduced by operational control into the software of the AC node. If $\mu = 1/Tobs$, then

$$\mu' = \frac{1}{T'obs} = \frac{1}{Tobs + \sigma'} \qquad (3.10)$$

where Tobs, T'obs - service time of one application without operational control and with it.

A formula has been obtained to determine the number of processed applications, after which periodic control will not introduce temporary redundancy into the operation of the software of the AC node. This formula looks like this

$$n = \frac{Tpk}{\frac{\beta z - \beta p}{\lambda} - Tok}, \quad \frac{\beta z - \beta p}{\lambda} > Tok \qquad (3.11)$$

where, $\lambda$ – intensity of receipt of applications; Tpk – is the time of performing periodic control implemented in the BCD, Current is the total time of operational control; $\beta z$ – the given value of the load factor, $\beta p$ – its real value.

When formula (3.11) was obtained, it was assumed that during the operation of the adaptive switching node, due to the non-stationarity of the flow of requests, the actual network load may have a value $\beta p$ less than $\beta z$, i.e.

$$\beta p < \beta_3 \qquad (3.12)$$

and the value of $\beta_3$ (the loading factor of the AC node software using operational and periodic control) is less.

$$\beta' p \leq \beta p + \lambda \sigma' \qquad (3.13)$$

Using the right side of inequality (3.12) and formula (3.13), we determine the average time constraints for a one-time execution of control and restoration tools

$$\beta p + \lambda \sigma' \leq \beta z, \quad \sigma' \leq \frac{\beta z - \beta p}{\lambda}$$

In this regard, $\sigma'$ is summed from the costs of operational control (Current) and the remaining time ($\sigma_{pk}$)

$$Tok + \sigma_{pk} \leq (\beta z - \beta p)/\lambda$$

or

$$\sigma_{pk} \leq (\beta z - \beta p)/\lambda - Tok \qquad (3.14)$$

Periodic control execution time ($Tpk$) may exceed $\sigma_{p\kappa}$ to n me therefore

$$Tpk/\sigma_{pk} = (\beta z - \beta p)/\lambda - Tok \qquad (3.15)$$

The parameter n in formula (3.15) is the average number of serviced requests, after which the launch of periodic control does not impose temporary redundancy on the software of the AC node.

The performance of the analytical model and the discussion of the results will be considered using an example. Let: $Tpk = 0.003c$, $Tok = 0.0009c$, $\beta p = \mathbf{0.60}$, $\beta z = 0.65$, $\lambda = 40$, $\mu = 66.66$, then $\mathbf{n} = (0.003/(0.65–0.6)/40 – 0.0009) = 9.23$.

The resulting $\mathbf{n}$ shows that after 10 serviced requests, it is possible to perform periodic control with minimal time costs.

In another example, it is possible to plot the dependence of the interval of periodic control on the intensity of receipt of requests for $\beta z = \mathbf{0.8}$, $\mu = 50$, Tpk = 0.003c, Tок = 0.00078c and different $\lambda$: 30; 31; 32; 33; 34; 35; 36; 37; 38; 39 Accordingly received: 5, 6; 7; 9; 11; 14; 21; 36; 110; 2803.

In the formula (3.11) n depends on $\lambda$, for $\lambda \rightarrow 0$, mean $n \rightarrow 0$. Therefore

$$\boldsymbol{Tmin} = n/\lambda \qquad (3.16)$$

This shows that when $\lambda$ is less than 40, it is possible to perform periodic control without compromising the operation time of the unit. The time interval for the launch of periodic control Tmin is determined by the ratio of the number of serviced requests (n) to the intensity of requests received ($\lambda$).

The readiness of the AC node software using control and recovery tools is determined by the formula:

$$Krq = (1 - P_{11})(1 - Kpok) \qquad (3.17)$$

where, **Kpok** - coefficient of loss of efficiency due to operational control.

The graph diagram shown in Fig. 1 can be used to analyze the functioning of both the entire software of the AC node and a single unit.

For the case of functioning of the entire software of the AC node, when the load of the node software $\beta$ is summed from the load of each block $\beta i$, ($i = 1, k$ where k - number of node blocks)

$$\beta = \beta_1 + \beta_2 + \ldots + \beta k \qquad (3.18)$$

or

$$\frac{\lambda}{\mu} = \frac{\lambda_1}{\mu_1} + \frac{\lambda_2}{\mu_2} + \ldots + \frac{\lambda_k}{\mu_k}$$

And

$$Tobs = \frac{\sum_{i=1}^{k} \frac{\lambda i}{\mu i}}{\lambda} \qquad (3.19)$$

The processing time for applications of the l-th block can be calculated by the formula

$$T'obs = 1/\mu i \tag{3.20}$$

## 4 Discussion

Many CSs are based on the packet switching method [23–26]. However, in recent years, very close attention has been paid to the creation of networks with hybrid switching methods, which combine the capabilities of several switching methods: channels, messages, and packets. At the same time, hybrid switching, which combines the methods of circuit switching (CS) and packet switching (PS), makes it possible to efficiently transmit displaced traffic. These methods include fixed threshold hybrid switching, floating threshold hybrid switching, and adaptive switching.

The adaptive switching method, which allows you to dynamically redistribute the bandwidth of the path between the CS and the PS, depending on the network traffic, is the most efficient in comparison with other hybrid switching methods [27, 28].

Based on the above considerations, the architecture of the AC node can be represented by elements of the physical, logical and software structure. The elements of the physical structure for the AC node are: multiplexers, modems, adapters, computer facilities (RAM, processor, input-output channels, etc.). The logical and program structure is mainly made up of software applications: the operating system of the AC node, data flow control programs, programs for the logical connection of the processing process, information transfer with a physical device, storage data structures and logical connection between them, etc.

In the AC node, each path and subscriber line are duplex, reception and transmission are carried out simultaneously.

In the general algorithm of functioning of the AC node, the execution of each function by any block is carried out using the data of the AC node. At a throughput of 40 packets/s, the packet switching unit accesses the required internal data structures of the adaptive switching node 40 times per second. Such a number can be more than 144 thousand accesses to the main memory of the computer (during one hour of operation of the block), since all internal data is stored in the common memory area (PLO) of the computer.

The fault-tolerant mechanism allows some kinds of errors, limitations. It cannot handle some fatal errors or situations with a huge number of errors. In [29], under the assumption that the fault reach is a Poisson process, a fault-tolerant model of an embedded system is approximately proposed. In the analysis of fault-tolerant planning, breadth-first methods are used to construct real-time system error scenarios. In addition, the key new algorithm proposed in the paper is designed to calculate the reliability of the system. The results of the experiment show the feasibility of the proposed evaluation method.

The fault-tolerant mechanism allows some kinds of errors, limitations. It cannot handle some fatal errors or situations with a huge number of errors. In [29], under the assumption that the fault reach is a Poisson process, a fault-tolerant model of an embedded system is approximately proposed. In the analysis of fault-tolerant planning, breadth-first methods are used to construct real-time system error scenarios. In addition, the key new algorithm proposed in the paper is designed to calculate the reliability of the system. The results of the experiment show the feasibility of the proposed evaluation method.

Currently [29], embedded software operating in safety-critical systems such as avionics, mission calculation and vehicle control is mainly used to collect information from external stimuli and respond to various interferences in a timely manner environment. To meet the requirements for its critical properties, especially reliability, it is necessary to accurately assess the fault tolerance capability of the real-time system, otherwise failure to meet the time requirements can lead to system failures, which can lead to catastrophic consequences. Reliability [30] is the ability of a system or component to perform its assigned functions under specified conditions for a certain period of time.

A typical example of them is described in [31]. A symmetrical computing system with three identical computers and copies of the programs implemented on them, which controls the railway traffic in real time, failed only 7 times in three years of operation, 5 of them due to errors in the programs.

Real-time systems can be divided into hard real-time systems, in which the consequences of timing violations can be catastrophic, and soft real-time systems, in which the consequences are relatively tolerable. In hard real-time systems, it is important that tasks are completed on time even in the event of a failure [32]. Examples of hard real time systems are space station control systems, autopilot systems, and critical care patient monitoring systems. In soft real-time systems, it is more important to detect a fault as soon as possible than to mask it. Examples of soft real-time systems are all kinds of applications for booking airline tickets, banking and e-commerce.

A fault-tolerant system must continue to work, despite the failure of some of its parts, it must have spare capacity to run. There are two ways to make the system more fault tolerant [33]. Hardware: This method relies on adding additional redundant hardware to the system to make it fault-tolerant. Software: This method relies on duplication of code, process, or even messages, depending on the context.

A typical example of the application of the above methods can be an autopilot system on board a large passenger aircraft [34].

A passenger aircraft usually consists of a central autopilot system with two other backups. This is an example of providing system resiliency by adding redundant hardware.

## 5 Conclusion and Suggestions

Embedded electronic devices may operate in an undefined environment. Electromagnetic interference, voltage fluctuations, and high or low temperatures can easily cause intermittent or permanent failures in semiconductor devices, potentially leading to operational errors in a real-time system. To cope with such a situation, real-time systems usually have a fail-safe mechanism.

There are two main approaches to solving the problem of reliability of computing systems, the first of which is aimed at achieving failure-free operation, and the second - fault-tolerant operation, both of which apply to both hardware and software. These approaches complement each other.

Both approaches were considered in the work and an analytical model was developed that allows evaluating the usefulness of the functioning of both autonomously executed blocks of an adaptive switching node and the entire node software with and without control and recovery tools. The implemented program for calculating the reliability indicators of the software of the AC node makes it possible to obtain on a computer various dependences of the throughput and readiness of the software of the adaptive switching node. Software-computed data results show that the use of monitoring and recovery tools significantly increases throughput while reducing the probability of being in a failure state by more than ten times. This increases the fault tolerance of switching nodes.

# References

1. Sebastian, M., Ernst, R.: Modelling and designing reliable on-chip-communication devices in MPSoCs with real-time requirements. In: 13th IEEE International Conference on Emerging Technologies and Factory Automation, pp. 1465–1472 (2008)
2. Anderson, T., Knight, J.C.: A framework for software fault tolerance in real-time systems. IEEE Trans. Softw. Eng. SE-9(3), 355–364 (1983)
3. Krishna, C.M., Singh, A.D.: Reliability of checkpointed real-time systems using time redundancy. IEEE Trans. Reliab. 42(3), 427–435 (1993)
4. Bums, A., Punnekkat, S., Strigini, L., Wright, D.R.: Probabilistic scheduling guarantees for fault-tolerant real-time systems. In: Dependable Computing for Critical Applications, pp. 361–378 (1999)
5. Broster, I., Burns, A., Rodriguez-Navas, G.: Probabilistic analysis of CAN with faults. In: 23rd IEEE Real-Time Systems Symposium, pp. 269–278 (2002)
6. de A. Lima, G.M., Burns, A.: An effective schedulability analysis for fault-tolerant hard real-time systems. In: 3rd Euromicro Conference on Real-Time Systems, pp. 209–216 (2001)
7. de A. Lima, G.M., Burns, A.: An optimal fixed-priority assignment algorithm for supporting fault-tolerant hard real-time systems. IEEE Trans. Comput. 52(10), 1332–1346 (2003)
8. Li, J., Yang, F., Lu, Y.: A feasible schedulability analysis for fault-tolerant hard real-time systems. In: Proceeding of the 10th IEEE International Conference on Engineering of Complex Computer Systems, pp. 176–183 (2005)
9. Li, J., Yang, F., Tu, G., Cao, W., Lu, Y.: Schedulability analysis for fault-tolerant hard real-time tasks with limited priority levels. In: The 4th International Conference on Autonomic and Trusted Computing, pp. 529–538 (2007)
10. Li, J., Yang, F., Lu, Y.: Schedulability analysis for fault-tolerant hard real-time tasks with arbitrary large deadlines. In: The 6th International Symposium on Parallel and Distributed Computing, pp. 149–156 (2007)
11. Wu, Z., Wang, L., Yang, G., Zheng, Z.: Schedulability analysis for fault-tolerant group-based preemptive scheduling. J. Pervasive Comput. Commun. 1(3), 71–76 (2005)
12. Sebastian, M., Ernst, R.: Reliability analysis of single bus communication with real-time requirements. In: 15th IEEE Pacific Rim International Symposium on Dependable Computing, Shanghai, pp. 3–10 (2009)
13. Gui, S., Luo, L.: Reliability analysis of real-time fault-tolerant task models. Des. Autom. Embed. Syst. 17(1), 87–107 (2013). https://doi.org/10.1007/s10617-013-9120-7
14. Izosimov, V., Pop, P., Eles, P., Peng, Z.: Design optimization of time- and cost-constrained fault-tolerant distributed embedded systems. In: Proceedings of Design, Automation and Test in Europe, pp. 864–869 (2005)

15. Eles, P., Izosimov, V., Pop, P., Peng, Z.: Synthesis of fault-tolerant embedded systems. In: Proceedings of the Conference on Design, Automation and Test in Europe, pp. 1117–1122 (2008)

16. Головкин, Б.А.: Многовариантное программирование и его применение, Автомат. и телемех. выпуск **7**, 5–39 (1986)

17. Вентцель, Е.С.: Исследование операции. Советское радио, p. 551 (1972)

18. Овчаров, Л.А.: Прикладные задачи теории массового обслуживания. Машиностроение, p. 324 (1969)

19. Вентцель, Е.С.: Исследование операций: принципы, методология. Наука, p. 207 (1980)

20. Вентцель, Е.С., Овчаров, Л.А.: Прикладные задачи теории вероятностей.– Радио и связь, p. 416 (1983)

21. Мартин, Дж.: Системный анализ передачи данных. II – том.- Мир, p. 431 (1975)

22. Шарейко, Л.А.: Проблема эффективности вычислительных сетей и пути ее повышения. АН СССР. –Научный совет по комплексной проблеме кибернетики, p. 72 (1981)

23. Глушков, В.М.: и др. Сети ЭВМ,- Связь, p. 280 (1977)

24. Геленбе, Е.: Модель восстановления информации методом кратных контрольных точек. Автоматика и телемеханика, **4**, 142–151 (1979)

25. Якубайтис, Э.А.: Архитектура вычислительных сетей.- Статистика, p. 279 (1980)

26. Якубайтис, З.Я.: Информационно-вычислительные сети. Финансы и статистика (1984)

27. Самойленко, С.И.: Эффективность информационного обмена в сетях ЭВМ. Проблемы МСНТИ. МЦНТИ, №. 2, pp. 76–84 (1981)

28. Самойленко, С.И.: Оценка эффективности адаптивной коммутации в сетях интегрального обслуживания. Вопросы кибернетики. Проблемы теории вычислительных сетей/Под ред.Самойленко С.И,- АН СССР. Научный совет по комплексной проблеме кибернетики (1983)

29. Chen, X., Hou, W., Zhang, Y.: Reliability Evaluation of Embedded Real-Time System Based on Error Scenario. From the Book Current Trends in Computer Science and Mechanical Automation, vol. 2. De Gruyter Open Poland (2022).https://doi.org/10.1515/9783110584998-056

30. IEEE: 610.12-1990 - IEEE Standard Glossary of Software Engineering Terminology, pp 1–84 (1990)

31. Ихара, Х., Фукуока, К., Кубо, Ю., Ёкота, Ц.: Отказоустойчивая вычислительная система с тремя симметричными вычислительными машинами. ТИИЭР **66**(10), 68–89 (1978)

32. Persya, C., Gopalakrishnan, T.R.: Fault tolerant real time systems. In: International Conference on Managing Next Generation Software Application (MNGSA 2008), Coimbatore (2008)

33. Kumar, A.: Scheduling for Fault-Tolerant Distributed Embedded Systems, IEEE Computer (2008)

34. Autopilot (2007). http://en.wikipedia.org/wiki/Autopilot

# Artificial Intelligence Software Architecture in the Field of Cardiology and Application in the Cardio Vessel Project Using CJM and Customer Development Methods

Dilafruz Nurjabova[1], Qulmatova Sayyora[2]([✉]), and Pardayeva Gulmira[1]

[1] Tashkent University of Information Technologies Karshi Branch "Software Engineering", 180118 Karshi, Uzbekistan
[2] Deparment of "Digital Economy and Information Technologies", Tashkent State University of Economics, 49, Uzbekistan Av., 100003 Tashkent, Uzbekistan
squlmatova@mail.ru

**Abstract.** The article is devoted to the task of automating tasks for the Cardio Vessel project, on the basis of which a platform is designed—an independent model of object-oriented software architecture within the framework of a model-oriented approach for the Cardio Vessel project in UML and the CJM and customer development projects is proposed. The article formalizes the problem of UML class diagrams, sequence diagrams, and precedents and offers mathematical models based on the Navier—Stokes method for defining the function of structural semantics of UML class diagrams and descriptions of semantically equivalent transformations. Algorithms for transforming Star UML class diagrams and calculating object-oriented metrics are also proposed. The paper presents a UML software tool that allows analysis using UML class diagrams. In conclusion, the CJM and customer development methodology for UML class diagrams using the Star UML software tool have been developed.

**Keywords:** software design · software architecture · CJM · customer development · UML · Sequence diagram · class diagram · Object diagram

## 1 Introduction

17.5 million people die from cardiovascular diseases every year. More than 75% of these deaths occur in low- and middle-income countries. According to these statistics, early heart attacks and cardiovascular diseases can be prevented by 80%. Treatment of cardiovascular diseases and proper diagnosis are very expensive. The coronographic "golden diagnostic method" is widely used in Uzbekistan at the Research Institute of Cardiology. This work has been studied by such scientists as Alfio Quarteroni, Manzoni A., Vergara S., F. N. Vande Vose, Eindhoven, Italy and the Netherlands. However, since problems in the network of atherosclerotic vessels in the treatment of cardiovascular diseases still exist, doctors need software. In Uzbekistan, the "golden diagnostic method"

© The Author(s), under exclusive license to Springer Nature Switzerland AG 2023
Y. Koucheryavy and A. Aziz (Eds.): NEW2AN 2022, LNCS 13772, pp. 57–72, 2023.
https://doi.org/10.1007/978-3-031-30258-9_6

of coronography is widely used in the Research Institute of Cardiology. In accordance with the Decree of the President of the Republic of Uzbekistan dated February 26, 2003 "On measures for further reform of the healthcare system" PR-3214 dated February 26, 2003 and Resolution of the Cabinet of Ministers No. 140 dated March 17, 2003, the Research Institute of Cardiology and the 15th City Clinical Hospital were established on the basis of the Decree of the President of the Republic of Uzbekistan No. PF-5216 dated October 30, 2017 (National Database of Legal Documents, October 30, 2017, No. 17.06.5216/0187) with additions and amendments. The Republican Center for the Development of Medical Education of the Ministry of Health of the Republic of Uzbekistan's project "Improvement of the healthcare system (Health-3)" Collection of Clinical Protocols on Cardiovascular Diseases for Doctors of District and City Medical Associations according to the Order of the Minister of Health No. 57 dated February 1, 2016 PR. The main purpose of the organization of RICM is to provide qualified cardiological care to the population at the level of international standards through the introduction of modern methods of treatment and diagnosis of cardiac patients into the practice of healthcare. At the Institute of Scientific Expertise in Cardiology of Uzbekistan, the main analyses necessary for the patient can be performed directly in the laboratory, which reduces the time of the patient's stay in the hospital. Such examinations include: daily ECG monitoring; a test with physical activity on a bicycle ergometer and treadmill; determination of EchoECG; cholesterol and its fractions; sugar profile; determination of glycated hemoglobin; study of platelet aggregation activity; and study of endothelial functions. Direct cooperation with the trauma center named after V. Vohidov allows carrying out complex examinations necessary for the patient (coronary angiography, myocardial scintigraphy to assess the reserve of coronary circulation) and treatment methods (coronary angioplasty and stenting). But the software for solving the above problem helps solve 85% of the problems in cardiology.

Why is this topic relevant? There are many people in the world suffering from diseases of the cardiovascular system. Our fathers and mothers, great-grandmothers and great-grandfathers, a newborn child got sick with some kind of heart symptom or a person got sick and many suffered. In order to solve this problem, we used customer journey mapping, customer development, SWOT analysis, and UML. All data and results were used in the competition Tumaris.Tech.

Tumaris.Tech is one of the largest projects implemented by IT Park Uzbekistan in cooperation with the United States Agency for International Development (USAID). It was launched in July 2020. The Tumaris.Tech program fully supports women's business initiatives. The project consists of several components. It aims to increase the involvement of women in the ICT ecosystem and includes areas ranging from BPO (Business Process Outsourcing) development to education for women aspiring freelancers, startup development, and investment training. In two years, the project has borne fruit in the form of 30 startups and more than 200 girls have had the opportunity to get an IT education. Currently, the project is expanding throughout Central Asia, and now representatives of Kazakhstan, Kyrgyzstan, Turkmenistan, and Tajikistan can participate in Tumaris.Tech programs. I am a listener and a winner of this Tumaris.Tech start-up center gaining more knowledge and skills. I am participating in my start-up project "Cardio Vessel" and this project is about creating a two-phase model based on hemodynamic laws in the calculation of blood velocity in thrombi and plaques in cardiovascular diseases and the expression of blood through filtration problems.

To solve this problem and compile the Customer Journey Map, Customer Development, SWOT analysis, and UML design, each component was thoroughly considered, an analysis was made in the form of tables and diagrams, and the articles of some scientists and specialists in the Scopus database were studied. It is understood that each part is meant by Customer Journey Map, Customer Development, SWOT analysis, and UML design. [1] in his article to suggest that the level of customer satisfaction with tourist accommodation is an important prerequisite when the goal is to build a loyal relationship with this type of facility. The study involved 239 participants (50% women) who have been using tourist sites for the past 2 years and have been studying here for the first part [1, 4]. We are considering our project "Cardio Vessel" to create a Customer Journey Map, knowing that the main pain points of the client as a type of patient are what problems in cardiology exactly will need to be studied and proposed. Other scientists: [2–4] offer implementation from the customer's path to the path of consumption: the approach of consumer culture to the study of value creation in practical consumption, behavior when searching for information at the stage of the customer's path after purchase and the management of customer experience: on the way to the implementation of a developing marketing concept [1, 9]. In our case, the client should be offered the elimination of pain in which all patients meet a doctor's visit on time. In the following examples, we considered all the pains of the doctor and the client. The doctor consciously accepts the patient, knowing that the program works according to the assigned tasks and accepts according to the numerical method where diagrams in UML are suggested.

Scientists like [26–30] in their articles, they offered to work with UML models in graphical form and offered to design from the best point of view to create a software architecture for the project, and we used the best modeling tools in UML. Scientists also investigated using a mathematical model. A small business is always built on the behavior and habits of its clients [1, 9]. These are international corporations and monopolists who have the resources to dictate their rules to the market and retrain people. Small business is about something else—about servicing what is already there.

The main user of the chatbot is not an entrepreneur, but his client. Therefore, the card is based on the behavior of this very client [1, 9].

Small businesses have something to respond to every action, inaction, wish and client's question. We emphasize that this is not about satisfying any whim, not about "the customer is always right", but only about embedding business in customer behavior. Taking into account the interests and limitations of the business, of course.

By the way, this is a typical problem—ignoring the client's behavior or misunderstanding his entire path. The business does something, but it does not fully understand how this something relates to the client's life. This is partly why CJM is so popular, which is forced by its format to straighten the client's path and decompose it into steps [1, 9].

Customer Journey Map (CJM) is a detailed and beautiful table that step—by-step describes the user's path to your product, from desire to completion of the transaction and even after!

In this project we will consider the disease of cardiac problems and description in UML. In order to create software in the framework of the architecture, we link the project with CJM [1, 9].

## 2 Methods

The UML language provides users with an easily perceivable and expressive visual modeling language specifically designed for the development and documentation of models of complex systems for a variety of purposes. The constructive use of the UML language is based on an understanding of the general principles of modeling complex systems and the features of the process of object-oriented analysis and design in particular [25, 30]. The choice of expressive means for constructing models of complex systems determines the tasks that can be solved using these models. At the same time, one of the basic principles of constructing models of complex systems is the principle of abstraction, which states that one should include in the model only those aspects of the designed system that are directly related to the performance of the system's functions or its intended purpose. At the same time, all minor details are omitted so as not to overly complicate the process of analysis and research of the resulting model. Another principle of constructing models of complex systems is the principle of multi-delity [25, 30]. This principle is a statement that no single model can adequately describe various aspects of a complex system. In software architecture, it is divided into 2 parts so that we can represent systems. These are dynamic and static parts. In the dynamic part, we will use a sequence diagram. The reason why the system is a dynamic system is that we have to take into account every piece of information that comes to us, which is variable. The data is changing, but we need to analyze how the processes within the system have changed in the chain. The server in the hospital was considered the hospital because the projects we are implementing, architectures, are basically diagrams needed to represent the Cardio Vessel project using these dynamic diagrams [25, 30].

So the mountain hospital is the first object, the district is the second object in the hospital, the admin server is divided into the third object, doctors-into the fourth object, and doctors-into the fifth object. The first object we have is Podgorny. We used Lifeline to present the hospital as a lifeline regarding the realization of our facility in this life. This means that in order for us to program our dynamic system as a process, each process uses the states in which we implement its program code. This means that Lifeline is a Life Line, the first of which has become linear. All these lines on the Sequence Diagram are a lifeline. Patient going is a patient who is going to look for a doctor. We send the message via FindDoctor so we can find a doctor. The main task of Link is to find a FindDoctor, that is, a doctor, if we focus on the main part of the interaction here. We find the doctor through the message. Here we also have 2 different asynchronous messages and a creative message. All messages are different from each other, and that's what we represent. In order for us to use Link, we need to have internet access because it has to work with the internet. We represent it as Link. When we look further, we see that the long-tailed Massage is shown then eating the Searchingdoctor. That means we've found the doctor. Then we send a message to the Replyto doctor, and then the Replyto doctor also responds to us. Replyto's task is to respond to the sent message in the Fig. 1. At the end, we used the DataBase database [25, 30]. This is done through the database. Note that at the top of the rectangle, two diagonals passing through its center are valid. The actor will look like this on the sequence diagram.

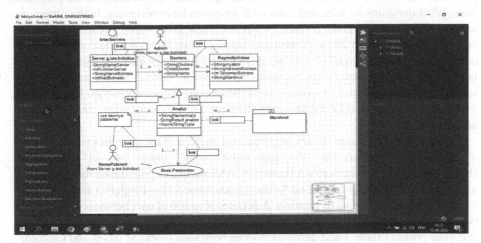

**Fig. 1.** A Class Diagram

It will be easy to write a program if we create an executable architecture in our environment before writing one [10, 24]. We know that if we use START UML from the real original version that was registered and not from the Demo version, of course we can make it an expert in other programming languages such as Python, PHP, Java, etc. (Fig. 2).

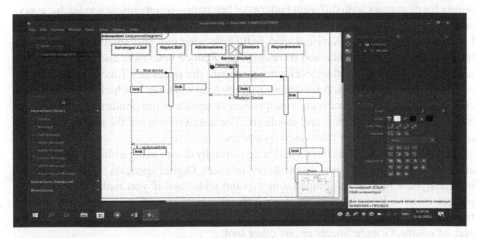

**Fig. 2.** Sequence Diagram

This is an analytics tool needed to understand the client, improve his experience and, of course, earn more by increasing conversion and brand loyalty.

The customer path map is a scenario of interaction between a potential buyer and your e-commerce project. It is based on large-scale analytics data, takes into account the psychology of consumer behavior, and shows what the user is doing at each stage [10, 24]. What solutions to his tasks he is waiting for and how he reacts to the proposed ones, what questions he asks, and even what emotions he experiences, In the future, we will use Cardio Vessel in the project. In this document given Table 1. Customer Development, Doctors (from 28 to 45 men and women, https://docs.google.com/document/d/1P3zdSsVGLJ60J87tqmTgRvGYwgdhQEVMkAd0Xi6gJA/edit?usp=sharing) about making friendly user design. As can been this document Table 2. SWOT analysis, Doctors (from 28 to 45 men and women, https://docs.google.com/document/d/1M4bx2j8b9wEjnuo9vPu0FTCsh4JAZ0bLkh-vmdKJBhI/edit?usp=sharing) who can participated and shown.

The client's travel map is very important for startups at the analytics stage (Fig. 3).

The map is needed to understand what must be in the MVP (https://lushrussia.com/export/w/Oxana/p/2CASE/m/Sparks.png?theme=default&isexport=true&isBranding=false&hasArtifactHeader=true&viewId=jleFx) and what will need to be added first of all as it grows. A detailed scenario of user behavior will help not only to prioritize but also to attract investors—it will show who, how, and why they will use your project (Table 1 and Table 2). As can been seen from the tables and Customer development below, conclusion of doctors give finally decision. This result influence MPV finally product for Cardio Vessel.

The Table 2 below provides an overview of certain relevant international projects characteristics in each project concerned and compared with each other parameters.

The path map for a stable business will help improve service and increase revenue because customer orientation at each stage increases all key performance indicators (KPIs): Simplify the path to the target action. Fewer obstacles—more orders and higher conversion. Increase audience reach. Additional options for interaction at important points for customers with different patterns of behavior—a convenient service for everyone. Increase brand loyalty. Positive user experiences result in more repeat customers. Find the growth points. A visual map will show what can and should be changed to improve the user experience and increase sales. Reduce your risks and your costs. You will be able to invest in the development of only the necessary functionality and the necessary marketing tools. A Customer Journey Map is a table in which each step of the customer on the way to receiving your product or service corresponds to descriptions of his goals, actions, questions, and emotions. The last two lines are the problems that the consumer may face when choosing you and their solutions.

A rough version of the client's path map is usually drawn using a blackboard, marker, and stickers, or here, as here "on the knee" in Excel. Digital agencies turn such "drafts" into analytical reports-infographics in a brand style, and if you make CJM for your project, it can look like literally anything. You can remotely work as a team with templates from the paid Touchpoint Dashboard service or the free Miro, use Canvanizer or Trello, and, of course, Google Sheets or any other tool.

A Customer Journey Map (CJM) is a detailed and beautiful table that step-by-step describes the user's path to your product, from desire to completion of the transaction and even after!

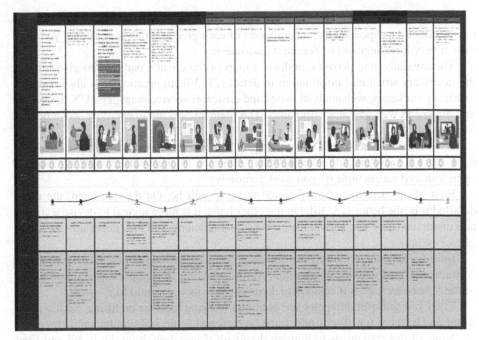

**Fig. 3.** CJM for the Cardio Vessel project

This is an analytics tool needed to understand the client, improve his experience and, of course, earn more by increasing conversion and brand loyalty. The most important and large-scale stage To build a Customer Journey Map, you will need everything you can squeeze out of your web analytics, from all the components of the sales funnel to heatmaps and session recordings. We use Google Analytics data, Hotjar session recordings, and Yandex. Metrica also offers survey creation and feedback form processing services. Inquire with customers and managers, observe how competitors are faring, monitor mentions on social media, hold focus groups, and so on. You need to know in every detail who your customers are, how they think, and what they want.

The second part of the preparation is the most interesting. All the data received must be packed into "characters". This is what collective images of the main representatives of your target audience are called. "Persona" displays a group of people of the same age, gender, and wealth, as well as those with similar professions, hobbies, and many others. Depending on the specifics of your business, one or more characteristics will be more important than others. For example, if you are developing a navigator for the sights of the city, then the most important thing becomes lifestyle. The product should be equally convenient for those who just want to take a walk with children, those who are interested in cultural centers, and those who go to a conditional concert and crave "adult" entertainment.

A Customer Journey Map (CJM) is a detailed and beautiful table that step-by-step describes the user's path to your product, from desire to completion of the transaction and even after!

You can draw separate CJMS for each person or split all the lines into several to take into account the expectations and emotions of each group. If this is not done, you may miss a very large segment of potential customers.

Theoretically, one person can draw a map of the client's path if you give him all the necessary structured information in detail [25, 30]. In practice, it is always easier to attract marketers, web analysts, sales and customer service managers, UX designers, and managers who will make decisions. The main thing is not to overdo it—6–8 people will be enough.

By the time of the scheduled meeting, all specialists should already have access to the collected analytics data. Now all that remains is to arm yourself with a marker or open a shared access table (if you work remotely).

First of all, determine how detailed the map will be. On the one hand, the more detailed it is, the better [25, 30]. On the other hand, it is more logical to devise a simple and understandable way to find the most critical moments and then delve into the study of each stage.

In order for everyone to figure out what needs to be done in practice, the first two columns are filled with the whole team. At the same time, it is important to act on behalf of the "character", even if customers do not behave as you would like.

Then you can split into pairs and continue working together on filling. So it will go faster and be more fun. The results must be reviewed again and supplemented together.

Now all that remains is to digitize the result if you drew it on the board and send it to everyone involved in case they want to add something within a couple of days. Additionally, be sure to show the card to the focus group of clients and other employees whose opinions you would like to hear.

## 3   Conclusion

Most often, it is deviations from the main route that pose the greatest difficulty for users. It's one thing to walk a section of the way in a bad mood; another thing is to find yourself in a situation in which movement is simply impossible.

As an example, consider the CJM of an attending physician who works with patients connected to a remote blood pressure monitoring program and in cardiology. We have a detailed case study of the project itself.

The doctor observes the patient as usual, i.e., through regular appointments, analysis of changes, and correction of appointments. In addition to therapy, the patient also receives a wearable device for monitoring blood pressure. The data from the device is fed into the information system, and the doctor can work with it both during the appointment and between appointments.

It is difficult to describe the work of a doctor in the form of a traditional CJM, because his actions depend on the situation. Simply put, the path is not linear at all. It includes branches and loops. Despite this, the doctor-patient system works, and we don't even need to accurately display this process on the map. It is documented and regulated, and the doctor and his superior are directly responsible for its implementation. What is in our interest then?

Our interest is to help the doctor cope with situations that do not require medical competence at all. Simply put, working with deviations.

Take a look at CJM. It looks like a complex, confusing, but still working mechanism. And that's exactly what we need [25, 30]. We do not need to thoroughly understand the workings of this mechanism; its complexity is due to medical regulations and treatment plans. The doctor himself ensures the operability of this mechanism. But not everything. Some points on the map are outside of what the doctor can influence.

Naturally, it is not simple enough to identify deviations or offer general solutions. The map sets the starting point for finding a solution for each item. Somewhere a tool is needed, somewhere a technical solution, somewhere the connection of service personnel is required, and somewhere a doctor's training or additional instructions.

The result of working through CJM in this format is the elimination of all "exit points." In other words, we insure the doctor against unforeseen situations.

Was it possible to visualize the same information in a traditional way? Absolutely, yes. But the point of visualization is not to put the data on a standardized canvas. Its purpose is to help the reader perceive information by focusing it on the important [25, 30].

Techies think of solutions. For example, often an IT developer boldly and fairly declares that he has a universal platform for something. For example, for monitoring. What to monitor at the same time—what difference does it make? The core is one thing, and you can screw up any interface. That's right, as long as we're talking about technology, not about the product [25, 30].

The product is a very specific thing. You need to have a certain expertise (usually there is one) and courage (it's more difficult here) to pack a super functional solution into a narrow and extremely specific tool. The product framework is explicitly defined in the diagram. Who is to blame and what to do? We begin to correct errors. A Customer Journey Map is a very powerful tool for improving your product. If you are creating a map for a startup, you will be able to immediately release an MVP, taking into account the specifics of the target audience and refining it while remaining faithful to customer orientation (Fig. 4).

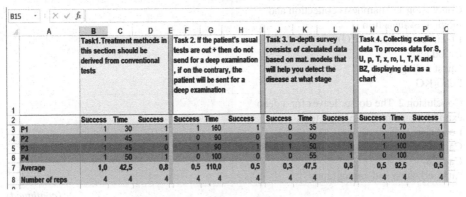

**Fig. 4.** Metric of Mathematical modeling

**Table 1.** Research questions, Doctors (from 28 to 45 men and women)

| Research questions | Answers |
|---|---|
| Question 1. If you want to display your tests, go to the apps, describe your actions, and complete the task: Collect medical history and check up<br>Electrocardiogram (ECG)<br>Blood tests<br>Chest radiography. Echo-KG<br>All parameters must be entered<br>1. Coronary artery angioplasty<br>2. Stenting action | Answer 1. Medical history and medical examination<br>Electrocardiogram (ECG)<br>Blood tests<br>Chest radiography<br>Echo-KG |
| Question 2. You want to display the tests in the app, send a doctor to check up, describe your actions and complete the task, and the doctor will go for a deep examination: Functional lung tests<br>Load test<br>Cardiac magnetic resonance imaging (MRI)<br>Cardiac catheterization and angiography | Answer 2. In the system, it is necessary to display all the existing data on deep examination: Functional pulmonary tests<br>Load test<br>Cardiac magnetic resonance imaging (MRI)<br>Cardiac catheterization and angiography |
| Question 3. You should send the patient for an in-depth examination 1. Coronary classiography, 2. Myocardial scintigraphy to assess the reserve of coronary circulation | Answer 3. The sent patients should be deeply iced and all the apparatuses should be displayed to get the result. Existing parameters S, U, p, t, x, $r_0$, L, T, K, and BZ, data displayed as a diagram |
| Question 4. The nurse outputs data to check the correctness of parameters related to blood vessel diseases | Answer 4. Representation of the model and algorithm as a result graphically and numerically. i-grouping of parameters related to the disease |
| **Key findings** | |
| Conclusion 1. Anamnesis collection and medical examination<br>Electrocardiogram (ECG)<br>Blood tests<br>Chest radiography<br>Echo-KG | |
| Conclusion 2. The doctor leaves for a deep examination: Functional lung tests<br>Load test<br>Cardiac magnetic resonance imaging (MRI)<br>Cardiac catheterization and angiography | |

(*continued*)

Table 1. (*continued*)

| Research questions | Answers |
|---|---|
| Conclusion 3. Sent patients need to be deeply iced and withdraw all the apparatuses to get the result. There are parameters S, U, p, t, x, $r_0$, L, T, K, and BZ, displaying data as a diagram. Treats each patient carefully and on the data. Allows you to adequately describe the dynamics and integrals of cardiac activity | |
| Output 4. Representation of the model and algorithm as a result graphically and numerically. i-grouping of parameters related to the disease. The general circulatory system allows you to model a closed blood network of the system, including hundreds and thousands of vascular segments. Provides fundamentally new opportunities for virtual analysis | |

If you are developing a Customer Journey Map for a stable business that needs growth, then you can start correcting errors immediately after filling out the table (Table 3). First, create separate detailed tasks for all priority issues and assign those responsible. Secondly, to make a long-term strategy to simplify the user's path and increase his comfort. Thirdly, do not forget to update the map every time a task has been completed or you notice a new pattern of customer behavior [25, 30].

Improving your product and customer interaction with it is a continuous process, without which the company will not be able to maintain the popularity and love of consumers.

## 4 Discussion

The description of all the processes taking place in the heart is an extremely difficult task. The model, which describes in detail the processes occurring in the heart and cardiovascular system, includes many parameters and variables. However, such a model is not convenient for practical use in cardiology. In this regard, they are usually limited to constructing simplified models (Fig. 5) reproducing the basic functions of the heart, allowing them to obtain physiologically real flows in the vascular system and make a number of assumptions.

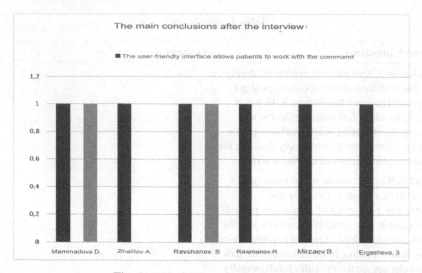

**Fig. 5.** Main findings after the interview

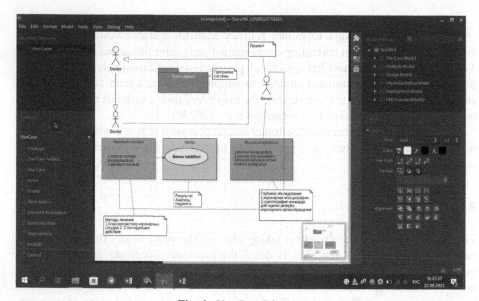

**Fig. 6.** Use Case Diagram

The first is part of the beginning. At first, we will use Terminator. Next, in the section Receiving and processing data of cardiac and vascular parameters, we will use the Data object. Because the reason why data is called data information is because data information is a variable [10, 24]. Therefore, we also include in this section a summary of our Cardio Vessel project in the Fig. 6 and Fig. 7.

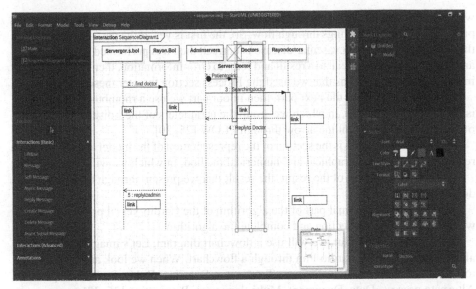

**Fig. 7.** Sequence Diagram

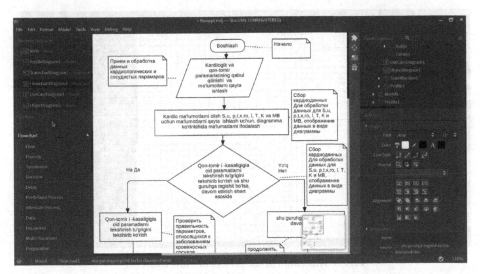

**Fig. 8.** The algorithm of the project in the flowchart (a)

Next, we get the card data S, u, p, t, x, $r_o$, l, T, K and for the database, for data processing, the data representation in the form of a diagram is the function that we need. We need to insert a function into this section. But we didn't present it as a function, because the information consists of a very large part. Therefore, we have compiled a short link algorithm and put it in the Process part in the Fig. 8 and Fig. 9.

Next, we will have a Decision part in which we will enter a condition. In it, we have to check the correctness of the parameters associated with vascular i-disease and check whether they belong to this group or not. This means that we will divide this part into 2 parts. We express our strings through flow. So, the first is yes, if the parameter check for the presence of the I—th vascular disease is correct, then it is performed in the yes part, and if not, it should not lead to a result and refer to error information, then it is performed in the no part. This means that we used the Process section to enter these conditions.

Now we move on to the next part, then in our part we use a rhombus. Our rhombus is located in Preparation, in which we group the parameters of the i-disease and consist of an arrow and represent the arrow through FLOW [25, 30].

And then our section is the section of the representation of the model and algorithmic result in the form of a graphical and numerical method, in which we will use Process.

The next part is part of the result, the result that we present through a section of the document.

Our last part is the final part of the algorithm of the Cardio Vessel project, in which we use the Terminator section and complete the algorithm.

In this cardio-Fun blur, we will use a flowchart diagram. Let's imagine a flowchart algorithm for blurring cardio-Fun through a flowchart. When we look at the Flowchart toolbar, it consists of: Flow, Process, Terminator, Decision, Delay, Predefined process, Alternate process, Data, Document, Multi-document, Preparation [25, 30].

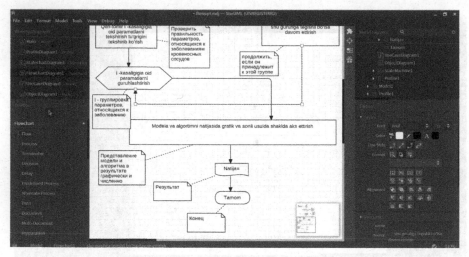

**Fig. 9.** Algorithm of the project in Flow Chart (b)

# References

1. Ciavolino, E., Lagetto, G., Montinari, A., et al.: Customer satisfaction and service domains: a further development of PROSERV. Qual. Quant. **54**, 1429–1444 (2019). https://doi.org/10.1007/s11135-019-00888-4
2. Schau, H.J., Akaka, M.A.: From customer journeys to consumption journeys: a consumer culture approach to investigating value creation in practice-embedded consumption. AMS Rev. **11**(1–2), 9–22 (2020). https://doi.org/10.1007/s13162-020-00177-6

3. Pizzutti, C., Gonçalves, R., Ferreira, M.: Information search behavior at the post-purchase stage of the customer journey. J. Acad. Mark. Sci. **50**, 981–1010 (2022). https://doi.org/10. 1007/s11747-022-00864-9

4. Schweidel, D.A., Bart, Y., Inman, J.J., et al.: How consumer digital signals are reshaping the customer journey. J. Acad. Mark. Sci. (2022). https://doi.org/10.1007/s11747-022-00839-w

5. Homburg, C., Jozić, D., Kuehnl, C.: Customer experience management: toward implementing an evolving marketing concept. J. Acad. Mark. Sci. **45**(3), 377–401 (2015). https://doi.org/ 10.1007/s11747-015-0460-7

6. Murali, S., Balasubramanian, M., Choudary, M.V.: Investigation on the impact of the supplier, customer, and organization collaboration factors on the performance of new product development. Int. J. Syst. Assur. Eng. Manag. (2021). https://doi.org/10.1007/s13198-021-01064-4

7. Morgan, T., Anokhin, S.A., Song, C., Chistyakova, N.: The role of customer participation in building new product development speed capabilities in turbulent environments. Int. Entrepreneurship Manag. J. **15**(1), 119–133 (2018). https://doi.org/10.1007/s11365-018-0549-9

8. Fang, X., Zhou, J., Zhao, H., Chen, Y.: A biclustering-based heterogeneous customer requirement determination method from customer participation in product development. Ann. Oper. Res. **309**(2), 817–835 (2020). https://doi.org/10.1007/s10479-020-03607-7

9. Stormi, K., Lindholm, A., Laine, T., Korhonen, T.: RFM customer analysis for product-oriented services and service business development: an interventionist case study of two machinery manufacturers. J. Manag. Gov. **24**(3), 623–653 (2019). https://doi.org/10.1007/ s10997-018-9447-3

10. Viktorovich, S.S., Vladimirovna, S.N.: Study of the influence of the properties of the walls of blood vessels on the hemodynamics of the cardiovascular system. Bulletin PSU im. Sholom Aleichem, no. 2 (2011). https://cyberleninka.ru/article/n/issledovanie-vliyaniya-svoystv-ste nok-sosudov-na-gemodinamiku-serdechnososudistoy-sistemy. Accessed 03 Nov 2020

11. Shilko, S.V., Kuzminsky, Yu.G., Borisenko, M.V.: Mathematical model and software for monitoring of cardiovascular system. Проблемы физики, математики и техники **3**(8) (2011)

12. Kiselev, I.N., et al.: Personalization of parameters and validation of the model of the human cardiovascular system. Math. Biol. Bioinform. **10**(2), 526–547 (2015). https://doi.org/10. 17537/2015.10.526

13. Sindeev, S.V., Frolov, S.V.: Modeling of hemodynamics of the cardiovascular system in cerebral aneurysm. Matem. Model. **28**(6), 98–114 (2016)

14. Simakov, S.S.: Modern methods of mathematical modeling of blood flow using averaged models. Comput. Res. Model. **10**(5), 581–604 (2018)

15. Aptukov, A.V., Shevelev, N.A., Dombrovsky, I.V.: Mathematical modeling of the process of deformability of blood vessels with pathology in angioplasty. Russian J. Biomech. **2** (1999). https://cyberleninka.ru/article/n/matematicheskoe-modelirovanie-pro tsessa-deformiruemosti-krovenosnyh-sosudov-s-patologiey-pri-angioplastike. Accessed 03 Nov 2020

16. Vladimirovich, L.A., Aleksandrovich, B.I.: Dependence of the strength of welded blood vessels on the diameter, thickness and Young's modulus of the wall. Biomed. Eng. Electron. **2**(6) (2014). https://cyberleninka.ru/article/n/zavisimost-prochnosti-svarennyh-krovenosnyh-sosudov-ot-diametra-tolschiny-i-modulya-yunga-stenki. Accessed 11 Mar 2020

17. Tygliyan, M.A., Tyurina, N.N.: A mathematical model for the passage of a hemodynamic impulse through bifurcation points. Keldysh Institute preprints, im. M. V. Keldysha **062**, 18 (2017)

18. Chernyavsky, M.A., et al.: Computer simulation in the assessment of hemodynamic parameters after stent implantation in patients of the AORT. Mod. Probl. Sci. Educ. **5** (2018). http://www.science-education.ru/ru/article/view?id=28070. Accessed 03 Nov 2020

19. Tregubov, V.P., Zhukov, N.K.: Computer simulation of blood flow in the presence of vascular pathologies. Russian J. Biomech. **2** (2017). https://cyberleninka.ru/article/n/kompyuternoe-modelirovanie-potoka-krovi-pri-nalichii-sosudistyh-patologiy. Accessed 03 Nov 2020

20. Vladimirovich, F.S., Ogly, A.N.E., Andreevich, K.A., Vyacheslavovich, S.S.: Approaches to zero-dimensional modeling of the cardiovascular system and their use in assessing cerebral circulation. Izvestiya TulGU. Tech. Sci. **10** (2018). https://cyberleninka.ru/article/n/pod hody-k-nulmernomu-modelirovaniyu-serdechno-sosudistoy-sistemy-i-ih-ispolzovanie-pri-otsenke-mozgovogo-krovoobrascheniya

21. Vyacheslavovich, S.S., Vladimirovich, F.S., Yuryevich, P.A.: Physician's decision-making support system in assessing the preoperative state of patients with acute cerebrovascular accident. Vestnik TSTU **4** (2017) https://cyberleninka.ru/article/n/sistema-podderzhki-pri nyatiya-resheniy-vracha-pri-otsenke-predoperatsionnogo-sostoyaniya-bolnyh-s-ostrymi-nar usheniyami-mozgovogo. Accessed 03 Nov 2020

22. Sindeev, S.V., Frolov, S.V., Liepsch, D., Balasso, A.: Modeling of flow alterations induced by flow-diverter using multiscale model of hemodynamics. Вестник ТГТУ №. 1 (2017). https://cyberleninka.ru/article/n/modeling-of-flow-alterations-induced-by-flow-div erter-using-multiscale-model-of-hemodynamics. дата обращения 03. Nov 2020

23. Teregulov, Yu.E., Mayanskaya, S.D., Teregulova, E.T.: Changes in the elastic properties of arteries and hemodynamic processes. PM **2**(103) (2017). https://cyberleninka.ru/article/n/izm eneniya-elasticheskih-svoystv-arteriy-i-gemodinamicheskie-protsessy

24. Yakhontov, S.V., Kulemzin, A.V., Chufistova, O.N.: Mechanisms and factors of interaction between the links of the cardiovascular system during transient processes (analytical review, part 1). Vestnik TSPU **3** (2010). https://cyberleninka.ru/article/n/mehanizmy-i-faktory-vza imodeystviya-zveniev-serdechno-sosudistoy-sistemypri-perehodnyh-protsessah-analitich eskiy-obzor-chast-1

25. Torre, D., Genero, M., Labiche, Y., et al.: How consistency is handled in model-driven software engineering and UML: an expert opinion survey. Softw. Qual. J. (2022).https://doi.org/10. 1007/s11219-022-09585-2

26. Fernández-Sáez, A.M., Chaudron, M.R.V., Genero, M.: An industrial case study on the use of UML in software maintenance and its perceived benefits and hurdles. Empir. Softw. Eng. **23**(6), 3281–3345 (2018). https://doi.org/10.1007/s10664-018-9599-4

27. Wei, R., Zolotas, A., Hoyos Rodriguez, H., Gerasimou, S., Kolovos, D.S., Paige, R.F.: Automatic generation of UML profile graphical editors for Papyrus. Softw. Syst. Model. **19**(5), 1083–1106 (2020). https://doi.org/10.1007/s10270-020-00813-6

28. Ciccozzi, F., Malavolta, I., Selic, B.: Execution of UML models: a systematic review of research and practice. Softw. Syst. Model. **18**(3), 2313–2360 (2018). https://doi.org/10.1007/ s10270-018-0675-4

29. Kraas, A.: On the automation-supported derivation of domain-specific UML profiles considering static semantics. Softw. Syst. Model. **21**, 51–79 (2021). https://doi.org/10.1007/s10270-021-00890-1

30. Amálio, N., Briand, L., Kelsen, P.: An experimental scrutiny of visual design modelling: VCL up against UML+OCL. Empir. Softw. Eng. **25**(2), 1205–1258 (2019). https://doi.org/10.1007/s10664-019-09784-9

# Using Discretization and Numerical Methods of Problem 1D-3D-1D Model for Blood Vessel Walls with Navier-Stokes

Dilafruz Nurjabova[1], Qulmatova Sayyora[2]([✉]), and Pardayeva Gulmira[1]

[1] Tashkent University of Information Technologies Karshi Branch "Software Engineering", 180118 Karshi, Uzbekistan
[2] Department of "Digital Economy and Information Technologies", Tashkent State University of Economics, 49, Uzbekistan Av., 100003 Tashkent, Uzbekistan
squlmatova@mail.ru

**Abstract.** This article describes a three-dimensional model of fluid flow a mathematical model of the circulatory system for the cardiovascular system and provides a basic framework for the mathematical representation of cumulative medical parameters such as total vascular area, blood volume, self-regulation, and effects on the upper and inner heart. This article presents a mathematical model of the circulatory system for the cardiovascular system and is the basis for a mathematical view of aggregated medical parameters such as total vascular area, blood volume, self-regulation, and effects on the upper and inner state of the heart. Concepts are given. Linear dependence of mathematical concepts, differential, integral differential, as well as logical-dynamic equations, Navier-Stokes problems, and mathematical apparatus for their practical application are given and the principle of operation of the program based on this mathematical model has used UML diagrams which consist of results of Navier-Stokes. The program given is the numerical results of Navier-Stokes 2D and 3D integral and differential equations on the basic diagram U, V, W, and parameters. In mathematical terms, linear dependencies, differential, integral, and differential equations are used.

**Keywords:** Linear dependence · Integral-differential equations · Logical-dynamic equations · General vascular zone · Self-regulation · Influence on the upper and working heart · Medical parameters

## 1 Introduction

Cardiovascular diseases are the leading cause of death in the world. Atherosclerosis is the most common among them. Because of the disease, several arteries are often affected at once, therefore the influence and development of the pathological process must be considered in the vascular network. To eliminate stenosis, stenting of the arteries is performed. Another serious complication of cardiovascular disease is pulmonary embolism. The cause of thromboembolism is floating blood clots that form in the lower extremities and move with the blood flow. To prevent this complication (to stop blood

© The Author(s), under exclusive license to Springer Nature Switzerland AG 2023
Y. Koucheryavy and A. Aziz (Eds.): NEW2AN 2022, LNCS 13772, pp. 73–82, 2023.
https://doi.org/10.1007/978-3-031-30258-9_7

clots) special implant cava filters are placed in the inferior vena cava. Other patholo-gies require surgical intervention, for example, aneurysms, and malformations. Thus, an important problem of modern medicine is the creation of effective methods of treatment and prevention. Mathematical modeling plays an increasing role in their development and numerical calculations of blood flow in the network of vessels with pathologies. They allow predicting surgical operations, optimizing the shape of implants, and inves-tigating their influence on hemodynamics. Researchers are given some concrete ideas from published articles.

Maria Hadjinicolaou, Eleftherios Protopapas in their article "Separability of Stokes Equations in Axisymmetric Geometries" on May 29, 2020, in the "Journal of Applied Mathematics and Physics" suggested the flow of blood plasma through a swarm of red blood cells in capillaries is modeled as an axisymmetric Stokes flow in inverted spheroidal single cells with solid-liquid. The solid inner spheroid is a swarm particle, while the outer spheroid surrounds the spheroid and contains a similar amount of fluid, which corresponds to the volume fraction of the swarm fluid.

C. Bui, N. Pham, A. Vo, A. Tran, A. Nguyen, T. Le, in his article "Time Series Forecasting for Healthcare Diagnosis and Prognostics with the Focus on Cardiovascular Diseases" on 24 September 2017, predicted time series was a thriving field of science due to its popularity in real-world applications, but at the same time was a challenge in method development.

Jeffrey L. Kibler, Mindy Ma, and Maria M. Llabre in their article "Body mass index concerning cardiovascular recovery from psychological stress among trauma-exposed women" in the European Archives of Psychiatry and Clinical Neuroscience volume 270 pages 589–596 (2020) delayed cardiovascular recovery has been associated with greater heart disease risks. However, relative to stress reactivity, cardiovascular recovery has been understudied. Further, few studies have examined associations of recovery with modifiable factors that might inform efforts to enhance recovery. In addition, several studies have examined the links between recovery and modifiable factors that could contribute to recovery efforts. The focus of the present study was whether body mass index (BMI) was associated with recovery from two stressful tasks (speech and mental arithmetic). Based on the conceptualization that obesity can lead to impaired recovery from stress, we also investigated whether a higher BMI explains the previously reported association between increased PTSD symptoms and delayed recovery. The sample con-sisted of 50 affected civilian women aged 19–49 years (M ± SD = 30 ± 8). Stressful tasks were followed by 15-min rest periods after task completion. Cardiovascular recov-ery was measured as the percentage of return to baseline; recovery measures consisted of heart rate (HR), cardiac output (CO), systolic blood pressure (SBP), and diastolic blood pressure (DBP). The severity of PTSD was based on structured interviews. To solve problems in which one-dimensional and three-dimensional models are interfaced, as a rule, algorithms of two classes are used: methods that iterate between subdomains for example, [1, 2], or splitting methods for example, [3]. As already mentioned, meth-ods that iterate between subdomains require large computational costs and are more often used with the vortex form of writing the Navier-Stokes equations. Therefore, for computational experiments, we use the following splitting scheme at each time step [17, 20].

Let $\bar{u}^n$, $\bar{p}^n$, $S^n$, un, and $p^n$ values for the corresponding parameters in time $t = tn$. Suppose that the time step $\Delta t$ is constant and the same in the one-dimensional and three-dimensional models $\tau_{n+1} = \frac{0.9}{S^n_{max}}$:

$$\Delta t \leq \min_n \frac{0.9}{S^n_{max}} \tag{2.40}$$

Using these values, we calculate $\bar{u}\,n + 1$, $\bar{p}\,n + 1$, $S\,n + 1$, $u\,n+1$ и $p\,n+1$ and ($t = tn + 1$) in three stages:

Step 1. Will printeries $\partial \frac{\partial S}{\partial t} + \frac{\partial (Su)}{\partial x} = \varphi(t, x, S, \bar{u})$,

$$\frac{\partial \bar{u}}{\partial t} + \frac{\partial (\bar{u}^2/2 + \bar{p}/p)}{\partial x} = \psi(t, x, S, \bar{u}),$$

on the interval $\Omega$ up 1D in $t \in [tn, tn + 1]$ this $\bar{u}(tn + 1)$ at the point $x = a$ and the condition for the free flow at the point $x = b$.

Step 2. According to (2.36), calculate u in using

$$\{\bar{u}, \bar{p}, S\} = \left\{ \bar{u}^{-n+1}, \bar{p}^{-n+1}, S^{n+1} \right\}$$

Find $\bar{p}^*$ and $S^*$ as a linear extrapolation $\bar{p}|x = d$ and $S|x = d$ with layers of time tn and tn-1 layer tn + 1. If n = 1, we put $\bar{p}^* = 0$ and $S^* = \hat{S}$. We solve the Navier-Stokes problem in $\Omega3D$ concerning for un + 1, pn + 1:

$$\begin{cases} \frac{1}{2\Delta t}\left(3u^{n+1} - 4u^n + u^{n-1}\right) + w \cdot \nabla u^{n+1} \\ \qquad -v\Delta u^{n+1} + \nabla p^{n+1} = f^{n+1} \\ \qquad\qquad \text{div } u^{n+1} \\ u^{n+1}\big|_{\Gamma_{in}} = u_{in}, \quad u^{n+1}\big|_{\Gamma_0} = 0 \\ \left(-v\frac{\partial u^{n+1}}{\partial n} + p^{n+1}n\right)\Big|_{\Gamma_{out}} = \bar{p}^*n \end{cases} \tag{2.41}$$

where $w = 2\,un - u\,n - 1$, if the task is linearized, and $w = u + 1$ in the nonlinear case.

Step 3. Find $\bar{u}^{n+1}|x = d$ from

$$\bar{p}^*S^*\bar{u}^{n+1} + \frac{\rho}{2}S^*\left(\bar{u}^{n+1}\right)^3\Big|_{x=b} = \bar{p}^* \int_{\Gamma_{out}} u^{n+1} \cdot nds + \frac{\rho}{2}\int_{\Gamma_{out}} \left|u^{n+1}\right|^2 (u^{n+1} \cdot n)ds \tag{2.42}$$

For on the x on representations $\bar{u}^{n+1}|x = d$
of using and words (2.26) and

$$S^*\bar{u}^{n+1} = \int_{\Gamma_{out}} u^{n+1} \cdot nds \tag{2.43}$$

Now, using $\bar{u}^{n+1}$ for the boundary conditions at the point $x = d$ and the free flow condition at the point $x = e$, we integrate (1.1) for $t \in [tn, tn + 1]$ and we find $\bar{u}^{n+1}$, $\bar{p}^{n+1}$, $S^{n+1}$ in $\Omega_{1D}^{down}$ [18.23].

## 2   Methods

### 2.1   Solving the 1D-3D-1D Problem with Different Time Steps in One-Dimensional and Three-Dimensional models

The time step in the one-dimensional model of global blood circulation is bounded from above $\tau_{n+1} = \frac{0.9}{S^n_{max}}$ and is variable. In practice, it turns out to be quite small, about 10-4-10-5 cm. Given that the solution of the Navier-Stokes equations at each time step is quite time-consuming, it is advisable to recalculate the three-dimensional fluid flow less often than the one-dimensional one [11, 17, 20] (Figs. 1 and 2).

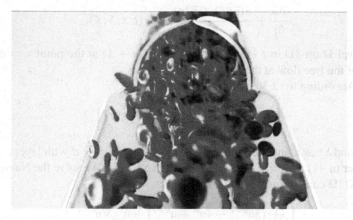

**Fig. 1.** Blood flow of vessel

**Fig. 2.** Blood flow of vessel with thrombus

Of particular interest are algorithms with a variable time step and for a three-dimensional model of fluid flow, for example, decreasing with increasing velocity or its derivative [11, 15, 17, 20]. However, in this paper we will limit ourselves to the case when the time step for the Navier-Stokes equations $\Delta t_{3D}$ is constant and greater than the time step in a one-dimensional model of global blood circulation, the algorithm described below will be used for numerical experiments in next steps. $\Delta t_{1D}^k, k = 1, 2, \ldots$:

$$\Delta t_{3D} \geq \max_m \Delta t_{1D}^m$$

Now let know the solution $u^p$ and $p^n$ to time $t = t_n = n\Delta t_{3D}$ and $-{}^{mn}, \overline{p}^{mn}, S^{mn}$ to $t = t_{mn}$, such that $t_{mn} \leq\ \leq t_n < t_{mn} + \Delta t_{1D}^{mn}$. To find solutions $u^{n+1}$ and $p^{n+1}$ when t $= t_{n+1} = t_n + \Delta t_{3D}$ and $\overline{u}^m, \overline{p}^m, S^m, m_n < m \leq m_{n+1}$ $m_{n+1}$ is determined by the ratio t $m_{n+1} + 1 \leq t_{n+1} < t\ m_{n+1} + \Delta t_{1D}^{mn+1}$, we will use the following algorithm:

Step 1. According to (2.36) compute $u_{in}$ using the values obtained by extrapolation $\{\overline{u}^{mn}, \overline{p}^{mn}, S^{mn}\}$ and $\{\overline{u}^{mn-1}, \overline{p}^{mn-1}, S^{mn-1}\}$ layer $t_{n+1}$ Find $\overline{p}^*$ and $S^*$ as a linear extrapolation $\overline{p}|_{x=d}$ and $S|_{x=d}$ with layers of time $t_{mn}$ and $t_{mn-1}$ per layer $t_{n+1}$. We solve the Navier-Stokes problem (2.41) in $\Omega_{3D}$ with respect to $u^{n+1}, p^{n+1}$.

Calculate $\overline{u}|_{x=d}$ when $t = t_{n+1}$ using $u^{n+1}, p^{n+1}$ and the condition of the pairing three-dimensional and one-dimensional solutions (2.42) (you can also use the condition $\hat{u}_{\Gamma_{out}} = u|_{x=d}$ or (2.43)).

Step 2. $m = m_{n+1}, \ldots, m_{n+1}$ calculate the blood flow in one-dimensional areas, with $t = t_m$:

Will printeries (1.1) on the interval $\Omega_{1D}^{up}$ in $t \in [t_{m-1}, t_m]$ this $\overline{u}(t_m)$ at the point $x = a$ and the condition for the free flow at the point $x = b$.

Find $\overline{u}^m|_{x=d}$ as interpolation of $\overline{u}|_{x=d}$ when $t = t_n$ and $t = t_{n+1}$. Now, using $\overline{u}^m$ for the boundary conditions at the point $x = d$ and the free flow condition at the point $x = e$, we integrate (1.1) for $t \in t_{m-1}, t_m]$ and we find $\overline{u}^m, \overline{p}^m, S^m$ in $\Omega_{1D}^{down}$.

Because $t = 0$ initialization of the model is defined, the implementation of this algorithm is also necessary for solutions $u^1, p^1$ and $\overline{u}^m, S^m, \overline{p}^m$ for $m \leq m_1$.

Doing this, for example, you can perform the following actions:

For $m = 1, \ldots, m1$, integrate

$$\partial \frac{\partial S}{\partial t} + \frac{\partial (Su)}{\partial x} = \varphi\left(t, x, S, \overline{u}\right),$$

$$\frac{\partial \overline{u}}{\partial t} + \partial \frac{(\overline{u}^2/2 + \overline{p}/p)}{\partial x} = \psi(t, x, S, \overline{u}),$$

on the interval $\Omega_{1D}^{up}$ and $\Omega_{1D}^{down}$ 1D and $\Omega$ down $t \in [tm - 1, tm]$ with a given $\overline{u}$ $(tm)$ at the point $x = a$, the condition of a free drain at the point $x = e$ and the standard system of boundary conditions for the model of the global circulation (1.11), (1.12), (1.6) at the points $x = b$ and $x = d$. The influence of the three-dimensional model of the fluid flow is not taken into account in this case.

According to (2.36), we calculate u in using the values $\{\overline{u}m1, \overline{p}m1, Sm1\}$, put $\overline{p} = \overline{p}^*m1 \mid x = d$ and $S^* = Sm1 \mid x = d$.

Let's solve the Navier-Stokes problem (2.41) in $\Omega_{3D}$ concerning $u1, p1$.

This 1D-3D-1D structure consisting of two one-dimensional vessels and a three-dimensional region located between them can be part of a full-fledged graph of the cardiovascular system. In this case, a standard system of boundary conditions is used at the junctions with the vascular tree (at the points x = a and x = e) in the node.

$\Omega_{1D}^{up}$ and   $\Omega_{1D}^{down}$ with a vascular tree (at points $= a$ and $= e$) is used standard system of boundary conditions

$$p_k(S_k(t.x_k)) - p_{node}(t) = \varepsilon_k R_k S_k(t, x_k) u_k(t, x_k).$$

$$\sum_{i=1}^{K} \varepsilon_i S_i(t, x_k) u_i(t, x_i) = 0.$$

$$\omega_i \left( \frac{dV}{dt} \right)_i = \omega_i \left( \frac{\partial V}{\partial t} + \lambda_i \frac{\partial V}{\partial x} \right) = \omega_i g_i \ i = 1, 2,$$

at the node (Fig. 3).

**Fig. 3.** Blood flow of vessel with thrombus and plaques

## 3   Conclusion

This article shows a three-dimensional model of fluid flow is considered and numerical methods for Navier-Stokes equations. Provides an overview of existing conditions for conjugation of one-dimensional and three-dimensional flow models liquids. For two-scale models using these conditions, the analysis of the energy balance has been carried out. It is shown that the energy estimate is valid only for conditions

$$\left( -\nu \frac{\partial u}{\partial n} + pn \right)\big|_{\Gamma_{out}} = \bar{p}|_{x=d} n,$$

$$\int_{\Gamma_{out}} u \cdot n ds = S\bar{u}|_{x=d}$$

$$-\nu \frac{\partial u}{\partial n} + (p + \frac{\rho}{2}|u|^2)n) = (\bar{p} + \frac{\rho}{2}\bar{u}^2)\big|_{x=d} n \ \text{on} \ \Gamma_{out}$$

which are natural for the Navier-Stokes equations, written in vertex form. For the used convective form of the Navier-Stokes equations, a new boundary condition

$$\bar{p} \int_{\Gamma_{out}} u \cdot n ds + \frac{\rho}{2} \int_{\Gamma_{out}} |u|^2(u \cdot n) ds = ?(\bar{p}S\bar{u} + \frac{\rho}{2} S\bar{u}^3)\big|_{x=d}$$

is proposed. For two-scale models with such a boundary condition and the requirement of continuity normal component of stress tensor (2.30) at the junction of regions of different dimensions, a theorem on the energy estimate is derived and a splitting scheme for numerical solution.

## 4  Results

An important advantage of this approach to modeling blood flow is the absence of an assumption u n $\leq$ 0 at the inflow boundary into the three-dimensional region at all times, where u is the three-dimensional velocity and n is the outward normal to the surface. The resulting equation simultaneously expresses both the balance of forces and the balance of momentum (momentum), since the left side of the equation (the product of acceleration by the mass of a unit of volume) is equal to the rate of change of the momentum in a unit of volume, and the right side of this equation is equal to the flow of momentum, included in the unit of volume, due to the action of external forces. To define a typical problem, one chooses a bounded spatial region and a starting time and then imposes boundary and initial conditions by referencing the exact solution appropriately. As a result, the piston in the cylinder with a larger diameter will transmit the pressure force, in so many times greater than the force applied to the piston in a cylinder with a smaller diameter, how many times is the cross-section of cylinder 1 larger than a cylinder.

In the Ethier reference, a calculation is made for the cube centered at (0,0,0) with a "radius" of 1 unit, and over the time interval from t = 0 to t = 0.1, with parameters a = PI/4 and d = PI/2, and with Dirichlet boundary conditions on all faces of the cube [4–6]. This table presents the Minimum, Maximum, and pressure UVWP samples solution. Estimate the range of velocity and pressure at the initial time T = 0, using a region that is the cube centered at (0, 0, 0) with "radius" 1.0, Viscosity NU = 0.25 [4–6] (Table 1).

Table 1. Estimate the range of velocity

| Magnitude | Minimum | Maximum |
| --- | --- | --- |
| U:= x | −3,08103 | 1,39472 |
| V:= y | −3,06036 | 1,32415 |
| W:= z | −3,06278 | 1,41037 |
| P: | 0,0250229 | 5,31825 |

Estimate the range of velocity and pressure at the initial time T = 0, using a region that is the cube centered at (0, 0, 0) with "radius" 1.0, Viscosity NU = 0.25 [4–6] (Table 2).

Estimate the range of velocity and pressure at the initial time T = 0, using a region that is the cube centered at (0, 0, 0) with "radius" 1.0, Viscosity NU = 0.25, at the initial time T = 0, using a region that is the cube centered at (0, 0, 0) with "radius" 1.0, Parameter A = 0.785398, Parameter D = 1.5708 [4–6] (Table 3 and Figs. 4 and 5).

**Table 2.** Estimate the range of velocity

| Magnitude | Minimum | Maximum |
|-----------|---------|---------|
| U:= x | −1.99845 | 1.9992 |
| V:= y | −1.99727 | 1.99955 |
| W:= z | −0.995313 | 0.995265 |
| P: | −3.95736 | −0.0081647 |

**Table 3.** Estimate the range of velocity

| Magnitude | Minimum | Maximum |
|-----------|---------|---------|
| U:= x | 0 | 3.55271e-15 |
| V:= y | 0 | 2.88658e-15 |
| W:= z | 0 | 2.66454e-15 |
| P: | 0 | 4.44089e-16 |

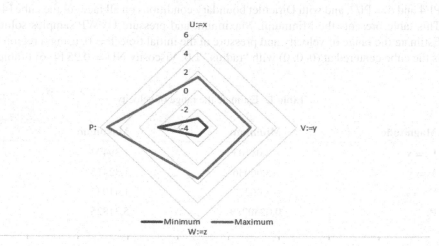

**Fig. 4.** Estimate the range of velocity

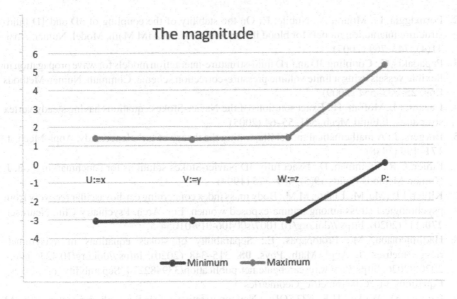

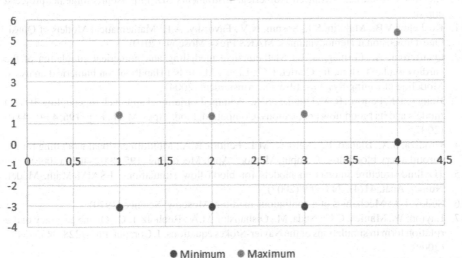

**Fig. 5.** Estimate the range of velocity min, max

# References

1. Formaggia, L., Gerbeau, J.F., Nobile, F., Quarteroni, A.: On the coupling of 3D and 1D Navier-Stokes equations for flow problems in compliant vessels. Comput. Methods Appl. Mech. Eng. **191**, 561–582 (2001)

2. Formaggia, L., Moura, A., Nobile, F.: On the stability of the coupling of 3D and 1D fluid-structure interaction models for blood flow simulations. ESAIM Math. Model. Numer. Anal. **41**(4), 743–769 (2007)

3. Papadakis, G.: Coupling 3D and 1D fluid-structure-interaction models for wave propagation in flexible vessels using a finite volume pressure-correction scheme. Commun. Numer. Methods Eng. **25**, 533–551 (2009)

4. Bazant, M., Moffatt, H.: Exact solutions of the Navier-Stokes equations having steady vortex structures. J. Fluid Mech. **541**, 55–64 (2005) .

5. Burgers, J.: A mathematical model illustrating the theory of turbulence. Adv. Appl. Mech. **1**, 171–199 (1948)

6. Ethier, C.R., Steinman, D.: Exact fully 3D Navier-Stokes solutions for benchmarking. Int. J. Numer. Methods Fluids **19**(5), 369–375 (1994)

7. Kibler, J.L., Ma, M., Llabre, M.M.: Body mass index concerning cardiovascular recovery from psychological stress among trauma-exposed women. Eur. Arch. Psychiatry Clin. Neurosci. **270**(11) (2020). https://doi.org/10.1007/s00406-019-01054-5

8. Hadjinicolaou, M., Protopapas, E.: Separability of stokes equations in axisymmetric geometries. J. Appl. Math. Phys. **08**, 315–348 (2020). https://doi.org/10.4236/jamp. 2020.82026. https://www.researchgate.net/publication/339482274_Separability_of_Stokes_ Equations_in_Axisymmetric_Geometries

9. Pernice, M., Walker, H.F.: NITSOL: a Newton iterative solver for nonlinear systems. SIAM J. Sci. Comput. **19**(72), 302–318 (1998)

10. Electronic resource: Advanced Numerical Instruments 3D. http://sourceforge.net/projects/ ani3d/

11. Koshelev, V.B., Mukhin, S.I., Sosnin, N.V., Favorsky, A.P.: Mathematical Models of Quasi-One-Dimensional Hemodynamics. MAKS Press, Moscow (2010)

12. Quarteroni, A., Formaggia, L.: Mathematical modelling and numerical simulation of the cardiovascular system. In: Ciarlet, P.G., Lions, J.L. (eds.) Handbook on numerical analysis, Modeling of Living Systems. Elsevier, Amsterdam (2004)

13. Blanco, P.J., Feijoro, R.A., Urquiza, S.A.: A unified variational approach for coupling 3D–1D models and its blood flow applications. Comput. Methods Appl. Mech. Eng. **196**, 4391–4410 (2007)

14. Urquiza, S.A., Blanco, P.J., Vernere, M.J., Feijoro, R.A.: Multidimensional modelling for the carotid artery blood flow. Comput. Methods Appl. Mech. Eng. **195**, 4002–4017 (2006)

15. 1D fluid-structure interaction models for blood flow simulations. ESAIM Math. Model. Numer. Anal. **41**(4), 743–769 (2007)

16. Sedov, L.I.: Mechanics of a continuous medium. Moscow: Science (1970)

17. Layton, W., Manica, C.C., Neda, M., Olshanskii, M.A., Rebholz, L.G.: On the accuracy of the rotation form in simulations of the Navier-Stokes equations. J. Comput. Phys. **228**, 3433–3447 (2009)

18. Olshanskii, M.A.: A low order Galerkin finite element method for the Navier-Stokes equations of steady incompressible flow: a stabilization issue and iterative methods. Comput. Methods Appl. Mech. Eng. **191**, 5515–5536 (2002)

19. Blanco, P.J., Deparis, S., Malossi, A.C.I.: On the continuity of mean total normal stress in geometrical multiscale cardiovascular problems. J. Comput. Phys. (2013)

20. Konstantinovna, D.T.: Numerical modeling of blood flow in the presence of vascular implants or pathologies, Moscow, October 2013

# Numerical Simulation of a Flow in a Two-Dimensional Channel on the Basis of a Two-Liquid Turbulence Model

Zafar Mamatkulovich Malikov[1], Farrukh Kholiyorovich Nazarov[1(✉)],
Bekzod Sultonmurodovich Toshpulov[2],
and Bakhromjon Alisherovich Abdurakhmonov[3]

[1] Institute of Mechanics and Seismic Stability of Structures of the Academy of Sciences of the Republic of Uzbekistan, Tashkent, Uzbekistan
farruxnazar@mail.ru
[2] Department of Mathematical Methods in Economics, Tashkent State University of Economics, Tashkent, Uzbekistan
[3] Department of Physics, Mathematics and Information Technology, The Tashkent Pharmaceutical Institute, Tashkent, Uzbekistan

**Abstract.** The article presents the results of a numerical study of the flow structure in a two-dimensional channel at high Reynolds numbers. A feature of such flows is that the flow is turbulent. It is known that many turbulence models are based on the solution of systems of Navier-Stokes equations averaged over Reynolds. Such models are called RANS models. These models are based on the Boussinesq hypothesis, where turbulent stresses are assumed to be proportional to the strain rate of the averaged velocities. In addition, a hypothesis is made that turbulence is isotropic. However, studies of the turbulent flow structure have shown that turbulence is anisotropic. Therefore, to calculate anisotropic turbulent flows, models are used that do not use the Boussinesq hypothesis. One of such directions in turbulence modeling is Reynolds stress methods. These methods are complex and require rather large computational resources. Recently, another model of turbulence has been developed, which is based on a two-fluid approach. The essence of this approach is that a turbulent flow is represented as a heterogeneous mixture of two fluids that perform relative motion. In contrast to the Reynolds approach, the two-fluid approach makes it possible to obtain a closed system of turbulence equations using two-fluid dynamics. Therefore, while empirical equations are used for closure in RANS models, in the two-fluid model the equations used are exact equations of dynamics. One of the main advantages of the two-fluid model is that it is able to describe complex anisotropic turbulent flows. Therefore, in this paper, we used the two-fluid turbulence model for testing and the Reynolds stress method for comparison. In this work, numerical results are obtained for the longitudinal velocity profiles, turbulent stresses, as well as the coefficient of friction in a flat channel. The results are compared with known experimental data. In addition, the paper also presents the numerical results of the Reynolds stress method EARSM-WJ. The results are obtained for Reynolds numbers Re = 5600, Re = 13700 and Re = 13750.

Y. Koucheryavy and A. Aziz (Eds.): NEW2AN 2022, LNCS 13772, pp. 83–92, 2023.
https://doi.org/10.1007/978-3-031-30258-9_8

**Keywords:** Navier-Stokes equations · Two-fluid model · Reynolds number · ERSM-WJ turbulent model · Turbulent stresses

# 1 Introduction

As is known, most of the flows that are interesting from a practical point of view are turbulent. There are many definitions reflecting the nature of turbulence. However, none of them can convey the essence of such a complex phenomenon. Although from a physical point of view, the origin of turbulence is the instability of the considered flow [1].

To date, turbulence remains one of the priority areas of science and one of the most complex objects of study in hydromechanics [2]. Throughout the history of its study, many different methods and approaches have been proposed [3–5], which represent the most promising areas of science of the corresponding period of time. The theory of turbulence continues to develop to this day. More and more new approaches to its study appear [6], and the number of models proposed for a better understanding of its properties, as well as the mechanisms of its occurrence and existence, is growing. To date, there are more than one hundred turbulence models with different approaches. All these models have many empirical constants and auxiliary functions that complicate the numerical calculation in the calculation. The ERSM-WJ turbulence model is one such turbulence model. The model consists of nine partial differential equations, which complicates the solution of the problem in its numerical calculation. Due to this, the estimated time of the ERSM-WJ turbulent model is twice as long as compared to the two-fluid turbulence model.

The need to study turbulent flows is explained by the fact that they are the predominant form of motion, both in nature and in technology. The presence of turbulence in technical devices has a strong impact on the performance, durability, and other important characteristics of structures [3, 7]. Therefore, the study of non-stationary phenomena characteristic of turbulent flows can explain the processes occurring in them and greatly facilitate the work on the creation of new devices.

The main element of many technical systems in which turbulent flows are present are diffusers - channels with an increase in static pressure in the direction of flow [8]. Diffusers are an integral part of jet engines, test facilities, in particular wind tunnels, they are used in turbines, pumps, fans, compressors and other machines. The main purpose of diffusers is the conversion of kinetic energy obtained by accelerating the flow and its subsequent expansion into an increase in static pressure. The need to obtain high coefficients of pressure recovery in diffusers often forces the use of geometric parameters at which the flow is either on the verge of separation or under conditions close to it [9, 10].

In this case, the diffuser acts as a self-excited oscillator with quasi-periodic formation and entrainment of separated regions; a regime called unsteady separated flow arises [11, 12], which greatly complicates a detailed study of flows in diffusers. Despite the extensive accumulated material on the hydrodynamics of turbulent separated flows [13, 14], there remains a need to develop reliable and universal methods capable of predicting the hydrodynamic parameters of flows of this kind.

Physical and mathematical formulation of the problem

In this study, the geometry of the considered two-dimensional channel is shown in Fig. 1 [15]. This problem is a classic example for testing new turbulence models.

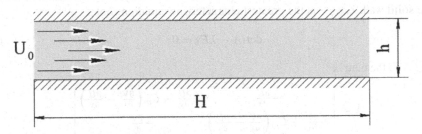

**Fig. 1.** Two-dimensional channel.

The channel length is 100 h, where h is the channel width. This length is chosen to form a fully developed turbulent flow. The number of control volumes CV = 6000. The grid is chosen to be uniform over the channel width, and the first point from the wall should be in the logarithmic sublayer when modeling using the wall law. The same rule must be taken into account when calculating other configurations using the wall law.

To describe the motion of a turbulent fluid in a two-dimensional channel, as mentioned above, a two-fluid model of turbulence is used. The unsteady system of turbulence equations according to the two-fluid model in the Cartesian coordinate system has the following form [16, 17]:

$$\begin{cases} \dfrac{\partial U}{\partial t} + U\dfrac{\partial U}{\partial x} + V\dfrac{\partial U}{\partial y} + \dfrac{\partial P}{\partial x} = \dfrac{1}{Re}\left(\dfrac{\partial^2 U}{\partial x^2} + \dfrac{\partial^2 U}{\partial y^2}\right) - \dfrac{\partial u\vartheta}{\partial y}; \\[2mm] \dfrac{\partial V}{\partial t} + U\dfrac{\partial V}{\partial x} + V\dfrac{\partial V}{\partial y} + \dfrac{\partial P}{\partial y} = \dfrac{1}{Re}\left(\dfrac{\partial^2 V}{\partial x^2} + \dfrac{\partial^2 V}{\partial y^2}\right) - \dfrac{\partial u\vartheta}{\partial x} - \dfrac{\partial \vartheta\vartheta}{\partial y}; \\[2mm] \dfrac{\partial u}{\partial t} + U\dfrac{\partial u}{\partial x} + V\dfrac{\partial u}{\partial y} = (C_m - 1)\dfrac{\partial U}{\partial y}\vartheta + \dfrac{\partial}{\partial y}\left(v_{xy}\dfrac{\partial u}{\partial y}\right) - K_f u; \\[2mm] \dfrac{\partial \vartheta}{\partial t} + U\dfrac{\partial \vartheta}{\partial x} + V\dfrac{\partial \vartheta}{\partial y} = -C_m\dfrac{\partial U}{\partial y}u + \dfrac{\partial}{\partial y}\left(v_{yy}\dfrac{\partial \vartheta}{\partial y}\right) - K_f\vartheta; \\[2mm] \dfrac{\partial U}{\partial x} + \dfrac{\partial V}{\partial y} = 0. \end{cases} \tag{1}$$

Here

$$v_{xy} = 3v + 2\left|\frac{u\vartheta}{def(U)}\right|, \quad v_{yy} = 3v + 2\left|\frac{\vartheta\vartheta}{def(U)}\right|,$$

$$def(U) = \sqrt{2\left(\left(\frac{\partial U}{\partial x}\right)^2 + \left(\frac{\partial V}{\partial y}\right)^2\right) + \left(\frac{\partial V}{\partial x} + \frac{\partial U}{\partial y}\right)^2}, \quad C_m = 0.2, K_f = C_s \cdot \lambda_{max} + C_{s0} \cdot \frac{|\vartheta|}{d}$$

In the above equations, $U, V-$ are the dimensionless longitudinal and transverse components of the average flow velocity, respectively, $P-$ is the dimensionless hydrostatic pressure, $u, \vartheta-$ are the relative dimensionless longitudinal and transverse components of the fluid velocity, $v_{xy}, v_{yy}-$ effective molar viscosities, d – is the nearest distance to the solid wall, $\lambda_{max}-$ is the greatest characteristic equation root

$$\det(A - \lambda E) = 0 \tag{2}$$

where A is the matrix

$$A = \begin{vmatrix} -\frac{\partial U}{\partial x} & -\frac{\partial U}{\partial y} - C_m\left(\frac{\partial V}{\partial x} - \frac{\partial U}{\partial y}\right) \\ -\frac{\partial V}{\partial y} + C_m\left(\frac{\partial V}{\partial x} - \frac{\partial U}{\partial y}\right) & -\frac{\partial V}{\partial y} \end{vmatrix}$$

The largest root of the characteristic equation is

$$D = \frac{\partial U}{\partial y}\frac{\partial V}{\partial x} - \frac{\partial U}{\partial x}\frac{\partial V}{\partial y} + C_m(1 - C_m)\left(\frac{\partial V}{\partial x} - \frac{\partial U}{\partial y}\right)^2,$$

$$\begin{cases} \lambda_{max} = \sqrt{D}, & D > 0 \\ \lambda_{max} = 0, & D < 0 \end{cases}$$

Constant coefficients are $C_s = 0.7825, \quad C_{s0} = 0.306$.

For the numerical implementation of system (1), it is necessary to choose an appropriate computational grid. The numerical results obtained will also depend on the chosen grid [18]. One of the conditions for obtaining satisfactory results is the thickening of the grid near the solid surface. Many turbulence models such as k–ω, SST k–ω, and Reynolds stress methods require a very fine mesh near the wall, which leads to certain difficulties for their application in engineering problems.

Solution method. It is well known that the numerical solution of problems on the motion of a viscous incompressible fluid based on the Navier-Stokes equations is complicated not only by their nonlinearity, but also by the absence of an explicit equation for determining pressure. Therefore, an approach that uses the natural physical variables "velocity-pressure" looks preferable. In this work, for the difference approximation of the initial equations, the SIMPLE control volume method [18] was used. In this case, the viscous terms were approximated by the central difference, and for the convective terms, a scheme against the flow of the second order of accuracy was used.

For the numerical implementation of system (1), the following conditions were set at the input for relative velocities:

$$u = 0.05, \quad \vartheta = 0$$

No-slip conditions were imposed on the walls. Extrapolation conditions [19] were used at the output. The optimal transverse pitch was $\Delta y = 0.0005$ and longitudinal $\Delta x = 0.5$. The integration was carried out with a time step $\Delta t = 0.01$.

The discussion of the results. On Fig. 2 shows graphs of comparison of calculated and experimental data. For comparison, these figures also show the numerical results of the Reynolds stress turbulence model EARSMWJ. Dots show experimental data [20].

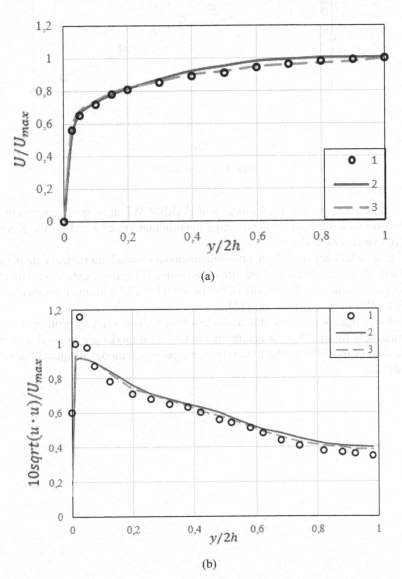

(a)

(b)

**Fig. 2.** Profiles of velocity, Reynolds stresses $uu$ and $u\vartheta$. Fig. (a) – experiment, Fig. (b) – two-fluid model, Fig. (c) – EARSM-WJ

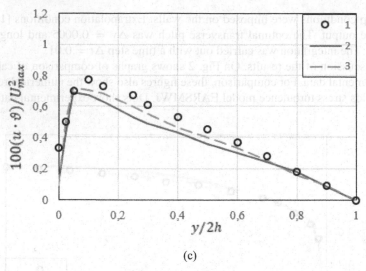

(c)

**Fig. 2.** (*continued*)

As can be seen, the two-fluid model and EARSM-WJ show good agreement with the experimental data, both for the average longitudinal velocity and for the Reynolds stress components $uu$ and $u\vartheta$.

To study turbulence models in a two-dimensional channel, numerical data obtained using the direct modeling method are often used instead of experimental data. Therefore, in fig. Figure 3 compares the results of the two-fluid model with the numerical results of DNS for Reynolds numbers and [15].

The lower figures show the dimensionless longitudinal velocity profiles. It can be seen from these figures that the results of the two-fluid model are in good agreement with the data of the DNS method, therefore, the proposed model adequately describes the "wall" law.

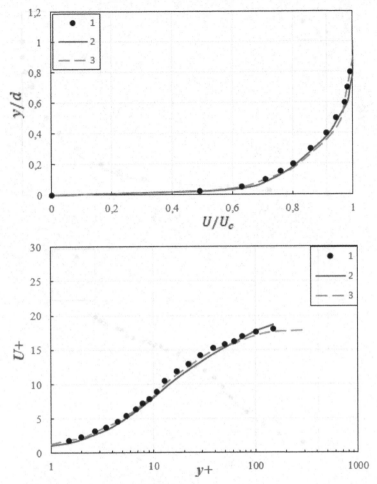

**Fig. 3.** Rice. 3. Profiles of velocities and dimensionless velocities for a two-dimensional channel. 1—DNS (Kim), 2—two-fluid model, 3—Low-Re CLS

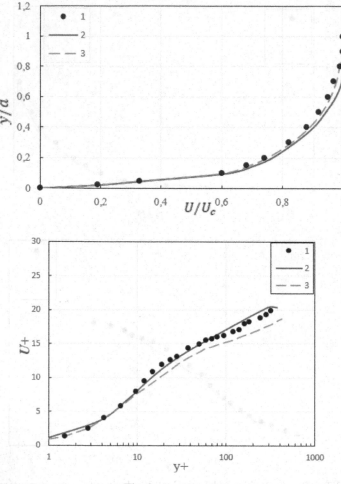

**Fig. 3.** (*continued*)

## 2   Conclusions

The paper presents the numerical results of studying the flow of an incompressible viscous fluid in a two-dimensional channel using a two-fluid turbulent model, as well as the EARSM-WJ Reynolds stress method. It is shown that the results obtained for the two-fluid model are in good agreement with the experimental data. Comparing the two-fluid model with the turbulent stress method, which is currently considered the best RANS model in predicting turbulent flows in two-dimensional channels, one can say that the accuracy of the two-fluid model is at least as good. However, the numerical implementation of the new model requires a much smaller computational resource compared to the Reynolds stress method, which is essential for calculations. Therefore, the two-fluid model can be recommended for solving practical work where complex anisotropic flows occur.

# References

1. Smirnov, Ye.M.: Techeniya vyazkoy zhidkosti i modeli turbulentnosti: metody rascheta turbulentnykh techeniy. Sankt – Peterburg (2010)
2. Fon Karman G Aerodinamika. Izbrannyye temy v ikh istoricheskom razvitii, p. 208. NITS Regulyarnaya i khaoticheskaya dinamika, Izhevsk (2001)
3. Gostey, A.D., Khalil, Ye.Ye., Uaytlou, Dzh.G.: Raschet dvumernykh turbulentnykh retsirkuly-atsionnykh techeniy. Turbulentnyye sdvigovyye techeniya, pp. 247–269. Mashinostroyeniye, Moscow (1982)
4. Reynolds A J. Turbulent flows in engineering applications, 408 p. Energy, Moscow (1978)
5. Bradshaw, P.: Turbulence, 343 p. Mashinostroenie, Moscow (1980)
6. Frick, P.G.: Turbulence: Models and Approaches: A Course of Lectures. At 2. h. Perm: PGTU, 244 p. (1998)
7. Juraev, G., Rakhimberdiev, K.: Mathematical modeling of credit scoring system based on the Monge-Kantorovich problem. In: 2022 IEEE International IOT, Electronics and Mechatronics Conference, IEMTRONICS 2022 Proceedings (2022)
8. Juraev, G., Rakhimberdiev, K.: Modeling the decision-making process of lenders based on blockchain technology. In: International Conference on Information Science and Communications Technologies: Applications, Trends and Opportunities, ICISCT 2021, pp. 1–5 (2021)
9. Juraev, G., Rakhimberdiev, K.: Prospects of application of blockchain technology in the banking. In: International Conference on Information Science and Communications Technologies: Applications, Trends and Opportunities, ICISCT 2022, pp. 1–5 (2022)
10. Karimov, M., Arzieva, J., Rakhimberdiev, K.: Development of approaches and schemes for proactive information protection in computer networks. In: International Conference on Information Science and Communications Technologies: Applications, Trends and Opportunities, ICISCT 2022, pp. 1–5 (200)
11. Tashev, K., Arzieva, J., Arziev, A., Rakhimberdiev, K.: Method authentication of objects information communication systems. In: International Conference on Information Science and Communications Technologies: Applications, Trends and Opportunities, ICISCT 2022, pp. 1–5 (2022)
12. Arzieva, J., Arziev, A., Rakhimberdiev, K.: Application of random number generators in solving the problem of user authentication in blockchain systems. In: International Conference on Information Science and Communications Technologies: Applications, Trends and Opportunities, ICISCT 2022, pp. 1–5 (2022)
13. Smit, P.: Turbulentnoye techeniye pri simmetrichnom vnezapnom rasshirenii ploskogo kanala. Teoreticheskiye osnovy **100**(3), 200–206 (1978)
14. Amano, R.S.: Turbulentnoye techeniye pri rezkom rasshirenii truby. Aerokosmicheskaya tekhnika (6), 41–47 (1986)
15. Gogish, L.V., Stepanov, G.Yu.: Turbulent separated flows, 368 p. Nauka, Moscow (1979)
16. Restivo, A., Uaytlo, Dzh.KH.: Kharakteristiki turbulentnogo techeniya za simmetrichnym ploskim vnezapnym rasshireniyem. Teoreticheskiye osnovy inzhenernykh raschetov **100**(3), 163–166 (1978)
17. Yun, A.A., Krylov, B.A.: Raschet i modelirovaniye turbulentnykh techeniy s yeploob-menom, smesheniyem, khimicheskimi reaktsiyami i dvukhfaznykh techeniy v programmnom komplekse Fastest-3D: Uchebnoye posobiye. - M.: Izd-vo MAI, 2007. – 116 s
18. Malikov, Z.M., Nazarov, F.Kh.: Study of turbulence models for calculating a strongly swirling flow in an abrupt expanding channel. Comput. Res. Model. **13**(4), 793-805 (2021). https://doi.org/10.20537/2076-7633-2021-13-4-793-805

19. Numerical study of flow in a plane suddenly expanding channel based on Wilcox and two-fluid turbulence models. In: MSTU 2021 Journal of Physics: Conference Series, vol. 1901, pp. 012039, 1–9. IOP Publishing (2021). https://doi.org/10.1088/1742-6596/1901/1/012039
20. Patankar, S.V.: Numerical Heat Transfer and Fluid Flow. Taylor & Francis (1980)

# Application Fuzzy Neural Network Methods to Detect Cryptoattacks on Financial Information Systems Based on Blockchain Technology

G. U. Juraev[1], Rakhimberdiev Kuvonchbek[1], and B. Toshpulov[2(✉)]

[1] National University of Uzbekistan, Tashkent 100174, Uzbekistan
[2] Tashkent State University of Economics, Tashkent 100066, Uzbekistan
toshb8310@gmail.com

**Abstract.** In this article, an intelligent method for identifying possible threats to other information systems based on blockchain technology has been developed. This intelligent method is built on the basis of the theory of fuzzy neural network and uses a database trained to detect cryptoattacks on information systems. The system performs complex calculation and decision-making process by studying the given data. Verifies the authenticity of blockchain blocks and transactions. Forms a risk database of the general information system and applies security measures accordingly. In addition, the article presents the risks to financial information systems and their types, models for identifying risks to information security. A fuzzy neural network-based method for determining possible risks has been developed. The results were obtained by implementing the Matlab package program. In the conclusion of the study, the safety and economic efficiency of this method has been proven.

**Keywords:** Cryptoattack · artificial intelligence · intelligent · blockchain · decision-making process · risk · fuzzy neural network · neural network · information security · distributed information system · information system · electromagnetic

## 1 Introduction

It is known that issues of improvement of information systems, wide use of digital technologies, development of information protection methods and algorithms and their improvement are important all over the world. In particular, in the Republic of Uzbekistan, the consistent penetration of information technologies into many areas serves the growth of the country's economy [1].

The growth of business entities in the conditions of the market economy requires the improvement of financial relations between them. Therefore, many reforms are being carried out to develop the banking sector, which is one of the important links of the country's economy. For this purpose, a number of decrees and decisions have been

© The Author(s), under exclusive license to Springer Nature Switzerland AG 2023
Y. Koucheryavy and A. Aziz (Eds.): NEW2AN 2022, LNCS 13772, pp. 93–104, 2023.
https://doi.org/10.1007/978-3-031-30258-9_9

adopted by the government of Uzbekistan. In particular, great attention is paid to ensuring the implementation of the Decree of the President of the Republic of Uzbekistan No. 5992 of May 12, 2020 "On the strategy of reforming the banking system of the Republic of Uzbekistan for 2020–2025" [1].

The role of lending systems in the development of business entities is undoubtedly of great importance. However, at the same time, the ever-increasing demand for credit in the country creates problems such as non-timely repayment of loan funds, default, credit risk and fraud in the industry. Therefore, the introduction of blockchain technology in the field of lending will reduce the weight of such problems and create an opportunity to effectively use the preferential loan funds allocated by the country.

An overview of the effective credit system based on blockchain technology is presented in the following figure (Fig. 1).

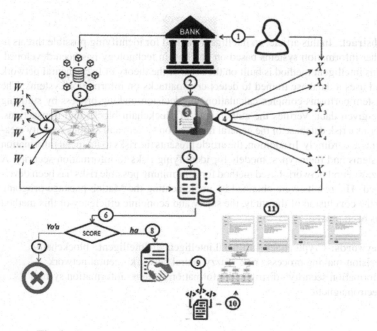

**Fig. 1.** Secure lending system based on blockchain technology

Figure 1 shows the strategy for protecting financial information using blockchain technology. We can intelligently analyze customers using neural networks or fuzzy neural networks in part 4 of this system. We can also identify risks to financial data on the blockchain network [1].

Currently, the business processes of most companies are built taking into account the geography of their points of presence. An example can be companies that have their branches, representative offices and divisions in all territories of the country of presence and beyond. This also applies to public administration processes. The structure of state authorities is distributed over all territories of the Republic of Uzbekistan, respectively, their structural elements are located in the regions and subjects of the country. In this regard, modern information systems in most cases are complex geographically distributed (territorially distributed) systems with their own IT infrastructure, information processing technology and information technologies that implement business processes or public administration processes [2].

Another example of the growth of information leaks is the annual reports "Hi-Tech Crime Trends" of the international company Group-IB, which talks about the activity of socalled progovernment organizations involved in cybercrime (attacks) in the interests of their states. According to the report "Hi-Tech Crime Trends 2020–2021", there is an increase in the growth of cyberattacks using spyware, ransomware, backdoors, an increase in attacks on banks and an increase in financial fraud using social engineering. At the same time, the motive of cybercriminals remains the same - theft of money or information for which you can get financial profit [3].

According to Positive Technologies analytical data, in Q3 2021, there was an increase in the number of incidents by 2.7% compared to the previous period, an increase in the share of APT attacks from 63% to 70%, as well as an increase in attacks and the use of ransomware. Figure 2 shows a graph of the growth in the number of incidents in 2020 and 2021, presented by Positive Technologies [4].

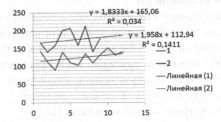

**Fig. 2.** Graph of the number of incidents in 2020 and 2021.

To ensure information security, it is necessary to: determine the goals and objectives of the information system; explore business processes in the information system (functional subsystems, modules and their functions); identify all users of the information system (hereinafter referred to as IS); roles and powers of users in IS (access rights), a list of information technologies that ensure the execution of business processes (IT infrastructure, software, including information security tools, models and methods of user access to IS, etc.). Directly in terms of information security, it is necessary to determine the actual violator in the IS, determine the list of actual threats to information security (modeling information security threats), design and implement an information security system (information protection system), and also conduct a qualitative assessment of the effectiveness of the information protection system on a regular basis [3].

The effectiveness of an information security system is understood as its ability to withstand threats to information security, i.e. the effectiveness of the information security system characterizes the level of security of the information system. Based on the foregoing, the purpose of the study is to improve the quality of evaluating the effectiveness of protection systems for geographically distributed information systems by determining the necessary and sufficient evaluation indicators using promising technologies that make it possible to most effectively solve such problems, namely: determining the best operating parameters of adaptive fuzzy neural production systems, such as most suitable for solving such problems, fuzzy inference algorithms and the use of Data Science technologies when processing large amounts of data.

## 2 Literature Review

The problems of information security in information systems, including the assessment of the effectiveness of the information security system, the assessment of the compliance of the information security system, are reflected in the works of Juraev G.U., Gvozdika Ya.M., Desyatova A.D., Kolomoitsev. G.U. Juraev, A.V. Kabulov from Uzbek scientists on issues of information protection methods and development of cryptographic algorithms. We can cite the scientific works of At the same time, effective methods of protecting financial information are presented in the scientific works of researcher K. Rakhimberdiev [8, 9, 13]. Including, the work of Gvozdik Y.M. research work is devoted to the evaluation of the information security system of automated systems. Functional requirements and safety assurance requirements of the guiding document were chosen as indicators (criteria) for evaluation [2].

Existing methods and techniques for determining (modeling) actual threats to information security and evaluating the effectiveness of an information security system cannot be applied at all stages of the life cycle of a geographically distributed information system; they do not take into account in aggregate such indicators as: IT infrastructure of a geographically distributed information system, actual threats information security, information security requirements, a list of information security tools and their cost, as important indicators in the performance of such tasks [14].

## 3 Methodology

The work uses the methods of implicit enumeration, probability theory and mathematical statistics, dynamic programming, the theory of adaptive fuzzy neural production systems, fuzzy inference algorithms.

## 4 Methodology for Determining Actual Threats to Information Security

### 4.1 Steps to Identify Potential Threats to Financial Information

To effectively determine the list of relevant UBIs, the following steps must be sequentially performed: the following steps must be performed sequentially:

1. Determining the main goals and tasks of information systems.
2. Conduct an analysis of business processes performed by the information system.
3. Conduct an analysis of the protected information processed in the information system.

4. Determine the risks (cyber risks) and negative consequences in the event of these risks.
5. Determine the objects of influence in the information system - elements of the tertiary information system (information assets).
6. Determine the sources of threats to information security (actual offenders), assess the level of their capabilities and motivation.
7. Determine the list of possible threats to information security in information systems, taking into account IT infrastructure and information processing technology.
8. Determine possible ways and scenarios for the implementation of information security threats in information systems - tactics, techniques and procedures.
9. Determine the final list of actual threats to information security, for the neutralization of which it is necessary to develop information protection systems.

## 4.2 Types of Financial Information Security Threats

When compiling the list of information security threats, the following types of threats should be considered:

– threats that are not attacks;
– threats that are attacks.

In the process of data processing of personal and regionally distributed information systems, attacks on the data of individuals and organizations are divided into the following types:
Threats of information leakage through technical channels:

• Threats of unauthorized access to information processed in a geographically distributed information system;
• Threats of special impacts on a geographically distributed information system;
• Threats of information leakage through technical channels include;
• Threats of information leakage through the acoustic channel;
• Threats of information leakage through the visual-optical channel;
• Threats of information leakage through the channel of side electromagnetic;
• Radiation and interference (PEMIN).

Since regionally distributed TRIS does not have voice input functions, there is no risk of acoustic (speech) data leaking directly into regionally distributed information systems.
Unauthorized access (UA) threats are associated with the actions of intruders who have access to TDIS, including TDIS users who implement threats directly in TDIS, as well as intruders without access to TDIS, who implement threats from external public communication networks and (or) international information exchange.
The implementation of UA threats to information can lead to the following types of violation of its security:

• breach of confidentiality;

- violation of integrity;
- violation of accessibility;
- breach of authenticity;
- violation of non-repudiation;
- violation of accountability, authenticity and credibility.

## 5 Choosing a Model for Determining Actual Threats to Information Security

A study of adaptive fuzzy neural production systems ANFIS (adaptive neuro-fuzzy inference system) was carried out using Sugeno-Takagi, Takagi-Sugeno-Kang, Wang-Mendel and Mamdani fuzzy inference algorithms [3]. It is noted that the dependence of the error on the number of rules when checking on a test sample is less for the ANFIS network with the Takagi-Sugeno-Kanga fuzzy inference algorithm. In this regard, to determine the actual IST, the adaptive fuzzy neural production system ANFIS [4] was chosen, based on the fuzzy inference system of Takagi-Sugeno Kang (hereinafter referred to as TSK).

A fuzzy neural network algorithm based on the following rules is used to solve this problem:

$$R_t : IFs_iISA_{i1}AND...ANDs_jISA_{ij}AND...ANDs_{im}ISA_{im}, THEN$$
$$y = d_{i0} + d_{i1}s_1 + d_{i2}s_2 + d_{i3}s_3 + ... + d_{ij}s_j \quad i = 1, ..., n \tag{1}$$

or

$$y = d_{i0} + \sum_{j=1}^{m} d_{ij}s_j \quad i = 1, ..., n \tag{2}$$

To do this, a rule base was formed to determine the actual IST. An example of filling the rule base based on the data set formed in this work is shown in Table 1.

**Table 1.** Fragment of the rule base of the methodology for determining actual VBI

| | Type of intruder | IT - infrastructure | Implementation scenario | TO (THEN) |
|---|---|---|---|---|
| 1 | External intruder with low potential, Internal intruder with low potential | VMWare 6.5 virtual machine (VMWare Workstation), | T1.3 T1.4 T1592.004 T1205 | Threat of unauthorized access to protected virtual machines from other virtual machines (IST.079) |

*(continued)*

**Table 1.** (*continued*)

| | Type of intruder | IT - infrastructure | Implementation scenario | TO (THEN) |
|---|---|---|---|---|
| 2 | External intruder with high potential | Mobile device based on iOS (Android), | T3.1 T7.4 T1204 T1399 | List malware control threat applications running on a mobile device |
| 3 | External intruder with medium potential | Means of protection Information 12.x (Cisco IOS), 15.x (Cisco IOS), Version | T6.1 T7.21 T1562 T1056 | The threat of unauthorized impact on the information security tool (IST.187) |

The number of rules n for the case of determining the actual IST based on is 222. The rules are presented in Table 1 as a single one, in fact, it represents a set of rules consisting separately by the type of intruder, the type of ISTool (information security tool) (for example, SecretNet, Dallas Lock, etc...) and impact. The data set was already formed taking into account these nuances. Responsible – a collection of data from IS IT infrastructure data taken from IST models and UA design decisions [6].

The end result of determining the relevance of IST is calculated by the totality of indicators of the methodology for determining the actual IST, described in Sect. 2.3 of this work.

ANFIS is based on the following provisions [7]:

- Input variables are crisp;
- Membership functions (hereinafter referred to as FF) are defined by the Gaussian function:

$$\mu_{A_{ij}}(s_j) = e^{\frac{-s_j^2 + 2s_j q_{ij} - q_{ij}^2}{2p_{ij}}} \qquad (3)$$

where, $s_j$ - input networks, $p_{ij}$, $q_{ij}$ - configurable FP settings.

- Larsen's fuzzy implication is a fuzzy product;
- T-norm is a fuzzy product;
- Composition is not produced;
- The defuzzification method is the centroid method.

After the defuzzification process to calculate the output variable, the functional dependence has the following form [7]:

$$
y' = \frac{\sum\limits_{i}^{n}\left(\left(d_{i0}+\sum\limits_{j=1}^{m}d_{ij}s_j\right)\prod_{j}^{m}\mu_{A_{ij}}\left(s_j'\right)\right)}{\sum\limits_{i=1}^{n}\prod_{j}^{m}\mu_{A_{ij}}\left(s_j'\right)} = \frac{\sum\limits_{i}^{n}\left(d_{i0}+\sum\limits_{j=1}^{m}d_{ij}s_j\right)\prod_{j}^{m}e^{\left[-\left(\frac{s_j'-p_{ij}}{q_{ij}}\right)^2\right]}}{\sum\limits_{i=1}^{n}\prod_{j}^{m}e^{\left[-\left(\frac{s_j'-p_{ij}}{q_{ij}}\right)^2\right]}}.
$$

(4)

Expression 1 underlies the ANFIS network using the TSK algorithm, which includes five layers:

The first layer performs fuzzification of input crisp variables:

$$
s_j' \quad j = 1, ..., n
$$

(5)

The elements of the second layer calculate the values of the powers of the FP $\mu_{A_{ij}}\left(s_j'\right)$ given by the Gaussian functions with the parameters $p_{ij}, q_{ij}$.

The third layer generates the values of functions $\left(d_{i0}+\sum\limits_{j=1}^{m}d_{ij}s_j\right)$, which are multiplied by the results of calculations by the elements of the second layer.

The first element of layer 4 is necessary to activate the conclusions of the rules in accordance with the values aggregated in the 3rd layer, the degrees of membership of the prerequisites of the rules. The second element of the fourth layer performs additional calculations for the subsequent defuzzification of the result of the ANFIS network. This layer consists of one normalizing element and produces defuzzification of the results of the ANFIS network. ANFIS TSK contains 2 parametric layers (layer 1 and 3). The parameters that can be configured during the training of the ANFIS network are:

- in 1st layer – nonlinear parameters, $p_{ij}, q_{ij}$ FP of the fuzzifier;

- in the 3rd layer - parameters $d_{i0}$ and $d_{i1}$ of linear functions $\left(d_{i0}+\sum\limits_{j=1}^{m}d_{ij}s_j\right)$ from the conclusions of the rule base.

In the presence of n rules and m-input variables, the number of parameters of the 1st layer is equal to $2nm$, and $2-n(m+1)$. The total total number of adjustable parameters is $n(3m+1)$. At the next step of the proposed method, the parameters $d_{i0}$ and $d_{i1}$ of linear functions are calculated under the condition of fixed values of the parameters $p_{ij}, q_{ij}$.

The parameters $c_{i0}$ and $c_{i1}$ are found by solving a system of linear equations.

We represent the output variable from expression 1 in the following form:

$$
y' = \sum\limits_{i=1}^{n}w_j'\left(d_{i0}+\sum\limits_{j=1}^{m}d_{ij}s_j\right)
$$

(6)

where

$$w'_j = \frac{\prod_j^m \mu_{A_{ij}}\left(s'_j\right)}{\sum_{i=1}^n \prod_j^m \mu_{A_{ij}}\left(s'_j\right)} = \frac{\prod_j^m e^{\left[-\left(\frac{s'_j - p_{ij}}{q_{ij}}\right)^2\right]}}{\sum_{i=1}^n \prod_j^m e^{\left[-\left(\frac{s'_j - p_{ij}}{q_{ij}}\right)^2\right]}} = const \quad (7)$$

ANFIS network training algorithm using the TSK algorithm.

With K training examples $s_1^{(k)}, s_2^{(k)}, s_3^{(k)}, ..., s_m^{(k)}, y^{(k)}$, where $k = 1, ..., K$ and replacing the values of the output variables $y'(k)$ with the values of the reference variables $y^{(k)}$, we obtain a system of $K$ linear equations of the form:

$$\begin{bmatrix} w_1^{'(1)} & w_1^{'(1)} s_1^{(1)} & ... & w_1^{'(1)} s_m^{(1)} & w_n^{'(1)} & w_n^{'(1)} s_1^{(1)} & ... & w_n^{'(1)} s_m^{(1)} & 0 \\ w_1^{'(2)} & w_1^{'(2)} s_1^{(2)} & ... & w_1^{'(2)} s_m^{(2)} & w_n^{'(2)} & w_n^{'(2)} s_1^{(2)} & ... & w_n^{'(2)} s_m^{(2)} & 0 \\ ... & ... & ... & ... & ... & ... & ... & ... & ... \\ w_1^{'(k)} & w_1^{'(k)} s_1^{(k)} & ... & w_1^{'(k)} s_m^{(k)} & w_n^{'(1)} & w_n^{'(k)} s_1^{(k)} & ... & w_n^{'(k)} s_m^{(k)} & 0 \end{bmatrix} \times \begin{bmatrix} d_{10} \\ ... \\ d_{1m} \\ ... \\ d_{n0} \\ ... \\ d_{nm} \end{bmatrix} = \begin{bmatrix} y^{(1)} \\ y^{(2)} \\ ... \\ y^{(k)} \end{bmatrix} \quad (8)$$

where $w_1^{'(k)}$ is the aggregated degree of truth of the premises according to the ith rule when presented with the k-th input vector $s_1^{(k)}, s_2^{(k)}, s_3^{(k)}, ..., s_m^{(k)}$.

So 2 in shorthand:

$$W \times D = y \quad (9)$$

The matrix W has dimension equal to $K \times (m + 1)n$, while the number of rows k is much greater than the number of columns: $K \times (m + 1)n$. The solution of this system of equations can be carried out in one step using the pseudo-inversion of the matrix $W$:

$$D = W^+ y = \left(W^T \bullet W\right)^{-1} W^T y \quad (10)$$

After determining the linear parameters ij, we fix and calculate the actual output signals of the network for all examples, for which we use a linear relationship:

$$y' = \begin{bmatrix} y^{(1)} \\ y^{(2)} \\ ... \\ y^{(k)} \end{bmatrix} = W \bullet D \quad (11)$$

define the error vector:

$$e = y' - y \quad (12)$$

we refine the parameters:

$$p_{ij}^{(k)}(t+1) = p_{ij}^{(k)}(t) - C\frac{dE^{(k)}(t)}{dp_{ij}^{(k)}}$$

$$q_{ij}^{(k)}(t+1) = q_{ij}^{(k)}(t) - C\frac{dE^{(k)}(t)}{dq_{ij}^{(k)}}$$

(13)

The structure of the fuzzy neural production network ANFIS using the TSK algorithm is shown in Fig. 3.

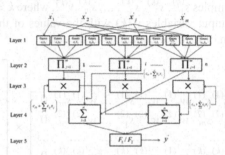

**Fig. 3.** ANFIS network using the TSK algorithm

In order to carry out calculations and determine the actual UBI, in this work, the computer program "Model of Threats and the Intruder" was developed in the Python 3 programming language, and the calculations were carried out in the MATLAB environment to compare and illustrate studies.

### 5.1 Determination of Parameters in the Best Model

With the initial initial data and parameters of the ANFIS network, the network training error was 3.6–3.7. During the experiments, it was found that with certain parameters of the ANFIS network, cleaning and transformation of the initial data set, the training error decreases.

  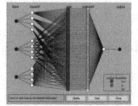

**Fig. 4.** ANFIS settings in the MATLAB environment and the distribution of training data

**Fig. 5.** Structure of the ANFIS network

As a result of training the ANFIS network with the parameters shown in Figs. 4 and 5, with the generated data set, the network training error reached values in the range of 0.018–0.026, which is the best result of the method compared to the existing ones.

# 6   Result

This chapter proposes a method for determining relevant IST in TDIS, the effectiveness of which, in comparison with known methods, is achieved by the following indicators: the number of determined actual IST in TDIS increased by 4,8%, and the reduction in financial costs for the purchase of SRT from 14,8 to 28,2%.

In the work, experiments were carried out for a comparative analysis of the work of the proposed methodology and known classification methods for solving such problems. As a comparative characteristic, the accuracy of determining the actual IST in TDIS was used (classification accuracy). The results of the comparative analysis are shown in Table 2.

**Table 2.** Comparative analysis

|  | Neural network | Fuzzy neural network |
|---|---|---|
| Accuracy of determination of actual IST in TDIS (%) | 69,7 | 79,6 |

Figure 6 shows a graph of a comparative analysis of methods for solving the problem in the research article.

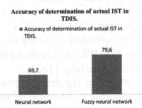

**Fig. 6.** Graph of a comparative analysis of methods for solving the problem

Thus, for the given conditions of the problem (the generated data set after cleaning, transformation, selection of the most useful and created new more representative features) and the indicators for determining the actual IST determined in the work, the proposed method is the best in comparison with the existing ones.

# 7   Conclusion

The use of systems based on the theory of adaptive fuzzy neural development and fuzzy decision-making methods is considered to be highly effective in detecting attacks on the blockchain network and information systems. In particular, the fuzzy neural network-based system detects attacks using necessary and sufficient indicators, which is different from the methods used to detect real threats to blockchain systems. Hypothetically excludes automated and expert errors and increases the number of blockchain attacks to

4.8%. This intelligent method makes it possible to reduce the size of means of detection of attacks on information systems. As a result, spending on crypto-attack detection tools will be reduced from 14.8% to 28.2%. From this, the economic and safety efficiency increases significantly.

## References

1. Rakhimberdiyev, K.B., Mardonov, A.A.: The use of intellectual analysis systems and blockchain technology in improving the bank lending system. Theoretical and methodological aspects of improving the statistical analysis of the development of the digital economy. Institute of Personnel Training and Statistical Research under the State Statistics Committee of the Republic of Uzbekistan, Tashkent, pp. 371–376 (2022)
2. Маслова, Н.А.: Методы оценки эффективности систем защиты информационных систем. Искусственный интеллект, pp. 253–264 (2008)
3. Десницкий, В.А., Сахаров, Д.В., Чечулин, А.А., Ушаков, И.А., Захарова, Т.Е.: Защита информации в центрах обработки данных, Санкт-Петербург (2019)
4. Росс, Г.В.: Моделирование производственных и социально-экономических систем и использованием аппарата комбинаторной математики. – М.: Мир, 176 С (2001)
5. Юсупов, Р.М.: Наука и национальная безопасность. 2-е издание, переработанное и дополненное. - СПб.: Наука, 369 С (2011)
6. Миняев, А.А., Юркин, Д.В., Ковцур, М.М., Ахрамеева, К.А.: Сертификация средств защиты информации: учебное пособие. СПбГУТ. – СПб., 80 С (2020)
7. Круглов, В.В., Дли, М.И., Годунов, Р.Ю.: Нечеткая логика и искусственные нейронные сети. – М.: Физматлит. 224 С (2001)
8. Круглов, В.В.: Искусственные нейронные сети. Теория и практика/В.В. Круглов, В.В. Борисов.- М.: Горячая линия – Телеком. 382 С (2002)
9. Juraev, G., Rakhimberdiev, K.: Mathematical modeling of credit scoring system based on the Monge-Kantorovich problem. In: 2022 IEEE International IOT, Electronics and Mechatronics Conference, IEMTRONICS 2022 Proceedings (2022)
10. Juraev, G., Rakhimberdiev, K.: Modeling the decision-making process of lenders based on blockchain technology. In: International Conference on Information Science and Communications Technologies: Applications, Trends and Opportunities (ICISCT 2021), pp. 1–5 (2022)
11. Juraev, G., Rakhimberdiev, K.: Prospects of application of blockchain technology in the banking. In: International Conference on Information Science and Communications Technologies: Applications, Trends and Opportunities (ICISCT 2022), pp. 1–5 (2022)
12. Karimov, M., Arzieva, J., Rakhimberdiev, K.: Development of approaches and schemes for proactive information protection in computer networks. In: International Conference on Information Science and Communications Technologies: Applications, Trends and Opportunities (ICISCT 2022), pp. 1–5 (2022)
13. Tashev, K., Arzieva, J., Arziev, A., Rakhimberdiev, K.: Method authentication of objects information communication systems. In: International Conference on Information Science and Communications Technologies: Applications, Trends and Opportunities (ICISCT 2022), pp. 1–5 (2022)
14. Arzieva, J., Arziev, A., Rakhimberdiev, K.: Application of random number generators in solving the problem of user authentication in blockchain systems. In: International Conference on Information Science and Communications Technologies: Applications, Trends and Opportunities (ICISCT 2022), pp. 1–5 (2022)
15. Abdullaev, T., Juraev, G.: Application three-valued logic in symmetric block encryption algorithms. J. Phys. Conf. Ser. **2131**(2), 022082 (2021)

# Method Authentication of Objects Information Communication

Rakhimberdiev Kuvonchbek[⊠] (iD)

Tashkent State University of Economics, Tashkent 100066, Uzbekistan
qquuvvoonn94@gmail.com

**Abstract.** In this article, the issue of authentication of objects of information and communication systems based on mutual authentication, models of authentication of users of information and communication systems, the use a five-level authentication model in the control of access to computer systems, the use of blockchain technology in solving the problem of identification and authentication basics, working principle of Blockstack and uPort authentication protocols based on Blockchain technology, advantages and disadvantages of Blockstack, uPort authentication protocols are analyzed. In the given thesis questions of the authentication of objects of information-communication systems on the basis of mutual authenticate are considered. Also, the article considers the results obtained on the development of a model and algorithm for protecting an information system using two-factor authentication based on the generation of a one-time password. The proposed mathematical model of the information security system for user authentication based on the generation of a one-time password is described.

**Keywords:** Cryptoattack · time stamp · blockchain · handshake · information security · information system · cryptocurrencies · banking systems · authentication · identification

## 1 Introduction

Banks play a huge role in the economic life of society, they are often called the circulatory system of the economy. Due to their specific role, since their appearance, they have always attracted criminals. By the 1990s, banks switched to computer processing of information, which significantly increased labor productivity, accelerated settlements and led to the emergence of new services. However, computer systems, which no bank can currently do without, are also the source of completely new threats, previously unknown [9].

This problem is especially relevant in the Republic of Uzbekistan. Republic of banks software (software) is developed specifically for each bank, and the ABS device is largely a trade secret. The availability of computer technology has led to the spread of computer literacy among the general population. This, in turn, caused numerous attempts to interfere in the work of state and commercial, in particular banking, systems, both with malicious intent and out of purely "sporting interest". Many of these attempts were

Y. Koucheryavy and A. Aziz (Eds.): NEW2AN 2022, LNCS 13772, pp. 105–116, 2023.
https://doi.org/10.1007/978-3-031-30258-9_10

successful and caused significant damage to the owners of information and computing systems [7, 8].

It is difficult to imagine a modern bank without an automated information system. The computer on the desk of a bank employee has long become a familiar and necessary tool. The connection of computers between themselves and more powerful computers, as well as with computers of other banks is also a necessary condition for the successful operation of the bank - the number of operations that must be performed in a short period of time is too large. The level of equipment with automation tools plays an important role in the bank's activities and, therefore, directly affects its position and income. Increasing competition between banks leads to the need to reduce the time for making settlements, increase the range and improve the quality of services provided.

These data indicate that the most common violations, such as attacks by hackers or the theft of computers with valuable information, occur most often, but the most ordinary ones arising from daily activities. At the same time, it is intentional attacks on computer systems that cause the greatest one-time damage, and protection measures against them are the most complex and expensive. In this regard, the problem of ABS protection optimization is the most relevant in the field of information security of banks [8].

According to the National 129 Computer Crime Data Center (Los Angeles, USA), computer crimes are most often committed by programmers, students, and input operators. Table 1 shows the main types and subjects of threats to computer systems.

**Table 1.** Main types and subjects of threats to computer systems

| Type of threats | Operator | Organizer | Programmer | Engineer (technical) | User | Competitor |
|---|---|---|---|---|---|---|
| Changing codes | Yes | No | Yes | No | No | No |
| Copying Files | Yes | No | Yes | No | No | No |
| File shredding | Yes | Yes | Yes | No | Yes | Yes |
| Program Assignment | No | No | Yes | Yes | No | Yes |
| Espionage | Yes | Yes | Yes | No | No | Yes |
| Eavesdropping installation | No | No | Yes | Yes | No | Yes |
| Sabotage | Yes | Yes | Yes | Yes | No | Yes |
| Selling data | Yes | Yes | Yes | No | Yes | No |
| Theft | No | Yes | Yes | No | Yes | Yes |

From the point of view of professional readiness, the subjects of computer crimes are usually divided into persons who commit crimes:

– "non-technical";
– "technical", requiring a minimum of special knowledge;
– "high-tech", possible subject to a thorough knowledge of computer technology;

Practice shows that the majority of category "a" crimes are committed by employees with a secondary education who are unfamiliar with computer technology. However, these people are distinguished by two qualities: they have access to a computer and know what functions it performs in their organization. "Non-technical" crimes are committed mainly by stealing the password to access files of information stored in machine memory. With a password and certain skills, you can enter classified files, change their content, and so on.

## 2 Literature Review

Foreign scientists Edna Elizabeth, S. Niveta [1], Fazeh Sadat Babamir, Murvet Kirchi [2], Yi Yu, Jingsha He, Nafei Zhu, Fanbo Tsai, Mohammed Salman dealt with the tasks of information security, access control and authentication based on the second factor. Patan [16] and others. An important part is also the protection of information stored in databases and software and hardware for processing and transmitting information. A significant contribution to the development of this direction was also made by foreign scientists Meshcheryakov R.V. [3], Iskhakov A.Yu. [4], Poltavtseva M.A. [5] and others. In connection with the above, the topic of this article on the development and research of an authentication algorithm for users of information and communication systems based on two stages is relevant. In this dissertation, a one-time password is used as two stages.

## 3 Methodology

The protection of information systems is an urgent task, since they are used to record, process and store data in such systems of various companies. One of the main methods of protecting an information system is user identification based on an additional means of protection during authentication.

## 4 Authentication Models for Bank Lending Platforms

### 4.1 Authentication System Based on Generation of One-Time Password for Bank Lending Platforms

In the course of the study, user authentication methods based on the generation of a one-time password were considered to conduct the efficiency of the algorithms.

One-time passwords OTP (One - Time Passwords) - are generated for a single entry into the information system using software or hardware security methods [9]. The invulnerability of these passwords is based on the use of a given time interval. In this regard, the problem of intercepting the generated one-time password is being solved.

To provide two-factor authentication in information systems, one-time passwords are often used in a group with stored passwords. In the general case, this algorithm looks like this (Fig. 1).

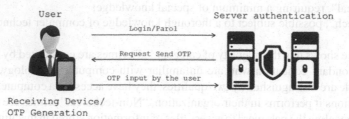

**Fig. 1.** Two-factor authentication scheme using one-time passwords

The use of one-time passwords for two-factor authentication is carried out as follows:

– user credentials are entered (login/password);
– credentials are sent to the authentication server;
– credentials are sent to the authentication server;
– on the server side, a request is generated that generates a one-time code and sends it to devices;
– a one-time password is entered by the user and transmitted to the server;
– the server checks the similarity of passwords;
– verification is satisfactory, authentication is considered successful.

The main sources of one-time passwords used in information systems are the following:

1. Software tokens that generate one-time passwords using a secret key and the current time (OS system time). User secret keys are usually stored on the server, but additional storage can be used if necessary.
2. Software tokens that generate one-time passwords using a secret key and the current time (OS system time). User secret keys are usually stored on the server, but additional storage can be used if necessary.
3. Recording pre-generated one-time passwords or Scratch card. Each time you log into the system, you will need to enter a new generated one-time password with the specified number.

The most common authentication methods are software tokens, which are more in demand and do not require additional costs.

## 4.2 Development of a Two-Factor Authentication Algorithm

A two-factor authentication algorithm has been developed to protect information in information and communication systems, which allows using a combination of permanent and temporary (one-time) passwords. The user chooses a permanent password. A temporary password is generated according to certain algorithms and is valid for a certain time [2].

Additional software is used to obtain a one-time password. One-time password generation is possible online. In this mode, the additional software sends a request to the authorization server to generate a temporary password.

To obtain a one-time password, it is generated on the server side and presented to the user in additional software. A one-time password can contain a specific expiration date up to one minute.

One-time password generation is performed based on the result of a selected specific trigonometric function, which will have a number of variable parameters.

The functions will be combined into an array of 256 by 256 values, their number is 65536. The choice of the trigonometric function and its initial parameters is based on the result of calculating the SHA256 hash function. Also, any type of hash function can be used to calculate the trigonometric function and its initial parameters. The input string for computing the hash function is a combination of the user's credentials, the current point in time, and an additional secret string. The resulting hash function is divided into separate numbers, which will be indices for choosing a trigonometric function and initial data [6].

Before obtaining a one-time numeric password, it is necessary to perform a one-time initialization of the algorithm using the following parameters: $F(t)$ and $W$, where $F(t)$ is the function for obtaining the system time/date, which gives the value $t$, and w is the generated secret word.

The one-time numeric password is calculated using the formula:

$$P_{password} = T(K, N) \tag{1}$$

where $P_{password}$ is the result of the calculated numeric password; $T$ is a function for calculating a one-time numeric password based on user identification based on the entered parameters $K$ and $N$: $K$ is the user's login; $N$-user password.

We expand the function $T(K, N)$ as follows:

$$T(K, N) = Q_{ij}(d, e, f, x, y, s_1, s_2) \tag{2}$$

where $Q_{ij}$ is an array of functions ti,j for computing a one-time numeric password:

$$Q_{ij} = \begin{pmatrix} t_{11} & t_{12} & \cdots & t_{1j} \\ t_{21} & t_{22} & \cdots & t_{2j} \\ \cdots & \cdots & \cdots & \cdots \\ t_{i1} & t_{i2} & \cdots & t_{ij} \end{pmatrix} \tag{3}$$

where $i, j$ is the position of the functions in the array $Q_{ij}$; $d, e, f, x, y, s_1, s_2$ are the parameters of the function to calculate from the array $Q_{ij}$. The position of the function in the array $Q_{ij}$ and its parameters are the result of obtaining a certain number from the generated hash.

Then we find the values of the function parameters (3):

$$i = M(H, \delta_1), \ j = M(H, \delta_2), \ d = M(H, \delta_3), \ e = M(H, \delta_4), \ f = M(H, \delta_5),$$
$$x = M(H, \delta_6), \ y = M(H, \delta_7), \ s_1 = M(H, \delta_8), \ s_2 = M(H, \delta_9)$$

where $M(H, \delta_k)$ is the function of obtaining; $\delta_k$ is the values from the hash $H$.

We calculate the hash from the results obtained:

$$H = F(K, N, t, W) \tag{4}$$

where $F(K, N, t, W)$ is the hash calculation function based on the input parameters $K, N, t, W$; $t$ is the current system time/date, w is the generated secret word.

The one-time password generation algorithm proposed in the dissertation work using an authenticator program and a mobile phone is based on the one-time key generation model for user authentication based on the second factor.

To implement the described algorithm, the SHA256 hash function is used. This hashing algorithm was created by the US National Security Agency (NSA, National Security Agency). Hash functions turn a certain set of elements into a fixed length value and are used to authenticate the user [13]. SHA256 is used to compress digital data to a length of 2.31 exabytes.

Consider an example of obtaining a one-time password. The input data will be the following values: 1) **user login:** Blockchainuser1; 2) **user password:** pass14word; 3) **current time/date:** 25 September 202218:20:38; 4) **secret signs**: UzBCS$.

The input string for calculating the hash will take the form and the result of the hash function will be the following expression Table 2:

**Table 2.** Password and Login hash value calculation

|   | User login | User pass word | Current time/date | Secret string | Password string | Password hash value (SHA 256) |
|---|---|---|---|---|---|---|
| 1 | Blockch ainuser1 | pass14word | 25 september 202218:20:38 | UzBCS$ | Blockchainuser1p ass14word202209 25182038UzBCS$ | cc20291b0ef11d415 7716cce5c2a0f56bdf 461754b232ca91b70 2e0cf85ebf92 |
| 2 | Blockch ainuser2 | pass14word | 25 september 202219:27:39 | Quvca$ | Blockchainuser2p ass14word202209 25192739Quvca$ | a78878c29f65665b7 b72eda9bb8c8764e1 6a73e534a371b8068 2b25337371825 |
| 3 | Blockch ainuser3 | pass14word | 25 september 202220:25:48 | Rakhi% | Blockchainuser3p ass14word202209 25202548Rakhi% | 774f3c6f2341fdbba2 0fd35cd1a5c890522 5c4ab1b5254124d93 0e9b98a78176 |
| 4 | Blockch ainuser4 | pass14word | 25 september 202221:28:56 | Bakht& | Blockchainuser4p ass14word202209 25212856Bakht& | 33e56ba0f2785a377 9be73b6bf9633a486 c658f11837fa0dc2af 5f336f9de368 |

The first characters of the result are used to select the trigonometric function. The resulting numbers "cc,20" must be translated from the hexadecimal number system to the decimal system, the resulting values "204, 32" will be indexes for selecting a trigonometric function from an array of dimension $256 \times 256$. Let's say, for example, the following function will be selected for this index:

$$T_{\text{trigonometric function}} = \frac{\sin^3(x) + \sin(x^2)}{s_1/s_2} \tag{5}$$

where $s_1$ and $s_2$ are the initial parameters.

As the initial parameters, we take two hexadecimal numbers from the end of the hash function value, and as the value of $x$, we take a hexadecimal number from position 10. Then they will take the following values:

$$s_1 = 191(bf), \quad s_2 = 146(92), \quad x = 15(0f) \tag{6}$$

Then the result of the function will be as follows:

$$T_{\text{trigonometric function}} = \frac{\sin^3(15) + \sin(225)}{\frac{191}{146}} = \frac{\sin^3(15) + \sin\left(15^2\right)}{\frac{191}{146}} = -0,500760797575664$$

As a one-time password, we take the numbers after the decimal point, starting from the 5th position and 6 digits long. Then the one-time password is the number 607975.

The proposed two-factor authentication system can be used in the company's information system as an additional security barrier in electronic document management. It is based on the combined use of two authentication factors, which significantly increases the security of information use by users connecting to information systems via secure and unsecured communication channels [10].

### 4.3 Creating Generators for Generating a One-Time Password for Two-Factor Authentication

At the first stage of creating a one-time password, input data was used, where the secret word was entered by the user from the keyboard independently. When researching the algorithm, it became necessary to create a secret word generator. This implementation method will strengthen the protection of the input data when generating a one-time password.

To form a secret string, a generator has been developed that allows you to randomly form words. Dictionaries of words were not used, as words stored in the dictionary are easier to crack.

The secret word generator is based on the use of the Latin alphabet of uppercase and uppercase characters in a total amount equal to 52. The length of the generated word is 5 characters.

For optimization, it is possible to use such methods as [11]:

- a complete bust;
- application of mathematical models;
- analytical study of the system;
- combinatorics method;
- using software tools;

To analyze the durability of the generator, a full search method was used. This method takes into account the length of the string and the search speed per second. The search speed is affected by the characteristics of the software and hardware. The characteristics of the software include antivirus programs, screen protection, operating systems, etc. The characteristics of the equipment include the bandwidth of the data bus, the speed of information storage, network bandwidth, availability of virtualization, etc. These characteristics significantly affect the speed of the algorithm and cannot exceed the iteration rate of 1000000 per second. A 64-core processor can iterate through 1,000,000 words per second.

In the developed user authentication algorithm based on the second factor, the secret word generator works according to the algorithm described above and generates words consisting of 5 characters. The search speed was taken 100,000 words per second, which can be sorted by a 4-Core i7 Processor, which is optimal for using processing on a personal computer [11].

The number of options is calculated by the formula (7), and the search time is calculated by the formula (8):

$$P = E^n \qquad (7)$$

where $P$ is the number of variants; $E$ is the number of characters; n is the length of the string.

$$PQ = \frac{P}{V} \qquad (8)$$

where $PQ$ – is the search time; $P$ – is the number of options; $V$ – is the search speed.

$$P = E^n = 52^5 = 380204032$$

$$PQ = \frac{P}{V} = \frac{380204032}{100000} = 3802, 04032\,\text{s} = \frac{3802, 04032}{60} = 63, 3673\,\text{min} \approx 63\,\text{min}$$

An example of generator analysis is presented in Table 3.

Durability is determined by the measure of time estimation, which is used to select (recognize) a password, while taking into account the number of attempts made in order to guess the password. Also, the durability determines the dependence of the function on the length of the password in characters, its randomness and unpredictability.

**Table 3.** Results of private key length and decryption time

| Number of signs | Number of options | Search speed | Length | Search time seconds |
|---|---|---|---|---|
| 1 | 52 | 100000 | 5 bits | 0,00052 |
| 2 | 2704 | 100000 | 10 bits | 0,02704 |
| 3 | 140608 | 100000 | 15bits | 1,40608 |
| 4 | 7311616 | 100000 | 21 bits | 73,11616 |
| 5 | 380204032 | 100000 | 26 bits | 3802,04032 |
| 6 | 19770609664 | 100000 | 31 bits | 197706,09664 |
| 7 | 1028071702528 | 100000 | 36 bits | 10280717,02528 |
| 8 | 53459728531456 | 100000 | 42 bits | 534597285,31456 |

*(continued)*

**Table 3.** (*continued*)

| Number of signs | Number of options | Search speed | Length | Search time seconds |
|---|---|---|---|---|
| 9 | 2779905883635710 | 100000 | 47 bits | 27799058836,35710 |
| 10 | 144555105949057000 | 100000 | 52 bits | 1445551059490,5700 |
| 11 | 75168655093509700000 | 100000 | 57 bits | 75168655093509,700 |
| 12 | 3908770064862500000000 | 100000 | 63 bits | 3908770064862500000 |
| 13 | 203256043372850000000000 | 100000 | 68 bits | 2032560433728500000 |
| 14 | 10569314255388200000000000 | 100000 | 73 bits | 10569314255388200000 |
| 15 | 549604341280187000000000000 | 100000 | 78 bits | 5496043412801870000000 |
| 16 | 28579425746569700000000000000 | 100000 | 84 bits | 285794257465697000000000 |
| 17 | 1486130138821620000000000000000 | 100000 | 89 bits | 14861301388216200000000000 |
| 18 | 77278767218724500000000000000000 | 100000 | 94 bits | 772787672187245000000000000 |
| 19 | 4018495895373670000000000000000000 | 100000 | 99 bits | 40184958953736700000000000000 |
| 20 | 208961786559431000000000000000000000 | 100000 | 105 bits | 2089617865594310000000000000000000 |

Random passwords are generated by random selection of any number of characters and font type with the possible use of text cases. Then the choice of any symbol from some set of symbols is equally probable. The strength of a random password depends on the entropy of the random number generator used, and pseudo-random number generators are often used. The use of limited entropy is used in software libraries that are used to generate random numbers; standard dictionaries can also be used. Applications for creating one-time passwords result in a generated password consisting of a certain length of characters [13]. To determine the complexity of a random password, measured in terms of information entropy, is calculated using formula 9:

$$P_{entropy} = \log_2 E^K = K \log_2 E = K \left( \frac{\log E}{\log 2} \right) \tag{9}$$

where $P_{entropy}$ is the result, measured in bits, $E$ is the number of possible characters; $K$ is the number of characters in the password.

## 5  Result

In the developed authentication algorithm for users of information and communication systems, based on the generation of a one-time password, a secret string generator has been created, which is one of the input parameters. This secret word generator uses 52 characters of 26 uppercase and 26 uppercase Latin letters, calculated in accordance with formula 9.

Table 3 shows that 5 characters are sufficient to generate the secret word, since the secret word is just one of the parameters for hash generation. Due to the fact that, in accordance with the developed two-factor authentication algorithm, a one-time password is generated every 20 s, the probability of breaking the generated secret word is very small. If you use the brute force method to check the strength of the algorithm, then with an increase in the number of characters in the password, the number of brute force options increases. We take 52 characters as a basis, and the speed is 1,000,000 words per second (these characteristics are higher than those of commonly used personal computers, for example, in IIVT). Table 4 shows the results of entropy calculation.

**Table 4.** Entropy calculation results

| Number of signs $n$ | Number of options | Length | Entropy |
|---|---|---|---|
| 1 | 52 | 5 bits | 5,700439718 bits |
| 2 | 2704 | 10 bits | 22,80175887 bits |
| 3 | 140608 | 15bits | 51,30395746 bits |
| 4 | 7311616 | 21 bits | 91,20703549 bits |
| 5 | 380204032 | 26 bits | 142,510993 bits |
| 6 | 19770609664 | 31 bits | 205,2158299 bits |
| 7 | 1028071702528 | 36 bits | 279,3215462 bits |
| 8 | 53459728531456 | 42 bits | 364,828142 bits |
| 9 | 2779905883635710 | 47 bits | 461,7356172 bits |
| 10 | 144555105949057000 | 52 bits | 570,0439718 bits |
| 11 | 7516865509350970000 | 57 bits | 689,7532059 bits |
| 12 | 390877006486250000000 | 63 bits | 820,8633194 bits |
| 13 | 20325604337285000000000 | 68 bits | 963,3743124 bits |
| 14 | 1056931425538820000000000 | 73 bits | 1117,286185 bits |
| 15 | 54960434128018700000000000 | 78 bits | 1282,598937 bits |
| 16 | 2857942574656970000000000000 | 84 bits | 1459,312568 bits |
| 17 | 148613013882162000000000000000 | 89 bits | 1647,427079 bits |
| 18 | 7727876721872450000000000000000 | 94 bits | 1846,942469 bits |
| 19 | 401849589537367000000000000000000 | 99 bits | 2057,858738 bits |
| 20 | 20896178655594310000000000000000000 | 105bits | 2280,175887 bits |

We can compare the results of Table 4 in the following graph. In this, we can compare secret word length and entropy metrics (Figs. 2 and 3).

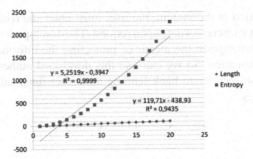

**Fig. 2.** Secret word length and entropy metrics

**Algorithm 1.** As a result of the generator, we get a string function in JavaScript, which will be processed on the server side.

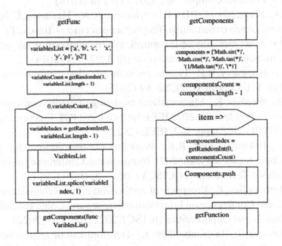

**Fig. 3.** Algorithm getFunc and getComponents function

## 6 Conclusion

An algorithm has been developed to enhance the means of protecting information in an information system. The algorithm is based on the choice of a certain trigonometric function and a number of variable parameters. The choice of parameters is based on the result of the SHA256 hash function. The input string for the hash function is the user's credentials, the current GMT time, and an additional secret string. An analysis of the stability of the developed secret word generator was carried out using the brute force method, as well as a trigonometric function generator based on random array formation. From the result of the calculation of the function, a temporary code is generated, which is displayed only in the user's mobile application, linked to the online system login. For successful authorization in the system, the user must enter the received code after an authorization attempt with correct data upon request. The developed model and algorithm makes it possible to strengthen the means of protecting the information system based on two-factor authentication. So we can use this developed authentication algorithm to ensure information security in bank lending and other financial systems based on blockchain technology.

## References

1. Edna Elizabeth, N., Nivetha, S.: Design of a two-factor authentication ticketing system for transit applications. In: IEEE Region 10 Conference (TENCON), pp. 2496–2502. Singapore (2016)
2. Babamir, F.S., Kirci, M.: Dynamic digest based authentication for client–server systems using biometric verification. Future Gener. Comput. Syst. **101**, 112–126 (2019)
3. Yu, Y., He, J., Zhu, N., Cai, F., Pathan, M.S.: A new method for identity authentication using mobile terminals. Procedia Comput. Sci. **131**, 771–778 (2018)
4. Исхаков, А.Ю., Мещеряков, Р.В., Шелупанов, А.А., Исхаков, С.Ю.: Современные методы и способы идентификации. Теория и практика. – Томск: ТГУСУР 114 (2016)
5. Исхаков, А.Ю: Система двухфакторной аутентификации на основе QR кодов. Безопасность информационных технологий **3**, 97–101 (2014)
6. Evseev, S.P., Tomashevskyy, B.P.: Two-factor authentication methods threats analysis. Radio Electron. Comput. Sci. Control 1(32), 52–59 (2015)
7. Juraev, G., Rakhimberdiev, K.: Mathematical modeling of credit scoring system based on the Monge-Kantorovich problem. In: 2022 IEEE International IOT, Electronics and Mechatronics Conference (IEMTRONICS), pp. 1–7. IEEE (2022)
8. Umarovich, J.G., Bakhtiyorovich, R.K.: Modeling the decision-making process of lenders based on blockchain technology. In: 2021 International Conference on Information Science and Communications Technologies (ICISCT), pp. 1–5. IEEE (2021)
9. Juraev, G., Rakhimberdiev, K.: Prospects of application of blockchain technology in the banking. In: International Conference on Information Science and Communications Technologies: Applications, Trends and Opportunities (ICISCT 2022), pp. 1–5 (2022)
10. Karimov, M., Arzieva, J., Rakhimberdiev, K.: Development of approaches and schemes for proactive information protection in computer networks. In: International Conference on Information Science and Communications Technologies: Applications, Trends and Opportunities (ICISCT 2022), pp. 1–5 (2022)
11. Tashev, K., Arzieva, J., Arziev, A., Rakhimberdiev, K.: Method authentication of objects information communication systems. In: International Conference on Information Science and Communications Technologies: Applications, Trends and Opportunities (ICISCT 2022), pp. 1–5 (2022)
12. Arzieva, J., Arziev, A., Rakhimberdiev, K.: Application of random number generators in solving the problem of user authentication in blockchain systems. In: International Conference on Information Science and Communications Technologies: Applications, Trends and Opportunities (ICISCT 2022), pp. 1–5 (2022)
13. Sulak, F.: Cryptographic random testing of block ciphers and hash functions. Publication of the Middle East Technical University Ph.D. Examinations, pp. 7–39 (2011)

# TEDCTSSA: Trust Enabled Data Collection Technique Based Sparrow Search Algorithm for WSN-Based Applications

Walid Osamy[1,2] , Ahmed M. Khedr[3,5] , Ahmed Salim[4,5] ,
and Ahmed Aziz[1,6(✉)]

[1] Computer Science Department, Faculty of Computers and Artificial Intelligence,
Benha University, Benha, Egypt
walid.osamy@fci.bu.edu.eg
[2] Unit of Scientific Research, Applied College, Qassim University,
Unaizah, Qassim, Kingdom of Saudi Arabia
w.elsherif@qu.edu.sa
[3] Computer Science Department, University of Sharjah,
Sharjah 27272, UAE
akhedr@sharjah.ac.ae
[4] Department of Computer Science, College of Sciences and Arts, Al-methnab,
Qassim University, P. O. Box 931, Buridah 51931, Al-mithnab,
Kingdom of Saudi Arabia
a.salem@qu.edu.sa
[5] Faculty of Science, Zagazig University, Zagazig, Egypt
amkhedr@zu.edu.eg
[6] Tashkent State University of Economics, Tashkent, Uzbekistan
a.mohamed@tsue.uz

**Abstract.** Wireless sensor networks (WSNs) are typically used to monitor and detect diverse objects in realistic environments, where security remains a major concern. Estimating the trust between WSN nodes increases the security of the network, and so enhances node-to-node communication. Here, we introduce a Trust Enabled Data Delivery Technique based Sparrow Search Algorithm (SSA) for WSN-based applications (TEDCTSSA). In TEDCTSSA, a nature-inspired based SSA and secure cluster head (CH) selection method based on node's trust value and energy is proposed. For the efficient selection of CH, our fitness function takes into account node remaining energy and trust value. The simulation results reveal that the suggested method is more energy-efficient, provides a longer average network lifetime, and selects the most trustworthy nodes than other works in the literature.

**Keywords:** Data collection · Swarm Algorithms · Trust · Clustering · Internet of Things · Wireless Sensor Networks

© The Author(s), under exclusive license to Springer Nature Switzerland AG 2023
Y. Koucheryavy and A. Aziz (Eds.): NEW2AN 2022, LNCS 13772, pp. 117–132, 2023.
https://doi.org/10.1007/978-3-031-30258-9_11

# 1    Introduction

Wireless Sensor Networks (WSNs) is one of the prominent technology that has made rapid progress recently [1–8,19,20]. Simply WSNs can be described as a single system that glue low-power embedded components, sensors, wireless module, and distributed data processing. It is made up of a large number of low cost static or dynamic sensor nodes (SNs) that can perform real-time perceiving, monitoring, and gleaning data from the defined target in specific locations. WSN has the potential to create a plethora of applications for military, disaster relief services. Self-organization capability of WSN makes it has unlocked up a variety of application possibilities [9]. WSNs primary benefits are its low price and distributed intelligence. They save money on installation and maintenance since they use low-cost devices that don't require wire. WSN distributed intelligence could pave the way for the creation of a variety of applications that aid in real-time traffic safety [10].

Internet of Things (IoT) is a combination of various technologies such as WSN, cloud computing, data information, big data [11,12]. WSNs already be integrated into IoT [13,14] because IoT has a large number of connected sensor nodes. The main task of IoT components is to capture, collect, store and transmit data to base stations (BS) [15]. The problem of retrieving data across large distributed wireless networks is an obstacle in the development of IoT technologies [16,17]. Therefore, it is highly required to find creative technologies that extend the life of network [18].

Clustering is a logical way of arranging sensor nodes (SNs) based on a set of pre-defined criteria into a set of groups called clusters for optimal network energy usage and enhancing WSNs lifetime. One of the most appropriate approaches to identify faulty nodes or malicious nodes in WSNs is trust management. It provides robustness to the network and ensures the secure delivery of data as well as secure resource sharing [22–24]. To achieve enhanced data security, we adopted a clustering method that incorporates trust management and it is aware of energy consumption and trustworthiness of nodes. As the choice of a suitable CH with sufficient residual energy is crucial for the network's overall performance.

The goal of this study is to create a trust-based WSN clustering method for a WSN-based application. Based on the node's various trust parameters and residual energy, this study proposes an energy-efficient and safe CH selection mechanism. The following will summarize our paper's contributions:

1. A new clustering method that safely selects CHs using trust parameters for a WSN-based application is developed.
2. A new fitness function that considers residual energy and trust value weighted by the number of SNs that satisfy thresholds conditions for the selection of CHs is designed.
3. For the efficient selection of CH, one of the recent SI optimization approaches, the Sparrow Search Algorithm, is used.
4. A comprehensive comparison between our proposed TEDCTSSA approach and other existing clustering work is given.

The rest of the paper is organized as follows. Section 2 provides the literature review of some related works. Section 3 provides the Problem Formulation and System Model, Sect. 4 describes the proposed TEDCTSSA. Section 5 presents our simulation results. Finally, Sect. 6 concludes our work.

## 2  Related Work

WSNs are a data-monitoring technology that is becoming increasingly popular which make them ideal for various applications since they lower the cost of deployed devices while also lowering installation expenses by removing the need for wired infrastructure. Several research publications have discussed clustering in WSN. LEACH is the first clustering method devised, and it selects CH based on probability. Because of the practical challenges with LEACH, an upgraded LEACH with a more practical set-up step has been proposed. Improved LEACH [25] builds clusters using Adaptive On-demand Weighting (AOW), which is a trade-off between total energy and residual energy as well as competition range. Currently, more than 60 enhanced variants of LEACH protocols have been proposed [26]. The authors of [27] introduced MG-LEACH, an upgraded LEACH that includes a new phase called set building, which occurs before the set-up and steady-state phases in the basic LEACH. Due to the threshold, network density, and residual energy, the new phase creates sub-groups via communicating with BS. However, because every round requires communication with BS, this strategy adds a load. Furthermore, the burden of the CH has not been evenly distributed.

In [28], a proposed a clustering method ELEACH to improve the LEACH protocol's ability to transfer sensed data from source nodes to the sink. The ELEACH procedure is identical to the LEACH except that the distance between the sink and the SNs is also taken into account while choosing CHs. This reduces energy usage by lengthening the network's lifespan. The technique in [29] stabilizes the construction of clusters in WSN, and the CH election is accomplished using a few factors such as the optimal cluster count, remaining energy of the SNs, and threshold. The authors of [30] proposed a WSN clustering algorithm to improve energy consumption and WSN lifetime by selecting CHs based on balancing the number of nodes in clusters, remaining power, and determining abandoned nodes to submit their data to the sink. Then, CHs select the best way to the sink.

The majority of research on energy-aware cluster-based approaches is predicated on the assumption that all SNs are trustworthy. As a result, the selection of a CH is mostly determined by the energy level of a single node. However, in the actual scenario, malicious or compromised nodes have an equal potential to function as CH, resulting in poor network performance [31]. As a result, because SNs are typically installed in hostile areas, security is an important and challenging issue in Cluster-based WSN [32]. To address these concerns, a substantial body of work based on various encryption techniques, such as [33–39], has sought to solve the problem of safe clustering in WSNs, focusing on issues like CH selection criteria, dynamic key change, complexity, and so on.

SLEACH [33] is the first attempt to design a secure clustering model. In SLEACH, the sink-hole, HELLO flooding, and selective forwarding attacks are all avoided in this model. SLEACH suffers from memory requirements as well as network performance and lifetime issues. Following this, a new model [36, 40] was recently developed to overcome these restrictions and handle the memory size issue. Homomorphic encryption and elliptic curve cryptography are used in this concept. It is extremely difficult to implement cryptography-based procedures in SNs since they are resource-constrained and low-cost small devices. As a result, various research works on trust-aware approaches have been introduced with the goal of improving network lifetime and performance in WSNs [21, 41–43].

STELR proposed in [52] to overcome security concerns in WSNs. STELR employ emperor penguin optimization (EPO) algorithm for the selection of cluster head and for data aggregation. Based on Elephant Herd Optimization, a trust-based security method is built in [53]. The proposed routing selects routes to destination based on the trust values, thus, finding optimal secure routes for transmitting data.

The work in [44] presented GradeTrust, a secure routing system based on node trust degrees. A clustering-based secure routing protocol was proposed in [45] to protect against different types of attacks. While the CHs require permanent energy supply equipment, resulting in high WSN layout requirements. The beta reputation and direct trust (BRDT) model is utilized for secure communication in WSNs to reduce energy usage in the BRDT model [46]. Large overlapping communication ranges among CHs, on the other hand, frequently lead to an excessive number of CHs, wasting energy. A lightweight and fast deployable trust-based secure routing protocol (TBSRP) was introduced in [47] to reduce the computational complexity of the SNs. TBSRP can detect and isolate misbehaving nodes. The TBSRP's goal is to find the shortest path that includes all trustworthy nodes, discover packet forwarding misbehaviour caused by malicious or malfunctioning nodes, and divert traffic to more secure paths.

HiTSeC is a trust-based CH selection methodology for WSN that is recently introduced by the authors of [51]. For the selection of CHs, they used the Bat Optimization Algorithm. Each node in HiTSeC is responsible for monitoring the behaviour of its cluster neighbours. CHs are also in charge of assessing each member's trustworthiness depending on the results of other members' assessments. The values are then forwarded to BS to be finalized and malicious nodes detected.

In our proposed work, we will pick CHs using one of the most recent SI optimization techniques, the sparrow Swarm algorithm. For the most efficient selection of CHs, we will take into account each SN's trust value and residual energy. And the goal of this research is to provide a safe WSN clustering technique for WSN-related applications that extends the network lifetime compared to previous studies.

## 3    Problem Formulation and System Model

This section discusses the problem formulation, and system model that are used in the proposed strategy.

## 3.1   Problem Formulation

The clustering concept works by electing leaders among the sensor nodes. These leaders then gather information from members of their cluster, perform data aggregation, and then report the aggregated data to the sink. Nonetheless, being a CH could use considerable energy, so rotating it instead of fixing it could provide significant energy savings. The ability to control the energy distribution in a network, in order to guarantee a longer lifetime for the network, is among the most important criteria for determining the efficiency of a clustering protocol design for distributed WSNs. Designing a protocol capable of uniformly distributing energy within a network is not an easy task. On the other side, security is a crucial and challenging topic in Cluster-based WSN. The entire network may contain both normal and malicious nodes, and malicious or compromised SNs have the same ability to function as CH, leading to poor network performance. As a result, one of the most difficult aspects of choosing CH is determining which SN is the most trusted by all CMs. So, the goal of this research is to provide a trust-based CH selection technique for WSN-based that extends network lifetime as well as ensure that resources in the network are used efficiently and effectively by implementing a protocol that can distribute energy consumption equally across all nodes.

## 3.2   System Model

The following considerations guide the development of the proposed framework. $n$ sensor nodes are distributed randomly in with dimension $R \times R$ and a fixed BS. The energy model used is same as that of [25, 27–29, 51] because it is the generally known model used in several research works. We are following the trust model inspired by the work in [51]. The suggested trust model in [51] calculates the trust value of every SN in two tiers. In the first-tier normal SN and CH calculate the trust value and it is called node tier. BS calculates the trust value in the second tier, which is known as the BS tier.

The network is built with the following assumptions:

1. The SNs are capable of self-localization [48–50].
2. All SNs are static and a unique ID is assigned to every node.
3. All SNs can listen and cooperate with other neighbors whose lie within their communication transmission range.
4. Environmental data (for example, humidity or temperature) is gathered by SNs and then SNs send it to their CHs.

# 4   TEDCTSSA: Trust Enabled Data Delivery Based Sparrow Search Algorithm

In this section, we will discuss our proposed TEDCTSSA technique for trust-based WSN clustering. TEDCTSSA uses and modifies the SSA for efficient WSN clustering.

The clustering problem can be regarded as an optimization problem because it seeks to find the best solution among all possible solutions. Optimization is the process of maximizing or minimizing an objective function in order to find a solution to a complex or difficult problem. Meta-heuristic algorithms have emerged as a promising method for solving complicated optimization problems. The SSA [25] is one of the most recent nature-inspired meta-heuristic search algorithms, which is naturally inspired by the social behaviour of sparrows. The design of SSA was motivated by the anti-predation and foraging behavior of sparrows. Some of its qualities include good resilience, great stability, and rapid convergence. This technique has a lot of potential for refinement and may be used to handle real-world issues like non-linear optimization and reducer design. Based on their foraging behaviors, the SSA algorithm divides sparrows into two groups: producers and scroungers. Producers are responsible for identifying sources of food, whereas scroungers are responsible for collecting food from producers. Sparrows on the outskirts of the group are more vulnerable to attack, therefore they assemble towards the center. Sparrows in the flock's center will approach their neighbors to lessen the risk of being attacked. A sparrow warns when it detects danger, and the entire sparrow flock escapes. More details about SSA can be founded in [25].

The TEDCTSSA clustering model proposed in this study is based the SSA. Our optimization goal in TEDCTSSA clustering algorithm is to choose a set of SNs to work as CHs that have a higher average trust value and maximize network lifetime.

The major objectives of this clustering technique are to extend the network lifetime, choose the most trustworthy SNs to be CHs. A real-valued vector ($\in [0,1]$) is used to represent each sparrow (SSA works in continuous space). However, we consider an individual's binary representation in our approach, in which the index represents the SN id and the 0 value indicates that the SN is not a CH, while the 1 value indicates that the SN is a CH. The transformation procedure is as follows:

$$B(x) = 1 \qquad \text{if x} > 0.5, \qquad \text{otherwise} \qquad 0 \qquad (1)$$

TEDCTSSA includes the CH election and Cluster formation processes, and after $t$ time when the energy level of one or more CHs fall below a user-defined threshold, it restarts the clustering process.

The whole process of the TEDCTSSA can be described as follows:

1. The CH selection process will be started by the BS, where the BS broadcasts a message requesting every SN to send their IDs, residual energy level, list of neighbours, and estimated trust values for their neighbours.
2. From the the obtained trust values for each SN, BS determines the final trust value for each SN.
3. BS generates a final list which includes SN id ($N_{id}$), final trust value ($TR_i$), residual energy ($RE_i$), and the number of neighbours which is called the list of candidate's information.

4. BS picks a set of trusted SNs as the CHs in the network using the following TEDCTSSA clustering algorithm.
   - Initialize the SSA parameters that includes maximum iterations count, number of sparrows, producers count, danger sparrows count, alarm value, and safety threshold.
   - Initialize the sparrow positions to create a search space.
   - Repeat the following up to maximum iteration
     (a) Using Eq. (1), convert the real-valued population to a binary population
     (b) For each solution (sparrow) $s_i$ in the population; evaluate the fitness value of each sparrow using Eq. (5).
     (c) Sort the population based on the fitness value of each sparrow and arrange them as producers and scroungers.
     (d) If this iteration is the first iteration, set *best_solution* as the first sparrow and *best_fitness* as its fitness value. Otherwise, Update *best_solution* and *best_fitness* to the first sparrow if it has fitness value higher than the current *best_fitness*.
     (e) Update the position of sparrows as follows:
        i. Updating Producers Location: During each round, the producer's position is changed as follows:

$$x_{i,j}^{t+1} = \begin{cases} x_{i,j}^t.exp(\frac{-i}{\alpha.T_{max}}), & \text{if R2} < \text{ST} \\ x_{i,j}^t + Q.L, & \text{otherwise} \end{cases} \quad (2)$$

where t is the number of iterations, and $T_{max}$ is the maximum number of iterations. The location of the $i^{th}$ sparrow in the $j^{th}$ dimension is $x_{i,j}^t$. A random number $\alpha \in (0,1]$, the alert value is R2, and $R2 \in [0,1]$. The safety threshold is $ST \in [0.5,1]$. Q is a normal-distributed number created at random. A matrix $(1 \times d)$ with all members equal to 1 is denoted by the letter L. When $R2 < ST$, it signifies there are no predators in the feeding environment at this moment, enabling the producer to do extensive searches. When $R2 \geq ST$, it means that some of the population's sparrows have detected predators and have warned their fellow sparrows. At this moment, all sparrows must flee to safer feeding places.

        ii. Updating Scroungers Location: Scroungers make up the rest of the sparrow population, which maintains a watchful check on the producers. They will leave their current site and fly to better foraging grounds if they perceive the producer has found better food. The positions of the scroungers have been revised as follows:

$$x_{i,j}^{t+1} = \begin{cases} Q.exp(\frac{x_{worst}^t - x_{i,j}^t}{i^2}), & \text{if } i > n/2 \\ x_P^{t+1} + |x_{i,j}^t - x_P^{t+1}|.A^+.L, & \text{otherwise} \end{cases} \quad (3)$$

where, $x_p$ denotes the producer's best position, and $x_{worst}$ is the present global worst location. A is a $1 \times d$ matrix (each element with value 1 or $-1$ at random) and $A^+ = A^T(AA^T)^{-1}$. When $i > n/2$, it indicates that the $i^{th}$ scroungers with lesser fitness did not receive food, were extremely hungry, and had to fly somewhere to obtain more food.

iii. Detection and Early Warning Behavior: The colony's sparrows have a scouting and early warning system. In general, sparrows who are aware of the predator make up 10% to 20% of the colony. The following is the mathematical model's description:

$$x_{i,j}^{t+1} = \begin{cases} x_{best}^t + \beta.|x_{i,j}^t - x_{best}^t|, \text{if } f_i > f_g \\ x_{i,j}^t + K.(\frac{|x_{i,j}^t - x_{worst}^t|}{(f_i - f_w) + \epsilon}), \text{if } f_i = f_g \end{cases} \quad (4)$$

where $x_{best}$ represents the present global optimal position. $\beta$ is a normally distributed random (mean 0, variance 1). It is used as a step control parameter. Current sparrow individual's fitness value is $f_i$, & $K \in [0, 1]$ is a random number. The current global best is $f_g$. The worst fitness value is $f_w$. $\epsilon$ is the smallest constant used to prevent zero value in denominator. When $f_i > f_g$, the sparrows are on the border of the population and are particularly prone to attack. $f_i = f_g$ indicates that middle-of-the-population sparrows are danger aware and must be near to neighboring sparrows to avoid being preyed on. K is a step control factor that defines the direction of the sparrow's movement.

(f) Finally goto step 4.

– Return *best_solution* and *best_fitness*. *best_solution* contains the best-selected clusters.

5. Following the selection of CHs, BS selects the nearest non-CHs from an elected CH to be its CMs.

6. A message is delivered to each SN designated as a CH to advise it of its selection, as well as to the other non-CHs SNs to inform them of their linked CHs.

7. CMs should submit their sensed data to their CH regularly which aggregate, and then send the aggregated data to BS. For data accuracy review the CH includes with the disseminated data its ID along with the IDs of its CMs.

8. BS starts a new CH election procedure by broadcasting a new election message to all CHs after $t$ time or when the energy level of one or more CHs falls below a user-defined threshold. Then, using Steps 2–7, each CH should collect the relevant election information from SNs in its cluster and submit it to the BS, which will select the new CHs.

The following section provides the fitness function that used in the clustering algorithm.

**Fitness Function.** TEDCTSSA chooses CHs based on residual energy and trust value. In TEDCTSSA, the best solution is one with the lowest fitness value, implying that our optimization goal is to minimize the value of the fitness function. Our fitness function is represented by the following equation.

$$F = (\sum_{i=1}^{ch} \frac{1}{1 + RE_{ch}}) * \frac{1}{CR+1} + (\sum_{i=1}^{ch} \frac{1}{1 + TR_{ch}}) * \frac{1}{CT+1} \qquad (5)$$

The CR is the number of CHs whose residual energy is greater than or equal to the residual energy threshold. The CT is the number of live CH nodes whose trust value is greater than or equal the trust threshold. CRT is the number of live CHs whose satisfy both of the two thresholds. RE is the residual energy and TR is the trust value. $ch$ represents the total number of CHs.

The TEDCTSSA clustering approach selects CHs using the SSA. The fitness function stated in Eq. 5 is used to analyse each solution in the clustering process. The best solution is the one with the lowest fitness value.

## 5    Simulation Results

The performance evaluation of the proposed work is obtained based on MAT-LAB. The trust value of SNs is computed as a value in $(0,1)$, while, malicious node's percentage is set to 10%. We consider heterogeneous setting for SN energies, the percentage of the advanced SNs is set to 10% with initial energy for the advanced SN is 1 $J$ and 0.5 $J$ for the normal SNs.

We consider 100 SNs are randomly scattered in the region of size 100 × 100 meters square with BS at the (100,100) with 10% as percent of CHs with $E_{th}$ = 0.05 and $T_{th} = 0.5$.

The following are the the performance metrics that we are follow:

1. Network Lifetime: These are the total number of SNs, those have not yet exhausted all of their energy and have enough energy to continue communication operation. Network lifetime can calculated as the FND (first node dies), HND (half node dies) and LND(last node dies) The time period until the first SN becomes dead in the network field is termed as FND or Stability Period.

2. Average Trust Value of CHs (ATV):

$$ATV = \frac{\sum_{i=1}^{r_{last}} AT(r)}{r_{last}}, \qquad (6)$$

where $AT(r)$ is the average trust value of $chs$ (total trust values of CHs divided by the number of CHs) at round $r$ and $r_{last}$ is the round number at which the last SN dies.

In this section, we compare the performance of the proposed approach with the performance of existing algorithms HiTSeC [51] (minimum number of CHs = 1 and maximum number of CHs = $p * n$ ), Improved-Leach [25], MG-LEACH [27], RCH-LEACH [29] and Enhanced-LEACH [28] with Trust threshold 0.5 and using the above performance metrics and setting.

The main goal of WSN clustering is to extend the life of the network by lowering the number of SNs that die during its operation. The number of alive SNs over rounds is used to compute the lifetime of the WSN.

Figures 1, 2 and 3 show the network lifetime over round. The figure show that the lifetime of WSN using TEDCTSSA is significantly better than HiT-SeC, Improved-Leach, MG-LEACH, RCH-LEACH, and Enhanced-LEACH over rounds. While the results also illustrate that Enhanced-LEACH starts to have dead SNs before HiTSeC, Improved-Leach, MG-LEACH, and RCH-LEACH. These figures clearly show that TEDCTSSA's first SN dies outperformed all of these algorithms. We can notice clearly, that TEDCTSSA has a superior lifetime of the network under FND compared with HiTSeC, Improved-Leach, MG-LEACH, RCH-LEACH, and Enhanced-LEACH up to 41%, 139% 28%, 25 and 400%, respectively. TEDCTSSA enhanced the network lifetime for HND comparing to HiTSeC, Improved-Leach, MG-LEACH, RCH-LEACH, and Enhanced-LEACH up to 15%, 14% 11%, 12% and 16%, respectively. This figure shows that the stability period of TEDCTSSA is significantly longer than that of HiTSeC, Improved-Leach, MG-LEACH, RCH-LEACH, and Enhanced-LEACH. This is because new fitness function, which selects CHs with high residual energy and trust value. It is also clear from the results that the stability period of Enhanced-LEACH is very short when compared to other protocols.

The time interval between the time slot when the first SN becomes dead and the time slot when the last SN becomes dead is called the instability period. TEDCTSSA enhanced the instability period comparing to HiTSeC, Improved-Leach, MG-LEACH, RCH-LEACH, and Enhanced-LEACH up to 80%, 93% 84%, 87% and 84%, respectively.

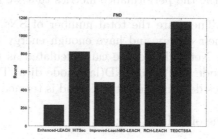

**Fig. 1.** Network Lifetime in terms of FND.

In this test the network energy consumption is evaluated, and the Residual Energy (RE) which can be used to estimate how efficiently network energy is used. Figure 4 show the average residual energy over round. Figure 4 shows that all of the protocols consume around the same amount of average residual energy.

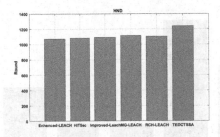

**Fig. 2.** Network Lifetime in terms of HND.

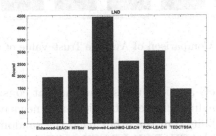

**Fig. 3.** Network Lifetime in terms of LND.

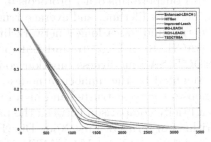

**Fig. 4.** Average residual energy per round.

TEDCTSSA is intended to ensure the trustworthiness of CHs, and this goal is achieved by using a defined fitness function, which causes the algorithm to select SNs with trust values greater than or equal to trust threshold to be the CHs. The average trust value of various protocols is compared in Fig. 5. This figure clearly shows that the average trust value of Improved-Leach, MG-LEACH, RCH-LEACH, and Enhanced-LEACH is less than the trust threshold 0.5, whereas HiTSeC and TEDCTSSA only select CHs with an average trust value more than the trust threshold. This is because the fitness function in HiT-SeC and TEDCTSSA picks CH with a trust value larger than the trust threshold.

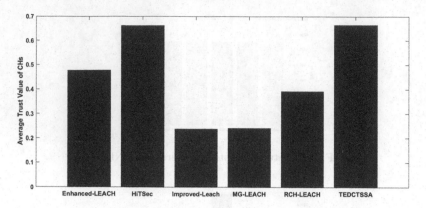

**Fig. 5.** Comparison of Average Trust Value of CHs.

In summary, HiTSeC applies fitness function that considers only the degree of the node to select the final cluster set which has a negative impact on the network lifetime, and stability. On the other hand the random selection of CHs in Improved-Leach, MG-LEACH, RCH-LEACH and Enhanced-LEACH algorithms leads to low average trust value because random selection increases the probability of selecting untrusted CHs, which prolongs instability period and decreases the stability. TTEDCTSSA outperforms other protocols in, stability, instability, average residual energy, network lifetime, and average trust value of CHs, i.e., TEDCTSSA uses less energy, and has a longer network lifetime than HiTSeC, Improved-Leach, MG-LEACH, RCH-LEACH, and Enhanced-LEACH. For the selection of CHs in TEDCTSSA, our fitness function considers both residual energy and trust value weighted by the number of nodes that pass energy and trust thresholds, so it chooses the most trusted and high residual energy SNs as the CHs. Table 1 shows a briefly comparison between the proposed TEDCTSSA and other existing algorithms in terms of First Node Die (FND), Half Node Die (HND), Last Node Die and Average Trust Value (ATV).

**Table 1.** Compare TEDCTSSA with existing algorithms

|                | FND    | HND  | LND    | ATV  |
| -------------- | ------ | ---- | ------ | ---- |
| **Enhanced-LEACH** | 231.8  | 1071 | 1942.4 | 0.48 |
| **HiTSeC**         | 821.8  | 1082 | 2218.2 | 0.67 |
| **Improved-LEACH** | 485.6  | 1091 | 4436   | 0.24 |
| **MG-LEACH**       | 905.6  | 1113 | 2602   | 0.24 |
| **RCH-LEACH**      | 924.6  | 1104 | 3019.4 | 0.39 |
| **Proposed**       | 1159.8 | 1239 | 1436.8 | 0.67 |

# 6   Conclusion

In this paper, we introduced Trust Enabled Data Delivery Technique using Sparrow Search Algorithm for WSN (TEDCTSSA), a nature-inspired and secure CH selection method for WSN based on a node's trust value. For selecting CHs in TEDCTSSA. Our fitness function takes two parameters into account: residual energy and trust value to yield trusted and energy-efficient CHs. Also, we used Sparrow Search Algorithm to search a set of nodes with residual energy and trust value. The simulation results show that our proposed TEDCTSSA is more stable, trustworthy, and energy-efficient than HiTSeC, Improved-Leach, MG-LEACH, RCH-LEACH, and Enhanced-LEACH, and has a longer network lifetime. The proposed TEDCTSSA outperforms the existing algorithms (HiTSeC, Improved-Leach, MG-LEACH, RCH-LEACH and Enhanced-LEACH) up to 0.41, 1.39, 0.28,0.25 and 4, respectively in terms of FND. TEDCTSSA shows the best HND comparing to HiTSeC, Improved-LEACH, MG-LEACH, RCH-LEACH and Enhanced-LEACH up to 15%, 14%, 11%, 12% and 16%, respectively in terms of HND. The proposed work can be extend by considering nodes with different transmission radius and study its effect.

# References

1. Aziz, A., Osamy, W., Khedr, A.M., Singh, K.: Energy efficient scheme for data gathering in internet of things based heterogeneous wireless sensor networks. Wireless Pers. Commun. **114**, 1905–1925 (2020). https://doi.org/10.1007/s11277-020-07454-4

2. Osamy, W., El-sawy, A.A., Khedr, A.M.: SATC: a simulated annealing based tree construction and scheduling algorithm for minimizing aggregation time in wireless sensor networks. Wireless Pers. Commun. **108**(2), 921–938 (2019). https://doi.org/10.1007/s11277-019-06440-9

3. Khedr, A.M.: Effective data acquisition protocol for multi-hop heterogeneous wireless sensor networks using compressive sensing. Algorithms **8**(4), 910–928 (2015)

4. Aziz, A., Osamy, W., Khedr, A.M.: Effective algorithm for optimizing compressive sensing in IoT and periodic monitoring applications. J. Netw. Comput. Appl. **126**(15), 12–28 (2019)

5. Osamy, W., El-Sawy, A.A., Khedr, A.M.: Effective TDMA scheduling for data collection in tree based wireless sensor networks. Peer-to-Peer Netw. Appl. **13**, 796–815 (2020). https://doi.org/10.1007/s12083-019-00818-z

6. Osamy, W., Salim, A., Khedr, A.M., El-Sawy, A.A.: IDCT: intelligent data collection technique for IoT-enabled heterogeneous wireless sensor networks in smart environments. IEEE Sens. J. **21**(18), 21099–21112 (2021). https://doi.org/10.1109/JSEN.2021.3100339

7. Aziz, A., Singh, K., Osamy, W., et al.: An efficient compressive sensing routing scheme for internet of things based wireless sensor networks. Wireless Pers. Commun. **114**, 1905–1925 (2020). https://doi.org/10.1007/s11277-020-07454-4

8. Aziz, A., Salim, A., Osamy, W.: Adaptive and efficient compressive sensing based technique for routing in wireless sensor networks. In: Proceedings of INTHITEN (IoT and its Enablers) (2014)

9. Huanan, Z., Suping, X., Jiannan, W.: Research on technology of wireless sensor network. In: Kountchev, R., Mahanti, A., Chong, S., Patnaik, S., Favorskaya, M. (eds.) Advances in Wireless Communications and Applications. SIST, vol. 190, pp. 109–114. Springer, Singapore (2021). https://doi.org/10.1007/978-981-15-5697-5_13

10. Losilla, F., Garcia-Sanchez, A.-J., Garcia-Sanchez, F., Garcia-Haro, J., Haas, Z.J.: A comprehensive approach to WSN-based ITS applications: a survey. Sensors 11(11), 10220–10265 (2011). https://doi.org/10.3390/s111110220

11. Haupt, J., Bajwa, W.U., Rabbat, M., Nowak, R.: Compressed sensing for networked data: a different approach to decentralized compression. IEEE Sig. Process. Mag. 25(2), 92101 (2008)

12. Ulusoy, A., Gurbuz, O., Onat, A.: Wireless model-based predictive networked control system over cooperative wireless network. IEEE Trans. Ind. Inf. 7(1), 4151 (2011)

13. Al-Kashoash, H.A., Kharrufa, H., Al-Nidawi, Y., Kemp, A.H.: Congestion control in wireless sensor and 6LoWPAN networks: toward the internet of things. Wireless Netw. 25(8), 4493–4522 (2018). https://doi.org/10.1007/s11276-018-1743-y

14. Rahmani, A.M., et al.: Exploiting smart e-health gateways at the edge of healthcare internet-of-things: a fog computing approach. Future Gener. Comput. Syst. 78, 641–658 (2018)

15. Dhumane, A.V., Prasad, R.S.: Multi-objective fractional gravitational search algorithm for energy efficient routing in IoT. Wireless Netw. 25(1), 399–413 (2019). https://doi.org/10.1007/s11276-017-1566-2

16. Palopoli, L., Passerone, R., Rizano, T.: Scalable offline optimization of industrial wireless sensor networks. IEEE Trans. Ind. Inf. 7(2), 328329 (2011)

17. Li, S., Xu, L., Wang, X.: Compressed sensing signal and data acquisition in wireless sensor networks and internet of things. IEEE Trans. Ind. Inf. 9(4), 2177–2186 (2013)

18. Kavitha, M., Geetha, B.G.: An efficient city energy management system with secure routing communication using WSN. Cluster Comput. 22, 13131–13142 (2019). https://doi.org/10.1007/s10586-017-1277-6

19. Osamy, W., Khedr, A.M., Salim, A., AlAli, A.I., El-Sawy, A.A.: Recent studies utilizing artificial intelligence techniques for solving data collection, aggregation and dissemination challenges in wireless sensor networks: a review. Electronics 11(3), 313 (2022). https://doi.org/10.3390/electronics11030313

20. Osamy, W., Khedr, A.M., Salim, A., Al Ali, A.I., El-Sawy, A.A.: A review on recent studies utilizing artificial intelligence methods for solving routing challenges in wireless sensor networks. Peer J. Comput. Sci. 8, e1089 (2022). https://doi.org/10.7717/peerj-cs.1089

21. Aziz, A., Osamy, W., Khedr, A.M., Salim, A.: Iterative selection and correction based adaptive greedy algorithm for compressive sensing reconstruction. J. King Saudi Univ. - Comput. Inf. Sci. 34(3), 892–900 (2022)

22. Dhulipala, V.R.S., Karthik, N.: Trust management technique in wireless sensor networks: challenges and issues for reliable communication: a review. CSI Trans. ICT 5(3), 281–294 (2017). https://doi.org/10.1007/s40012-017-0169-5

23. Fang, W., Zhang, W., Chen, W., Pan, T., Ni, Y., Yang, Y.: Trust-based attack and defense in wireless sensor networks: a survey. Wireless Commun. Mob. Comput. 2020, 1–20 (2020)

24. Yan, Z., Zhang, P., Vasilakos, A.V.: A survey on trust management for internet of things. J. Netw. Comput. Appl. 42, 120–134 (2014)

25. Singh, S.K., Kumar, P., Singh, J.P.: A survey on successors of LEACH protocol. IEEE Access 5, 4298–4328 (2017). https://doi.org/10.1109/access.2017.2666082

26. Ren, P., Qian, J., Li, L., Zhao, Z., Li, X.: Unequal clustering scheme based LEACH for wireless sensor networks. In: 2010 Fourth International Conference on Genetic and Evolutionary Computing (2010). https://doi.org/10.1109/icgec.2010.30
27. Ouldzira, H., Lagraini, H., Mouhsen, A., Chhiba, M., Tabyaoui, A.: MG-LEACH: an enhanced leach protocol for wireless sensor network. Int. J. Electr. Comput. Eng. (IJECE). **9**, 3139 (2019). https://doi.org/10.11591/ijece.v9i4.pp3139-3145
28. Abu Salem, A.O., Shudifat, N.: Enhanced LEACH protocol for increasing a lifetime of WSNs. Pers. Ubiquit. Comput. **23**(5), 901–907 (2019). https://doi.org/10.1007/s00779-019-01205-4
29. Panchal, A., Singh, L., Singh, R. K.: RCH-LEACH: residual energy based cluster head selection in LEACH for wireless sensor networks (2020). https://doi.org/10.1109/ICE348803.2020.9122962
30. Daanoune, I., Baghdad, A., Ballouk, A.: Improved LEACH protocol for increasing the lifetime of WSNs. Int. J. Electr. Comput. Eng. (IJECE). p-ISSN 2088–8708, e-ISSN 2722–2578 (2020). https://doi.org/10.11591/ijece.v11i4.pp3106-3113
31. Rajeswari, A.R., Kulothungan, K., Ganapathy, S., Kannan, A.: Trusted energy aware cluster based routing using fuzzy logic for WSN in IoT. J. Intell. Fuzzy Syst. **40**(5), 9197–9211 (2021). https://doi.org/10.3233/jifs-201633
32. Elsayed, W., Elhoseny, M., Sabbeh, S., Riad, A.: Self-maintenance model for wireless sensor networks. Comput. Electr. Eng. (2017). https://doi.org/10.1016/j.compeleceng.2017.12
33. Xiao-yun, W., Yang, L., Ke-fei, C.: SLEACH: secure low-energy adaptive clustering hierarchy protocol for wireless sensor networks. Wuhan Univ. J. Nat. Sci. **10**(1), 127–131 (2005). https://doi.org/10.1007/bf02828633
34. Oliveira, L.B., et al.: SecLEACH-on the security of clustered sensor networks. Sig. Process. **87**(12), 2882–2895 (2007). https://doi.org/10.1016/j.sigpro.2007.05.016
35. Yin, J., Madria, S.K.: ESecRout: an energy efficient secure routing for sensor networks. Int. J. Distrib. Sens. Netw. **4**, 67–82 (2008). https://doi.org/10.1080/15501320802001101
36. Elhoseny, M., Elminir, H., Riad, A., Yuan, X.: A secure data routing schema for WSN using elliptic curve cryptography and homomorphic encryption. J. King Saud Univ. - Sci. **28**, 262–275 (2015). https://doi.org/10.1016/j.jksuci.2015.11.001
37. Reegan, A.S., Kabila, V.: Highly secured cluster based WSN using novel FCM and enhanced ECC-ElGamal encryption in IoT. Wireless Pers. Commun. **118**(2), 1313–1329 (2021). https://doi.org/10.1007/s11277-021-08076-0
38. Ganesh, S., Amutha, R.: Efficient and secure routing protocol for wireless sensor networks through SNR based dynamic clustering mechanisms. J. Commun. Netw. **15**(4), 422–429 (2013). https://doi.org/10.1109/jcn.2013.000073
39. Huang, L., Li, J., Guizani, M.: Secure and efficient data transmission for cluster-based wireless sensor networks. IEEE Trans. Parallel Distrib. Syst. **25**(3), 750–761 (2014). https://doi.org/10.1109/tpds.2013.43
40. Elhoseny, M., Yuan, X., El-Minir, H.K., Riad, A.M.: An energy efficient encryption method for secure dynamic WSN. Secur. Commun. Netw. **9**(13), 2024–2031 (2016). https://doi.org/10.1002/sec.1459
41. Jerusha, S., Kulothungan, K., Kannan, A.: Location aware cluster based routing in wireless sensor networks. Int. J. Comput. Commun. Technol. 36–41 (2015). https://doi.org/10.47893/IJCCT.2015.1271
42. Sahoo, R.R., Singh, M., Sardar, A.R., Mohapatra, S., Sarkar, S.K.: TREE-CR: trust based secure and energy efficient clustering in WSN. In: 2013 IEEE International Conference ON Emerging Trends in Computing, Communication and Nanotechnology (ICECCN) (2013). https://doi.org/10.1109/ice-ccn.2013.6528557

43. Yan, L., Pan, Y., Zhang, J.: Trust cluster head election algorithm based on ant colony systems. In: 2010 Third International Joint Conference on Computational Science and Optimization (2010). https://doi.org/10.1109/cso.2010.205
44. Airehrour, D., Gutierrez, J., Ray, S.K.: GradeTrust: a secure trust based routing protocol for MANETs. In: 2015 International Telecommunication Networks and Applications Conference (ITNAC) (2015). https://doi.org/10.1109/atnac.2015.7366790
45. Wang, T., Zhang, G., Yang, X., Vajdi, A.: A trusted and energy efficient approach for cluster-based wireless sensor networks. Int. J. Distrib. Sens. Netw. **12**(4), 3815834 (2016). https://doi.org/10.1155/2016/3815834
46. Priayoheswari, B., Kulothungan, K., Kannan, A.: beta reputation and direct trust model for secure communication in wireless sensor networks. In: Proceedings of the International Conference on Informatics and Analytics - ICIA-16 (2016). https://doi.org/10.1145/2980258.2980413
47. Ahmed, A., Bakar, K.A., Channa, M.I., Haseeb, K.: Countering node misbehavior attacks using trust based secure routing protocol. Telkomnika (Telecommun. Comput. Electr. Control). **13**, 260–268 (2015). https://doi.org/10.12928/TELKOMNIKA.v13i1.1181
48. Silmi, S., Doukha, Z., Moussaoui, S.: A self-localization range free protocol for wireless sensor networks. Peer-to-Peer Netw. Appl. **14**(4), 2061–2071 (2021). https://doi.org/10.1007/s12083-021-01155-w
49. Sabale, K., Mini, S.: Localization in wireless sensor networks with mobile anchor node path planning mechanism. Inf. Sci. **579**, 648–666 (2021)
50. Lalama, Z., Boulfekhar, S., Semechedine, F.: Localization optimization in WSNs using meta-heuristics optimization algorithms: a survey. Wireless Pers. Commun. 1–24 (2021). https://doi.org/10.1007/s11277-021-08945-8
51. Gaber, T., Abdelwahab, S., Elhoseny, M., Hassanien, A.E.: Trust-based secure clustering in WSN-based intelligent transportation systems. Comput. Netw. **146**, 151–158 (2018). https://doi.org/10.1016/j.comnet.2018.09.015
52. Rajesh, L., Mohan, H.S.: EPO based clustering and secure trust-based enhanced LEACH routing in WSN. In: Karrupusamy, P., Balas, V.E., Shi, Y. (eds.) Sustainable Communication Networks and Application. LNDECT, vol. 93, pp. 41–54. Springer, Singapore (2022). https://doi.org/10.1007/978-981-16-6605-6_3
53. Veerapaulraj, S., Karthikeyan, M., Sasipriya, S., Shanthi, A.S.: An optimized novel trust-based security mechanism using elephant herd optimization. Comput. Syst. Sci. Eng. **44**(3), 2489–2500 (2023)

# ISTOA: An Improved Sooty Tern Optimization Algorithm for Multilevel Threshold Image Segmentation

Reham R. Mostafa[1], Ahmed M. Khedr[2], and Ahmed Aziz[3,4($\boxtimes$)]

[1] Department of Information Systems, Mansoura University, Mansoura, Egypt
reham_2006@mans.edu.eg
[2] Computer Science Department, University of Sharjah, Faculty of Science, Fayoum University, Sharjah 27272, United Arab Emirates
akhedr@sharjah.ac.ae
[3] Tashkent State University of Economics, Tashkent, Uzbekistan
a.mohamed@tsue.uz
[4] Computer Science Department, Faculty of Computers and Artificial Intelligence, Benha University, Benha, Egypt

**Abstract.** This paper introduces an improved version of well-known Sooty Tern Optimization Algorithm (STOA). The improved version combines Opposition based learning (OBL) to introduce the Improved Sooty Tern Optimization Algorithm (ISTOA). The OBL strategy increases population diversity and avoids falling into local solutions. The efficiency of the proposed ISTOA is verified on multilevel threshold segmentation based on the objective functions of Kapur, and its performance is compared with the original algorithm and another metaheuristic algorithm. Experimental results reveal that the proposed ISTOA outperforms other algorithms in terms of fitness, peak signal-to-noise ratio, structural similarity, and segmentation findings.

**Keywords:** Sooty Tern Optimization Algorithm (STOA) · Opposition-based learning (OBL) · multilevel thresholding · image segmentation · Kapur's entropy

## 1 Introduction

Image segmentation is an important pre-processing step in most image analyzing-based applications, which serves the purpose of breaking down the image into meaningful homogeneous pieces or objects depending on the nature of the problem, so that the data can be analyzed more easily [1,2]. Several segmentation methods are available in the literature, and the process of image segmentation can be accomplished in different ways [3,4]. Thresholding-based segmentation is one of the most fundamental methods for performing image segmentation because it involves less calculations and is more effective [5,6].

© The Author(s), under exclusive license to Springer Nature Switzerland AG 2023
Y. Koucheryavy and A. Aziz (Eds.): NEW2AN 2022, LNCS 13772, pp. 133–148, 2023.
https://doi.org/10.1007/978-3-031-30258-9_12

Thresholding partitions the image into groups that can distinguish between object pixels and background pixels. Bi-level thresholding and multilevel thresholding are the two image thresholding approaches. With bi-level thresholding, the image is split into two classes (background and foreground), and hence cannot be used for grayscale or color images since it produces a binary image as a segmented result. Contrarily, multi-level thresholding splits the image into diffferent classes that correspond to various objects and backgrounds by selecting a number of thresholds. This technique extracts more information from the resulting segmented images and is widely adopted. However, the computational complexity increases with the increase in the number of segmentation levels.

Obtaining the optimal threshold values is one of the most difficult tasks in thresholding-based segmentation. For this, parametric and non-parametric methods are utilized. The parametric approaches rely on mathematical functions to estimate the histogram (for eg. Gaussian mixture). Non-parametric approaches rely on statistical criteria or entropy measurements to choose the appropriate thresholds. Kapur's Thresholding approach, which relies on the principle of maximizing entropy to measure class homogeneity, is a popular statistical entropy-based thresholding approach [7]. This method shows good performance in bi-level thresholding segmentation; however, when extended to multi-level threshold segmentation, it cannot give the same performance because multi-level thresholding is more complex and computationally expensive.

The field of image segmentation has been subjected to a great deal of research over the past few decades, and it has been discovered that multilevel image thresholding using traditional methods requires more time because it iteratively searches for the best results to optimize the objective function [8,9]. Meanwhile, meta-heuristic methods are found to be more efficient and hence acquires a lot of attention in handling different optimization problems [10–14]. Well-known meta-heuristic methods that are successfully used in multilevel thresholding include Fruitfly optimization algorithm (FOA) [15], Moth-flame optimization (MFO) [16], Black widow optimization (BWO) [17], Chimp optimization algorithm (ChOA) [18], and Krill Herd Optimization (KHO) [19]. In addition, hybrid approaches such as modified grasshopper optimization algorithm (MGOA) [20], modified firefly algorithm (MFA) [21], hybrid tunicate swarm algorithm (TSA-LEO) [22], modified remora optimization algorithm (MROA) [23], and hybrid artificial ecosystem-based optimization and differential evolution (AEODE) [24] are also utilized by researchers to enhance the effectiveness.

One of the latest metaheuristic algorithms, the Sooty Tern Optimization Algorithm (STOA), which imitates the sooty tern's natural migratory and attack patterns, is found to outperform other well-known competitors on a multitude of scientific and technical benchmark problems in numerous domains as a result of its features such as simple structure, fewer parameters and fast convergence [25–27]. However, this algorithm's single search guidance approach and position updating mechanism make it difficult to locate the global optimal solution and is vulnerable to population diversity loss while handling with complex optimization issues [28,29]. Therefore, to address these shortcomings, this paper proposes an improved version of the STOA algorithm, named as, ISTOA by exploiting the Opposition-based learning (OBL) strategy. In particular, the OBL is utilized in the initialization and updating stages of the basic STOA algorithm to improve its population diversity, therefore empowering the exploration capability.

The proposed ISTOA is then employed to solve the multi-level thresholding image segmentation challenges. Employing Kapur's entropy objective function, the proposed ISTOA and the state-of-the-art methods are individually tested using various metrics to demonstrate the performance and efficacy of ISTOA for this problem. For example, peak signal-to-noise ratio (PSNR), the mean and standard deviation of fitness and structural similarity index (SSIM) are computed to analyze the performance.

The main contributions of this study are summarized as follows:

- An improved version of the original STOA, named ISTOA, is proposed for multilevel thresholding segmentation problems.
- OBL strategy is integrated into the original STOA to solve its limitations, and it is applied in (1) the initialization phase to enhance the first generation and (2) the update stages of STOA to improve solutions.
- Employing Kapur's entropy objective function, the proposed ISTOA is tested using various metrics to demonstrate the performance and efficacy of ISTOA in solving the multi-level thresholding image segmentation challenges
- The proposed ISTOA method is tested with the state-of-the-art techniques using well-known grayscale images.

## 2   Methods

### 2.1   Sooty Tern Optimization Algorithm (STOA)

After studying the sooty tern's behavior in the nature, Dhiman and Kaur devised the STOA algorithm [25] through modeling the behavior of attacking and migration for this unique type of creature. Sooty terns eat a wide variety of prey. During their migration (discovery), they travel in teams to find the richest areas and use aerial navigation to pinpoint their prey during attacks. To avoid a collision, they tend to keep a safe distance between each other. Birds in a flock follow the path of the strongest/best bird in the flock and adjust their positions accordingly. STOA represents both exploration and exploitation in a search space mathematically as follows:

- The goal of migration behaviour (Exploration) is to calculate the distance between search agents meeting two criteria.
  - The avoidance of Collision between each agent and its neighbours

$$\vec{C_i} = S_A \times \vec{P_i}(t) \tag{1}$$

where $\vec{C_i}$ is the agent position that avoids collisions, $\vec{P_i}(t)$ is the search agent $i$'s position in iteration $t$, while the movement of the agent in search space is noted as $S_A$ and is calculated as follows:

$$S_A = C_f \times \left( Z \times \left( \frac{C_f}{\text{Tmax}} \right) \right) \tag{2}$$

where $Tmax$ is maximum iterations count, $Z = 1, 2, \ldots, Tmax$, and $S_A$ is adapted by the controlling variable $C_f$ which is initialized at 2 and decreases linearly to 0 over time.

- The movement of search agents in the direction of the best neighbor. The movement $M_i$ of agent $P_i$ towards best agent is determined as follow:

$$\overrightarrow{M_i} = C_B \times \left( \overrightarrow{P_{bst}}(t) - \overrightarrow{P_i}(t) \right) \tag{3}$$

where $\overrightarrow{P_{bst}}$ denotes the best agent, $C_B$ is a random variable utilized for greater exploration which is calculated as below:

$$C_B = 0.5 \times R_{\text{and}} \tag{4}$$

where $R_{\text{and}}$ is a random number in the range $[0, 1]$.

- Then, agent's position is updated according to the best agent as follow:

$$\overrightarrow{D_i} = \overrightarrow{C_i} + \overrightarrow{M_i} \tag{5}$$

where $\overrightarrow{D_i}$ is the agent's new position that satisfy the two criteria.

- In the attacking behavior (exploitation) of sooty terns, they adjust their velocity and angle during attack. These creatures enhance their altitude during attacks by flapping their wings in the following ways:

$$s_x' = R_{\text{rad}} \times \sin(i) \tag{6}$$

$$s_y' = R_{\text{rad}} \times \cos(i) \tag{7}$$

$$s_z' = R_{\text{rad}} \times i \tag{8}$$

$$r = u \times e^{kv} \tag{9}$$

where variable $i$ falls within the range of $[0 \leq i \leq 2\pi]$, and $R_{\text{rad}}$ denotes the radius of each spiral turn. The spiral form is defined by the constants $u$ and $v$, and the base of the natural logarithm is $e$. The position of the agent is then updated as given below:

$$\overrightarrow{P_i}(t) = \left( \overrightarrow{D_i} \times (s_x' + s_y' + s_z') \right) + \overrightarrow{P_{bst}}(t) \tag{10}$$

## 2.2  Opposition-Based Learning (OBL)

OBL is a strategy that has been adopted as an effective technique for improving various optimization methods [30]. Meta-algorithms usually achieve fast convergence to optimal solutions when the initial population of solutions is close to the optimal solution space; Otherwise, late convergence is expected. The main idea of the OBL strategy is to select a new set of solutions from the existing ones by taking the opposition and then comparing the fitness value of these solutions to determine a better candidate solution to reach the optimal solution. To demonstrate OBL strategy more precisely, assume that $X_i$ is a solution of N-dimension, then the opposite solution $\bar{X}_l$ can be determined as given below:

$$\bar{X}_i = (ub + lb) - X_i \tag{11}$$

where the dimension's upper and lower bounds are $ub$ and $lb$, respectively. The two solutions ($X_i$ and $\bar{X}_i$) are often compared by their fitness values during the optimization process, with the optimal solution being stored and the other being discarded.

## 3    Proposed ISTOA Method

A thorough explanation of the proposed ISTOA optimization strategy is given in this section. It begins with a review of the original STOA algorithm inadequacies and then moves on to the steps of the proposed ISTOA that works on improving the initial solutions to the problem.

### 3.1    Shortcomings of the Original Algorithm

Dhiman and Amandeep developed STOA algorithm by mathematical modelling the sooty tern's migration and attack behaviours to solve optimization problems. STOA's structure is straightforward and simple to apply. Nonetheless, STOA's flaws are also glaring. In STOA, for instance, only the best individual controls the update of other individuals' locations throughout the migrating and attacking phases, resulting in robust local exploitation but a weaker global exploration capability. It's possible that this search method can't escape a local optimal solution, leading to a loss of population diversity and an untimely halt in evolutionary progress in the population.

Accordingly, this paper introduces an improved STOA algorithm (ISTOA) to address the original STOA algorithm's shortcomings and enhance its search capabilities. ISTOA is based on employing the OBL method to increase the population's diversity and improve search efficiency.

### 3.2    Architecture of Proposed ISTOA Method

In this section, we present the proposed ISTOA method, which takes advantage of STOA's strengths and fine-tuning it for the multilevel threshold image segmentation problem. In ISTOA method, OBL strategy is used to increases population diversity and enhances solutions quality. Figure 1 depicts the framework of the proposed ISTOA. The following is an illustration of the proposed ISTOA algorithm's steps (Algorithm 1):

- Step one involves generating an initial population $X$ with size $N$ by a random generation function, as stated in the following equation:

$$X_i = lb + \text{rand}_i(ub - lb) \quad i = 1, 2, \ldots, N \tag{12}$$

where $X_i$ represents a particle's initial position vector, the dimension's upper and lower bounds are $ub$ and $lb$, respectively, $N$ is the total particles count, and $\text{rand}_i$ is a random vector over the interval $[0, 1]$.

- The second step involves using the OBL method to create a new population $\bar{N}$ by taking the opposite of $N$ using Eq. (11), where $N$ denotes the initial population. Then by using the objective function, evaluate N and $\bar{N}$ populations, compare the fitness of $N$ and $\bar{N}$, and finally select the best $N$ solution and the global best outcome with the maximum fitness $P_{bst}$.
- In the third step, solutions in both exploitation and exploration phases are updated.
- The fourth step is carried out to assess the previous step's generated solutions for improving the solution's quality in the following iterations. In light of this, ISTOA evaluates and compares the fitness of each solution in the current population with its opposite solution, then updating the current best global solution.
- In fifth step, the proposed method continue with the iterations until the stopping requirement is satisfied.

---

**Algorithm 1** . Pseudo-code of ISTOA algorithm.

---

1: **Input:** Size of Population (N), maximum Iterations (Tm), dimension of problem (dim)
2: **Output:** Best search agent $\overrightarrow{P_{bst}}$
3: Generate the initial population of solutions $X$
4: Apply OBL on the population $X$ using Eq. (11) and create $\bar{X}$
5: Evaluate the objective function (fitness) of $X$ and $\bar{X}$ and return the best $N$ solutions
6: $\overrightarrow{P_{st}}(z) :\leftarrow$ best search agent
7: Determine the initial parameters $S_A$ and $C_B$ using Eq. (2) and Eq. (4), respectively.
8: **for** $t = 1 : Tm$ **do**
9:     **for** $i = 1 : N$ **do**
10:         Update the positions of search agents, Eq. (10).
11:     **end for**
12:     Update $S_A$ and $C_B$ parameters.
13:     **for** $i = 1 : N$ **do**
14:         Evaluate $X_i$ after update using fitness function
15:         Create the opposite using OBL strategy using Eq. (11)
16:         **if** fitness $(\bar{X}_l) >$ fitness $(X_i)$ **then**
17:             Set $X_i = \bar{X}_t$
18:         **end if**
19:     **end for**
20:     Update $\overrightarrow{P_{bst}}$ if a better solution exists than the preceding optimum solution.
21:     $t = t + 1$
22: **end for**
23: Return $\overrightarrow{P_{bst}}$.

---

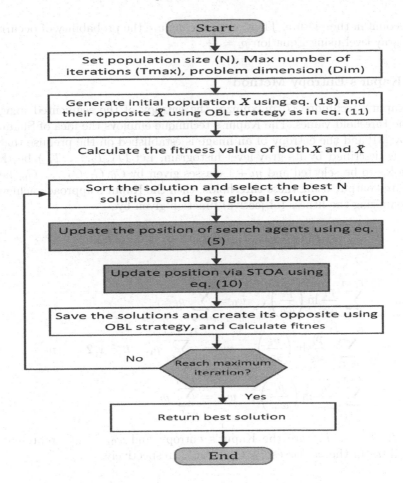

**Fig. 1.** Flowchart of ISTOA method

# 4    Application of Proposed Method in Image Segmentation

The fundamental goal of image segmentation, which involves dividing an image into several segments, is to make the objects' representation in the image simpler for subsequent processing. The critical aspect of using the multilevel thresholding image segmentation process is to determine the optimal thresholds for segmenting images more accurately. To discover the best thresholds, Kapur's entropy-based method is a well-known one. The entropy approach of Kapur is briefly described in this section.

Consider that the function $f(x, y)$ describes an image as a 2D gray-level intensity function, where the gray level is specified as a value in the range of $\{0, 1, 2, \ldots, L-1\}$. Let $n_i$ be the pixels count at intensity $i$ and $N$ be the total pixels count in the picture. Then, we can compute the probability of occurrence of $ith$ gray level using Equation $p_i = \frac{n_i}{N}$.

## 4.1 Kapur's Entropy Method

The Kapur's technique [7] maximizes the entropy of the segmented image to find the threshold values. The Kapur's technique employs the idea of Shannon's entropy [31] and the entropy of an image is established on the premise that the image is described by its gray-level histogram. Let $(T_1, T_2, \ldots, T_m)$ be the $m$ thresholds to be selected and $m + 1$ classes given by $C_0, C_1, C_2, \ldots, C_m$ be the segmented output using these thresholds, then the Kapur's approach achieves it by maximizing the fitness (objective) function given by:

$$f(T_1, T_2, \ldots T_m) = E_0 + E_1 + \cdots + E_m \tag{13}$$

where

$$E_0 = -\sum_{i=0}^{T_1-1} \frac{p_i}{\omega_0} \ln\left(\frac{p_i}{\omega_0}\right), \quad w_0 = \sum_{i=0}^{T_1-1} p_i$$

$$E_k = -\sum_{i=T_k}^{T_{k+1}-1} \frac{p_i}{\omega_k} \ln\left(\frac{p_i}{\omega_k}\right), \quad w_k = \sum_{i=T_k}^{T_{k+1}-1} p_i, \quad k = 1, 2, \ldots, m-1 \tag{14}$$

$$E_m = -\sum_{i=T_m}^{L-1} \frac{p_i}{\omega_m} \ln\left(\frac{p_i}{\omega_m}\right), \quad w_m = \sum_{i=T_m}^{L-1} p_i$$

where $E_0, E_1, \ldots, E_m$ are the Kapur's entropy and $\omega_0, \ldots, \omega_m$ represent the probabilities of the $m$ classes $C_0, C_1, \ldots, C_m$, respectively.

## 4.2 Experimental Setting

Here, we provide a brief summary of the proposed ISTOA method's experimental setting. For comparison of ISTOA with state-of-the-art methods, segmentation is performed on four standard test images as given in Fig. 2. This figure also shows the histogram, which reveals the feature of each image, respectively. We adjust the swarm parameters to their original versions [32], with the population number equal to 30, iterations equal to 350 and the dimension set to the threshold level. All parameters are chosen based on the recommendations provided in [33]. Different threshold values (i.e., 2, 3, 4, and 5) were examined for testing the performance. ISTOA's performance was evaluated by employing it to a number of different images with varying shapes, contents and morphologies. The trials were carried out on a machine "Core i7 and 16 GB of RAM operating on MS Windows 10" using Matlab 2022a.

Three metrics are used to test the methods' performance and segmented images' quality at various thresholds: (1) PSNR: Peak signal-to-noise ratio, (2) SSIM: Structural similarity, and (3) FSIM: Feature similarity.

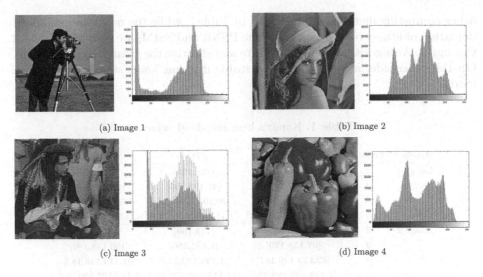

(a) Image 1                    (b) Image 2

(c) Image 3                    (d) Image 4

**Fig. 2.** Images used for Testing

- **PSNR** is a key quality metric for determining the quality difference between the actual and the segmented image, and is given by:

$$PSNR = 20 \log_{10} \frac{255}{RMSE}$$

$$RMSE = \sqrt{\frac{\sum_{i=1}^{M} \sum_{j=1}^{N} ((I(i,j) - \text{Seg}(i,j))^2)}{M \times N}}$$

(15)

where the Root-mean-square error is denoted by $RMSE$ and $M \times N$ is the size of actual $(I)$ and segmented $(Seg)$ images.

- **SSIM** measures the structural similarity between actual image and the segmented result, and is given by:

$$\text{SSIM}(I, \text{Seg}) = \frac{(2\mu_I \mu_{\text{Seg}} + c_1)(2\sigma_{I,Seg} + c_2)}{\left(\mu_I^2 + \mu_{\text{Seg}}^2 + c_1\right)\left(\sigma_I^1 + \sigma_{\text{Seg}}^2 + c_2\right)}$$

(16)

where $\mu_I$ and $\mu_{Seg}$, $\sigma_I$ and $\sigma_{Seg}$ are the mean intensities and standard deviations of actual $(I)$ and segmented image $(Seg)$ respectively. $c_1$ and $c_2$ are the two constants utilized and $\sigma_{I,Seg}$ denotes the covariance between the original and the segmented image.

## 4.3   Results and Analysis

The proposed ISTOA method's obtained results, which depends on maximizing the Kapur's objective (fitness) function, are shown and discussed in this section. The best thresholding values chosen by the proposed ISTOA method, and the other competing methods are provided in Table 1, while the mean and standard deviation of fitness results, as well as the PSNR and SSIM, are shown in Tables 2 through 4. An algorithm is more accurate and effective the greater its mean value. On the other side, a method is more stable if it has lower standard deviation (Std).

**Table 1.** Kapur's best threshold values.

| Image | Threshold | CSA | STOA | ISTOA |
|-------|-----------|-----|------|-------|
| Image 1 | 2 | [128,193] | [128,193] | [128,193] |
|         | 3 | [44,104,193] | [42,103,196] | [49,107,194] |
|         | 4 | [44,97,146,197] | [20,103,194,253] | [45,98,146,198] |
|         | 5 | [19,102,193,193,254] | [1,114,130,195,243] | [22,54,93,137,198] |
| Image 2 | 2 | [113,169] | [113,169] | [113,169] |
|         | 3 | [97,138,179] | [1,132,256] | [100,138,180] |
|         | 4 | [82,113,146,181] | [1,132,132,245] | [91,114,149,183] |
|         | 5 | [1,113,132,169,256] | [11,113,134,170,227] | [1,113,132,166,254] |
| Image 3 | 2 | [39,126] | [39,126] | [39,126] |
|         | 3 | [39,113,180] | [38,103,180] | [39,116,180] |
|         | 4 | [39,43,131,235] | [37,87,132,183] | [39,88,127,184] |
|         | 5 | [39,43,124,131,234] | [1,39,39,122,253] | [37,72,109,147,183] |
| Image 4 | 2 | [75,146] | [75,146] | [74,146] |
|         | 3 | [74,145,228] | [1,117,256] | [91,150,230] |
|         | 4 | [54,91,150,228] | [1,117,118,254] | [33,131,186,228] |
|         | 5 | [1,75,117,146,244] | [1,75,117,146,235] | [3,70,121,146,256] |

According to the mean values of fitness results, it is evident from Table 2 that the proposed ISTOA method ranks first by 11 higher fitness values over the 16 experiments, and CSA ranks second by 5 higher fitness values, while STOA algorithm obtains no higher fitness cases. Regarding Std, the proposed ISTOA method ranks first with the greatest number of minimum Std cases, followed by CSA in second place, and STOA in third place.

The mean and standard deviation (Std) of PSNR for the four images created by employing the three methods are shown in Table 3. For the Mean values, the proposed method comes in the first place and has a higher PSNR in 14 cases, followed by STOA in second place with two higher cases and CSA algorithms in third place with no higher PSNR in any case. Concerning Std, the proposed ISTOA method ranks first with greatest count of minimum Std cases, followed by STOA in second place, CSA in third place.

**Table 2.** Kapur's Mean and Standard deviation of fitness values across all tested images

| Image | Threshold | CSA | | STOA | | Proposed | |
|---|---|---|---|---|---|---|---|
| | | Mean | Std | Mean | Std | Mean | Std |
| Image 1 | 2 | **17.5558** | 2.06E-13 | 17.11136 | 0.519725 | 17.19544 | 0.504624 |
| | 3 | 21.38576 | 0.982432 | 19.87576 | 0.885812 | **21.81801** | 0.078577 |
| | 4 | 25.21846 | 0.625734 | 24.37805 | 0.958806 | **26.12154** | 0.252828 |
| | 5 | 29.48468 | 1.14295 | 27.20748 | 1.18442 | **29.63289** | 0.724502 |
| Image 2 | 2 | 17.03484 | 0.611469 | 17.03323 | 0.61109 | **17.14924** | 0.037919 |
| | 3 | 20.56994 | 0.815462 | 19.69109 | 0.000262 | **21.1548** | 0.137067 |
| | 4 | **24.73093** | 0.286742 | 24.50153 | 0.725333 | 24.33922 | 0.411376 |
| | 5 | **28.70852** | 1.255404 | 27.31797 | 0.997621 | 28.55348 | 0.634359 |
| Image 3 | 2 | 17.30864 | 0.998807 | 17.5138 | 0.736448 | **17.63564** | 0.109859 |
| | 3 | 21.20307 | 1.443434 | 19.74133 | 0.630937 | **22.27329** | 0.166536 |
| | 4 | 24.79111 | 0.125934 | 24.60414 | 1.106496 | **26.28296** | 0.278034 |
| | 5 | **29.18395** | 1.214901 | 27.62566 | 1.454673 | 29.13778 | 0.944997 |
| Image 4 | 2 | 18.07261 | 0.679731 | 18.07234 | 0.679668 | **18.21187** | 0.01248 |
| | 3 | 21.55944 | 0.986609 | 20.77932 | 7.51E-05 | **22.59753** | 0.081352 |
| | 4 | 26.26566 | 0.363378 | 25.75909 | 1.054293 | **26.55** | 0.191723 |
| | 5 | **30.56329** | 1.21936 | 29.22576 | 1.360352 | 30.3025 | 0.495047 |

**Table 3.** Kapur's Mean and Standard deviation of PSNR values across all tested images

| Image | Threshold | CSA | | STOA | | Proposed | |
|---|---|---|---|---|---|---|---|
| | | Mean | Std | Mean | Std | Mean | Std |
| Image 1 | 2 | 13.52295 | 0.029349 | **13.82708** | 0.525026 | 13.54315 | 1.275365 |
| | 3 | 14.84067 | 2.607781 | 8.425955 | 4.143082 | **15.15779** | 1.166562 |
| | 4 | 14.46338 | 4.186817 | 13.36953 | 2.870681 | **18.45681** | 1.456351 |
| | 5 | 15.94591 | 3.440903 | 9.035205 | 4.45955 | **19.07049** | 2.190547 |
| Image 2 | 2 | 13.28543 | 1.897049 | 13.43025 | 1.931593 | **13.85702** | 0.224417 |
| | 3 | 13.95631 | 2.432201 | 11.42443 | 0.028941 | **16.24088** | 0.495904 |
| | 4 | 13.57458 | 2.150211 | 12.43808 | 2.089056 | **17.15214** | 2.511381 |
| | 5 | 14.94526 | 2.829781 | 11.95597 | 1.253131 | **16.92647** | 2.278464 |
| Image 3 | 2 | 14.55879 | 1.870321 | **15.01989** | 2.02631 | 14.90765 | 0.881547 |
| | 3 | 15.16061 | 2.587669 | 12.032 | 1.570574 | **16.48377** | 0.8198 |
| | 4 | 14.59759 | 1.785155 | 14.1119 | 3.161682 | **19.20616** | 0.933479 |
| | 5 | 14.8584 | 2.690316 | 12.02569 | 2.393571 | **18.49641** | 2.393311 |
| Image 4 | 2 | 15.86704 | 2.36468 | 15.93745 | 2.380845 | **16.3911** | 0.107183 |
| | 3 | 14.1427 | 3.150277 | 11.69754 | 0.000746 | **17.83841** | 1.040616 |
| | 4 | 14.19408 | 2.801337 | 14.01343 | 3.369567 | **19.10059** | 1.693164 |
| | 5 | 16.50709 | 2.54388 | 13.40539 | 2.743542 | **18.75105** | 2.079722 |

The mean and Std of the SSIM for the 16 experiments are depicted in Table 4. The findings show that the proposed ISTOA method ranks first with 15 higher SSIM cases, followed by STOA with one case in second place, and finally CSA algorithm with no higher SSIM cases. Concerning Std, the proposed ISTOA method ranks first with the greatest count of minimum Std cases, followed by STOA in second place, and CSA in third place.

**Table 4.** Kapur's Mean and Standard deviation of SSIM values across all tested images

| Image | Threshold | CSA | | STOA | | Proposed | |
|---|---|---|---|---|---|---|---|
| | | Mean | Std | Mean | Std | Mean | Std |
| Image 1 | 2 | 0.528728 | 0.000481 | **0.558458** | 0.030709 | 0.539477 | 0.062649 |
| | 3 | 0.59179 | 0.104582 | 0.218991 | 0.253527 | **0.622369** | 0.024412 |
| | 4 | 0.547807 | 0.194444 | 0.537501 | 0.172748 | **0.672799** | 0.034769 |
| | 5 | 0.625107 | 0.108607 | 0.26044 | 0.271194 | **0.700862** | 0.029751 |
| Image 2 | 2 | 0.553418 | 0.128275 | 0.559435 | 0.129724 | **0.588407** | 0.011861 |
| | 3 | 0.584649 | 0.113666 | 0.466463 | 0.001977 | **0.693013** | 0.019908 |
| | 4 | 0.578996 | 0.104082 | 0.511189 | 0.133398 | **0.726127** | 0.095011 |
| | 5 | 0.630653 | 0.126133 | 0.49365 | 0.062446 | **0.717272** | 0.080526 |
| Image 3 | 2 | 0.556244 | 0.112132 | 0.584845 | 0.136026 | **0.585121** | 0.054728 |
| | 3 | 0.59476 | 0.150898 | 0.377223 | 0.099385 | **0.681431** | 0.034131 |
| | 4 | 0.552897 | 0.108154 | 0.514625 | 0.205164 | **0.783169** | 0.028532 |
| | 5 | 0.565725 | 0.155526 | 0.394112 | 0.143846 | **0.748879** | 0.101141 |
| Image 4 | 2 | 0.593228 | 0.136761 | 0.598848 | 0.138101 | **0.634767** | 0.010216 |
| | 3 | 0.518889 | 0.148796 | 0.403876 | 0.000249 | **0.696609** | 0.042919 |
| | 4 | 0.526184 | 0.131395 | 0.528332 | 0.190703 | **0.742105** | 0.051971 |
| | 5 | 0.633742 | 0.12238 | 0.493175 | 0.134977 | **0.739688** | 0.064132 |

For each of the test benchmark images, the histograms and the segmented result generated by the proposed ISTOA method with different values of threshold $[Th = 2, 3, 4, 5]$ are shown in Table 5. These images demonstrate that even in complex settings, the classes in the histogram are generated uniformly. The histogram for Image 3 is the hardest to segment. The complexity is due to the different peaks that are present in the distribution of the pixels, which could provide multiple classes or even make choosing the best thresholds challenging.

**Table 5.** Segmented images at different thresholds

| Image | th=2 | th=3 | th=4 | th=5 |
|---|---|---|---|---|
| Image 1 | | | | |
| Image 2 | | | | |
| Image 3 | | | | |
| Image 4 | | | | |

# 5   Conclusions and Future Work

This paper introduced an alternative multilevel thresholding image segmentation approach based on Sooty Tern Optimization Algorithm (STOA) performance, which emulates sooty terns behavior. An improved version of STOA (ISTOA) is proposed in this paper which depends on using the opposition-based learning (OBL) method to enhance population diversity and prevent stuck-in-local solutions. The proposed algorithm has been evaluated to solve the multilevel threshold image segmentation problem, which aims to define the optimal threshold value, which increases Kapur's function. The study concluded that the proposed ISTOA method's performance is better than that of the STOA and SOA algorithms.

# References

1. Osamy, W., Khedr, A.M., Salim, A., Agrawal, D.P.: Sensor network node scheduling for preserving coverage of wireless multimedia networks. IET Wirel. Sens. Syst. **9**(5), 295–305 (2019)
2. Khalifa, B., Khedr, A.M., Al Aghbari, Z.: A coverage maintenance algorithm for mobile WSNs with adjustable sensing range. IEEE Sens. J. **20**(3), 1582–1591 (2019)
3. Milletari, F., Navab, N., Ahmadi, S.A.: V-net: fully convolutional neural networks for volumetric medical image segmentation. In: 2016 Fourth International Conference on 3D Vision (3DV), pp. 565–571. IEEE (2016)
4. Tengfei, S., Zhang, S.: Local and global evaluation for remote sensing image segmentation. ISPRS J. Photogramm. Remote. Sens. **130**, 256–276 (2017)
5. Dirami, A., Hammouche, K., Diaf, M., Siarry, P.: Fast multilevel thresholding for image segmentation through a multiphase level set method. Signal Process. **93**(1), 139–153 (2013)
6. Omar, D., Khedr, A.M.: SEPCS: prolonging stability period of wireless sensor networks using compressive sensing. Int. J. Commun. Netw. Inf. Secur. **11**(1), 1–6 (2019)
7. Kapur, J.N., Sahoo, P.K., Wong, A.K.: A new method for gray-level picture thresholding using the entropy of the histogram. Comput. Vis. Graph. Image Process. **29**(3), 273–285 (1985)
8. Sahoo, P.K., Soltani, S.A.K.C., Wong, A.K.: A survey of thresholding techniques. Comput. Vis. Graph. Image Process. **41**(2), 233–260 (1988)
9. Hammouche, K., Diaf, M., Siarry, P.: A comparative study of various meta-heuristic techniques applied to the multilevel thresholding problem. Eng. Appl. Artif. Intell. **23**(5), 676–688 (2010)
10. Osamy, W., El-Sawy, A.A., Khedr, A.M.: Effective TDMA scheduling for tree-based data collection using genetic algorithm in wireless sensor networks. Peer-to-Peer Networking Appl. **13**(3), 796–815 (2020)
11. Khedr, A.M., Osamy, W.: Mobility-assisted minimum connected cover in a wireless sensor network. J. Parallel Distrib. Comput. **72**(7), 827–837 (2012)
12. Khedr, A.M.: Effective data acquisition protocol for multi-hop heterogeneous wireless sensor networks using compressive sensing. Algorithms **8**(4), 910–928 (2015)
13. Mostafa, R.R., Ewees, A.A., Ghoniem, R.M., Abualigah, L., Hashim, F.A.: Boosting chameleon swarm algorithm with consumption AEO operator for global optimization and feature selection. Knowl. Based Syst. **246**, 108743 (2022)

14. Elaziz, M.A., et al.: Triangular mutation-based manta-ray foraging optimization and orthogonal learning for global optimization and engineering problems. Appl. Intel. **53**, 1–30 (2022)
15. Huang, C., Li, X., Wen, Y.: An OTSU image segmentation based on fruitfly optimization algorithm. Alex. Eng. J. **60**(1), 183–188 (2021)
16. Abd El Aziz, M., Ewees, A.A., Hassanien, A.E.: Whale optimization algorithm and moth-flame optimization for multilevel thresholding image segmentation. Expert Syst. Appl. **83**, 242–256 (2017)
17. Houssein, E.H., Helmy, B.E.D., Oliva, D., Elngar, A.A., Shaban, H.: A novel black widow optimization algorithm for multilevel thresholding image segmentation. Expert Syst. Appl. **167**, 114159 (2021)
18. Eisham, Z.K., Haque, M.M., Rahman, M.S., Nishat, M.M., Faisal, F., Islam, M.R., et al.: Chimp optimization algorithm in multilevel image thresholding and image clustering. Evolving Syst. 1–44 (2022)
19. Resma, K.B., Nair, M.S.: Multilevel thresholding for image segmentation using krill herd optimization algorithm. J. King Saud Univ. Comput. Inf. Sci. **33**(5), 528–541 (2021)
20. Liang, H., Jia, H., Xing, Z., Ma, J., Peng, X.: Modified grasshopper algorithm-based multilevel thresholding for color image segmentation. IEEE Access **7**, 11258–11295 (2019)
21. He, L., Huang, S.: Modified firefly algorithm based multilevel thresholding for color image segmentation. Neurocomputing **240**, 152–174 (2017)
22. Houssein, E.H., Helmy, B.E.D., Elngar, A.A., Abdelminaam, D.S., Shaban, H.: An improved tunicate swarm algorithm for global optimization and image segmentation. IEEE Access **9**, 56066–56092 (2021)
23. Liu, Q., Li, N., Jia, H., Qi, Q., Abualigah, L.: Modified remora optimization algorithm for global optimization and multilevel thresholding image segmentation. Mathematics **10**(7), 1014 (2022)
24. Ewees, A.A., et al.: Modified artificial ecosystem-based optimization for multilevel thresholding image segmentation. Mathematics **9**(19), 2363 (2021)
25. Dhiman, G., Kaur, A.: STOA: a bio-inspired based optimization algorithm for industrial engineering problems. Eng. Appl. Artif. Intell. **82**, 148–174 (2019)
26. He, J., Peng, Z., Cui, D., Qiu, J., Li, Q., Zhang, H.: Enhanced sooty tern optimization algorithm using multiple search guidance strategies and multiple position update modes for solving optimization problems. Appl. Intel. **53**, 1–37 (2022)
27. Ali, H.H., Fathy, A., Kassem, A.M.: Optimal model predictive control for LFC of multi-interconnected plants comprising renewable energy sources based on recent sooty terns approach. Sustain. Energ. Technol. Assessments **42**, 100844 (2020)
28. Jia, H., Li, Y., Sun, K., Cao, N., Zhou, H.M.: Hybrid sooty tern optimization and differential evolution for feature selection. Comput. Syst. Sci. Eng. **39**(3), 321–335 (2021)
29. Mostafa, R.R., El-Attar, N.E., Sabbeh, S.F., Vidyarthi, A., Hashim, F.A.: ST-AL: a hybridized search based metaheuristic computational algorithm towards optimization of high dimensional industrial datasets. Soft Comput. 1–29 (2022)
30. Tizhoosh, H.R.: Opposition-based learning: a new scheme for machine intelligence. In: International Conference on Computational Intelligence for Modelling, Control and Automation and International Conference on Intelligent Agents, Web Technologies and Internet Commerce (CIMCA-IAWTIC 2006), vol. 1, pp. 695–701. IEEE (2005)
31. Shannon, C.E.: A mathematical theory of communication. Bell Syst. Tech. J. **27**(3), 379–423 (1948)

32. Arcuri, A., Fraser, G.: Parameter tuning or default values? an empirical investigation in search-based software engineering. Empir. Softw. Eng. **18**(3), 594–623 (2013)
33. Sepas-Moghaddam, A., Yazdani, D., Shahabi, J.: A novel hybrid image segmentation method. Prog. Artif. Intell. **3**(1), 39–49 (2014). https://doi.org/10.1007/s13748-014-0044-7

# Implementing Digital Transformation in the Logistics System of Uzbekistan

Shadibekova Dildor[1]([⊠]) and Ismoilov Narimonjon[2]

[1] "Business management and Logistics", Tashkent State University of Economics, Tashkent,
Uzbekistan
d.shadibekova@tsue.uz
[2] Tashkent State University of Economics, Tashkent, Uzbekistan

**Abstract.** In the development of the economy of every country, the logistics
system, which is its lifeblood, is very important. By optimizing the movement of
finished products and raw materials in the domestic market, an effective logistics
system ensures the delivery of goods and services in favorable conditions and at
low prices for customers and stimulates competition in the market. In the foreign
market, it increases the country's economic competitiveness and accelerates the
process of integration into the world economy. It is very important to organize an
effective logistics system for our developing country.

**Keywords:** Digitization · Logistics Industry · Logistics Management ·
Globalization · Cutting-edge technologies

## 1 Introduction

Implementation of digital transformation in the logistics industry of Uzbekistan is a hot
trend, nowadays. Modern information technologies have a great impact on the economy
and society, as a result of which the current economy and people's lifestyle are changing.
As the current and future modernization of the transport sector, it is worth emphasizing
the development of new types and methods of relations between transport organizations
and consumers and their wide use. Digitization of the transport sector will serve to
optimize transport and logistics costs. Modern information systems are characterized
by the creation of a single information space for all participants of interactions. The
vastness of the territory of our country and the need to cover the most remote areas
with transport services increase the dependence of the transport infrastructure on high
information technology. Improving the efficiency of logistics is especially relevant in
our country, which is geographically disadvantaged and does not have direct access to
seaports, which is the cheapest mode of transport, even though bordering countries.

## 2 Digital Transformation Occurring in Logistics

Implementation of digital transformation in the logistics industry of Uzbekistan is a hot
trend, nowadays. Modern information technologies have a great impact on the economy

Y. Koucheryavy and A. Aziz (Eds.): NEW2AN 2022, LNCS 13772, pp. 149–155, 2023.
https://doi.org/10.1007/978-3-031-30258-9_13

and society, as a result of which the current economy and people's lifestyle are changing. As the current and future modernization of the transport sector, it is worth emphasizing the development of new types and methods of relations between transport organizations and consumers and their wide use. Digitization of the transport sector will serve to optimize transport and logistics costs. Modern information systems are characterized by the creation of a single information space for all participants of interactions. The vastness of the territory of our country and the need to cover the most remote areas with transport services increase the dependence of the transport infrastructure on high information technology. Improving the efficiency of logistics is especially relevant in our country, which is geographically disadvantaged and does not have direct access to seaports, which is the cheapest mode of transport, even though bordering countries.

The use of digital and intelligent information technologies in the management of the transport sector brings several useful functions. For example, thanks to the active use of information technology, the acceptance of new orders, as well as the delivery process and transportation of goods, management of warehouses and fleet of vehicles are significantly accelerated. As a result of increasing the speed of these processes, the order fulfillment period is shortened from the customer's point of view, the flow of paper documents is reduced, the role of the human factor is reduced, which leads to a decrease in material costs. Due to the quick response to the customers, the demand of the consumers is satisfied, it guarantees the stability of the execution of the orders and fully meets the requirements of today's modern market economy.

As mentioned above, truck maintenance in the US is hard to imagine without Tablet, I-pass, Prepass, Samsara and GPS gadgets. The use of these modern gadgets in logistics and transport enterprises of our country will give very good results.

For example, the I-pass is now widely used throughout the United States. This gadget shows truck drivers that they have traveled on toll roads, how far they have traveled and the amount of the toll. The peculiarity of the gadget is that the driver does not make payments for the toll road, instead of the driver, the I-pass gadget, which can connect to the bank card online, does it. The widespread use of this system throughout our country in the coming years will save the time spent on delivering goods and prevent excessive efforts required of the driver.

It is no secret that starting from 2020, the weight of the cargo will be measured at weighing stations after the cargo transported across the country exceeds a certain ton. This system already exists in foreign countries, for example, in the United States, it is implemented as follows. Trucks equipped with the Prepass gadget can move without stopping at toll stations, that is, when the signal from the gadget goes to the weight calculation system, the payment is automatically deducted, and the reference indicating the weight is displayed electronically on the driver's phone. This gadget is very effective in saving time and preventing disputes between drivers (related to waiting in line).If the truck is not equipped with a gadget, the driver will first receive the order to load the cargo, then make the payment, and when it is his turn to weigh the cargo, it is no exaggeration to say that he will lose at least 30–50 min of time. This modern system is now very necessary for the logistics sector of our country, and the efficiency of its use is very high.

For the customer and the supplier, the condition of the cargo, the distance traveled and the level of safety are always considered important factors. Currently, various GPS devices are used in the practice of cargo transportation in our country. However, these GPS devices only allow you to determine the location of a moving truck. Currently, the Samsara device, one of the modern forms of monitoring that is entering the world practice, provides many opportunities for both the driver and the customer.

For the driver the below mentioned features can be helpful:

– Full data recording source.
– Continuous technical monitoring of the truck.
– Power of attorney stating that the cargo has been delivered.

For the customer:

– Monitoring of the condition of the load through a video camera;
– Allows you to determine the location of the truck.

Figure 1st below shows the working principle of the Samsara device. This device is connected to the driver's phone via Bluetooth and provides an opportunity to monitor the condition of the cargo and technical monitoring of the truck. The customer, in turn, can access the Samsara interface using the Internet and track the status and location of his cargo online through his password.

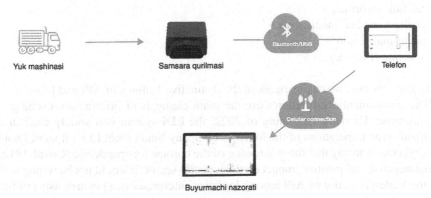

**Fig. 1.** Samsara gadget work algorithm

In today's competitive era where businesses aim to stay ahead of the market, they require their systems and software programs to work in sync and work as a coordinated whole. Proper integration provides companies with increased productivity, more efficient use of data and new opportunities, and allows key business processes to play well together.

Thus, the use of modern integration approaches such as application programming interfaces (APIs) and their flexibility, regular expansion are attracting the attention of many logistics enterprises. Thus, the use of modern integration approaches such as application programming interfaces (APIs) due to their flexibility and regular expansion are currently attracting the attention of many logistics enterprises.

For the past fifty years, Electronic Data Interchange (EDI) has been a critical tool for keeping all partners and processes in the loop as shipments make their round trips from point A to points B, C, and D. With half a century of success, EDI deserves serious credit for this.

Electronic Data Interchange (EDI) is the concept of exchanging paper-based data over the Internet. There are separate EDI standards created for the respective industries (X12, EDIFACT, IATA, etc.). The main idea of the concept is that the received data is always processed by software. Therefore, each EDI standard strictly defines the available document types, their format and the rules for interpreting them. The main advantages of EDI are as follows:

- Task automation.
- Ability to send documents.
- Compatibility with conventional technology.

API is one of the main integration approaches today. APIs complement traditional B2B technologies such as electronic data exchange and managed file transfer. As for logistics firms, API technology offers real-time, two-way connectivity and communication, which is essential for third-party logistics. Key features of the API include:

- Real-time information.
- Simultaneous communication.
- Ease of integration.
- Economic efficiency.

In Fig. 2 below, we can learn about the distinctive features of API and EDI.

The above-mentioned features are the main elements of information exchange in the enterprise. Until the beginning of 2022, the EDI system was widely used in the organization and operations of the logistics company Smart Fleet LLC. It would not be an exaggeration to say that the emergence of the coronavirus pandemic (Covid-19) had a great negative and positive impact on the logistics sector. It would not be wrong to say that the widespread use of API among logistics enterprises is a positive aspect of this pandemic.

The 4 main reasons for developing API integration are:

- Real-time data transfer
- Reducing integration costs
- More scalability
- Confirmation of data exchange

During 2021, most foreign logistics companies used highly customizable and scalable e-commerce platforms such as Shopify, Woo Commerce or Magento, Transflo to

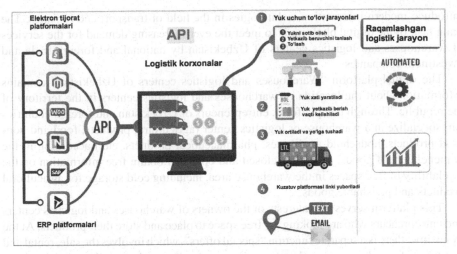

**Fig. 2.** Specific features of API and EDI

automate many back office and logistics operations tasks. With the help of robust enterprise resource planning platforms such as SAP, Oracle, Netsuite or Microsoft Dynamics, small businesses have digitized most of their processes.

It should be noted that many innovative developments in the field of logistics are being implemented in our country today. In order to facilitate the implementation of international transportation and increase transparency, an automated online system for the distribution of foreign multilateral permit forms has been launched. Licensing of cargo and passenger transportation activities has been transferred to a fully electronic form. This system made it possible for entrepreneurs to obtain a license remotely. Currently, in cooperation with the Commodity Exchange, a special electronic trading platform for the provision of cargo transportation services in road transport - the single platform "mytransport.uz" will be fully launched in August of this year.

On this platform, it is possible to purchase internal and external cargo transportation services through an electronic trading platform.

Until today, the purchase of passenger tickets was carried out through electronic systems created separately for each type of transport (for buses - avtoticket.uz, for air transport - uzairways.com, for railway transport e-ticket.railway.uz). In order to create more convenience for passengers, a single "Uztrans" portal was created, which allows you to buy tickets for bus, railway and air transport "online", and it was launched in test mode from May 1 this year, and the creation of its mobile application is currently underway. is being done.

When it comes to modern platforms, the creation of the digital platform "Warehouses and Logistics Centers of Uzbekistan" by the Logistics Association of Uzbekistan with the support of the Ministry of Transport of the Republic of Uzbekistan in mid-2021 is a clear example of the fact that our country is at a new stage of development in this field. The purpose of creating the platform is to increase the volume of foreign trade operations, create favorable conditions for doing business, attract foreign investments to the construction of new and modern warehouses and logistics centers in Uzbekistan, and introduce modern information technologies in the field of transport and logistics. The main task of the digital platform is to meet the ever-increasing demand for the services of warehouses and logistics centers of Uzbekistan by national and foreign trade and investment companies.

The digital platform "Warehouses and logistics centers of Uzbekistan" contains information about the location of warehouses and logistics centers in the territory of the republic. Through this platform, entrepreneurs of Uzbekistan and foreign countries can specialize in a warehouse or logistics center (agricultural products, food and non-food products, household appliances, pharmaceutical products, etc.) according to the nomenclature of goods, as well as closed and open can obtain free information on the availability of free spaces in the warehouse area, including cold storage for agricultural products and perishable goods.

This platform serves the interests of the owners of warehouses and logistics centers and entrepreneurs who are looking for free space to place and store their products. At the same time, there is a separate function "special offers", which involves the sale, rental and purchase of warehouses, warehouse equipment, loading and unloading equipment, as well as receiving applications for storage. This information platform meets the principles of "single window", in which the participants of transport and trade logistics can see and receive the necessary information and services related to the storage of goods in one place in electronic form. This information resource is useful for production and trading companies, entrepreneurs (cargo owners) and transport companies (carriers), as well as companies and organizations that provide services related to cargo forwarding, insurance and customs clearance.

The digital platform created in cooperation with experts of the Ministry of Transport serves to organize efficient transport and warehouse services, create a competitive environment and favorable conditions for the activities of transport and logistics companies, as well as improve and develop the cargo transportation system.

At the same time, this platform combines information on warehouses and logistics centers operating in Uzbekistan, their size and specialization, equipment and service level, compliance with international standards and generally recognized classifications. It also serves as an information base for analyzing the situation and development prospects of Uzbekistan's warehouse logistics, which, in turn, serves as a basis for the formation and development of development forecasts. The following norms are the basis for the creation of such platforms and their wide use in the activities of logistics enterprises in our country. Decree No. PF-4947 of the President of the Republic of Uzbekistan of February 7, 2017 on the Action Strategy for the further development of the Republic of Uzbekistan, February 25, 2019 "The position of the Republic of Uzbekistan in international ratings and indices" to ensure the implementation of the tasks specified in paragraph 6 of the decision PQ-4210 "On measures to improve the position of Decree No. PF-5953 on the implementation of the action strategy in the five priority directions "in the year of the development of science, enlightenment and digital economy", as well as to further increase the effectiveness of the ongoing reforms, priority direction on creation of conditions for comprehensive and rapid development of society and economy, modernization of our country and liberalization of all spheres of life in order to implement:

1. Development of the fundamental bases of increasing competitiveness through digitization of the economy in the service sector.
2. Creation of software that enables digitization of the economy in the service sector.
3. Priorities such as the creation of a single electronic platform for digitalization of the economy in the service sector have been defined.

## 3   Conclusion

Today, there are a number of problems in the transport infrastructure of the Republic, information about roads, facilities, posts, logistics centers, railway stations, airports, bus stations, as well as road, railway, air- lack of a system for monitoring information on cargo and passenger transportation on the road, non-existence of flat and differential tariff plans for regions in the process of using public transport of the population, outdated road transport infrastructure, as well as the very low level of use of information and communication technologies in this direction is one of the important problems facing the sector.

If we look at developed foreign countries, we can see that the above-mentioned processes were fully implemented several years ago. In particular, the transport sector is fully automated in the USA, Germany, France, England, Turkey, Singapore, UAE, China, Malaysia, Korea, Japan and other countries. As a result, we can see that the transport sector has developed in every way over the years, and the processes are implemented through digital technologies. By the present time, we can witness that these countries are moving to a new stage using artificial intelligence based on the Smart City concept.

## References

1. Karriyeva, Ya.K.: Effectiveness of the international transport logistics system in the process of globalization. Monograph. TDIU. Economics T. (2013)
2. Karriyeva, Ya.K, Ismailov, N.: Introduction of modern technologies for digitization in the field of transport. "Prospects for the development of the transport sector: problems and ways to overcome them" collection of theses, pp. 102–105 (04 August 2020)
3. Shadibekova, D.: Prospective Development Analysis of Small Business and Entrepreneurship of Uzbekistan, pp. 1733–1743 (2020)
4. Shadibekova, D., Ismailov, N.: Development of digital logistics and transport during globalization. ICFNDS 2021, December 15, 16, Dubai, United Arab Emirates © 2021 Association for Computing Machinery, pp. 863–867 (2021)

# Numerical Modeling of Vertical Axis Wind Turbines Using ANSYS Fluent Software

Muzaffar Muhiddinovich Hamdamov[1(✉)], Akram Ismoilovich Ishnazarov[2], and Khusniddin Abdujalilovich Mamadaliev[3]

[1] Institute of Mechanics and Seismic Stability of Structures of the Academy of Sciences of the Republic of Uzbekistan, Tashkent, Uzbekistan
mmhamdamov@mail.ru

[2] Mathematical Methods in Economics Tashkent State University of Economics, Tashkent, Uzbekistan
a.ishnazarov@tsue.uz

[3] Tashkent University of Information Technologies named after Muhammad Al-Khwarizmi, Tashkent, Uzbekistan

**Abstract.** The main objective of this study is to perform numerical simulations to test the performance of a vertical axis wind turbine in the low wind speed state of the east coast of Uzbekistan as indicated elsewhere with an average annual wind at a cut-off wind speed of 5 m/s. The aim is to develop wind energy technologies that can maximize the power extracted from the turbine in low wind conditions and to accelerate the penetration of wind energy technologies in Uzbekistan. The main problem of mathematical modeling of vertical axis wind turbines within the framework of the ANSYS Fluent software package is the choice of a turbulence model.

**Keywords:** Global Wind Energy · wind turbines · numerical models · RANS models · Power · kinetic energy · HAWT and VAWT turbines · ANSYS Fluent

## 1 Introduction

World energy consumption has been growing exponentially over the past few decades, mainly due to an increase in energy demand from developing and developed countries associated with the growth of the world's population and increasing personal demand. The economic, social and technological growth of a country is closely linked to the availability of energy. This is especially true for developing countries. Energy has undoubtedly become a basic human need in the modern era and will remain so in the distant future. The main energy consumers are the residential, commercial/institutional, industrial and transport sectors. In Fig. 1 shows the growth in energy supply from 1971 to 2013, as well as a breakdown of energy production by type of source according to the International Energy Agency (IEA) [1]. The same figure shows that from 1971 to 2013, most of the world's energy was still produced from fossil fuels such as coal, oil/oil, and natural gas. Although energy sources such as nuclear power, hydropower and renewables are

Y. Koucheryavy and A. Aziz (Eds.): NEW2AN 2022, LNCS 13772, pp. 156–170, 2023.
https://doi.org/10.1007/978-3-031-30258-9_14

growing, they still make up a small part of the total supply. On fig. Figure 2 shows a breakdown of energy in Canada published by Natural Resources Canada (NRCan) [2]. As before, almost 90% of all energy produced comes from fossil fuels. As you know, these energy sources are limited and, more importantly, they produce large amounts of greenhouse gases (GHGs), which in turn damage our environment and exacerbate the effects of climate change.

There are two common sources of energy: renewable and non-renewable. Until now, most of the energy demand is covered by non-renewable energy sources such as oil, coal and natural gas, which generate electricity through combustion technologies and cannot be renewed. In the renewable energy sector, wind energy represents the most mature technology. In March 2007, the European Council approved a mandatory target to meet 20% of EU energy consumption from renewable energy sources by 2020 [3]. Meanwhile, in 2008, the US Department of Energy (DOE) published a report looking at the technical feasibility of using wind power to generate 20% of the national electricity demand by 2030 [4]. In the last 25 years, global wind power capacity has increased rapidly, reaching 159,213 MW at the end of 2009. The wind power growth rate was 31.7%, the highest since 2001. Throughput doubles every three years. Figure 1 shows the total installed wind power worldwide.

The need for a sustainable and efficient source of renewable energy is highly demanded and meeting this need has been a goal for decades. There are a number of renewable energy sources available such as solar, wind, geothermal, hydro, biomass and tides. Interest in these cleaner and renewable energy sources has increased as they reduce dependency on other limited energy sources, as well as significantly reduce greenhouse gas exposure, helping to fight climate change.

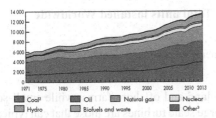

**Fig. 1.** Total world supply of primary energy from 1971 to 2013 by fuel type (Mtoe).

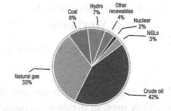

**Fig. 2.** Primary Energy Production in Canada by Source in 2013. "Other Renewable Energy" includes

Wind, solar, wood/wood waste, biofuels and municipal waste [2]. Wind power has shown great potential as a sustainable solution and its production has grown significantly in recent years. In Fig. 3 shows the growth of wind power capacity on a global scale, published by the Global Wind Energy Council (GWEC) [3]. Wind energy has been used as an additional source of energy, as well as a replacement for other energy sources. The numerous types of wind turbines in terms of size and application make them a very flexible power source. The most common way to extract energy from wind is wind turbines. The only stage at which wind turbines pollute the environment is before the installation stage. Once installed, turbines produce negligible greenhouse gases for the rest of their life cycle. Since their first use, wind turbines have undergone incredible technological advances, and even today there is still much room for improvement and development. Wind turbines have become more efficient and much larger since their invention thanks to advances in aerodynamics, construction and materials design (Fig. 4).

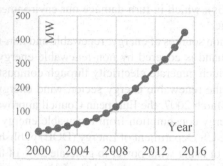

**Fig. 3.** Global cumulative installed wind capacity, 2000–2015 [3]

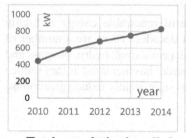

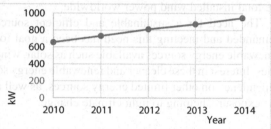

a. Total cumulative installed          b. Total units installed Worldwide
   capacity Worldwide

**Fig. 4.** Global installed energy capacity and units [5]

Large-scale wind turbines are used for land and offshore farms, while small-scale turbines are used in urban environments. Large scale turbines are those that can typically produce 100kW or more, as shown in Fig. 5, while the small turbines shown in Fig. 6, produce less than this threshold. It should be noted that whether a turbine is considered large or small for accreditation purposes, the turbine footprint is used as a criterion instead. Until now, large wind turbines have been favored as they tend to be more efficient and produce significantly more power. However, recent advances in small wind turbines have made them more attractive, especially as distributed power generation is quite an attractive concept as it is a much cheaper solution as electricity can be produced on site or close to where it is consumed. In this way, typical problems faced by large scale turbines such as transportation, transmission cables and maintenance costs can be avoided. The growth of small wind turbines in terms of capacity and number of units can be seen in Fig. 7 published by the World Wind Energy Association (WWEA) [5].

Wind energy can be used by various turbines, which are classified according to the axis of rotation. The main types are shown in Fig. 7. This includes horizontal axis wind

**Fig. 5.** Example of large wind turbines (a) Siemens G2 2.3 MW [6], (b) Éole Rotor Darrieus 4.3 MW [7]

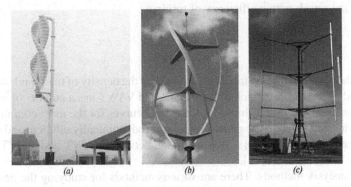

**Fig. 6.** Examples of small wind turbines (a) Helix Wind 5 kW Savonius [8], (b) Quiet Revolution 7.5 kW [9], (c) WHI 70 kW [10]

turbines (HAWT), whose rotation axes are parallel to the oncoming wing, and vertical axis wind turbines (VAWT), whose rotation axes are perpendicular to the oncoming wind. Generally, HAWTs are used more for large scale power generation while VAWTs are used for small to large applications. The two most common types of VAWT are the Savonius turbine, which is a drag-based turbine, and the Darrieus wind turbine, which is a lift-based turbine. There are also a number of different types of Darrieus VAWTs, the most common being the Darrieus rotor, H-Rotor Darrieus (H-Darrieus) and Helical Darrieus shown in Fig. 8.

All Darier type turbines have an airfoil profile for the blade cross-section, but differ in blade shape. An example of a HAWT, a Darrieus VAWT, a Savonius VAWT, a Helicoidal VAWT, and an H-rotor VAWT can be seen in Fig. 5(a) and (b) and Fig. 6(a), (b) and (c), respectively.

The following two dimensionless parameters are commonly used to describe the performance and operating conditions of a VAWT. The first is the tip speed ratio (TSR), which is the ratio of the blade tip speed to the free wind speed.

$$\lambda = TSR = \frac{\omega R}{u_\infty}$$

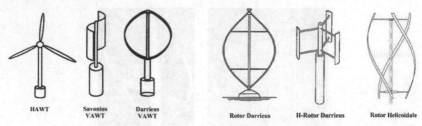

**Fig. 7.** Main types of wind turbines [11]     **Fig. 8.** Various Darier wind turbines [12]

where ω—turbine angular velocity, R—turbine radius, a $U_\infty$—flow velocity. Secondly, the power factor (CP), which is the ratio of the extractable power to the available power (available kinetic energy per unit time) with the oncoming wind. Power factor is a measure of the aerodynamic efficiency of turbines.

$$C_p = \frac{2P}{\rho u_\infty^3 S}$$

where P is the power extracted from the turbine, ρ is the density of the liquid, and S is the area covered by the turbine. Each of the HAWT and VAWT has a number of advantages and disadvantages. On Fig. 9 shows typical power curves for the most common turbine types, showing that HAVTs are generally more aerodynamically efficient and operate at much higher TSRs than VAWTs. A comparison between HAWT and VAWT has been explored by Eriksson et al. [13].

VAWT analysis methods. There are various methods for studying the performance of a VAWT. Two main categories involve the use of either experimental or numerical methods. These methods are presented in Fig. 9. Experimental analysis is carried out in wind tunnels, and numerical analysis is carried out by simulating the fluid phenomenon. Numerical models can be broken down into computational aerodynamics and computational fluid dynamics (CFD). Aerodynamic models are significantly faster than CFD models, but lack accuracy in predicting VAWT performance, especially when the turbine is running at low TCP. Airfoil models were previously the most common simulation method because the resources required to perform CFD simulations were too expensive; however, with the current advances in computing power, CFD modeling has become much more attractive. For CFD simulations, the Navier-Stokes equations are discretized and solved, giving much more room for accurate results, but the disadvantage is higher computational cost and time. Even in CFD, there are various methods for modeling flow; The most common for engineering applications are Reynolds-averaged Navier-Stokes (RANS) models with turbulence modeling because they can predict VAWT performance with reasonable accuracy. This will be the analysis method of choice for this dissertation because it provides sufficient accuracy at a reasonable computational cost. Other more accurate CFD models are eddy simulation, where turbulence is now allowed and only eddies smaller than the grid size are modeled. Although Eddy Simulations are more accurate than RANS models, they require significantly more computational effort. Single eddy simulation (DES) is a hybrid of large eddy simulation (LES) and RANS models. Finally, the most accurate and computationally expensive is Direct Numerical

Simulation (DNS) where the Navier-Stokes equations are completely solved without any simulation, which is the reason why it is computationally expensive since the required grid and time step are extremely accurate. Xin et al. [14] provide more details on most of the methods presented here, with related studies done by Daria VAWT. It should be noted that not all existing RANS models have been presented here, but only those that are commonly used for VAWT analysis.

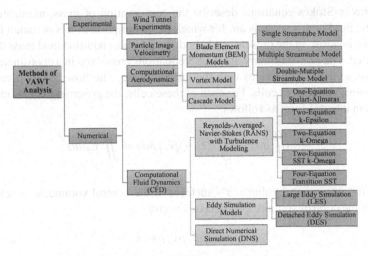

**Fig. 9.** Summary of VAWT Analysis Methods

New turbine concepts. Using a similar idea of expanding the region of maximum power of the VAWT, Ponta et al. [15] analyzed a Variable Geometry Oval Trajectory (VGOT) Darrieus wind turbine using a dual multiple flow model, where they showed very little improvement in aerodynamic efficiency compared to the classic H-Darrieus VAWT. They also showed that the performance of the turbine was independent of the number of blades, but very sensitive to the direction of the headwind.

A new turbine concept has been explored by Kinsey et al. [16], where it consists of a pair of oscillating hydrofoils moving along a sinusoidal path. Kinsey et al. presented a computational methodology in [17] that agreed very well with their experimental data shown in [16]. They used ANSYS Fluent [18] to solve 2D and 3D models of non-stationary Reynolds-Averaged-Navier-Stokes (URANS) equations. After examining various turbulence models for calculating turbine performance, they showed that the single-equation Spalart-Allmaras (SA) model performed very similarly to the dual-equation k-ω shear stress transfer (SST) model. Nonconformal sliding grids were used to simulate oscillatory motion within a dynamically moving grid. Sliding meshes are used to simulate the pitching motion, while the dynamic mesh is used for the lifting motion. In [15], they showed that it is possible to limit losses occurring in 3D simulation space, such as tip vortices, from their 2D prediction to about 10% using end plates and a blade length ratio greater than 10. Gauthier et al. [19] investigated the effect of blocking on the same oscillating wing hydrokinetic turbine (OFHT) using CD-Adapco STAR CCM + finite volume code with overset mesh technique. They showed that blocking effect increase and extractable power are linearly related for blocking up to 40% and also provide a correlation factor to account for this mentioned blocking effect.

CFD against aerodynamic models. Delafine et al. [20] compared the performance of a Darrieus rotary turbine using 3D CFD modeling of the SST k-ω model with other aerodynamic models such as dual flow tube and vortex models. They showed that 3D modeling accurately predicted turbine behavior, while aerodynamic models predicted power for all TSR values.

The Navier-Stokes equations describe the conservation of mass, momentum, and energy. The fluid in this study is air, for which the assumption of a Newtonian fluid is a valid approximation. In the present work, body forces, heat addition, and mass diffusion are neglected. The non-stationary 3D RANS equations are solved in a coordinate system mounted on a casing that rotates with the turbine blade. The flow field is divided into several control volumes or cells. For each of these cells, the governing equations can be expressed in integral form as follows:

$$\frac{d}{dt} \iiint_{\vec{v}} \vec{q} d\vec{v} + \iint_{s} \left( \vec{E} - q\vec{v}_v \right) \vec{n} ds = \iint_{s} \tilde{E}_v \vec{n} ds$$

$\vec{v}-$ deforming control volume, $s-$ surfaces of the control volume, $\vec{v}_v-$ velocity of surfaces of the control volume, $q-$ molasses vector

$$q = \rho, \rho u, \rho v, \rho w, e.$$

$\rho-$ density, $\rho u$, $\rho v$, $\rho w-$ momentum components in each principal direction, $e-$ total energy per unit volume.

The value of e is the sum of the internal energies $\frac{p}{\gamma-1}$, kinetic energy $\frac{\rho(u^2+v^2+w^2)}{2}$, $p-$ static pressure.

All of the above velocity components are in an inertial Cartesian frame of reference. Vector q can be considered as the state of flow characteristics averaged over the cell. Quantities $E_1$ and $E_v$ are inviscid and viscous flows, respectively, and are defined as follows:

$$\vec{E}_1 = \vec{F}_1 + \vec{G}_1 + \vec{H}_1,$$
$$\vec{E}_v = \vec{F}_v + \vec{G}_v + \vec{H}_v.$$

The PDE form of the Navier-Stokes equations can be obtained by applying conservation principles to an infinitesimal fluid element fixed in space. Under the additional assumption of the absence of body forces, external heat supply and mass diffusion, the three-dimensional Navier-Stokes equations can be written in the following compact form as a vector form in an inertial Cartesian system:

$$\frac{\partial \vec{q}}{\partial t} + \frac{\partial \vec{F}_1}{\partial x} + \frac{\partial \vec{G}_1}{\partial y} + \frac{\partial \vec{H}_1}{\partial z} = \frac{\partial \vec{F}_v}{\partial x} + \frac{\partial \vec{G}_v}{\partial y} + \frac{\partial \vec{H}_v}{\partial z}$$

$$
\vec{F}_1 = \left\{ \begin{array}{c} \rho \\ \rho u^2 + p \\ \rho u v \\ \rho u w \\ u(e+p) \end{array} \right\}, \quad
\vec{G}_1 = \left\{ \begin{array}{c} \rho \\ \rho u v \\ \rho v^2 + p \\ \rho v w \\ v(e+p) \end{array} \right\}, \quad
\vec{H}_1 = \left\{ \begin{array}{c} \rho \\ \rho u w \\ \rho v w \\ \rho w^2 + p \\ w(e+p) \end{array} \right\},
$$

$$
\vec{F}_v = \left\{ \begin{array}{c} 0 \\ \tau_{xx} \\ \tau_{yx} \\ \tau_{zx} \\ E_x \end{array} \right\}, \quad
\vec{G}_v = \left\{ \begin{array}{c} 0 \\ \tau_{xy} \\ \tau_{yy} \\ \tau_{zy} \\ E_y \end{array} \right\}, \quad
\vec{H}_v = \left\{ \begin{array}{c} 0 \\ \tau_{xz} \\ \tau_{yz} \\ \tau_{zz} \\ E_z \end{array} \right\}.
$$

The pressure property P is related to internal energy through:

$$
p = \rho R T = \rho(\gamma - 1)\tilde{e} = (\gamma - 1)\left[ e - \frac{\rho(u^2 + v^2 + w^2)}{2} \right].
$$

$$
\left\{ \begin{array}{l}
\dfrac{\partial \rho}{\partial t} + \dfrac{\partial \rho}{\partial x} + \dfrac{\partial \rho}{\partial y} + \dfrac{\partial \rho}{\partial z} = 0, \\[2mm]
\dfrac{\partial \rho u}{\partial t} + \dfrac{\partial \left(\rho u^2 + p\right)}{\partial x} + \dfrac{\partial \rho u v}{\partial y} + \dfrac{\partial \rho u w}{\partial z} = \dfrac{\partial \tau_{xx}}{\partial x} + \dfrac{\partial \tau_{xx}}{\partial y} + \dfrac{\partial \tau_{xx}}{\partial z}, \\[2mm]
\dfrac{\partial \rho v}{\partial t} + \dfrac{\partial \rho u v}{\partial x} + \dfrac{\partial \left(\rho v^2 + p\right)}{\partial y} + \dfrac{\partial \rho v w}{\partial z} = \dfrac{\partial \tau_{yx}}{\partial x} + \dfrac{\partial \tau_{yy}}{\partial y} + \dfrac{\partial \tau_{yz}}{\partial z}, \\[2mm]
\dfrac{\partial \rho w}{\partial t} + \dfrac{\partial \rho u w}{\partial x} + \dfrac{\partial \rho v w}{\partial y} + \dfrac{\partial \left(\rho w^2 + p\right)}{\partial z} = \dfrac{\partial \tau_{zx}}{\partial x} + \dfrac{\partial \tau_{zy}}{\partial y} + \dfrac{\partial \tau_{zz}}{\partial z}, \\[2mm]
\dfrac{\partial e}{\partial t} + \dfrac{\partial u(e+p)}{\partial x} + \dfrac{\partial v(e+p)}{\partial y} + \dfrac{\partial w(e+p)}{\partial z} = \dfrac{\partial E_x}{\partial x} + \dfrac{\partial E_y}{\partial y} + \dfrac{\partial E_z}{\partial z}.
\end{array} \right.
$$

$\tau_{xx}$, $\tau_{xy}$, $\tau_{xz}$, $\tau_{yx}$, $\tau_{yy}$, $\tau_{yz}$, $\tau_{zx}$, $\tau_{zy}$, $\tau_{zz}$ — stress tensor components determined using the Stokes relations and the Boussinesq hypothesis.

$$
\begin{cases}
\tau_{xx} = (\lambda + 2\mu)u_x + \lambda v_y + \lambda w_z, \\
\tau_{xy} = \mu(u_y + v_x), \\
\tau_{xz} = \mu(u_z + w_x), \\
\tau_{yy} = \lambda u_x + (\lambda + 2\mu)v_y + \lambda w_z, \\
\tau_{yz} = \mu(v_z + w_y), \\
\tau_{zz} = \lambda u_x + \lambda v_y + (\lambda + 2\mu)w_z.
\end{cases}
$$

$$
\begin{cases}
E_x = u\tau_{xx} + v\tau_{xy} + w\tau_{xz} + k\dfrac{\partial T}{\partial x}, \\[2mm]
E_y = u\tau_{xy} + v\tau_{yy} + w\tau_{yz} + k\dfrac{\partial T}{\partial y}, \\[2mm]
E_z = u\tau_{xz} + v\tau_{yz} + w\tau_{zz} + k\dfrac{\partial T}{\partial z}.
\end{cases}
$$

Using the Stokes hypothesis, the value $\lambda$ can be eliminated from the equation with this relation:

$$
\lambda = -\frac{2}{3}\mu
$$

Value $\mu$ — molecular viscosity coefficient. In turbulent flows, this viscosity is increased by adding "turbulent viscosity" - $\mu_t$. Molecular viscosity $\mu$ is a property of a fluid, so it can be considered constant if the temperature does not change significantly.

This study uses Sutherland's law to evaluate laminar viscosity. Similarly, $k$ represents thermal conductivity and is the sum of molecular and effective conductivity. It is defined as:

$$
k = \frac{c_p \mu}{\text{Pr}} + \frac{c_p \mu_t}{\text{Pr}_t} = c_p \left( \frac{\mu}{\text{Pr}} + \frac{\mu_t}{\text{Pr}_t} \right).
$$

Here Pr — Prandtl number, ($\text{Pr} = 0.72$), a $\text{Pr}_t$ — turbulent Prandtl number ($\text{Pr} = 0.8$).

Dimensionlessness of the governing equations. In this work, all simulations are performed in dimensionless form. Dimensionless parameters $L_R$ — base length, $a_\infty$ — free stream speed, $\rho_\infty$ — density of a fluid in free flow, $\mu_\infty$ — molecular viscosity of the liquid.

$$
x^* = \frac{x}{L_R}, \quad u^* = \frac{u}{a_\infty}, \quad t^* = \frac{t a_\infty}{L_R}, \quad \mu^* = \frac{\mu}{\mu_\infty}, \quad \varepsilon^* = \frac{\mu_\infty \omega}{\rho_\infty a_\infty^4}, \quad y^* = \frac{y}{L_R},
$$

$$
v^* = \frac{v}{a_\infty}, \quad \rho^* = \frac{\rho}{\rho_\infty}, \quad k^* = \frac{k}{a_\infty^2}, \quad z^* = \frac{z}{L_R}, \quad w^* = \frac{w}{a_\infty}, \quad p^* = \frac{p}{\rho_\infty a_\infty^2},
$$

$$
\omega^* = \frac{\mu_\infty \omega}{\rho_\infty a_\infty^2}.
$$

**Modeling of Turbulence.** Turbulent flows are characterized by fluctuating velocity fields. These fluctuations mix transportable quantities, such as momentum, energy, and species concentration, and cause fluctuations in transportable quantities. Since these oscillations can be small scale and high frequency, they are too computationally expensive to be directly modeled in practical engineering calculations. Instead, the instantaneous (exact) governing equations can be time averaged, ensemble averaged, or otherwise modified to eliminate small scales, resulting in a modified set of equations that are computationally less expensive to solve. However, the modified equations contain additional unknown variables, and turbulence models are needed to define these variables in terms of known quantities.

$$\text{Re} = \frac{\rho V D}{\mu}$$

where D is a characteristic length scale (eg chord length for airfoil sections), namely the undisturbed flow velocity and $\mu$ is the dynamic viscosity. In fact, this is the ratio of inertial (convective) and viscous forces. When the Reynolds number is low (less than 1200), the flow is considered laminar. When the flow becomes turbulent, the movement of the fluid looks disorganized and the particles move along a tortuous path. In this study, for a flow velocity of 10 m/s, the Reynolds number was calculated to be approximately 4 × 106. This confirms that the flow is completely turbulent. To evaluate whether the flow is either compressible or incompressible, the Mach number was calculated and found to be less than 0.3, making the flow incompressible.

ANSYS Fluent provides the following options for turbulence models.

- Model Spalart-Allmaras
- k-ε models (standard, renormalizable group (RNG), realizable)
- k-ω models (standard, zero voltage transfer (SST))

  Transitional SST models

- Reynolds Stress Models (RSM)
- Single Eddy Simulation Model (DES)
- Large Eddy Simulation Model (LES)

The choice of a turbulence model will depend on considerations such as the physics covered by the flow, established practice for a particular class of problems, the level of accuracy required, the computational resources available, and the amount of time available for simulation. To make the most appropriate choice of model for an application, it is necessary to understand the capabilities and limitations of the various options.

The modified $k - \varepsilon$ model is a semi-empirical model [21–24] based on model transfer equations for the turbulence kinetic energy k and its dissipation rate. The model transport equation for k is derived from the exact equation, while the model transport equation for ε was derived using physical reasoning and bears little resemblance to its mathematically exact counterpart. When deriving the k-ε model, it was assumed that the flow is complete and the effect of molecular viscosity is negligible. Thus, the modified value of $k - \varepsilon$ is valid only for fully turbulent flows.

Turbulence kinetic energy k and its dissipation rate $\varepsilon$ are obtained from the following transport equations:

$$
\begin{cases}
\dfrac{\partial}{\partial t}(\rho k) + \dfrac{\partial}{\partial x_j}(\rho k u_j) = \dfrac{\partial}{\partial x_j}\left[\left(\mu + \dfrac{\mu_t}{\sigma_k}\right)\dfrac{\partial k}{\partial x_j}\right] + G_k + G_b - \rho\varepsilon - 2\rho\varepsilon M_t^2 + S_k, \\[3mm]
\dfrac{\partial}{\partial t}(\rho\varepsilon) + \dfrac{\partial}{\partial x_j}(\rho\varepsilon u_j) = \dfrac{\partial}{\partial x_j}\left[\left(\mu + \dfrac{\mu_t}{\sigma_\varepsilon}\right)\dfrac{\partial\varepsilon}{\partial x_j}\right] + \\[3mm]
\rho C_1 S\varepsilon - \rho C_2 \dfrac{\varepsilon^2}{k + \sqrt{\nu\varepsilon}} + C_{1\varepsilon}\dfrac{\varepsilon}{k}C_{3\varepsilon}G_b + S_\varepsilon.
\end{cases}
$$

Here we use the notation

$$
C_1 = \max\left[0.43, \frac{\eta}{\eta + 5}\right], \eta = S\frac{k}{\varepsilon}, S = \sqrt{2S_{ij}S_{ij}}, \mu_t = \rho C_\mu \frac{k^2}{\varepsilon}, C_\mu = \frac{1}{A_0 + A_S \frac{kU^*}{\varepsilon}},
$$

$$
U^* \equiv \sqrt{S_{ij}S_{ij} + \tilde{\Omega}_{ij}\tilde{\Omega}_{ij}}, \Omega_{ij} = \overline{\Omega}_{ij} - 2\varepsilon_{ijk}\omega_k, A_S = \sqrt{6}\cos\phi, \phi = \frac{1}{3}\cos^{-1}\left(\sqrt{6}W\right),
$$

$$
W = \frac{S_{ij}S_{jk}S_{ki}}{\tilde{S}^3}, \tilde{S} = \sqrt{S_{ij}S_{ij}}, S_{ij} = \frac{1}{2}\left(\frac{\partial u_j}{\partial x_i} + \frac{\partial u_i}{\partial x_j}\right), G_k = -\rho\overline{u_i'u_j'}\frac{\partial u_j}{\partial u_i}, S \equiv \sqrt{2S_{ij}S_{ij}},
$$

$$
G_b = \beta g_i \frac{\mu_t}{\Pr_t}\frac{\partial T}{\partial x_i}, \Pr_t = 1/a_t, a_0 = 1/\Pr = k/\mu c_p, \beta = -\frac{1}{\rho}\left(\frac{\partial\rho}{\partial T}\right)_p,
$$

$$
G_b = -g_i \frac{\mu_t}{\rho\Pr_t}\frac{\partial\rho}{\partial x_i}, M_t = \sqrt{\frac{k}{a^2}}, a = \sqrt{\gamma RT}.
$$

Empirical Constants $k - \varepsilon$ models take standard values: $C_{1\varepsilon} = 1.44$, $C_2 = 1.9$, $\sigma_k = 1.0$, $\sigma_\varepsilon = 1.2$, $A_0 = 4.04$.

**Aerodynamic Power.** The characteristics of a wind turbine depend on its aerodynamic features.

The electric power of the wind turbine is related to the aerodynamic power through the wind energy utilization factor $\xi$:

$$
P = \xi P_A
$$

Real $\xi$ vertical-axis settings varies within 0.25–0.4. The maximum possible value of the wind energy utilization factor, determined by calculation according to Zhukovsky-Betz, is equal to $\xi = 0, 593$. In practice, this value cannot be obtained due to the resulting losses.

Aerodynamic power is the energy of the oncoming wind flow transmitted to the wind wheel in 1 s:

$$
P_A = \frac{mv^2}{2} = \frac{\rho sv^3}{2},
$$

where $P_A$ – aerodynamic power, W

$\rho$ – density of air passing through the rotor (assumed to be 1.2041 kg/m$^3$ in dry air at a temperature of 20 °C and a pressure of 101325 Pa);

$v$ – wind flow speed before meeting with the rotor, m/s;

$m$ – mass of air moving through the rotor in 1 s, kg;

$V$ – volume of air passing through the rotor in 1 s, m$^3$;

$S$ – wind-swept area of a wind turbine.

The area swept by the wind for vertical-axis installations is:

$$S = \frac{\pi D^2}{4}, \ m^2$$

where $D$ – wind wheel diameter.

For calculations, we need the technical characteristics of the wind generator. Rated power of wind turbine-5 kW,

Nominal wind speed 10 m/s. From the formula $P_9 = \xi P_A P = \xi P_A$ find the ideal aerodynamic power $P_A$ with an ideal wind utilization factor according to Zhukovsky:

$$P_A = \frac{P_9}{\xi_{\text{эк}}} = \frac{5000}{0,593} = 8432\,W$$

From the formula $P_A = \frac{mv^2}{2} = \frac{\rho s v^3}{2},\ W$ find the swept area of the rotor s:

$$s = \frac{2P_A}{\rho v^3} = \frac{2 \cdot 8432}{1,2041 \cdot 1000} = 14\,m^2$$

In reality, the swept area should be 33–35% larger than the ideal, since the actual wind utilization does not exceed 65–67% of the ideal.

$$S_{real} = S \cdot 1,33 = 14 \cdot 1,33 = 18,6\,m^2$$

From the formula $S = \frac{\pi D^2}{4},\ m^2$ find the diameter of the rotor D:

$$D = \sqrt{\frac{4S}{\pi}} = \sqrt{\frac{4 \cdot 18,6}{3,14}} = 4,9\,m.$$

The outer diameter of the wheel is found by the formula:

$$D_{\text{calc}} = \sqrt{\frac{8N}{C_p \rho v^3 \pi \eta_{\text{эл}} \eta_{\text{мех}}}} = 3,63\,m.$$

where $C_p$ – coefficient at the working point is accepted $C_p = 0,4$.

Rounding up the value $D_{calc} = 4$ m.

The radius of the wind wheel, respectively $R = 2$ m.

Thus, the developed wind turbine has the following aerodynamic characteristics:

- aerodynamic power $P_A = 8432\,\text{W}$;
- swept area of the wind turbine $S = 18,6\,\text{m}^2$;
- rotor diameter $D = 4\,\text{m}$.
- wind wheel outer diameter $D_{calc} = 4\,\text{m}$.

A quality mesh has been created for concealed and unprotected turbines. The number of selected nodes for the wind turbine simulation study was 188,000. The mesh was an independent study with three different meshes (coarse mesh with 94,000 nodes, medium mesh with 188,000 nodes, and fine mesh with 365,000 nodes) and the simulation results were compared with the difference between the results simulations obtained with medium and fine meshes were less than 1.5%. Based on this grid-independent study, a mean grid was chosen for this numerical study. The Control Volume Based Finite Difference Method is used to solve a system of partial differential equations defining the conservation of mass, momentum, and turbulent flow. In this CFD analysis, the SIMPLER algorithm is used to solve explicitly for the velocity and pressure fields. SIMPLE (a revised version of the SIMPLE algorithm) is a semi-implicit method used as a numerical procedure for solving the Navier-Stokes equation [15–17]. A SIMPLE algorithm uses the relationship between velocity and pressure corrections (pressure-velocity relationship algorithm) to enforce the continuity equation (conservation of mass) and obtain the pressure field (Fig. 10).

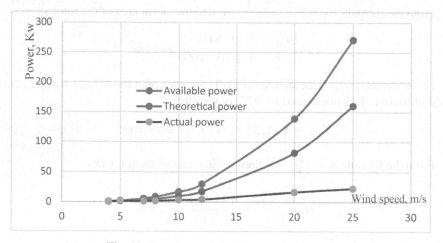

**Fig. 10.** Power output at different wind speeds.

# References

1. Abbott, I., Von Doenhoff, A., Stivers, L.: Report no. 824 summary of airfoil data. Langley Field (1945). https://ntrs.nasa.gov/archive/nasa/casi.ntrs.nasa.gov/19930090976.pdf
2. Abe, K.I., Ohya, Y.: An investigation of flow fields around flanged diffusers using CFD. J. Wind Eng. Ind. Aerodyn. **92**(3–4), 315–330 (2004). https://doi.org/10.1016/j.jweia.2003.12.003

3. World Wind Energy Association (WWEA). World Wind Energy Report 2009. http://www.wwindea.org

4. World Energy Outlook 2009. http://www.iea.org

5. Alam, F., Golde, S.: An aerodynamic study of a micro scale vertical axis wind turbine. Proc. Eng. **56**, 568–572 (2013). https://doi.org/10.1016/j.proeng.2013.03.161

6. Ali, A., Alam, F., Djamovski, V., Watkins, S.: A review of power generation from wind in Australia. In: Proceedings of the 9th International Conference of Mechanical Engineering (ICME2011). ANSYS Inc. (2011). ANSYS-FLUENT Theory Guide, 15317(November), 724–746

7. Aranake, A.C., Lakshminarayan, V.K., Duraisamy, K.: Computational analysis of shrouded wind turbine configurations using a 3-dimensional RANS solver. Renew. Energy **75**, 818–832 (2015). https://doi.org/10.1016/j.renene.2014.10.049

8. Balduzzi, F., Bianchini, A., Carnevale, E.A., Ferrari, L., Magnani, S.: Feasibility analysis of a Darrieus vertical-axis wind turbine installation in the rooftop of a building. Appl. Energy **97**, 921–929 (2012). https://doi.org/10.1016/j.apenergy.2011.12.008

9. Barth, T., Jespersen, D.: The design and application of upwind schemes on unstructured meshes. In: 27th Aerospace Sciences Meeting (1989). https://doi.org/10.2514/6.1989-366

10. Bazilevs, Y., et al.: 3D simulation of wind turbine rotors at full scale. Part I: geometry modeling and aerodynamics. Int. J. Numer. Methods Fluids **65**(1–3), 207–235 (2011). https://doi.org/10.1002/fld.2400

11. Bet, F., Grassmann, H.: Upgrading conventional wind turbines. Renew. Energy **28**(1), 71–78 (2003). https://doi.org/10.1016/S0960-1481(01)00187-2

12. Chen, J., Yang, H., Yang, M., Xu, H., Hu, Z.: A comprehensive review of the theoretical approaches for the airfoil design of lift-type vertical axis wind turbine. Renew. Sustain. Energy Rev. **51**, 1709–1720 (2015). https://doi.org/10.1016/j.rser.2015.07.065

13. Bird, R.B., Stewart, W.E., Lightfoot, E.N.: Transport Phenomena. Revised Second Edition (2007)

14. Global Wind Energy Council: Global Wind Statistics 2017. Brussels(2018). http://gwec.net/wp-content/uploads/vip/GWEC_PRstats2017_EN-003_FINAL.pdf

15. Hansen, M., et al.: A global Navier-Stokes rotor prediction model. In: 35th Aerospace Sciences Meeting and Exhibit (1997). https://doi.org/10.2514/6.1997-970

16. Hsiao, F.-B., Bai, C.-J., Chong, W.-T.: The performance test of three different horizontal axis wind turbine (HAWT) blade shapes using experimental and numerical methods. Energies **6**(6), 2784–2803 (2013). https://doi.org/10.3390/en6062784

17. Grauers, A.: Efficiency of three wind energy generator systems. IEEE Trans. Energy Convers. **11**(3), 650–655 (1996). https://doi.org/10.1109/60.537038

18. Gaden, D.L.F., Bibeau, E.L.: A numerical investigation into the effect of diffusers on 114 the performance of hydro kinetic turbines using a validated momentum source turbine model. Renew. Energy **35**(6), 1152–1158 (2010). https://doi.org/10.1016/j.renene.2009.11.023

19. Igra, O.: Research and development for shrouded wind turbines. Energy Convers. Manage. **21**(1), 13–48 (1981). https://doi.org/10.1016/0196-8904(81)90005-4

20. Ilk, R.: High-speed aerodynamic characteristics of four thin naca 63-series airfoils. Moffett Field. Innovations I Offshore Wind Turbines I MHI VestasTM (1947). http://www.mhivestasoffshore.com/innovations/. Accessed 5 Mar 2018

21. Hamdamov, M., Khujaev, I., Bazarov, O., Isabaev, K.: Axisymmetric turbulent methane jet propagation in a wake air flow under combustion at a finite velocity. In: IOP Conference Series: Materials Science and Engineering this Link is Disabled, vol. 1030, no. 1, p. 012163 (2021)

22. Hamdamov, M., Mirzoyev, A., Buriev, E., Tashpulatov, N.: Simulation of non-isothermal free turbulent gas jets in the process of energy exchange. In: E3S Web of Conferences, vol. 264, p. 01017 (2021)

23. Fayziev, R.A., Hamdamov, M.M. Model and program of the effect of incomplete combustion gas on the economy. In: ACM International Conference Proceeding Series, pp. 401–406 (2021)
24. Khujaev, I.K., Hamdamov, M.M.: Axisymmetric turbulent methane jet propagation in a co-current air flow under combustion at a finite velocity. Herald of the Bauman Moscow State Technical University, Series Natural Sciencesthis link is Disabled, no. 5, pp. 89–108 (2021)
25. SHadimetov, Kh.M., Akhmedov, D.M.: Approximate solution of a singular integral equation using the Sobolev method. J. Lobachevsky Math. 43(2) pp 496–505 (2022)

# "i'll wait 4 ur answr!" A Study on Modern Style of Cyber-Writing and User Reactions

Urmanov Bahromjon[1]([✉]), Shin Hoyoung[2], Abdullaev Munis[3], Suleimanov Farrukh[4],
Uktamova Durdona[1], Sulaymanov Samandarboy[1], Bakhodirova Durdona[1],
Norboyeva Nafisa[3], and Yusupova Dilbar[3]

[1] Department of International Business Administration, Tashkent State University of Economics, Tashkent, Uzbekistan
urmanov1983@gmail.com
[2] Department of Management Information Systems, Yeungnam University, Gyeongsan-si, Gyeongsangbuk-do, South Korea
[3] Department of Digital Economy and Information Technologies, Tashkent State University of Economics, Tashkent, Uzbekistan
[4] Foundation of the Joint Program TSUE and IMC Krems, Tashkent State University of Economics, Tashkent, Uzbekistan

**Abstract.** The present era of technology brought a new phenomenon in text messaging and writing in the cyber world with a "modern style" that breaks the rules of conventional written language and offers self-created symbols of expression. Previous research has investigated the effects on the literacy attainment of children and even adults. This study is distinct from previous studies in that it explored the effects of the modern style of texting on feelings and reactions of foreigners of different ages in South Korea who well possess English language skills and the differences between users and non-users of the modern style. The findings of this study demonstrate that younger and older people have significantly different feelings and reactions about the new style. When younger people receive a modern message, they feel happy and comfortable, while older people feel a little angry and confused by abbreviations and emoticons. Users and non-users of the modern style differ in feelings and reactions, as well. Users feel happy and fine when they receive a message in the modern style from people even younger than they are, while non-users do not feel happy, but rather they feel a little angry and bad when they receive a message in the modern style from people who are younger than they are. These findings are worth considering for all users when communicating with people at work and outside work through computer-mediated communication (CMC) tools; for education institutions when teaching virtual behavior; and for researchers when developing deeper research on this issue.

**Keywords:** Computer mediated communication · cyber-writing · textism · abbreviations · emoticon usage · text messaging · user reactions

## 1 Introduction

Text messaging through all kinds of computer-mediated technologies became an incredible way to keep in touch with people in modern society. It makes people much closer to and aware of each other wherever they are in the world in a fast and cheap way. Today people communicate with each-other by text-messaging through instant messaging applications, smartphone and computer-based instant messaging and SNS applications. Especially, Covid-19 pandemic period made people spend most of their time at home and increased use of these tools for communication, being in touch with each other, and social support (Paykani et al. 2020). There were 2.94 billion monthly active users (as of 31 March 2021) in Facebook, Twitter had 229 million active users DAU (Q1 2022). Even in 2017, 375 million subscribers actively used Instagram to share posts, pictures and videos either publicly or privately (https://techcrunch.com/2017/02/01/fac ebook-q4-2016-earnings/). Currently over 2 billion users are using WhatsApp Messenger in 2022 (https://backlinko.com/whatsapp-users). Telegram instant messaging service reached 700 million monthly active users in 2022 (https://telegram.org).

Currently, we see messages or writings in the cyber world such as: "can u cum 2 my haus 2nite 4 dinner?:)" -instead of "Can you come to my house tonight for dinner?" or "cud u plz explain dis?" instead of "Could you please explain this?". These differ greatly from formal language and mostly occur in phone messaging, Messengers and instant messaging applications. We can call this trend or phenomenon "text speak" or the modern style of writing in the cyber world or cyber writing. The modern style of writing includes using text abbreviations, textism, stickers and, emoticons; creating self-emoticons using available keyboard symbols; changing letters to write words as they sound; and not paying attention to grammatical, orthographic, phonetic, spelling, punctuation, capitalization, and other rules of language (Vosloo 2009).

It is a modern trend for users to feel lazy or not to pay attention to write properly. Instead, some even enjoy writing without rules and using abbreviations, emoticons, and self-made characters that are understood only in a particular society or age group. Users also approach SMS language with a metalinguistic awareness and a robust sense of play (Thurlow 2003). Indeed, emoticons could facilitate users with the opportunity to deliver their emotions and feelings without having to activate their webcam showing their faces or write them in words (Anthony and Nicolas 2021). However, not all users can easily understand various emoticons. There is a proficiency difference among specific users, especially between more general user groups. Furthermore, different emoticons can give ambiguous meanings, especially, when used without other additional information (Michal et al. 2020). And, due to some reasons emoticons without text can be deceptive and might give misunderstanding while some texts seem to be more comprehensible with emoticons (McHaneya and George 2021). Wood et al. (2014) claim that people text message in this manner because of character restrictions imposed by those tools similar to the case of phone text messaging. Modern writing or text messaging in the cyber world includes self-made styles and conventional language rules. Abbreviations, textisms, emoticons and, keyboard characters to express emotions and feelings are examples of using modern self-made styles of writing. Not following grammatical, spelling, orthographic, capitalization and punctuation rules are examples of not using conventional language rules.

Some text messaging includes acronyms and symbols, rebus abbreviations and other phonetically based variants. Texting corresponds much to spoken language (Plester et al. 2008). According to Tayebinika and Puteh (2012), extensive use of abbreviations has become common, and such abbreviations generally do not conform to the standard English rules in writing and spelling. This can endanger children's actual literacy because they have read less than older people whose spelling skills are already well established (Woronoff 2007). Similar to this research, mainstream researchers on this field initially focused on effects on the literacy of children and teenagers. The results of a study on different literacy levels of text speak users and non-text speak users showed no significant differences between the two groups in standardized literacy levels (Dourin and Davis 2009). Thurlow (2003) discussed what young people mainly use text messaging for and to what extent they prefer to implement such a method of text messaging. Results found that young people mainly use text messaging for informational-relational, chain message, practical arrangement, social arrangement, informational-practical, salutary, friendship maintenance, sexual and romantic purposes by manipulating conventional discursive practices with linguistic creativity and communicative competence in their pursuit of intimacy and social intercourse. Other researchers studied a sample of 86 children aged 10 to 12 focusing on the effects of their mobile phone text messaging. The results showed that the children's texting experience increased writing but not reading speed. However, better literacy skills were associated with greater textese reading speed and accuracy (Kemp and Bushnell 2011). In contrast, Wood et al. (2014) examined the interrelationships between 243 children and undergraduate students' grammatical violations made when text messaging and their performance on assessments of spoken and written grammatical understanding, orthographic processing and conventional spelling ability. Some children's phonological awareness led to good reading attainment even though they used textism when messaging. (Elbro 1997; Goswami 2002).

Defining the new modern trend of text messaging using text message language, Hsu (2013) explored the relationship between the use of text messaging language and the literacy skills of dyslexic and normal students. Emoticon usage and its effects were also discussed in many studies. Researchers investigated the impacts of emoticons on message interpretation in CMC and concluded that unnecessary and overuse of emoticons when messaging will reduce its impact (Walther and D'Addario 2001). A study empirically investigated the effect of emoticons in simplex and complex task-oriented communication by IM applications. The authors concluded that employees are likely to use emoticons in text messages in the workplace when communicating with colleagues (Vosloo 2009).

Almost all studies of modern text messaging investigate whether there is a negative or positive effect of modern text messaging on the literacy attainment of elementary school children, adolescents, teenagers, and university students and how to address this issue. However, very few studies of the modern style of messaging focused on its effect on users' feelings and how people of different ages and different usage patterns react to text messaging. Furthermore, most researchers included only traditional phone text messaging. Therefore, we see a gap in the research and a need to conduct an exploratory study to investigate how the modern style of writing in the cyber world affects people of different ages who use and do not use this style. We also include phone messaging and all kinds of instant messaging applications and messengers such as WhatsApp, Telegram, KakaoTalk, Viber and, IMO, Yahoo Messenger, Google Hangouts, Facebook Messenger and others.

## 2 Research Questions

We define our research questions as follows:

Q1-1. How do people of different ages feel about the modern style of writing in the cyber world?

Q1-2. How do people of different ages differ in feeling and reaction when they receive a modern-style message through phone messaging and any type of IM application from people of different ages?

Q2-1. How do users and non-users differ in general feelings about the modern style of writing in the cyber world?

Q2-2. How do users and non-users differ in feeling and reaction when they receive a modern-style message through any type of CMC technology in the cyber world from people of different ages?

## 3 Methodology

*Pilot Test*

To conduct a research survey, we gave respondents some examples of modern style messages. A pilot test was held in three steps:

Step 1. We studied previous related research papers concerning CMC and selected several examples of modern style writing (messages).

Step 2. We met with education experts and discussed the examples we gathered. They helped us select 14 messages.

Step 3. The 14 messages were given to 30 people of different ages to sort as "easy", "medium" and "hard" to read and understand.

Step 4. Using a statistical technique (number of most responses), we were able to select the ultimate 3 "easy", "medium", and "hard" messages in CMC for people to read and understand. We used these messages as our survey examples and shuffled them as follows:

    ⓐ   plz tink about it. I'll wait 4 ur answr! Txt me a msg suun! ~
    ⓑ   wot he askin' iz really hi 4 me
    ⓒ   LOL!!! how com!! De owner saz its lil lo :(

    Above ⓐ, ⓑ, and ⓒmight occur in following contexts of dialogues:
ⓐ

A: Hi, dude! How are you?

B: Good, thanks! How about you?

A: Me, too. Tomorrow is a festival. Why don't we go to downtown together? And we would enjoy the festival.

B: Ok, let me think. These days I am busy with my finals.

A: Please, think about it! I will wait for your answer. Text me a message soon! (ⓐ**plz tink about it. I'll wait 4 ur answr! Txt me a msg suun!~**).
B: Okay, I will.

ⓑ

A: Hey, Bob! Can you offer me another designer?
Bob: How was the one I sent you yesterday?
A: I liked his work. But, what he asking is really high for me (ⓑ**wot he askin' iz really hi 4 me**).
Bob: Don't worry! We will see some more options from other ones.
A: Okay, that would be a good idea.

ⓒ

A: Bella, did you move to your new room?
Bella: No, unfortunately.
A: Why? What happened?
Bella: The owner says 500 dollars per month is little low.
A: LOL! How come the owner says it's little low?! (ⓒ**LOL!!! how com!! De owner saz its lil lo:()**).

During our pilot test, using the interview method (Seidman 2013), we also asked why the respondents (non-users of modern style) do not use the modern style of writing. Of all offered reasons, we selected the most common ones to use in our survey questionnaire to explore why people do not use the modern style of writing in the virtual world.

**Table 1.** Demographics of Survey Respondents (N = 221).

| Distribution | | Number (%) |
|---|---|---|
| Gender | Male | 143 (64.7%) |
| | Female | 78 (35.3%) |
| Age | under 29 | 74 (33.5%) |
| | 30–39 | 83 (37.6%) |
| | over 40 | 64 (29.0%) |
| Country | English speaking country | 152 (68.7%) |
| | Other country | 69 (31.3%) |
| Number of daily writings in the cyber world | under 20 | 45 (20.4%) |
| | 20–50 | 48 (21.7%) |
| | 50–100 | 56 (25.3%) |
| | over 100 | 72 (32.6%) |

*(continued)*

**Table 1.** (*continued*)

| Distribution | | Number (%) |
|---|---|---|
| Daily time spent writing in the cyber world | under 30 min | 42 (19.0%) |
| | 30 min–1 h | 64 (29.0%) |
| | 1 h–2 h | 64 (29.0%) |
| | over 2 h | 51 (23.1%) |
| Number of people that a person chats with a day | Less than 5 people | 36 (16.3%) |
| | 5–10 people | 50 (22.6%) |
| | 10–20 people | 43 (19.5%) |
| | More than 20 people | 92 (41.6%) |

*Participants*

We conducted online survey in South Korea for three months in summer, 2021 to reach foreign people of different ages. We targeted only international students, office employees, and academic foreigners such as teachers and professors. Furthermore, since our study and survey language is English, we chose the respondents who are from English speaking countries or fluent in English and used it when messaging and chatting in the virtual world.

We received 221 valid answers for data analysis. Table 1 given above shows the demographic characteristics of the survey respondents in terms of gender, age, country, daily time spent writing in the virtual world, number of daily writings in the virtual world, and number of people chatted with or written to daily. Of all respondents, 64.7% were men, and 35.3% were women. Out of 221 respondents, 152 (68.7%) were from English speaking countries. 69 respondents (31.3%) were from other countries that they use English daily because of being international students or employees. Most respondents (37.6%) were in the age group of 30–39; 33.5% were younger than 29, and 72 of the 221 respondents (32.6%), that is, almost one-third of them, believed that they send more than 100 writings a day. We considered each time the "send" button is pressed –to be one "writing" rather than one message. If we had asked respondents how many messages they send a day, they might have considered only traditional phone messages.

# 4   Results

Descriptive statistics

Descriptive statistics organize, summarize, and present data in a convenient and informative-descriptive way. Although descriptive statistics outline various features of the collected data, synthesizing the results with other inferential statistics is beneficial to reveal study findings (Hsu 2013). Therefore, we provide several descriptive statistics to find appropriate answers to our research questions.

Descriptive statistics in Table 2 reveal some facts about our survey respondents' opinions about the modern style of writing using CMC. More than half of the respondents

(57%) use the modern style when writing in the cyber world. This means that they use at least one of the aspects of the modern style of messaging. In the survey questionnaire, we asked them to check "yes" if they use at least one of the aspects of modern style of writings. In contrast, 43% of the respondents (95 out of 221) do not use any type of modern style. We included some reasons from previous research (Wood et al. 2014) and our pilot test to suggest why or why not people choose to use the modern style.

Most users (56%) use this style to save time and chat quickly. Respondents who do it because of their friends represented the second largest portion of the users (25.4%). The third reason was usage for fun (18.3%); this is identical to the playfulness seen in modern computer technology use among young users (Lin and Li 2014). A very small number of users (2.4%) indicated that they use the modern style to save money, and a few others said that they use the modern style of writing for other reasons. For non-users of the modern style of writing, we found that most of them (34.7% of the non-users) do not use the modern style because they do not like it or annoyed with it; 28 respondents (29.5%) stated that they to prefer to follow the writing rules of the language, while 25.3% of the non-users consider that writing in such a manner would be disrespectful towards others. Only 10% of the non-users had other reasons message. If we had asked respondents how many messages they send a day, they might have considered only traditional phone messages.

**Table 2.** Descriptive Statistics of Survey Respondents Opinions about Modern Style of Writings in the Virtual World.

| Question Type | | Number (%) |
| --- | --- | --- |
| Using modern style when writing in the cyber world | Yes | 126 (57.0) |
| | No | 95 (43.0) |
| Reasons for using modern style | To save money | 3 (2.4) |
| | To save time | 56 (44.4) |
| | For fun | 23 (18.3) |
| | Because friends are using | 33 (25.4) |
| | Other reasons | 12(9.5) |
| Reasons for not using modern style | Just do not like | 33 (34.7) |
| | Respect others | 24 (25.3) |
| | Want to follow the rules of writing | 28 (29.5) |
| | Other reasons | 10 (10.5) |

Descriptive statistics of the variables of feelings used in this study are summarized in Table 3. These variables describe the following five feelings users experience when they receive a message in the modern style with any of the CMC tools: happiness, anger, familiarity, surprise, and confusion. The results indicate that when respondents receive a message (or writing) in the modern style, they tend to feel happy (mean of 3.11) and not angry (mean of 2.44). Items marked with a star are reversed-items such as "angry", with a 5-point scale from angry to not angry at all. We can consider most people to feel "not angry at all". In contrast, familiarity (mean of 3.76) had a relatively higher level than all other feelings variables. This means that everyone in the survey has encountered or received this kind of message (or writing) through CMC tools before, regardless of how they feel. Thus a lot of people are very familiar with them. Furthermore, people see and receive this kind of message daily, and they do not fell surprised (mean of 2.40). Those who do not like this style might get a little annoyed, but they do not feel surprised. Confusion also shows a considerably high mean value (2.66). From this reverse-item, we can see that people are not very confused when they receive a message in the modern style in CMC tools. This fits with the high value for familiarity because of people see this kind of message every day if they use CMC to communicate with others.

**Table 3.** Descriptive statistics of feelings when people receive a modern style message.

| Feeling | Mean | Standard Deviation |
|---------|------|--------------------|
| happy | 3.11 | 1.11 |
| angry | 2.44 | 1.41 |
| familiar | 3.76 | 1.44 |
| surprised | 2.40 | 1.55 |
| confused | 2.66 | 1.46 |

MANOVA and post hoc analysis

We used multivariate analysis of variance (MANOVA) because we wanted to know two things: 1) differences in general feelings (happy, angry, familiar, surprised and confused) within three age groups (younger than 29, 30–39 and, older than 40) and feelings (on a five-point scale from bad to fine) when respondents receive a modern style message (or writing) from someone in one of the three age groups (younger than the respondent, the same age as the respondent or, older than the respondent); 2) differences in the general feelings of users and non-users of the modern style and their feelings when they receive a modern style message from someone in one of the three age groups (given above). Table 4 illustrates the results of MANOVA testing, and the post hoc analysis. Significant differences were discovered between groups for all the indicators.

The results for the indicators of the three age groups were as follows: 1) happy (F = 49.082), angry (F = 28.661), familiar (F = 12.149), surprised (F = 16.216), confused (F = 22.969); 2) for these age groups, when they receive a modern-style message from someone: younger (F = 27.273); the same age (F = 21.377), or; older (F = 15.709). Even though the notable differences showed that at least one group mean differed from the others, we conducted post hoc analysis to identify which groups' means differ significantly. We used the Tukey post hoc analysis method because of its wide usage in analysis of variance (Cronk 2004) among other post hoc analyses. Post hoc analysis showed that respondents younger than 29 feel happier than older people when they see a modern message; respondents older than 40 feel angrier than respondents in the younger groups; respondents younger than 29 are very familiar with the modern style, and people aged 30–39 and older than 40 seem to be equally familiar. As for "surprised", people older than 40 are responsive and get more confused than younger people. These three age groups' feelings (bad to fine) also differ as follows: respondents younger than 29 (rather than older respondents) feel fine when they receive a modern-style message from someone in any age group (younger, same age or older than they are). That means that older people (aged 30–39 and older than 40) feel bad when they receive from younger people.

**Table 4.** ANOVA and post hoc analysis.

|  |  | F | Post hoc comparison |
|---|---|---|---|
| Age | Feeling |  |  |
|  | Happy | 49.082*** | 20 > 30 > 40 |
|  | Angry | 28.661*** | 20 < 30 < 40 |
|  | Familiar | 12.149*** | 20 > 30 = 40 |
|  | Surprised | 16.216*** | 20 < 30 < 40 |
|  | Confused | 22.969*** | 20 < 30 < 40 |
|  | Receive Age |  |  |
|  | Younger | 27.273*** | 20 > 30 > 40 |
|  | Same | 21.377*** | 20 > 30 > 40 |
|  | Older | 15.709*** | 20 > 30 > 40 |
| Users and nonusers | Feeling |  |  |
|  | Happy | 221.850*** | Yes > No |
|  | Angry | 470.177*** | Yes < No |
|  | Familiar | 572.995*** | Yes > No |
|  | Surprised | 528.098*** | Yes < No |
|  | Confused | 558.875*** | Yes < No |
|  | Receive Age |  |  |
|  | Younger | 413.049*** | Yes > No |
|  | Same | 505.913*** | Yes > No |
|  | Older | 407.439*** | Yes > No |

The results for the indicators of users and non-users were as follows: 1) for feelings: happy (F = 221.850), angry (F = 470.177), familiar (F = 572.995), surprised (F = 528.098), confused (F = 558.875); 2) for users and non-users when they receive from someone: younger (F = 413.049), same age (F = 505.919), older (F = 407,439). Post hoc analysis results helped us determine which groups' means differ significantly. The results show that for general feelings, users more than non-users feel familiar and happy; most non-users feel angry, surprised and confused. Non-users might be expected to feel angry, surprised and confused because they do not use the modern style of writing in the virtual world. Furthermore, post hoc analysis shows that users feel fine when they receive a modern-style message from people whether younger, the same age or older than they are, while non-users feel bad when they receive from people younger or the same age as they are.

## 5 Discussion and Conclusions

Previous studies on modern messaging have focused mainly on violations of language rules when text messaging and relationships between those violations and their causes; other studies have investigated whether there is a negative or positive effect of modern text messaging on the literacy attainment of elementary school children, adolescents, teenagers, and university students and how to address this issue. Different from them, we conducted an exploratory study to investigate how the modern style of writing in the cyber world affects people of different ages who use and do not use this kind of style. While previous studies included only traditional phone messaging and instant messaging, the present study included all kinds of tools in the virtual world. The present study includes people of different ages. As most of our survey respondents (57.0%) use the modern style of writing in the cyber world, we were able to draw two main conclusions based on our research questions.

First, regarding our first research question, data analysis demonstrated that people of different ages feel differently about the modern style of writings. In general, younger people feel happy, while older people (older than 40) feel a little angry because of their concern about the low level of literacy skills among the younger population. Middle-aged respondents feel neutral: not so happy and not so angry. Some of them even feel comfortable with the modern style. People in the younger and middle-aged groups do not tend to feel confused or surprised, while people older than 40 do feel confused and surprised. They also react differently, when they receive a modern style message. Younger respondents feel fine when they receive such a message from someone of any age. Middle-aged people feel a little bad when they receive a modern message from people who are younger than they. Older people feel bad when they receive modern messages from younger people and even peers. Thus, we can conclude that people should be careful when writing via CMC tools to older people, as this might negatively affect their relationships. It is better to follow the conventional language rules.

Second, regarding our second research question, the results reveal that the feelings of users and non-users of the modern style differ. Because users are familiar with this style, they feel much happier, not surprised and not confused. They use the modern style of messaging. In contrast, non-users feel angry and cannot tolerate this modern style; they feel uncomfortable, surprised and confused because of their unfamiliarity with the style. Some of them stated that modern style of writing may spoil the language and lead to disrespect and illiteracy. In the questionnaire, they mentioned these kind of reasons in the "Why don't you use modern style ow writing?" section "other reasons" part (see Appendix).

Users and non-users differ significantly in their response to receiving a modern-style message. Most of the users feel all right when they get such a message from people younger than they and they can understand and easily cope. Some of them encourage the style's use to save time and improve social relationships, particularly in the work-place mentioned in the "other reasons" part of "why do you use modern style of writing?" section in the questionnaire (see Appendix). We suggest that people write to other users in a modern style, and there will be no harm. However, non-users feel bad when they receive a modern message from younger people or even from people of the same age. They require more respect and formality in writing. Therefore, we should be careful when writing to people who do not usually use the modern style of messaging. Otherwise, we may lose a good relationship or make them anxious.

Our study is not free of limitations. We could reach only a small number of respondents. Future researchers should seek a larger sample of the population for more complete responses. Future researchers can include some other variables such as social status, other reasons for using or not using the modern style of messaging, and other feelings.

The findings of our exploratory study provide contributions for future researchers to carry out deeper empirical study. First, we opened a new direction in this field of research so that future researchers can develop an empirical model to investigate other aspects of the modern style of writings and its consequences. Second, practitioners such as behavioral education instructors and teachers, social studies and program developers might benefit from our findings, and human resource managers at work-places can use our results when creating a virtual work chat room that is socially healthy.

# References

Anthony, Ch., Nicolas, M.: The recognition of emotions beyond facial expressions: comparing emoticons specifically designed to convey basic emotions with other modes of expression. Comput. Hum. Behav. **118**, 106689 (2021)

Cronk, B.: How to Use SPSS: A Step-by-Step Guide to Analysis and Interpretation. Pyrczak Publishing, Glendale (2004)

Drouin, M., Davis, C.: R u txting? Is the use of text speak hurting your literacy? J. Lit. Res. **41**, 46–67 (2009)

Elbro, C.: Early linguistic abilities and reading development: a review and a hypothesis. Reading Writing: Interdisc. J. **8**, 453–485 (1997)

Goswami, U.: Phonology, reading development, and dyslexia: a cross-linguistic perspective. Ann. Dyslexia **52**, 1–23 (2002)

Hsu, J.L.: Exploring the relationship between the use of text message language and the literacy skills of dyslexic and normal students. Res. Dev. Disabil. **34**, 423–428 (2013)

Kemp, N., Bushnell, C.: Children's text messaging: abbreviations, input methods and links with literacy. J. Comput. Assist. Learn. **27**, 18–27 (2011)

Lin, T.T.C., Li, L.: Perceived characteristics, perceived popularity, and playfulness: youth adoption of mobile instant messaging in China. China Media Res. **10**(2), 60–71 (2014)

Michal, P., Fumito, M., Naoto, I.: A method for automatic estimation of meaning ambiguity of emoticons based on their linguistic expressibility. Cogn. Syst. Res. **59**, 103–113 (2020)

Plester, B., Wood, C., Bell, V.: Txt msg n school literacy: does texting and knowledge of text abbreviations adversely affect children's literacy attainment? Literacy **42**, 132–213 (2008)

https://techcrunch.com/2017/02/01/facebook-q4-2016-earnings/

https://backlinko.com/whatsapp-users

https://telegram.org

McHaneya, R., George, J.F.: Influence of emoticons on deception detection: an empirical exploration. Telemat. Inform. Rep. **1–4**, 100001 (2021)

182     U. Bahromjon et al.

Seidman, I.: Interviewing as qualitative research. A Guide for Researchers in Education and the Social Sciences. Fourth Edition. Teachers College Press. Teachers College Columbia University New York and London (2013)

Tayebinika, M., Puteh, M.: Txt msg n English language literacy. Procedia Soc. Behav. Sci. **66**, 97–99 (2012)

Thurlow, C.: Generation txt? The sociolinguistics of young people's text-messaging. Discourse Analysis Online (2003). http://extra.shu.ac.uk/daol/articles/v1/n1/a3/thurlow2002003-paper.html

Paykani, T., Zimet, G.D., Esmaeili, R., Khajedaluee, A.R., Khajedaluee, M.: BMC Public Health **20**, Article number 1650 (2020)

Vosloo, S.: The effects of texting on literacy: modern scourge or opportunity? An issue paper from the Shuttleworth Foundation (2009). http://bomedia.pbworks.com/f/Positive%20Texting

Walther, J.B., D'Addario, K.P.: The impacts of emoticons on message interpretation in computer – mediated communication. Soc. Sci. Comput. Rev. **19**, 324–424 (2001)

# Improvement of Information Support in Intelligent Information Energy Systems

Gayrat Ishankhodjayev[1], Murodjon Sultanov[1]([✉]) [iD], Rano Parpiyeva[2], and Nafisa Norboyeva[2]

[1] Institute of Energy Problems, Chingiz Aytmaotv str., 2-B, Tashkent, Uzbekistan
Energetika_in@umail.uz
[2] Tashkent State University of Economics, Islam Karimov str., 49, Tashkent, Uzbekistan
info@tsue.uz

**Abstract.** The article presents the results of a system analysis of the processes of functioning of existing energy systems. Based on these results of system analysis, problems and shortcomings of the processes of functioning of energy systems were identified, to eliminate which it was proposed to improve the functioning of the information support of intelligent information systems in the energy sector. In this paper, the principles and requirements for the creation and application of information support based on the common information model and unified modeling language are formed, and a block diagram of an enlarged algorithm for the formation of management decisions based on the common information model in an intelligent information energy system is developed, which shows the functional relationships between databases, knowledge and tasks of management processes. Using the methods of system analysis and the methodology for forming a common information model, a block diagram of information support and a generalized information model of intelligent information energy systems have also been developed. To solve the problems of functioning and development of a unified energy system, an adequate information model has been developed, which is built on the basis of a multidimensional, hierarchical information system consisting of subsystems united by many functional links. It is these connections that make it possible to assess the functional state of subsystems and the system as a whole. In this paper, a new integration mechanism for organizing information interaction of heterogeneous information systems of a single energy system is considered.

**Keywords:** system analysis · model · task · algorithm · decision making · information model · intelligent system · information support

## 1 Introduction

At present, the existing unified energy system (UES) of the republic, created more than sixty years ago, is a unique organizational and technical facility, the structure and management of which is built according to a hierarchical principle, which ensured a balanced unity of generation, distribution and consumption of electricity in the territorial context to ensure energy security of the regions and the possibility of intersystem exchange of

Y. Koucheryavy and A. Aziz (Eds.): NEW2AN 2022, LNCS 13772, pp. 183–195, 2023.
https://doi.org/10.1007/978-3-031-30258-9_16

power and energy flows in normal and emergency modes to improve the efficiency of the energy interconnection. At the same time, it should be noted that the UES, which was created a long time ago, needs a serious modernization of fixed assets and renewal, both in terms of replacing physically and morally obsolete equipment, and in the application of new technologies and equipment, information and diagnostic systems. The restructuring of the energy sector, the market conditions for the functioning of the energy industry bring their own characteristics and problems. To solve these problems, the use of an intelligent information energy system (IIES) is required, which ensures a reduction in costs in the production and transmission of electricity, a decrease in the level of losses in the transport of heat and electricity, and optimization of the size and placement of reserve capacities. The use of the IIES in the energy sector and the reform of the national energy sector pose new important tasks for the development of the UES of the republic. Modernization of energy management will lead to the financial independence of the fuel and energy complexes, which is provided by funds received for the production and transportation of energy. With an increase in the number of enterprises of fuel and energy complexes and a decrease in the size of each separately, in comparison with pre-reform vertically integrated enterprises of fuel and energy complexes, the risks and significance of management decisions increase significantly. The responsibility of enterprises of fuel and energy complexes for their own energy consumption increases the importance of energy saving issues, reducing excess energy losses and improving the quality of energy metering systems. Modernization of equipment and improvement of information technologies require more focused attention to the formation of the scientific and technical policy of the enterprise of fuel and energy complexes. Building the structure of the IIES is primarily associated with building a system model, in which both the traditional elements of the control system and the knowledge processing models implemented by the intelligent system should be defined. In an intelligent control system, new elements compared to a traditional control system are all intelligent transformations or knowledge management elements that are associated with the implementation of artificial intelligence, i.e. using technologies of expert systems, database, goals and knowledge, decision making, associative memory, fuzzy logic, semiotic networks, structural dynamics control, etc. [1].

For the efficient and reliable functioning of energy facilities (energy associations, power systems, grid and generating enterprises), it is necessary to create and implement modern information management systems. During the last quarter of a century, domestic information systems have undergone a progressive evolution, both in terms of the development of theoretical principles for their construction, and in the field of implementation of these systems. A significant contribution to this difficult work was made by V.A. Barinov, A.I. Bartolomey, F.D. Goldenberg, A.F. Bondarenko, V.V. Bushuev, V.P. Vasin, V.A. Venikov, N.I. Voropay, V.E. Vorotnitsky, A.Z. Gamm, A.F. Dyakov, Yu.S. Zhelezko, A.G. Zhuravlev, N.I. Zelenokhat, Gustav Olsson, Gianguido Piani, V.I. Idelchik, G.L. Kemelmacher, I.N. Kolosok, V.G. Kitushin, JI.A. Koshcheev, L.A. Krumm, Yu.N. Kucherov, Yu.Ya. Lyubarsky, M.I. Londer, K.G. Mityushkin, V.L. Nesterenko, V.G. Ornov, Yu.I. Morzhin, M.A. Rabinovich, S.I. Palamarchuk, V.I. Rozanov, Yu.N. Rudenko, V.A. Semenov, S.S. Smirnov, Yu.A. Tikhonov, Yu.A. Fokin, E.V. Tsvetkov, M.I. Londer, A.P. Chepkasov and others [1–6].

At present, with the development of high-performance computer technology, information systems (IS) are an effective means of solving systemic problems. The works of M.K. Chirkova, S.P. Maslova, V.N. Petrov, D. Mark, K. McGowan. The issues of developing information systems for various purposes by methods of system analysis using modern object-oriented programming languages and database technologies are widely covered in the works of V.P. Agaltsov, K.Yu. Bogachev, V.I. Vasilyeva, B.G. Ilyasov, E. Jordan, D.M. Mutushev and others. To a lesser extent, this affected the problems of creating adapted methods for developing special information systems for agricultural complexes. Separate aspects devoted to the methods of system analysis and decision-making on the creation and deployment of information systems for monitoring the parameters of agricultural complexes for smart grid technologies are considered in the works of C.C. Liu, D.A. Pierce, K.Y. Lee, Z.A.Vale, B.B. Kobets, I.O.Volkova and others. In this direction, there is also a certain number of legal documents, both international and domestic, partially describing the direction of development of standards in the field of intelligent grid [7–10].

## 2 Methodology

Under the ability of the system to make decisions independently, it is necessary to understand the ability of the system to receive and analyze information, understand it and draw new conclusions (filling it up), formulate conclusions, i.e. "think", helping the natural intellect - a person, who, in turn, correcting, "improves" the adopted integrated solution.

It should be noted here that there are automatic machines or just a mechanical, electronic relay that react to the presence or absence of a signal or, when monitoring parameters, work according to the "good - bad" principle. This is also a decision, but we will refer them to information and computing systems with a low level of "intellectualization".

In this regard, under the intellectual information system we will understand a system capable of making a decision in the conditions of: a) the need to process and analyze a large array of information database; b) limited information; c) uncertainty; d) multidimensional space; e) the need to recognize the situation (images, scenes, etc.); f) different stages of the life cycle of objects (processes) - design, production, operation; g) dynamic, evolving, non-stationary facts that affect the solution of the problem; h) formalization and representation of knowledge; i) adaptation, self-learning, self-organization, etc.

Thus, if an information-computing system has the necessary mathematical, algorithmic, software and instrumental support in making a decision under the above conditions, then we will assume that it has intellectual support in solving a wide class of various problems.

In other words, we can formally write:

$$IIES = < MS, AS, PS, IS >_{(a,b,....,i)},$$

where $MS, AS, PS, IS$ - respectively mathematical, algorithmic, software and information support; $<>|_{()}$ - stands for condition.

All existing IIES can be divided into two classes: general purpose and specialized. General-purpose IIES include those that not only perform specified procedures; but on the basis of meta search procedures, they generate and execute procedures for solving new specific problems. The technology of using such systems is as follows. The user-operator (expert) generates knowledge (data and rules) describing the selected application (applications, subject area). Then, based on this knowledge, the given goal and the initial data, the meta procedures of the system generate and execute the procedure for solving a specific problem.

Specialized IIES include those that solve a fixed set of tasks predetermined during system design. To use such systems, it is required to fill them with data corresponding to the selected application (applied tasks, subject area).

The construction of the IIES structure is primarily associated with the construction of a system model, in which both traditional elements of the control system and the knowledge processing models implemented by the intelligent system should be defined. In an intelligent control system, new elements compared to a traditional control system are all intelligent transformations or knowledge management elements that are associated with the implementation of artificial intelligence, i.e. using technologies of expert systems, database, goals and knowledge, decision making, associative memory, fuzzy logic, semiotic networks, structural dynamics control, etc.

Consider the block diagram of the enlarged algorithm for the formation of management decisions in the IIES, which is presented in Fig. 1.

In this system, the information input block is designed to enter numerical data, text, speech, which come (depending on the task being solved) from the user, the external environment, the control object. At the next stage, information is sorted, analyzed, interpreted, and the necessary information is selected for solving problems and recorded in a database (DB). DB - a set of tables that store, as a rule, symbolic and numerical information about the objects of the subject area. On the basis of this information, the tasks of the IIES are formulated. At the next stage, models and algorithms for solving the functional tasks of the IIES are developed, reliable management decisions are formed and promptly transferred to the control object of the IIES.

For the effective functioning of the IIES, information is needed about the state of the controlled object, the environment, and the accepted control actions. The necessary conditions for the functioning of the IIES, the optimal volumes of information that are promptly received by various control units, the distribution of information flows in time and space, which significantly depends on the optimality of building information support (IS).

The main functions of the IS IIES are the functions of collecting, controlling, transforming, storing, making reliable decisions, distributing and transmitting information from sources to its consumers. The block diagram of the IS developed to determine the composition of the IIES database elements and their interrelations in order to provide the possibility of building rational information and computing processes, choosing the direction for ensuring information compatibility of the components interacting in the IIES, as well as rational organization of reliable decision-making processes.

The main functions of the IS IIES are the functions of collecting, controlling, transforming, storing, making reliable decisions, distributing and transmitting information from sources to its consumers. The block diagram of the IS developed to determine the composition of the IIES database elements and their interrelations in order to provide

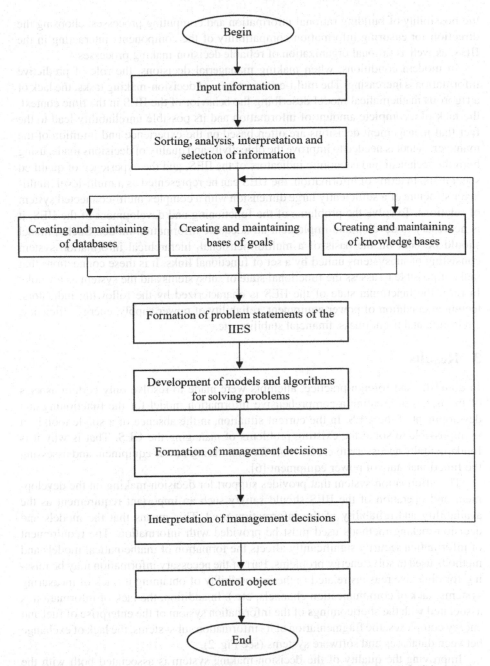

**Fig. 1.** Block diagram of an enlarged algorithm for the formation of management decisions in the IIES.

the possibility of building rational information and computing processes, choosing the direction for ensuring information compatibility of the components interacting in the IIES, as well as rational organization of reliable decision-making processes.

In modern conditions, when making managerial decisions, the role of predictive information is increasing. The multi-criteria nature of decision-making tasks, the lack of a rigorous mathematical model describing the behavior of the IIES in the time context, the lack of a complete amount of information and its possible unreliability lead to the fact that management decisions are often based on the experience and intuition of the manager. A tool is needed to improve the objectivity and quality of decisions made, using both the technical and economic indicators of the IIES, and the experience of qualified specialists. In terms of information, the UES can be represented as a multi-level, multi-layer structure of a sufficiently large dimension with a complex multi-connected system of relations. To solve the problems of the functioning and development of the IIES, it is necessary to develop and implement an adequate information model. Such a model should be built on the basis of a multidimensional, hierarchical information system consisting of subsystems united by a set of functional links. It is these connections that make it possible to assess the functional state of subsystems and the system as a whole. In turn, the functional state of the IIES is characterized by the following indicators: technical condition of power equipment, reliability of power supply, energy efficiency, environmental friendliness, financial stability, etc.

## 3  Results

In domestic and foreign practice, attempts were made to resolve only certain aspects of the issues of creating a comprehensive information model for the functioning and development of the UES. In the current situation, in the absence of a single toolkit, it is impossible to solve the existing problems of managing the UES. That is why it is fundamentally necessary to create tools for monitoring power equipment and assessing the functional state of power equipment [6].

The information system that provides support for decision-making on the development and operation of the IIES should satisfy such an important requirement as the availability and reliability of the information used. This means that the models and decision-making methods used must be provided with information. The requirement of information security significantly affects the formation of mathematical models and methods used to solve energy problems. Part of the necessary information may be missing for objective reasons related to the impossibility of obtaining it (lack of measuring systems, lack of communication channels, etc.). In addition, the lack of information is associated with the shortcomings of the information system of the enterprise of fuel and energy complexes, the fragmentation of its information subsystems, the lack of exchange between databases and software systems (see Fig. 2).

Improving the quality of the decision-making system is associated both with the improvement of its information security, and with the development of mathematical methods of decision-making.

Information support of the tasks of synthesis and operation of the IIES is proposed to be considered based on the information model. Modern requirements for the representation and use of information in the IIES make it expedient to use a new information

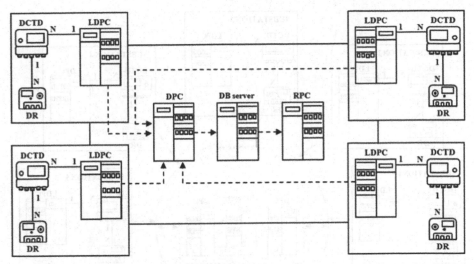

**Fig. 2.** Exchange of information in IIES (DCTD-data collection and transmission device; LDPC-local data processing center; DR-data recorder; RPC-request processing center; DB-database).

technology - the so-called Common Information Model (CIM) - systems. The generalized information model CIM - hereinafter CIM - is a certain conceptual model for describing various objects (subjects) of the surrounding world, using object-oriented terminology. If until recent years the concepts of object-oriented technology were related to programming languages (C++, Java, etc.), then CIM expands these concepts to describe data, deliberately using such terminology of object-oriented programming as classes, properties, methods, etc. associations. In essence, CIM is an information model, the task of which is a single unified representation of data structures, regardless of the source of data origin and the purposes of their use (see Fig. 3).

As already noted CIM - the model uses a standard object-oriented visual representation. The main elements of the CIM model are classes, associations, and packages. The class is the main element of the CIM model. A class is an abstract description of some objectively existing entity of an electric power system. Examples of classes are «transformer», «load», «ac line», «dc line», «measurement», etc. The fundamental difference between the concept of a class in CIM and object-oriented programming languages is that in CIM a class describes only an interface and is completely independent of both the computer technology platform and the implementation. The main properties of a class are encapsulation, polymorphism, and associations. Encapsulation means concentrating all the properties of a class as its attributes within the class declaration. Polymorphism means that the same symbolic attribute name can be used in different classes, but the class name must be unique.

Association means the possibility of connecting classes to each other, that is, any pair of classes can be connected by an association, which in turn is also a class. Associations represent a semantic relationship between two classes, with the help of which one class can obtain information about the attributes and associations of another class. An association has two association ends, each attached to one of the association classes.

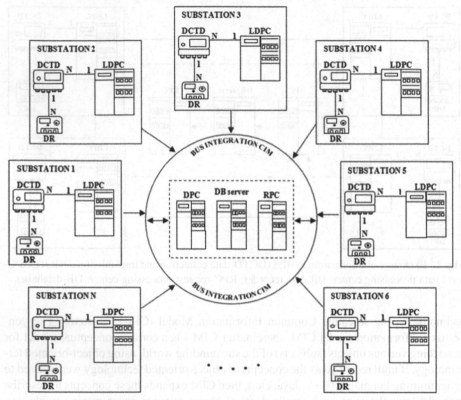

**Fig. 3.** Relationship diagram when applying the CIM model in IIES (DCTD-data collection and transmission device; LDPC-local data processing center; DR-data recorder; RPC-request processing center; DB-database; CIM- common information model).

The end of an association may be marked with a label called «role name» or «role». In the CIM model, the role name almost always contains the class name, and in some cases simply repeats it. The end of the association (role) also has a multiplicity, which indicates how many objects of the class can participate in this association.

In this paper: - a new integration mechanism for organizing information interaction of heterogeneous information systems of the UES - the so-called CIM-systems - is considered; - Investigated the benefits of using such systems; - Analyzed the methodology for building CIM models in relation to energy applications, as well as data access interfaces in CIM systems.

In the future, work will be carried out to adapt international standards for CIM systems to the real UES, a number of methodological documents will be developed that determine the possibility, rules and techniques for building information models, for the first time CIM for interactive creation of information models [11–14].

The CIM can be used in a variety of ways. Ideally, task information is organized so that it can be used by disparate groups of people. This can be achieved with an information model that represents the details needed by people working in a particular field. An information model requires a set of legal assertion types or syntax to capture a representation, and a set of expressions to control general aspects of the domain (in this case, complex computer systems). Because of the general focus, the Distributed Management Task Force (DMTF) refers to this information model as the CIM, the Common Information Model. For information about the current core and general circuits developed using this metamodel, contact the DMTF.

Management schemas are the building blocks for management platforms and management applications such as device configuration, performance management, and change management. CIM structures the managed environment as a set of interconnected systems, each of which consists of separate elements. The CIM provides a set of classes with properties and associations that provide a well-understood conceptual framework for organizing information about the managed environment. We suggest that any programmer who writes code to work with an object schema, or any schema developer who intends to put new information into a managed environment, should have a good knowledge of the CIM.

Because the CIM is not implementation-specific, it can be used to exchange control information in a variety of ways; four of these methods are shown in Fig. 4. These communication methods can be used in combination in the control application.

The constructs defined in the model are stored in the database repository. These constructs are not instances of an object, relationship, etc. Rather, they are definitions for establishing objects and relationships. The metamodel used by the CIM is stored in the repository, which becomes the representation of the metamodel. The metamodel constructs are mapped to the physical schema of the target repository. The repository is then populated with classes and properties expressed in the base model, general model, and extension schemas.

For a database management system (DBMS) application, the CIM is mapped to the physical schema of the target DBMS (for example, relational). The information stored in the database consists of actual construct instances. Applications can exchange information when they have access to a common DBMS and the display is predictable. For application objects, the CIM is used to create a set of application objects in a particular language. Applications can exchange information when they can communicate with application objects. For exchange parameters, the CIM, expressed in some consistent syntax, is a neutral form for exchanging control information through a standard set of object application programming interfaces (API). The exchange occurs through a direct set of API calls or through exchange-oriented APIs that can create the corresponding object in the local implementation technology [15].

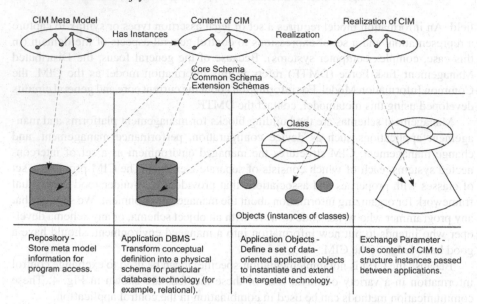

**Fig. 4.** Four Ways to Use CIM

# 4   Discussion

The CIM framework is an approach to systems and network management that applies the basic techniques for structuring and conceptualizing the object-oriented paradigm. This approach uses a single modeling formalism that, together with a basic set of object-oriented constructs, supports the collaborative development of an object-oriented schema across multiple organizations. The article describes an object-oriented metamodel based on the Unified Modeling Language (UML). This model includes expressions for common elements that must be clearly represented in control applications (for example, object classes, properties, methods, and associations). This document does not describe specific CIM implementations, APIs, or communication protocols.

A meta-schema is a formal definition of a model, defining terms for expressing a model, its usage, and semantics. The UML defines the structure of the meta-schema. It assumes that you are familiar with UML notation and basic object-oriented concepts in the form of classes, properties, methods, operations, inheritance, associations, objects, cardinality, and polymorphism.

The CIM meta-schema provides a framework for defining CIM schemas and models. The CIM meta schema defines the meta elements that have attributes and the relationships between them. For example, a CIM class is a meta element that has attributes such as the name of the class, and relationships such as a generalization relationship to a superclass, or ownership relationships to its properties and methods. A CIM meta schema is defined as a custom UML model using the following UML concepts:

– CIM meta-elements are represented as UML classes (a UML class meta-class defined in Unified Modeling Language: Superstructure);

– CIM meta elements can use single inheritance, which is represented as a UML generalization (the UML generalization meta class defined in Unified Modeling Language: Superstructure);

– Attributes of CIM meta-elements are represented as UML properties (a meta-class of UML properties defined in Unified Modeling Language: Superstructure);

– Relationships between CIM meta-elements are represented as UML associations (UML association meta-class defined in the Unified Modeling Language: superstructure) whose association ends belong to the related meta-classes. The reason for this ownership is that UML association meta classes cannot own attributes or operations. Such relationships are defined in the Association Ends sections of each meta element definition.

Languages that define CIM schemas and models (for example, the CIM Managed Object Format) shall use as their basis the meta-schema defined in this subclause, or an equivalent meta-schema.

The meta schema that describes the actual run-time objects on the CIM server is outside the scope of this CIM meta schema. Such a meta-schema may be closely related to the CIM meta-schema defined in this subclause, but there are some differences. For example, a CIM instance specified in a schema or model following that CIM meta-schema can specify property values for a subset of the properties provided by its defining class, while a CIM instance on a CIM server always has all of the properties provided by the defining class.

The methodology for generating a CIM model of power supply system objects is presented below.

1. Highlighting voltage levels and designating them as objects of the "VoltageLevel" class.
2. Grouping the elements of the power supply circuit according to the voltage level.
3. Allocation of AC power line segments into a set of objects of the AC Line Segment (ACLineSegment) class.
4. Combining objects of the AC Line Segment (ACLineSegment) class into objects of the Line class according to a geographical feature.
5. Converting transformers into a set of objects of classes "Power transformer (PowerTransformer)", "Transformer winding (TransformerWinding)" and "TapChanger" provided that the transformer is with a split winding.
6. Fixing the connection between the objects of the class "Transformer winding (TransformerWinding)" and the corresponding object of the class "Voltage level (VoltageLevet)".
7. Converting the current-carrying equipment of the power supply circuit into the corresponding network elements from the "Network Elements (Wires)" package of the CIM model. Namely, the load break switches are replaced by objects of the class "Breaker", the disconnector - "Disconnector", the bus section - "Busbar Section".
8. Connection of objects derived from the class "Conductive Equipment (ConductingEquipment)" of the CIM model to each other through objects of the class

"ConnectivityNode" of the "Topology" package based on information from the power supply scheme about the physical connection of the elements to each other.

9.  Adding objects of the "Terminal" class of the "Core" package for each connection between the "ConductingEquipment" and "ConnectivityNode" objects, which will add objects of the "Measurement" class and store meter readings.

10. Fixing the connection between the objects of the class "Measurement" of the package "Measuring (Meas)" with the objects of the class "Terminal" based on the power supply scheme. Namely, measuring transformers of current, voltage, etc. are replaced by a combination of objects of classes "Terminal" and "Measurement" with the corresponding type of measured value. The "Measurement" class is used to represent state variables that take place in technological processes. This class aggregates a set of objects of the "MeasurementValue" class, which allows you to store indicators of the measured value [16–18].

11. Formation of a list of objects (attributes and belonging to the class and package of the CIM model) of the CIM model to be added to the database in the form

$$OL = \{ ol_i | i = 1, \ldots, n \}$$

where $n$ is the number of model elements;

$ol_i = (A_{id}, A_1, A_2, \ldots, A_m, D_j)$ - $i$ - th model object;

$A_{id}$ - attribute identifier (name) of the object;

$A$ - object attribute;

$m$ - the number of object attributes;

$D_j$ - CIM model class, $j = 1, \ldots, k$;

$k$ - number of CIM model classes.

## 5   Conclusion and Suggestions

The analysis of structural models of information systems for monitoring the parameters of energy complexes for smart grid technologies was carried out based on the CIM model and UML deployment diagrams. One of the most important requirements for the developed information model is the most complete description of the subject area, taking into account future expansion and the addition of new types and elements of the model. The CIM provides a standard way of representing power system resources as object classes and attributes, and their relationships. The CIM model simplifies the integration of the production and transmission control system. Integration is facilitated by the fact that the CIM defines a common language to enable applications to access or exchange information, regardless of how such information is represented within applications. The technique for generating a CIM model of objects of the power supply system is a sequence of steps that leads the power supply scheme to an object-oriented CIM model. Through the use of the CIM model, the developed and information models of IS for managing the parameters of energy complexes can be used as a methodological basis for creating larger-scale distributed ISs that combine several energy complexes.

# References

1. Barinov, V.A., Gamm, A.Z., Kucherov, Y.N., et al.: Automation of dispatch control in the electric power industry. Moscow Power Engineering Institute Publishing House, Moscow (2000)
2. Goldenberg, F.D.: New technologies in the dispatching control of the power system of Israel. In: The Collection. Energy systems management - new technologies and the market, Syktyvkar 2004, pp. 123–130 (2004)
3. Dyakov, A.F., Lyubarsky, Y.Y., Ornov, V.G., Semenov, V.A., Tsvetkov, E.V.: Intelligent systems for operational management in power associations, p. 236. Moscow Power Engineering Institute Publishing House, MEI Publishing House, Moscow (1995)
4. Lyubarsky, Y.Y., Morzhin, Y.I.: The concept of intelligent operational information systems for automated control systems for energy systems, pp. 16–22. Publishing house Agro-Print, Moscow (2002)
5. Vasiliev, V.I., Ilyasov, B.G.: Intelligent control Systems: Theory and Practice, p. 392. Radiotehnika, Moscow (2019)
6. Mutushev, D.M.: Methods for providing access to object-oriented databases based on relational systems standards, Ph.D. thesis, Moscow Power Engineering Institute (1998)
7. Liu, C.C., Pierce, D.A.: Intelligent system applications to power systems. IEEE Comput. Appl. Power 10(4), 21–22 (1997). https://doi.org/10.1109/67.625369
8. Lee, K.Y.: Tutorial on intelligent optimization and control for power systems: an introduction. In: Proceedings of the 13th International Conference on, Intelligent Systems Application to Power Systems, pp. 2–5 (n.d.). https://doi.org/10.1109/ISAP.2005.1599235
9. Vale, Z.A.: Intelligent Power System. In: Wiley Encyclopedia of Computer Science and Engineering. John Wiley & Sons, Inc., Hoboken (2009). https://doi.org/10.1002/978047005 0118.ecse196
10. Vale, Z.A., Morais, H., Khodr, H.: Intelligent multi-player smart grid management considering distributed energy resources and demand response. In: IEEE PES General Meeting, pp. 1–7 (2010). https://doi.org/10.1109/PES.2010.5590170
11. Ishankhodjayev, G.Q., Sultanov, M.B., Nurmamedov, B.B.: Issues of development of intelligent information electric power systems. Mod. Innov. Syst. Technol. 2(2), 0251–0263 (2022). https://doi.org/10.47813/2782-2818-2022-2-2-0251-0263
12. Ishankhodjayev, G., Sultanov, M., Sultanov, D., Mirzaahmedov, D.: Development of an algorithm for optimizing energy-saving management processes in intelligent energy systems. In: International Conference on Information Science and Communications Technologies: Applications, Trends and Opportunities, ICISCT 2021 (2021). https://doi.org/10.1109/ICI SCT52966.2021.9670247
13. Ishankhodjayev, G., Sultanov, M., Mirzaahmedov, D., Azimov, D.: Optimization of information processes of multilevel intelligent systems. In: ACM International Conference Proceeding Series (2021). https://doi.org/10.1145/3508072.3508212
14. Ishankhodjayev, G., Sultanov, M.: Creation and application of intelligent information electric power system. Probl. Energy Resour. Sav. 2, 50–64 (2022)
15. Common Information Model (CIM) Infrastructure. (2012). Distributed Management Task Force standard, p. 186
16. Kraleva, R.S., Kralev, V.S., Sinyagina, N., Koprinkova-Hristova, P., Bocheva, N.: Design and analysis of a relational database for behavioral experiments data processing. Int. J. Online Eng. (IJOE) 14(02), 117 (2018). https://doi.org/10.3991/ijoe.v14i02.7988
17. Storey, V.C.: Relational database design based on the entity-relationship model. Data Knowl. Eng. 7(1), 47–83 (1991). https://doi.org/10.1016/0169-023X(91)90033-T
18. Tsalenko, M.S.: Relational database models. Algorithms and organization of solving economic problems, M.: Statistics, pp. 18–32 (1997)

# The Assessment of the Effectiveness
# of the Development of Digital Technologies
# in Commercial Banks of Uzbekistan

Fayzieva Muyassarzoda[✉] (iD)

Tashkent State University of Economics, Tashkent 100066, Uzbekistan
m.fayzieva@tsue.uz

**Abstract.** The aim of this assessment is to assess the effectiveness of the digital development of commercial banks in Uzbekistan. To accomplish the aim of this assessment, identifying the highest ranked banks in the effectiveness of digital development in commercial banks in Uzbekistan was chosen as the objective of this assessment by the researcher. The following methods were used in this assessment: survey, comparative analysis, index, correlation, statistical tables, and figures. In the end of the assessment, "Uzmilliybank" JSC, "Uzsanoatkurilishbank" JSC, "Ipoteka-bank" JSCMB, "Asakabank" JSC, and "Anor Bank" JSCS were ranked the highest positions among the banks that are effective digitally developed banks in Uzbekistan. Based on the indicators of the assessment, the level of development of digital technologies and the level of development of innovative digital technologies in commercial banks in Uzbekistan were determined. As well, the classifications of the groups on the digital technology offerings and on the effectiveness of the digital development of the commercial banks in Uzbekistan were formed in accordance with five categories of "very strong," "strong," "medium," "weak," and "very weak." The strategy for the effective development of the offerings of digital technologies in commercial banks of Uzbekistan was recommended for the banks that were ranked in "very weak" and "weak" positions on the list of the offerings of digital technologies by the banks. In the process of the research, a regression model was also created to predict the effectiveness of the digital development of commercial banks in Uzbekistan.

**Keywords:** digital technologies · commercial banks · effectiveness

## 1 Introduction

The approval of the strategy for reforming the banking system of the Republic of Uzbekistan for 2020–2025 by the Decree of the President of the Republic of Uzbekistan No. DP-5992 of May 12, 2020 became an important basis for conducting modern banking business in local commercial banks and strengthening the competitive environment in the banking sector.

Increasing the attractiveness and quality of banking services, expanding the scope of remote services using modern information technologies, increasing the types of digital services and products, and moderately digitizing traditional banking activities are currently the most important strategic goals of commercial banks in Uzbekistan. In the banking sector, digital transformation is one of the priority goals of banking business in the strategic planning of banking business activity, and therefore the assessment of the development of digital technologies in commercial banks is a relevant task [1, 2].

The fact that commercial banks are constantly assessing the overall effectiveness of their activities is principally limited to the determination of general financial and economic effectiveness indicators. The study of the impact of digital technologies on overall effectiveness, the evaluation of the effectiveness of the implementation of digital technologies in commercial banks, or the evaluation of the development of digital technologies remains out of the attention of bank officials.

The aim of this assessment is to assess the effectiveness of the digital development of commercial banks in Uzbekistan and the objective of this assessment is to identify the highest ranked banks in effective digital development in commercial banks in Uzbekistan.

## 2  Methodology

The following methods were used in this assessment: survey, comparative analysis, index, correlation, statistical tables, and figures. In order to assess the effectiveness of the development of digital technologies in 33 commercial banks of the Republic of Uzbekistan, an assessment conducted in the Republic of Belarus [3] was used as a basis. 27 types of products and services based on digital technologies was sent to the employees of commercial banks through social networks in the form of a questionnaire. Besides, based on their feedback, it was also studied whether other digital services and products that were used in the business activities of commercial banks were available or not where they worked.

The results were calculated and summarized in the Excel office program. The effectiveness of digital development in commercial banks in Uzbekistan was assessed based on index methods [4–6]. In this assessment, the results of the assessment of the use of digital technologies in the commercial banks of Uzbekistan, the net profit indicators of the commercial banks of Uzbekistan as of July 1, 2022 [7] and the system of relative normalized indicators (1–3) [3], which takes the value from 0 to 1, were used.

*The index of offered digital technologies by the bank, $Of_i$, is calculated using (1) formula:*

$$Of_i = \frac{T_i}{max\{T_i\}} \tag{1}$$

Here,

$T_i$ –a complex indicator of digitization of bank $i$;

$max\{T_i\}$- the maximum value in the range of complex indicators of banks digitization.

*The index of the net profit of the bank, $Inc_i$, is calculated in line with (2) formula:*

$$Inc_i = \frac{Inc_i}{max\{Inc_i\}} \tag{2}$$

Here,

$Inc_i$ - the net profit indicator of the bank for the reporting period (month, year);

$max \{Inc_i\}$ – the maximum value in the range of the net profit indicators of the bank for the reporting period (month, year).

The index of the effectiveness of digital development of the bank, $Eff_i$, is calculated based on the method of "vector development:"

$$Eff_i = \sqrt{\frac{1}{2}(Of_i^2 + Inc_i^2)} \qquad (3)$$

## 3 Results and Analysis

The assessment of the use of digital technologies was implemented according to the results that was based on 27 types of digital technologies, as mentioned above, and 8 types of digital services and products indicated by the survey participants (cash withdrawal "Quant", online conversion, online international money transfer, online account opening, online plastic card opening, receiving international money transfers through a mobile application, collection of credit debt from plastic cards opened by other banks, and mobile programs) but not specified in the questionnaire that was sent to the respondents.

In the assessment rating, the top five the following banks ranked the highest positions on the index of the effectiveness of digitally development of the bank:

- Uzsanoatqurilishbank JSC and Asakabank JSC with 34 points;
- Anor Bank JSC with 32 points;
- Kishloqqurilishbank JSCB and "Agrobank" JSCB with 28 points;
- Xalq Bank JSC and Ipoteka Bank JSCMB with 27 points;
- Uzmilliybank JSC, Microcreditbank JSCB, Turonbank JSC, Aloqabank JSC, and Poytaxt Bank JSC with 24 points.

Commercial banks use the following digital technologies the most among digital technologies that were listed in the survey: remote banking services—100%; issuance of bank payment cards—97%; online money transfers—100%; online deposit—85%; API interface—97%; online conversion—85%; and mobile applications—97%.

After the process of assessing the use of digital technologies in the commercial banks of Uzbekistan, indicators of digital development in the commercial banks of Uzbekistan were determined, that is, the indicators of the index of the net profit of the bank ($Inc_i$), the indicators of the index of offered digital technologies by the bank ($Of_i$), and the indicators of the index of the effectiveness of digital development of the bank ($Eff_i$). According to these indicators, the top five positions in the net profit of the banks were ranked by Uzmilliybank JSC, Ipoteka-bank JSCMB, Kapitalbank ATIB, Uzsanoatkurilishbank JSC, and Trustbank JSC. In compliance with the index of offered digital technologies by the bank, the top five positions were taken by Uzsanoatkurilishbank JSC, Asaka-bank JSC, Anor Bank JSC, Agrobank JSC, and Kishloqkurilishbank JSC. As a result, "Uzmilliybank" JSC, "Uzsanoatkurilishbank" JSC, "Ipoteka-bank" JSCMB, "Asaka-bank" JSC, and "Anor bank" JSCs took high-ranking positions based on the index of the effectiveness of digital development of the banks ($Eff_i$).

"Uzsanoatkurilishbank" JSC was the sole bank that kept its ranking position in the top five according to three indicators of the indexes (Table 1).

**Table 1.** The indicators of digital development in the commercial banks of Uzbekistan

| Banks | Net profit of the bank during the reporting period, billion soums (Q2) 2022) [7] | The net profit index of the bank | The index of offered digital technologies by the bank | Bank rating | The index of the effectiveness of digital development of the bank | Bank rating |
|---|---|---|---|---|---|---|
| Uzmilliybank | 986,0 | 1 | 0,705882 | 5 | 0,865526 | 1 |
| Ipoteka-bank | 608,4 | 0,617 | 0,794118 | 4 | 0,711112 | 3 |
| Kapitalbank | 486,8 | 0,494 | 0,5 | 10 | 0,496866 | 14 |
| Uzsanoatqurilishbank | 416,5 | 0,422 | 1 | 1 | 0,767605 | 2 |
| Trustbank | 329,3 | 0,334 | 0,352941 | 13 | 0,343589 | 26 |
| Hamkorbank | 318,0 | 0,322 | 0,441176 | 12 | 0,386428 | 19 |
| Qishloq qurilish bank | 273,3 | 0,277 | 0,823529 | 3 | 0,614422 | 6 |
| Ipak yo'li Bank | 258,8 | 0,262 | 0,647059 | 7 | 0,49375 | 15 |
| Xalq Bank | 206,3 | 0,209 | 0,794118 | 4 | 0,580689 | 8 |
| Orient Finance Bank | 195,6 | 0,198 | 0,676471 | 6 | 0,498481 | 13 |
| Aloqabank | 110,9 | 0,112 | 0,705882 | 5 | 0,505431 | 9 |
| Davr-bank | 87,9 | 0,089 | 0,529412 | 9 | 0,379621 | 20 |
| KDB Bank Uzbekistan | 86,2 | 0,087 | 0,294118 | 15 | 0,216966 | 32 |
| Universal Bank | 82,4 | 0,083 | 0,558824 | 8 | 0,399542 | 17 |
| InFinbank | 81,8 | 0,083 | 0,529412 | 9 | 0,378919 | 21 |
| Agrobank | 77,5 | 0,079 | 0,823529 | 3 | 0,58497 | 7 |
| Asia Alliance Bank | 71,2 | 0,072 | 0,558824 | 8 | 0,398433 | 18 |
| Turonbank | 56,1 | 0,057 | 0,705882 | 5 | 0,500753 | 10 |
| Ziraat bank Uzbekistan | 40,3 | 0,041 | 0,5 | 10 | 0,354733 | 24 |
| Mikrokreditbank | 33,8 | 0,034 | 0,705882 | 5 | 0,499722 | 11 |
| Apelsin bank | 23,7 | 0,024 | 0,5 | 10 | 0,353962 | 25 |
| Madad Invest Bank | 23,1 | 0,023 | 0,323529 | 14 | 0,229369 | 30 |
| Asaka Bank | 21,7 | 0,022 | 1 | 1 | 0,707278 | 4 |

(*continued*)

**Table 1.** (*continued*)

| Banks | Net profit of the bank during the reporting period, billion soums (Q2 2022) [7] | The net profit index of the bank | The index of offered digital technologies by the bank | Bank rating | The index of the effectiveness of digital development of the bank | Bank rating |
|---|---|---|---|---|---|---|
| Tenge Bank | 15,6 | 0,016 | 0,529412 | 9 | 0,374518 | 22 |
| Poytaxt Bank | 12,4 | 0,012 | 0,705882 | 5 | 0,499213 | 12 |
| Iran "Soderot" bank | 5,1 | 0,005 | 0,352941 | 13 | 0,249594 | 29 |
| Savdogar bank | 4,0 | 0,004 | 0,323529 | 14 | 0,228788 | 31 |
| Ravnak-bank | −7,2 | −0,007 | 0,647059 | 7 | 0,457569 | 16 |
| Hi Tech Bank | −7,9 | −0,008 | 0,470588 | 11 | 0,332804 | 27 |
| Anorbank | −18,5 | −0,019 | 0,941176 | 2 | 0,665644 | 5 |
| Uzagroexportbank | −20,7 | −0,021 | 0,176471 | 16 | 0,125663 | 33 |
| Turkistonbank | −22,9 | −0,023 | 0,352941 | 13 | 0,250107 | 28 |
| TBC bank | −80,4 | −0,081 | 0,5 | 10 | 0,358224 | 23 |

The correlation analysis of the indicators of digital development of the banks was also conducted by the researcher. Based on the results of the correlation analysis, there was a weak but positive correlation between the index of offered digital technologies by the bank and the net profit index of the bank ($r = 0.264$, $p > .05$). Furthermore, a high and positive correlation between the index of the effectiveness of digital development of the bank and the net profit index of the bank ($r = 0.620$, $p < .001$). Moreover, very high positive correlations ($r = 0.910$, $p < .001$) were identified between the index of the effectiveness of digital development of the bank and the index of offered digital technologies of the bank (Table 2).

The following regression model was created to predict the effectiveness of the digital development of commercial banks in Uzbekistan:

$$Eff = 0.011 + 0.313 Inc + 0.664 Of \qquad (4)$$

**Table 2.** The matrix of the correlation indicators of the digital development in the commercial banks of Uzbekistan

| Variables | | 1. The net profit index of the bank | 2. The index of offered digital technologies by the bank | 3. The index of the effectiveness of digital development of the bank |
|---|---|---|---|---|
| 1. The net profit index of the bank | Pearson's r | — | | |
| | p-value | — | | |
| 2. The index of offered digital technologies by the bank | Pearson's r | 0.264 | — | |
| | p-value | 0.138 | — | |
| 3. The index of the effectiveness of digital development of the bank | Pearson's r | 0.620*** | 0.910*** | — |
| | p-value | <.001 | <.001 | — |

* $p < .05$, ** $p < .01$, *** $p < .001$

The coefficient of determination of the regression model was high, $R^2 = 0.983$, and it signifies that 98.3% of the index of the effectiveness of digital development of the bank was explained by the independent variables of the model, that is to say, "the net profit index of the bank" and "the index of offered digital technologies by the bank". The correlation between the independent variables and the dependent variable was very high and positive, that is $R = 0.992$. The adjusted $R^2$ was 0.982, which indicated the high reliability of the linear regression model. The coefficients of the general linear model were statistically significant ($p < .001$) and have the following economic meaning: an increase in the index of offered digital technologies by the bank (Of) by 1 percentage point affects the index of the effectiveness of digital development (Eff) by 0.664 percentage point; also, an increase in the net profit index of the bank (Inc) by 1 percentage point allows the index of the effectiveness of digital development (Eff) to increase by 0.313 percentage point.

The results of the obtained regression analysis verify the high importance of digital technologies in ensuring the competitiveness of banks.

Based on the results of the assessment of the use of digital technologies in the commercial banks of Uzbekistan, the level of development of digital technologies in the commercial banks of Uzbekistan was developed (Fig. 1).

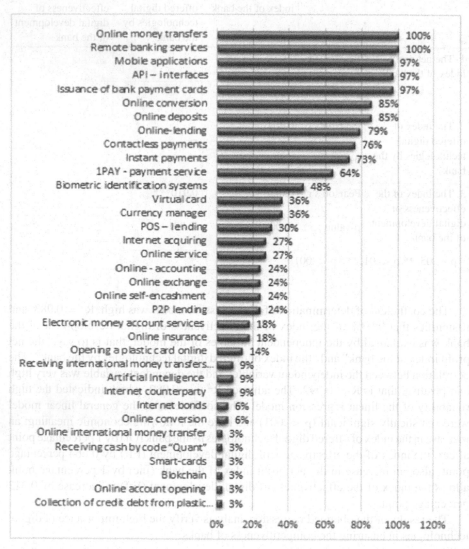

**Fig. 1.** The level of development of digital technologies in the commercial banks of Uzbekistan

Based on the results of Fig. 1, the level of development of innovative digital technologies in commercial banks in Uzbekistan was also created. In line with, the level of development, the following digital technologies were used less frequently than other innovative digital technologies that were highlighted in the survey list: blockchain, smart cards, receiving cash by code "Quant", online-international money transfer, receiving international money transfers through a mobile application, using artificial intelligence and electronic money account services (Fig. 2).

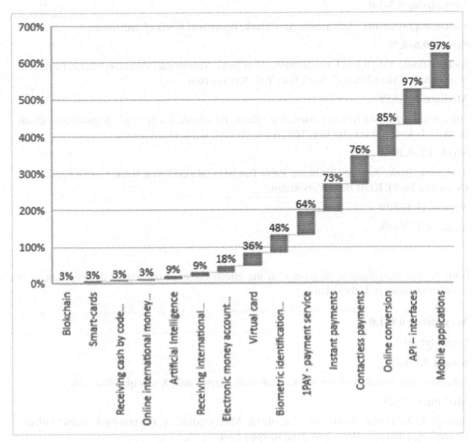

**Fig. 2.** The level of development of innovative digital technologies in commercial banks in Uzbekistan

Based on the indicators of digital development in commercial banks of Uzbekistan (Table 1), the classification of groups on the digital technology offerings of the commercial banks in Uzbekistan was formed. In this classification, "Uzsanoatkurilishbank" JSC, "Asakabank" JSC, "Anor bank" JSC, "Agrobank" JSC, "Kishloqkurilishbank" JSC took position in the group of "Very strong" banks (Table 3).

Along with the digital development indicators for commercial banks in Uzbekistan, the classification of the groups on the effectiveness of the digital development of the commercial banks in Uzbekistan was developed. In this classification, "Uzmilliybank" JSC was included in the group of "Very strong" banks and "Uzsanoatqurilishbank" JSC, "Ipoteka-bank" JSCMB, "Asakabank" JSC, "Anar bank" JSC, and "Kishloqkurilishbank" JSC took position in the group of "Strong" banks (Table 4).

**Table 3.** The classification of groups on the digital technology offerings of the commercial banks in Uzbekistan

| |
|---|
| **Very strong 0.8–1.0** |
| Uzsanoatqurilishbank, Asakabank, Anor Bank, Agrobank, Kishloqkurilishbank |
| **Strong 0.6–0.79** |
| Ipoteka-Bank, Xalq bank, Uzmilliybank, Aloqabank, Turonbank, Microcreditbank, Poytaxt bank, Bank "Orient Finans", Bank Ipak Yuli, Ravnaq-bank |
| **Medium 0.4–0.59** |
| Universal Bank, Asia Alliance Bank, Davr Bank, InFinbank, Tenge Bank, Kapitalbank, Ziraat Bank Uzbekistan, Bank Apelsin, TBC Bank, Hi Tech Bank, Hamkorbank |
| **Week 0.2–0.39** |
| Trastbank, Bank "Saderat" Tashkent, Bank Turkistan, Madad Invest Bank, Garant bank (Savdogar bank), KDB Bank Uzbekistan |
| **Very week 0–0.19** |
| Uzagroexportbank |

**Table 4.** The classification of groups on the effectiveness of the digital development of the commercial banks in Uzbekistan

| |
|---|
| **Very strong 0.8–1.0** |
| Uzmilliybank |
| **Strong 0.6–0.79** |
| Uzsanoatqurilishbank, Ipoteka-Bank, Asakabank, Anor Bank, Kishloqkurilishbank |
| **Medium 0.4–0.59** |
| Agrobank, Xalq bank, Aloqabank, Turonbank, Microcreditbank, Poytaxt bank, Bank "Orient Finans", Kapitalbank, Bank Ipak Yuli, Ravnaq-bank |
| **Week 0.2–0.39** |
| Universal Bank, Asia Alliance Bank, Hamkorbank Davr Bank, InFinbank, Tenge Bank, TBC Bank, Ziraat Bank Uzbekistan, Bank Apelsin, Trastbank, Hi Tech Bank, Bank Turkistan, Bank "Saderat" Tashkent, Madad Invest Bank, Garant bank (Savdogar bank), KDB Bank Uzbekistan |
| **Very week 0–0.19** |
| Uzagroexportbank |

## 4  Discussion and Conclusion

The findings of this study are that the high-ranking banks were identified based on the assessment of the effectiveness of the digital technologies in commercial banks of Uzbekistan. This assessment depends to the indicators of offerings of the digital technologies by the banks and at the same time the indicators of the net profit of the banks. The banks that are effectively developing digitally have been identified in line with these indicators. In compliance with the assessment results, "Uzmilliybank" JSC, "Uzsanoatkurilishbank" JSC, "Ipoteka-bank" JSCMB, "Asakabank" JSC, and "Anor Bank" JSCS ranked in the high position on the list of digitally developing banks.

With regard to using the digital technologies that are offered by the banks to their customers, the most commonly used digital technologies were: remote banking services—100%; issuance of bank payment cards—97%; online money transfers—100%; online deposit—85%; API interface—97%; online conversion—85%; and mobile applications—97%.

In order to improve the effectiveness of the digital development of banks in Uzbekistan, we suggest using "benchmarking" processes in practice. "Benchmarking" is the process of measuring one's company's performance against the best in one or another industry [8]. The most basic concept of benchmarking is learning from others [9, 10]. In the process of benchmarking, an organization studies the knowledge and experience of another organization, assesses the performance, determines the strengths and weaknesses, and chooses the right strategy to improve the results [11]. The purpose of the benchmarking process is to improve the effectiveness of the organization in response to customer requirements. According to the results of Table 1, Uzmilliybank JSC, Uzsanoatqurilishbank JSC and Ipoteka-bank JSCMB were suitable partners for benchmarking processes in increasing the effectiveness of digital development in the banking sector of Uzbekistan.

The strategy for the effective development of the offerings of digital technologies in commercial banks of Uzbekistan was suggested for the banks that they ranked "very weak" and "weak" positions on the list of the offerings of digital technologies by the banks:

- to change traditional business models to digital business models;
- creation of a clear strategy based on three main components: the customer, new information technologies, and quality service, taking into account the directions of innovation, process, and product development in the creation of business models;
- to involve bank customers in the process of creating of the strategy for the effective development of the offerings of digital technologies in the bank;
- formation of mutually beneficial relations with the Central bank, commercial banks, Fintech and IT companies;
- to outsource of innovations;
- to train qualified human resources with new skills in digital technologies, in human resources management, and in understanding customer needs;
- to change business culture along with the development of human resources;
- to expand cooperation with higher education institutions and online platforms in the continuous improvement of staff qualifications;
- introduction of digital technologies as a separate project;
- recognition of digital technologies as the predominant value of the bank;
- to create an ecosystem based on digital channels;
- to create innovative digital products designed to meet the financial needs of customers within 24 h;

- creation of a separate organizational structure in the development of innovative technologies;
- to establish a Committee within the Bank Council for the purpose of monitoring and promoting digital transformation processes;
- to attract qualified specialists from leading foreign financial institutions to leadership positions;
- reorganization of the management bank and strategy to meet the requirements of the new business model;
- to use of social networks widely as a marketing tool for the extensive introduction of effective banking services;
- to introduce of convenient digital technologies based on the needs of customers;
- to expand and develop the functional capabilities of remote banking services;
- to study and in-depth analysis of the financing of programs and projects down to the lower layers;
- to study the demand of population for digital products and services and make appropriate changes to the strategy of the bank;
- integration of bank data with the database of relevant state organizations and their effective use;
- modernization of the infrastructure of the bank continuously;
- to adapt of the organizational culture in the bank for the speed of digital changes;
- improvement of the marketing system in order to increase the interest and confidence of customers in banking services;
- to improve the quality of digital banking services and products, introducing convenient online and automatic payment services and products for customers;
- to diagnose information and communication technologies in the banking system and adapt them to modern requirements;
- development of a roadmap for the introduction of digital services and products;
- creation of new digital products and services in accordance with regional and marketing strategies for further development in market conditions;
- to establish and develop cooperation relations with professional organizations on the introduction of innovative IT technologies;
- to introduce and improve the system of remote identification of users;
- to constantly assess the effectiveness of the introduction of digital technologies.

# References

1. Goyipnazarov, S., Fayzieva, M.K.: The assessment of the strategic roles of human resources professionals in the banking sector in Uzbekistan. Архив научных исследований 2(1), (2022). http://journal.tsue.uz/index.php/archive/article/view/763
2. Fayzieva, M.: The role of human capital in ensuring the participation of women scientists in science. Конференции (2021)
3. Шумский, Д.С.: Оценка развития цифровых технологий в банках Республики Беларусь. Научные труды Белорусского государственного экономического университета, Вып. 14, Министерство образования Республики Беларусь, Белорусский государственный экономический университет 501–509 (2021)

4. Забродская, КА.: Инфокоммуникационные технологии как фактор обеспечения инно вационной конкурентоспособности банков на рынке безналичных расчетов. Вестник Белорусского государственного экономического университета **4**, 28–37 (2016)
5. Хроменкова, М.С.: Методика оценки использования инновационных технологий бан ками на рынке безналичных платежей Республики Беларусь. Вестник Белорусского государственного экономического университета **3**(134), 99–108 (2019)
6. Забродская, К.А.: Методологические подходы к оценке уровня развития инфокоммун икационных технологий и услуг, Веснік сувязі111(1), 25–29 (2012)
7. Тижорат банклари 2022 йилнинг 1-ярим йиллигида канча соф фойда олгани маълум б ўлди. https://bankers.uz/news/net-profit-i-half-2022
8. William, S.: Productions/Operations Management, 5th edn. Irwin Publishing Company, Burr Ridge (1996)
9. Khalilov, M.Sh., Samadov, S.I., Musayev, O.Sh., Eshkuziev, O.O., Mirzaliev, S.M., Turayev, N.M.: Social functions of entrepreneurship in Uzbekistan. In: The 5th International Confer-ence on Future Networks and Distributed Systems, pp. 685–687 (2021)
10. Eshbayev, O.A., Mirzaliev, S.M., Rozikov, R.U., Kuzikulova, D.M., Shakirova, G.A.: NLP and ML based approach of increasing the efficiency of environmental management operations and engineering practices. In: IOP Conference Series: Earth and Environmental Science, vol. 1045, No. 1, p. 012058, IOP Publishing (2022)
11. Avezimbetovich Sharipov, K., Alisherovna Abdurashidova, N.: Benchmarking strategy for industrial enterprise development. In: The 5th International Conference on Future Networks and Distributed Systems, pp. 318–322 (2021)

# The Study of the Impact of the Digital Economy on the Growth of E-Government Services in Uzbekistan

Muyassarzoda Fayzieva(✉) ⓘ, Mirzaliev Sanjar ⓘ, Sharipov Kongratbay ⓘ,
Yuldashev Maksudjon ⓘ, Bakiyeva Iroda ⓘ, Kamilova Iroda ⓘ,
and Oqmullayev Ravshan ⓘ

Tashkent State University of Economics, Tashkent, Uzbekistan 100066
{m.fayzieva,k.sharipov,i.bakiyeva,i.khusnitdinovna,
r.oqmullayev}@tsue.uz

**Abstract.** This research is dedicated to studying the impact of the digital economic infrastructure of Uzbekistan on the growth of e-government services. As for the research methodology, analyzing the indicators of the EGDI index of Uzbekistan; statistical analysis; analysis and synthesis; correlation tests; and linear and multiple regression analyses were used to achieve the aim of this research. Based on the results of this research, very high and positive correlations were identified between "the number of e-applications of citizens" and 12 independent variables; the most explanatory factors of "the number of e-applications of citizens" were determined by "the number of computers connected to the Internet at enterprises and organizations" and "the number of mobile cellular base stations by region (thousand pieces); the highest model accuracy of the economic-mathematical models was (2) and (3) economic-mathematical models; it was found that five independent factors have the greatest influence on the number of applications sent to users via government portals.

**Keywords:** digital economy · digital economy infrastructure · e-government · e-government services · law base

## 1 Introduction

In our country, the reforms for the development of extensive digitalization of economic sectors and regions are not regulated for a single year or by a single legal document, but complex measures are implemented with several Resolutions and Decrees of the President of the Republic of Uzbekistan and the Cabinet of Ministers of the Republic of Uzbekistan. In particular:

– Decree of the President of the Republic of Uzbekistan of March 2, 2020 No. DP-5953, "On the State Program for the Implementation of the Action Strategy in Five Priority Areas of Development of the Republic of Uzbekistan in 2017–2021 in the "Year of Development of Science, Enlightenment, and Digital Economy";

Y. Koucheryavy and A. Aziz (Eds.): NEW2AN 2022, LNCS 13772, pp. 208–217, 2023.
https://doi.org/10.1007/978-3-031-30258-9_18

- Resolution of the President of the Republic of Uzbekistan of April 28, 2020 No. RP-4699, "On Measures for the Wide Implementation of the Digital Economy and Electronic Government;
- Resolution of the Cabinet of Ministers of the Republic of Uzbekistan of June 15, 2021 No. 373, "On Measures to Further Improve the Rating Assessment System of the State of Development of the Digital Economy and Electronic Government;
- Decree of the President of the Republic of Uzbekistan of October 5, 2020 No. DP-6079, "On Approval of the Strategy "Digital Uzbekistan-2030" and Measures for its Effective Implementation;
- Resolution of the President of the Republic of Uzbekistan of February 17, 2021 No. RP-4996 "On Measures to Create Conditions for Accelerated Implementation of Artificial Intelligence Technologies;
- and other legal documents that are related to the introduction of digital economy in the various industries and sectors in Uzbekistan.

The results of reforms in the digital economy and e-government of Uzbekistan are being recognized by international organizations. In particular, the E-Government survey of the United Nations (UN) is a product of the UN Department of Economic and Social Affairs, and the department has been publishing E-Government survey information continuously since 2003. According to the 2016–2022 ratings of the E-Government Development Index for Uzbekistan, Uzbekistan took 80th place in 2016, 81st place in 2018, 87th place in 2020, and 69th place in 2022. From the results of 2022, it is known that Uzbekistan rose 18 places in the EGDI index rating.

On the basis of the laws aimed at the development of the digital economy and e-government adopted in recent years, significant positive changes are being made in the indicators of the infrastructure of the digital economy in our country. In addition to this, the development in the field of information and communication technologies and the knowledge of its application by citizens of the country are increasing with the effects of the digital economy in the Republic of Uzbekistan. As a result, a significant part of the applications sent by the inhabitants of the country to state agencies and organizations are done electronically.

The aim of the research is to study the impact of digital economic infrastructure on the growth of e-government services in Uzbekistan.

## 2  Literature Review

### 2.1  Digital Economy

The digital economy includes information and communications technology, e-commerce, and digitally delivered services, software, and information [1]. New ideas of "digital economy" in the international financial markets, the thoughts of the information and communication modernization and market liberalization represented by the Internet are merged into new ideas of "digital economy" [2]. A digital economy has emerged, generating new forms of productivity, services, and information that could create more value for more people under different conditions.

## 2.2 E-Government

The understanding of e-government and the value it is supposed to create requires an understanding of public sector management. Although both public and private organizations exist to serve people, their concerns are different [3]. [4] argue that policies for e-government can be evaluated according to their ability to increase the public administration's capacity of producing public value for citizens as users, customers, policy makers and as operators of public administration. [5] argues that e-government encompasses the following four main groups of stakeholders: citizens, businesses, governments (other governments and public agencies) and employees. The electronic transactions and interactions between government and each group constitute the following e-government web of relationships: G2C, G2B, G2G, and G2E.

## 2.3 E-government Services

E-government services are believed to make overall government processes more efficient as a result of improved connectivity and ease of access [6]. By converting from traditional to online services citizens can access e-government services 24 h per day, and it also presents benefits of efficiency, cost reduction, and quality [7].

## 3 Research Methodology

In this research, the E-Government Development Index (EGDI) of Uzbekistan and the ranking of its dimensions were analyzed. Statistical analysis, analysis and synthesis, correlation tests, linear and multiple regression analyses, as well as statistical tables and graphs were used as research methods.

The data collection methods are both secondary and primary. Secondary data came from journals, reports, books, book chapters, and other sources, while primary data came from correlation, regression, and hypothesis tests. The correlation analyses were tested by Jeffrey's Amazing Statistics Program, and the regression analyses were performed using the Excel program.

Three research variables were formulated in the conceptual framework of this research, as shown in Fig. 1: mediator (the legal basis related to the introduction and development of the digital economy and e-government in the country); independent variables (the factors of the digital economic infrastructure); and dependent variable (the number of e-applications of citizens).

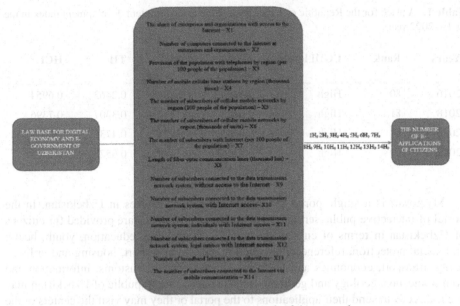

**Fig. 1.** The Conceptual Framework of the research

## 4   Results and Analysis

As mentioned above, the aim of the research is to study the impact of digital economy infrastructure on the growth of e-government in Uzbekistan. In order to obtain the research aim, the following data were analyzed and studied comparatively: a place for the Republic of Uzbekistan in the E-Government development index in the 2016–2022 years; the number of applications which were sent by individuals and legal entities between 2017 and 2022; the number of users of the portal of interactive public services in Uzbekistan in 2022; the indicators of the use of ICT in enterprises and organizations; the indicators of the telecommunication infrastructure of Uzbekistan; data transmission network indicators; research variables; Pearson correlation coefficients; regression statistics; and economic-mathematical models of factors.

According to the 2016–2022 rating indicators of the E-Government Development Index, in 2016, Uzbekistan took 80th place, 81st place in 2018, 87th place in 2020, and 69th place in 2022 among countries with a high EGDI level. The indicator of the EGDI index is inextricably linked with the indicators of the dimensions that consist of the EGDI index. According to the measurements that consist of the EGDI index, the online service index (OSI) of Uzbekistan was 0.69 in 2016, 0.79 in 2018, 0.78 in 2020, and 0.74 in 2022. The human capital index (HCI) of Uzbekistan also has constant growth indicators, which was 0.69 in 2016, 0.7396 in 2018, 0.7434 in 2020, and 0.78 in 2022. The telecommunication infrastructure index (TII) of Uzbekistan was 0.25 in 2016, 0.33 in 2018, 0.47 in 2020, and it increased sharply to 0.66 (Table 1).

**Table 1.** A place for the Republic of Uzbekistan in the E-Government development index in the 2016–2022 years

| Years | Rank | EGDI level | EGDI index | OSI | TII | HCI |
|---|---|---|---|---|---|---|
| 2016 | 80 | High | 0.5434 | 0.6884 | 0.2463 | 0.6954 |
| 2018 | 81 | High | 0.6207 | 0.7917 | 0.3307 | 0.7396 |
| 2020 | 87 | High | 0.6665 | 0.7824 | 0.4736 | 0.7434 |
| 2022 | 69 | High | 0.7265 | 0.7440 | 0.6575 | 0.7778 |

My.gov.uz is a single portal for interactive public services in Uzbekistan. In the portal of interactive public services, 346 government services are provided for citizens of Uzbekistan in terms of citizenship, family and children, education, youth, health and social protection, references, jurisdiction, culture and sport, housing and utilities, realty, transport, economics and business, licensing, taxes, customs, information and communication, ecology and geology, etc. Citizens of the Republic of Uzbekistan may use it directly to send their applications to the portal or they may visit the centers of the portal.

Since 2017, plenty of e-applications have been sent by a large number of individuals and legal entities through the portal of my.gov.uz and the centers. According to Fig. 2, between 0, 0341 and 9,1 mln. Applications were sent through the portal of my.gov.uz between 2017 and 2022, which means that in the period of 6 years the number of e-applications grew 277 times. With regard to the applications that were sent through the

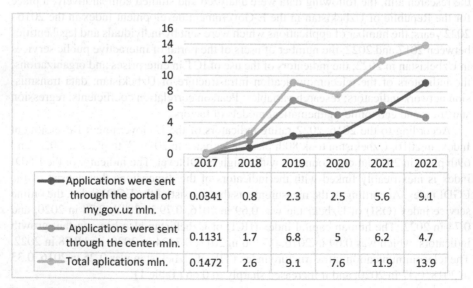

| | 2017 | 2018 | 2019 | 2020 | 2021 | 2022 |
|---|---|---|---|---|---|---|
| Applications were sent through the portal of my.gov.uz mln. | 0.0341 | 0.8 | 2.3 | 2.5 | 5.6 | 9.1 |
| Applications were sent through the center mln. | 0.1131 | 1.7 | 6.8 | 5 | 6.2 | 4.7 |
| Total aplications mln. | 0.1472 | 2.6 | 9.1 | 7.6 | 11.9 | 13.9 |

**Fig. 2.** The number of applications which were sent by individuals and legal entities between 2017 and 2022 [8]

center, between 0, 1131 and 4,7 mln. Applications were sent between 2017 and 2022; this means that in the period of 6 years, the number of applications went up 42 times. In other words, the interest of citizens in using e-government services is six times higher than that of using government services directly (Fig. 2).

Based on the data of the State Committee of the Republic of Uzbekistan on Statistics [9], the share of enterprises and organizations with access to the Internet decreased from 21,6% to 17,5% (the difference is 4,1%). The number of computers connected to the Internet at enterprises and organizations increased from 223 907 to 538 933 (the difference is 335 026). The indicator of the provision of the population with telephones by region (per 100 people of the population) was reduced from 5,7 in 2015 to 4,7 in 2021. The remaining indicators noted the growth between the 2015–2021 years (Table 5).

Data transmission network indicators are provided by the State Committee of the Republic of Uzbekistan on Statistics [9]. There are seven indicators, and these indicators have been growing noticeably between 2015 and 2021. Specifically, the number of subscribers connected to the data transmission network system (including the Internet) increased from 18 339,7 in 2015 to 29 500,2 in 2021 (61% growth), the number of subscribers connected to the data transmission network system, which without access to the internet dropped from 10 000,6 in 2015 to 6 513,1 in 2021, which means that 65% improved. In addition to this, the number of subscribers connected to the data transmission network system with Internet access increased sharply from 8 339,1 in 2015 to 22 987,2 in 2021, namely, there is a rise of 276% or almost 3 times (Table 5).

Dependent variable and independent variables of this research were adjusted in Table 2 for to test the correlation and regression analyses. In Table 3, the coefficients of Pearson correlation and p-values of dependent and independent variables are provided by the authors of this research paper. There are very high and positive correlations were identified between the number of e-applications and the number of computers connected to the Internet at enterprises and organizations ($r = 0.990$, $p < .029$), between the number of e-applications and the number of mobile cellular base stations by region (thousand piece) ($r = 0.978$, $p = .004$), between the number of e-applications and the number of subscribers connected to the data transmission network system (legal entities with Internet access) ($r = 0.953$, $p = .012$), between the number of e-applications and the number of broadband Internet access subscribers ($r = 0.957$, $p = .011$), between the number of e-applications and the number of subscribers connected to the Internet via mobile communication ($r = 0.959$, $p = .010$).

**Table 2.** The variables of the research

|  | Y | X1 | X2 | X3 | X4 | X5 | X6 | X7 | X8 | X9 | X10 | X11 | X12 | X13 | X14 |
|---|---|---|---|---|---|---|---|---|---|---|---|---|---|---|---|
| 2017 | 0,0341 | 27,2 | 310 459 | 4,7 | 20 | 69,5 | 22 504,5 | 34,5 | 24,5 | 9 439,80 | 11 168,00 | 10 764,3 | 403,7 | 498,5 | 10 258,8 |
| 2018 | 0,8 | 27,5 | 358 003 | 4,7 | 24,1 | 66,6 | 21 954,5 | 40,4 | 26,6 | 6 963,20 | 13 321,70 | 12 883,3 | 438,4 | 622,2 | 12 668,6 |
| 2019 | 2,3 | 26,2 | 413 417 | 4,6 | 26,1 | 71,0 | 23 846,7 | 48,8 | 36,6 | 6 071,50 | 16 386,20 | 15 750,8 | 635,4 | 725,4 | 15 651,2 |
| 2020 | 2,5 | 21,1 | 441 913 | 4,5 | 31,7 | 75,9 | 25 971,3 | 58,4 | 68,6 | 6 456,40 | 19 981,00 | 19 241,3 | 739,7 | 1 080,0 | 17 946,5 |
| 2021 | 5,6 | 17,5 | 538 933 | 4,7 | 45,9 | 83,1 | 29 022,4 | 65,8 | 118,0 | 6 513,10 | 22 987,20 | 22 112,1 | 875,1 | 1 457,5 | 20 991,8 |

**Table 3.** The results of Pearson's correlation

| Variable | | Y | X1 | X2 | X3 | X4 | X5 | X6 | X7 | 9X8 | X9 | X10 | 1X11 | X12 | X13 | 1X14 |
|---|---|---|---|---|---|---|---|---|---|---|---|---|---|---|---|---|
| Y | Pearson's r | — | -0.915 | 0.990 | -0.073 | 0.978 | 0.930 | 0.955 | 0.944 | 0.955 | -0.620 | 0.949 | 0.949 | 0.953 | 0.957 | 0.959 |
| | p-value | — | 0.029 | 0.001 | **0.907** | 0.004 | 0.022 | 0.011 | 0.016 | 0.012 | **0.265** | 0.014 | 0.014 | 0.012 | 0.011 | 0.010 |

In this research, the linear regression analysis was conducted in order to determine the highest explanatory factor in relation to the dependent variable. That is to say, the variation in Y variable that was explained by X variables was identified by using the coefficient of determination R2 in regression analysis in Excel by the researchers. According to table 8, the highest variations in Y - "the number of e-applications of citizens" are explained by X2 – "the number of computers connected to the Internet at enterprises and organizations," and "the number of mobile cellular base stations by region (thousand piece), 98% and 96%, respectively (Table 4).

In line with the coefficients of intercept and slopes of every independent variable, 12 economic-mathematical models were created for predicting the number of e-applications that will be sent by users in the future and their goodness-of-fit (model accuracy) measure was identified with adjusted R squares. The p-values of X3 and X9 independent variables were high than 0.05 and for that reason the economic-mathematical models for these factors were not created by the researchers. Based on Table 4, the highest model accuracy of the economic-mathematical models was (2) and (3).

**Table 4.** Regression statistics and economic-mathematical models of factors

| | X1 | X2 | X3 | X4 | X5 | X6 | X7 | X8 | X9 | X10 | X11 | X12 | X13 | X14 |
|---|---|---|---|---|---|---|---|---|---|---|---|---|---|---|
| Multiple R | 0,915028 | 0,98959 | 0,073119 | 0,978364 | 0,930487 | 0,954923 | 0,944202 | 0,954566 | 0,619518 | 0,9491 | 0,948534 | 0,953143 | 0,957075 | 0,959251 |
| R² | 0,837276 | 0,979288 | 0,005346 | 0,957196 | 0,865806 | 0,911878 | 0,891518 | 0,911195 | 0,383803 | 0,900791 | 0,899716 | 0,908481 | 0,915993 | 0,920163 |
| Adjusted R² | 0,783034 | 0,972384 | -0,3262 | 0,942928 | 0,821075 | 0,882503 | 0,855357 | 0,881594 | 0,178404 | 0,867721 | 0,866288 | 0,877975 | 0,88799 | 0,893551 |
| p-value | 0,029352 | 0,001273 | **0,906985** | 0,003808 | 0,02177 | 0,011411 | 0,015689 | 0,011546 | **0,265061** | 0,013679 | 0,013907 | 0,01209 | 0,010607 | 0,009814 |
| Intercept | 2,293524 | -1,39236 | 1,850027 | -0,6969 | -3,62148 | -2,71245 | -0,99804 | -0,10564 | 1,642099 | -0,86368 | -0,86854 | -0,72669 | -0,41991 | -0,94085 |
| X1 | -2,17734 | 2,343068 | -1,46754 | 1,705132 | 4,565504 | 3,6645 | 1,857026 | 1,09021 | -1,65242 | 1,733955 | 1,738473 | 1,595951 | 1,36508 | 1,817181 |
| Equation | (1) Y=2,293524-2,17734X1 | (2) Y=2,343068X2-1,39236 | | (3) Y=1,705132X4-0,6969 | (4) Y=4,565504X5-3,62148 | (5) Y=3,6645X6-2,71245 | (6) Y=1,857026X7-0,99804 | (7) Y=1,09021X8-0,10564 | | (8) Y=1,733955X10-0,86368 | (9) Y=1,738473X11-0,86854 | (10) Y=1,595951X12-0,72669 | (11) Y=1,36508X13-0,41991 | (12) Y=1,817181X14-0,94085 |

**Table 5.** The indicators of the factors of the digital economic infrastructure of Uzbekistan

| Indicators | 2015 | 2016 | 2017 | 2018 | 2019 | 2020 | 2021 |
|---|---|---|---|---|---|---|---|
| The share of enterprises and organizations with access to the Internet, at the end of the year (as a percentage) | 21,6 | 25,9 | 27,2 | 27,5 | 26,2 | 21,1 | 17,5 |
| Number of computers connected to the Internet at enterprises and organizations (at the end of the year, units) | 223 907 | 271 357 | 310 459 | 358 003 | 413 417 | 441 913 | 538 933 |
| Provision of the population with telephones by region, (at the end of the year; per 100 people of the population | 5,7 | 5,6 | 4,7 | 4,7 | 4,6 | 4,5 | 4,7 |
| Number of mobile cellular base stations by region, thousand piece | | | 20 | 24,1 | 26,1 | 31,7 | 45,9 |
| The number of subscribers of cellular mobile networks by region (at the end of the year; per 100 people of the population) | 66 | 66,8 | 69,5 | 66,6 | 71 | 75,9 | 83,1 |
| The number of subscribers of cellular mobile networks by region (at the end of the year; thousands of units) | 20666,10 | 21265,40 | 22504,50 | 21954,50 | 23846,70 | 25971,30 | 29022,40 |
| The number of subscribers with Internet (at the end of the year; per 100 people of the population) | 26,6 | 30,2 | 34,5 | 40,4 | 48,8 | 58,4 | 65,8 |
| Length of fiber-optic communication lines (thousand km) | 20 | 22,1 | 24,5 | 26,6 | 36,6 | 68,6 | 118 |
| Number of subscribers connected to the data transmission network system, including the Internet, thousand units | 18 339,7 | 19 532,1 | 20 607,8 | 20 284,9 | 22 457,7 | 26 437,4 | 29 500,2 |
| -without access to the Internet | 10 000,6 | 9 905,3 | 9 439,8 | 6 963,2 | 6 071,5 | 6 456,4 | 6 513,1 |
| -with Internet access | 8 339,1 | 9 626,8 | 11 168,0 | 13 321,7 | 16 386,2 | 19 981,0 | 22 987,2 |
| -individuals with Internet access | 8 073,6 | 9 279,0 | 10 764,3 | 12 883,3 | 15 750,8 | 19 241,3 | 22 112,1 |
| -legal entities with Internet access | 265,5 | 347,8 | 403,7 | 438,4 | 635,4 | 739,7 | 875,1 |
| Number of broadband Internet access subscribers | 466,3 | 511,5 | 498,5 | 622,2 | 725,4 | 1 080,0 | 1 457,5 |
| The number of subscribers connected to the Internet via mobile communication | 7 793,7 | 9 022,9 | 10 258,8 | 12 668,6 | 15 651,2 | 17 946,5 | 20 991,8 |

# 5  Conclusion

In the 2021–2022 years, the number of e-applications rose drastically in relation to the use of government services by individuals and legal organizations in Uzbekistan, based on the development of a legislative basis in the fields of digital technologies and e-government [10–13]. The majority of opportunities are established and formulated by Uzbekistan's government in relation to e-government services for use by Uzbek citizens.

These established opportunities exist in line with the factors of digital economic infrastructure. Approved and adopted legal documents caused a rapid rise in Uzbekistan's telecommunication infrastructure indicators and, as a result, increased citizen literacy in information and communication technologies. The number of oral and written applications from Uzbek citizens to government organizations has decreased as all processes have been converted to digital format. Individuals and organizations are saving a lot of their money, time, and energy as a result of these reforms. In the period of 2021–2022, the number of e-applications is increasing continuously, and it is a positive change, which is related to the indicators of digital infrastructure.

The findings of this research are:

- there is a very high and positive correlation with the number of e-applications of citizens and digital economy infrastructure factors, besides the factors of "the provision of the population with telephones by region" and "the number of subscribers connected to the data transmission network system without access to the Internet";
- the factors that most explain the variation in Y "the number of e-applications of citizens" are "the number of computers connected to the Internet at enterprises and organizations" and "the number of mobile cellular base stations by region (thousand pieces")", 98% and 96%, respectively;
- the highest model accuracy of the economic-mathematical models is (2) and (3) economic-mathematical models.
- the following factors have the greatest influence on the number of applications sent to users via government portals: the number of computers connected to the Internet at enterprises and organizations; the number of mobile cellular base stations by region (thousand piece), the number of subscribers connected to the data transmission network system (legal entities with Internet access); the number of broadband Internet access subscribers; and the number of subscribers connected to the Internet via mobile communication.

Based on the results of hypotheses testing, there are statistically significant effects among the factors of digital economy infrastructure and the number of e-applications of citizens of Uzbekistan except "the provision of the population with telephones by region" and "the number of subscribers connected to the data transmission network system without access to the Internet".

In a nutshell, the factors of the digital economy infrastructure have the highest impact on the growth of e-government services and to make citizens more ICT literate in Uzbekistan. Correspondingly, the power in the developing of digital economy infrastructure is the digital economy legislative base of Uzbekistan.

## References

1. Babbitt, T.G., Brynjolfsson, E., Kahin, B.: Understanding the digital economy: data tools, and research. Acad. Manag. Rev. **26**(3) (2001). https://doi.org/10.2307/259191
2. Zheng, Q.: Introduction to E-commerce. In: Introduction to E-commerce (2009). https://doi.org/10.1007/978-3-54

3. Twizeyimana, J.D., Andersson, A.: The public value of E-Government – a literature review. Gov. Inf. Q. **36**(2) (2019). https://doi.org/10.1016/j.giq.2019.01.001
4. Castelnovo, W.: A stakeholder-based approach to public value. In: Proceedings of the European Conference on E-Government, ECEG (2013)
5. Ndou, V.D.E.: Government for developing countries: opportunities and challenges. Electron. J. Inf. Syst. Dev. Ctries. **18**(1) (2004). https://doi.org/10.1002/j.1681-4835.2004.tb00117.x
6. Lin, F., Fofanah, S.S., Liang, D.: Assessing citizen adoption of e-Government initiatives in Gambia: a validation of the technology acceptance model in information systems success. Gov. Inf. Q. **28**(2) (2011). https://doi.org/10.1016/j.giq.2010.09.004
7. Linders, D.: From e-government to we-government: defining a typology for citizen coproduction in the age of social media. Gov. Inf. Q. **29**(4) (2012). https://doi.org/10.1016/j.giq.2012.06.003
8. Single portal of interactive public services. https://my.gov.uz/ru/site/statistic
9. The Sate Committee of the Republic of Uzbekistan on Statistics. https://stat.uz/en/official-statistics/tsifrovaya-ekonomika-eng
10. Sh. Khalilov, M., I. Samadov, S., Sh. Musayev, O., O. Eshkuziev, O., M. Mirzaliev, S., M. Turayev, N.: Social Functions of Entrepreneurship in Uzbekistan. In: Proceedings of the 5th International Conference on Future Networks & Distributed Systems, pp. 685–687 (2021)
11. Mirzaliev, S.M., Homidov, H.H., Sharipov, K.A., Kholikova, N.A.: Perspectives of use of agricultural drones in Uzbekistan. In: IOP Conference Series: Earth and Environmental Science, vol. 1045, no. 1, p. 012147. IOP Publishing, June 2022
12. Goyipnazarov, S.B., Ngah, N., Fayzieva, M.K., Azizan, A.A., Khalique, M.: Assessment of the strategic roles of HR professionals in the development of the E-Banking system in the banking sector of Uzbekistan. In: Proceedings of the 5th International Conference on Future Networks and Distributed Systems (ICFNDS 2021), 15, 16 December 2021, Dubai, United Arab Emirates, ACM, New York, NY, USA, p. 6 (2021). https://doi.org/10.1145/3508072.3508221
13. Khancharovna, F.M.: The importance of the application of human resources management in the management of public sector. Integr. Sci. Educ. Pract. Sci. Methodical J. **3**(2), 50–58 (2022)

# Deep Learning Algorithm for Classifying Dilated Cardiomyopathy and Hypertrophic Cardiomyopathy in Transport Workers

Rashid Nasimov[1] , Nigorakhon Nasimova[2] , Karimov Botirjon[1(✉)] ,
and Munis Abdullayev[1]

[1] Department of Digital Economy and Information Technologies, Tashkent State University of Economics, Tashkent, Uzbekistan
botir.karim1@gmail.com
[2] Tashkent University of Information Technologies named after Muhammad al-Khwarizmi, Tashkent, Uzbekistan

**Abstract.** Automatic classification of the different types of cardiomyopathies is desirable, but has been done less with a convolutional neural network (CNN). The aim of this study was to evaluate currently available CNN models for the classification of cine magnetic resonance images (cine-MR) of cardiomyopathies. In this paper, we developed an echo-based wrinkled neural network algorithm for automatic classification of cardiomyopathies. Dilated cardiomyopathy (DCM) is a heart muscle disease with enlargement of the left ventricle or both ventricles and systolic dysfunction. It is an important cause of sudden cardiac death and heart failure and is the most common indication for heart transplantation. MRI of the heart diagnoses severe heart diseases such as myocardial damage and valve problems. This algorithm allows classification of dilated (DCM) cardiomyopathy and hypertrophic cardiomyopathy (HCM) in transport workers with 96.4% accuracy. With the improvement of this approach, it is possible to develop an intelligent system and expert systems to help make decisions aimed at early detection, classification and diagnosis of symptoms of heart disease in transport industry workers.

**Keywords:** Cardiomyopathy · dilated cardiomyopathy · hypertrophic cardiomyopathy · deep learning · classification · echocardiogram · convolutional neural network · softmax · kNN

## 1 Introduction

Despite the widespread introduction of information technologies in the classification, diagnosis and treatment of diseases in medicine, cardiovascular diseases remain the area with the highest rates of morbidity and mortality in the world [1]. Heart disease has a significant impact on a person's overall health, living a full life, and life expectancy. The number of heart diseases is also increasing as the population grows and the average life expectancy increases. Scientists are proposing innovative information technology-based approaches to successfully overcome these challenging situations, which have become

Y. Koucheryavy and A. Aziz (Eds.): NEW2AN 2022, LNCS 13772, pp. 218–230, 2023.
https://doi.org/10.1007/978-3-031-30258-9_19

more complex in recent years. In particular, there is growing interest in using algorithms, which are able to work as the human visual system in solving the problem, based on AI for the classification and diagnosis of cardiovascular diseases based on images [2, 3].

In recent years, the proliferation of artificial intelligence (AI) based algorithms in rapidly digitized sectors of developed and developing countries, as well as measures to improve the efficiency of each sector, have increased at the level of public policy.

In modern diagnostic centers, the process of diagnosing some heart diseases using existing techniques of visual analysis of Echo takes a long time. In many cases, due to the similarity of features in the images, the accuracy of visual differentiation and diagnosis is impaired. However, recent advances in machine learning show that software applications based on deep learning algorithms have the ability to automatically classify medical images with the highest degree of accuracy and distinguish the phenotypes that are more difficult to visually recognize for specialists. The development of deep learning algorithms for the accurate classification and diagnosis of heart disease, in particular cardiomyopathy (CM) diseases, which is difficult to visually detect and diagnose according Echo, is a hot topic today.

CM is a general term for diseases of the heart muscle in which the heart muscle becomes thinner or thicker. CM diseases are characterized by impaired blood flow throughout the heart for the above reasons. If CM is not detected or treated promptly, it can lead to heart failure, irregular heartbeat (arrhythmias) and sudden death. HCM and DCM are recognized as the most common and dangerous types of CM today.

In the case of HCM, the heart muscle becomes thinner and the heart's ability to pump blood throughout the body is reduced, or in the case of DCM, the heart muscle thickens and the ability to pump enough blood throughout the body is also reduced. Statistically, HM diseases are mainly caused by thinning or thickening of the left chamber. In practice, in some cases thinning or thickening of the muscles progressed into the right chamber as the disease progressed.

Here introduces the paper, and put a nomenclature if necessary, in a box with the same font size as the rest of the paper. The paragraphs continue from here and are only separated by headings, subheadings, images and formulae. The section headings are arranged by numbers, bold and 10 pt. Here follow further instructions for authors. Currently, cardiovascular diseases, in particular CM, can be diagnosed using the following tools:

- Electrocardiography;
- Blood tests;
- Stress tests;
- Holter monitoring;
- Radiograph;
- Computed tomography;
- Magnet resonance imaging;
- Echocardiography.

As mentioned above, the most commonly used methods for the purposes of distinguishing, classifying, and correctly diagnosing the symptoms of heart disease is echocardiography, because echocardiogram (Echo) provides detailed information about changes in the heart compared to others. In practice, it is often used ECG for primary diagnostic procedures. Inconsistent changes in electrocardiogram (ECG) signals or the absence of symptoms, or the formation of electrical signals similar to the heart of a healthy person, make it difficult to correctly diagnose CM in this way.

Since the diagnosis of CM diseases using blood tests, stress tests and Holter monitoring takes a long time, echocardiography remains the best tool for diagnosing CM.

Chest radiographs play an important role in assessing the early stages of some heart diseases, such as heart enlargement and heart failure. Unlike X-ray, computed tomography is one of the great approaches in detecting CM. This method is targeted in the evaluation of coronary arteries, in the description of the CM phenotype, in the determination of heart volume and function. Magnetic resonance imaging can be used to evaluate and treat patients who have had a heart attack due to a severely narrowed artery. In turn, with the help of echocardiography it is possible to systematically determine the size, volume, wall thickness and mass of the atria and ventricles in short period of time and without harm.

In experiments, CM symptoms in some cases may be similar with symptoms of other heart diseases, for example, myocardial infarction. The accuracy of diagnosing maybe depreciates due to abstract and blurry shapes in images. Therefore, for the diagnosis of CM based on Echo, it is necessary to have sufficient skills and knowledge of specialists. During a pandemic, the insufficiency of highly qualified personnel on a global scale pose serious problems. In solving such problems, scientists are working on the AI-based automatic classification and diagnosis algorithms.

In the last 10 years, AI algorithms have covered many areas of digital signal processing. Machine learning, in turn, is a major area of AI. Machine learning based programs have the ability to recognize and classify hidden features more easily and with greater accuracy than humans, especially deep learning algorithms. Therefore, in recent years, programmers and professionals (for example, healthcare workers) have been working together to collect Echo based data base [2–4]. Unlike machine learning, deep learning requires a large amount of data to solve tasks correctly and to be highly accurate of the results.

Currently, many researches are being done to improve this area, for example:

1. Echo first step issues;
2. Issues of measurement and evaluation of cardiac parameters;
3. Problems of detection of pathologies of the heart.

Echo first step issues. These issues include reducing noise levels on demand and classifying the cardiac view [2–6]. So far, many issues in this area have been resolved, but applying the deep learning algorithms into this area, there is an opportunity to further increase the level of accuracy. By expanding the Echo-based dataset, it is possible further improve the accuracy of deep learning algorithms.

Measurement and evaluation of cardiac parameters issues. This scientific direction covers the processes of segmenting the heart, calculating the size of its parts (LV, RV, Atria, Aorta, Interior Vena Cava) and measuring the functional parameters of the heart (Ejection fraction, ESV, etc.). These parameters are typically calculated using machine learning algorithms [7]. In 2018, an Echonet database was created that contains a very large amount of video data, classified according to the cardiac parameters such as EF, ESV, and EDV. Due to the limited capabilities of machine learning algorithms in solving the set of tasks in such a database, there was a need to solve the problem of using deep learning algorithms. The EF, ESV, and EDV features are classified using a 3D convolution network with great accuracy [8].

Problems of detection of the heart pathologies. The third type of problem includes recognition cardiac abnormalities, irregular blood flow, improper opening and closing of valves, regional wall motion abnormalities, and the automatic classification of diseases [9–15]. Although this field has been of great interest to researches of recent years, these issues have not yet been fully explored. The reason is that the performance of the assigned tasks remains complicated.

In short, the convolution model has recently been widely used to solve problems in all three, directions, especially in data mining [2–4, 27]. This indicates that the convolutional neuron network (CNN) model has a higher level of image processing performance than machine learning methods. The CNN method requires a large-scale Echo database to classify the result with high accuracy. In this article, Echo database consist of images captured from echocardiogram videos.

By solving the problem of automatic interpretation of Echo, it is possible to make accessible these medical services even for non-qualified-specialist and prevent the emerging complications. Echocardiogram data consists of images and videos, and features that many people find difficult to identify. The increasing number of characters and character interdependencies complicate the development of machine learning algorithms and their computational processes. Therefore, as mentioned above, the efficiency of using deep learning algorithms to solve such problems is high [21].

International researchers are proposing new algorithms of the CNN model for echocardiogram image processing. For example, LSTM and 3D methods are currently used in Echo video processing [9]. For cardiac image segmentation and for reducing the noise level in the image a new algorithm called Generative adversarial networks was developed, with its help good results are achieved [10, 11]. In order to divide the heart into segments, a semi-supervised learning method is used [12]. Although the performance accuracy of this method is low, it is important that this method does not require a data classification process. The development of such algorithms makes it possible to work with large amounts of unclassified data and effectively classify it in the future. Also, another very effective new algorithms of deep learning are proposed to improve classification efficiency [13, 25, 26]. In this study, pyramid local attention neural network was proposed, which allows the comparison of data in adjacent pixels with the improvement of network performance in segmentation. Moreover, this approach is a fully automated system that allows not only to distinguish cardiac parameters, but also to diagnose the disease [22].

The algorithms proposed by J. Zhang, G. N. Balaji, A. Madani and A. Ghorbani have a number of advantages, and the need for such systems has been increasing in recent years [14–17]. Therefore, a number of studies are being conducted to perform multiple tasks with deep neural networks, for-instance Zang et al. [14] algorithms capable of cardiac view identification, image segmentation, quantification of structure and function, prediction of cardiac diseases: heart failure, hypertrophic cardiomyopathy, cardiac amyloidosis, and pulmonary hypertension. Balaji et al. developed an algorithm for distinguishing DCM, HCM and a healthy heart based on the PLAXview of Echo [15]. In this study, the researchers used back propagation neural network (BPNN), Support vector machines (SVM), and combined k-nearest neighbors (k-NN) algorithms of machine learning. Because their approaches are mainly based on machine learning methods, a feature extraction phase was performed before each classification process. In this study, the classification accuracy reached 92.04%. Another researcher used U-net and transfer learning methods to differentiate HCM from healthy heart Echo. The accuracy of the algorithm based on the approach proposed by them was 91.21% [16].

The main problems to achieve the high classification accuracy is the lack of a database. It is a fact that most of databases consist of completely unclassified data. So, they must be separated manually, which takes a lot of time and efforts or classified one is not accessible publicly. Furthermore, most Echo images are very large in size and technically require a large resource for training processes. In short, classified, open-access and consisting of small files databases are very rare today. One of the most popular is Echonet. It is an open-access database consisting of low-resolution (112 × 112) and classified videos. However, the Echo videos in this database were not classified by disease, but rather by the patient's gender, age, Ejection fraction (EF), End-systolic volume (ESV), and End-diastolic volume (EDV) values. This database also provides only Apical 4-chamber (A4C) cardiac view, there is no other cardiac views (Apical two-chamber (A2C), Parasternal long axis (PLAX), Parasternal short axis (PSAX) images, which are very important for diagnosis).

## 2 Materials and Methods

In the general cases, Echo can have 30 different cardiac view [9]. However, not all of these views are used to diagnose a specific disease. Often it is sufficient to use 4 different views to diagnose the disease: PSAX (parasternal short axis), PLAX (parasternal long axis), A2C (apical two chambers) and A4C (apical four chambers). In practice, PSAX and A4C are mainly used to diagnose CM disease. In particular, the following changes are taken into account in the diagnosis of HCM in two-dimensional (2D) echocardiogram images [18] (Fig. 1):

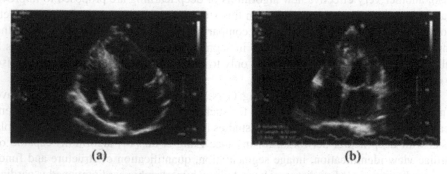

(a)                                    (b)

**Fig. 1.** a) RV wall thickness; b) LA scale

Another common type of CM disease, called DCM, can be identified by the size of the left ventricle in A4C images. This is one of the main symptoms, and it is known that the diagnostic sensitivity based on left ventricular dilatation is >112% [19] (Fig. 2):

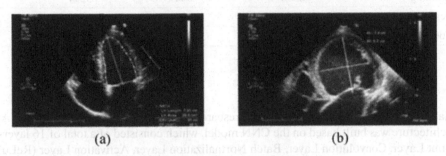

(a)                                    (b)

**Fig. 2.** a) DCH and b) HCM.

In this study Echo videos from the Internet, as well as videos from the Echonet data base were used to develop an Echo-based dataset. First of all, HCM and DCM videos were collected from sites that have been recommended and trusted [23, 24]. The collected videos included Echo and also redundant frames, so only 2–5 s video frames with Echo were clipped from the videos for developing the data set. Thereafter, the video frames were cropped to fit the size of the video frames to separate only the heart image by reducing various noises (signs, recordings, patient information) in the Echo. The images were cropped into a square shape, considering that changing the image size from a rectangular view to a square view would affect the image quality. When converting a rectangular image to a square shape, it is important to avoid changing the shape and size of the walls of the heart and ventricles in the image. These parameters contain values that are critical for diagnosis [18, 19].

After collecting videos from internet, videos from Echo net database were selected. The above-mentioned diagnostic criteria (based on A4C cardiac view) of DCM were used to extract DCM video data from the Echo net database.

After that the clipped videos were divided into frames: 112 × 112 × 1 resolution grayscale images. As a result, a data set of 3,530 images was developed. Then dataset was split into 2 parts: training and testing. The feature extraction process was done manually. The reason of manually feature extraction is that in the automatic case there is a possibility that frames belonging to the same video will fall into both folders, which can lead to an incorrect evaluation of the performance of the algorithm. That is, while the classification accuracy is high during the test process, in practice the classification accuracy of such a network may decrease. Subsequent paragraphs, however, are indented. This situation can be considered as overfitting of the network. The distribution of images in the data set is given in Table 1.

**Table 1.** The number of total images allocated in the disease section for training and test.

| Name of class | DCM | HCM | Total |
|---|---|---|---|
| Training | 2350 | 944 | 3294 |
| Testing | 140 | 96 | 236 |
| Total | 2490 | 1040 | 3530 |

## 3  Our Study

Matlab 2019a was used to conduct this research and achieve the intended results. An architecture was built based on the CNN model, which consisted of a total of 16 layers: Input Layer, Convolution Layer, Batch Normalization Layer, Activation Layer (ReLu), Fully Linked Layer, Softmax, and Output Layer. Details of the parameters of these layers are given in Table 2 (Figs. 3 and 4).

**Table 2.** CNN architecture layer parameters.

| Name of blocks | Number of Convolution layer filter | Size of Convolution layer filter | Dropout (%) |
|---|---|---|---|
| Input | | | |
| Conv Block | 64 | 3 | 5 |
| Conv Block | 128 | 2 | 20 |
| Conv Block | 256 | 3 | 40 |
| Conv Block | 64 | 1 | 5 |
| Conv Block | 8 | 2 | 0 |
| Output | | | |

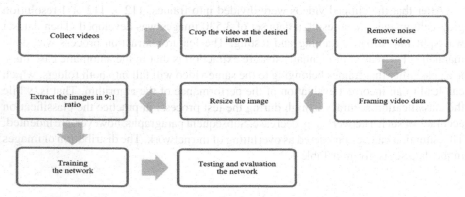

**Fig. 3.** The dataset development workflow and data mining process is shown

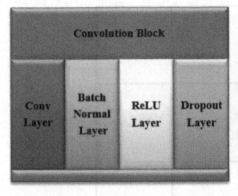
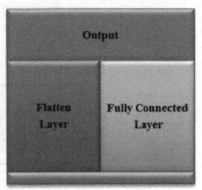

**Fig. 4.** Full description of Conv Block and Output Block is shown

In this study, Adam's optimization method was used to optimize the neural network. The network's learning rate was set at 0.0001, batch size 32, SquaredGradientDecay-Factor value was 0.95, GradientDecayFactor value was 0.95, L2Regularization value was 0.001 and Epsilon value was 0.001. The selected values achieved the highest performance in other similar scientific studies [20]. The duration of the network training was a total of 15 epochs. In order to prevent overfitting of the network we used Dropout layer after each Convolutional block, which is composed of Convolutional, Batch Normalization and ReLU layers. These Dropout out layer is tuned to drop neurons according to filter numbers, for clarity, higher coefficient of Dropout function was used for the layer with higher number of filter. For example, for layer in which filter number is equal 256, Dropout coefficient was 0,4, but for layer with 64 filters, Dropout coefficient was merely 0,05.

## 4  Results

During the training of the CNN model, the classification accuracy of the network reached 96,6%. After that, confusion matrix was constructed to calculate the other parameters of the network (Fig. 5). The sensitivity, specify, and F1-score of the network were determined using a confusion matrix, Table 3.

**Table 3.** Values of statistical parameters evaluating the accuracy of the network

| Statistic parameters | DCM | HCM |
|---|---|---|
| Specificity | 91.7 | 100 |
| Sensitivity | 100 | 91.7 |
| Precise | 94.6 | 100 |
| F1-score | 97.2 | 95.7 |
| Accurity | 96.6 | 96.62 |

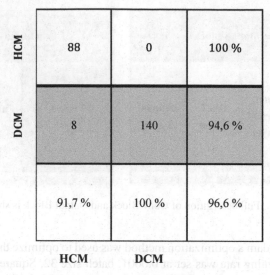

|  | | |
|---|---|---|
| **HCM** 88 | 0 | 100 % |
| **DCM** 8 | 140 | 94,6 % |
| 91,7 % | 100 % | 96,6 % |

**HCM**    **DCM**

**Fig. 5.** Confusion matrix

The following formulas were used to determine these indicators:

$$\text{Sensitivity} = TP/(TP + FN) \tag{1}$$

$$\text{Specifity} = TN/(TN + FP) \tag{2}$$

$$\text{Precision} = TP/(TP + FP) \tag{3}$$

$$\text{F1-score} = (2 * \text{Precision} * \text{Sensitivy})/(\text{Precision} + \text{Sensitivy}) \tag{4}$$

$$\text{Accuracy} = (TP + TN)/(TP + TN + FP + FN) \tag{5}$$

Although there were almost 2.5 times more DCM images in the dataset than HCM images, it can be seen that the network sensitivity and F1-score were very close to each other when distinguishing between the two classes.

## 5  Discussion

Research shows that today there are more than 14 types of CM, and the problem of classifying them on the basis of Echo is very difficult. Nevertheless, to date, many algorithms have been proposed that allow early detection of the most common and life-threatening type of HCM among the population and distinguish it from other types of CM. In particular, Balaji et al. developed an algorithm that distinguishes HCM from DCM, and this algorithm includes several processes [15]. In the first step, the authors used speckle reducing anisotropic diffusion filter (SRAD), and adaptive histogram equation

(AHE) techniques to reduce noise in A4C echocardiogram view. Then, step by step, first the left ventricular region, then the features (LV parameters, shape, and statistical features) required for image classification were subdivided using the FCM threshold. In the final step, the isolated features are classified using machine learning algorithms such as BPNN, SVM, and combined kNN. Among these methods, the highest result was shown by BPNN, whose classification accuracy reached 90.20%, sensitivity 85.71% and specificity 92.54%. However, it is noteworthy that the structure of this method is very complex and time consuming.

An algorithm has been proposed by U-net to differentiate HCM from healthy heart electrocardiography by retraining the network [16]. Based on the proposed algorithm, a semi-supervised generative adversarial network model was developed using an unnamed dataset, and it showed a result of 92.3%. At another study, the ability to predict all phenotypes using an Inception-Resnet-v110-based architecture was developed [17]. Based on the proposed approach, the accuracy of HCM in the left ventricle reached 75%. In a study by J. Zhang et al., a CNN model was developed that differentiated left ventricular hypertrophy from a healthy heart [14]. The study used a dataset containing 260 videos collected by specialists. The approach proposed by J. Zhang et al. provides an opportunity to differentiate 3 other diseases in addition to HCM. The network proposed by them registers these diseases only separately, that is, the disease can be distinguished from the normal state only. Moreover, the authors emphasized the impossibility of distinguishing 3 diseases from each other. This is a drawback of the proposed approach. A comparative analysis of all relevant scientific studies is also presented in Table 4.

The proposed algorithm differs from other algorithms in the Table 4 with its higher accuracy. Furthermore, this algorithm does not require a feature extraction process for image classification. Although the accuracy in Ghorbani's work is lower, in contrast to our proposed work, they classify video data rather than image, which is an important advantage [17]. Due to the small size of the data set, in our study, images were processed intellectually, not video data. This aspect will be taken into account in our future works.

**Table 4.** Comparative analysis of algorithms for differentiation of DCM and HCM on the basis of Echo.

| Authors | Distinguished diseases and types | The size of the data set (unit) | Database type | The area of the heart studied in the data set | Accuracy of the result (%) |
|---------|----------------------------------|--------------------------------|---------------|----------------------------------------------|----------------------------|
| J. Zang et al. [14 | Left ventricle HCM/normal | 260 | video | PLAX, A4C, A2C, A3C | 93 |
| G. N. Balaji et al. [15] | HCM/ DCM/normal | 60 (4–6s 46 fps) | image | PSAX | 90.2 |

(*continued*)

**Table 4.** (*continued*)

| Authors | Distinguished diseases and types | The size of the data set (unit) | Database type | The area of the heart studied in the data set | Accuracy of the result (%) |
|---|---|---|---|---|---|
| A. Madani et al. [16] | HCM/normal | 455 | image | A4C | 92.3 |
| A. Ghorbani et al. [17] | HCM/normal | >2. 6mln | image | A4C | 75 |
| Proposed algorithm | HCM/DCM | 3530 | image | A4C | 96.6 |

## 6  Future Research

To diagnose DCM and HCM, it is necessary to take into account changes in at least 3 different manifestations of the heart area. In our future work, we aimed to build a network architecture that simultaneously analyzes several different images using the global fully connected layer of CNN model. It was decided to form a data set that was large enough to achieve the goal and contained images of at least 3 different cardiac view.

## 7  Conclusion

In this work, Echo video data were collected, and a data set based on video-based Echo images has been developed. Convolutional neural network architecture focused on the training Echo-based-dataset was built, and the data set was trained. Based on the developed model, the problem of classification of DCM and HCM was solved. The classification accuracy of the proposed model reached 96.6%.

## References

1. Wilkins, E., et al.: European cardiovascular disease statistics 2017. European Heart Network, Brussels (2017)
2. Liu, S., et al.: Deep learning in medical ultrasound analysis: a review. Engineering **5**, 261–275 (2019)
3. Kusunose, K.: Steps to use artificial intelligence in echocardiography. J. Echocardiogr. **19**, 21–27 (2021)
4. Akkus, Z., et al.: Review artificial intelligence (AI)-empowered echocardiography interpretation: a state-of-the-art review. J. Clin. Med. **10**, 1391 (2021)
5. Ali, M., Ramy, A., Mohammad, M., Rima, A.: Fast and accurate view classification of echocardiograms using deep learning. NPJ Digit. Med. **1**, 6 (2018)
6. Balaji, G.N., Subashini, T.S., Chidambaram, N.: Automatic classification of cardiac views in echocardiogram using histogram and statistical features. Proc. Comput. Sci. **46**, 1569–1576 (2015)

7. Matthias, S., et al.: A machine learning algorithm supports ultrasound naïve novices in the acquisition of diagnostic echocardiography loops and provides accurate estimation of LVEF. Int. J. CVD Imaging **37**, 577–586 (2021)

8. Ouyang, D., et al.: EchoNet-dynamic: a large new cardiac motion video data resource for medical machine learning. In: 33rd Conference on Neural Information Processing Systems (NeurIPS 2019), Vancouver, Canada (2019)

9. Ulloa, A., Jing, L., et al.: A deep neural network to enhance prediction of 1-year mortality using echocardiographic videos of the heart (2018)

10. Abdi, A.H., Tsang, T., Abolmaesumi, P.: GAN-enhanced conditional echocardiogram generation. In: 33rd Conference on Neural Information Processing Systems (NeurIPS 2019), Vancouver, Canada (2019). arXiv:1911.02121v2 [eess.IV]

11. Teng, L., Fu, Z., Yao, Y.: Interactive translation in echocardiography training system with enhanced Cycle-GAN. IeeeOnIeee Eng. Med. Biol. Soc. Sect. **8**, 106147–106156 (2020)

12. Ta, K., et al.: A semi-supervised joint learning approach to left ventricular segmentation and motion tracking in echocardiography. In: Proceedings of the IEEE International Symposium on Biomed Imaging, April 2020, pp. 1734–1737 (2020)

13. Liu, F., et al.: Deep pyramid local attention neural network for cardiac structure segmentation in two-dimensional echocardiography. Med. Image Anal. **67** (2021)

14. Zhang, J., Gajjala, S., et al.: Fully automated echocardiogram interpretation in clinical practice: feasibility and diagnostic accuracy. Circulation **138**, 1623–1635 (2018)

15. Balaji, G.N., Subashini, T.S., Chidambaram, N.: Detection and diagnosis of dilated cardiomyopathy and hypertrophic cardiomyopathy using image processing techniques. Eng. Sci. Technol. Int. J. **016,4**(19), 1871–1880 (2016)

16. Madani, A., Ong, J.R., Tibrewal, A.: MRK mofrad deep echocardiography: data-efficient supervised and semisupervised deep learning towards automated diagnosis of cardiac disease. NPJ Digit. Med. **1**, 59 (2018)

17. Ghorbani, A., et al.: Deep learning interpretation of echocardiograms. NPJ Digit. Med. 1–14 (2020)

18. Smith, N., Steeds, R., Masani, N., Sharma, V.: A systematic approach to echocardiography in hypertrophic cardiomyopathy: a guideline protocol from the British Society of Echocardiography. Echo Res. Pract. **2**(1), G1–G7 (2015)

19. Mathew, T., Williams, L., et al.: Diagnosis and assessment of dilated cardiomyopathy: a guideline protocol from the British society of echocardiography. Echo Res. Pract. **4**(2), G1–G13 (2017)

20. Nasimov, R., Muminov, B., Mirzahalilov, S., Nasimova, N.: Algorithm of automatic differentiation of myocardial infarction from cardiomyopathy based on electrocardiogram. In: 2020 IEEE 14th International Conference on Application of Information and Communication Technologies (AICT), pp. 1–5 (2020)

21. Nasimov, R., et al.: A new approach to classifying myocardial infarction and cardiomyopathy using deep learning. In: 2020 ICISCT, pp. 1–5 (2020)

22. Nasimova, N., Muminov, B., Nasimov, R., Abdurashidova, K., Abdullaev, M.: Comparative analysis of the results of algorithms for dilated cardiomyopathy and hypertrophic cardiomyopathy using deep learning. In: 2021 International Conference on Information Science and Communications Technologies (ICISCT), pp. 1–5 (2021). https://doi.org/10.1109/ICISCT52966.2021.9670134

23. https://www.123sonography.com

24. https://medtube.net/radiology/medical-videos

25. Turgunov, A., Zohirov, K., Rustamov, S., Muhtorov, B.: Using different features of signal in EMG signal classification. In: 2020, ICISCT, pp. 1–5 (2020). https://doi.org/10.1109/ICISCT50599.2020.9351392

26. Turgunov, A., Zohirov, K., Nasimov, R., Mirzakhalilov, S.: Comparative analysis of the results of EMG signal classification based on machine learning algorithms. In: 2021 International Conference on Information Science and Communications Technologies (ICISCT), pp. 1–4 (2021). https://doi.org/10.1109/ICISCT52966.2021.9670108
27. Musaev, M., Rakhimov, M.: Accelerated training for convolutional neural networks. In: 2020 International Conference on Information Science and Communications Technologies (ICISCT), pp. 1–5 (2020). https://doi.org/10.1109/ICISCT50599.2020.9351371

# eCommerce Benchmarking: Theoretical Background, Variety of Types, and Application of Competitive-Integration Benchmarking

Faridakhon Abdukarimovna Khamidova[1] (ID)
and Shakhzod Sherzodovich Saydullaev[2(✉)] (ID)

[1] Tashkent Financial Institute, 60A, Amir Timur Avenue, Tashkent, Uzbekistan
[2] Tashkent State University of Economics, 49, Islam Karimov Str., Tashkent, Uzbekistan
saydullaev0077@gmail.com

**Abstract.** Benchmarking around the world is pushing organizations to learn from each other and develop how it is done, creating unique examples of excellence in this area. Today, interest is constantly growing and there is a high need to study the experience of successful benchmarking studies. This article discusses the history of the emergence, the theoretical basis of benchmarking and analyzes its types. The article also studied and analyzed the method of competitive integration benchmarking for e-commerce enterprises of the Republic of Uzbekistan.

**Keywords:** benchmark · height mark · competitive analysis · best-in-class solutions · eCommerce companies · Comparative Critical SWOT Analysis

## 1 Introduction

Today, in the era of globalization of business, companies are aware of the need for a comprehensive and detailed study and subsequent use of the best achievements of competitors for their own survival. Benchmarking as a search for standards for learning and implementation of experience has become a worldwide movement.

The concept of "benchmarking" appeared in a number of economic concepts relatively recently. It is generally accepted that the concept of benchmarking originated in the late 50s when Japanese specialists visited leading companies in the US and Western Europe in order to study and subsequently use their experience [1].

Of course, comparative analysis originated long before modern ideas about management methods and systems. So, in China as early as the 4th century BC, Sun Tzu [2] wrote in his writings: "If you know the enemy and know yourself, then your victory is beyond doubt." For many centuries, mankind has assessed the strength and weaknesses of others in order to avoid situations that could lead to undesirable consequences.

Officially, the term "benchmarking" appeared in 1972 at the Institute for Strategic Planning of Cambridge (USA). Today there are different interpretations of the term "benchmarking".

© The Author(s), under exclusive license to Springer Nature Switzerland AG 2023
Y. Koucheryavy and A. Aziz (Eds.): NEW2AN 2022, LNCS 13772, pp. 231–243, 2023.
https://doi.org/10.1007/978-3-031-30258-9_20

## 2    Theoretical Overview

Most researchers view benchmarking as a process of identifying, learning, and adapting the best practices and experiences of other organizations to improve their own organizations. Comparison is carried out by organizations both with similar processes in their industry and regardless of industry affiliation, in their own country and abroad. The most common understanding of the term "benchmarking" comes from the English words "bench" (level, height) and "mark" (mark). This phrase is interpreted in different ways: "reference mark", "height mark", "reference comparison", etc. As a result, "benchmarking" is compared with a "landmark", or "standard", adhering to continuous improvement of processes.

In the studies of foreign scientists, many definitions of the category of benchmarking are given, revealing its content. The earliest and most famous definition was made by R.Camp [3], the founder of classical benchmarking. In his opinion, "Benchmarking is a constant process of studying and evaluating goods, services and production experience of the most serious competitors or those companies that are recognized leaders in their fields".

Another author, G.Watson [4], lists systematic and continuous measurement as one of the most important characteristics of benchmarking: assessment of enterprise processes and their comparison with the processes of leaders' enterprises in order to obtain information useful for improving their own characteristics.

R.Grant calling benchmarking a comparison method refers to reengineering tools and defines its purpose as comparing the principles of the company's work with the most successful examples from the practice of other organizations in order to identify changes that could lead to high-quality results [5].

An interesting definition of benchmarking was given by the CEO of AlliedSignal, L.Bossidy [6], who understands it as the analysis of specific techniques, borrowing the benefits obtained from the analysis of the experience of other companies, and using the best practices introduced from outside in his own company. Here is another definition given by G.Anand and R.Kodali [7]: "Benchmarking is a continuous, systematic process of comparing one's own performance, expressed in terms of productivity, quality, and organization of work processes, with enterprises and institutions that are "best".

### 2.1   Research Setting

Competitive analysis, SWOT analysis, scientific abstraction deduction, classification, generalization, comparative, theoretical interpretation, and analytical methods were used in the methodology of this article, as a result of the bibliographic study, the direct and indirect factors affecting them, and the prospects for further development were identified.

### 2.2   Purpose of the Study

As a result of studying the cases and experiences of developed countries, it is planned to study the theoretical basis of benchmarking, as well as the mechanisms for applying competitive integration benchmarking.

# 3 Discussion

The development of benchmarking is closely related to how the essence of the concept of "quality" was recognized. There are several stages in changing the conceptual approaches to quality.

The functional understanding of quality was linked to economic processes. At the beginning of the 20th century, the science of product quality management in the production process appears. For enterprises, the most important condition for success is ensuring the quality of their products. The term "quality" is applicable both to products and to the sphere of management and organization. Many experts call the quality of products a mirror of the work of the enterprise since it can be seen in it the level of development of scientific and technological progress in the technologies used, materials, and the qualifications of the personnel involved.

In this regard, the concept of sorting inspection of product quality was born and dominated for a long time. It is characterized by checking the quality of finished products. This was typical for all countries, including ours. The very understanding of quality was mainly of a technocratic approach, while the emphasis was on the quality of the final product [8]. Later came the realization that this is a costly concept. With such a conceptual approach, only partial application of product benchmarking is possible, the main purpose of which was to compare one's own products with those of competitors. However, due to the lack of information on the flow of processes, the use of the experience and knowledge of other organizations is extremely difficult.

In a later period and at the present time, a new understanding of the concept of "quality" is being affirmed as a set of properties of an object that determine its suitability to satisfy the established or implied expectations of consumers. As a result, the idea of quality priority is being affirmed in world production. Organizations are beginning to realize that customer satisfaction is key to their business success. However, the satisfaction of market demands cannot be carried out at any cost, it is necessary to ensure this at the lowest possible cost [9].

From this position, the most important is the quality of the process, in which product quality is only one of the elements or components of a holistic concept.

A distinctive feature of the modern stage, which began approximately in the 70 - 80s of the XX century, can be considered a sharp increase in competition between organizations and enterprises. This led to the emergence and development of competitiveness benchmarking, which was clearly manifested in the early 80s of the XX century when competitive relations are established between various departments of the organization, which very often leads to contradictions and complications in relationships. Each division performs its functions and tasks assigned to it by top management. Functions typically include marketing, sales, design, manufacturing, human resources, customer service, administration, and control. Functions in the organization, at the enterprise, are divided according to the types of independent tasks, which leads to the emergence of organizational barriers between functions, thereby reducing the manageability and efficiency of work as a whole.

The third generation of benchmarking is associated with the development of functional, or general, benchmarking, when enterprises study the experience not of their competitors, but of leading organizations outside their sector or industry.

The fourth generation is associated with the development of strategic benchmarking, which is based on the process of comparing organizations, firms, and processes competing in the same field of activity, aimed at identifying "strengths" and "weaknesses", and comparing the characteristics of your organization with similar parameters of direct competitors.

The further development of benchmarking is associated with a change in the idea of an organization as a single whole mechanism that can be effectively managed only on the basis of a correctly made decision. The decision-making process takes place only on the basis of comprehensive and accurate information, provided that the overall efficiency of the enterprise is ensured.

At this stage, strategic benchmarking becomes global. Global benchmarking should be understood as a process of cooperation between organizations, regardless of their industry affiliation, aimed at studying, exchanging, and practical use of the best world practices.

The development of benchmarking methods has led to the fact that by now the main classification of benchmarking types has been formed [10].

Thus, benchmarking is a process that promotes learning and understanding of an organization and its processes. This allows organizations to identify key processes that need improvement and seek best-in-class solutions to match.

Benchmarking applications vary in purpose and style. Table 1 shows the different types of benchmarking [11].

**Table 1.** Benchmarking styles.

| Types of benchmarking | Focus of comparison | Advantages | Disadvantages |
|---|---|---|---|
| Internal | Primarily within the company departments, business units, and sister companies | Relatively easy to access information Transferability of processes should be simple | Processes might not be the best in class |
| Competitive | Made with a direct competitor and can be benchmarked processes, products, services, etc | If successful can lead to step changes and productive results | Difficult to access information |
| Functional and generic | Focused on a specific function of a process (functional) or against the whole process (generic) | Can create partnerships and rewards with other organizations It decreases the difficulty of accessing information | The processes or functions might not be applicable to the process where it is intended to be applied |
| Strategic | A benchmark of strategies (market, technology, costs, etc.) | It illustrates a competitive strategy | One fundamental factor for becoming first class is the development of the strategy, strategy cannot be imitated |

Table 2 shows that all benchmarking models go through five main steps:

(1)  planning;
(2)  analysis and data collection;
(3)  comparison and results;
(4)  change;
(5)  verification and maturity.

**Table 2.** Benchmarking stages.

|  | Hypothesis |
|---|---|
| **Phase 1**<br>**Planning** | Talking about planning the organization of the entire benchmarking procedure, starting with the areas under study and ending with the implementation stage of the research results.<br>The systematic organization of control and planning is an integral part of the whole procedure, otherwise, it makes no sense to carry it out, since it will be doomed to failure.<br>It is necessary to adhere to the specified sequence of stages of development of benchmarking processes:<br>• to determine the object of research;<br>• develop a plan for obtaining the necessary informative data;<br>• coordinate and approve the plan with the specialists of the enterprise;<br>• get approval and take care of the maintenance of the project by the management staff of the enterprise;<br>• make a plan for calculating comparative performance indicators |
| **Phase 2**<br>**Analysis and data collection** | It involves dividing the obtained indicators into two components: direct, measurable indicators of the high performance of the company; ways, techniques, and methodologies to achieve similar results<br>Direct data collection occurs during mutual visits to companies, open exchange of information, and negotiations. To make comparisons, it may be necessary to present the information obtained in the same way as it is presented within the organization. For example, if the technical characteristics of a product are compared, then the set of these characteristics may differ for different manufacturers. Characteristics will need to be brought to a single "base". |
| **Phase 3**<br>**Comparison and results** | In the third stage, leaders in the industry of interest and outside it are identified. The choice should not be limited to obvious, direct competitors. It is often useful to achieve parallel competitors that do not put pressure on the enterprise under study. On the other hand, parallel competitors always have the potential to become direct in the long run.<br>It is interesting to study companies from other business areas. Undoubtedly, information about world experience will be invaluable. Ideally, the list of leading companies should not be more than a dozen, or even less. But it must be creative, that is, it is better to select successful enterprises according to the principle of diversity. |

*(continued)*

**Table 2.** (*continued*)

|  | Hypothesis |
|---|---|
| **Phase 4**<br>**Change** | Now the task is to eliminate errors in their own work. To improve the quality of work, it is necessary to identify weaknesses (logistical problems, high costs, low level of the implementation system). Then you can copy the style and method of work of the leader, but here it is important to remain yourself.<br>Most companies, based on the results of benchmarking, use the Twenty Keys revolutionary transformation program developed by the Japanese professor Iwao Kobayashi. |
| **Phase 5**<br>**Verification and maturity** | This is usually the most difficult phase of research that the benchmarking process involves. If the procedure was successful, detailed answers to the following questions should be obtained:<br>Is the company ready to introduce new technologies, and to what level of their use is it ready to reach?<br>What actions should the company decide to achieve in order to improve its performance and get as close as possible to the results of a partner?<br>What time and material resources will be needed for this?<br>When addressing these issues, it is necessary to take into account the fact that not all technologies, tools, and methods that work in one enterprise may suit its partner. |

## 4 Findings

### 4.1 Variety of Types of Benchmarking Relationships

Currently, in its most general form, benchmarking is called the activity of searching, identifying, and mastering the best business practices.

But today, several types of social relations that have an unequal economic and legal nature and a different composition of subjects fit this definition.

The development of an exhaustive classification of benchmarking relationship types is based on the application of two specific classification criteria:

– the structure of benchmarking relationships;
– range of benchmarking subjects.

The structure of benchmarking relationships reflects a combination of active and passive positions (role functions) of benchmarking subjects.

In benchmarking relationships, subjects can take active (evaluating) and passive (evaluating) positions, expressed in the corresponding role functions, which are combined in different ways in subjects depending on the type of benchmarking relationship.

An active benchmarking position is implemented in the role function of a "provider" of benchmarking, the holder of all benchmarking processes, who collects the necessary information and directly performs a benchmark comparison. At the same time, in some cases of providing benchmarking services, it is necessary to distinguish between the functions of the "provider" of benchmarking and the "customer, initiator" of benchmarking.

"Benchmarking Provider" - a person who evaluates and compares the parameters of entrepreneurial activity of several entrepreneurial structures. "Benchmarking customer" - a person in whose interests (to ensure competitiveness) benchmarking is carried out, whose parameters of entrepreneurial activity are subject to benchmarking.

A passive benchmarking position is characteristic of the role status of the firm that is the object of comparison. At the same time, a passive role status may imply the role function of an "informant", a carrier of primary internal information that provides the requested information to the "provider" of benchmarking (in particular, by filling out questionnaires).

"Benchmarking Informant" - a "standard" and other person providing information for comparison.

A passive role status may not imply the function of an "informant" if the "provider" of benchmarking does not contact the carrier of primary information, relying on other sources of information, for example, when benchmarking is carried out secretly (Fig. 1).

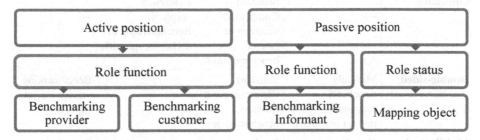

**Fig. 1.** Role functions and statuses of benchmarking participants.

According to the criterion of structure (a combination of role functions in participants), benchmarking is divided into:

– external;
– mixed;
– internal;
– mutual.

External benchmarking is a system of relations in which the active and passive positions of the benchmarking participants do not completely coincide, i.e., benchmarking is carried out in relation to two or more business structures by a third independent party. In external benchmarking, the "provider" is not the "informant".

Mixed benchmarking is a system of relations in which the active and passive positions of the benchmarking participants partially coincide, i.e. benchmarking is carried out by one business structure ("provider") in relation to its indicators ("self-informer") and indicators of another business structure ("informant") – "classic" two-sided, non-reciprocal benchmarking.

Internal benchmarking is a system of relations in which active and passive positions completely coincide in one subject of benchmarking (unilateral benchmarking), i.e. benchmarking is carried out by an entrepreneurial structure ("provider") in relation to its own divisions ("self-informer") or a holding in relation to business structures under its unified corporate control.

Mutual benchmarking is a system of relations in which the active and passive positions of the benchmarking participants completely coincide in each subject (with more than one subject), i.e. benchmarking is carried out by both business structures in relation to their indicators and indicators of another business structure (bilateral, mutual benchmarking - partner benchmarking).

**Table 3.** Types of benchmarking relationships depending on the criteria for the range of subjects and the structure of relationships.

| Benchmarking type | Mutual | Mixed | Internal | External |
|---|---|---|---|---|
| **One-sided** | — | Standard Competitive intelligence (secret benchmarking) | Reference (explicit) Benchmarking of divisions, spin-offs | — |
| **Double-sided** | Mutually beneficial (win-win), partner (explicit) | Standard Classic, explicit (process benchmarking) | — | Benchmarking service (secret, explicit) |
| **Multilateral** | Cartel, Affiliate | Leader benchmarking, Beginner Benchmarking | — | Associative, benchmarking service, media rating |

The range of benchmarking subjects indicates the number of parties involved in the benchmarking relationship, i.e. the number of subjects that implement the role functions of the benchmarking provider and/or benchmarking informant (Table 3).

According to the criterion of the range of subjects, the benchmarking relations are divided into [12]:

– One-sided;
– Double-sided;
– multilateral.

The table shows that the imposition of classes of benchmarking relations according to the specified criteria led to the formation of types of benchmarking that do not exist in practice. Thus, external and mutual benchmarking, by definition, cannot have only one participant (one-sided).

The table also shows the types of benchmarking that are not used by business structures, in particular, the relations of double-sided (mixed) and multilateral (mutual, partnership, cartel) benchmarking are studied.

## 4.2 The Method of Competitive-Integration Benchmarking

It should be noted that at the institutional stage of benchmarking development, the acquisition of competitive advantages should be organized as a new business strategy of an enterprise based on cooperation and interaction, where the achievement of more successful competitors and leading organizations from various industries, mainly international best practices, should be studied on the basis of competitive integration benchmarking.

At the same time, competitive integration benchmarking should be understood as an analysis of the activities of competitors, based on interaction and cooperation, in order to combine and form qualitatively new business processes based on the experience of leading international organizations in this industry to improve competitive advantages at the international level. Thus, a new constituent element is included in the concept of competitive integration benchmarking - interaction, which allows you to improve your own performance based on the already achieved results of competitors and determines the essence of competitive integration benchmarking.

The main content of competitive integration benchmarking is to study and adapt best practices, mainly foreign ones, to the conditions of your own enterprise by identifying reference organizations that have achieved significant success in the studied functional areas on the basis of partnerships. Thus, competitive integration benchmarking involves the active interaction of partners exchanging information about the business processes of their own enterprises, as well as mutually beneficial cooperation with competing enterprises or other subjects of the benchmarking institute for joint study and development of foreign best practices.

In order for benchmarking to develop into a civilized way of determining its market position in the industrial market in the business environment, it is necessary to develop its clear, step-by-step process, revealing the main content of competitive integration benchmarking, which will take into account Uzbek specifics. In this regard, the mechanism of the competitive-integration benchmarking process based on the "benchmarking wheel" model is represented by a sequence of stages of the audit, planning, monitoring, analysis, adaptation, and coordination (Fig. 2).

Directly in competitive integration benchmarking, competitive advantage analysis is applicable, since benchmarking itself involves the process of assessing the parameters of enterprises in the course of their comparison, where the results of enterprises are compared, but most importantly, indicators of the competitiveness of enterprises, products of activity. The toolkit here is not a simple analysis of the strengths and weaknesses of the enterprise, but a SWOT analysis by comparing the degree of effectiveness of the key success factors of competitors' enterprises using graphical methods for interpreting the results, that is, a comparative critical SWOT analysis. Thus, a comparative critical SWOT analysis is a comparative analysis of key indicators or critical success factors of the enterprise under study and competitors.

The practical application of comparative critical SWOT analysis was considered on the basis of retailers in the Tashkent territory. The purpose of the study was to identify

Internal audit

Process planning

- Selecting the object of the benchmarking process
- Building a benchmarking team
- Selection of benchmarking partners
- Development of a data collection and analysis plan

Organization of the benchmarking process

- Determination of the form of the process
- Development of questionnaires and questionnaires for data collection

Observation

- Data collection
- Documentation of partner processes

Data analysis

- Finding breaks in data
- Development of implementation recommendations

Adaptation

- Formation of the implementation team
- Development of the implementation program
- Realization of the implementation program

Continuous improvement

**Fig. 2.** Competitive integration benchmarking process model.

the competitive advantages of their own enterprise in relation to competitors' enterprises and to identify areas for improvement.

The goal was achieved by solving the following tasks:

1. Identify the main competitors of the enterprise.
2. Conduct a survey of experts on key success factors.
3. Build a diagram.

Using the method of interviewing experts, information was obtained reflecting the critical success factors of a retail enterprise and their importance, in addition, using a questionnaire survey of respondents and experts, information was obtained reflecting the opinions of consumers about the severity of these success factors in each retail enterprise under consideration. The sample was 10 people based on 1% of the general population. The questionnaire of consumers and experts served as a tool for collecting information.

As a result, a competitiveness polygon was formed, which is a graphical connection of assessments of the position of the enterprise and competitors in the most significant areas of activity - key success factors, shown in Fig. 3.

Analysis of ratings for the most important attributes in the eyes of the respondents revealed the following situation. The location of the store is of paramount importance for consumers, the importance index is 0.127. It should be noted that the Mediapark enterprise scored the highest number of points - 9.5. According to the respondents, this factor is also most fully represented in the Elmakon enterprise. The next most important factor is the quality of the product (0.124). The leaders here are Mediapark and Elmakon (9.7), followed by Ishonch (9.0) and Texnomart (8.8) with a small margin. An insignificant indicator of this factor in the company "Idea" (8). An important factor is also considered the quality of service (0.122), the most pronounced in the enterprises "Elmakon" (8), "Mediapark" (8), and "Idea" (8), the least of all these factors is manifested in the enterprises "Ishonch" (7) and "Texnomart" (7) (Table 4).

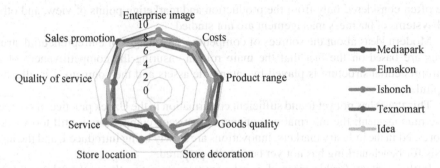

**Fig.3.** Diagram of Comparative Critical SWOT Analysis of Retail Businesses in Uzbekistan

**Table 4.** Retail businesses indicators.

| Indicators | Mediapark | Elmakon | Ishonch | Texnomart | Idea |
|---|---|---|---|---|---|
| Enterprise image | 9 | 9 | 8 | 7 | 7,5 |
| Costs | 8,5 | 8,5 | 9 | 7,5 | 8 |
| Product range | 9,5 | 8 | 9 | 8 | 8 |
| Goods quality | 9,7 | 9,5 | 8,5 | 8,2 | 8 |
| Store decoration | 8 | 7 | 6 | 9 | 8 |
| Store location | 6 | 4 | 8 | 4 | 3 |
| Service | 9 | 9 | 9,4 | 8 | 8,5 |
| Quality of service | 8 | 8 | 7 | 7 | 8 |
| Sales promotion | 9,5 | 9 | 9 | 9 | 9 |

Thus, a comparative critical SWOT analysis successfully complements the industry analysis. Their use in the aggregate makes it possible to assess both the situation in the industry as a whole and the position of the enterprise under study in it. In addition, the combination of these methodological tools allows you to take a look from a dynamic perspective, that is, not only assess the current state but also quite clearly foresee a qualitative picture in the future, taking into account the active position of the enterprise in relation to changing its strategic position.

The above chart shows how companies differ from each other when choosing the same benchmarks and analyzing based on benchmarking. We found out that benchmarking is a very powerful type of analysis, in which any company can determine its weaknesses and strengths.

Currently, none of the Uzbek business structures can refuse the processes of their competitive positioning and the use of tools for comparative assessment of their competitiveness. Despite the huge variety of forms and methods of competition, all companies are trying to develop a unique strategy of behavior in the market, using their competitive advantages in resources to achieve the highest rates of real industry competitiveness.

Unfortunately, now the tasks of increasing the competitiveness of business structures are often considered only from the production and marketing points of view, and other subsystems of business management are not studied.

Modern ideas about the sources of competitive advantages of entrepreneurial structures are based on the fact that the main role in ensuring the competitiveness of an entrepreneurial structure is played by intangible assets and the company's intellectual capital.

This thesis has not yet found sufficient confirmation in the Uzbek practice of competitive management: the information connection between competitors is still too weakly expressed in the industry markets, innovations are slowly being introduced, and the legal basis for benchmarking has not yet been fully prepared.

In this context, further research is relevant to systematize the methodological tools of benchmarking in relation to assessing and managing the competitiveness of business structures.

# References

1. Blakeman, J.: Benchmarking: Definitions and Overview (2002). https://www4.uwm.edu/cuts/bench/bm-desc.htm
2. Tzu, S.: The Art of War - Floating Quote. https://www.goodreads.com/quotes
3. Camp, R.C.: Benchmarking: The Search for Industry Best Practices That Lead to Superior Performance. ASQC Industry Press, Milwaukee, Wisconsin (1989)
4. Watson, G.: The Benchmarking Workbook: Adapting Best Practices for Performance Improvement. Productivity Press, Portland (1992)
5. Grant, R.: Contemporary Strategy Analysis: Concepts, Techniques Applications. Blackwell, Oxford (1995)
6. Bossidy, L.: Execution: Goal Achievement System. Alpina Publisher, Russia (2011)
7. Anand, G., Kodali, R.: Benchmarking the benchmarking models. Benchmarking: Int. J. **15**, 257–291 (2008)
8. Alstete, J.: Measurement benchmarks or 'real' benchmarking: An examination of current perspectives. Benchmarking An International Journal **15**(2), 178–186 (2008)
9. Eftimov, T., Korosec, P.: Benchmarking theory. In: Deep Statistical Comparison for Meta-heuristic Stochastic Optimization Algorithms. Natural Computing Series, pp. 15–21. Springer, Cham (2022). https://doi.org/10.1007/978-3-030-96917-2_3
10. Stapenhurst, T.: The Benchmarking Book. Routledge, Milton Park (2009)

11. Fernandez, P., McCarthy, I., Rakotobe-Joel, T.: An evolutionary approach to benchmarking. Benchmarking Int. J. **8**(4), 281–305 (2001)
12. Rigby, D., Bilodeau, B.: Management Tools and Trends. Bain and Company, Boston (2009)

# Cryptocurrencies as the Money of the Future

Shokirov Mirkamol[✉] and Eshov Mansur

Tashkent State University of Economics, Tashkent 100066, Uzbekistan
7465092m@gmail.com, m.eshov@tsue.uz

**Abstract.** This article discusses, the role of cryptocurrency in the economy, its negative and positive aspects, the attitude of the population to cryptocurrencies, and the analysis of indicators of the current state of cryptocurrency, the possibility of qualifying it as money, electronic money, currency values, information and other property, cryptocurrency as "other property", as well as economic comments on the possibility of consideration as money from the point of view are presented. At the same time, the possibility of cryptocurrency as a substitute for money in private law relations has been explored. Also, the main focus of the article is on how close to reality the views of cryptocurrency as the money of the future are.

**Keywords:** Cryptocurrency · virtual currency · crypto assets · bitcoin · blockchain · L Block · Solana · BAT · Yearn finance · Shiba Inu · cryptocurrency market · means of payment · virtual money circulation · Lucky Block · future money · cryptocurrency future · the most reliable types of cryptocurrency · digital economy

## 1 Introduction

Relevance of the topic of the research: Along with the concept of "money circulation", economic and legal category such as "money" also plays an important role in the functioning of financial relations. In parallel with the development and modification of traditional forms of money, their substitutes - money surrogates - are developed, which are arbitrarily introduced into the economy by private organizations for mutual settlements. Today, due to the active development of the Internet, in addition to the technological innovation of processing and the improvement of modern encryption tools, the most popular type of monetary surrogates are digital settlement tools in the form of cryptocurrencies - the most popular and at the same time, the least studied instruments in the field of money circulation within the framework of local science and the world economy in general. Such payment instruments, on the one hand, represent a unique and contradictory phenomenon in the modern financial services market, and on the other hand, a global system that is rapidly developing day by day. A clear proof of this is that there are currently more than 1,300 types of money surrogates in the form of cryptocurrencies. From the point of view of economic functionality, monetary surrogates can be considered in part as an economic and legal category of "money".

In fact, money surrogates replace real money in settlements between economic entities, transactions for payments for rendered services and purchased goods, and payment

Y. Koucheryavy and A. Aziz (Eds.): NEW2AN 2022, LNCS 13772, pp. 244–251, 2023.
https://doi.org/10.1007/978-3-031-30258-9_21

of obligations to the state. In practice, the release of money substitutes is a source of negative economic processes, such as an increase in quantitative indicators for non-payment of wages, a significant deformation of the cost of goods (works, services). This is accompanied by the deviation of prices from the base value, the formation of closed financial systems, the subsequent increase in the number of transactions based on the barter scheme, and the flourishing of corruption.

Taking into account the above, today the problem of functioning of money surrogates in the form of cryptocurrencies together with the corresponding means of payment should be recognized as very urgent.

Importance of research cryptocurrency as a form of money surrogate in the system of modern economic relations and solving the problem of its future.

The task of research work presented the main ideas about cryptocurrencies, their features, advantages and disadvantages.

According to the account books, by 2030, digital currency users are expected to rise to 200 million. According to Deutsche Bank, digital currency may eventually replace cash one day as demand for anonymity and decentralized payment methods increases.

## 2 Literature Analysis from Topic Surface

Cryptocurrency is a type of virtual currency, its issuance and accounting is based on cryptographic protection methods, which is characterized by a high level of security. After the rapid development of digital currency in 2021, many people included the concept of crypto in their future investment. In 2021, the market capitalization of cryptocurrency was 800 billion dollars. By 2022, it will nearly triple to $2.25 trillion.

With around 16,000 digital coins currently in circulation, the crypto market is experiencing tremendous volatility. Let me touch on a few types of cryptocurrencies that are expected to make a name for themselves in the crypto market in the coming years:

1. Bitcoin is the world's first decentralized cryptocurrency launched in 2009 and is the largest and most widely used. The market capitalization will be 786 billion dollars by the beginning of January 2022. Many people have heard of Bitcoin, but very few understand how it works. Bitcoin and blockchain are not the same thing. Blockchain is a tool that records and stores Bitcoin transactions. It is often defined as an immutable public ledger that securely links blocks of encrypted transaction data on a network. Ether, secondly, runs on the Ethereum blockchain like all other cryptocurrencies. According to some estimates, the total value of cryptocurrencies is around 2 trillion dollars. However, in 2022, the value of Bitcoin and other virtual currencies has fallen.
2. Lucky Block (L Block) is the best cryptocurrency to buy in 2022. Lucky Block is truly the best cryptocurrency to buy in 2022. When deciding which cryptocurrency to add to your wallet, you should first consider the coin's novelty and whether it has the potential to increase in value in the future. In short, this digital asset project is trying to revolutionize the global cryptocurrency market.

   Binance Smart Chain Lucky Block is one of the scalable networks in the market, which aims to promote projects without worrying about transaction fees and network time delays.

3.  Solana - One of the most popular cryptocurrencies of the past year. 2. Solana is one of the most popular cryptocurrencies of the past year. Solana is the best cryptocurrency to buy and invest in 2022, founded in 2020, within a few years it has become one of the most popular and powerful blockchains on the market. Solana relies on Proof of History (PoH). As a result of this alternative direction, blockchain has emerged as one of the most scalable areas in the industry. Solana is currently the fastest blockchain on the market with a transaction rate of 60,000 transactions per second (TPS).
4.  Basic Attention Token (BAT) is one of the most likely projects of 2022. (BAT) is one of the projects of 2022. It is the next token in the list of top five cryptos. Brave browser is protected by BAT token. Brave is a decentralized browser that lets users choose what to watch.
5.  Yearn finance - 2022 is known for its strong growth rate
6.  Shiba Inu is the best meme to buy in 2022

Cryptocurrencies operate independently of central banks and government agencies, but of course they are not immune from global banking systems and markets. In addition to market risk, cryptocurrencies are still the subject of many debates in the industry. Critics say that the cryptocurrency market is very difficult to regulate because it is regulated. Not tied to a central bank or sovereign body. Thus, cryptocurrencies, and Bitcoin in particular, are still effective tools for those who wish to use them to launder money, purchase illicit goods, and circumvent capital controls. Despite these controversies, the popularity and use of cryptocurrencies has grown rapidly in recent years and could take a toll on the global economy over the next few years. As a result, many companies, financial institutions and investors are trying to calculate the economic benefits that can be derived from the use of cryptocurrencies. For example, according to Gartner, by 2024, at least 20% of large enterprises will use cryptocurrencies for payments, storage of value and collateral, which is the current financial industry. And disrupts business models. Stablecoins more than quintupled last year, from $29 billion to $163 billion. Its popularity is due to its stability of value and its ability to support more efficient and transparent value transfers than traditional payment networks. Gartner's vice president, author of the company's 2022 Predictions: Prepare for Blockchain-Based Digital Disruption report, told ZDNet that cryptocurrencies are about 3- He said it will be available for sale in 5 years. Retail Payments Investors will be keen to use cryptocurrencies as an investment vehicle, hedge against inflation and as an alternative to gold over the next few years. He told ZDNet that cryptocurrencies will be available for sale in about 3–5 years. Retail Payments Investors will be keen to use cryptocurrencies as an investment vehicle, hedge against inflation and as an alternative to gold over the next few years. He told ZDNet that cryptocurrencies will be available for sale in about 3–5 years. Retail Payments Investors will be keen to use cryptocurrencies as an investment vehicle, hedge against inflation and as an alternative to gold over the next few years.

## 3   Metrology

In the study of this research work, all the sources stated in electronic and written form were studied and analyzed. In order to study the opinion of the population regarding the research, a survey was conducted on Facebook and Telegram social networks and the opinion of the population was evaluated.

## 4 Result Discussion

We know that cryptocurrencies are very volatile. Despite Bitcoin's current value, there are several reasons why investors and companies are willing to forego the potential benefits of cryptocurrencies. This goes beyond speculative buying in anticipation of the price of virtual currency. The reason some investors and companies are interested in cryptocurrencies is their entry into decentralized finance (DeFi). "Companies want to join the trend. Even hedge funds are investing more in cryptocurrencies." Banks must provide the services required by these companies and act as custodians of digital assets. This is a global phenomenon, not just in the US. "DeFi is starting to attract institutional money. Cryptocurrencies make up about 0.08% of assets in existence, but some studies suggest that 7% of assets held by hedge funds, for example, will be in cryptocurrencies within five years. This would be," - approximately $31,187, which is much lower than $68,223 on November 10, 2021. It should be noted that the cryptocurrency market has seen a lot of volatility in the last few months, especially during this period, when strong cryptocurrencies such as Bitcoin fell by up to 50%. Has caused many experts to start worrying whether bitcoin will continue to dominate the crypto market. CoinGecko data shows that bitcoin's market share has also declined. Before the beginning of 2020, bitcoin controlled 70% of the crypto market. Now it is down to 42%. If we look at it in dollar terms, then the total value of Bitcoin in the entire crypto market is 1600 billion dollars.

Choosing the right cryptocurrency can have a significant impact on the success of your cryptocurrency investment.

Lucky Block is indeed the best cryptocurrency to buy in 2022. When deciding which cryptocurrency to add to your wallet, you should first consider the coin's novelty and whether it has the potential to increase in value in the future. In short, this digital asset project is trying to revolutionize the global cryptocurrency market.

Binance Smart Chain Lucky Block is one of the scalable networks in the market, which aims to promote projects without worrying about transaction fees and network time delays.

Crypto-asset trading has been widely recognized since 2017, but many may have a perception that it is on the decline due to stock market leaks, but as the coronavirus continues to wreak havoc around the world, cryptocurrency trading is once again in the spotlight. Returned to the center. In particular, Bitcoin, which was around $800,000 in April 2020, has risen to $6 million in 2021, about a year later, and interest in cryptocurrency trading has revived.

Crypto asset (virtual currency) market in 2021. All major currencies such as Bitcoin and Ethereum are bullish or strong. 2021 will also be characterized by positive news about cryptoassets, such as the growth of the decentralized financial system called DeFi and the widespread use of non-volatile tokens called NFTs, which have increased the price of related currencies. All of this has elevated the status of crypto-assets and given the opportunity for many to discover new useful values.

Bitcoin (BTC) current chart

If you look at the chart of Bitcoin, a cryptocurrency market participant, you can once again observe the strength of its price action (Fig. 1).

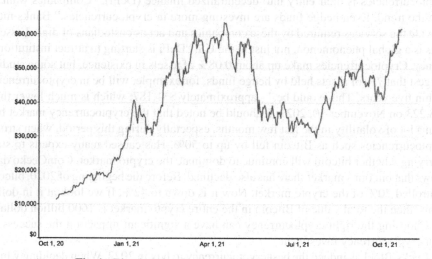

**Fig. 1.** Bitcoin Price October 18, 2020 - October 18, 2021.

From around August 2020, the growth is spectacular, leading to a dramatic explosion of crypto assets. Bitcoin is also a symbol of the image and value of cryptoassets. The

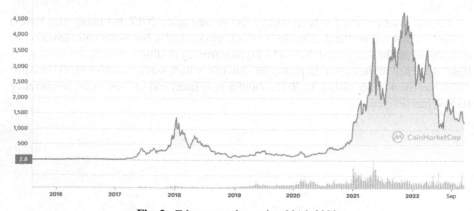

**Fig. 2.** Ethereum price action 2016–2022.

high price continued from October to November 2021, but this was due to the expected increase due to the listing of the Bitcoin ETF in the United States. Next, let's look at the chart for the same period of Ethereum, which is recognized as an altcoin (a general term for all cryptographic assets except Bitcoin). (Fig. 2).

The price action is very similar to the Bitcoin chart. Since Ethereum is a large entity with the second largest market capitalization after Bitcoin, it tends to move in line with the price movements of crypto assets in general.

Therefore, in January 2022, Russia issued a report on the regulation of cryptocurrencies, which led to a decrease in the value of all crypto assets, including Ethereum.

Ripple (XRP)- Ripple (XRP) is known as a cryptocurrency aimed at speeding up and reducing the cost of international money transfers and payments. Unlike other crypto-assets, it is a currency with a centralized operating company and servers instead of a decentralized network. This seems to be the point at which the price starts to rise at the same time as Bitcoin and Ethereum, but it can be seen that there is a period of large fluctuations after that. Compared to the above two currencies, the ratio of buying and selling can be considered high due to investor speculation. In order to make big profits in a few years, it is necessary to start investing in cryptocurrencies that are not so well known at the moment. To invest, you need to choose a cryptocurrency exchange that deals with a large number of currencies and check the currencies that are traded. The currency for which the price increases varies by season, so choosing an exchange that works with a large number of currencies in advance is definitely a good choice.

Coincheck works with 17 types of cryptoassets and is known for the ease of use and performance of its smartphone app, so even beginners can easily view charts on their smartphones.

Recently, such Dogecoin has received a lot of attention, as Elon Musk, who is said to be the "richest man in the world", mentioned it on SNS. Elon Musk uploaded a photo of Dogecoin's symbol after talking about his future predictions for the crypto asset on social media. Because of this, Dogecoin was the focus of the richest people in the world and the price rose instantly. In fact, the price of Dogecoin increased almost nine times, from $5 to $44. Strax was created to facilitate such electronic payments, especially internet transactions. If it is put to practical use, it is likely to suddenly increase in value as a cryptoasset.

**"Trading volume"** is an important point when looking at the future potential of crypto-assets. Arguably, the more trading volume a virtual currency has, the more people buy and sell it, in other words, the more people recognize its value.

Positive in the monetary future of cryptocurrency role

- It is known that cryptocurrencies can be used not only for buying and selling, but also for transferring money. When considering the future potential of virtual currency (crypto assets), it is also necessary to consider whether it will be used for other purposes, such as sending and receiving money, in addition to trading. If it is used not only for trading purposes, but also for payments and money transfers, it is likely to become widespread in the future.
- Virtual currencies that are being actively pursued by governing bodies and development communities are expected to have the potential to improve the usability of the

system in the future. Suffered from system issues in managing many virtual currencies. Rather than leaving problems as they are, if there is a development community that makes improvements based on requests and times, it can continue to move in a good direction in the future. For example, Bitcoin has had many updates from the development community to solve system problems that cause delays in transfers. As a result, the currency split, but there was a desire to establish it as a better crypto-asset. The number of participants in the development community is also an indicator of the future potential of crypto assets. Altcoin Ethereum has more than 300 developers who joined the team in January. Developing a more user-friendly system will facilitate the development of a virtual currency project while many developers are actively engaged in discussions.

- One of the points of future potential of virtual currency is the proliferation of applications.
- Cryptocurrencies that have specific purposes beyond buying, selling, and storing may be more likely to spread in the future.
- In addition, Ethereum is expanding its fundraising method called STO (Security Token Offering).
- An STO is a method of raising funds by selling securities to investors. In the past, raising funds through ICOs was popular, but the system had many problems, such as fraud. STOs are expected to improve the problems of ICOs and spread as a financing method for virtual currencies in the future. XRP (Ripple) has partnered with more than 300 financial institutions and plans to implement fast international money transfers.
- In the future, the XRP system may be accepted as an alternative to the SWIFT international money transfer network.

In addition, virtual currency may be used in more familiar places in the future. The final point in exploring the future potential of virtual currency (crypto-assets) is legal regulation.

The establishment of regulations by law can change the position of virtual currency (crypto assets) for better or worse. As of July 16, 2021, virtual currencies (crypto assets) have higher taxes on trading income than securities and currencies. The prospect of how this tax system will change could be an important point in looking ahead.

Cryptocurrencies, if properly designed and implemented, have the potential to significantly improve payment systems;

Currently, the goals of cryptocurrency creators are fighting to support cryptocurrency as the money of the future, but none of the existing cryptocurrencies have been universally successful in fulfilling the role of "money".

*Factors hindering the development of cryptocurrency*

- Knowledge, use and understanding of crypto-currencies remain very underdeveloped in Europe and America
- Majority of citizens in all countries agree to continue issuing money by central banks.
- Most of the citizens of developed Europe and the USA do not own digital currencies either, because they consider it too risky. Our research shows that countries with a history of monetary stability are less open to new currencies such as cryptocurrencies.

– Acceptability and price stability play a key role in determining the preference for holding money, regardless of who issued it.

## 5   Conclusion

While theoretically analyzing the research, the report confirms the results of recent surveys and articles written by Facebook about the viability of cryptocurrencies. Consumers' willingness to trust cryptocurrencies is very negative, respondents from Europe and the US have less trust than other digital currencies, at the end of our research, in our Facebook survey, only 3% of 800,000 participants from Central Asian countries, especially Uzbekistan, have sufficient knowledge about this cryptocurrency and trust it. Confirmed.

Gone are the days of going to a bank branch to withdraw cash from an ATM, getting a mortgage, and shopping at a department store. For many, any financial transaction has now become a fully online experience, a trend accelerated by the COVID-19 pandemic over the past two years. The money of the future lives in the "sky" and increasingly powerful financial technology from smartphones and laptops is changing the concept of money. Modern discussions and debates about cryptocurrencies tend to confuse "money" with "payment systems" or mechanisms for processing and settling transactions; Cryptocurrency is the big future. Its initial stages are becoming a reality. Virtual currencies are challenging the financial institutions that operate them. 2021 will be a year of financial changes.

## References

1. Abramova, M.A.: Factors of development of circulation of electronic money and means of payment in the territory of the Republic of Uzbekistan/MA Abramova, SE Dubova, SV Krivoruchko // University news. Series: "Economics, finance and production management" 03(45), 3–13 (2020)
2. Ageev, A.I.: Cryptocurrencies, markets and institutions/AI Ageevs, EL Loginov. Economic strategies 20(1), 94–107 (2018)
3. Aksenov, V.S.: On the issue of interpretation of electronic money/BC Aksenov. Bulletin of the Russian State Humanities University. Series "Economy. Management. That's right" 10, 14–22 (2011)
4. Aksenov, D.A.: Directions and characteristics of the application of blockchain technology in the economy/DA Aksenov, AP Kuprikov, PA Sahakyan. Scientific and technical statements of St. Petersburg State Polytechnic University. Economic sciences 11(1), 30–38 (2018)
5. Andryushin, S.A.: Bitcoin, blockchain, file-money and features Evolution of monetary mechanism/SA Andryushin, VK Burlachkov. Finance and credit 23(31), 1850–1861 (2017)
6. Andryushin, S.A.: Changing the paradigm of the monetary system: from centralization to decentralization/SA Andryushin. Actual problems of economics and law 12(2), 204–220 (2018)
7. Anokhin, N.V.: Cryptocurrency as a tool of the financial market/NV Anokhin, AI Shmireva. Ideas and ideals 2(3), 37 (2018). FROM. 39–49. Author, F.: Article title. Journal 2(5), 99–110 (2016)
8. Pulatovich Eshov, M., Sabitxanovna Nasirkhodjaeva, D.: Development prospects for digital economy development in Uzbekistan. In: The 5th International Conference on Future Networks & Distributed Systems (2021)

# A Data Security Technique Combining Asymmetric Cryptography and Compressive Sensing for IoT Enabled Wireless Sensor Networks

Ahmed Aziz[1,6]($\boxtimes$), Ahmed M. Khedr[2,3], Ahmed Salim[2,4], and Walid Osamy[1,5]

[1] Computer Science Department, Faculty of Computers and Artificial Intelligence, Benha University, Benha, Egypt

[2] Mathematics Department, Zagazig University, Zagazig, Egypt
akhedr@sharjah.ac.ae

[3] Computer Science Department, University of Sharjah, Sharjah 27272, UAE

[4] Department of Computer Science, College of Sciences and Arts, Al-methnab, Qassim University, Buraydah, Saudi Arabia

[5] Department of Applied Science, College of Community in Unaizah, Qassim University, Buraydah, Saudi Arabia

[6] Tashkent State University of Economics, Tashkent, Uzbekistan
a.mohamed@tsue.uz

**Abstract.** Reducing the amount of data transmitted and protecting devices from the adversary environment are the major challenges faced in the development of the Internet of Things (IoT) network. Compressive sensing (CS) offers the major advantage of performing lightweight encryption and compression at the same time, making it energy efficient. Like any private key algorithm, the CS encryption method has problems with key distribution and management. Public key algorithms, on the other hand, do not have these problems and provide a high level of security. However, public key algorithms increase the cost of communication that leads to a decrease in network lifetime. In this paper, we propose an efficient technique that achieves a high level of security with minimum energy consumption. The proposed technique utilizes the advantage of public-key algorithms to provide a high level of security and reduces communication costs by using the CS method. The simulation results indicate that the proposed security approach is effective in achieving better performance in security with minimal communication cost, along with prolonging network lifetime. In addition, the proposed technique makes it possible to use public-key algorithms for securing the IoT network efficiently.

**Keywords:** Security · Asymmetric Cryptography · Compressive Sensing · Wireless Sensor Networks · Network lifetime · Communication cost

© The Author(s), under exclusive license to Springer Nature Switzerland AG 2023
Y. Koucheryavy and A. Aziz (Eds.): NEW2AN 2022, LNCS 13772, pp. 252–268, 2023.
https://doi.org/10.1007/978-3-031-30258-9_22

# 1   Introduction

The most essential aspect of the IoT model is considered to be Wireless Sensor Networks (WSNs). The usage of wireless sensors and IoT innovations in various applications (e.g. e-health, transportation, etc.) is among the most promising market segments in the future [1–3]. IoT sensor nodes have the main task of detecting data and then transmitting it to the base station (BS). One of the dominant factors affecting the energy consumption of IoT devices is the data transmission process. In addition, wireless transmission of data using unsecure channels make it very easy to eavesdrop. Security and energy efficiency are therefore the keys to the growth of IoT. The encryption of the data transmitted between the sensors and the BS usually allows for confidentiality. Two groups of encryption algorithms namely symmetrical and asymmetrical key algorithms are commonly used. Data encryption algorithms dependent on symmetric (private) keys such as DES and AES [4] do not require complex computation and storage. However, these algorithms require a key exchange technique between the sender and the receiver. Otherwise, the keys have to be saved in advance. So when installed in outdoor locations, sensors could be vulnerable to hacking [5,6]. On the other hand, asymmetric (public) key-based data encryption algorithms such as RSA and ECC [8] can accomplish an increased security level.

In CS, if the signal is sparse either naturally or using a domain transformer, it may be effectively sampled at less than the rate of the Nyquist theory. According to CS theory, the raw data $x$ is transformed to the compressed data y by matrix $\Phi$. It is identical to block ciphers encryption, with $x$ being the plain text, $y$ being the cipher text, and matrix $\Phi$ the secret key. The CS compression and reconstruction process can therefore be considered correspondingly to be encryption and decryption, i.e., both compression and encryption are performed simultaneously, making it more energy efficient. The concept behind CS encryption is that the pseudo-random key (seed) that is utilized to produce the sensing matrix $\Phi$ is not accessible by the intruder. The drawback of the CS encryption method comes from the reality that the CS encryption method acts as a private key scheme, where communication on either sides had to agree on the same key that was considered to be one of the biggest challenges faced by these types of algorithms. However, using public key algorithms, this problem can be addressed, but it increases the computational cost or communication data traffic.

Public-key algorithms are used in IoT-based WSNs in two scenarios: first, each sensor node generates its own public and private key to encrypt and decrypt data, which increases computation and complexity, and reduces network life. Thus, the first scenario cannot be applied to the IoT network. Second, BS generates the keys and sends the public key to the entire network to encrypt sensor data [19]. Then the sensors send the encrypted data to the cluster head for data aggregation. The problem with this scenario is that cluster heads cannot aggregate sensor data without decrypting the data, i.e. they need a private key, which leads to an increase in data traffic and communication costs. In this paper, our aim is to address the gap in previous works by proposing an efficient data security technique for IoT that integrates the public key algorithms with the CS method.

Our contributions can be summarized as follows:

1. The proposed technique utilizes CS's advantage in achieving load balancing during data aggregation. It achieves good security performance and load balancing by using a public algorithm and data vector size reduction by using hybrid CS.
2. Due to the energy constraint of the sensor node, our technique shifts all complex computing and data decryption to the BS side, which has no energy problem.
3. We use hybrid CS instead of plain CS, which leads to the elimination of unnecessary high traffic at the early stages of transmissions, which reduces power consumption.
4. The proposed technique not only depends on CS for data encryption, but also uses a public-key algorithm, so that CPA attacks can not affect our technique and there is no need to change the CS matrix in each iteration as any CS data encryption algorithm consumes more power during matrix sharing between BS and sensors.

The remainder of the paper is arranged accordingly: In Sect. 2, we describe the background knowledge. Related work is briefly reviewed in Sect. 3. The proposed security technique is described in Sect. 4. Section 5 provides the details of simulation of the proposed technique as well as comparison with current methods. The paper's conclusion is set out in Sect. 6.

## 2   Compressive Sensing (CS)

The general architecture for CS is defined as: we provide $N$ sensor nodes for sensing data from any field and then sending it to a BS. Let matrix $x(x \in R^{N \times 1})$ reflect the reading of sensors, where each row $x$ denotes a sensor node's data. The $x$ matrix has a sparse representation in the $\Psi$ transformer domain where $\Psi$ is $N \times N$ transformation matrix, i.e., $x = \Psi k$ where $k$ is a vector of coefficients. To put it another way, $x$ is labeled $S$-sparse if it has $S$ non-zero values and $N - k$ zero values. As per the CS theory, if $M$ is the size of the measurement and $S$ is the sparse level, then BS only requires $M \geq S \log (N / S)$ to reproduce original sensors reading $x$ from the CS measurements $y$, such that $y = \Psi x$, where $y \in R^{(M \times 1)}$ and $\Phi$ is $M \times N$, $M \gg N$, CS random matrix (Bernoulli, Gaussian, etc.).

CS can be applied for data aggregation in the IoT network as Plain CS [20–27], or Hybrid CS technique [28,29]. In plain CS, each sensor generates the corresponding coefficient of CS matrix for data compression and subsequently sends M samples to the cluster head (CH). The CH then uses CS to compress the received samples and sends $M$ samples to the BS as illustrated in Fig. 1. Each node sends $M$ samples even if the data size is shorter than $M$ which leads to unwanted high traffic at the early stages of transmission.

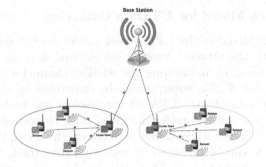

**Fig. 1.** Plain CS technique.

A hybrid CS technique was therefore proposed to overcome this limitation of plain CS technique. In the hybrid CS technique, every node sends their data without CS to the CH, which decides whether or not to use the CS, according to the size of the data received. If the size is greater than M, CS will be used to send M to BS, otherwise it will send M to BS without the CS, as shown in Fig. 2.

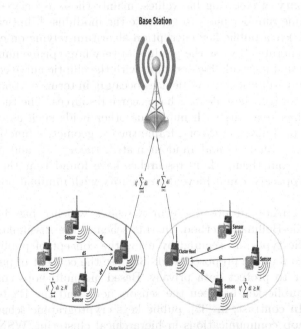

**Fig. 2.** Hybrid CS technique.

## 2.1 CPA Attack Model for CS Data Gathering

In this section, we describe the CPA attack model for CS data gathering. In CPA attack model, the attacker knows both original data $x$, by measurement and the cipher data $y$, by monitoring the wireless channel and he/she tries to obtain the secret key $\Phi$. Moreover, $x$ can be controlled by CPA attack using different ways; for example, the CPA attackers select one node as a target and then they increase the noise value for the target node by adding radiation source near to that node. The attackers target is to obtain the secret key $\Phi$ from $x$ and $y$. The secret key $\Phi$ can be obtained by repeating the attack $N$ times in order to get $N$ different values of $(x, y)$. Then, the attacker will recover the secret key $\Phi$ by solving with the least squares method $\acute{\Phi} = argmin_{\Phi}||y - \Phi x||_2$.

## 3 Related Work

In this section, we present the related works in the field of IoT-based WSNs and CS reconstruction and their application. Related research includes many important contributions. Rivest - Shamir - Adleman (RSA) is an algorithm used for encrypting and decrypting messages. RSA uses prime numbers widely to calculate both public and private keys. The effectiveness of this method depends on the complexity of factoring big values, mainly those associated with finding the correct prime number pairs to generate the modulus. Elliptical curve cryptography (ECC) is a public key encryption algorithm relying on elliptical curve theory. ECC generates keys as the product of very large prime numbers, instead of the conventional method of generation, with the elliptic curve equation. However, they are not suitable for IoT devices because, in terms of computing power, memory, and storage, these devices have scarce resources. The theoretical foundation of CS has relations with numerous other fields such as computational linear algebra, optimization theory, frame theory, geometric functional analysis, applied harmonic analysis and random matrix theory [7], and also addresses methodologies from them. Many researches have found that the Compressive Sensing (CS) approach can achieve data security with minimal power consumption [9,10].

In [37], the authors proposed a security scheme which is based on ECC algorithm and Diffie-Hellman method. In this scheme, the dissimilar unicast and broadcast traffic types are secured by using the concept of public and private keys. The authors of the proposed work [33], use the concept of public key algorithms in order to protect data privacy. Based on multi-hops communication, [34] uses the public key between the sensors node and the BS to secure data transmission. In contrast, in [35], public keys cryptographic scheme is used to secure single hop communications in hierarchical clustering WSN. In [36], the number of computations in each round is reduced by using the concept of the private key algorithm.

Using cellular automata (CA) rules, asymmetric key cryptography technique of block cipher is proposed in [4]. The above algorithms provide data privacy and security. However, due to their high computational complexity, they cannot be considered as security solution for sensor devices which have limited power and storage. To address these limitations, CS is being used as an encryption technique to compress and encrypt sensor's data, which provides data privacy and security with energy efficiency.

Based on CS data encryption, many works have been proposed. The work proposed in [11] was the first work to present CS as the method of data encryption, where the CS matrix was used as the private key, and the compressed sample was considered as the encrypted-text (cipher) of plain data. In addition, the CS data encryption method was used to defeat the brute force attack and proved that the method of CS encryption could beat the attack.

The authors analyzed the CS data encryption method in [11,12] which expresses CS as a private key cryptosystem. The security performance of CS in the wiretap channel was discussed in [13]. The CS encryption method was proposed in [14] for applications used for outsourcing. The authors of [12] have shown that if the intruders use improper encryption matrix for decrypting the data, the initial data sparsity will be lower than that of the decrypted data. In [15], without concentrating on computational feasibility, Cambareri et al. demonstrated that CS is not completely safe by carrying out a statistical study.

The researchers used chaotic sequences in [16] to produce the measurement matrix. [17] was the first to address CPA attacks, wherin the authors developed a hidden sparsifying basis called Fractional Fourier Transform. However, this approach was not feasible in sensors with power and storage limitations. Although the CS method achieves an acceptable security level, it still faces security threats like CPA attack [18]. However, CS encryption method has some drawbacks also, for instance, it is considered as a private key scheme where the private key is the CS matrix which has problems in key storage and management.

The proposed security technique in this paper is based on public key algorithm to encrypt data from the sensors. In addition, the proposed technique uses the advantage of the hybrid CS approach in achieving the data traffic load balancing during the aggregation phase to enhance the way the public algorithms are used in IoT network, to achieve high protection with minimum energy consumption.

## 4   The Proposed Security Technique

In this section, we explain the main idea of the proposed technique which consists of three stages: Key Sharing and Data Encryption, Hybrid CS Data Aggregation, and Data Recovery. We assume that the network is structured into a number of clusters using some cluster-based algorithm such as the LEACH algorithm [8], so that in each cluster there is one node acting as Cluster Head (CH) and others as Cluster members (CMs). Figure 3 shows the flow diagram of our Security technique. The procedures of the proposed security technique stages are described in Algorithm 1.

## 4.1   Key Sharing and Data Encryption Stage

The CS method, as described above, achieves an acceptable level of security, but faces key management and distribution challenges that make it not preferable to provide security solution for many applications that require a high level of security, such as military applications.

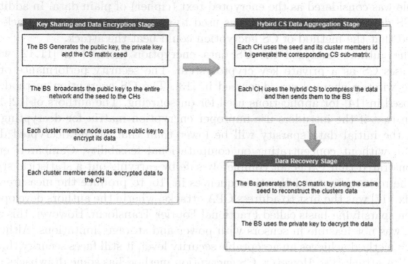

**Fig. 3.** Flow diagram: Overall process operations in the proposed technique

A direct solution to these problems is to apply public key algorithms where the BS sends only the public key to the entire network and keeps the private one to itself. Later, every sensor node utilizes this public key to encrypt its data and sends them to its CH which then sends them to the BS. So by using Public key algorithms, the key distribution problem is solved and if the attackers capture any sensor node, they cannot recover the data without the private key. However, the CHs cannot aggregate the cipher data received from the sensors without knowing the private key, which leads to the increase in data communication traffic and decrease in network lifetime dramatically, as the CHs send the data to the BS without any aggregation.

On the other hand, the hybrid CS method has a major effect on data traffic load balancing. Thus, the proposed technique utilizes the high security of public-key algorithms and the advantage of the hybrid CS method in data traffic load balancing in order to achieve high security with minimal power consumption. In our proposed technique, the BS uses RSA algorithm [37] to generate the public key $k_p$ and the private key $k_{pr}$ for data encryption and decryption respectively. Then, the BS broadcasts the global seed for CS matrix generation to every CH, followed by the public key $k_p$ to the entire network. This scenario will be applied only once before any transmission from both sides. Each sensor $i$ uses $k_p$ to encrypt its data $d_i$ into cipher data $c_i$ such that $c_i = E(d_i, k_p)$. Each sensor $i$ sends $c_i$ to the CH. The procedures of this stage is shown in Figs. 4 and 5.

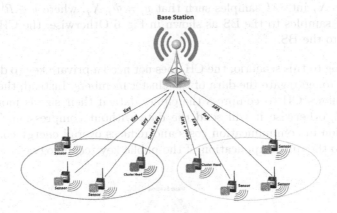

**Fig. 4.** Key Sharing and Data Encryption Stage (Key sharing)

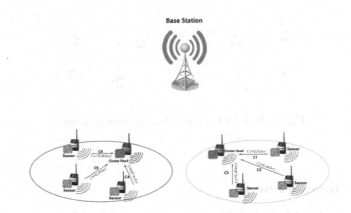

**Fig. 5.** Key Sharing and Data Encryption Stage (Encryption)

### 4.2 Hybrid CS Data Aggregation Stage

At this stage, the proposed technique strives to overcome the drawback of public key algorithms that do not allow the CH to perform a data aggregation. This problem is addressed by the proposed technique using the hybrid CS method. Each CH shall perform the following procedure:

1. Collect ciphered vector $X_j = [c_1, c_2, \ldots, c_j)]$.

2. Use the received global seed from the BS along with its cluster member's id to construct the corresponding CS sub-matrix $\Phi_j$ such that $|\Phi_j| = |j|$.
3. If the size of $X_j$ is bigger than or equal to $M$, i.e., $|X_j| \geq M$, use $\Phi_j$ to compress $X_j$ into $M$ samples such that $y_j = \Phi_j X_j$, where $y \in R^{(M \times 1)}$, and sends $M$ samples to the BS as shown in Fig. 6 Otherwise, the CH sends $X_j$ directly to the BS.

According to this scenario, the CH does not need a private key to decrypt the cipher data to aggregate the data of the cluster members. Instead, the proposed technique allows CH to compress the cipher data if their size is more than or equal to $M$, otherwise it will send the data without compression. This leads to a reduction in communication costs and reduces overall energy consumption compared to the direct application of the public key technology.

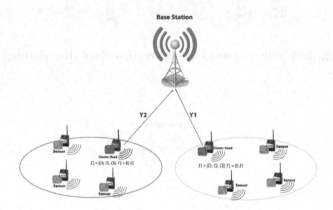

**Fig. 6.** Hybrid CS Data Aggregation process.

### 4.3   Data Recovery Stage

At this stage, the BS receives two types of data: ciphered compressed samples $y = [y_1, y_2, \ldots, y_i]$ and ciphered uncompressed data $X = [X_1, X_2, \ldots, X_j]$ such that $i \neq j$. The BS differentiates between them on the basis of the size of received data; if it is equal to $M$, then it is ciphered compressed samples, otherwise it is ciphered uncompressed data. First, BS tries to reconstruct the ciphered compressed samples $y = [y_1, y_2, \ldots, y_i]$ to decrypt them using the private key $k_{pr}$ . It uses the same global seed to generate the CS matrix $\Phi$ to solve the $||l||_1$-norm minimization problem as

$$R = argmin||R||_1, subject \ \ to \ \ y = \Phi R \tag{1}$$

Within the CS framework, Eq. 1 can be solved efficiently using any greedy algorithm such as Orthogonal Matching Pursuit (OMP) in [38], Subspace Pursuit in [40], or COSAMP in [39] to recreate d from only $M$. Finally, the BS uses the private key $k_{pr}$ to decrypt vector $\hat{R}$ and vector $X$ to obtain the plain text $\hat{d}$ such that $\hat{d} = D([\hat{R}, X], k_{pr})$ and then take a decision depending on the network data $d$. Algorithm 1 outlines the procedures of the proposed security technique stage.

---

**Algorithm 1.** The proposed Security Scheme
***
   *Key Sharing and Data Encryption Stage:*
   BS generates the public key $k_p$, the private key $k_{pr}$ and the CS matrix global seed.

   BS sends the global seed to the CHs and broadcast $k_p$ to the entire network.
   **for** each node i **do**
      use $k_p$ to encrypt its data $d_i$ into cipher data $c_i$ such that $c_i = E(d_i, k_p)$.
      send $c_i$ to the CH.
   **end for**
      *Hybrid CS Data Aggregation Stage:*
   **for** each cluster $j$ of the CH do the following **do**
      collect the cipher data from its cluster members into vector $X_j$.
      Use the global seed and cluster member's id to generate the CS sub-matrix $\Phi_j$.
      **if** $|X_j| \geq M$ **then**
         Use $\Phi_j$ to compress$X_j$ vector into $M$ samples such that $Y_j = \Phi_j X_j$.
         Send $Y_j$ to the BS.
      **end if**
   **end for**
      *Data recovery stage:*
   BS uses the same global seed to generate the CS matrix $\Phi$.
   BS uses any reconstruction algorithm to solve Eq. 1 in order to obtain $\hat{R}$.
   BS uses the private key $k_{pr}$ to decrypt vector $\hat{R}$ and vector $X$, then obtains the plain text $\hat{d}$
   such that $\hat{d} = D([\hat{R}, X], k_{pr})$.

---

# 5   Simulation Results and Discussion

In this section, we provide simulation results for evaluation and comparison of the effectiveness of the proposed technique with P. Hu's algorithm [41], wherein the authors used plain CS method for data encryption and a direct RSA-1024 algorithm for data encryption, in terms of communication cost, network lifetime and security level. The implementation was done in MATLAB R2015a. All evaluations in this section depend on real dataset [31]. This data set contains data collected from 54 sensors of different environmental data such as humidity, temperature, light, and voltage. In our evaluation, we assume that a number of sensor nodes are randomly distributed to monitor the voltage field. We used the Leach algorithm [8] to group these nodes into clusters, where the $N$ network nodes are divided into a number of clusters. In each cluster, the CMs send their data to the CH, then each CH aggregates, and send their data to the BS as shown in Fig. 7. Additionally, Fig. 8 displays the voltage data before (time domain) and after the DCT transformer is applied.

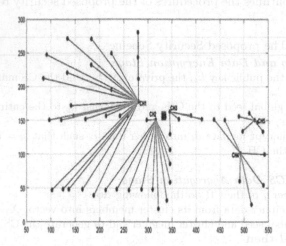

**Fig. 7.** Random distribution network in cluster based using leach algorithm.

## 5.1   Network Lifetime

The size of the network region is taken as $100m \times 100m$, the number of sensor nodes varies from 50 to 200 with increments of 50 nodes, and the BS is at the centre. We are considering the same energy parameters used by [29] to send a $l - bit$ message for a distance $d$ and the radio power consumption is :

$$E_{Tx}(l, d) = \begin{cases} lE_{elec} + l\epsilon_{fs}d^2 & d < d_0 \\ lE_{elec} + l\epsilon_{mp}d^4 & d \geq d_0 \end{cases} \tag{2}$$

To obtain this message, the radio expend is:

$$E_{Rx}(l) = lE_{elec} \tag{3}$$

The parameters used for the simulated model is given below:

$$E_{elec} = 50nJ/bit,$$
$$\epsilon_{fs} = 10pJ/bit/m^2,$$
$$\epsilon_{mp} = \frac{13}{1000}pJ/bit/m^4, \tag{4}$$
$$d_0 = \sqrt{\frac{\epsilon_{fs}}{\epsilon_{mp}}}.$$

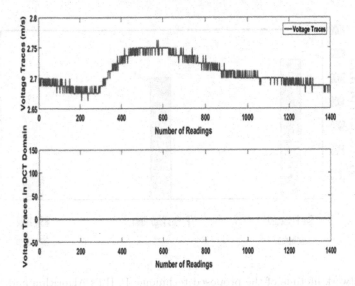

**Fig. 8.** Voltage traces in DCT domain

The energy factor associated with super nodes = $2J$, advanced nodes = $1.25J$, and for normal nodes = $0.5J$. We measured the network life time until half of the nodes die. Figure 9 compares the lifetime of the proposed technique, P. Hu's algorithm and the RSA-1024 algorithm. In P. Hu's algorithm and RSA-algorithm, half-node death occurred earlier than the proposed algorithm, and Fig. 9 also illustrates the effectiveness of the proposed algorithm in achieving high security and extending the network lifetime more than the other two algorithms. This is because the proposed algorithm requires the key sharing only once before any communication between the BS and sensor nodes starts, and does not add any additional information to the sensor data in each round like any other algorithm. Furthermore, our algorithm relies on hybrid CS method for data compression and aggregation which has an advantage over plain CS method to maximize network lifetime.

In P. Hu's algorithm, the authors have improved the traditional method of CS data encryption, but according to their security technique, some additional information must be transmitted between the BS and the sensor nodes that add to the data transmission overhead. In addition, the algorithm also relies on a simple CS compression and aggregation method that causes unnecessary traffic at an early stage of transmission. Both of these factors lead to a decrease in network life. It is also clear from the same figure that the RSA-1024 displays the worst performance in terms of network lifetime, because the behavior of public algorithms that increases computation and complexity make them unpreferable for IoT network.

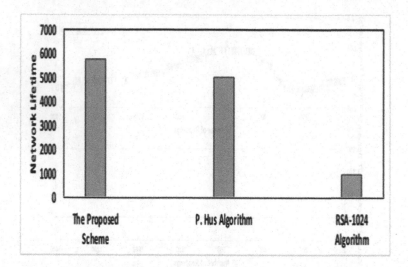

**Fig. 9.** Network lifetime of the proposed technique, P. Hu's Algorithm and RSA-1024 Algorithm.

## 5.2   Communication Cost

In this section, we evaluate our technique in terms of network load balancing with a different compression ratio (4% and 5%). Figure 10 shows that the proposed technique achieves a slightly lower cost of communication than P. Hu's algorithm because our proposed algorithm depends on hybrid CS data aggregation, but both algorithms' communication cost increases as the network size increases. Compared to the others, the RSA-1024 algorithm achieves the highest communication costs since there is no data aggregation in CHs and causes high data traffic. Changes in the compression ratio do not affect the efficiency of the proposed technique which, as shown in Fig. 11, still achieves lower communication costs compared to others.

## 5.3   Security Improvement

Compared with private key algorithms, it is clear that public key algorithms provide better performance in security. As a result, our proposed technique for data encryption, which relies on the RSA algorithm, achieves greater security than the P. Hu's algorithm, in which authors rely on CS data encryption, which is considered to be a private key algorithm.

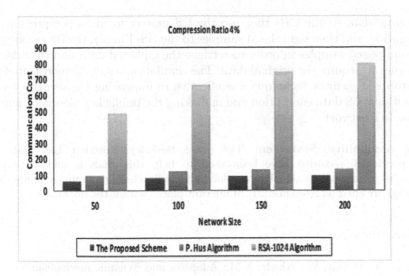

**Fig. 10.** Communication Cost vs. Network size when the compression ratio is 4%.

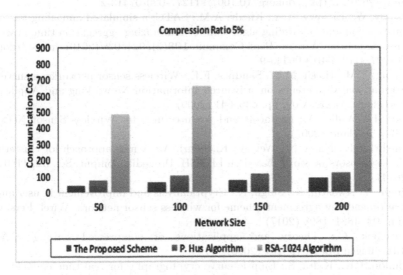

**Fig. 11.** Communication Cost vs. Network size when the compression ratio is 5%.

## 6    Conclusion

In this paper we have introduced an efficient data security scheme that modifies the standard public key algorithms by using the hybrid CS approach for data compression and aggregation to achieve high security and network load balancing. The proposed technique consisted of three steps, with BS generating public and private keys in the first stage and then transmitting a public key to the entire network for data encryption. During the second stage, the sensors send the cipher data to the CHs that use the CS matrix for data compression and aggregation, and then send the M samples to the BS. Finally, the BS reconstructs the compressed samples in order to retrieve the ciphered data and then decrypt it in order to acquire the original data. The simulation results demonstrated that the proposed security technique was effective in improving the security level of conventional CS data encryption and in making the public key algorithm suitable for the IoT network.

**Data Availibility Statement.** The [Intel Berkeley Research Lab Data Set] data previously recorded have been used to help this analysis and are accessible at [http:/db.csail.mit.edu/labdata/labdata.html]. These preliminary studies (and datasets) are cited as reference [31] in relevant places within the document.

# References

1. Aziz, A., Osamy, W., Khedr, A.M.: Adaptive and dynamic mechanism for round length determination in cluster based wireless sensor networks. Wireless Pers. Commun. (2020). https://doi.org/10.1007/s11277-020-07413-z
2. Osamy, W., El-sawy, A.A., Khedr, A.M.: SATC: a simulated annealing based tree construction and scheduling algorithm for minimizing aggregation time in wireless sensor networks. Wireless Pers. Commun. **108**(2), 921–938 (2019). https://doi.org/10.1007/s11277-019-06440-9
3. Huang, Y.M., Hsieh, M.Y., Sandnes, F.E.: Wireless sensor networks: a survey. In: International Conference on Advanced Information Networking and Applications Workshops, WAINA'09, pp. 636–641 (2009)
4. Karl, H., Willig, A.: Protocols and Architectures for Wireless Sensor Networks. Wiley, England (2007)
5. Khediri, S.E., Nasri, N., Wei, A., Kachouri, A.: A new approach for clustering in wireless sensors networks based on LEACH. Procedia Comput. Sci. **32**, 1180–1185 (2014)
6. Singh, A., Awasthi, K., Singh, K.: Cryptanalysis and improvement in user authentication and key agreement scheme for wireless sensor network. Wirel. Pers. Commun. **94**, 1881–1898 (2017)
7. Kutyniok, G.: Theory and applications of compressed sensing. GAMM-Mitteilungen **36**(1), 79–101 (2013)
8. Dhillon, P.K., Kalra, S.: Elliptic curve cryptography for real time embedded systems in IoT networks. In: 5th International Conference on Wireless Networks and Embedded Systems (WECON), Rajpura, pp. 1–6 (2016)
9. Orsdemir, A., Altun, H.O., Sharma, G., Bocko, M.F.: On the security and robustness of encryption via compressed sensing. In: MILCOM'08, pp. 1–7. IEEE (2008)
10. Rachlin, Y., Baron, D.: The secrecy of compressed sensing measurements. In: 46th Annual Allerton Conference on Communication, Control, and Computing, pp. 813–817. IEEE (2008)
11. Aderohunmu, F.A., Deng, J.D., Purvis, M.K.: A deterministic energy efficient clustering protocol for wireless sensor networks. In: Proceedings of the 7th IEEE International Conference on Intelligent Sensors, Sensor Networks and Information Processing (IEEE-ISSNIP), pp. 341–346 (2011)

12. Aderohunmu, F.A., Deng, J.D., Purvis, M.K.: Enhancing clustering in wireless sensor networks with energy heterogeneity. Int. J. Bus. Data Commun. Netw. **7**(4), 18–32 (2011)

13. Qing, L., Zhu, Q., Wang, M.: Design of a distributed energy-efficient clustering algorithm for heterogeneous wireless sensor networks. Comput. Commun. **29**(12), 2230–2237 (2006)

14. Chatterjee, M., Das, S.K., Turgut, D.: WCA: a weighted clustering algorithm for mobile ad hoc networks. Clust. Comput. **5**(2), 193–204 (2002)

15. Smaragdakis, G., Matta, I., Bestavros, A.: SEP: a stable election protocol for clustered heterogeneous wireless sensor networks. In: Proceeding of the International Workshop on SANPA (2004)

16. Kumar, D., Aseri, T.C., Patel, R.B.: EEHC: energy efficient heterogeneous clustered scheme for wireless sensor networks. Comput. Commun. **32**(4), 662–667 (2009). ISSN 0140–3664

17. Mizher, M.A., Al-Sharaeh, S.H., Ang, M.C., Abdalla, A.M., Mizher, M.A.: Centroid dynamic sink location for clustered wireless mobile sensor networks. J. Theor. Appl. Inf. Technol. **73**(3), 481–491 (2015)

18. Mamalis, B., Gavalas, D., Konstantopoulos, C., Pantziou, G.: Clustering in wireless sensor networks, RFID and sensor networks: architectures, pp. 324–353. Protocols, Security and Integrations (2009)

19. Gulen, U., Alkhodary, A., Baktir, S.: Implementing RSA for wireless sensor nodes. Sensors **19**(13), 28–64 (2019)

20. Thomas, M., Thomas, J.A.: Elements of Information Theory, (Wiley Series in Telecommunications and Signal Processing). Wiley-Inter science (2006)

21. Omar, D., Khedr, A.M.: Prolonging stability period of wireless sensor networks using compressive sensing. Int. J. Commun. Networks Inf. Secur. (IJCNIS) **11**(1), 1–6 (2019)

22. Omar, D., Khedr, A.M., Agrawal, D.P.: Optimized clustering protocol for balancing energy in wireless sensor networks. Int. J. Commun. Networks Inf. Secur. (IJCNIS) **9**(3), 367–375 (2017)

23. Omar, D., Khedr, A.M.: ERPLBC: energy efficient routing protocol for load balanced clustering in wireless sensor networks. Ad Hoc Sens. Wireless Netw. **42**, 145–169 (2018)

24. Khedr, A.M.: Effective data acquisition protocol for multi-hop heterogeneous wireless sensor networks using compressive sensing. Algorithms **8**(4), 910–928 (2015). https://doi.org/10.3390/a8040910

25. Khedr, A.M., Omar, D.M.: SEP-CS: effective routing protocol for heterogeneous wireless sensor networks. Ad Hoc Sensor Wireless Netw. **26**, 211–232 (2015)

26. Aziz, A., Singh, K., Osamy, W., Khedr, A.M.: An efficient compressive sensing routing scheme for internet of things based wireless sensor networks. Wireless Pers. Commun. **114**(3), 1905–1925 (2020). https://doi.org/10.1007/s11277-020-07454-4

27. Saini, P., Sharma, A.K.: E-DEEC: enhanced distributed energy efficient clustering scheme for heterogeneous WSN. In: 1st International Conference On Parallel, Distributed and Grid Computing (PDGC 2010), Solan vol. 2010, pp. 205–210 (2010)

28. Javaid, N.: An energy-efficient distributed clustering algorithm for heterogeneous WSNs. EURASIP J. Wireless Commun. Network. **2015**(1), 1–11 (2015)

29. Heinzelman, W., Chandrakasan, A., Balakrishnan, H.: An application-specific protocol architecture for wireless microsensor networks. IEEE Trans. Wireless Comm. **1**(4), 660–670 (2002)

30. Tian, J., Liu, T., Jiao, H.: Entropy weight coefficient method for evaluating intrusion detection systems. In: 2008 International Symposium on Electronic Commerce and Security, Guangzhou City, pp. 592–598 (2008)
31. Intel Berkeley Researc Lab (2020).http://db.lcs.mit.edu/labdata/labdata.html.2
32. Hengqiang, S., Helong, Y.: Application of entropy weight coefficient method in environmental assessment of soil. In: World Automation Congress 2012, Puerto Vallarta, Mexico, pp. 1–4 (2012)
33. Wang, Q.: Assessment of the sustainable development capacity with the entropy weight coefficient method. Sustainability 7(10), 13542–13563 (2015)
34. Shaji, M.: Distributed energy efficient heterogeneous clustering in wireless sensor network. In: 2015 5th International Conference on Advances in Computing and Communications (ICACC), Kochi, pp. 130–134 (2015)
35. Javaid, N., Qureshi, T.N., Khan, A.H., Iqbal, A., Akhtar, E., Ishfaq, M.: EDDEEC: enhanced developed distributed energy-efficient clustering for heterogeneous wireless sensor networks. Procedia Comput. Sci. 19, 914–919 (2013)
36. Boubiche, D.E., Boubiche, S., Bilami, A.: A cross-layer watermarking-based mechanism for data aggregation integrity in heterogeneous WSNs. IEEE Commun. Lett. 19(5), 823–826 (2015)
37. Abdallah, W., Boudriga, N., Kim, D., An, S.: An efficient and scalable key management mechanism for wireless sensor networks. In: 2015 17th International Conference on Advanced Communication Technology (ICACT) (2015)
38. Tropp, J., Gilber, A.: signal recovery from random measurements via orthogonal matching pursuit. IEEE Trans. Inform. Theory 53(14), 4655–4666 (2007)
39. Needell, D., Tropp, J.A.: CoSaMP: iterative signal recovery from incomplete and inaccurate samples. Appl. Comput. Harmon. Anal. 26(3), 301–321 (2009)
40. Wei, D., Olgica, M.: Subspace pursuit for compressive sensing signal reconstruction. IEEE Trans. Inf. Theor. 55(5), 2230–2249 (2009)
41. Hu, P., Xing, K., Cheng, X., Wei, H., Zhu, H.: Information leaks out: attacks and countermeasures on compressive data gathering in wireless sensor networks. IEEE, pp. 1258–1266 (2014)

# Energy Efficient and Secure Scheme Based Compressive Sensing Method for Internet of Vehicles

Ahmed Aziz[1,2]([☒]) and Maha Ibrahim[1]

[1] Tashkent State University of Economics, Tashkent, Uzbekistan
a.mohamed@tsue.uz
[2] Computer Science Department, Faculty of Computers and Artificial Intelligence,
Benha University, Benha, Egypt

**Abstract.** The Compressive Sensing (CS) technique based solutions are increasingly finding application in the field of IoV and WSNs motivated by the benefits of concurrent implementation of lightweight encryption and compression, which offers security and enhancement of WSN lifetime. The CS based solutions still face certain major challenging issues concerned with Key Distribution and Chosen Plain-Text Attacks (CPA). We introduce in this paper, a lightweight framework by instigating a scheme that generates and exchanges the key between the WSN nodes and the BS with the objective of enhancing security and efficiency. It enhances the security by resisting the Chosen Plaintext Attack using the newly introduced algorithm, "Data Compression with Encryption", which allows the WSN nodes to use a secret value for generating secret compressed samples. Furthermore Mobile Distributed Clustering Algorithm (MDCA) which is based on the use of predicted combined criteria metric is proposed for node clustering. The simulation results using experimentally collected data from real sensors placed at Intel Berkeley Research Lab show that the introduced scheme decrypts data with a small error in case of real user with correct seed, however, the decryption of the same data by an adversary produces the resultant data with considerably larger error. Moreover, the proposed framework succeeds to prolong the WSN lifetime when compared to other encryption algorithms.

**Keywords:** IoT · WSNs · IoV · Computer Security

## 1 Introduction

Internet of Things (IoT) provides networking to connect people, things, applications, and data through the Internet to enable remote control, management, and interactive integrated services. Based on IoT, now everything is going to be connected. In addition, predictions are made that there will be 50 billion 'things' connected to the Internet by 2020. So, Internet of Things study is very important

© The Author(s), under exclusive license to Springer Nature Switzerland AG 2023
Y. Koucheryavy and A. Aziz (Eds.): NEW2AN 2022, LNCS 13772, pp. 269–289, 2023.
https://doi.org/10.1007/978-3-031-30258-9_23

[1]. Actually, Wireless Sensor Networks (WSNs) is considered the most important element in the IoT model. Utilization of wireless sensors devices and other IoT technologies in transportation applications are one of the most promising market segments in the future [2–4]. That is because, the numbers of vehicles have been increased which leads to increase growth the traffic problems.

IoT technology can replace the traditional traffic problems solutions such as CCTV cameras and speed trackers, which have bad performance when the number of vehicles become huge, by using the concept of Internet of vehicles (IoV) in which the vehicles can be able to work and communicate seamlessly. The basic Idea of IoV is that, on each vehicle there number of sensors are deployed for various purposes such as monitor the vehicle metrics, Tyre pressure, car lock, etc. and then send these data to intermediate embedded board which we can called it process stage in which this board process and take decision either send the data to the BS or not depend on some threshold values.

Then main task of IoV sensors nodes is to sense the data then send them to the base station (BS). Therefore, security and energy efficiency are of major importance issues in IoV [5]. Encrypt the transmitted data between sensors and the BS usually makes the security possible. There are two types of encryption algorithms which are known as asymmetric and symmetric key algorithms. The data encryption algorithms based on symmetric key like DES and AES [7], although they don't require huge computational power and storage, but key exchange scheme is still required or keys have to be pre-stored. So sensors can be easily compromised when placed in outdoor environments.

Moreover, the data encryption algorithms based on asymmetric key like RSA and ECC [6] achieve high level of security. But they are not preferable for IoV devices because, these devices have limited resources, in terms of processing power, memory, and storage. Thus presently, many research noted that the Compressive Sensing (CS) [9,10] method can achieve the data security with minimum power consumption. In CS, the signal can be successfully sampled less than the rate of Nyquist theory, if the signal is sparsed by natural or by transformer. According to CS theory, the original data $x$ is converted to the compressed sample $y$ by using matrix $\Phi$. This operation is very similar to block ciphers encryption one, where $x$ is the plaintext, $y$ is considered the ciphertext and the matrix $\Phi$ is the key. So the CS compression and reconstruction process can be considered as encryption and decryption respectively i.e., both of data encryption and compression are execute in the same time, so energy efficiency becomes possible. The idea behind CS encryption method relies on the fact that the attacker does not have the pseudo-random key(seed) which used to generate the sensing matrix $\Phi$. But CS encryption method is facing a lot of challenges such as CS attacks like Chosen Plain Text Attack (CPA) [13] which aims to predict the CS matrix, and CS matrix seed sharing problem that is because CS can be consider as private key scheme where both sender and the receiver must have the same key to encrypt and decrypt the sensors data. To address these challenges, many CS encryption schemes have been proposed which based on one-time sensing assumption i.e., the CS matrix which considered secret key is used only once in each iteration. However, However, they didn't provide enough explanation on how the secret values are exchanged in secure manner by the legitimate users.

On the other hand, the use of the WSN potential provides efficient and costs effective solutions for several problems. However, it is necessary to implement mechanisms or procedures to deal with the sensors' constraints. Due to the limitation of their physical size, the sensors tend to have storage space, energy supply and communication bandwidth so limited that every possible means of reducing the usage of these resources is aggressively sought.

The use of clustering techniques has been proposed to help solve some of those constraints, by allowing the organization of the sensors in a hierarchical manner, grouping them into clusters and assigning specific tasks to the sensors in the clusters, before forwarding the information to higher levels. A cluster in WSN means to interconnect the sensor nodes hierarchically in order to improve their performance. Clusters provide reliability by having sensors taking over the workload of failing sensors. Clusters also improve data aggregation mechanisms, reduce the workload of each sensor to save energy and thus increase the overall lifetime of the system The creation of clusters in a WSN field is generally done taking into account the proximity between the sensors, measured through the radio frequency signal they emit. Clustering helps solve some of the sensors' constraints by: reducing the cost of transmitting data to base stations, reducing the power consumption in the devices, facilitating the gathering of sensed data, maximizing the routing process execution and allowing scalability, i.e., the concept of clustering is very useful in different contexts of WSN.

Mobility in wireless sensor networks has attracted a lot of attention in the recent years and has introduced unique challenges in aspects like resource management, coverage, routing protocols, security, etc. Thus, the next evolutionary step for sensor networks is to handle the mobility effect in all its forms. Most of clustering protocols currently used or proposed for WSN assume that the nodes are stationary [45, 46]. However, in applications like habitat monitoring (animal tracking) or search and rescue, that assumption makes those clustering mechanisms invalid, since the static nature of sensors is not real. One of the reasons for the sensors to be taken as stationary is because that assumption facilitates the simplification of the clustering protocols, making them have a very low overhead. It also avoids having to manage the mobility patterns of the sensors and allows saving more energy, since the localization information that the network has to manage is very low.

Thus this paper aims to address all mentioned above challenges by proposing secure key sharing which allows sender and receiver to share the CS seed in secure way. in addition, the proposed security scheme apply one-time sensing method without sharing CS seed in each iteration. Moreover, we propose a Mobile Distributed Clustering Algorithm (MDCA) which is based on the use of predicted combined criteria metric. In MDCA algorithm, the IoV nodes calculates its combined criteria metric according to connectivity, coverage, mobility and residual energy, after that each sensor node uses its history combined criteria information to predict the current combined criteria based on heuristic predictors. The IoV node with the highest Predicted combined criteria in its $r - hop$ neighborhood will become the cluster-head We highlight contributions of this paper and list them as follows:

- The proposed framework improves security by introducing a new scheme that generates and exchanges the key between the WSN nodes and the BS. In this method, every WSN node uses simple chaotic map and generate a random number, whereas two random numbers are generated by the BS ($e_2$ and $g_s$): The first one ($g_s$) is acting as the CS matrix seed which should be shared by both sides to encrypt and decrypt sensors data and the second one ($e_2$) is used by the BS to perform the sharing process during the proposed Key Exchange algorithm. This scenario will be applied only once before any transmission by both sides.
- The proposed scheme provides security enhancement by withstanding the CP-attack (CPA) using the newly introduced algorithm, "Data Compression with Encryption", which allows the WSN nodes to use secret value to generate secret compressed samples.
- The proposed scheme improves security by withstanding the Known Plaintext Attack (KPA) using the proposed Key Regeneration algorithm with which the BS and the WSN nodes regenerate the CS matrix seed dynamically and independently in every iteration.
- Propose Mobile Distributed Clustering Algorithm (MDCA) which is based on the use of predicted combined criteria metric.

The paper is further arranged as mentioned below:

Section 2 describes the related researches. Section 3 describes the proposed approach in detail. In Sect. 4, we provide the performance results of our approach and the comparison with the existing algorithms. In Sect. 5, the conclusion is presented.

## 2    Related Work

Both data privacy and security have equal significance in IoT technology since a wide variety of vital applications (e.g. transportation) relies on low power and low data connectivity sensors to send secret and important information [14]. Normally, a data encryption scheme can provide security between the IoT parties. Based on the encryption scheme, a lot of researches have been proposed such as [15–21]. In [15], the authors proposed an ECC and Diffie-Hellman based method that can be applied on different levels of network. [16] proposed confidentiality and integrity algorithm uses a homomorphic encryption with symmetric key for protecting the data privacy. Suganthi et al. [17] presented a key-management strategy that uses three categories of keys shared by every sensor node. Kadri et al. [18] proposed an algorithm that uses a symmetric key between sensor and BS and uses multi hop transmission, targeted to achieve minimum energy consumption, better scalability and high security. In [19], the authors presented a symmetric key cryptographic scheme, having hierarchical clustering WSN which uses single hop transmission. The main target of the scheme is to reduce probability of eavesdropping and connectivity probability. In [20], the authors proposed a symmetric key algorithm to reduce the number of operations per round and time. In this approach, some steps of the round function are merged and blended by randomly generated mixing bijection. The authors of [21] presented a cryptographic technique based on symmetric key which uses cellular automata rules (CA rules) for encryption and decryption of sensor data. All above algorithms succeeded to provide data privacy and security however due to their high computational complexity, they cannot be considered as security solution for IoT devices which have limited power and storage.

To address these limitations, presently CS is used as encryption technique to compress and encrypt sensor's data which achieve data privacy, security, and energy efficiency. Based on CS data encryption, a lot of works have been proposed such as [8,22–29]. In [22], CDG algorithm (Compressive Data Gathering) has been proposed, that uses CS method for data gathering in large-scale networks. Each node adopts the global seed to perform encryption and compression of its data, this seed is updated in each round by the BS to change the CS matrix. In [23], the authors improved the security level of CDG by proposing Secure CDG (SCDG). In each round of SCDG, the BS and the WSN nodes generates global seed using hash function. However, communication cost of SCDG is high because according to SCDG security mechanism in each round, some information is needed to be shared between BS and sensors. In [39], CS based security strategy for data collection (SeDC) is proposed where the authors integrated between CS and public key algorithms to achieve high security level. However, performing computations such as encryption and compression beside the public key size at each node lead to decrease the network lifetime. In [24], the authors proposed algorithm that uses CS for security. They used random linear projections to generate the compressed samples for use as cipher-text. In [25], the authors used CS to find solution for authentication and tamper detection problems. The key generation can be accomplished using RSS (Received Signal Strength) based techniques as presented in [26,27]. However, the generated keys using such techniques are applicable for conventional cryptographic encryption algorithms such as ECC and RSA. Another work presented in [8,28,29] used channel measurements for generating keys suitable for CS-based cryptography, which doesn't make use of any strategy distribution of keys. However, the above techniques cannot be used in IoT because they involve large number of steps for key generation which is difficult to be performed successfully in resource-constrained WSN nodes as it can result in increased power consumption. In contrast to this, our proposed framework realize all such complex mathematical computations for generation and exchange of keys using BS.

The proposed algorithm in [30] shows that the decrypted data will be sparser than that of the actual data, when an attacker tries to encrypt the data with a wrong encryption matrix. While [31] provides an insight that CS cannot be considered as immaculately secure, [32] shows that the measurement matrix can facilitate secure computations from attacks such as brute force attack and Cipher text Only Attack(COA). Even though the encryption methods using CS can offer computational secrecy to withstand attacks such as COA and brute-force attack, these schemes do not handle the case of CP-Attack (Chosen Plain-Text Attack). The CP-Attack (CPA) scenario was first addressed in [11] where the author used Fractional Fourier Transform (FRFT) as the secret sparsifying basis. However, the complexity of this method restricted its applicability on power and storage constrained sensor nodes. The authors of [12] proposed another solution to address the CPA, efficient in terms of computation and memory, using chaotic sequences as secret values. However, they didn't provide enough explanation on how the secret values are exchanged in secure manner by the legitimate users. In addition to this, chaotic system is also used in [33] to overcome challenges such as low-cost sampling and confidentiality preservation. In [34], the authors used CS method for securing the interaction between IoT and cloud system. Secure CS method for image encryption is proposed in [35] where the CS method combined with stream cipher method is used. In [36], LFSR technique is used to generate secure CS matrix. The wireless physical layer security is used for generating secure CS matrix in [37]. The work in [38] visually secures the image data based on CS method where the image is first transformed into coefficient matrix, then it is encrypted by CS and finally the ciphered image is embedded into carrier image.

All of the above methods and techniques are acting as private key algorithms and they are suffering from key distribution challenge. Moreover, all of the previous works are vulnerable to KPA attack because they used single CS matrix during their encryption and decryption process. We introduce in this paper, a lightweight CS security framework where a novel key sharing algorithm is proposed to address the key distribution challenge. Moreover, the proposed strategy improves security with its ability to withstand CPA using the proposed Data Compression with Encryption algorithm which allows the nodes to use a secret value to generate secret compressed samples. Finally, the proposed scheme provides resistance against the Known Plain-text Attack (KPA) using Key-Regeneration Algorithm. The notations used are provided in Table 1.

## 2.1 Security Model

In this section, we are addressing CS attacks models which called: Chosen Plain Text Attack (CPA) and Known Plain-text Attack (KPA).

**Chosen Plain Text Attack (CPA).** Through Chosen Plain Text Attack (CPA), it is possible for an adversary to tamper the sensing data $x$ of a sensor and take control over it by making changes in environmental conditions, resulting in false values for sensed data by the sensor, as desired by the adversary. For e.g., consider an environmental monitoring scheme, an attacker can alter the radiation value sensed by the sensor either by setting a source of radiation adjacent to the desired node (for intensifying the sensed value) or by creating a shield of radiation

**Table 1.** Notions Description

| Notation | Description |
|---|---|
| $x$ | Sensors readings |
| $\xi$ | Global seed |
| $S$ | Sparse level(number of non zeros values) |
| $\Psi$ | Transform matrix |
| $r$ | Number of round |
| $\Phi$ | Measurement matrix |
| $n_j.\alpha$ | Coefficient vector for node $n_j$ |
| $\Theta$ | $M \times N$ matrix such that $\Theta = \Phi\Psi$ |
| $n_j.y$ | Compressed vector for node $n_j$ |
| $y$ | Measurement vector(compressed samples) |
| $g$ | Sparse presentation of $x$ |

around the desired node (for decreasing the sensed value). [11] was the first work that dealt with CPA, in which the author used Fractional Fourier Transform (FRFT) as the secret sparsifying basis. However, the complexity of this method restricted its applicability on power and storage constrained sensor nodes. The authors of [12] proposed another solution to address the CPA, efficient in terms of computation and memory, using chaotic sequences as secret values. However, they didn't provide enough explanation on how the secret values are exchanged in secure manner by the legitimate users.

**Known Plain-Text Attack (KPA).** In KPA it is assumed that the attacker knows about the plain-text $x$ and the cipher-text $y$ and he/she tries to suggest the key, which is not the case in proposed work. Thus, we propose a novel and simple algorithm called key Re-generation algorithm which resists against KPA attack by changing the CS matrix in each round without sharing any information between the communication sides. Moreover, in [13], the performance evaluation is limited where we compared only with RSA and ECC algorithms, however, in our proposed scheme, a comprehensive evaluation is executed with and without CS based algorithms and the performance evaluation of the CS scheme is tested on image encryption.

## 3  The Proposed Energy Efficient and Security Scheme

This section, explain the proposed scheme which consists of two Algorithms: Mobile Distributed Clustering Algorithm (MDCA) and Lightweight CS Security Algorithm (LSS). MDCA aims to generate load balance cluster scheme. On the other hand, LSS aims to achieve high CS security performance and protect CS method from the proposed security models. The details of each algorithm can be descried as follows.

## 3.1 Mobile Distributed Clustering Algorithm

In this section, we present our proposed algorithm that enables to generate steady and balanced clusters. Every one of them has special properties that affect on the node these properties include mobility and energy.

- Mobility is an important factor in deciding the cluster-heads. In order to avoid frequent cluster-head changes, it is desirable to elect a cluster-head that does not move very quickly.
- Cluster-heads are responsible for coordinating among the cluster members, aggregating their collected data, and transmitting the aggregated data to the remote sink, directly or via multi-hop transmission mode. Since cluster-heads need to receive many packets and consume a lot of power for long range transmission, they are the ones whose energy is used up most rapidly in the cluster if they are elected for a long time. Therefor energy is an important factor.

The Criterion $C(s_i)$ of node$s_i$ properties at any time $t$ by the following formula:

$$C(s_i) = \frac{\gamma}{1 + M(s_i)} + \zeta \times REC(s_i),$$

where $\gamma + \zeta = 1$

The Criterion $C$ will be predicted at a current time $t_c$ as follows: Eq. 1 shows the formula to obtain Predicated Criterion $PC$

$$PC = \begin{cases} C_n, & \text{n is odd;} \\ \frac{t_c - t_{n-1}}{t_n - t_{n-1}}(C_n - C_{n-1}) + C_{n-1}, & \text{n is even.} \end{cases} \tag{1}$$

We introduce a parameter termed as cluster-hop, $r_{hop}$. Cluster-hop is defined as the maximum number of direct hops between a cluster head node and nodes at the cluster periphery. This dynamic parameter determines the dimensions of the clusters formed by the algorithm and serves as an input for the cluster formation process.

$MDCA$ consists of two phases; Information Update and Cluster Formation phase. In information update phase each node (Vehicle)calculates its predicted criteria $PC$. Then, based on the cluster-hop $r_{hop}$, the local $PC$ dissemination process is carried out. While in cluster formation phase, once the predicted combined criteria dissemination process is effectuated and the nodes have a weighted view of their neighborhood, the cluster organization can be performed thereby forming the physical clusters.

**Pase 1: Information Update.** Firstly, each node calculates its $PC$ (Algorithm 1, line 1). The second step of the algorithm is a method of disseminating the estimated $PC$ of nodes in its $r_{hop}$ neighborhood. The step-by-step operation of the algorithm is described in Algorithm 1. Once the algorithm has performed

$r_{hop}$ runs of local iterations using the exchanged messages, each node in the network will have information about the node which has the maximum $PC$ in its $r_{hop}$ neighborhood. The synchronization between nodes for the algorithm is not required since the node verifies (Algorithm 1, lines 9–12) for $PC$ information of neighboring nodes after a pre-defined wait period. This algorithm of Predicted Criterion Dissemination is efficient and allows the formation of larger clusters bounded by $r_{hop}$.

---

**Algorithm 1.** Predicted Criterion Algorithm(PCA)

---

1: Calculate $PC(s_i)$ using equation 1
2: $M_i.C \leftarrow PC(s_i)$
3: $M_i.Id \leftarrow i$
4: **while** $r_{cl} > 0$ **do**
5:     Transmit $M_i$ to $s_j$ $\forall s_j \in N(s_i)$.
6:     Wait a period of time to receive the $M_j$ from all $s_j \in N(s_i)$
7:     **if** all messages received **then**
8:         Determine maximum $M_j.C$.
9:         **if** $M_j.C > M_i.C$ **then**
10:             $M_i.C = M_j.C$
11:             $M_i.id = M_j.id$
12:         **end if**
13:     **end if**
14:     $r_{cl} = r_{cl} - 1$
15: **end while**

---

**Phase 2: Cluster Formation.** After the nodes have obtained a largest $PC$ using dissemination process; we move to the cluster formation phase which is a distributed process. We do not adopt a greedy approach of cluster formation where the largest $PC$ node advertises to other neighboring nodes to join their clusters. The objective is to form nearly equal sized and distributed clusters with self-decided cluster admissions. The steps of cluster formation procedure are described in Algorithm 2. Briefly MDCA algorithm runs as follows:

Each node $s_i$ which has the largest $PC$ value consider itself as cluster head and broadcast $CH$ message contains $PC(s_i)$ value, otherwise $s_i$ elects the node which has the largest $PCC$ value and send $My\_CH$ message (Algorithm 2, lines 1–7). If node $s_i$ received a $CH$ message, it registers the message and waits for all $CH$ messages. If there are multiple messages, choose node which has lower $PC$ value as cluster head and sends a $Join$ message to the source node (Algorithm 2, lines 8–13). The cluster head will keep information of all the nodes in its cluster in a cluster table and updates the cluster table depending on received $Join$ messages(Algorithm 2, lines 14–16).

---

**Algorithm 2. MDCA**

---

1: **if** $(M_i.id == i)$ OR ( $My\_CH$ message received) **then**
2:     $s_i$ considered as Cluster head
3:     Broadcast a $CH(C(s_i))$ message for all neighbors
4: **else**
5:     Select node $s_{j=M_i.id}$ as cluster head
6:     Broadcast a $My\_CH$ message to $s_j$
7: **end if**
8: **if** $s_i$ received $CH$ message **then**
9:     Wait a period of time
10:     **if** time expired **then**
11:        send $Join$ message to $s_j$ which has minimum $PC$
12:     **end if**
13: **end if**
14: **if** $s_i$ received $Join$ message from $s_j$ **then**
15:     Update the cluster table by $s_j$
16: **end if**

---

### 3.2 Lightweight CS Security Algorithm (LSS)

In the previous section, we have explained the ability of CS strategy to reduce the data size without involving complex mathematical computations which models it a convenient solution to reduce the data proceedings in IoT. Also, its potential to perform simultaneous compression and encryption makes it more attractive.

The actual data $x$ is transformed into the compressed sample $y$ with the help of $\Phi$. The step is identical to that of encryption using block ciphers, where $x$, $y$ and $\Phi$ represent plain text, cipher text and the key respectively. CS based encryption scheme works based on the fact that attacker cannot generate $\Phi$ (the sensing matrix) as he/she doesn't have the generator seed called pseudo-random key. The associated concerns are: the nodes and BS have to securely communicate the seeds to generate $\Phi$; at the same time CS based encryption scheme is vulnerable to CPA.

To address these challenges, we introduce lightweight CS security scheme that: (1) enables the nodes (Vehicles) and the BS to securely exchange the pseudo-random key in a simple way, and (2) introduces a new method to safeguard the CS scheme from CPA. We consider the scenario between one node, the BS and the attacker (refer Fig. 1, for simplicity. The proposed strategy has several benefits such as:

- The proposed strategy transferred all complex mathematical computations to BS.
- It doesn't require the keys to be pre-stored in the nodes.
- All operations done by the sensor nodes are simple and doesn't require additional energy or storage space.

The proposed scheme involves four stages: (1) Key generation, (2) Key exchange, and (3) Data Compression with Encryption.

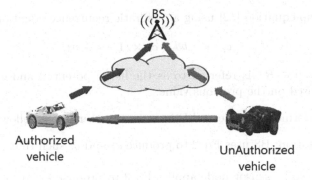

**Fig. 1.** The proposed scenario: Two legitimate sides (sensor node and BS) and one malicious side (Hacker).

**The Key Generation Stage.** We describe the performed tasks for generating keys by the WSN nodes and the BS as follows:

- **At the Base Station:** Bernoulli or Gaussian distribution matrix are the most favorable choice for CS strategy. Any technique for pseudo-random number generation uses a vector or a number to start its process (known as seed), which can either be selected randomly or initialized. Therefore, if the node and base station uses identical values for seed, then they will generate the identical random matrix $\Phi$ for data encryption/decryption. Main disadvantage about this is: if the adversary guesses this seed successfully, he/she will be able to produce same matrix. One goal of the proposed scheme is to generate this seed and make it difficult to be guessed by the attacker. We use 2D chaotic maps [43] to generate the seed $g_s$, as we assume there is no resource restrictions at BS.

  Chaos: It describes certain nonlinear dynamic systems that appears to be random and unpredictable. The 2-D Logistic mapping equations [40]:

  $$x_{i+1} = \mu_1 x_i (1 - x_i) + \gamma_1 y_i^2, \quad y_{i+1} = \mu_2 y_i (1 - y_i) + \gamma_2 (x_i^2 + x_i y_i). \quad (2)$$

  Here, $i$ denotes the count of iterations to produce $x_{i+1}$ and $y_{i+1}$. The $x_i$ and $y_i$ values are selected as start values to Eq. 2. The dynamic nature of 2D Logistic mapping is governed using the power equation parameters $\mu_1$, $\mu_2$, $\gamma_1$ and $\gamma_2$. Equation 2 increases the quadratic coupling of the items $x_i^2$, $y_i^2$, and $x_i y_i$ and enhances security. When $2.75 < \mu_1 < 3.4$, $0.15 < \gamma_1 < 0.21$, $2.7 < \mu_2 < 3.45$ and $0.13 < \gamma_2 < 0.15$, Eq. 2 attains chaotic-state and produces a chaotic-sequence in the range $(0, 1]$ [43].

- **At the WSN node:** CP-attack (CPA) can threaten CS scheme where the adversary can acquire the ciphertext $y$ for any plaintext $x$. To safeguard CS scheme from such an attack, the proposed scheme multiplies $y$ with secret values $S$ to generate a secret compressed sample $y'$. To produce $S$, the node generates a random value $e_1$ and multiples it with the received seed from BS $(g_s)$, i.e., $S = g_s \times e_1^{-1}$. For generating $e_1$, the node applies simple logistic chaotic map equation [12] using a quadratic recurrence equation.

$$c_{n+1} = bd \times c_n \times (1 - c + n).$$     (3)

Here, $bd \neq 0 \in R^+$ is referred to as the biotic potential and every value in Eq. 3 is based on the previous value.

The steps performed at node and BS can be summarized as follows:

- At Base Station: BS uses Eq. 2 to produce $e_2$ and $g_s$ such that $e_2 = x_{i+1}$ and $g_s = y_{i+1}$.
- At Sensor Node: sensor node applies Eq. 3 to produce $e_1$ s.t., $e_1 = c_{n+1}$ and computes its inverse $e_1^{-1}$ s.t., $e_1 * e_1^{-1} = 1$.

**The Key Exchange Stage.** The CS based strategy for encryption depends on an assumption that only the node and the base station possess identical values for seed to produce the same sensing matrix $\Phi$. However, this assumption faces serious problem if the adversary is listening to their communication channel. The base station and the node have to exchange the seed securely. To prevent this issue, we propose a Key Exchange Algorithm as presented in Algorithm 3.

The new algorithm permits safe and simple exchange of the seed between the base station and the node, as follows:

- BS computes and sends $k_1 = g_s^{e_2}$ to the node. If adversary obtains $k_1$ and uses it as the seed, it will provide him/her wrong results and makes it difficult to guess the $g_s$ because BS uses 2D chaotic map to produce this number.
- The node computes and sends $k_2 = k_1^{e_1}$ to BS. As $k_1$, the adversary will encounter the same difficulty, if he/she uses $k_2$.
- The BS calculates $k_3 = k_2^{1/e_2} = g_s^{e_1}$ and sends the value of $k_3$ to the node who can generate the seed by computing $g_s' = k_3 * {}^{1/e_1} = g_s$.
- Finally, BS and the node possess identical values of seed $g_s$; they initiate the succeeding phase. The steps involved in this phase is described in Fig. 2.

---

**Algorithm 3.** Key Exchange Algorithm

---

1: BS calculates $k_1 = g_s^{e_2}$
2: BS sends $k_1$ to the node
3: Node computes $k_2 = k_1^{e_1}$
4: Node transfers $k_2$ to the BS
5: BS computes $k_3 = k_2^{1/e_2} = g_s^{e_1}$
6: BS sends $k_3$ to the node
7: Node computes $g_s' = k_3^{1/e_1} = g_s$.
8: Finally both the node and BS possess the identical values for $g_s' = g_s$, and sensing matrix $\Phi$ is generated using $g_s$ as seed.

---

**Key Exchange Algorithm Procedure.** We present the mathematical steps of Algorithm 3 in this section.

– First as mentioned in key generation phase, the node produces $e_1$ and the BS produces $e_2$ and $g_s$ and sends $g_s$ to the node in safely.
– The BS computes and sends $k_1 = g_s^{e_2}$ to the node.
– Node uses $k_1$ to compute and sends $k_2 = (g_s^{e_2})^{e_1} = g_s^{e_1 e_2}$ to the BS.
– The BS calculates $k_3 = k_2^{1/e_2} = (g_s^{e_1 e_2})^{1/e_2} = g_s^{e_1}$, then sends $k_3$ to the sensor node
– Finally using $k_3$, the sensor node calculates $g_s' = k_3^{e_1} = (g_s^{e_1})^{1/e_1} = g_s$
– At the end, the node and BS possess identical values for seed $g_s' = g_s$.
– BS and the node initiate the next stage.

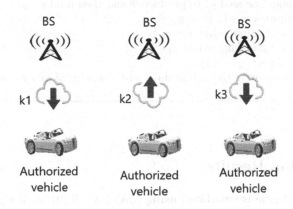

**Fig. 2.** Key Sharing Phase Procedures.

### 3.3   The Data Compression with Encryption Stage

As we discussed above, the node and BS possess identical value for seed. They use Algorithm 4 for encrypting the compressed data as follows:

– The node applies seed to produce the sensing matrix $\Phi$ for encrypting the compressed data to $y$.
– The node transfers this $y$ to BS to compute the secret compressed sample $y'$. A secret value $S$ is multiplied with $y$ to produce $y'$ (refer Eq. 4).

$$y' = y \times S \tag{4}$$

Here $S = g_s^{-1}$. The node then transfers $y'$ to the BS.
Now if the CPA attacker generates any plain text and send it to the sensor node which encrypts it and then send back $y'$ to attacker, he/she will generate wrong cipher text to his/her plain text and so attacker can never generate the correct matrix $\Phi$. Therefore, the proposed scheme succeeds to safeguard CS scheme from CPA.

- Finally, BS calculates the secret value $S$ s.t., $S = g_s^{-1}$ and recomputes $y$ from $y'$ (refer Eq. 5).

$$y = y' \diagup S. \tag{5}$$

- The BS applies the same seed $g_s$ to produce $\Phi$ for encrypting and reconstructing the actual data using $y$ with the help of any reconstruction algorithm such as OMP algorithm [41]. Without knowing this seed $g_s$, it is impractical to produce the same $\Phi$ and hence no one except BS can reproduce $y$.

---

**Algorithm 4.**: Data Compression with Encryption

1: The node calculates the $S$ s.t., $S = g_s^{-1}$.
2: The node applies the seed $g_s'$ to produce $\Phi$ and then produce $y$.
3: The node computes $y'$ s.t., $y' = y * S$
4: BS calculates the secret value $S = g_s^{-1}$
5: BS generates $\Phi$ by making use of $g_s$
6: BS recomputes $y$ s.t, $y' = y/S$
7: Lastly, the BS recovers the actual data with the help of any reconstruction algorithm.

---

# 4  Simulation Results

The proposed scheme is simulated using MATLAB R2015a. We provide in this section, the performance results of our scheme in terms of key generation sensitivity and security level against CPA attack. Furthermore, the results include comparison between the proposed scheme and SeDC, CDG, SCDG, ECEG and RSA-1024 algorithms for data encryption and network lifetime. All evaluations in this section depend on real data set of 54 sensor nodes at Intel Berkeley Research Lab [44]. Each WSN node detects the environmental temperature, light, humidity and voltage. In our evaluation, we assume that nodes are deployed randomly in the temperature field to monitor and measure this field. We used MDCA algorithm to organize these nodes into clusters, where the network nodes N are grouped into various clusters. The CMs of every cluster transfers their data to their respective CHs; the CHs perform aggregation and transfers the resultant data to BS. We used DCT transformer as the sparsifying domain as shown in Fig. 6. Separate observation matrix $\Phi$ is employed for each test sample, with entries drawn from zero mean and $1/N$ standard deviation Gaussian distribution. OMP [41] algorithm was implemented at the BS for reconstructing the plaintexts. The 2D chaotic maps parameters $\mu_1 = 3.33$, $\gamma_1 = 0.17$, $\mu_2 = 3.44$, and $\gamma_2 = 0.14$ are used (Fig. 3).

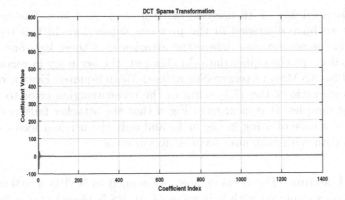

**Fig. 3.** Temperature traces in DCT domain.

**Analysis of Key Space.** The key space have to be significantly sized to withstand brute-force type of attacks. Key space size can be defined as the total count of distinct keys used for encryption. In our work, to produce the key (seed $g_s$), the BS adopted the 2D chaotic map with parameters $\mu_1, \gamma_1, \mu_2, \gamma_2, x_i$, and $y_i$. We employ precision equivalent to $10^{-14}$, therefore, the size of key space reaches $10^{84} \cong 2^{280}$, which is larger than $2^{128}$, i.e., the key space is relatively larger sized to withstand brute-force type of attacks.

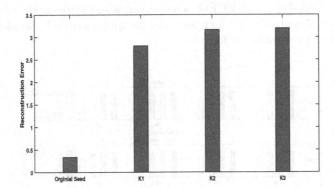

**Fig. 4.** Reconstruction Error over Intel Temperature trace in case of the seed value is Original seed, $k_1$, $k_2$ and $k_3$ respectively.

**Data Reconstruction.** In this part, we applied the proposed scheme to recover the signals obtained from temperature field, to explain the security offered by the developed approach. In the developed approach, the BS and the sensor nodes share a number of keys between them, including the seed in key exchange phase. The adversary may capture these keys and try to find the relation between them to guess the seed key or to use one of them as a seed key. The first case is difficult as we have discussed in the previous subsection. In this test, we are interested in the second case, where the attacker uses these keys one by one as the seed to decrypt the cipher data. In this test, the accuracy in reconstruction is provided by ANMSE (Average Normalized Mean Squared Error), referred to as the average ratio of the $\|L\|_2$ norm of the reconstruction error to $\|x\|_2$ over the 500 test samples. It is clear from Fig. 4 that the attacker fails to obtain the correct data in case of using $k_1$, $k_2$ or $k_3$ and only the original seed can recover the correct data with minimum reconstruction error.

**Network Lifetime.** The network area is assumed to be $100 \times 100\,\text{m}^2$, having 50 to 200 nodes deployed with increment of 50. BS is placed at $x = 50$, $y = 50$. CR varies from 10% to 20% with increment of 5. Here, we adopt the energy consumption model and parameters as proposed in [42].

Figure 5 shows the lifetime for the proposed scheme, CDG, SeDC and SCDG algorithms. It shows that the performance of the proposed scheme and CDG algorithm are equal and better than SCDG and SeDC algorithms because according to SCDG some extra information has to be transmitted between nodes and BS, which increases the data transmission overhead and unnecessary higher traffic and so decreases the network lifetime. However, in SeDC each sensor node do encryption and the compression which increases the computation beside the public key size that leads to decrease the network lifetime. Moreover, Fig. 6 shows the network lifetime performance in our proposed scheme, ECEG and RSA. It is clear that RSA-1024 and ECEG achieve the worst performance because the behavior of public algorithms increases the computation and complexity which make them not preferable for IoT.

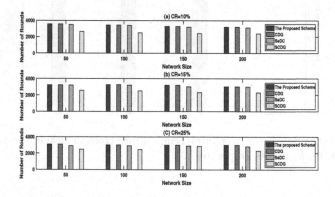

**Fig. 5.** Network lifetime versus Number of nodes

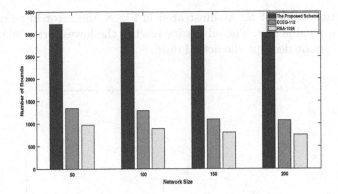

**Fig. 6.** Network lifetime in proposed scheme, ECEG and RSA.

**CPA Attacks Test.** Here, we present the test results of our scheme against CPA. We use the same specification as in [12] and we define two types of attackers: 1)oblivious and 2)non-oblivious.

**The Oblivious Attacker.** In this case, the adversary can initiate CPA successfully and obtains the ciphertext $y\prime$ that the nodes have transmitted. But he/she is not aware of the secret value $S$, and then by decrypting $y\prime$ using any reconstruction algorithm produce very high reconstruction error as shown in Fig. 7, so he/she can never succeed to decrypt the sensor data.

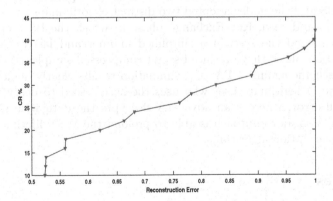

**Fig. 7.** The oblivious attacker: Compression Ratio vs. Reconstruction Error

**Non-oblivious Attacker.** Here, an adversary initiates CPA and know the secret value $S$. We assume that the adversary will guess $S\prime$ s.t., $S\prime = (1 - r) * S$, with $r = 5\%$ to $25\%$ (with incremental of 5) as the percentage (%) of deviation from the actual value of $S$. As illustrated in Fig. 8, the error in reconstruction is large for any value of $r$. The adversary reaches the lowest error when $r = 5\%$, but he/she cannot decrypt the actual data.

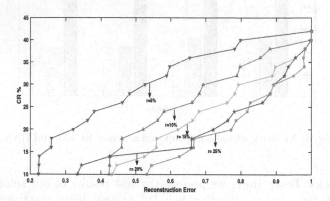

**Fig. 8.** The non-oblivious attacker: Compression Ratio vs. Reconstruction Error

## 5   Conclusion

We have presented a lightweight security scheme using CS-based encryption/decryption method. This scheme operates in three phases: Key-Generation phase, the BS and the nodes adopted two distinct chaotic maps to produce random numbers and seed, Key-Exchange phase in which the BS and the nodes securely exchanged the seed in a simplified manner and lastly, Compression with encryption phase that produced secret compressed samples to offer immunity to our scheme against CPA. The simulation results clearly depicts that our scheme allows a legitimate user who uses the actual seed to decrypt the data with a small error, whereas an adversary decrypts the data with significantly larger error. Also, our approach is able to prolong the WSN lifetime compared to existing encryption algorithms.

## References

1. Liu, X., Yang, Q., Luo, J., Ding, B., Zhang, S.: An energy-aware offloading framework for edge-augmented mobile RFID systems. IEEE Internet Things J. **6**, 3994–4004 (2018)
2. Zheng, J., Simplot-Ryl, D., Bisdikian, C., Mouftah, H.T.: The internet of things. IEEE Commun. Mag. **49**, 30–31 (2011)
3. Palopoli, L., Passerone, R., Rizano, T.: Scalable offline optimization of industrial wireless sensor networks. IEEE Trans. Ind. Inf. **7**(2), 328–329 (2011)

4. Lazarescu, M.T.: Design of a WSN platform for long-term environmental monitoring for IoT applications. IEEE J. Emerg. Sel. Top. Circuits Syst. **3**(1), 45–54 (2013)
5. Del-Valle-Soto, C., Mex-Perera, C., Monroy, R., Nolazco-Flores, J.: On the routing protocol influence on the resilience of wireless sensor networks to jamming attacks. Sensors **15**(4), 7619–7649 (2015)
6. Mollin, R.A.: An Introduction to Cryptography. CRC Press, Boca Raton (2006)
7. Vanstone, S.A., Menezes, A.J., Orschot, P.C.: Handbook of Applied Cryptography. CRC Press, Boca Raton (1999)
8. Fragkiadakis, A., Tragos, E., Traganitis, A.: Lightweight and secure encryption using channel measurements. In: 4th International Conference on Wireless Communications, Vehicular Technology, Information Theory and Aerospace, Aalborg, pp. 1–5 (2014)
9. Zhang, Y., Xiang, Y., Zhang, L.Y., Rong, Y., Guo, S.: Secure wireless communications based on compressive sensing: a survey. IEEE Commun. Surv. Tutor. **21**, 1093–1111 (2018)
10. Zhang, Y., Xiang, Y., Zhang, L.Y.: In Secure Compressive Sensing in Multimedia Data, Cloud Computing and IoT. Springer, Singapore (2019)
11. Zhang, L., Wong, K., Li, C., Zhang, Y.: Towards secure compressive sampling scheme. CoRR (2014)
12. Fragkiadakis, A., Kovacevic, L., Tragos, E.: Enhancing compressive sensing encryption in constrained devices using chaotic sequences. In: Proceedings of the 2nd Workshop on Experiences in the Design and Implementation of Smart Objects, pp. 17–22 (2016)
13. Aziz, A., Singh, K.: Lightweight security scheme for internet of things. Wirel. Pers. Commun. **104**(2), 577–593 (2019)
14. Tragos, E., et al.: Enabling reliable and secure IoT-based smart city applications. In: Proceedings of PERCOM, pp. 111–116 (2014)
15. Abdallah, W., Boudriga, N., Kim, D.: An efficient and scalable key management mechanism for wireless sensor networks. In: 17th International Conference on ICACT, India. IEEE (2015)
16. Othman, S.B., Bahattab, A.A., Trad, A., Youssef, H.: Confidentiality and integrity for data aggregation in WSN using homomorphic encryption. Wirel. Pers. Commun. **80**, 867–889 (2015)
17. Suganthi, N., Vembu, S.: Energy efficient key management scheme for wireless sensor networks. Int. J. Comput. Commun. Control **9**, 71–78 (2014)
18. Kadri, B., Feham, M., Mhammed, A.: Efficient and secured ant routing algorithm for wireless sensor networks. Int. J. Netw. Secur. **16**, 149–156 (2014)
19. Geetha, R., Kannan, E.: A hybrid key management approach for secure communication in wireless sensor networks. Indian J. Sci. Technol. **8**, 654–659 (2015)
20. Boubiche, D.E., Boubiche, S., Bilami, A.: A cross-layer watermarking-based mechanism for data aggregation integrity in heterogeneous WSNs. IEEE Commun. Lett. **19**, 823–826 (2015)
21. Roy, S., Karjeea, J., Rawata, U.S., Pratik, D., Deyb, N.: Symmetric key encryption technique: a cellular automata based approach in wireless sensor networks. Procedia Comput. Sci. **78**, 408–414 (2016)
22. Luo, C., Wu, F., Sun, J., Chen, C.: Compressive data gathering for large-scale wireless sensor networks, pp. 145–156. ACM (2009)
23. Hu, P., Xing, K., Cheng, X., Wei, H., Zhu, H.: Information leaks out: attacks and countermeasures on compressive data gathering in wireless sensor networks, pp. 1258–1266. IEEE (2014)

24. Candes, E.J., Tao, T.: Near-optimal signal recovery from random projections: universal encoding strategies. IEEE Trans. Inf. Theory **52**(12), 5406–5425 (2006)
25. Cossalter, M., Valenzise, G., Tagliasacchi, M., Tubaro, S.: Joint compressive video coding and analysis. IEEE Trans. Multimed. **12**(3), 168–183 (2010)
26. Premnath, S., et al.: Secret key extraction from wireless signal strength in real environments. IEEE Trans. Mob. Comput. **12**(5), 917–930 (2013)
27. Li, Z., Xu, W., Miller, R., Trappe, W.: Securing wireless systems via lower layer enforcements. In: Proceedings of WiSe, pp. 33–42 (2006)
28. Dautov, R., Tsouri, G.: Establishing secure measurement matrix for compressed sensing using wireless physical layer security. In: Proceedings of ICNC, pp. 354–358 (2013)
29. Fragkiadakis, A., Tragos, E., Makrogiannakis, A., Papadakis, S., Charalampidis, P., Surligas, M.: Signal processing techniques for energy efficiency, security, and reliability in the IoT domain. In: Mavromoustakis, C.X., Mastorakis, G., Batalla, J.M. (eds.) Internet of Things (IoT) in 5G Mobile Technologies. MOST, vol. 8, pp. 419–447. Springer, Cham (2016). https://doi.org/10.1007/978-3-319-30913-2_18
30. Rachlin, Y., Baron, D.: The secrecy of compressed sensing measurements. In: Proceedings of Allerton Conference on Communication, Control, and Computing, pp. 813–817 (2008)
31. Cambareri, V., Mangia, M., Pareschi, F., Rovatti, R., Setti, G.: Low-complexity multiclass encryption by compressed sensing. IEEE Trans. Signal Process. **63**, 2183–2195 (2015)
32. Rachlin, Y., Baron, D.: The secrecy of compressed sensing measurements. In: Proceedings of 46th Annual Allerton Conference on Communication, Control, and Computing, pp. 813–817 (2008)
33. Zhang, Y., et al.: Low-cost and confidentiality-preserving data acquisition for internet of multimedia things. IEEE Internet Things J. **5**, 3442–3451 (2017)
34. Xue, W., Luo, C., Lan, G., Rana, R.K., Hu, W., Seneviratne, A.: Kryptein: a compressive-sensing-based encryption scheme for the internet of things. In: Proceedings of the 16th ACM/IEEE International Conference on Information Processing in Sensor Networks (IPSN), pp. 169–180 (2017)
35. Pudi, V., Chattopadhyay, A., Lam, K.-Y.: Secure and lightweight compressive sensing using stream cipher. IEEE Trans. Circuits Syst. II Express Briefs **65**(3), 371–375 (2018)
36. George, S.N., Pattathil, D.P.: A secure LFSR based random measurement matrix for compressive sensing. Sens. Imaging **15**(1), 1–29 (2014)
37. Dautov, R., Tsouri, G.R.: Establishing secure measurement matrix for compressed sensing using wireless physical layer security. In: International Conference on Computing, Networking and Communications (ICNC), pp. 354–358. IEEE (2013)
38. Chai, X., Gan, Z., Chen, Y., Zhang, Y.: A visually secure image encryption scheme based on compressive sensing. Signal Process. **134**, 35–51 (2017)
39. Zhang, P., Wang, S., Guo, K., Wang, J.: A secure data collection scheme based on compressive sensing in wireless sensor networks. Ad Hoc Netw. **70**, 73–84 (2018)
40. Mallat, S.: A Wavelet Tour of Signal Processing. Academic Press, Cambridge (1999)
41. Tropp, J., Gilber, A.: Signal recovery from random measurements via orthogonal matching pursuit. IEEE Trans. Inf. Theory **53**(14), 4655–4666 (2007)
42. Abo-Zahhad, M., Farrag, M., Ali, A., Amin, O.: An energy consumption model for wireless sensor networks. In: International Conference on Energy Aware Computing Systems & Applications (ICEAC), pp. 1–4. IEEE (2015)

43. Liu, H., Zhu, Z., Jiang, H., Wang, B.: A novel image encryption algorithm based on improved 3D chaotic cat map. In: The 9th International Conference for Young Computer Scientists (2008)

44. Intel Berkeley Research Lab Data Set (2018). http://db.csail.mit.edu/labdata/labdata.html. Accessed 9 Apr

45. Aziz, A., Singh, K., Osamy, W., et al.: An efficient compressive sensing routing scheme for internet of things based wireless sensor networks. Wirel. Pers. Commun. **114**, 1905–1925 (2020). https://doi.org/10.1007/s11277-020-07454-4

46. Aziz, A., Salim, A., Osamy, W.: Adaptive and efficient compressive sensing based technique for routing in wireless sensor networks. In: Proceedings of INTHITEN (IoT and its Enablers) Conference, pp. 3–4 (2014)

# Impact of Digital Technologies on Women's Employment

Aziza Bakhramovna Irmatova and Malika Ilhomovna Akbarova$^{(\boxtimes)}$

Department of Human Resources Management, Tashkent State University of Economics,
Tashkent, Uzbekistan
{1a.irmatova,2m.akbarova}@tsue.uz

**Abstract.** Technology is an engine for growth with great potential to transform women's self-efficacy and social capital. This article focuses on women's employment within the context of the development of digital technologies and sheds light on the intersection of technology, self-efficacy and social capital in developing countries. The use of technology allows women to transform their social and economic lives by changing and reshaping processes that enable opportunities for growth and development—ultimately offering a bridge to close the many gaps in human socioeconomic development in developing countries. To this end, we offer several recommendations for women and organizations to expand their application of technological capabilities for their initiatives and directions for self-employment through Internet platforms. There are recommendations to increase the employment of women in the digital economy by removing barriers in the field of IT and strengthening their motivation through competitions and rewards.

**Keywords:** women's employment · digital technologies · information technologies · digital knowledge · SEM model · digital business · intellectual labor

## 1 Introduction

Globalization and acceleration of information processes in society have dramatically increased the importance of information labor in terms of its reception, processing, exchange, and storage. DT (Digital technologies) plays an important role in socioeconomic development, growth of GDP, human potential and employment, labor productivity and poverty reduction, especially for developing countries[1]. The phenomenon of DT is being accepted as an important tool to attract more women to the formal sector in developing countries.[2]

---

[1] R. Kozma. National policies that connect ICT-based education reform to economic and social development Hum. Technol., 1 (2) (2005), pp. 117–156, T. Irawan ICT and economic development comparing ASEAN member states Int. Econ. Econ. Policy, 11 (1–2) (2014), pp. 97–114.

[2] Simplice A. Asongu, Nicholas M. Odhiambo. Inequality and gender inclusion: Minimum ICT policy thresholds for promoting female employment in Sub-Saharan Africa, Telecommunications Policy, Volume 44, Issue 4, 2020, 101900, ISSN 0308–5961, https://doi.org/10.1016/j.tel pol.2019.101900. (http://www.sciencedirect.com/science/article/pii/S0308596119302976).

Y. Koucheryavy and A. Aziz (Eds.): NEW2AN 2022, LNCS 13772, pp. 290–298, 2023.
https://doi.org/10.1007/978-3-031-30258-9_24

Issues such as application of information technologies, creation of new modern jobs, and training of competitive personnel based on digital economy and their employment have been emphasized by the President of our country many times. In order to achieve progress, it is necessary for us to acquire digital knowledge and modern information technologies. This gives us the opportunity to take the shortest path to ascension. After all, nowadays, information technology deeply penetrates all areas of the world.[3]

Digital technologies include products capable of storing, manipulating, transmitting, and receiving information electronically in digital form. Digital technologies include computers, the Internet, radio, mobile phones, digital cameras, geographic information systems (GIS), tracking devices, global positioning systems (GPS), barcode scanners, and smart card readers.[4]

## 2  Literature Review

Digital trends such as social media, mobile services, cloud computing, the Internet and robotics have changed the ways of collaborating, designing products, matching complex demands and supplies, standards, and procedures (Autio et al. 2018, Giones and Brem 2017).

New arrangements from organizations caused problems in time management, lack of resources, and other social and psychological discomforts while individuals tried to manage the balance between private and work life (Machado et al. 2021).

The concept of digital technologies is often illustrated as the consequence of three separate but embedded elements: digital artefacts, digital platforms, and digital infrastructures (Nambisan 2017). Digital infrastructure collects digital technology equipment and systems that present collaboration, communication, and computing capacities (Rippa and Secundo 2019). Just as the human interactions with technological platforms are a tool for competitive advantage and fiscal gain, such technologies are a tool for women to improve their participation in the economy and their quality of life (Ojokoh, Zhang, Oluwadare, and Akintola 2013).

Innovations in the area of digital technology such as the Internet, cellphones, laptops, gadgets and platforms aimed at gathering, processing and preserving big data have penetrated into our life rapidly over the past three decades. For example, more than half of global population today has access to the Internet. Consequently, this implies that digitalization may have positive implications for quality of life and economy as communication and connectedness leads to the rise of e-commerce, e-governance and more employment prospects. Digitalization can reduce inequality, improve quality of financial services, increase inclusiveness and decrease transaction and coordination costs (Abdurakhmanova G. et al. 2021).

---

[3] Mirziyoyev Sh. M. Appeal to the Oliy Majlis of the President of Republic of Uzbekistan // official site of the President of Republic of Uzbekistan https://president.uz/uz/lists/view/3324.

[4] Alhassan A. Karakara, Evans S. Osabuohien. Households' ICT access and bank patronage in West Africa: Empirical insights from Burkina Faso and Ghana, Technology in Society, Volume 56, 2019, Pages 116–125, ISSN 0160-791X, https://doi.org/10.1016/j.techsoc.2018.09.010. (http://www.sciencedirect.com/science/article/pii/S0160791X18301635).

Regarding Internet use, Van Deursen and Van Dijk (A. Van Deursen, J. Van Dijk 2014) mention the need to acquire new skills when going online due to the enormous amount of data and people's growing dependency on the exploration of this information.

Another set of studies has focused on identifying the determinants of Internet uses (T. Penard, N. Poussing, B. Mukoko, T. Piaptie 2015; J.E. Prieger 2013). These studies show that socioeconomic factors such as age, income, and educational level influence the decision to use the Internet, but they do not influence the activities that users conduct online. Internet usage patterns like communication, entertainment, social networks, and e-commerce can be largely explained as dependent on digital skills (T. Garín-Munoz, R. Lopez, T. Perez-Amaral, I. Herguera, A. Valarezo 2019).

Self-efficacy is one's belief in their capacity to employ the necessary resources needed in a particular situation (Bandura 1997). In general, individuals exert more effort and become more persistent as self-efficacy increases and, in doing so, learn how to deal with task-related obstacles. This process of inner transformation occurs when a woman recognizes both her ability to define her self-interests and her entitlement to make her own decisions (Nussbaum 2001). Kay and Shipman (2014) go so far as to suggest that confidence matters as much as competence when it comes to success.

Women have a desire to use their authenticity, affective commitment, and passion to help other women, and stories act as a great enabler for women to empower other women (Crittenden and Bliton 2019).

Since digital technology affects the "rules and conditions of social interaction" (van Dijck and Poell, 2013, p. 3), it "redirects and reimagines what empowerment means for girls and women" (Banet-Weiser 2018, p. 17). The expectancy-value theory of achievement motivation can explain the fact that women rarely choose careers in computer-related fields (Croasdell, McLeod and Simkin 2011, Wigfield and Eccles 2000).

One of the most important trends of the last two decades has been the growing adoption of mobile phones worldwide. This phenomenon is considered an important vector of economic growth, especially in developing countries (Aker and Mbiti 2010).

## 3  Research Methodology

We found it appropriate to study the impact of digital technologies on the employment of women in our Republic, and to make scientifically based proposals on the basis of empirical analysis to attract women to a wider digital economy.

In order to test this hypothesis, we preferred to conduct the analysis using the SEM (Structural equation model) method. For our analysis, we obtained independent and connected indicators, illustrated in Table 1. These indicators were selected on the basis of foreign and domestic scientists' research, which are highlighted in the literature review. These indicators were obtained from the data of the State Statistics Committee of the Republic of Uzbekistan for 2008–2020. Primary data is provided in the appendix.

During 12 years, on average, 5,387.5 thousand women were employed in the economy. Of those, 63.75 were provided with telephone devices (per 100 permanent residents). Mobile phone subscribers consisted of 19.18 million people, whereas a number of computers per household was 36.3 (100 per permanent household). The residents,

**Table 1.** Statistical analysis of DT indicators related to women's employment

| № | Variables | Classification of Variables | Number of observations | Mean | Deviation from the standard | Min | Max |
|---|-----------|-----------------------------|------------------------|------|-----------------------------|-----|-----|
| 1 | $Y_a$ | Women employed in the economy | 12 | 5,387.5 | 554.5 | 4,583.8 | 6,189.2 |
| 2 | $X_{a1}$ | Provision of the population with telephone devices (per 100 permanent residents) | 12 | 63.75 | 16.2 | 22 | 87 |
| 3 | $X_{a2}$ | Number of mobile phone subscribers, thousand units | 12 | 19,180.6 | 5,226.75 | 5,873 | 25,442 |
| 4 | $X_{a3}$ | Number of computers per 100 households | 9 | 36.3 | 16.9 | 12 | 59 |
| 5 | $X_{a4}$ | Internet usage | 12 | 7,013,211 | 4,018,189 | 340,436 | 1.33e+07 |
| 6 | $X_{a5}$ | Average salary in the information industry | 9 | 1,687,390 | 828,355.2 | 741,256 | 3,329,592 |
| 7 | $X_{a6}$ | Number of banking institutions per 100,000 adult population | 8 | 9.8 | 2.3 | 7.9 | 14.8 |

who used the Internet made up 7,013,211 and the average fee for an information system was equal to 1,687,390 UZS.

## 4 Results

With the aid of STATA-15 application program, we managed to get a model of the following form, by constructing block diagrams of all variables through the SEM builder (see Fig. 1).

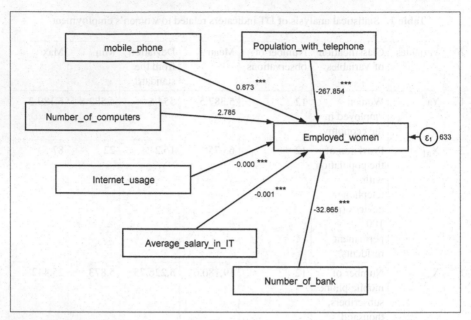

**Fig. 1.** SEM model of impact of digital technologies on women's employment Note: N = 12 (number of observations), *** − p < 0.001, R2 = 99.

Taking these factors into account, we constructed the regression equation below:

$$\hat{Y}_a = 7483,6 - 267,853X_{a1} + 0,872X_{a2} - 0,00004X_{a4} - 0,0007X_{a5} - 32,864X_{a6} + \varepsilon \tag{1}$$

The coefficients of the regression equation showed that all except $Xa_3$ were significant (p < 0.001).

The following indicators were used to check the adequacy of the model.

Based on R-squared values, the model was found to be 99% significant for all selected variables. In particular, changes in the percentage of women engaged in scientific research are explained by selected variables ($Xa_1$, $Xa_2$, $Xa_3$, $Xa_4$, $Xa_5$, $Xa_6$) in 99%.

- According to the result of the correlation analysis, there is multicollinearity in the sum of initial factors, i.e. high correlation between independent variables, and linear correlation between arguments. Bentley-Raykov multicorrelation coefficient between the obtained indicators was determined to be 0.99, which is explained by the existence of a relationship between all variables.
- The comparative comparison index (CFI) is equal to 1 and this is a very good indicator, which means that all obtained indicators are independent and do not duplicate each other.
- Root mean square error of approximation (RMSEA) is 0 (error is assumed to be 0.05), which means that errors in each variable in the calculations are equal to zero.

- Estat mindices (extended statistics reporting modification indices) command shows the most effective ways to adjust the variables so that the selected model has a better result. According to this, it turned out that our model is the most correct and optimal (no modification indices to report).

## 5   Discussion

Based on results of analysis of implemented SEM model, the following conclusions were reached.

It was determined that if provision with telephone devices per 100 permanent residents increases by 1 unit, the number of employed women in the economy will decrease by 267 and if number of banking institutions increases by 1 unit per 100,000 adult population the number of employed women will decrease by 32. Of course, the digitization process has a negative impact on employment. The widespread use of information technology brings technological changes, and creation of new professions and jobs. Therefore, it is necessary to increase digital literacy of women in advance.

It can be seen that changes in the average salary in Internet use and information sector have little effect on the employment of women, but in general, these indicators are also found to be inversely related. Overall, this indicates that the problem of women's employment with the help of Internet tools is getting worse, while the issues of Internet coverage are being implemented technically in the Republic. Therefore, special attention should be paid to the development of women's digital skills along with technical support for digital technologies.

It was found that if the number of mobile phone subscribers increases by one unit, the number of employed women increases by 0.8.

The regional analysis showed that the percentage of Internet users among women is in Surkhandarya (39.8%), Sirdarya (62.3%), Tashkent (65.3%), and Jizzakh (68.5%) regions. Also, in Surkhandarya, Sirdarya, and Tashkent regions, this indicator has changed a little in the last 3 years. On the contrary, in Andijan, Kashkadarya, Navoi, Fergana regions, it can be observed that the number of Internet users among women has increased sharply (see Fig. 2).

As a result of the research, it was found that the majority of mobile phone users in our republic are men (more than 95%). Women using mobile/cellular phones showed high rates in Tashkent city (97.4%), Surkhandarya (94.5%), Samarkand (94.1%), and Kashkadarya (94%) regions. It was found that the level of women's use of mobile phones is lower in Sirdarya (84.8%), Navoi (85.4%) and Jizzakh (86.7%) regions (see Fig. 3.)

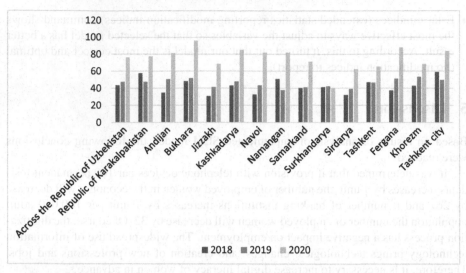

**Fig. 2.** Changes in the percentage of Internet users among women in Uzbekistan, %[5]

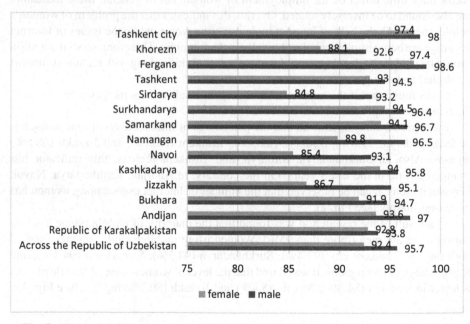

**Fig. 3.** Share of mobile phone users in Uzbekistan in 2020, by gender, % (See footnote 5)

Thus, the rapid innovative development of the country, especially in rural areas, the wide use of information technologies in providing employment to women deserves special attention. Therefore, it is necessary to improve the mechanisms of maintaining

---

[5] https://gender.stat.uz.

existing jobs and creating new jobs for women with the wide involvement of public and private investment projects aimed at creating remote jobs for women with higher education, professional knowledge and high qualifications.

It is desirable to support the development of women's initiatives and direct women to self-employment (e-commerce activities, copywriting, freelance, training system through Internet platforms (Zoom, Google Meet, etc.), etc.).

Supporting women in the development of digital skills and entrepreneurship in the field of digital business, increasing digital literacy, creating electronic platforms and affordable internet service packages for women entrepreneurs in remote districts, promoting women in STEM (Science, Technology, Engineering, Mathematics) and high-tech fields. To increase the participation of girls, it is possible to achieve an increase in the employment of women in the digital economy by removing barriers to education in the field of IT and by strengthening the motivation of girls through competitions and awards.

## 6 Conclusion

The rapid introduction of modern innovative technologies in the organization of women's work is an important condition for the prompt development of the Republic of Uzbekistan, which requires close support for reforms based on modern innovative ideas, developments and technologies, which ensure a quick and high-quality transition of the country to the ranks of leading countries.

Modern requirements for women's work are aimed at increasing its efficiency, using previously acquired work skills, and in the process of professional training and learning, showing their abilities, especially in new techniques, methods and methodologies of specialized and intellectual work.

These requirements should also apply to the following: finally choosing the means of intellectual labor activity, creating effective conditions that allow to increase its efficiency, expanding the opportunities for cooperation and communication as a necessary component of the integrated system of intellectual labor relations of a woman in her professional field.

The insufficient development of the information and communication network in Uzbekistan, the lack of qualified female specialists in this field, the insufficient level of coverage of the Internet network throughout the republic and the low speed of the Internet, as well as the limited access to communication, the Internet and computers for all segments of the population limit employment in this area.

## References

Autio, E., Nambisan, S., Thomas, L.D.W., Wright, M.: Digital affordances, spatial affordances, and the genesis of entrepreneurial ecosystems. Strateg. Entrep. J. **12**(1), 72–95 (2018)

Giones, F., Brem, A.: Digital technology entrepreneurship: a definition and research agenda. Technol. Innov. Manage. Rev. **7**(5), 44–51 (2017)

Machado, L.S., Caldeira, C., Perin, M.G., de Souza, C.R.B.: Gendered experiences of software engineers during the COVID-19 crisis. IEEE Softw. **38**(2), 38–44 (2021)

Nambisan, S.: Digital entrepreneurship: toward a digital technology perspective of entrepreneurship. Enterpren. Theor. Pract. **41**(6), 1029–1055 (2017)

Rippa, P., Secundo, G.: Digital academic entrepreneurship: the potential of digital technologies on academic entrepreneurship Technol. Forecast. Soc. Chang. **146**, 900–911 (2019)

Ojokoh, B., Zhang, M., Oluwadare, S., Akintola, K.: Women's perceptions and uses of information and communication technologies in Nigeria and China: a comparative analysis. Inf. Manage. Bus. Rev. **5**(4), 203–216 (2013)

Abdurakhmanova, G., et al.: Do human capital and economic development drive adoption of digital technologies across countries? Some correlational evidence. In: The 5th International Conference on Future Networks & Distributed Systems, pp. 702–705 (2021)

Van Deursen, A., Van Dijk, J.: The digital divide shifts to differences in usage. New Media Soc. **16**(3), 507–526 (2014). https://doi.org/10.1177/1461444813487959

Penard, T., Poussing, N., Mukoko, B., Piaptie, T.: Internet adoption and usage patterns in Africa: evidence from Cameroon. Technol. Soc. **42**, 71–80 (2015). https://doi.org/10.1016/j.techsoc. 2015.03.004

Prieger, J.E.: The broadband digital divide and the economic benefits of mobile broadband for rural areas. Telecommun. Policy **37**(6–7), 483–502 (2013). https://doi.org/10.1016/j.telpol. 2012.11.003

Garín-Munoz, T., Lopez, R., Perez-Amaral, T., Herguera, I., Valarezo, A.: Models for individual adoption of e-Commerce, e-Banking and e-Government in Spain. Telecommun. Policy **43**(1), 110–111 (2019). https://doi.org/10.1016/j.telpol.2018.01.002

Bandura, A.: Self-Efficacy: The Exercise of Control. Freeman, New York, NY (1997)

Nussbaum, M.C.: Women and Human Development: The Capabilities Approach. Cambridge University Press, Cambridge, UK (2001)

Kay, K., Shipman, C.: The confidence gap The Atlantic (2014). https://www.theatlantic.com/mag azine/archive/2014/05/the-confidence-gap/359815/

Crittenden, V., Bliton, K.: Direct selling: women helping women. In: V.L. Crittenden (Ed.), Go-to-Market Strategies for Women Entrepreneurs: Creating and Exploring Success, pp. 195–205. Emerald Group Publishing, Bingley, UK (2019)

van Dijck, J., Poell, T.: Understanding social media logic. Media Commun. **1**(1), 2–14 (2013)

Banet-Weiser, S.: Empowered - Popular Feminism and Popular Misogyny. Duke University Press, Durham (2018)

Croasdell, D., McLeod, A., Simkin, M.G.: Why don't more women major in information systems? Inf. Technol. People **24**, 158–183 (2011). https://doi.org/10.1108/09593841111137340

Wigfield, A., Eccles, J.S.: Expectancy-value theory of achievement motivation. Contemp. Educ. Psychol. **25**, 68–81 (2000). https://doi.org/10.1006/ceps.1999.1015

Aker, J.C., Mbiti, I.M.: Mobile phones and economic development in Africa. J. Econ. Perspect. **24**(3), 207–232 (2010)

# The Impact of Digitalisation on the Safe Development of Individuals in Society

Oksana Viktorovna Bondarskaya[1], Jamshid Sharafetdinovich Tukhtabaev[2]([✉]),
Rano Ramzitdinovna Akramova[3], Kholida Bekpulatovna Saidrasulova[4],
Uchkun Shirinov[5], and Zulaykho Tashboboyevna Kurbanova[6]

[1] Tambov State Technical University, Tambov, Russia
[2] Tashkent State University of Economics, Tashkent, Uzbekistan
jamshidtukhtabaev@gmail.com
[3] Tashkent Chemical - Technological Institute, Tashkent, Uzbekistan
[4] University of Gelogical Sciences, Tashkent, Uzbekistan
[5] Samarkand Institute of Economics and Service, Samarkand, Uzbekistan
[6] Termez Branch of the Tashkent Medical Academy, Termez, Uzbekistan

**Abstract.** Digital technologies are becoming an integral part of all aspects of human activity. The relevance of this article lies in the fact that in recent years the use of digitalization has been considered as one of the most promising tools at the macro and micro levels of sustainable economic development. This article is aimed at studying the problems associated with the introduction of digital technologies into human life and the development of scientific and practical proposals aimed at eliminating them. The Russian Federation, which implements modern digitalization processes, was chosen as the object of our study. The effective results achieved in the development and implementation of digital technologies are taken into account.

**Keywords:** digitalization · digitalization of the business sector · personality · growth rates of indicators · digital transformation · cyber attacks · government agencies · artificial intelligence

## 1 Introduction

One of the main goals of any State is to ensure high quality of life and safety of its citizens. In the XXI century, the process of digital technology development has accelerated. Digitalization has affected almost all spheres of people's lives. That is why the state should use digital tools to achieve its goals.

The development of digitalization is one of the main trends in modern Russia. It affects almost all spheres, introducing digital technologies into them and thereby improving the quality of life of the population. Digitalization technologies have been successfully implemented in our country for many years.

Y. Koucheryavy and A. Aziz (Eds.): NEW2AN 2022, LNCS 13772, pp. 299–309, 2023.
https://doi.org/10.1007/978-3-031-30258-9_25

## 2 Methodology

Digitalization of the business sector has a direct impact on economic growth, employment, and competitiveness. Figure 1 shows the dynamics of the digitalization indicator of commercial organizations.

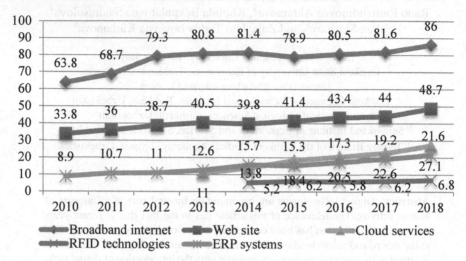

**Fig. 1.** Digitalization of business sector organizations (as a percentage of the total number of organizations) [1]

Having studied the dynamics of the indicators presented in Fig. 1, we can note a positive trend in the development of digitalization of organizations in the enterprise sector (Table 1).

**Table 1.** Absolute deviations and growth rates of indicators of digitalization of business sector organizations

| Indicators | 2011 | 2012 | 2013 | 2014 | 2015 | 2016 | 2017 | 2018 |
|---|---|---|---|---|---|---|---|---|
| **Absolute deviations** | | | | | | | | |
| Broadband Internet | 4.9 | 10.6 | 1.5 | 0.6 | -2.5 | 1.6 | 1.1 | 4.4 |
| Website | 2.2 | 2.7 | 1.8 | -0.7 | 1.6 | 2 | 0.6 | 4.7 |
| Cloud services | | | | 2.8 | 4.6 | 2.1 | 2.1 | 4.5 |
| RFID - technology | | | | | 1 | -0.4 | 0.4 | 0.6 |
| ERP-systems | 1.8 | 0.3 | 1.6 | 3.1 | -0.4 | 2 | 1.9 | 2.4 |
| **Growth rate** | | | | | | | | |
| Broadband Internet | 7.7 | 15.4 | 1.9 | 0.7 | -3.1 | 2.0 | 1.4 | 5.4 |

(*continued*)

**Table 1.** (*continued*)

| Indicators | 2011 | 2012 | 2013 | 2014 | 2015 | 2016 | 2017 | 2018 |
|---|---|---|---|---|---|---|---|---|
| Website | 6.5 | 7.5 | 4.7 | -1.7 | 4.0 | 4.8 | 1.4 | 10.7 |
| Cloud services | | | | 25.5 | 33.3 | 11.4 | 10.2 | 19.9 |
| RFID - technology | | | | | 19.2 | -6.5 | 6.9 | 9.7 |
| ERP-systems | 20.2 | 2.8 | 14.5 | 24.6 | -2.5 | 13.1 | 11.0 | 12.5 |

## 3  Results

In the period from 2010 to 2018, the use of broadband Internet by organizations increased by 22.2%. In 1018, there was a jump in the use of websites, in total they became more popular by 14.9% during the study period. The use of enterprise resource planning systems (ERP systems) increased by 12.7%.

The cloud infrastructure makes it possible to implement joint initiatives between financial organizations and organizations of other sectors of the economy, allowing you to quickly, in the shortest possible time, create new working business models and accelerate the introduction of new products to the consumer market. In the period from 2013 to 2018, the percentage of organizations using cloud services increased significantly from 11% to 27.1%, respectively, an increase of 17.1%.

RFID technologies are used to control the movement of goods in the warehouse and in the store, control working hours, identification of vehicles, automation of production. Despite the obvious growth of the presented indicators, the methods of automatic identification of objects (RFID systems) are not yet popular in our country. In the period from 2014 to 2018, the growth rate was only 1.6%.

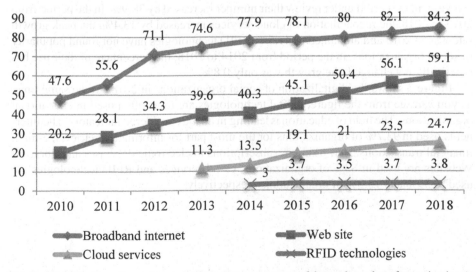

**Fig. 2.** Digitalization of social organizations (as a percentage of the total number of organizations)

Figure 2 shows data on indicators of digitalization of the social sphere. It includes the digitalization of educational institutions of higher education, organizations operating in the field of health and social services, culture, sports, leisure and entertainment.

The use of digital technologies in the work of social organizations makes it possible not only to improve the quality of services provided, but also to increase the correctness of forecasts, risk and threat assessments, as well as to optimize ways to neutralize them.

**Table 2.** Absolute deviations and growth rates of indicators of digitalization of the social sphere

| Indicators | 2011 | 2012 | 2013 | 2014 | 2015 | 2016 | 2017 | 2018 |
|---|---|---|---|---|---|---|---|---|
| **Absolute deviations** | | | | | | | | |
| Broadband Internet | 8 | 15.5 | 3.5 | 3.3 | 0.2 | 1.9 | 2.1 | 2.2 |
| Website | 7.9 | 6.2 | 5.3 | 0.7 | 4.8 | 5.3 | 5.7 | 3 |
| Cloud services | | | | 2.2 | 5.6 | 1.9 | 2.5 | 1.2 |
| RFID - technology | | | | | 0.7 | -0.2 | 0.2 | 0.1 |
| **ERP-systems** | | | | | | | | |
| Broadband Internet | 16.8 | 27.9 | 4.9 | 4.4 | 0.3 | 2.4 | 2.6 | 2.7 |
| Website | 39.1 | 22.1 | 15.5 | 1.8 | 11.9 | 11.8 | 11.3 | 5.3 |
| Cloud services | | | | 19.5 | 41.5 | 9.9 | 11.9 | 5.1 |
| RFID - technology | | | | | 23.3 | -5.4 | 5.7 | 2.7 |

Having studied the data in Table 2, we can note the constant growth of indicators. The use of broadband Internet in the period from 2010 to 2018 increased by 36.7%, the largest increase was in 2015, it amounted to 15.5%. The use of websites is also steadily growing, in the period under review their number increased by 38.9%. In the period from 2013 to 2018, the reconciliation of cloud services increased by 13.4%, the peak growth rate was in 2015 and amounted to 41.5%. RFID technologies have not found popularity in social organizations, in the period from 2014 to 2018, the percentage of their use has practically not changed, the growth was only 0.8%.

Figure 3 shows the digitalization of social organizations in 2018. At the same time, as you can see from the figure, digital technologies are most often used in educational organizations. The field of education is leading in all the considered indicators. The Internet is used in 92.7% of organizations for the most part for information retrieval, e-mail, financial transactions, staff training, subscriptions to electronic databases and libraries. Websites are used in 83% of organizations, cloud services and RFID technologies are used in 39% and 13.3% of organizations, respectively.

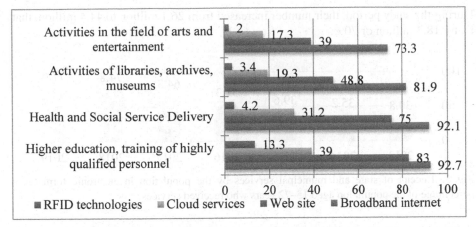

**Fig. 3.** Digitalization of the social sphere by type of activity (as a percent-age of the total number of organizations) in 2018

In second place is the healthcare system. In it, 92.1% of organizations use broadband Internet, mainly for searching information on the Internet, using e-mail, financial transactions, conferences and staff training. 75% of organizations have websites, cloud services and RFID technologies are used by 31.2% and 4.2% of organizations, respectively.

Digitalization of libraries, archives, museums and other cultural objects takes the third place. 87.9% of organizations have Internet, 48.8% have websites. Cloud services and RFID technologies were used by 19.3% and 3.4% of organizations in the year under study, respectively. At the same time, most of the material stored in libraries, archives and museums has been digitized. Figure 4 shows the constant growth of digitized copies.

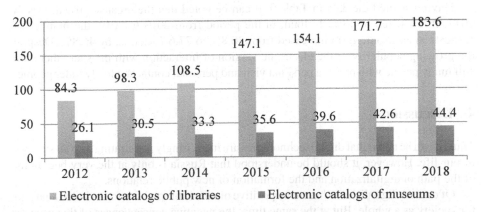

**Fig. 4.** Number of electronic catalogs, million units

In the period from 2012 to 2018, the number of electronic catalogues of libraries increased by 99.3 million units or by 117.8% and by 2018 amounted to 183.6 million copies. Electronic catalogues of museums have also become much more numerous.

During the study period, their number increased from 26.1 million to 44.4 million, that is, by 18.3 million or 70%.

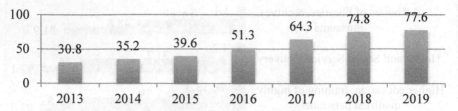

**Fig. 5.** Receipt of state and municipal services by the population in electronic form (as a percentage of the population aged 15–72 years who received services)

Figure 5 shows the dynamics of public and municipal services received by the population. Every year the number of people who have chosen the electronic form of appeal increases.

**Table 3.** Absolute deviation and growth rate of state and municipal services received by the population in electronic form [2]

| Indicators | 2014 | 2015 | 2016 | 2017 | 2018 | 2019 |
|---|---|---|---|---|---|---|
| Absolute deviations | 4,4 | 4,4 | 11,7 | 13 | 10,5 | 2,8 |
| Growth rate | 14,3 | 12,5 | 29,5 | 25,3 | 16,3 | 3,7 |

Having studied the data in Table 3, it can be noted that the greatest growth was in 2017, it amounted to 13%. In total, in the period from 2013 to 2019, the number of requests in electronic form increased from 30.8% to 77.6%, that is, by 46.8%. Despite the growing popularity of the electronic version of interaction with the state, there are still many people who prefer a personal visit and personal contacts, mostly older people.

## 4 Discussion

Thus, it can be noted that digital technologies are increasingly penetrating into all spheres of our life. However, it should be understood that Russia is only at the very beginning of the path of digitalization and the formation of new public relations.

Of course, digitalization has many positive manifestations, both for an individual and for society as a whole. But at the same time, the negative consequences of this process are already quite obvious. One of the most widespread threats to social security is the threat of unemployment, as a result of the release of a large number of jobs.

Digital technologies have made it possible to automate many processes, primarily related to simple physical labor. Artificial intelligence systems used in organizations increasingly displace specialists of average qualifications. In addition, digitalization affects workers' wages and leads to its reduction. According to the CMACP, the development of digitalization is able to displace 12.5 million people employed [3].

Also, at the moment, there is a danger of exceeding the pace of digitalization development over the pace of retraining of employees. As a result, the population that has failed to adapt to the new realities will lose their jobs.

Having studied Fig. 6, it can be seen that the majority of the population, namely 39.3%, has a low level of digital technology proficiency. 24.5% of the population has a basic level, 22.5% have not used the Internet in the last 3 months, and finally, only 11.9% of the population's skills are assessed above the basic level.

Since the digital transformation of society is directly related to the digitization, collection, processing and storage of various information, the information obtained as a result of these actions needs reliable protection. The rapid pace of digitalization increases the likelihood of new types of fraud. Cyber attacks on various commercial organizations, government agencies, socially significant objects, which, ultimately, negatively affects the security of an individual.

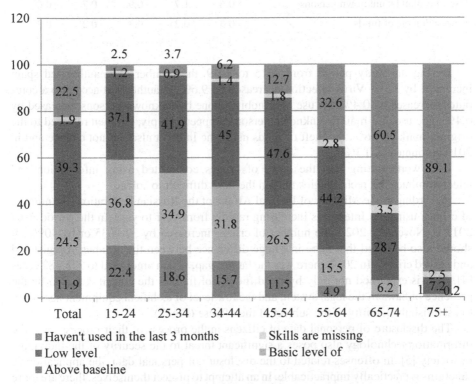

**Fig. 6.** The level of digital skills of the population by age groups in 2019 (as a percentage of the total population of the corresponding age group)

In addition, changes occurring during the transition to the digital economy can potentially lower the existing level of data security. As a result, important information can not
only be stolen, but also irretrievably lost.

As can be seen from Table 4, already today a large number of people are facing
threats to information security of varying severity and scale.

**Table 4.** Collision of the population with threats of information security when using the Internet
(as a percentage of the population aged 15–74 years) [4]

| Indicators | 2015 | 2016 | 2017 | 2018 | 2019 |
|---|---|---|---|---|---|
| Unauthorized mailing (spam) | 19 | 18,4 | 18,5 | 19,7 | 22,3 |
| Infection with viruses | 17.1 | 13.3 | 11.4 | 8.9 | 7.5 |
| Unauthorized access to the computer | 1.9 | 1.4 | 1.8 | 1.4 | 1.5 |
| Use of a mobile phone by unknown persons | 0.4 | 0.7 | 0.8 | 0.7 | 0.8 |
| Use of e-mail by unknown persons | 0.6 | 1.7 | 0.9 | 0.7 | 0.6 |
| Embezzlement of funds | 0.3 | 0.2 | 0.3 | 0.2 | 0.3 |

During the study period from 2015 to 2019, the number of unauthorized spam
increased by 3.3%. Virus infection decreased by 9.6%, unauthorized access to a computer increased by 0.4%, the use of a mobile phone by unknown persons increased by
0.4%. The use of e-mail by unknown persons dropped sharply, but then returned to the
original mark of 0.6%, the theft of funds using the Internet also did not change and in
2019 amounted to 0.3%.

It is worth noting that the types of crimes committed using information and
telecommunication technologies remain the most difficult to solve.

According to the Ministry of Internal Affairs of the Russian Federation, the number
of crimes using the Internet is increasing rapidly from year to year. In the period from
2017 to November 2020, the number of crimes increased by 370.635 or by 409%. It
should also be noted that there is a huge difference between the number of registered
and solved crimes. In 2020, there was the largest gap, which amounted to 375.482 cases
[4]. This is explained not only by the difficulty of finding the culprit, but also by the
presence of flaws in the legal system and the low level of technical equipment necessary
to establish the identity of the subject of the offense (Fig. 7).

The disclosure of personal data of citizens in the process of their processing using
information technology also poses a significant threat to the security of the individual
in society [5]. In offenses related to the disclosure of personal data, the application of
sanctions is practically impracticable. In an attempt to protect themselves, there are more
and more people who refuse to use the Internet.

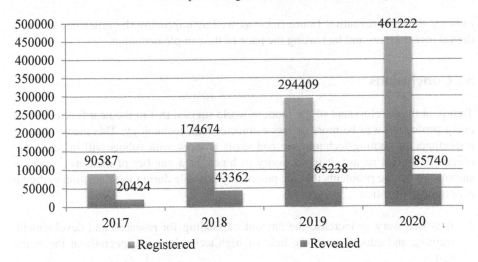

**Fig. 7.** Crimes committed using computer and telecommunication technologies

Figure 8 shows the dynamics of the percentage of the population that does not use the Internet for security reasons. The vast majority of them take this step because of their unwillingness to disclose personal data on the Internet. In the period from 2015 to 2019, the number of people who do not use the Internet increased by 1.9%.

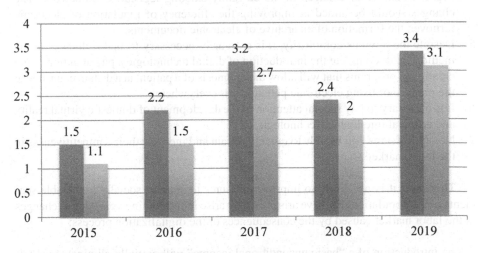

**Fig. 8.** The population that does not use the Internet for security reasons (as a percentage of the population aged 15–74 years who did not use the Internet) [6]

Thus, it can be noted that the processes associated with the digitalization of the country, despite many positive aspects, can cause significant risks. That is why it is extremely important to pay attention to the development of measures aimed at leveling existing threats, preventing future risks, as well as improving the efficiency of using digital technologies and increasing the pace of their implementation.

## 5 Conclusions

Trends in the development of the modern world suggest that in the near future, almost every profession will be more or less connected with technology. This means that the importance of owning technologies and skills to work with robots will increase significantly. In this regard, it is necessary to highlight a number of measures aimed at smoothing out the problems that are potentially possible during the transition to digital economic civilization.

1.  It is necessary to increase the amount of funding for research and development, training and education in the field of high technologies, especially at the initial stage.
2.  It is necessary to pay attention to stimulating certain areas for more active implementation of digital technologies.
3.  It is necessary to support such areas as import substitution, export of information technologies, ensuring equal conditions for Internet companies in Russia, development of access and data storage infrastructure, promotion of all types of mass digital communications and services.
4.  Make a number of changes to the currently existing legislative framework. The changes should be aimed at improving the efficiency of regulation of electronic turnover, the formation of an archive of electronic documents.
5.  Despite the obvious complexity, it is extremely necessary to make changes in the medical field: complete the introduction of digital technologies, pay attention to the creation of programs that will allow the diagnosis of a patient at a distance, introduce the practice of using electronic patient cards everywhere.
6.  It is necessary to pay special attention to the development of domestic virtual reality and artificial intelligence technologies.
7.  Not all Russians will be able to quickly retrain and increase their competitiveness in the labor market.

Therefore, it is necessary to improve measures to support socially vulnerable segments of the population that have arisen or may arise in the coming years due to changes in the labor market caused by the consequences of the digitalization process:

–  The introduction of a "basic unconditional income" will partially eliminate inequality in the distribution of income, but the resolution of related inflationary and other problems is required;
–  It is necessary to develop entrepreneurial activity as an alternative to employment;
–  Stimulating the active creation of new enterprises will increase the chances of retraining and further employment of the unemployed population;
–  Introduction of additional taxes. At the end of August 2020, the government Commission for Digital development approved the passport of the federal project "Artificial

Intelligence". In this regard, one of the measures may be the introduction of a tax on robots, which will allow collecting the necessary funds and redirecting them to help the population who lost their jobs in the process of automatization of production;
– Consider switching to a four-day work week or a six-hour work day.

It should be noted that digitalization is a relatively new, little-studied type of economic relations between subjects. But it is already quite obvious that digitalization will become the locomotive of the development of the modern economic and social sphere. Despite this, the process of digitalization in Russia demonstrates upward dynamics, which positively affects the quality of life of citizens and ensures the economic growth of the country.

# References

1. Abdrakhmanova, G.I., Vishnevsky, K.O., Gokhberg, L.M. et al.: Indicators of the digital economy: 2020: statistical collection / National research. unit Higher School of Economics. M.: HSE (2020). https://www.hse.ru/primarydata/ice2020
2. Tillaeva, B.R., et al.: Ways of development of agriculture and processing industry enterprises manufacturing cooperation. In: IOP Conference Series: Earth and Environmental Science, vol. 1043, no. 2022, p. 012024 (2022). https://doi.org/10.1088/1755-1315/1043/1/012024, https://iopscience.iop.org/article/10.1088/1755-1315/1043/1/012024
3. The official website of the Center for Macroeconomic Analysis and Short-term Forecasting (CMACP). http://www.forecast.ru/
4. Official website of the Ministry of Internal Affairs of the Russian Federation (Ministry of Internal Affairs of the Russian Federation). https://mvd.ru/. Official website of the International Independent Institute of Agrarian Policy (MINAP). http://minap.ru/analytics/Perspektivy-cifrovizacii/
5. Bondarskaya, T.A.: The quality of the regional economy: analysis and prospects. Socio-economic phenomena and processes, no. 9 (2016). https://cyberleninka.ru/article/n/kachestvo-regionalnoy-ekonomiki-analiz-perspektivy
6. Tukhtabaev, J.S., et al.: The role of industrial enterprises in ensuring food security. In: IOP Conference Series: Earth and Environmental Science, vol. 1043, no. 2022, p. 012023 (2022). https://doi.org/10.1088/1755-1315/1043/1/012023, https://iopscience.iop.org/article/10.1088/1755-1315/1043/1/012023

# Econometric Evaluation of the Efficiency of the Management of the Enterprise Through the Supply of Raw Materials in Oil Enterprises in the Conditions of the Digital Economy

Yuldashev Abdukhakim[✉] [ID], Uktamov Khusniddin, Mirzaliev Sanjar[ID], and Sharipov Kongratbay[ID]

Tashkent State University of Economics, Tashkent 100066, Uzbekistan
{ayuldashev,uktamov,k.sharipov}@tsue.uz

**Abstract.** Comprehensive measures are being implemented in the republic to develop the oil industry, to increase the volume of production and rise the range of finished products in order to meet the needs of the population. In particular, in the article, an econometric evaluation of the efficiency of enterprise management through the supply of raw materials in oil and oil enterprises in the conditions of the digital economy was carried out. The correlation coefficient of the factors affecting the management efficiency of JSC "Tashkent oil-oil combine" in the form of a joint enterprise and the change of the management efficiency of JSC "Tashkent oil-oil combine" in the form of a joint enterprise as a result of the influence of selected factors are reflected in the coefficients of the regression equation and the result of checking it with quality criteria. The regression equation coefficients and the result of checking it with quality criteria reflect the change of the management efficiency of "Yangiyol oil-oil" JSC with the participation of foreign investors as a result of the influence of selected factors. The multi-factor management efficiency of JSC "Tashkent oil-oil combine" in the form of a joint venture is forecasted for the years 2022–2026. In addition, conclusions and proposals were developed based on the econometric evaluation of the efficiency of enterprise management through the supply of raw materials in the conditions of the digital economy.

**Keywords:** oil enterprises · digital economy · "Tashkent oil-oil combine" JSC · raw material supply · management efficiency · econometric assessment · influencing factors

## 1 Introduction

Raw material inventory management of global oil and gas enterprises, in particular, material flow management as a profit center, enterprise and raw material inventory management, raw material placement management at processing enterprises, modeling of raw material inventory management at processing enterprises, management of raw material processing based on resource conservation, raw material supply economic relations with suppliers and processing enterprises, a number of scientific researches have been carried out in the direction of analysis of enterprises based on increasing the efficiency of raw material supply. In this process, one of the priorities is to conduct scientific research on improving the management of oil-oil enterprises based on the improvement of the efficiency of raw material supply [1].

Quantitative indicators of the management system save labor, etc.; indicators of financial efficiency of the management system; includes many factors such as time saving indicators.

Quality indicators of social effectiveness of management: increasing the scientific level of management; integrated level of management processes; training of managers; increase the level of validity of the decisions made; system controllability; job satisfaction; gain public trust; strengthen the social responsibility of the organization; environmental consequences. The effectiveness of quality indicators of the social efficiency of management can be characterized by easing and improving working conditions, improving the psychological environment in the team, establishing normal relations between managers and executives, etc. [2].

If, as a result of management rationalization, it is possible to achieve a high level of the above indicators, then there will be a positive shift in the organization of the management system and economic efficiency will be achieved. To improve the management of the organization, to introduce information technologies, a certain amount of investments is required, which requires the evaluation of the management of these investment projects. The aim of this research is to improve the supply of raw materials in the oil industry using digital technologies.

## 2 Literature Review

Induction, deduction and expert evaluation methods of scientific research were used in the course of the research.

Foreign scientists D. Bowersox, D. David Kloss, M. Christopher, D. Lambert, Dj. Stock, Michael R. Lindere, E. Harold, C. Skowronek, Thomas T. Stollkamp, D. Waters, D. Hadley, T. Whitin, E. Mate and others have been reflected in scientific research.

B. Anikin, V. Bautin, I. Bogomolova, D. Gavrilov, K. Kuznetsov, V. Lukinsky, E. Makarov, Yu. Nerush, V. Nikolaychuk, B. Plotkin, Yu. Salikov, V. Sergeev from the scientists of the CIS countries and others have made significant contributions to the study of raw material inventory management [3–5].

Some problems of raw material stock management of enterprises in Uzbekistan N. Yoldoshev, Ya. Karrieva, D. Rakhimova, Sh. Zaynutdinov, D. Suyunov, A. Hashimov, Sh. Ergashkhodjaeva, A. Fattakhov, T. Akramov, M. Eshov, G. Abdurakhmanova and others were studied in scientific research works [6, 7].

## 3 Data and Methodology

The article uses systematic analysis, expert assessment, synthesis, comparison, statistical analysis, SWOT-analysis, economic-mathematical modeling and econometric analysis (Table 1).

**Table 1.** Consumption of raw materials of JSC "Tashkent Oil-Oil Combine" as a joint venture and "Yangiyol Oil-Oil" JSC with participation of foreign investors

| Indicators | 2015 year | 2016 year | 2017 year | 2018 year | 2019 year | 2020 year | In 2020 compared to 2015 (±), % |
|---|---|---|---|---|---|---|---|
| JSC "Tashkent Yog-Moy" in the form of a joint venture | | | | | | | |
| Energy consumption million soums | 34987 | 35310 | 41700 | 64900 | 72688 | 74869 | 214,0 |
| Raw material consumption million soums | 26385 | 44761 | 54755 | 43211 | 48396 | 49848 | 188,9 |
| Total costs | 61372 | 80071 | 96455 | 108111 | 121084 | 126533 | 206,2 |
| Raw material volume tons | 51576 | 60530 | 49451 | 42260 | 50629 | 53160 | 103,1 |
| The volume of produced products is tons | 41580 | 41631 | 34749 | 33438 | 38191 | 40101 | -3,6 |
| Consumption of raw materials per unit of finished product, mln. Soum | 0,6 | 1,1 | 1,6 | 1,3 | 1,3 | 1,5 | 250,0 |
| JSC "Yangiyol Yog-Moy" with the participation of foreign investors | | | | | | | |
| Energy consumption million soums | 32499 | 30278 | 42539 | 47644 | 55267 | 56649 | 174,3 |
| Raw material consumption million soums | 30813 | 34161 | 49714 | 42326 | 47074 | 48721 | 158,1 |
| Total costs | 61176 | 70543 | 85170 | 96327 | 107281 | 111572 | 182,4 |
| Raw material volume tons | 53231 | 57672 | 56052 | 51678 | 53460 | 56133 | 105,5 |
| The volume of produced products is tons | 26139 | 28319 | 24516 | 22338 | 26472 | 27134 | 103,8 |
| Consumption of raw materials per unit of finished product, mln. Soum | 1,2 | 1,2 | 2 | 1,9 | 1,8 | 1,9 | 158,3 |

## 4 Results and Findings

In the research work, the efficiency of management was determined in the selected objects, and an econometric analysis of the factors affecting the effective management process in these enterprises was carried out. It is to help them determine which factors to focus on and what measures to develop in the development of the future perspective of the enterprise [8].

For this, first of all, the influence of factors such as production costs - X1, energy consumption - X2 and raw material consumption - X3 on the change of management efficiency - Y, calculated using the statistical data of the JSC "Tashkent Oil and Oil Combine" in the form of a joint venture for the years 2008–2020 we will perform an econometric analysis. First, we can check the degree of correlation between these factors and the resulting factor (strong or weak), conduct econometric analyzes and check the correlation coefficient based on the order of selection of factors (Table 2).

**Table 2.** Correlation coefficient of factors affecting management efficiency of JSC "Tashkent oil-oil combine" in the form of a joint venture

|    | Y | X1 | X2 | X3 |
|----|----|----|----|----|
| Y  | 1 |    |    |    |
| X1 | 0,779227 | 1 |    |    |
| X2 | 0,687639 | 0,574075 | 1 |    |
| X3 | 0,781067 | 0,649826 | 0,526122 | 1 |

From the data in Table 2 above, it can be seen that the resulting factor is related to the management efficiency of JSC "Tashkent oil-oil combine" in the form of a joint venture[10], including all factors, including production costs - X1 $(r_{Y,X1} = 0,779227)$ energy consumption – X2 $(r_{Y,X2} = 0,687639)$ and raw material consumption - X3 $(r_{Y,X1} = 0,781067)$ was found to be correctly connected with average density. Among the selected factors $(r_{X1,X3} = 0,6498 < 0,8; r_{X1,X2} = 0,5741 < 0,8; (r_{X2,X3} = 0,5261 < 0,8)$ conditionally, multicollinearity was not observed, and the process can be continued using Eviews software, which is now widely used in conducting econometric analyzes (Table 3).

**Table 3.** The results of checking the regression equation coefficients and its quality criteria on the change of the management efficiency of JSC "Tashkent oil-oil combine" in the form of a joint venture as a result of the influence of selected factors

| Variable | Coefficient | Std. Error | t-Statistic | Prob. |
|----------|-------------|------------|-------------|-------|
| LNX1 | −0,00771 | 0,216697 | −0,03557 | 0.0311 |
| LNX2 | −0,01445 | 0,147317 | −0,0981 | 0.0069 |

*(continued)*

**Table 3.** (*continued*)

| Variable | Coefficient | Std. Error | t-Statistic | Prob. |
|---|---|---|---|---|
| LNX3 | 0,350867 | 0,13009 | 2,69711 | 0.0473 |
| C | 1,3842 | 4,851573 | 0,28531 | 0.0191 |
| | | | $t_{jad} = 2,262157$ | |
| R-squared | 0.924230 | Mean dependent var | | 4.155419 |
| Adjusted R-squared | 0.767693 | S.D. dependent var | | 0.386273 |
| S.E. of regression | 0.417406 | Akaike info criterion | | 1.338143 |
| Sum squared resid | 1.568047 | Schwarz criterion | | 1.511974 |
| Log likelihood | -4.697932 | Hannan-Quinn criter | | 1.302413 |
| F-statistic | 65.42555 | Durbin-Watson stat | | 1.961808 |
| Prob(F-statistic) | 0.000074 | $F_{jad} = 8,8123$ | | |

According to the data of Table 3 above, we have logarithmized the index of factors, taking into account that there is a large difference between the indicators of the selected factors and the indicator of Management efficiency. According to these values, only from the parameters $t_{X3} = 2.697$ from being $t_{JAD} < t_{X3}$ according to the inequality, the significance of the raw material consumption – X3 parameter follows. In fact, remaining parameters are checked according to MAPE < 10 very close reliable (Mean Absolute Percentage Error) and TIC < 1 (Tayl inequality coefficient - an alternative measure of Tayl forecast accuracy) criteria (Fig. 1) [10].

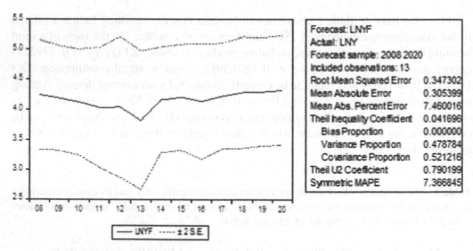

**Fig. 1.** Result of MAPE and TIC criteria of parameter X1 and X2

Based on the data presented in Fig. 1 above, MAPE = 7.46 < 10 and TIC = 0.042 < 1, the significance of parameters X1 and X2 was proved. Now the regression equation is based on Fisher's criterion of significance when $\alpha = 0.05$ $k1 = 8$; $k2 = 3$ $F_{JAD} = 8,81$ from equality to $F_{JAD} < F_{account}$. According to the condition $F_{xиcoб} = 65,4$ from equality and DW = 1.96 Since there is no autocorrelation, the regression Eq. (1) defined below:

$$LnY = 0,35LnX3 - 0,01LnX1 - 0,01445LnX2 + 1,4 \qquad (1)$$

is reliable and adequate, this regression Eq. (1) is exponentiated to get rid of the logarithm, and regression Eq. (2) becomes:

$$Y = \frac{X3^{0,35} * e^{1,4}}{X1^{0,01} * X2^{0,01445}} \qquad (2)$$

If we give an economic interpretation to this regression Eq. (2), it is found that if production costs and energy consumption in the enterprise are reduced by 100%, the efficiency of enterprise management will increase by 0.014% and 0.02%, respectively. However, if the raw material consumption is increased by 100%, the management efficiency is found to increase by 0.47%. In turn, it is appropriate to provide the enterprise with raw materials as much as possible while promoting the relations of economic cooperation in the management of the enterprise, and in this regard, any available opportunity should be used [11].

## 5 Discussion

Now, according to the factors selected for the object analyzed above, the management efficiency calculated using the statistical data of the New Road oil-oil enterprise for the years 2008–2020 - factors such as production costs - X1, energy consumption - X2 and raw material consumption - X3 for the change of Y We will perform an econometric analysis of the effect [12]. First, we can check the correlation coefficient between these factors and the resulting factor (strong or weak) by conducting econometric analyzes and the order of selection of factors (Table 4).

**Table 4.** Correlation coefficient of factors affecting the management efficiency of "Yangiyol Yog-Moy" JSC with the participation of foreign investors

|  | Y | X1 | X2 | X3 |
|---|---|---|---|---|
| Y | 1 | | | |
| X1 | 0,82415 | 1 | | |
| X2 | 0,880117 | 0,794133 | 1 | |
| X3 | 0,983351 | 0,697799 | 0,735471 | 1 |

From the data in Table 4 above, it can be seen that all factors, including production costs, are related to the management efficiency factor of JSC "Yangiyol oil-oil" with the participation of foreign investors [13] - X1 ($r_{Y,X1} = 0,82415$) energy consumption - X2 ($r_{Y,X2} = 0,880117$) and raw material consumption - X3 ($r_{Y,X1} = 0,983351$) with is found to be correctly connected in strong density. Among the selected factors ($r_{1,X3} = 0,7941 < 0,8$; $r_{1,X2} = 0,6978$; ($r_{2,X3} = 0,7355 < 0,8$) conditionally, multicollinearity was not observed, and the process can be continued using the Eviews program, which is now widely used in conducting econometric analyzes (Table 5).

**Table 5.** The result of checking the regression equation coefficients and quality criteria on the change of the management efficiency of "Yangiyol oil-oil" JSC with the participation of foreign investors as a result of the influence of selected factors

| Variable | Coefficient | Std. Error | t-Statistic | Prob |
|----------|-------------|------------|-------------|------|
| LNX1 | 0.675208 | 0.04289 | 15.74278 | 0.0000 |
| LNX2 | −0.06084 | 0.027348 | −2.2247 | 0.0532 |
| LNX3 | −0.24515 | 0.03102 | −7.90308 | 0.0000 |
| C | 0.284267 | 0.087672 | 3.242392 | 0.0122 |
| R-squared | 0.973849 | Mean dependent var | | 1.565319 |
| Adjusted R-squared | 0.965132 | S.D. dependent var | | 0.017584 |
| S.E. of regression | 0.003283 | Akaike info criterion | | −8.352205 |
| Sum squared resid | 9.70E-05 | Schwarz criterion | | −8.178375 |
| Log likelihood | 58.28933 | Hannan-Quinn criter | | −8.387935 |
| F-statistic | 111.7185 | Durbin-Watson stat | | 1.818960 |
| Prob(F-statistic) | 0.000000 | | | |

According to the data in Table 4 above, we logarithmized the index of factors, taking into account that there is a large difference between the indicators of the selected factors and the indicator of Management efficiency. According to these values, only from the parameters $t_{X1} = 15.74$ from being $t_{жад} < t_3$ according to the inequality, the significance of the parameter of production costs -X1 follows. In fact, the rest of the parameters are either insignificant or marginally checked according to the MAPE < 10 and TIC < 1 criteria (Fig. 2).

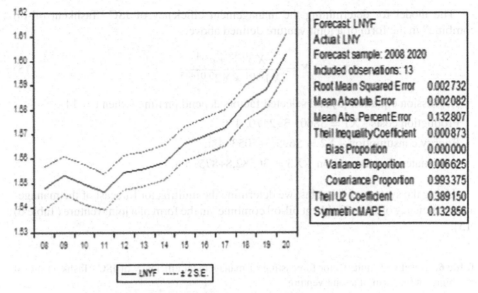

| | |
|---|---|
| Forecast LNYF | |
| Actual LNY | |
| Forecast sample: 2008 2020 | |
| Included observations: 13 | |
| Root Mean Squared Error | 0.002732 |
| Mean Absolute Error | 0.002082 |
| Mean Abs. Percent Error | 0.132807 |
| Theil Inequality Coefficient | 0.000873 |
| Bias Proportion | 0.000000 |
| Variance Proportion | 0.006625 |
| Covariance Proportion | 0.993375 |
| Theil U2 Coefficient | 0.389150 |
| Symmetic MAPE | 0.132856 |

**Fig. 2.** Result of MAPE and TIC criteria of parameter X2 and X3

Based on the data presented in Fig. 2 above, MAPE = 0.133 < 10 and TIC = 0.0009 < 1, the significance of parameters X1 and X2 was proved. Now the significance of the regression equation based on Fisher's criterion $\alpha = 0,05$ when k1 = 8; k2 = 3 at $F_{жад} = 8,81$ from equality to $F_{жад} < F_{хисоб}$. According to the condition $F_{хисоб} = 111,7$ from equality and DW = 1.82 Since there is no autocorrelation, the regression Eq. (3) defined below:

$$LnY = 0,6752LnX1 - 0,06LnX2 - 0,24515LnX3 + 0,284 \qquad (3)$$

is reliable and adequate, this regression Eq. (3) is exponentiated to get rid of the logarithm, and regression Eq. (4) becomes:

$$Y = \frac{X1^{0,6752} * e^{0,284}}{X2^{0,06} * X3^{0,24515}} \qquad (4)$$

If we give an economic explanation to this (4)-regression equation, if today the production costs in the enterprise are 100 mln. if it is increased to 334,000 soums, the efficiency of management will be increased by only 334,000 soums, which, in turn, requires the company to revise the future cost estimates and search for optimal cost options. Also, it was determined that if the consumption of energy and raw materials in the enterprise is reduced by 100 million, the management efficiency of the enterprise will increase by an additional 189,000 soums [14]. If we make a general conclusion based on the obtained results, taking into account the fact that raw materials are limiting the possibility of working at full capacity at the enterprise, it is appropriate to revise the economic cooperation agreements in the management of the enterprise and develop measures for the seasonal organization of production.

The model for determining the management efficiency of JSC "Tashkent oil-oil combine" in the form of a joint venture defined above:

$$Y = \frac{X3^{0,35} * e^{1,4}}{X1^{0,01} * X2^{0,01445}} \tag{5}$$

Regression equation (5) and selected factors depend on time (when t = 14):

Production costs - X1 = 38605,3+2470, 4*t;

Energy consumption – X2 = 5695,7+5053, 4*t;

Raw material consumption – X3 = 36582,8+875, 5*t.

Using the system of formulas, we determine the multifactor forecast of the management efficiency of JSC "Tashkent oil-oil combine" in the form of a joint venture (Table 6) [15].

**Table 6.** Results of multi-factor forecasting of management efficiency of JSC "Tashkent oil-oil combine" in the form of a joint venture

| Years | Management efficiency, mln. Soum | Production costs, mln. Sums | Energy consumption mln. Soums | Raw material consumption mln. Soums |
|-------|-------------|------------------|-------------|-------------|
| 2021 | 134,9 | 73190,9 | 76443,3 | 48839,8 |
| 2022 | 135,5 | 75661,3 | 81496,7 | 49715,3 |
| 2023 | 136, 2 | 78131,7 | 86550,1 | 50590,8 |
| 2024 | 136,9 | 80602,1 | 91603,5 | 51466,3 |
| 2025 | 137,5 | 83072,5 | 96656,9 | 52341,8 |
| 2026 | 138,2 | 85542,9 | 101710,3 | 53217,3 |

As can be seen in Table 6 above, in 2021 compared to 2020, the management efficiency of the enterprise is 134.9 mln. Soums, production costs 73190.9 mln. Soums, energy consumption is expected to be 76,443.3 million soums and raw material consumption is 48,839.8 million soums.

As a result of the multi-factor forecast of the management efficiency of JSC "Tashkent Oil and Oil Combine" in the form of a joint venture, the management efficiency of the enterprise in 2026 compared to 2021 is 102.4%, production costs are 116.8%, energy consumption is 133.1% and raw material consumption is It is expected to grow by 109 percent [16].

In 2021–2026, the size of the increase in the management efficiency of the enterprise by 102.4% is small compared to other factors, which means that it is necessary to increase the stock of raw materials in order to increase the management efficiency of the enterprise. Because the increase in the size of the production capacity of the enterprise proportionally leads to the increase of the management efficiency of the enterprise.

Multi-factor econometric analysis of management efficiency of "Yangiyol Yog-Moy" JSC with participation of foreign investors

$$Y = \frac{X1^{0,6752} * e^{0,284}}{X2^{0,06} * X3^{0,24515}} \tag{6}$$

model and selected factors depend on time (when $t = 14$):

Production costs - $X1 = 98791,3+16319,4*t$;

Energy consumption – $X2 = 43550,7+8891,4*t$;

Raw material consumption – $X3 = 64892,0+16847,2*t$.

Using the system of formulas, we determine the multi-factor forecast of the management efficiency of JSC "Yangi Yol Og-Moi" with the participation of foreign investors (Table 7).

**Table 7.** Results of multi-factor forecasting of the management efficiency of "Yangiyol Oil-Moy" JSC with the participation of foreign investors

| Years | Management efficiency, mln. Soum | Production costs, mln. Sum | Energy consumption mln. Soum | Raw material consumption mln. Soum |
|-------|----------------------------------|-----------------------------|------------------------------|-------------------------------------|
| 2021 | 155,1 | 327262,9 | 168030,3 | 300752,8 |
| 2022 | 157,6 | 343582,3 | 176921,7 | 317600 |
| 2023 | 160,1 | 359901,7 | 185813,1 | 334447,2 |
| 2024 | 162,6 | 376221,1 | 194704,5 | 351294,4 |
| 2025 | 164,9 | 392540,5 | 203595,9 | 368141,6 |
| 2026 | 167,2 | 408859,9 | 212487,3 | 384988,8 |

As can be seen from the table in Table 7 above, in 2021, compared to 2020, the management efficiency of the enterprise is 155.1 mln. Soums, production costs 327262.9 mln. Soums, energy consumption is expected to be 168,030.3 million soums and raw material consumption is 300,752.8 million soums.

As a result of the multi-factor forecast of the management efficiency of JSC "Yangiyol Oil-Moy" with the participation of foreign investors, it is expected that in 2026, compared to 2021, the management efficiency of the enterprise will increase by 107.8%, production costs by 124.9%, energy consumption by 126.5%, and raw material consumption by 128% [17, 18].

In 2021–2026, the 107.8% increase in the management efficiency of the enterprise is small compared to other factors, which means that it is necessary to increase the stock of raw materials in order to increase the management efficiency of the enterprise. Because the increase in the size of the production capacity of the enterprise proportionally leads to the increase of the management efficiency of the enterprise.

# 6 Conclusion

In conclusion, it can be said that the research conducted on improving the efficiency of raw material supply to the enterprise allowed the author to obtain the following results:

1. The organizational and economic mechanism of enterprise management was formed by providing raw materials to the production process of JSC "Tashkent oil-oil combine" JSC and "Yangiyol oil-oil" JSC with the participation of foreign investors.
2. The coefficients of the regression equation and its quality criteria were checked for the change of management efficiency of JSC "Tashkent oil-oil combine" JSC in the form of a joint venture and "Yangiyol oil-oil" JSC with the participation of foreign investors as a result of the influence of selected factors.
3. A multi-factor forecast of the management efficiency of the Tashkent oil-oil enterprise was made for 2021–2026. As a result of the multi-factor forecast of the management efficiency of the Tashkent oil-oil enterprise, in 2026, compared to 2021, the enterprise's management efficiency is expected to increase by 102.4%, production costs by 116.8%, energy consumption by 133.1%, and raw material consumption by 109%.

# References

1. Burkhanov, A.U., Eshmamatova, M.M.Q.: The ways for improvement of investment strategy in the period of digital economy. ACM International Conference Proceeding Series, pp. 655–662 (2021)
2. Burkhanov, A., Bakhodirovna, B.D.: Evaluation of economic potential of textile industry enterprises. Vlakna Textil **28**(2), 9–21 (2021)
3. Bobir, O.T.: Provincial features of industrial production dynamics in the research of textile enterprises' financial security in Uzbekistan. In: Popkova, Elena G. (ed.) ISC 2020. LNNS, vol. 368, pp. 601–610. Springer, Cham (2022). https://doi.org/10.1007/978-3-030-93244-2_66
4. Kholmuminov, S., Tursunov, B., Saidova, M., Abduhalilova, L., Sadriddinova, N.: Improving the analysis of business processes in digital era. In: ACM International Conference Proceeding Series, vol. 2021, pp. 775–789 (2021)
5. Yuldashev, N.K., Nabokov, V.I., Nekrasov, K.V., Tursunov, B.O.: Modernization and intensification of agriculture in the republic of Uzbekistan. In: 2020 E3S Web of Conferences, vol. 222, pp. 6033 (2020)
6. Tursunov, B., Umarova, G., Yusupov, S., Bekmuradova, N.: Methods for optimizing decision making in eliminating subjective psychological factors as a tool for ensuring the economic security of textile enterprises. J. Adv. Res. Dyn. Control Syst. **12**(5), 330–341 (2020)
7. Abdullaeva, B., et al.: Optimal variable estimation of a Li-ion battery model by fractional calculus and bio-inspired algorithms. J. Energ. Storage **54**, 105323 (2022). https://doi.org/10.1016/j.est.2022.105323
8. Khasanov, K.N., Baratova, D.A., Uktamov, K.F., Abdusattarova, D.B.: Improving the practice of attracting financial resources from the international capital market to the corporate sector of the economy. In: ICFNDS 2021: The 5th International Conference on Future Networks & Distributed Systems December, pp. 718–727 (2021). https://doi.org/10.1145/3508072.3508213

9. Sari, A., et al.: A novel combined power generation and argon liquefaction system; investigation and optimization of energy, exergy, and entransy phenomena. J. Energy Storage **50**, 104613 (2022). https://doi.org/10.1016/j.est.2022.104613. https://www.sciencedirect.com/science/article/pii/S2352152X22006296

10. Abdusamat ugli Dadabaev, U., Faxriddinovich Uktamov, K., Abdurakhimovich Isadjanov, A., Rustamovich Sodikov, Z., Sherkulovna Batirova, N.: Ways to improve integration of Uzbekistan in global financial services with the participation of Takaful companies in the conditions of development of the digital economy. In: The 5th International Conference on Future Networks & Distributed Systems, pp. 440–446 (2021). https://doi.org/10.1145/350 8072.3508159

11. Patra, I., et al.: Synthesis of efficient cobalt–metal organic framework as reusable nanocatalyst in the synthesis of new 1, 4-dihydropyridine derivatives with antioxidant activity. Front. Chem. **10**, 943 (2022). https://www.frontiersin.org/articles/10.3389/fchem.2022.932902/full?&utm_source=Email_to_authors_&utm_medium=Email&utm_content=T1_11.5e1_author&utm_campaign=Email_publication&field=&journalName=Frontiers_in_Chemistry&id=932902

12. Salah Aldeen, O.D.A., Mahmoud, M.Z., Majdi, H.S., Mutlak, D.A., Fakhriddinovich Uktamov, K.: Investigation of effective parameters Ce and Zr in the synthesis of H-ZSM-5 and SAPO-34 on the production of light olefins from naphtha. Adv. Mater. Sci. Eng. **2022**, 1–22 (2022). https://doi.org/10.1155/2022/6165180

13. Tukhtabaev, J.S., Uktamov, K.F., Tillaeva, B.R., Akramova, R.R., Goziyeva, A.A.: Ways of development of agriculture and processing industry enterprises manufacturing cooperation. In: IOP Conference Series: Earth and Environmental Science, vol. 1043, no. 1, p. 012024. IOP Publishing (2022). https://iopscience.iop.org/article/10.1088/1755-1315/1043/1/012024/pdf

14. Arenas, L.A.B., et al.: Solamen vaillanti mollusk powder as an efficient biosorbent for removing cobalt ions from aqueous solution: kinetic and equilibrium studies. Iranian Chemical Society. www.physchemres.org, https://repositorio.utp.edu.pe/bitstream/handle/20.500.12867/5831/L.Barboza_PCR_Articulo_eng_2022.pdf?sequence=1

15. Smaisim, G.F., et al.: Nanofluids: properties and applications. J. Sol-Gel Sci. Technol. **104**, 1–35 (2022). https://doi.org/10.1007/s10971-022-05859-0

16. Sun, X., et al.: Optimization of dyes and toxic metals removal from environmental water samples by clinoptilolite zeolite using response surface methodology approach. Sci. Rep. **12**(1), 1–14 (2022). https://www.nature.com/articles/s41598-022-17636-8

17. Dwijendra, N.K.A., et al.: Improving the transition capability of the low-voltage wind turbine in the sub-synchronous state using a fuzzy controller. Clean Energy **6**(4), 682–692 (2022). https://doi.org/10.1093/ce/zkac033

18. Sharipov, K.A., Abdurashidova, N.A.: Benchmarking strategy for industrial enterprise development. In: The 5th International Conference on Future Networks & Distributed Systems, pp. 318–322 (2021)

# The Impact of Digital Infrastructure, Foreign Direct Investment and Trade Openness on Economic Growth: In the Case of Uzbekistan

Lochinbek Amirov[1,3] and Nuriddin Avazov[2](✉) iD

[1] Faculty of Economics, Tashkent State University of Economics, 49 Islam Karimov Avenue, Tashkent 100066, Uzbekistan
[2] Tashkent State University of Economics, 49 Islam Karimov Avenue, Tashkent 100066, Uzbekistan
avazovnuriddin@tsue.uz
[3] Department of Macroeconomic Analysis and Forecasting, Tashkent State University of Economics, 49 Islam Karimov Avenue, Tashkent 100066, Uzbekistan

**Abstract.** This study assess the impact of digital infrastructure and macroeconomic environment on economic growth. Telephone subscriptions, mobile subscriptions, broadband subscriptions, internet subscribers and secure internet servers are chosen as the main indicators of digital infrastructure. FDI and trade openness are taken as indicators of the macroeconomic environment. In the study, the impact of independent variables on the dependent variable is evaluated with the help of the Least Squares (NLS and ARMA) model for the economy of Uzbekistan from 2010 to 2021. Indicators of digital infrastructure and indicators of macroeconomic environment are included in the model as independent variables, while the growth of GDP per capita is taken as a dependent factor.

According to the results of the model, there is a strong positive relationship between FDI and trade openness to economic growth. Some indicators of digital infrastructure have a positive effect, while some indicators have a negative effect during the analyzed period. According to the results of model, the indicators of digital infrastructure such as telephone subscriptions and internet subscribers have a positive effect on economic growth, while mobile subscriptions, broadband subscriptions and secure internet servers have a negative effect. As a result of the study, it is suggested that the country should focus on conducting an active FDI policy and increasing the number of reforms aimed at increasing the openness of trade. Also, the country should emphasize the quality of the digital infrastructure as the main direction of the development of the digital economy. Through this, the country can ensure sustainable economic growth.

**Keywords:** digital economy · FDI · economic growth · trade openness · GDP · digital infrastructure · macroeconomic environment · telephone subscriptions · mobile subscriptions · broadband subscriptions · internet subscribers · secure internet servers · ICT

Y. Koucheryavy and A. Aziz (Eds.): NEW2AN 2022, LNCS 13772, pp. 322–332, 2023.
https://doi.org/10.1007/978-3-031-30258-9_27

# 1   Introduction

The digital economy is developing as a result of the expansion of the ICT sector, the increasing role of digital technologies in people's daily lives and the increase of factors such as the number of Internet users, the types of digital services. The development of the digital economy leads to the reduction of poverty through the creation of new modern jobs, the formation of low-cost education and medical services. On the other hand, as a result of digitalization of the economy, production efficiency and labor productivity will increase. This directly affects supply based on increased production. This can rise the real volume of GDP and stimulate economic growth. The development of digital economy is directly related to the development of digital infrastructure. The level of digital economy is determined by the level of development of digital infrastructure.

In the conducted studies, it was determined that ICT has a positive effect on the economic growth of countries, and trade openness and foreign direct investment have a negative effect on economic growth [1]. However, in another study based on various econometric models, it was found that the ICT sector and foreign direct investments have a positive effect on economic growth [2].

The main purpose of this study is to assess the impact of the development of the digital economy, the openness of trade and the increase in the inflow of foreign direct investment on economic growth. In recent years, the government of Uzbekistan has been conducting an active investment policy, focusing its economic policy on increasing the level of openness of the economy and developing the digital economy, so this topic is the most relevant for the economy of Uzbekistan. In order to achieve these goals, the government implemented a number of reforms and developed several laws.

There are several views on the impact of foreign direct investment on economic growth. According to a study devoted to the analysis of the impact of foreign direct investment on individual sectors of the economy, foreign direct investment has a negative impact on growth in the primary sector when it has a positive effect on production [3]. In the research conducted on the example of Chinese provinces, it was determined that the transfer of foreign technologies is the main determining factor of economic growth [4]. In a study carried out in the case of India, the positive effect of direct investment on general growth was determined [5].

A study of Tunisian case found that ICT use has a long-term relationship with value added and increased economic growth. Also, this study shows that trade openness has a positive and significant effect on economic growth [6].

According to a study of EU member states, ICT infrastructure has a positive and strong impact on economic growth. In addition, according to the results of the research, it was found that the inflation rate, unemployment rate, trade openness level, government spending and foreign direct investment have a strong influence on economic growth in the EU countries [7].

According to studies carried out in the case of Asian countries, there is a strong and positive relationship between trade openness and economic growth. The results of this study shows that the increase in trade openness affects economic growth through capital accumulation and efficiency increase [8].

This study is aimed at assessing the impact of digital infrastructure key indicators, foreign direct investment and trade openness on economic growth for the economy of Uzbekistan. Different studies have obtained different results regarding the impact of these variables on economic growth. It has been proven in various studies that depending on the state of the economy and the analyzed period, the impact of these factors can be positive or negative.

## 2 Literature Review

The impact of the digital economy, the ICT sector and foreign direct investment on economic growth has been studied by scientists using different methods for different countries and different periods.

Based on econometric modeling, R. Bahrini and A. Qaffas found that information and communication technologies such as mobile phone, Internet use and broadband connection were the main factors of economic growth in the developing countries of the Middle East, North Africa and the Sahara region [9]. According to the results study for the period from 2007 to 2016, to stimulate economic growth, researchers suggested developing financial sectors, providing a more favorable regulatory and institutional environment, increasing the openness of the economy, and developing ICT infrastructure.

M. Belloumi and K. Touati, based on the implementation of the economic model, found that ICT and direct investments have a positive and significant effect on economic growth in the long term. In addition, according to the results of the research, they found that ICT indicators have a positive effect on the flow of foreign direct investments in the long term [10].

In the research conducted by N. Rakhmanova, N. Avazov and others, it was found that there is a strong connection between investment activity and macroeconomic stability in the case of Uzbekistan. According to research results, the increase in investment activity leads to the strengthening of macroeconomic stability [11].

According to the results of research conducted by B. Casella and L. Formenti, highly digitalized multinational companies have a greater chance of receiving direct investment than non-digitalized companies [12].

L.T. Ha and N.T.T. Huyen found that digitization plays an important role in stimulating the flow of direct investment in the short-term and long-term perspective based on research [13]. The research conducted by N. Avazov, L. Azimova and S. Khayitov analyzed the impact of digitization process and investments on structural changes of the economy. According to the results of the research, there is a strong connection between these factors and structural changes, and the change of these factors has a significant impact on the structural changes of the economy [14].

A study by Premila Nazareth Satyanand states that the development of the digital economy is linked to the Fourth Industrial Revolution and will drive sustainable development through resource-efficient products, technological inclusion and new green technologies. The directions of strategic attraction of direct investments in order to build and expand countries' digital economies have been studied [15].

Y. J. Choi and J. Baek studied the impact of foreign direct investment on economic growth in the case of India and based on the general factor efficiency of foreign direct investment found a positive effect on economic growth [5].

A study conducted by L. Duarte, Y. Kedong, and L. Huemei examines the relationship between foreign direct investment, economic growth, and financial development. According to the results of the research, in the case of Cape Verde, foreign direct investment has a positive effect on economic growth in the long term. It was also noted that domestic private loans are a factor that negatively affects foreign direct investment [16].

In a study conducted by J. Zhang et al. it was found that the impact of the digital economy on economic growth varies by region, but this impact is positive. According to the study, the main effects of the digital economy can be seen in helping to renew the industrial structure, providing general employment and reorganizing employment. The study examines the impact of the global pandemic of COVID-19 on the digitization of the economy. According to the results of the research, while the digital industry has achieved great growth during the global pandemic in countries such as Armenia, Israel, Latvia and Estonia, it has been found that the pandemic has a negative impact on the formation of the digital industry in countries such as Ukraine, Egypt, Turkey and the Philippines [17].

According to the results of the research conducted by S. Jiao and Q. Sun, it was found that digital economic development in China has a positive effect on the economic growth of cities, and employment is the main factor determining the impact of the digital economy on economic growth [18].

In most of the previous studies, it was determined that the digital economy and foreign direct investments had a positive effect on economic growth during the analyzed period. The most difficult process in conducting research is measuring the level of the digital economy. Various indicators have been used as proxies to measure the level of the digital economy in research. In some studies, the share of ICT products and services in GDP is considered as an indicator of the digital economy. We use five indicators of digital infrastructure in our research.

It is known that economic growth is influenced by many factors. Digital economy, trade openness and foreign direct investment were selected among the factors in this study. The reason for the selection of these factors is that today the government of Uzbekistan considers the quality of the digital economy, trade openness and investments as the main drivers of economic development. As a result, the economic policy is aimed at developing the digital economy, increasing trade openness and rising the volume of investments. Based on this, it is important to assess the impact of the digital economy, trade openness and investments on economic growth in the case of Uzbekistan. Also, the impact of the digital economy, trade openness and foreign direct investment on economic growth has been studied in many international studies. There is a basis for this study from previous studies.

M. Sinha and P. Sengupta [2], G. Zekos [19], V. Valentina and others [20], S. Abendin and P. Duan [21], A. M. Ciobanu [22], T. Shodiev and others [25], Kamal Upadhyaya and others [24], Z.H. Yin and C. H. Choi [25], Reza Sultanuzzaman [26] and other scientists' researches were studied. In these studies, scholars have used different methodologies to examine the relationships between foreign direct investment, the digital economy, trade openness, and economic growth. The research we conducted was based on the research cited above. It was formed based on the analysis of the studied literature on the theoretical basis of the research.

## 3 Data and Methodology

In this study, we used annual data to estimate the impact of selected factors (share of foreign direct investment in GDP, indicators of digital infrastructure, share of trade in GDP) on economic growth (growth of GDP per capita). The analysis period includes the period from 2010 to 2021. The reason why this period was chosen is that the economic policy in Uzbekistan was focused on actively attracting investments, creating an economy open to the outside world, and developing a digital economy. Due to the implemented reforms, today researchers emphasize that the impact of investments, trade openness and digital infrastructure on the development of the economy is strong. The data for the research was formed on the basis of official statistical indicators of the World Bank (World Development Indicators).

Scientists have studied the relationship between foreign direct investment, digital economy, trade growth and economic growth using various models. The results of the studies differed depending on the selected country, period and indicators. In this study, we will evaluate the impact of factors on economic growth by forming an econometric model. We use the Least Squares (NLS and ARMA) model on time series in this study. Economic growth per capita is taken as a dependent variable in the model. Table 1 shows the classification of the variables obtained for the study.

**Table 1.** Classification of variables.

|  | Variables | Measurement | Symbols | Source |
|---|---|---|---|---|
|  | **Dependent variable** | | | |
|  | Economic growth per capita | GDP per capita growth (annual %) | GR_GDP | WDI |
|  | **Independent variable** | | | |
| **Digital infrastructure** | Telephone subscriptions | Fixed telephone subscriptions (per 100 people) | FTS | WDI |
|  | Mobile subscriptions | Mobile cellular subscriptions (per 100 people) | MCS | WDI |
|  | Broadband subscriptions | Fixed broadband subscriptions (per 100 people) | FBS | WDI |
|  | Internet subscribers | Individuals using the Internet (% of population) | IUI | WDI |
|  | Secure internet servers | Secure Internet servers (per 1 million people) | SIS | WDI |

*(continued)*

**Table 1.** (*continued*)

|  | Variables | Measurement | Symbols | Source |
|---|---|---|---|---|
| **Macroeconomic environment** | Trade | Trade (% of GDP) | TR_GDP | WDI |
|  | Foreign direct investment | Foreign direct investment, net inflows (% of GDP) | FDI_GDP | WDI |

Digital infrastructure is formed based on five indicators. These indicators include telephone subscriptions, mobile subscriptions, broadband subscriptions, internet subscribers and secure internet servers. The main indicator of trade openness is the share of trade in GDP. In the model, the share of FDI in GDP is taken as an indicator of foreign direct investment. Trade and foreign direct investments act as a factor indicating the macroeconomic environment in the model.

Using an econometric model, we estimate the impact of each independent variable on economic growth. Based on this, the model for this study will look like this:

$$\text{GR\_GDP} = \alpha\text{FDI\_GDP} + \beta\text{TR\_GDP} + \gamma\text{FTS} + \delta\text{MCS} + \lambda\text{FBS} + \eta\text{IUI} + \mu\text{SIS} + c \tag{1}$$

Using this model, we estimate the impact of FDI, trade openness and digital infrastructure indicators on GDP per capita on the example of the economy of Uzbekistan. According to the model, the coefficient of each independent variable ($\alpha, \beta, \gamma, \delta, \lambda, \eta, \mu$) shows how much it affects economic growth (GR_GDP).

## 4   Analysis and Results

There are theoretical frameworks on the impact of digital infrastructure, trade openness, and foreign direct investment on economic growth. In Uzbekistan, trade, digital economy and FDI have a high impact on the economy, and these sectors are considered the main sectors of the country's economy. Currently, the main directions of the government's economic policy are the development of the digital economy, ensuring the openness of trade, strengthening macroeconomic stability and achieving high economic growth based on increasing the inflow of FDI.

As a result of the economic policy carried out in the country in recent years, the macroeconomic indicators of the country have recorded positive changes. GDP per capita was 5,365% in 2015, but in 2021, it recorded a sharp increase after the pandemic and the growth rate was 5,319% (Fig. 1).

The economic growth rate showed a tendency to decrease to 2,652% in 2017, and to -0,053% in 2020. The fall in economic growth in 2020 is explained by the situation related to the pandemic. Despite the strong impact of the global pandemic on the economy, thanks to the reforms implemented in 2021, the country was able to achieve high growth during this period.

The volume of inflow of foreign direct investments and its share in GDP also increased during the analyzed period. The share of FDI in GDP was 1,208% in 2015,

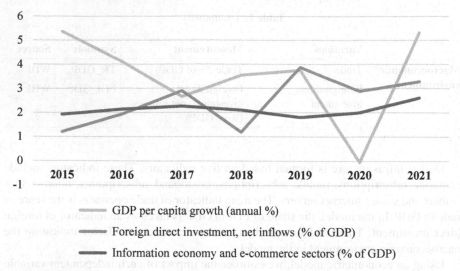

**Fig. 1.** Information about the digital economy, FDI and economic growth in Uzbekistan.

and this indicator increased to 3,867% by 2019. As a result of the negative impact of the pandemic on the economy, the FDI flow has a downward trend all over the world. This situation also affected the economy of Uzbekistan, and the share of FDI in GDP fell to 2,885%. After that, according to preliminary data, the share of FDI in GDP increased to 3,277%.

Information economy and e-commerce are one of the main indicators that determine the size of the digital economy. According to official statistics, the volume of this sector in 2015 was 1,927% of the country's GDP. As a result of reforms aimed at the development of the digital economy, the share of this sector in the GDP increased to 2,603% by 2021.

Table 2 shows the econometric analysis performed and the model results. According to this, some of the indicators of digital infrastructure have a positive effect on economic growth, while others have a negative effect.

According to the results of the Least Squares model, the econometric model showing the dependence of digital infrastructure, trade openness and FDI on economic growth in the economy of Uzbekistan is as follows:

$$GR\_GDP = 0,628FDI\_GDP + 0,148TR\_GDP + 0,007FTS - 0,032MCS - 0,479FBS + 0,273IUI - 0,029SIS - 6,256 \tag{2}$$

The model has an R-squared of 0,90 and an adjusted R-squared of 0.69. Accordingly, the independent variables included in the model can explain 69% of the dependent variable, i.e. economic growth.

According to the results of the model, three of the indicators of digital infrastructure have a negative impact on economic growth. Using an econometric model, it was determined that mobile subscriptions, broadband subscriptions and secure internet servers have a negative impact on economic growth during the analyzed period.

**Table 2.** Least Squares (NLS and ARMA) Model results.

Dependent Variable: GR_GDP
Method: Least Squares
Sample (adjusted): 2010 2021
Included observations: 12 after adjustments

| Variable | Coefficient | Std. Error | t-Statistic | Prob. |
|---|---|---|---|---|
| FBS | -0.478861 | 0.702400 | -0.681750 | 0.5443 |
| FTS | 0.007176 | 1.356446 | 0.005290 | 0.9961 |
| IUI | 0.273368 | 0.116185 | 2.352875 | 0.1000 |
| MCS | -0.032372 | 0.068186 | -0.474762 | 0.6674 |
| SIS | -0.029180 | 0.014692 | -1.986083 | 0.1412 |
| FDI_GDP | 0.628261 | 0.649556 | 0.967215 | 0.4048 |
| TR_GDP | 0.148316 | 0.059656 | 2.486182 | 0.0888 |
| C | -6.256399 | 11.19054 | -0.559080 | 0.6151 |

| | | | |
|---|---|---|---|
| R-squared | 0.909195 | Mean dependent var | 4.081115 |
| Adjusted R-squared | 0.697317 | S.D. dependent var | 1.654018 |
| S.E. of regression | 0.909984 | Akaike info criterion | 2.804484 |
| Sum squared resid | 2.484215 | Schwarz criterion | 3.093862 |
| Log likelihood | -7.424661 | Hannan-Quinn criter. | 2.622071 |
| F-statistic | 4.291129 | Durbin-Watson stat | 2.239306 |
| Prob(F-statistic) | 0.129375 | | |

Two of the indicators of digital infrastructure have a positive effect on economic growth. Accordingly, the positive effect of telephone subscriptions and internet subscribers on economic growth was determined. Of the digital infrastructure indicators, the most important and most influential factor is individuals using the internet. According to it, a one percent increase in the number of individuals using the Internet will increase economic growth by 0,273%. Also, a one percent increase in the number of telephone subscriptions leads to a 0,007% increase in economic growth.

Despite the fact that in some studies, the increase in the volume of broadband subscriptions, mobile subscriptions and secure internet servers has a positive effect on economic growth, according to the results of our research, these indicators of digital infrastructure have a negative effect on economic growth in the analyzed period. According to the results, a one-unit increase in broadband subscriptions can reduce economic growth by 0,478%, a one-unit increase in the number of mobile subscriptions can lead to a 0,032% decrease in the number of secure internet servers, and a one-unit increase in the number of secure internet servers can lead to a 0,029% decrease.

According to the results of the research, the macroeconomic environment had a positive effect on economic growth during the analyzed period. A one percent increase in the share of FDI in GDP leads to an increase in economic growth by 0,628%, and a one percent increase in the share of trade in GDP leads to an increase in economic growth by 0,148%.

In general, in the case of the Uzbekistan's economy, it was found that the variables selected as indicators of the macroeconomic environment have a positive effect on economic growth. Among the selected variables, the largest effect can be seen in FDI. That is, among the selected variables, the increase in the volume of FDI has the greatest impact on economic growth. The development of trade was also found to be a factor stimulating economic growth. Digital infrastructure indicators have also been found to have a positive effect on economic growth. It was found that some of the five indicators that make up the digital infrastructure have a negative effect on economic growth, and some have a positive effect. According to this, in the analyzed period, variables such as mobile subscriptions, broadband subscriptions and secure internet servers have a negative impact on economic growth, while factors such as telephone subscriptions and internet subscribers have a positive impact.

## 5 Conclusion and Recommendations

Developing the digital economy, creating an open economy, and achieving sustainable economic growth on the basis of increasing FDI flows into the economy are the main directions of economic policy in the countries of the world today. Many studies have found that digital infrastructure performance, FDI, and trade openness have strong effects on economic growth. According to them, the impact of these factors on economic growth is positive. One of the main indicators of the level of the digital economy is the digital infrastructure. Telephone subscriptions, mobile subscriptions, broadband subscriptions, internet subscribers and secure internet servers have been selected as indicators of digital infrastructure according to international research. We also used the above factors as indicators of digital infrastructure in this study. Trade openness and FDI are listed as indicators of the macroeconomic environment.

Based on econometric analysis, it was found that indicators of the macroeconomic environment have a positive and strong influence on economic growth. Based on this, the government of Uzbekistan is suggested to continue active investment and foreign trade policy. Because according to the results of the model, an increase in the share of FDI in GDP by one percent leads to an increase in economic growth by 0.628%. A one percent increase in the share of trade in GDP leads to an increase in GDP of 0.273%. In this case, it is possible to increase FDI flows based on increasing the efficiency of government free economic zones and small industrial zones. In theory, an increase in FDI stimulates production, which is directly related to an increase in trade. Based on the increase in the volume of production, it leads to an increase in sales by increasing the supply in the market.

Among the indicators of digital infrastructure, the factors of telephone subscriptions and internet subscribers have a positive effect on economic growth. It is recommended that the government take measures to increase the number of telephone subscriptions and the number of Internet users in order to develop the digital economy. Through this, the government can directly stimulate economic growth. It was found that factors such as mobile subscriptions, broadband subscriptions and secure internet servers had a negative impact on economic growth during the analyzed period. But theoretically, these factors have an important impact on the development of the digital economy. Research has shown that these factors have a positive effect on the development of the digital economy and economic growth.

In recent years, Uzbekistan has been achieving high economic growth. Even during the global pandemic, the country's economic growth rate did not drop significantly due to measures taken in the country. Also, in the period of recovery of the economy after the pandemic, the country experienced high economic growth, that is, in 2021, GDP growth was 7,1%, GDP growth per capita was 5,3%. According to studies, the main drivers of macroeconomic stability and high economic growth during this period were FDI, industrial development, the expansion of the scale of the digital economy, and the development of trade. Our research has confirmed that the digital economy, FDI and trade are the factors leading to high growth of Uzbekistan's economy. But while some indicators of digital infrastructure have been confirmed to have a positive effect on economic growth in other studies, in our study it was found that these indicators had a negative effect on economic growth in the analyzed period.

The main result of the study, namely the assessment of the impact of digital infrastructure, FDI and trade openness on economic growth, was achieved. But this study was carried out only in the case of Uzbekistan, and it is planned to increase the scope of the study by including other countries in the next studies. Also, expanding the data base for research, it is appropriate to evaluate the impact of factors on economic growth based on complex econometric models.

# References

1. Soomro, A.N., Kumar, J., Kumari, J.: The dynamic relationship between FDI, ICT, trade openness, and economic growth: evidence from BRICS countries. J. Asian Finan. Econ. Bus. 9(2), 295–303 (2022). https://doi.org/10.13106/JAFEB.2022.VOL9.NO2.0295
2. Sinha, M., Sengupta, P.P.: FDI inflow, ICT expansion and economic growth: an empirical study on Asia-Pacific developing countries. Glob. Bus. Rev. 23(3), 804–821 (2022). https://doi.org/10.1177/0972150919873839
3. Alfaro, L.: Foreign direct investment and growth: does the sector matter. Harvard Bus. School, 2003, 1–31 (2003). http://www.grips.ac.jp/teacher/oono/hp/docu01/paper14.pdf
4. Berthelemy, J.-C., Demurger, S.: Foreign direct investment and economic growth: theory and application to China. Rev. Dev. Econ. 4(2), 140–155 (2000). https://doi.org/10.1111/1467-9361.00083
5. Choi, Y.J., Baek, J.: Does FDI really matter to economic growth in India? Economies 5, 20 (2017). https://doi.org/10.3390/economies5020020
6. Dahmani, M., Mabrouki, M., Ben Youssef, A.: ICT, trade openness and economic growth in Tunisia: what is going wrong? Econ Change Restruct 55, 2317–2336 (2022). https://doi.org/10.1007/s10644-022-09388-2
7. Toader, E., Firtescu, B.N., Roman, A., Anton, S.G.: Impact of information and communication technology infrastructure on economic growth: an empirical assessment for the EU countries. Sustainability 10(10), 3750 (2018). https://doi.org/10.3390/su10103750
8. Trejos, S., Barboza, G.: Dynamic estimation of the relationship between trade openness and output growth in Asia. J. Asian Econ. 36, 110–125 (2015). https://doi.org/10.1016/j.asieco.2014.10.001
9. Bahrini, R., Qaffas, A.: Impact of information and communication technology on economic growth: evidence from developing countries. Economies 7(1), 21 (2019). https://doi.org/10.3390/economies7010021

10. Belloumi, M., Touati, K.: Do FDI inflows and ICT affect economic growth? an evidence from Arab countries. Sustainability 14, 6293 (2022). https://doi.org/10.3390/su14106293
11. Avazov, N.R., Rakhmanova, N.T., Kakhramonov, J.B., Azimova, N.N., Muratova, M.N.: Ensuring macroeconomic stability and increasing investment activity (a case of Uzbekistan). J. Contemp. Issues Bus. Gov. 27(2), 5128–5136 (2021). https://doi.org/10.47750/cibg.2021. 27.02.525, https://cibgp.com/article_10862.html
12. Casella, B., Formenti, L.: FDI in the digital economy: a shift to asset-light international footprints. Transnational Corporations, 25(1), 101–130 (2019). https://ssrn.com/abstract=337 3815
13. Ha, L.T., Huyen, N.T.T.: Impacts of digitalization on foreign investments in the European region during the COVID-19 pandemic. Dev. Stud. Res. 9(1), 177–191 (2022). https://doi. org/10.1080/21665095.2022.2074863
14. Nuriddin, A., Lola, A., Khayitov, S.: The impact of the digitalization process and investment on the structural changes of the economy. Rev. Geintec-Gestao Inovacao Tecnologias, 11(4), 2194–2207 (2021). https://doi.org/10.47059/revistageintec.v11i4.2264, https://www. revistageintec.net/index.php/revista/article/view/2264
15. Satyanand, P.N.: Foreign direct investment and the digital economy. ARTNeT on FDI Working Paper Series, No. 2, July 2021, Bangkok, ESCAP (2021). https://artnet.unescap.org/fdi
16. Duarte, L.D.R.V., Kedong, Y., Xuemei, L.:The relationship between FDI, economic growth and financial development in Cabo Verde. Int. J. Econ. Finan. Can. Cent. Sci. Educ. 9(5), 132–142 (2017). https://doi.org/10.5539/ijef.v9n5p132
17. Zhang, J., et al.: The impact of digital economy on the economic growth and the development strategies in the post-COVID-19 era: evidence from countries along the "belt and road." Front. Pub. Health 10, 856142 (2022). https://doi.org/10.3389/fpubh.2022.856142
18. Jiao, S., Sun, Q.: Digital economic development and its impact on econimic growth in China: research based on the prespective of sustainability. Sustainability 13(18), 10245 (2021). https://doi.org/10.3390/su131810245
19. Zekos, G.: Foreign direct investment in a digital economy. Eur. Bus. Rev. 17(1), 52–68 (2005). https://doi.org/10.1108/09555340510576267
20. Vukmirović, V., et al.: Foreign direct investments' impact on economic growth in Serbia. J. Balkan Near East Stud. 23(1), 122–143 (2021). https://doi.org/10.1080/19448953.2020.181 8028
21. Abendin, S., Duan, P.: International trade and economic growth in Africa: the role of the digital economy. Cogent Econ. Finan. 9(1), 1911767 (2021). https://doi.org/10.1080/23322039. 2021.1911767
22. Ciobanu, A.M.: The impact of FDI on economic growth in case of Romania. Int. J. Econ. Finan. 12(12), 1–81 (2021). https://doi.org/10.5539/ijef.v12n12p81
23. Shodiev, T., Turayey, B., Shodiyev, K.: ICT and economic growth nexus: case of central Asian countries. Procedia Soc. Sci. Humanit. 1, 155–167 (2021).https://doi.org/10.21070/ pssh.v1i.37
24. Upadhyaya, K.P., Pradhal, G., Dhakal, D., Bhandari, R.: Foreign aid, FDI and economic growth in east European countries. Econ. Bull. 6(13), 1–9 (2007). https://digitalcommons. newhaven.edu/economics-facpubs/15/
25. Yin, Z.H., Choi, C.H.: Has the internet increased FDI, economic growth, and trade? Evid. Asian Econ. Inf. Dev. 38(2), 192–203 (2022). https://doi.org/10.1177/0266666921999749
26. Sultanuzzaman, M.R., Fan, H., Akash, M., Wang, B., Shakij, U.S.M.: The role of FDI inflows and export on economic growth in Sri Lanka: an ARDL approach, Cogent Econ. Finan. 6(1), 1518116 (2018). https://doi.org/10.1080/23322039.2018.1518116. Maggie Chen (Reviewing editor)

# The Impact of the Financial Ratios on the Financial Performance. A Case of Chevron Corporation (CVX)

Bunyod Usmonov(✉) ᴵᴰ

Department of Financial Analysis and Audit, Tashkent State University of Economics, Tashkent, Uzbekistan
b.usmonov@tsue.uz

**Abstract.** The effect of financial ratios on financial performance of an American multinational energy corporation Chevron Corporation (CVX) was investigated in this paper for the period 1994 to 2020. In this paper current ratio (CR) and cash ratio (Cash R) represent the liquidity ratios, debt ratio (DR) and debt to equity ratio (DTER) represent the leverage ratios, while return on assets ratio (ROA) and return on equity ratio (ROE) shows the profitability ratios and earnings per share ratio (EPS) represents market value ratio. According to the results and the financial performance of the company, CVX faced financial problems, which shrank to negative due to the financial crisis and pandemic. However, this company is now the world's seventh-largest oil company based on revenue. The results depict that the earnings per share ratio (EPS), return on equity ratio (ROE) have a positive relationship, while the debt ratio (DR) has a negative association with the company's financial performance.

**Keywords:** Financial performance · Financial ratios · Liquidity ratios · Leverage ratios · Profitability ratios

## 1 Introduction

The negative consequences of the coronavirus pandemic in 2020 had impact not only particular countries but also affected the entire global economy including the oil industry. This situation has highlighted the urgency of preparing this article. Chevron is one of the top most developed oil companies in the United States and all around the globe as well. Originally, Frederick Tylerin was the founder of this company which penetrated more than 180 companies around the world. Plus, this company was acknowledged as one of the most lucrative oil companies between 1940 and 1970. It is worth mentioning that in 2020, it ranked fifth in the world with revenue of $ 146.5 billion and $ 136 billion. To begin with, as it is mentioned, Chevron company has a long, robust history, which began as a group of explorers and merchants established the Pacific Coast Oil Co. September 10, 1879. After 11 years, the Californian Company was bought by the trust for $ 761,000. Meanwhile, for Standard Oil, California was of interest not only as a source of raw materials and a sales market, but also as a port for entering the Asian

Y. Koucheryavy and A. Aziz (Eds.): NEW2AN 2022, LNCS 13772, pp. 333–344, 2023.
https://doi.org/10.1007/978-3-031-30258-9_28

market. In 1906, Pacific Coast and Iowa Standard merged into one company Standard Oil Company (California), or SoCal in brief and the capitalization of the new company increased from $ 1 million to $ 25 million. Another refinery was built in El Segundo near Los Angeles, thanks to which the company became the state leader in the production of kerosene, 80 percent of which was exported to Asia. In 1933, the company bought the rights to produce oil in Saudi Arabia for £ 5,000 a year. After World War II, it became clear that even both companies would not have enough capacity to develop such huge reserves, so 40% of the newly created joint venture Aramco (Arabian-American Company) was sold to other oil companies, SoCal and Texas Company each kept 30%. By the mid-1950s, Saudi Arabia accounted for a third of SoCal's production and two-thirds of SoCal's reserves, although the company also began producing oil in Venezuela and Sumatra, and large fields discovered in Texas and Louisiana. The 1973 oil crisis made SoCal's operations much more difficult, as Arabian oil quadrupled in price at once and the company (at least formally) lost control of it to the Saudi Arabian government. Related industries, the company in 1984 acquired a competitor of approximately equal oil reserves, Gulf Oil, and therefore changed its name to Chevron Corporation (the name Chevron has been used for several decades to sell oil products outside of California). The $ 13.2 billion purchase (the largest at the time) made Chevron the owner of the largest retail chain in the United States. In the early 1980s, oil began to fall in price, so Chevron acquired $ 12 billion in debt amid falling sales; the assets of Gulf in Canada and part of the gas station network were sold. In 2001, Chevron Corporation acquired Texaco for $ 45 billion, which changed the name to ChevronTexaco. In 2005, another oil company, Unocal Corporation, was bought for $ 18.4 billion, in connection with which the name of the company again became Chevron Corporation. In July 2020, Chevron agreed to purchase an oil and gas company, Noble Energy.

## 2 Problem Statement

A study done in America to compare the financial performance of the pre- and post-merger of the Chevron companies (2020) demonstrated that the major component in the financial and economic environment all over the world is corporate restructuring and importance of corporate fund. Companies in America have begun restructuring their operations for their core business activities. Thus, this study is conducted with the purpose of analyzing the financial performance of a Chevron company, from 1994–2020. The main focus of this study is the financial performance of the selected merged company based on performance from 1994 to 2020.

## 3 Research Questions

A number of questions relating to the problem statement have been developed.

The research questions are:

Q1. Do the liquidity ratios affect the company's financial performance?
Q2. Is there a relationship between the leverage ratio and the company's financial performance?
Q3. Do the profitability ratios have an impact on a company's financial performance?

# 4 Research Objectives

The primary goal of this research is to examine the financial performance of Chevron Corporation (CVX).

The objectives are:

1. to investigate the influence of liquidity ratios on the financial performance of the firm;
2. to analyze whether the leverage ratios effect the financial performance of a company;
3. to examine whether the profitability ratios impact the company's financial performance.

# 5 Significance of the Study

There is not enough study on the financial performance of oil company. As a result, this research could be used as a measurement to determine the financial performance of an oil company.

# 6 Scope of the Study

The analysis will concentrate on the company's financial performance, particularly between 1994 and 2020, as this may have significantly influenced the company's success. For the fifteen years from 1994 to 2020, data was gathered from CVX's Annual Report.

# 7 Literature Review

In general perspective, there are numbers of research studies have been carried out to identify and analyze the efficiency of capital in companies.

According to the investigations of Asmaul Husna and Ibnu Satria (2019) the return on asset and firm size have effects on firm value, while researching manufacturing companies listed in Indonesia Stock Exchange but debt to asset ratio, current ratio and dividend payout ratio did not affect to the firm value [3]. Moreover, it is suggested that companies paid more attention to that factors which influence the firm value. Furthermore, it is recommended to include the risk taking policy variable in order to take better test results.

Research done by James Sunday, K. (2011), informs that efficiency of capital in companies is crucial not only on its liquidity but also for its solvency [20]. Moreover, increasing capital efficiency provides financial stability of company and gives more and more opportunity of continuous growth by controlling the budget and development system of company.

Damodaran, A. (2012) research, contributing effective management of the company's capital is carried out by the value of debt capital and equity. Furthermore, researcher cited that the equity and debt capital play the major role in its effective management [21].

From the perspective of Leland, H. E. (1994) capital structure of companies is crucial in determining the value of their debt capital and its equity in order to value efficiency of not only equity but also companies value [22]. Researcher finds out that increase in debt capital gives more efficiency and moreover, company will generate plans according to its strategy.

Research paper from Burkhanov, A., & Begalova, D. B. (2021) gives information that efficiency of the company would be established by the effective capital management from which company would take more and more assets to its future and provide higher level of effective capital management [23].

Looking to the papers of Feng-Li Lin and Tsangyao Chang (2011) using model to test whether there is a 'threshold' debt ratio which causes there to be asymmetrical relationships between debt ratio and firm value in listed companies of Taiwan [8]. It is recommended by the test results which are consistent with the trade-off theory, and gives suggestion that there is a static amount of debt which prompts managers to find the 'optimal capital structure' and at the same time maximizes firm value when the benefits of debt equal the marginal cost of debt of course.

Looking to the Aswath Damodaran (2007) research, the author determined that there has been a move in corporate fund and valuation, which had a greater emphasis on excess returns in assessing a company's worth [4]. Moreover, there are models related to determining the relationship between growth and value; which the author describes that higher growth firms were assigned higher values unless more recent iterations growth cannot be valued. And as a result, by examining accounting and cash flow measures of returns, the prediction is determined to forecast any business management with financial ratios.

Aripin, Norhani and Abdulmumuni, Ogirima (2020) investigated the relationship between financial leverage and financial performance of Nigerian manufacturing firms and found out that firms' profitability is the firms' capital structure framework known as financial leverage was affected among the internal organizational factors [2]. According to the researchers, Nigerian manufacturing firms economic power is positively and significantly associated with financial performance, measured as return on equity (ROE). In the next level, these firms with the return on equity (ROE) index are positively associated with a moderate level of debt ratio. All in all, it is recommended that Nigerian manufacturing firms should apply the agency theory of optimal debts financing to fix their financial constraint and low-performance issues.

From the perspective of Mimelientesa Irman and Astri Ayu Purwati (2020) who's research conducted to the Indonesian Stock Exchange companies for the 5 years period from 2011 to 2017, to find out whether the Current Ratio (CR), Debt to Equity Ratio (DTER), and Total Asset Turnover effect on Return on Assets (ROA). As a consequence, the study found that Total Asset has a significant positive effect on Return on Assets (ROA) while the Current Ratio (CR) which has a significant effect on Return on Assets (ROA), Debt to Equity Ratio (DTER) has not considerable negative effect on Return on Assets (ROA) [10].

The study, which is organized by Basaria Christina Marito, Andam Dewi Sjarif (2020), selected financial ratios in 18 manufacturing companies listed on the Indonesia Stock Exchange (IDX), such as current ratio as one of the liquidity ratios, debt-to-equity ratio as leverage ratios, and return on assets as profitability ratios to empirically investigate the firm's performance on stock return from the period 2012–2016 [5]. In conclusion of researchers, it is founded that firm's performance simultaneously influenced stock market return, however, witnessing decline for a long time.

The paper written by Novi Nurbadriyah, Suci Lymartha, Wulan Griyandani Lenggana, Mutia Yulita Amarilis, Dudi Abdul Hadi (2020) analyzes the cement industry of companies listed on the Indonesia Stock Exchange exactly, PT. Holcim Indonesia Tbk (SMCB) in 5 years period, from 2013 to 2018 which experienced financial distress and in the meaning of financial distress can be predicted using Return on assets (ROA), liquidity ratios (Current Ratio), and leverage ratios (Debt Equity Ratio) are all revealed [13]. During the investigation, it is analyzed using the method of data analysis from which researchers made summary that on the one hand, partly financial distress is influenced by return on assets, current ratio, and debt equity ratio, while, on the other hand, current ratio, concurrently return on assets, and debt to equity ratio witnessed simultaneous influence on financial distress in cement sub-sector companies.

While studying beverage companies listed on the Indonesia Stock Exchange (BEI) from 2016 to 2018, Eda Nuarta, I Gede Arimbawa, Mahmood Maarof Abdullah Alwan, Elok Damayanti, Joko Suyono determined that the Debt to Equity Ratio (DER) variable has a negative effect on Price Earning Ratio (PER) and Return on Equity (ROE) has a positive effect on Price Earning Ratio (PER), while the DAR variable has no effect on PER. And other variables Debt to Equity Ratio (DER), Debt to Asset Ratio (DAR), and Return on Equity (ROE) has a positive effect on Price Earning Ratio (PER).

Desi Ratnasari (2020) research analyzes the effect of Debt to Equity Ratio (DER) and Earning Per Share (EPS), which are taken as independent variables on Company Value at PT INDOSAT, TBK from the period 2004 to 2018 [7]. According to the research results, Earning Per Share (EPS) has no impact on firm value, Debt to Equity Ratio (DER) has no effect and no significant effect on firm value, as well as, Debt to Equity Ratio (DER) and Earning Per Share (EPS) simultaneously have no influence on firm value but analyzes showed it resulted for other variables.

While examining Süleyman Serdar Karaca and Arif Savsar's (2012) paper which is dedicated to the impact of financial ratios on firm value as an example of 36 Food-Drink-Tobacco and Basic Metal Industry firms between 2002 and 2009 [1]. As a consequence, it is found out a significant positive relation between receivables turnover and firm value, while there is a significant negative relation between inventory turnover and return on equity but there is no significant relation between the other ratios.

Based on the investigation of Prof. Roberto Moro Visconti (2018), two financial ratios Return on equity (ROE) and Return on assets (ROA) are considered as an important key factors [16]. And Return on equity is emphasized as a measure of business profitability with the impact of company investments to its profits while on the other hand, the return on assets (ROA) is described as an indicator of profitability of the company, from which the manager and the investor can make an idea of how effective the company's management assets are for profit generation. A research by Ida Bagus Raka

Suardana, I Nengah Dasi Astawa, Luh Kadek Budi Martini (2018) expresses opinion that ratio as used to estimate the ability to generate income or profit in a given financial period; simultaneously, the most significant rate of return, which determines the efficacy of financial institutions, is the return on assets (ROA) [9]. As an example of Banks, researchers concluded that there are kind of organizations which have a high rate of return on assets (ROA).

In the paper of Jií Strouhal, Petra Stamfestova, Alexander Kljucnikov, Zuzana Vincúrová (2018), return on assets (ROA) in various research studies measures financial performance. Financial ratios, such as asset return (ROA), may be scientifically examined and subjectively applied using information from financial statements and measures [11]. The influence of accounting standards on the data acquired and the precision with which return on assets (ROA) is calculated reflects the amount of income earned by a unit of currency (dollars, euros, etc.) throughout the reporting period.

In addition to this, Pertiwi Tan and Annaria Magdalena Marpaung approved the Return on equity (ROE) ratio as the profitability ratio, which is a measure of the ability of the company to make a profit and simultaneously determines the level of effective management and the right strategy of the company [14]. But researcher Mathuva (2009) studied the Capital structure and regulatory capital of French banks and discovered that bank profitability has a positive impact on capital ratio by using the return on assets (ROA) and return on equity (ROE) as a measure of a bank's profitability ten years period between 1998 and 2007. According to the author, however, there is positive relation to capital ratio. Still, also it is found that the capital ratio and equity had a negative association during the period studied. Molina-Azorín, J.F., Claver-Cortes, E., Lopez-Gamero, M.D. and Tari, J.J. (2009), studied financial performance and results that have a positive impact on financial performance is obtained as predominant. Moreover, the findings revealed that the set of firms and industries are varied [12].

Research by T.P.Nikolaeva and Pornpen Thippayana determined that companies profitability index, which evaluates its financial performance and effectiveness, can only be determined by a system of profitability indicators [15]. In addition to this, the company's profitability indicators serve to find efficiency and profitability, which is investigated by a listed company in the Thailand stock exchange market and confirmed by the authors that leverage ratios increase with firm size and decrease with profitability significantly. Another study by A.A. Zaitseva found out that financial indicator for investors and business owners is the profitability of their capital and accounts as an essential index for further development [19]. And to support this, the researcher using the DuPont model achieved that the return on equity is affected by certain factors. That, in the author's opinion, reflects profitability and growth in the company's value.

# 8 Research Methodology

In this study, all the data were determined through Chevron corporation's website in 25 years, from 1994 to 2019. Additionally, data is gathered from reliable sources and official websites: Journal for Financial Performance, Elsevier journals, Google Scholar, journals from Sciencedirect and others. As a method of the study, multiple regression analysis is used. In addition to this, the financial ratio is regressed by using the E-views program.

The model of the research is:

$$\text{NET INCOME(CVX)} = \alpha(\text{EPS}) + \alpha(\text{ROE}) + \alpha(\text{DR}) + \alpha \qquad (1)$$

where Net Income (CVX), is the Chevron Corporation financial performance; $\alpha$, is the constant Value; EPS$\alpha$, is the earnings per share ratio; $\alpha$(ROE), is the return on equity ratio; $\alpha$(DR), is the debt ratio.

## 9  Analysis and Interpretation

While analyzing, the multiple regression models test the relationship between the dependent and independent variables, including 26 observations. And in this model, the Chevron Corporation's financial performance (Net Income (CVX) is a dependent variable, and the return on equity ratio (ROE), debt ratio (DR) (leverage ratio) and the earnings per share ratio (EPS) (profitability ratios) are the independent variables. During the research, the regression model is analyzed by the least square method. The result (Table 1):

$$\text{NET INCOME(CVX)} = 14.5908 * (\text{EPS}) + 2.1549 * (\text{ROE}) - 0.0957 * (\text{DR}) + 10.033$$
$$\text{t st}(2.35) \qquad \text{tst (6.75)} \qquad \text{tst } (-7.89) \quad \text{tst}(35.41) \qquad (2)$$

**Table 1.** The impact of the financial ratios on the financial performance.

| Variable | Coefficient | Std. Error | t-Statistic | Prob |
|---|---|---|---|---|
| Earnings Per Share Ratio | 14.59082 | 6.208084 | 2.350294 | 0.0281 |
| Return On Equity Ratio | 2.154966 | 0.318927 | 6.756925 | 0.0000 |
| Debt Ratio | −0.095748 | 0.012124 | −7.897371 | 0.0000 |
| C | 10.03321 | 0.283268 | 35.41956 | 0.0000 |
| R-squared | 0.770265 | Mean dependent var | | 8.481968 |
| Adjusted R-squared | 0.738937 | S.D. dependent var | | 1.395295 |
| S.E. of regression | 0.712916 | Akaike info criterion | | 2.301733 |
| Sum squared resid | 11.18149 | Schwarz criterion | | 2.495286 |
| Log likelihood | −25.92252 | Hannan-Quinn criter | | 2.357469 |
| F-statistic | 24.58747 | Durbin-Watson stat | | 2.194742 |
| Prob(F-statistic) | 0.000000 | | | |

where adjusted R2: 0.7389; F-statistic: 24.587; Durbin-Watson statistic: 2.194; t-statistic is demonstrated in parentheses under the formula.

From the result above, it is evident that when the ROE, DR ratio are equal to zero, the financial performance (net income) of CVX in term of net income will be declined to $10.033 million. CVX's performance (net income) will increase by $14.5908 million when the EPS increases by $1. Moreover, the net income of CVX's performance will also have a positive result which increases of $0.0957 million when the DR decreases by $1. Furthermore, the company's financial performance will rise by $2.1549 million when the ROE increases by $1. It depicts a positive relationship between CVX with EPS and ROE, while there is a negative relationship between CVX and DR.

All the independent variables are significantly based on the 5% level of significance. Based on analysis via the individual significance test (t-statistic), it can be concluded that ROE is the variable that has a highly significant impact on CVX, followed by the EPS and DR. The objective of this study is therefore achieved: the ROE is identified as the main variable that impacts upon CVX (Table 2).

**Table 2.** Breusch-Godfrey Serial Correlation LM Test.

| F-statistic | 0.649137 | Prob. F(2,20) | | 0.5332 |
|---|---|---|---|---|
| Obs*R-squared | 1.584877 | Prob. Chi-Square(2) | | 0.4527 |
| Dependent Variable: RESID | | | | |
| Variable | Coefficient | Std. Error | t-Statistic | Prob |
| Earnings Per Share Ratio | −3.045449 | 7.267024 | −0.419078 | 0.6796 |
| Return On Equity Ratio | −0.005267 | 0.326228 | −0.016146 | 0.9873 |
| Debt Ratio | 0.000662 | 0.012337 | 0.053647 | 0.9577 |
| C | 0.017305 | 0.290412 | 0.059589 | 0.9531 |
| Resid(−1) | −0.199541 | 0.255628 | −0.780593 | 0.4442 |
| Resid(−2) | −0.212574 | 0.234125 | −0.907952 | 0.3747 |
| R-squared | 0.060957 | Mean dependent var | | −1.27E−15 |
| Adjusted R-squared | −0.173804 | S.D. dependent var | | 0.668775 |
| S.E. of regression | 0.724565 | Akaike info criterion | | 2.392685 |
| Sum squared resid | 10.49990 | Schwarz criterion | | 2.683015 |
| Log likelihood | −25.10491 | Hannan-Quinn criter | | 2.476290 |
| F-statistic | 0.259655 | Durbin-Watson stat | | 2.038348 |
| Prob(F-statistic) | 0.929793 | | | |

The Breusch–Godfrey test results are demonstrated above which is used to assess the validity of some modelling assumptions specific to the application of regression-like models based on the observed data. In particular, it checks for a series of correlations that are not included in the proposed model structure. At the same time, it indicates that it receives erroneous conclusions or sub-optimal estimates of model parameters from other tests. Here, the Breush-Godfrey test is a test for autocorrelation of errors in the regression model, which uses the residues of the model under consideration in the regression analysis, through which the test statistics are derived.

The most important part of the Breusch–Godfrey test data is the first part, which presents the two statistical tests: F-Statistic and the second one - R-squared and the probabilities associated with these tests. In addition, two tests null hypothesis illustrates that there is no serial correlation of the equation errors. The null hypothesis is rejected if the probability associated with the two tests is less than the level of relevance we are working on; therefore, we reject the non-existence of serial correlation.

From above, we can see that coefficients of EPS, ROA are negative, while for DR, it shows a positive result. And this for t-Statistics also accounted as same as coefficients results. Moreover, the results depict that F-statistic 0.65 and Obs*R-squared over 1.5 points while p-value equalled to 0.5, indicating autocorrelation for some order (Table 3).

**Table 3.** Heteroskedasticity Test: Breusch-Pagan-Godfrey.

| F-statistic | 0.854200 | Prob. F(3,22) | 0.4794 |
|---|---|---|---|
| Obs*R-squared | 2.712563 | Prob. Chi-Square(3) | 0.4381 |
| Scaled explained SS | 2.256824 | Prob. Chi-Square(3) | 0.5208 |
| Dependent Variable: RESID^2 | | | |
| Variable | Coefficient | Std. Error | t-Statistic | Prob. |
| C | 0.331337 | 0.268015 | 1.236265 | 0.2294 |
| Earnings Per Share Ratio | −5.196371 | 5.873804 | −0.884669 | 0.3859 |
| Return On Equity Ratio | − 0.397537 | 0.301754 | −1.317420 | 0.2013 |
| Debt Ratio | 0.010546 | 0.011471 | 0.919349 | 0.3679 |
| R-squared | 0.104329 | Mean dependent var | | 0.430057 |
| Adjusted R-squared | −0.017808 | S.D. dependent var | | 0.668602 |
| S.E. of regression | 0.674529 | Akaike info criterion | | 2.191033 |
| Sum squared resid | 10.00976 | Schwarz criterion | | 2.384586 |
| Log likelihood | −24.48343 | Hannan-Quinn criter | | 2.246770 |
| F-statistic | 0.854200 | Durbin-Watson stat | | 1.962796 |
| Prob(F-statistic) | 0.479356 | | | |

The above set of tests allows us to test several heteroskedasticity properties in the remnants of our equation. In doing so, the treatments of the most straightforward smallest squares are consistent with the existing heteroskedasticity. For clarity in our work, we need to model heteroskedasticity to obtain more efficient estimates of it.

According to the results, the p-value for the F-statistic shows that a significance level of 5% is commonly used for the Heteroskedasticity test, and it is considered heteroskedastic in our paper. Moreover, F-statistic and Obs*R-squared are accounted for 0.85 points and 2.71 points while t-Statistic for EPS and ROE is negative with −0.88 and −1.3 points; for DR, this index is about 0.91.

## 10 Conclusion

The results above concluded that all the independent variables (liquidity ratio, leverage ratio and profitability ratio) impact CVX. ROE has a robust positive relationship with CVX. This variable is essential as it is the most influential factor related to the company's financial performance. The following most significant variables are DR and EPS, which also impact a company's financial performance after the ROE. It is evident that profitability ratios are one of the main factors that impact significantly not only on liquidity and leverage ratios but also on the financial performance of the CVX. And these kind of findings are consistent with Vanitha and Selvam's (2010) investigations for a manufacturing firm in which profitability was the most important factor influencing financial performance following a merger [18]. Furthermore, according to Collins and Clark (2003), top managers are critical to a company's success [6]. According to our research, ROE is the most influential variable that affects a company's net income, which is expressed as an increase in a company's financial performance and an increase in profitability.

Moreover, results showed that if the two financial indicators, ROE and DR ratio, is equal to zero, the financial performance (net income) of CVX company will be decreased to $10.033 million. In addition, when the EPS increases by $1, CVX's net income would be increase by $14.5908 million. While analyzing our paper with Breusch–Godfrey and Heteroskedasticity tests that illustrated autocorrelation for some order and simultaneously, it is considered as heteroskedastic under the significance level of 5% of p-value. It should be noted that all the variables show a positive relationship with the CVX. As a result, it is assumed that the provision of financial results through the improvement of each part of the financial statements will play a crucial role in the population. In this case, to effectively manage the liquidity ratio, the CVX company must avoid payments and, at the same time, manage its current assets and current liabilities prudently. DR is essential; high DR means that a company has its long-term debts, and the probability of default in this type of company is high.

## References

1. KARACA, Süleyman Serdar; SAVSAR, Arif – J. Appl. Econ. Sci. 7 1(19)/ Spring 2012, 56–63(2012). https://www.econbiz.de/Record/the-effect-of-financial-ratios-on-the-firm-value-evidence-from-turkey-karaca-s%C3%BCleyman-serdar/10011139812
2. Aripin, N., Abdulmumuni, O.: Financial leverage and financial performance of Nigerian manufacturing firms. Int. J. Supply Chain Manage. (IJSCM), 9(4), 607–614 (2020). ISSN 2050-7399. https://ojs.excelingtech.co.uk/index.php/IJSCM/article/view/513
3. Husna, A., Satria, I.: Effects of return on asset, debt to asset ratio, current ratio, firm size, and dividend payout ratio on firm value. International J. Econ. Financ. Issues 9(5), 50–54 (2019). https://doi.org/10.32479/ijefi.8595
4. Aswath, D.: Return on Capital (ROC), Return on Invested Capital (ROIC) and Return on Equity (ROE): Measurement and Implications (2007). https://ssrn.com/abstract=1105499
5. Marito, B.C., Sjarif, A.D.: The impact of current ratio, debt to equity ratio, return on assets, dividend yield, and market capitalization on stock return (evidence from listed manufacturing companies in Indonesia stock exchange). Sci. J. PPI-UKM, 7(1), 10–16 (2020). ISSN No. 2356– 2536. https://doi.org/10.27512/sjppi-ukm/ses/a11052020

6. Collins, C.J., Clark, K.D.: Strategic human resource practices, top management team social networks, and firm performance: the role of human resource practices in creating organizational competitive advantage. Acad. Manag. J. **46**(6), 740–751 (2003). https://doi.org/10.2307/30040665

7. Ratnasari, D., Muniarty, P.: Debt to equity ratio (DER), earning per share (EPS) analysis of company value at PT Indosat. Tbk. Ilomata Int. J. Manage. **1**(3), 83–87 (2020). https://doi.org/10.52728/ijjm.v1i3.118

8. Lin, F.L., Chang, T.: Does debt affect firm value in Taiwan? A panel threshold regression analysis. Appl. Econ. **43**(1), 117–128 (2011). https://doi.org/10.1080/00036840802360310

9. Suardana, I.B.R., Astawa, I.N.D., Martini, L.K.B.: Influential factors towards return on assets and profit change. Int. J. Soc. Sci. Humanit. **2**, 105–116 (2018)

10. Irman, M., Purwati, A.A.: Analysis on the influence of current ratio, debt to equity ratio and total asset turnover toward return on assets on the otomotive and component company that has been registered in Indonesia stock exchange within 2011–2017. Int. J. Econ. Dev. Res. (IJEDR) **1**, 36–44 (2020)

11. Strouhal, J., Štamfestová, P., Ključnikov, A., Vincúrová, Z.: Different approaches to the ebit construction and their impact on corporate financial performance based on the return on assets: some evidence from Czech top100 companies. J. Competitiveness **10**(1), 144–154 (2018)

12. Molina-Azorín, J.F., Claver-Cortés, E., López-Gamero, M.D. Tarí, J.J.: Green management and financial performance: a literature review. Manage. Decis. **47**(7), 1080–1100 (2009). Nikolaeva T.P. Finance and credit. Training and metodology complex. -Moscow 2009.-p.198–199

13. Nurbadriyah, N., Lymartha, S., Lenggana, W.G., Amarilis, M.Y., Hadi, D.A.: The influence of return on asset, current ratio, and debt equity ratio on financial distress in cement sub-sector companies registered on IDX period 2013–2018. J. Solid State Technol. **63**(3), 4893–4902 (2020)

14. Tan, P., Marpaung, A.M.: The influence of funding policy, sales level and return on equity to the growth of companies. In: Article in Proceeding the International Conference on Accounting and Management Science, vol 1, no. 1, pp. 329–335 (2018)

15. Thippayana, P.: Determinants of capital structure in Thailand. Procedia–Soc. Behav. Sci. **143**, 1074–1077 (2014)

16. Moro Visconti, R.: Corporate Profitability: Return on Equity, Return on Investment, Modigliani & Miller Proposition II and Economic Value Added", SSRN Electronic Journal March 2018. pp.2–20 (2018)

17. Jouida, S., Hallara, S.: Capital structure and regulatory capital of French banks. Procedia Econ. Finan. **26**(2015), 892–902 (2015)

18. Vanitha, S., Selvam, M.: Financial performance of Indian manufacturing companies during pre and post merger. Int. Res. J. Financ. Econ. **20**(12), 7–35 (2010)

19. Zaitseva A.A.: To the question of assessing the factor analysis of return on equity, fundamental and applied research: current issues, achievements and innovations. In: Collection of Articles of the XXIV International Scientific and Practical Conference, pp. 43–46 (2019)

20. Sunday, K.J.: Effective working capital management in small and medium scale enterprises (SMEs).Int. J. Bus. Manage. **6**(9), 271 (2011). https://doi.org/10.5539/ijbm.v6n9p271

21. Damodaran, A.: «Investment valuation: Tools and techniques for determining the value of any asset», p. 992 Wiley; 3 (edn.) (2012)

22. Leland, H.E.: Corporate debt value, bond covenants, and optimal capital structure. J. Finan. **49**(4), 1213–1252 (1994). https://doi.org/10.1111/j.1540-6261.1994.tb02452.x

23. Usmanovich Burkhanov, A., Mansur qizi Eshmamatova, M.: The Ways for Improvement of Investment Strategy in the Period of Digital Economy. In: The 5th International Conference on Future Networks & Distributed Systems (ICFNDS 2021), pp. 655–662 Association for Computing Machinery, New York, NY, USA (2021)
24. Aktamugli, U.: The Analysis of Capital Performance Indicators in Joint Stock Companies: In: Case GM Uzbekistan, p. 6 (2019). http://ijrmbs.com/vol6issue4/usmonov.pdf

# The Impact of the Digitalisation of Payment Systems on the Profitability of Commercial Banks

Gaipov Jasur Bakhrom Ugli[✉]

Tashkent State University of Economics, Tashkent, Uzbekistan
j.gaipov@tsue.uz

**Abstract.** The article emphasizes the relevance of digitalization of the banking sector at the current stage of economic development, an attempt to summarize the problems of implementing digitalization in the banking system of Uzbekistan, the analysis of factors affecting the efficiency of commercial banks, which allowed to build an economic-mathematical model and determine the forecast indicators of the national payment system. The constructed model has confirmed presence of close direct dependence of results of introduction of remote banking and digitalization on financial results of commercial banks activity. It was concluded that the purpose of improving the profitability of commercial banks serves public policy, one of the most important directions of which is the implementation of consistent measures to improve the mechanism of digitalization of the banking sector, which ultimately will improve the efficiency and profitability of the banking sector and the national economy as a whole.

**Keywords:** electronic payment systems · Internet banking · remote banking

## 1 Introduction

Payment systems today represent an important mechanism for maintaining the efficiency of financial markets, and their security should therefore be an objective of public policy. The functions performed by payment systems are so important that, in modern times, scholars have identified them as one of the defining components in ensuring the sustainability of the banking system and the economy as a whole[1].

The state of payment systems in developed countries is currently characterised by a high level of technical and technological sophistication. Due to this, these payment systems meet the highest standards of speed and reliability of settlements. The experience of most Western European countries, the USA and Japan shows that gross and net settlement systems operate in parallel there, which complement each other and ensure

---

[1] Chernysheva M.V. (2015). The essence of payment systems and their importance in the development of the financial market // Problems of Modern Economics (Novosibirsk). №28–1. P. 31–35. URL: https://cyberleninka.ru/article/n/suschnost-platezhnyh-sistem-i-ih-znachenie-v-razvitii-finansovogo-rynka.

© The Author(s), under exclusive license to Springer Nature Switzerland AG 2023
Y. Koucheryavy and A. Aziz (Eds.): NEW2AN 2022, LNCS 13772, pp. 345–355, 2023.
https://doi.org/10.1007/978-3-031-30258-9_29

reliable functioning of these payment systems by limiting credit and systemic risks and reducing liquidity needs.

The use of the accumulated experience in Uzbekistan's banking practice will make it possible to improve the domestic system of non-cash settlements and bring it to a qualitatively new level.

In Uzbekistan's banking system the problem of specialized services for various types of payments has not yet become widespread, but, in our view, domestic credit institutions can, on the basis of foreign experience, introduce appropriate banking technologies into the practice of non-cash settlements.

One of the areas of active innovation in banking practice in Uzbekistan is the use of internet banking. For the time being, internet banking is mostly seen as an additional service of the bank, although many customers do not rule out the possibility of switching completely to internet banking if it would be more profitable for them than traditional banking. A common option is to position Internet banking as an auxiliary office to pay current bills. It requires minimal investment. The bank could limit itself to a relatively unsophisticated security system, as current account balances would be small, in addition deposit insurance schemes could be used to minimise operational risks.

Electronic payment systems that provide a modern approach to ATM cash transactions through plastic cards and electronic wallets are now well established in Uzbekistan. These include: JV Uzpaynet LLC, Better Chirchik LLC, Click LLC, Ekonet Mobile PE, Euro Mebel INDP, SSP- Maroqand, Sabina Aloka Business LLC, Toshkentgasavdo LLC, etc.[2]

The existence of a national payment system that meets the needs of economic agents for the rapid and secure transfer of funds is an important component of the infrastructure necessary for the successful functioning of a developed economy, which makes the establishment and development of well-functioning payment systems one of the main objectives of economic growth.

## 2 Research Methodology

In order to assess the current state of digitalization of payment systems in Uzbekistan and to determine the forecasts for their development, we conduct an econometric analysis of the efficiency of payment systems on the quantitative performance of several of the largest commercial banks in the country.

## 3 Results and Analysis of the Study

The profit of commercial banks as a financial result of their activities in the current context of economic development and digitalisation – the net profit of commercial banks (NPCB) (in billions of soums) – was chosen as the explanatory variable (regressor). The explanatory variables (regressors) are presented in Table 1.

---

[2] Olkhovskaya I.V. (2017). Development of payment systems in Uzbekistan // Science, Technology and Education. №3 (33). P. 89–91. URL: https://cyberleninka.ru/article/n/razvitie-platez hnyh-sistem-v-uzbekistane.

The research study analyzes the panel data for the period from 2018 to 2021 for nine largest commercial banks in Uzbekistan – National Bank, Uzpromstroybank, Microcreditbank, Hamkorbank, Asaka bank, Trustbank, Alokabank, Asia Alliance bank, Orient Finance bank, i.e. the study is based on a sampling method of 25% observation.

**Table 1.** Description of the explanatory variables of the model[3]

| № | Regressors | Unit of measure | Variable | Designation |
|---|---|---|---|---|
| 1 | Receipts via payment terminals | Billions of sums | Receipts via payment terminals | RPT |
| 2 | Receipts via the Interbank Payments System | Billions of sums | Receipts via the Interbank Payment System | RIPS |
| 3 | Number of users of e-banking systems | Unit | Number of users of remote banking systems | NURBS |
| 4 | Amounts of payments passing through the CB clearing system | Millions of sums | Amounts of payments passing through the Central Bank's clearing settlement system | APPTCBCSS |

A total of five variables, one explanatory and four explanatory, are used in the model, with a total of 180 observations (see appendix for details). The cost indicators, including CPI, have been adjusted to a comparable form (to 2021 prices).

Descriptive statistics allows us to determine the mean, median, maximum and minimum values, as well as the standard deviation of each factor from the mean (std. Dev. – Standard Deviation) and the skewness (Skewness). The latter shows that the most symmetrical distribution is observed for receipts via the Interbank Payment System (RIPS) and the most asymmetrical for receipts via payment terminals (RPT), which indicates shifts in the dynamics of the factors under study: a sharp increase in receipts via payment terminals associated with the spread of coronavirus infection and forced quarantine measures as well as general processes of digitalisation of the banking sector (Table 2).

---

[3] Constructed by the author.

**Table 2.** Comparative statistics[4]

|  | NPCB | RPT | RIPS | NURBS | APPTCBCSS |
|---|---|---|---|---|---|
| Mean | 305.0562 | 4749.580 | 50441.35 | 630890.1 | 1134961 |
| Median | 216.8640 | 4077.645 | 38295.38 | 448837.5 | 719820.0 |
| Maximum | 1006.233 | 17246.21 | 115672.4 | 2659554 | 5393394 |
| Minimum | 17.03070 | 1615.904 | 10583.56 | 16650.00 | 11101.12 |
| Std. Dev. | 305.7873 | 2653.511 | 32664.50 | 582741.8 | 1367888 |
| Skewness | 1.294254 | 2.983360 | 0.605688 | 1.503488 | 1.817738 |
| Kurtosis | 3.436513 | 14.74023 | 2.078270 | 5.410160 | 5.823030 |
| Jarque-Bera | 10.33638 | 260.1521 | 3.475525 | 22.27617 | 31.77927 |
| Probability | 0.005695 | 0.000000 | 0.175914 | 0.000015 | 0.000000 |
| Sum | 10982.02 | 170984.9 | 1815889 | 22712042 | 40858610 |
| Sum Sq. Dev. | 3272705 | 2.46E+08 | 3.73E+10 | 1.19E+13 | 6.55E+13 |
| Observations | 36 | 36 | 36 | 36 | 36 |

Let us investigate the degree of correlation between the variables by constructing a correlation matrix (Table 3).

**Table 3.** Correlation matrix (see Footnote 4)

|  | NPCB | RPT | RIPS | NURBS | APPTCBCSS |
|---|---|---|---|---|---|
| NPCB | 1.000000 | 0.259673 | 0.767756 | 0.654209 | 0.100046 |
| RPT | 0.259673 | 1.000000 | 0.307009 | 0.348652 | 0.077861 |
| RIPS | 0.767756 | 0.307009 | 1.000000 | 0.547717 | 0.147303 |
| NURBS | 0.654209 | 0.348652 | 0.547717 | 1.000000 | 0.283070 |
| APPTCBCSS | 0.100046 | 0.077861 | 0.147303 | 0.283070 | 1.000000 |

According to the results of the correlation analysis performed, all attributes act on the result in the positive direction. The most significant effect on banks' net income is effect of receipts through Interbank Payment System (RIPS) ($r = 0.77$) and number of users of Remote Banking Systems (NURBS) ($r = 0.65$). The other explanatory variables have a less significant impact. In addition, the correlation matrix showed that there is almost no multicollinearity between the explanatory variables.

---

[4] Constructed by the author using the Eviews software product.

Testing the series of explanatory variable Y for stationarity using the extended Dickey-Fuller test rejected the null hypothesis, which is that Y has a unit root, since Prob = 0.0006 (Table 4). Consequently, the series is stationary and a model can be constructed.

Table 4. Augmented Dickey-Fuller Test on NPCB[5]

| Variable | Coefficient | Std. Error | t-Statistic | Prob. |
|---|---|---|---|---|
| NPCB(-1) | −0.542084 | 0.143378 | −3.780799 | 0.0006 |
| C | 148.2494 | 61.94412 | 2.393276 | 0.0225 |
| R-squared | 0.302244 | Mean dependent var | | −17.19506 |
| Adjusted R-squared | 0.281099 | S.D. dependent var | | 305.9147 |
| S.E. of regression | 259.3790 | Akaike info criterion | | 14.00990 |
| Sum squared resid | 2220157 | Schwarz criterion | | 14.09878 |
| Log likelihood | −243.1733 | Hannan-Quinn criter | | 14.04058 |
| F-statistic | 14.29444 | Durbin-Watson stat | | 2.543296 |
| Prob(F-statistic) | 0.000624 | | | |

Three multiple regression models were built to examine panel data: a general (pooled) regression model without regard to panel data structure (Table 5), a fixed-effects (FE) model (Table 6) and a random-effects (RE) model (Table 7).

Table 5. Pooled regression model (POLS) (see Footnote 5)

| Variable | Coefficient | Std. Error | t-Statistic | Prob. |
|---|---|---|---|---|
| C | −50.21805 | 74.04200 | −0.678237 | 0.5027 |
| RPT | −0.005100 | 0.012709 | −0.401310 | 0.6909 |
| RIPS | 0.005535 | 0.001156 | 4.787015 | 0.0000 |
| NURBS | 0.000195 | 6.78E−05 | 2.868382 | 0.0074 |
| APPTCBCSS | −1.98E−05 | 2.38E−05 | −0.831100 | 0.4123 |
| R-squared | 0.676216 | Mean dependent var | | 305.0562 |
| Adjusted R-squared | 0.634437 | S.D. dependent var | | 305.7873 |
| S.E. of regression | 184.8845 | Akaike info criterion | | 13.40559 |
| Sum squared resid | 1059650 | Schwarz criterion | | 13.62552 |
| Log likelihood | −236.3005 | Hannan-Quinn criter. | | 13.48235 |

*(continued)*

---

[5] Constructed by the author using the Eviews 10 software product.

**Table 5.** (*continued*)

| Variable | Coefficient | Std. Error | t-Statistic | Prob. |
|----------|-------------|------------|-------------|-------|
| F-statistic | 16.18569 | Durbin-Watson stat | | 1.615248 |
| Prob(F-statistic) | 0.000000 | | | |

The FEM model does not take into account unmeasured individual differences between objects (effects), they are interpreted as an intervening parameter, and the evaluation aims to exclude them (Table 6).

**Table 6.** Fixed effects panel regression model (FEM) (see Footnote 5)

| Variable | Coefficient | Std. Error | t-Statistic | Prob. |
|----------|-------------|------------|-------------|-------|
| C | 131.1704 | 107.9752 | 1.214820 | 0.2368 |
| RPT | −0.013280 | 0.014354 | −0.925185 | 0.3645 |
| RIPS | 0.002459 | 0.002576 | 0.954810 | 0.3496 |
| NURBS | 0.000148 | 6.80E-05 | 2.180530 | 0.0397 |
| APPTCBCSS | 1.70E-05 | 1.99E-05 | 0.856292 | 0.4007 |
| Effects Specification | | | | |
| Cross-section fixed (dummy variables) | | | | |
| R-squared | 0.872900 | Mean dependent var | | 305.0562 |
| Adjusted R-squared | 0.806587 | S.D. dependent var | | 305.7873 |
| S.E. of regression | 134.4814 | Akaike info criterion | | 12.91493 |
| Sum squared resid | 415960.5 | Schwarz criterion | | 13.48675 |
| Log likelihood | −219.4687 | Hannan-Quinn criter | | 13.11451 |
| F-statistic | 13.16333 | Durbin-Watson stat | | 3.821766 |
| Prob(F-statistic) | 0.000000 | | | |

The REM model takes into account unmeasured individual differences between objects (effects) and assumes that the individual differences are random (Table 7).

**Table 7.** Random effects panel regression model (REM) (see Footnote 5)

| Variable | Coefficient | Std. Error | t-Statistic | Prob. |
|---|---|---|---|---|
| C | 8.229998 | 83.78632 | 0.098226 | 0.9224 |
| RPT | −0.014201 | 0.011890 | −1.194311 | 0.2414 |
| RIPS | 0.005007 | 0.001436 | 3.487547 | 0.0015 |
| NURBS | 0.000174 | 6.15E−05 | 2.832228 | 0.0081 |
| APPTCBCSS | 1.58E−06 | 1.86E−05 | 0.084600 | 0.9331 |
| Effects Specification | | | | |
| | | | S.D. | Rho |
| Cross-section random | | | 123.8264 | 0.4588 |
| Idiosyncratic random | | | 134.4814 | 0.5412 |
| Weighted Statistics | | | | |
| R-squared | 0.750372 | Mean dependent var | | 145.5744 |
| Adjusted R-squared | 0.739684 | S.D. dependent var | | 186.2747 |
| S.E. of regression | 139.4345 | Sum squared resid | | 602701.0 |
| F-statistic | 7.866200 | Durbin-Watson stat | | 2.652218 |
| Prob(F-statistic) | 0.000169 | | | |
| Unweighted Statistics | | | | |
| R-squared | 0.653740 | Mean dependent var | | 305.0562 |
| Sum squared resid | 1133205 | Durbin-Watson stat | | 1.410595 |

Use the Durbin-Woo-Hausman specification test to test the hypothesis that there is no correlation between individual effects and regressors, and choose either the random-effects model or the fixed-effects model (Table 8).

**Table 8.** Correlated Random Effects – Hausman Test (see Footnote 5)

| Test cross-section random effects | | | | |
|---|---|---|---|---|
| Test Summary | Chi-Sq. Statistic | Chi-Sq. d.f | Prob | |
| Cross-section random | 6.325571 | 4 | 0.1761 | |
| Cross-section random effects test comparisons: | | | | |
| Variable | Fixed | Random | Var(Diff.) | Prob |
| RPT | −0.013280 | −0.014201 | 0.000065 | 0.9089 |

(*continued*)

**Table 8.** (*continued*)

| Test cross-section random effects | | | |
|---|---|---|---|
| Test Summary | Chi-Sq. Statistic | Chi-Sq. d.f | Prob |
| Cross-section random | 6.325571 | 4 | 0.1761 |
| Cross-section random effects test comparisons: | | | |

| Variable | Fixed | Random | Var(Diff.) | Prob |
|---|---|---|---|---|
| RIPS | 0.002459 | 0.005007 | 0.000005 | 0.2336 |
| NURBS | 0.000148 | 0.000174 | 0.000000 | 0.3713 |
| APPTCBCSS | 0.000017 | 0.000002 | 0.000000 | 0.0276 |
| Cross-section random effects test equation: | | | | |

| Variable | Coefficient | Std. Error | t-Statistic | Prob |
|---|---|---|---|---|
| C | 131.1704 | 107.9752 | 1.214820 | 0.2368 |
| RPT | −0.013280 | 0.014354 | −0.925185 | 0.3645 |
| RIPS | 0.002459 | 0.002576 | 0.954810 | 0.3496 |
| NURBS | 0.000148 | 6.80E−05 | 2.180530 | 0.0397 |
| APPTCBCSS | 1.70E−05 | 1.99E−05 | 0.856292 | 0.4007 |
| | Effects Specification | | | |

| Cross-section fixed (dummy variables) | | | |
|---|---|---|---|
| R-squared | 0.872900 | Mean dependent var | 305.0562 |
| Adjusted R-squared | 0.806587 | S.D. dependent var | 305.7873 |
| S.E. of regression | 134.4814 | Akaike info criterion | 12.91493 |
| Sum squared resid | 415960.5 | Schwarz criterion | 13.48675 |
| Log likelihood | −219.4687 | Hannan-Quinn criter | 13.11451 |
| F-statistic | 13.16333 | Durbin-Watson stat | 3.821766 |
| Prob(F-statistic) | 0.000000 | | |

The Hausman test (Table 9) shows that the probability of accepting the null hypothesis that the REM is adequate is 17.5%, meaning that in our case the random-effects model is preferable.

The Hannan-Quinn and Akaike information criteria and the value of the adjusted coefficient of determination support the conclusion that, of all the models, the random effects model is more appropriate. This result is correct, as specific commercial banks were taken for the study, each of which has specific characteristics.

Let us test the model for quality and adequacy. The coefficient of determination (R-square = 0.75) indicates a sufficiently close relationship between y and the factors affecting it and that 75.4% of the variation of the dependent variable is explained by the four explanatory variables included in the model while only 24.6% is due to the influence of unmeasured or random factors. According to Fisher-Snedekor criterion at

$F_{\text{набл.}} \succ F_{\text{крит}}$ we can consider the model to be adequate. In our case, $F_{\text{набл}} = 7{,}87$, and $F_{\text{табл}} = 4{,}02$ with degrees of freedom $f_1 = m = 4, f_2 = n - m - 1 = 36 - 4 - 1 = 31$, which confirms the possibility of null hypothesis rejection and, thus, reliability of regression model at 0,05 significance level. According to Fisher's test this model is adequate.

Tabulated value of Student's t-test corresponding to confidence probability $\gamma = 0{,}95$ and given number of degrees of freedom $t_{\text{крит}} = t_{0,05;4} = 2{,}78$. Comparing calculated t-statistics of equation coefficients with tabulated value, we conclude that with only two explanatory variables RIPS and NURBS, regression equation coefficients are statistically significant.

The standard deviations for the coefficients at the explanatory variables indicate low variability in the data. In general, it can be stated that the obtained regression coefficients are statistically significant and therefore they can be used in a linear regression equation for further analysis and forecasting.

The model with random effects REM (Table 7) confirms the fact of the greatest statistical significance of the variables RIPS – receipts through the Interbank Payment System and NURBS – the number of users of e-banking systems. The model suggests that the largest increase in net profit of commercial banks is due to growth of revenues through the Interbank Payment System. If the latter increase by 1 billion soums (assuming that other indicators remain unchanged), the net profit of commercial banks will increase by 5.01 million soums. If the number of users of e-banking systems increases by 1 unit, the net profit will increase by 174 thousand soums.

The positive correlation between the net profit of commercial banks and the volume of revenues through the Interbank System and the number of users of e-banking systems further confirms the positive impact of the digitalisation processes of the banking sector.

The model with random effects is constructed as follows:

$$NPCB = 8{,}23 - 0{,}014 \cdot RPT + 0{,}005 \cdot RIPS + 0{,}0002 \cdot NURBS + 0{,}000002 \cdot APPTCBCSS \qquad (1)$$

Based on the panel data model, it is possible to forecast the net income of one of the nine commercial banks of Uzbekistan participating in the study. In addition, a longer-term forecast can be experimentally carried out to see by which year, all other things being equal, Uzbekistan's banking system will enter the category of countries with high profitability and digitalization of the banking sector.

Based on the analysis, a forecast of the most important performance indicators of Orient Finance Bank of Uzbekistan for the coming years was carried out (Table 9).

**Table 9.** Forecast of OFB performance dynamics in 2021–2026 [6]

| Years | The bank's net profit, UZS billion | Receipts via payment terminals, UZS billion | Receipts through the Interbank Payments System, UZS billion | Number of users of e-banking systems, units | Amounts of payments passing through the Central Bank clearing system, UZS billion |
|---|---|---|---|---|---|
| 2021 (actual) | 300,0 | 3 181,4 | 22 025,3 | 364 323,0 | 1 453 492,1 |
| 2022 | 342,1 | 3 565,1 | 18 863,9 | 465 310,0 | 1 996 883,7 |
| 2023 | 388,4 | 4 053,7 | 14 587,6 | 569 684,8 | 2 481 887,9 |
| 2024 | 412,6 | 4 542,3 | 10 311,3 | 674 059,6 | 2 966 892,1 |
| 2025 | 436,9 | 5 030,8 | 6 035,0 | 778 434,4 | 3 451 896,3 |
| 2026 | 534,7 | 5 519,4 | 1 758,7 | 882 809,2 | 3 936 900,5 |

## 4   Conclusions and Proposals

Based on the results of the predictive panel data model, it has been found that with a 75% probability, Orient Finance Bank's net profit will barely exceed 530 billion soums by 2026, which will exacerbate the bank's lagging behind larger commercial banks in Uzbekistan. This, in turn, requires the implementation of strategic measures to increase the number of users of e-banking systems. At the same time, the model showed that revenues through the Interbank Payment System will decline year on year. The goal of improving the profitability of commercial banks is also served by government policy, one important area of which should be the implementation of consistent measures for the digitalisation of the banking sector. The econometric model has shown that this requires:

1. Formation of mechanisms to facilitate the growth in the number of users of e-banking systems, creating conditions for a new qualitative growth in the digitalisation of the banking sector.
2. Increase in revenues through payment terminals, clearing system of Central Bank settlements, etc., which will increase the financial sustainability of commercial banks.
3. Increased competitiveness, independence and profitability of commercial banks. This is possible through further liberalization of the banking sector, as outlined in the New Uzbekistan Development Strategy 2022–2026[7].

---

[6] Developed by the author on the basis of an econometric REM model constructed using panel data.

[7] Presidential Decree No. UP-60 of 28.01.2022 "On the New Uzbekistan Development Strategy for 2022–2026" https://www.lex.uz/ru/

While the coronavirus pandemic and quarantine that took everyone by surprise has significantly accelerated digitalisation in all areas of human life and society, including the banking sector, research suggests that this process is not proceeding efficiently enough. In particular, observations by experts at the Boston Consulting Group, a global consulting firm working with many business and social leaders, confirm that only one in five banks in the world is engaged in a systematic transition to digital technology[8]. At the same time, practice has long shown the benefits of switching to automated business processes – banks earn more and become more competitive. According to research by experts of one of the largest international financial conglomerates Citi Group, digitalization helps save up to half of operating costs through the introduction of technology that will reduce the number of offices and jobs. Accenture research shows that the most digitally advanced banks increase their return on capital by an average of 0.9%. Banks that do not use business process automation reduced the same figure by 1.1% on average[9].

Thus, the issue of improving the mechanism to stimulate digitalization of the banking sector through a consistent government policy, as well as switching banks from a passive strategy to a development strategy, remains a key one. There is a need for systematic work to introduce modern and innovative technologies in the banking sector, with the ultimate goal of increasing net profits, which will improve the efficiency and profitability of the banking sector and the national economy as a whole.

# References

1. Ol'hovskaya, I.V.: Development of payment systems in Uzbekistan. Nauka, tekhnika i obrazovanie **3**(33), 89–91 (2017). https://cyberleninka.ru/article/n/razvitie-platezhnyh-sistem-v-uzbekistane
2. Chernysheva, M.V.: The essence of payment systems and their importance in the development of the financial market. Problemy sovremennoj ekonomiki (Novosibirsk) **28**–1, 31–35 (2015). https://cyberleninka.ru/article/n/suschnost-platezhnyh-sistem-i-ih-znachenie-v-razvitii-finansovogo-rynka
3. Presidential Decree No. UP-60 of 28.01.2022 "On the New Uzbekistan Development Strategy for 2022–2026" https://www.lex.uz/ru/.
4. Boston Consulting Group information and analysis website https://www.bcg.com/
5. Accenture information and analysis website https://plusworld.ru/

---

[8] Boston Consulting Group information and analysis website https://www.bcg.com/.

[9] Accenture information and analysis website https://plusworld.ru/.

# The Main Aspects and Benefits of Digital Transformation of Business Entities

Qosimova Dilorom Sabirovna and Nutfulloev Tolib G'olibo'g'li[✉]

Department of Business Administration and Logistics, Tashkent State University of Economics,
Tashkent 100100, Uzbekistan

**Abstract.** The article considers the analysis of modern trends in digitalization processes and business transformation in digital way. The digitalization of business activity has now become one of the central trends in the development of enterprises. Digital solutions have a main impact on business processes and models, and their use is driven by changes in consumer interests, the availability of technology, and a positive economic effect. The Covid-19 pandemic has showed that businesses need to begin rapidly using digital tools in organizing business activities, which contributes to a progressive digital transformation of business. The authors highlight the distinctive features of business digitalization and its digital transformation. The fact that digital transformation affects the activities of many business structures, regardless of the scale of the business, is noted. Additionally, the authors describe the main aspects and benefits of business transformation by using digital technologies.

**Keywords:** digital transformation · business entities · entrepreneurship · digitalization · consumer behavior · competitiveness · competition

## 1 Introduction

World experience has convincingly demonstrated that information and communication technologies today are the most essential components of the sustainable effective development of modern enterprises and businesses. The development of the most important areas of high-tech production, as well as the creation of innovative products, is due to the development of IT, on which the success and competitiveness of both individual enterprises and the country's economy as a whole depend. According to World Bank studies, in 2021, most economically developed countries, due to the use of IoT and communication technologies in the industrial sector, as well as an increase in the number of Internet users (compared to 2017 by 15%), achieved an increase in GDP by an average of 3–3.9%, and per capita income – by 7.2% [2].

At the current phase of development of the world industry, main attention is paid to scientific research on improving market mechanisms for the effective development of industries and sectors of the national economy based on the effective use of information and communication technologies. Of particular relevance are the ongoing research on improving the mechanism for financing innovations in this activity, the effective use

Y. Koucheryavy and A. Aziz (Eds.): NEW2AN 2022, LNCS 13772, pp. 356–362, 2023.
https://doi.org/10.1007/978-3-031-30258-9_30

of digital technologies in various industries, the transformation of approaches to ensuring the competitiveness of industrial enterprises, and the improvement of methods for assessing competitiveness in the industrial complex.

In the context of the transition to a digital economy in Uzbekistan, market methods for increasing the competitiveness of industrial enterprises are becoming one of the main factors in the growth of economic sectors. "An important condition for the dynamic development of the Republic of Uzbekistan is the accelerated introduction of modern innovative technologies in the economy, social and other spheres with the widespread use of science and technology" [1]. In this regard, it becomes relevant to develop scientifically based proposals and recommendations for the active implementation of information and communication technologies in the activities of enterprises, the theoretical justification of methodological approaches to increasing the competitiveness of the economy and innovation activity based on the national concept of innovative development.

## 2    Materials and Methods

This article uses data from the State Statistics Committee of the Republic of Uzbekistan and also internet sites. The statistics collected were analyzed using a comparison method as well as in the econometric analysis section of the article.

The adaptation of enterprises to external conditions and high competition requires digital transformation. In the book by A. Prokhorov and L. Konik, said to digital transformation, technologies that companies can use are considered. There are four factors to be changed: strategy, technology, people, processes [5]. The authors do not only highlight the factors, but also consider them in dynamics by maturity levels: initial, managed and optimized transformation.

In the dissertation research Y.I. Gribanov [6], submitted for the degree of Doctor of Economics, the factors constraining digital transformation are given. The author divides them into external and internal. Internal refers to: resource, organizational, psychological barriers and the human factor.

More accurate recognition under the influence of digital transformations implies three organizational aspects: from the outside, with the improvement of the client's experience and the change of his entire life cycle; on the inside, the impact on business objectives, basic leadership and hierarchical structures; and in general, when all business sections and opportunities are influenced, usually leading to completely new business models [7].

## 3    Results

As a result of increased competition in the conditions of the market economy in Uzbekistan, businesses are rapidly transitioning to digitalization, and the number of enterprises providing such services is also increasing. By 2021, the share of software spending in GDP will be 0.09% and 633.4 billion, made up the value of sums. The total value of computer programming and related services increased continuously between 2015 and 2021, this figure was 142.5 billion Uzbek sums in 2015, and 2721.5 billion Uzbek sums by 2021 (see Fig. 1) [3].

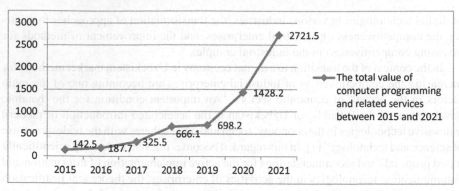

**Fig. 1.** The total value of computer programming and related services between 2015 and 2021 (in billion sums).

We can see from the above graph that over the last two years, the total value of computer programming and related services has almost doubled, and in 2020 it is 1428.2 billion and in 2021 it is 2721.5 billion. This shows digital transformation and using IoT becoming more popular among entrepreneurs in Uzbekistan. Since, it gives more opportunity achieving success in business world.

The maintenance of the role of digital business transformation is confirmed by a joint study of key performance indicators conducted by Capgemini Consulting and the MIT Sloan School of Management (School of Management at the Massachusetts Institute of Technology) [4]. As the results of this study showed that digital transformation cannot simply be ignored, as the decrease in profits in this case compared to competitors will be 24% per year.

The results of those companies that carried out digital transformations depended on accompanying the digital transformation of the business with parallel improvement of management, that is, they are directly related to the proactive management of the company by its top management. Thus, the profit of firms grows by an average of 26% if technologies and new management methods are used together. If only to improve management, without resorting to digital technologies, then the profit of firms grows by 9%. If you invest only in technology, forgetting about the necessary changes in management, profit does not grow at all, but falls by 11% (Table 1) [4].

**Table 1.** The results of the introduction of digital technologies in the company

| Option | Technology | New management methods | Profit |
|--------|-----------|------------------------|--------|
| 1 | − | − | 24% reduction compared to competitors |
| 2 | + | − | 11% decrease |
| 3 | − | + | Growth by 9% |
| 4 | + | + | Growth by 26% |

Thus, investment in technology with inefficient management will not only not have a positive impact on the business, but, on the contrary, will lead to disastrous results, and the driving force behind digital transformation is not only new digital technologies, but also leadership focused on the introduction of new technologies, processes and using modern management methods. [4].

Based on a regression model:

$$ROA = \beta_0 + \beta_1 FinLev + \beta_2 ProAsset + \beta_3 Liquidity + \beta_{p4} Inv + \beta_5 FirmSize +$$
$$+ \beta_6 MarShare + \beta_7 Exporting + \beta_8 ITUsage$$

An econometric analysis of the competitiveness of textile industry enterprises using IT (AMUDARYOTEX LLC, Kuvatekstil LLC, Art Soft Tech LLC, Nortex LLC) was carried out. The results of the econometric analysis of the competitiveness of these enterprises are presented in Table 2 [8].

**Table 2.** Descriptive statistics of competitiveness factors of textile enterprises

| Variables | Obs | Mean | Std. Dev | Min | Max |
|---|---|---|---|---|---|
| Return on assets | 16 | 0.385 | 0.0794145 | 0.27 | 0.51 |
| Financial leverage | 16 | 0.601875 | 0.0943199 | 0.45 | 0.8 |
| Production asset | 16 | 0.61 | 0.0832666 | 0.44 | 0.72 |
| Liquidity | 16 | 1.119375 | 0.3537507 | 0.6 | 1.74 |
| Investments | 16 | 0.578125 | 0.120345 | 0.3 | 0.78 |
| Firm Size | 16 | 7.463125 | 0.621908 | 6.1 | 8.3 |
| Market share | 16 | 7.82375 | 1.518139 | 5.1 | 9.4 |
| Export | 16 | 0.4375 | 0.5123475 | 0 | 1 |
| Use of IT | 16 | 6.25 | 0.7745967 | 5 | 7 |

For the econometric analysis of the competitiveness of industrial enterprises, the author made 16 observations (4-year indicators of each of the above companies were studied). Common variables considered were: return on assets, financial leverage, productive assets, liquidity, investments, firm size, market share, exports, IT use. Their mean value is shown in the second column, standard deviation – in the 3rd column, minimum and maximum values – in the 4th and 5th columns, respectively. Use of IT has main role in winning competition because it gives more opportunity and clear vision.

## 4   Discussion

Digital transformation of business processes is most often carried out in the areas of e-commerce, IT and fintech. Its implementation enables companies to:

• increase productivity and reduce business costs;

- improving the quality of work planning and business management;
- improve customer service and provide consumers with better and more convenient products;
- creating a positive brand image and achieving leadership positions in its market segment.

Digital business transformation is carried out to create an updated, sustainable business model for companies that are able to operate effectively in today's digital economy and adapt to their changes.

Examples of digital business transformation can be the development of:

- integrated Internet marketing and business promotion strategies;
- new sites using modern technologies;
- effective mobile applications for various platforms;
- CRM systems to manage content or customer interactions.

There are several strategic directions to help realize the digital transformation of business processes. These include:

- digitalization of business processes (digitalization of business) – the transition of companies to electronic platforms. With the help of business digitalization, it is possible to significantly reduce the number of steps required to complete a specific task by replacing the activities of the company's personnel with the work of software solutions;
- data management (Big Data, Data Analytics, Data Science) – work with large volumes of information using neural networks, machine learning and other artificial intelligence technologies. With the help of data management, it is possible to draw up models of customer behavior, predict demand and form preferences – this allows you to adapt products and services to the needs of specific consumers;
- customer centricity – when developing their products, companies build a business model, focusing on the client and his needs. At the same time, the client-centric model also takes into account the value of each client for the company;
- digital partnership – the creation by the company, together with partners, of a common digital infrastructure (a set of technologies and computing, telecommunication and network capacities) to solve the tasks;
- innovation – continuous study and testing of new business lines, products and solutions. This strategy involves the active use of modern digital channels and systems;
- value management – with the help of this strategy, measures are taken to adapt and personalize products, taking into account changing user requirements for them. At the same time, the value of the product for customers is the convenience of its use, the possibility of obtaining the necessary services, the continuous improvement of the product and the work of the company on the service.

Moreover, digitalization is not only enough to win in competition, but also using new methods of management is essential since we saw above in Table 1 how new management methods effected in company by integrating IT, growth by 26%. Before using digital technologies in business entities, business processes must be properly established, because technologies are only accelerators. if the business processes are not set up correctly, these digital technologies can be the reason for the failure of the enterprise.

We have considered that the use of IT technologies in business is of great importance in the fight against competition, in particular, we have seen that its importance level is almost equal to factors such as the company's market share and its size.

# 5 Conclusion

The transformation of the digital economy regulates the transformation of human and society. Any switches in terminology and theoretical apparatus occur under the leverage of innovative processes, new formats of business processes and ecosystem relation. Actualization and clarification of terminology and conceptual apparatus makes it possible to carry out professional management activities in the context of digitalization.

Company digitalization is not an absolute benefit for the business, but rather a challenge coming from the external environment. Business with sufficiently developed management benefit from digitalization, while firms with weak management suffer from a digital leap in their development. In this sense, it can be argued that the digitalization of a company is a neutral accelerator of the level of development of a company, and therefore can have both positive and negative consequences for it. The main approach to the introduction of digital technologies in a company should be the "company-technologies" approach, when digitalization is considered as an integral element of the company's strategic management, a tool to increase the efficiency of its functioning. Digital transformation is hard to define since it is so very dissimilar for every business sectors. But, in general terms, it is demonstrated as incorporating digital technology into all enterprise sectors. The result is a radical change in how enterprises function and work with customers. It is a fundamental reconsidering of how a company utilizes technology in conjunction with processes and people to change enterprise performance.

# References

1. Decree of the President of the Republic of Uzbekistan dated September 21, 2018 No. UP-5544 "On approval of the strategy of innovative development of the Republic of Uzbekistan for 2019–2021" (as amended and supplemented but as of September 27, 2020). Assembly Legislative in the Republic of Uzbekistan. September 24 (2018)
2. Minges, M.: Exploring relationship between broadband and economic growth. WDR (2015)
3. Data from the State Statistics Committee of the Republic of Uzbekistan. www.stat.uz
4. MIT Sloan Management Review, Strategy, Not Technology, Drives Digital Transformation Becoming a Digitally Mature Enterprise (2015)
5. Prokhorov, A., Konik, L.: Digital Transformation. Analysis, Trends, World Experience. 2nd ed. KomNewsGroup LLC, 368 p. (2019)
6. Gribanov, Y.I.: Digital transformation of socio-economic systems based on the development of the institution of service integration: Ph.D. Economy SCIENCES: 08.00.05: defended 03.10.19: approved. 03.10.19. St. Petersburg, 355 p. – Bibliography, pp. 284–320 (2019)
7. Hess, T., Benlian, A., Matt, C., Wiesböck, F.: Options for formulating a digital transformation strategy. MIS Q. Exec. **15**(2), 123–139 (2016)

8.  Matchanova, F.A.: Market methods for increasing the competitiveness of industrial enterprises based on IT: Ph.D. Economy Sciences: 08.00.03 – Tashkent (2022)
9.  Sobirovna, Q.D., Abdugafarovich, S.A., Bulturbayevich, M.B.: Improvement of the strategy of vertical integration in industrial enterprises. Am. J. Econ. Bus. Manage. 2(3), 63–68 (2019)
10. Kosimova, D.: Improvement of the strategy of vertical integration in industrial enterprises. Arxiv nauchnix issledovaniy (13) (2020)
11. Kosimova, D.S., Adashev, A.U.: Directions to increase productivity competitiveness in industrial enterprises. Econ. Innov. Technol. 17 (2019)
12. Sobirovna, D.K., O'rinboyevich, A.A.: Directions for increasing product competitiveness in industrial enterprises. Asian J. Multidimens. Res. 8(7), 29–35 (2019)
13. Kosimova, D.: Improving Human Resource Management in the Oil and Fat Industry Based on Structural Changes (2020)
14. Qosimova, D.K.: Use of modern innovative technologies in teaching English. Acad. Res. Educ. Sci. 2(10), 380–383 (2021)
15. Kosimova, D., Mukhtorova, I.: Modern migration processes in the context of regional contradictions on the example of Uzbekistan. Arxiv nauchnix issledovaniy 2(1) (2022)
16. Sobirovna, K.D., Gafurovich, A.N., Abdugafarovich, S.A.: Forming a management system of organizational culture of the enterprise. NVEO – Nat. Volatiles Essential Oils J. 4271–4278 (2021)
17. Qosimova, D.K.: Innovative methods of teaching foreign languages and their methodological analysis. Acad. Res. Educ. Sci. 2(10), 384–387 (2021)

# The Influence of the Capital Structure of State Enterprises on the Profitability of the Enterprise

Choriev Fazliddin Ishquvvatovich[✉]

Department of Macroeconomic Analysis and Forecasting, Tashkent State
University of Economics, Tashkent, Uzbekistan

**Abstract.** The study examined the relationship between the capital structure and profitability of SOEs. A literature review on the relationship between firm profitability and capital structure has shown that there is a positive, negative or neutral relationship between profitability and capital structure. It also showed that there is no reliable evidence of what the optimal capital should be. Regression analysis was used to study the relationship between capital structure and profitability. Also, average profitability and debt ratios were used to determine whether SOEs depended on debt and targeted budget transfers. It was determined that there is no dependence of short-term debt funds on profitability in making decisions on the capital structure of enterprises with a state share, and that long-term debt funds and state-targeted funds have a significant negative effect. Also, long-term debt accounts for an average of 43% of the total capital, and target incomes make up 53% of the company's own funds.

**Keywords:** capital structure · profitability · short-term debt funds · long-term debt · SOEs

## 1 Introduction

The capital structure decision is the selection of a mix of sources of financing, consisting of debt and equity financing. Ross et al. (2001) defined a firm's capital structure decision as "the choice of how much debt the firm should raise relative to its equity." They argue that capital structure describes a firm's borrowing policy.

This refers to a mix of long-term debt and equity financing (Brealey et al. 2009). Abor (2005) defined the capital structure as a "mix of different securities". A common concept in the above definitions is that a firm's capital structure decision is its choice of debt-equity ratio. At the heart of capital structure decisions is the search for an optimal capital structure. It aims to maximize return on capital and shareholder value. The enterprise may not provide opportunities to ensure economic stability in the use of its own funds and short-term debt funds.

The terms "firm value," "shareholder value," "shareholder wealth," and "profitability" are used interchangeably in the study because they all constitute measures that describe the creation of shareholder wealth. It can be understood that the main concept of the results of the main activities of organizations is to increase the company's wealth,

© The Author(s), under exclusive license to Springer Nature Switzerland AG 2023
Y. Koucheryavy and A. Aziz (Eds.): NEW2AN 2022, LNCS 13772, pp. 363–368, 2023.
https://doi.org/10.1007/978-3-031-30258-9_31

as a result of which the income of the primary stakeholders of the enterprise will increase accordingly. Ross et al. (2009, p. 432) support this view: "Managers should choose the capital structure that they believe will have the highest firm value because that capital structure will be most beneficial to the firm's shareholders."

The decision on the capital structure of the enterprise is very important, because a wrong decision can affect the profitability of the company, which leads to a decrease in shareholder value and vice versa. In this case, managers are required to determine the limits of financial insecurity of enterprises in terms of financial activity.

The primary objective of financial decisions is to maximize shareholder wealth. In other words, the objective of a firm's financial decisions is to increase the value of its stock (or share price). As stated by Ross et al. (2001), the objective of financial decisions is to maximize the market value of available owners' capital. According to them, good financial decisions increase the market value of owners' capital and bad financial decisions decrease it.

The impact of capital structure decisions on profitability and firm value is that it increases the present value of capital through the use of debt. However, it is necessary to determine the optimal values that allow stable growth of enterprises by finding the limit indicators of loan funds according to research. Excessive use of debt can lead to a decline in the value of businesses due to financial distress and the increased likelihood of a firm's credit rating downgrade. Therefore, a potential effect of capital structure policy is that it can increase both the firm's profits and losses – a double-edged sword, argued by Ross et al. (2001). The main purpose of this study is to study the impact of capital structure decisions on the profitability of state-owned enterprises. Seeks to identify how firms use capital structure decisions to create or destroy shareholder value in terms of profitability.

## 2   Literature Review

Capital structure decisions discuss theories that have no implications for cost of capital and cost of profitability. The choice of the mix of debt and equity financing is not significant for the value of the firm. That is, the value of the firm is the same regardless of the capital structure (Ross et al. 2009). This argument was promoted by Modigliani and Miller (MM). They argue that shareholders have the option to challenge management's choice of capital structure or to reinvest their existing assets. As a result, the firm's capital structure cannot increase or decrease the value of the firm.

What makes capital structure important comes from two key variables: the tax advantage of using debt and the risk of bankruptcy from using large amounts of debt. In this case, it is required that enterprises determine the limit amount of debt funds and conduct the correct debt policy. Increasing the company's income by expanding the available opportunities in debt financing leads to an increase in the profit for the shareholder. However, firms may not be able to pay debts due to wrong financial policies and may face financial difficulties. The resulting increase in costs reduces the profits available to shareholders.

Optimal capital structure leads to a further discussion of what level of capital structure a firm should choose to maximize shareholder value. Ross et al. (2009) argue that managers should choose the capital structure that they believe will have the highest firm value, as this capital structure will be most beneficial to the firm's shareholders. The reason shareholders invest in a firm is to increase their wealth. Any rational investor prefers financial decisions that maximize his wealth, and this capital structure is the optimal level of capital structure.

Bankruptcy occurs when the value of a firm's assets is equal to or less than the value of its debt. In general, as a company's debt increases, so does the likelihood of financial distress and eventual bankruptcy. Excessive use of debt capital leads to a debt crisis in which a firm has difficulty repaying its debt. If timely corrective action is not taken, the firm will eventually go bankrupt. In this case, companies can look for opportunities to get out of their financial difficulties by attracting additional debt funds. Companies that want to eliminate debt through debt can rarely get out of a financial crisis.

Bankruptcy costs are direct or indirect costs. Direct costs associated with bankruptcy may include legal fees, accounting fees, service fees, and administrative fees (Brealey et al. 2009).

Many studies have proven the negative relationship between profitability and financial structure. Abor (2007a), Abor (2007b) concluded that capital structure has a negative relationship with the profitability of enterprises. In their work, Fama and French (1998) concluded that there is a negative relationship between taxes, financing decisions, debt, value and profitability. They argue that, on balance, the downside of yield debt offsets any other benefits of debt. Yogendrarajah and Thanabalasingham (2011) suggest that firms that finance their investment activities with retained earnings are more profitable than those that finance them with debt capital, suggesting a negative relationship between profitability and capital structure in manufacturing companies. The results of Abor and Biekpe (2005) show that profitability is significantly negatively related to bank debt ratio.

Another theory used to predict optimal structure is agency theory. Agency relations arise because shareholders are separated from the management of enterprises. This also creates a situation of conflict of interest called the agency problem.

According to the agency problem, shareholders expect managers to act to maximize the value of their investment when they pursue their own best interests. We find that these conflicting interests can ultimately lead to situations that predict the optimal capital structure.

## 3 Methodology

The main variables we examine in this study are profitability (dependent variable) and capital structure (independent variable) ratios. In this study, our profitability ratio is defined as return on equity (ROE). It is defined as earnings before interest and taxes (EBIT) divided by equity (shareholders' equity and reserves). Equity is equal to the company's net assets (Assets minus liabilities).

We use EBIT because it is independent of the leverage effects of capital structure decisions and it excludes the effects of interest and taxes. Capital Structure Ratios – We used three capital structure ratios: short-term debt-total equity ratio, long-term debt-to-total equity ratio, and total debt-to-total equity ratio. In addition, another variable was introduced through the ratio of the target revenues allocated for state enterprises to their own funds.

Short-term debts are considered as all items included in the current liabilities section of the financial statements of the listed company. Long-term debt includes items listed as long-term liabilities, and total debt is the sum of short-term and long-term debt. Total capital is equal to the sum of equity, long-term and short-term debt, which is also equal to the total assets of the company.

In general, regression analysis was used to study the relationship between capital structure and profitability of state-owned enterprises. We also used the analysis to examine whether the relationship between capital structure and profitability is positive or negative, and how SOEs rely on debt financing.

$$ROE_{i,t} = b_0 + b_1 X_{1,t} + b_2 X_{2,t} + b_3 X_{3,t} + b_4 X_{4,t} + E_{i,t} \qquad (1)$$

## 4  Research and Results

According to the results of the correlational analysis of the results of the research, we can see the links between the profitability of the enterprises in relation to the share of the debt funds of the enterprises through the following tables (Table 1).

**Table 1.** Correlation matrix.

|       | Y     | $X_1$ | $X_2$ | $X_3$ |
|-------|-------|-------|-------|-------|
| Y     | 1     |       |       |       |
| X1    | −0.13 | 1     |       |       |
| $X_2$ | −0.82 | 0.02  | 1     |       |
| $X_3$ | −0.64 | 0.74  | 0.68  | 1     |
| X4    | −0.54 | 0.83  | 0.38  | 0.86  |

As a result of the correlation analysis of the example of the state enterprise, we can see that the correlation between the profitability of the enterprise (Y) and the share of short-term debt funds of the enterprise (X1) is negative and very insignificant. In addition, long-term debt of enterprises (X2), the ratio of the amount of total debt (X3) to the total capital volume, and we can see the share of the company's target income in relation to its own funds (X4) have significant negative effects on the company's profitability.

Taking these analyzes into account, when performing regression analysis, we do not perform regression analysis due to the fact that there is no dependence of the share of short-term debt funds of enterprises on the profitability indicator of an enterprise with a state share. Then we perform regression analysis of the independent variable long-term debt funds. The correlation index for independent $(X_2)$ and dependent (Y) variables was $R = 0.82$, the regression coefficient was $R^2 = 0.66$, and the one-factor regression equation was formed as follows (Table 2):

**Table 2.** Regression analysis results

| Y | Coef | Std. Err | T | P(t) |
|---|------|----------|---|------|
| X2 | −0.262 | 0.076 | −3.45 | 0.014 |
| _cons | 0.1169 | 0.027 | 4.29 | 0.005 |

$$Y_2 = 0.12 - 0.263X_2 + 0.076 \tag{2}$$

That is, if long-term debt funds increase by 1 compared to the total capital, the profitability of the enterprise decreases by −0.26. We check the validity of the results of this regression analysis. In this case, we rely on the F-test. According to the results of the F-test, when the calculated value of F is greater than the table value of F, we can see the validity of the non-regressive equation. According to our first regression model, F calculation is equal to 11.8 and F table is equal to 6. Our first equation is valid according to the F-test result.

We check the significance of the regression coefficient using the T-student test. According to the result of the t-test, we can see that the value of the t-table is 2.44 and is smaller than the value of the t calculation. According to the test result, the regression coefficient is significant.

According to the results of the correlation analysis, the regression equations of the independent variables are as follows:

$$Y_3 = 0.09 - 0.14X_3 + 0.07 \tag{3}$$

$$Y_4 = 0.06 - 0.09X_4 + 0.06 \tag{4}$$

We will check the validity of these regression equations and the significance of the regression coefficients. In this case, we rely on the above tests. The F-test and T-test conditions for the regression equation based on the independent variable X3 were not satisfied. The condition was not satisfied for the independent variable X4. In conclusion, we can say that then our two regression equations are not significant.

The results of the correlation analysis of the relationship between profitability and short-term debt show that, contrary to the conclusions of Abor (2005), there is a statistically insignificant negative relationship between the profitability of the enterprise and short-term debt for state-owned enterprises. This means that it is inefficient for state-owned enterprises to raise short-term debt funds, and state-owned enterprises can raise such debt funds to stimulate short-term working capital or to cover shortterm receivables.

Relationship between profitability and long-term debt The results of regression show a significant negative relationship between profitability and long-term debt for a state-owned enterprise. It means that long-term debt capital is relatively expensive for state-owned enterprises, as its use has a negative impact on revenue growth. Based on the long-term development strategies of the enterprise, it is advisable to use long-term low-interest bank loans or investments attracted under the guarantee of loans to stimulate its activities.

However, the target income of the state enterprise's own funds shows a significant negative correlation with the profitability of the enterprise, and it is aimed to regulate the real market prices of the main target income through state intervention. The result of this activity has a negative impact on the profitability of enterprises. In short, expensive long-term debt and developing economic conditions reduce profitability for SOEs.

# 5 Conclusion

In this study, we found that long-term debt has a negative effect on the profitability of the company using a regression model in making decisions on the capital structure of state-owned enterprises. It also showed that there is a statistically negative relationship between profitability and the share of target debt funds in own capital funds. The considered state share revealed a statistically significant negative relationship between profitability and total debt at the overall level of existing enterprises.

The capital structure of state-owned enterprises is the main proposals to be implemented in this regard, while diversifying the composition of shareholders and maintaining the share of the main shares in important state-owned enterprises. In addition, maintaining financial stability by using other methods of management. Attracting state-owned commercial banks to control packages of state-owned enterprises. As a result, it is ensured that state-owned enterprises have opportunities for sustainable growth rather than high-profit activities. In this case, it ensures the arrival of members engaged in business-based activities within the board of shareholders of state-owned enterprises. In addition, based on the compatibility of goals, an investment environment is formed for enterprises.

# References

Abor, J.: The effect of capital structure on profitability: an empirical analysis of listed firms in Ghana. J. Risk Finance 6(5), 438–445 (2005)

Abor, J.: Debt policy and performance of SMEs: evidence from Ghanaian and South African firms. J. Risk Finance 8(4), 364–379 (2007)

Abor, J.: Industry classification and the capital structure of Ghanaian Firms. Stud. Econ. Finance 24(3), 207–219 (2007)

Abor, J., Biekpe, N.: What determines the capital structure of listed firms in Ghana. Afr. Finance J. 7(1), 37–48 (2005)

Brealey, R.A., Myers, S.C., Marcus, A.J.: Fundamentals of Corporate Finance, 6th ed., pp. 440–463. McGrawHill/Irwin, New York (2009). Bryman, A.: Triangulation (n.d.)

Fama, French (1998). http://www.financeprofessor.coml. Accessed 07.11.11

Ross, S.A., Westerfield, R.W., Jaffe, J.F., Jordan, B.D.: Corporate Finance: Core Principles and Applications, 2nd edn. McGraw-Hill/Irwin, New York (2009)

Ross, S.A., Westerfield, R.W., Jordan, B.D.: Essentials of Corporate Finance, 3rd edn. McGraw-Hill, New York (2001)

Yogendrarajah, R., Thanabalasingham, S.: The Effect of Profit Margin on Capital Structure. Manufacturing Companies of Colombo Stock Exchange (CSE), Sri Lanka (2011)

Choriev, F.: Advantages of centralized models in the management of a state-owned enterprise. Econ. Educ. 23(2), 55 (2022). https://doi.org/10.55439/ECED/vol23_iss2/a55

# Exploring the Development of China's Digital Trade in the Context of the Domestic and International Double Cycle

Shufeng Cong[1], Lee Chin[1(✉)], and Piratdin Allayarov[2]

[1] School of Business and Economics, Universiti Putra Malaysia, UPM, Serdang, Malaysia
leechin@upm.edu.my
[2] Department of Mathematical Methods in Economics, Tashkent State University of Economics, Tashkent, Uzbekistan

**Abstract.** China's market advantages have been more apparent under the dual domestic and international circulation strategy, and the holding of the 2021 Global Digital Trade Conference has further encouraged international collaboration in this area. China has the second-largest digital economy in the world, and its digital trade, cross-border e-commerce, and digital service trade are all growing quickly, as is the level of rivalry between businesses. In this paper, the current state of China's digital trade development is examined from the standpoint of China's digital trade growth inside the double cycle, the issues and their root causes are compiled, and then practical solutions are suggested. To encourage the systematization of digital trade in China, the development of sophisticated digital services, and the specialization of talent development in digital trade.

**Keywords:** domestic and international dual cycle strategy · digital trade · cross-border e-commerce · digital services trade · digital trade talents

## 1 Introduction

### 1.1 Research Background

In early 2020, the trade of many countries was greatly affected by the COVID-19 and the development of the world economy was not optimistic. The pandemic also affected China's economic development, but due to the efficient and rapid response measures taken by China to minimize the losses under the impact of the pandemic and effectively resume production and life. The Central Committee of the Party originally advocated in 2020 to create a new development pattern of dual domestic and foreign cycles to promote one another to deal with and lessen the effects of the pandemic on our economy. In the twenty-first century, China's digital trade will grow to be a significant component of global trade and a key driver of economic growth.

Y. Koucheryavy and A. Aziz (Eds.): NEW2AN 2022, LNCS 13772, pp. 369–380, 2023.
https://doi.org/10.1007/978-3-031-30258-9_32

## 1.2  Purpose of the Research

In the context of the much-discussed local and worldwide double cycle, digital trade has merged as the most promising type of trade. Due to the abundance of trade goods in our nation, international trade is encouraged to grow. The research begins with China as the beginning point, and this paper concentrates on cross-border e-commerce, digital service trade, and digital trade talent training, which are extensions of digital trade and effective ways to boost the level of the national economy.

## 1.3  Research Significance

Theoretical significance: Nowadays, digital trade is a concern for countries all over the world, because digital trade is no longer restricted by geography and time, especially under the influence of pandemics, the traditional trade is restricted to different degrees. The existing research focuses more on cross-border e-commerce, digital services, or digital trade rules rather than a holistic analysis of digital trade. Studying the fundamentals of digital commerce, examining the challenges it faces as it develops, and outlining the appropriate countermeasures to address those challenges are important in the context of the double cycle to maximize the contribution of digital trade to China's economic growth.

Practical significance: In the post-epidemic era, digital trade has ushered in new development opportunities, and digital trade has made up for the shortcomings of traditional trade. Our country has guaranteed the stability of the supply chain among expanding domestic market demand and take the advantages of the huge domestic market, which also provides more stable product guarantee for the development of digital trade, promotes the construction of economic integration of Asian regional cooperation, and also provides guarantee for the sustainable development of our economy.

# 2  Overview of China's Development in Digital Trade

## 2.1  What is Digital Trade?

Digital trade is still in its infancy, so digital trade does not have a unified definition and measurement, and there is no unified standard for statistics. Regarding digital trade, China and the United States are more comprehensive in their understanding, and the United States was the first to study digital trade, and the United States expanded the definition of digital trade in 2017, arguing that digital trade includes not only online trade in goods and services but also all trade activities related to data flow and intelligent manufacturing, as well as cross-border e-commerce platforms. According to the Digital Trade White Paper published by China's ICT Institute in 2019, digital trade refers to a type of trade in which information technology plays a role in the trade process. Its content not only covers online promotion, transaction settlement, and other types of physically facilitated trade, but also digital service trade realized through information technology. The definition of digital trade used in China and the United States is more accurate since it takes current information technology and everyday life into account.

## 2.2  The Expansion of Digital Trade in China

According to Fig. 1, China's digital trade trial operation in 2006, the global digital trade industry alliance was born in Guangzhou.

The establishment of Beijing Digital Trade Base in 2009 marked the beginning of a new phase in the development of China's digital trade. In 2015, the emergence of new retail, unmanned vending, and fingerprint payment, with digital trade actively promoting the deep integration of China's real economy with the Internet. In 2016, the establishment of the China Digital Currency Research Institute, with digital trade accelerating the research and development of China's legal digital currency and financial innovation presenting diversified modes and tools. In 2017 China's first digital trade development research report was officially released - "Shanghai Digital Trade Development Research Report", providing valuable experience for digital trade in other regions of China.

In early 2020, the trade of many countries was greatly affected by the COVID-19 and the development of the world economy was not optimistic. The pandemic also affected China's economic development, but due to the efficient and rapid response measures taken by China to minimize the losses under the impact of the pandemic and effectively resume production and life. The Central Committee of the Party originally advocated in 2020 to create a new development pattern of dual domestic and foreign cycles to promote one another to deal with and lessen the effects of the pandemic on our economy. In the twenty-first century, China's digital trade will grow to be a significant component of global trade and a key driver of economic growth.

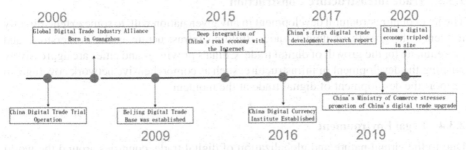

**Fig. 1.** China's digital trade stage map. Source: Compiled by authors

The National Information Network[1] and the State Ministry of Commerce[2] released separate documents in 2018 and 2019 to promote the thorough upgrade of China's digital trade and the use of digital trade to accelerate the growth of the global economy. China's digital economy will reach leapfrog development in 2020, and the state of development will continue to rise. According to the Ministry of Industry and Information Technology of China, the size of China's digital economy has increased from 11 trillion RMB to

---

[1] China National Internet Information Office, Digital China Construction Development Report (2018). http://www.cac.gov.cn/.

[2] Ministry of Commerce of China, China Digital Trade Development Report 2020. http://www.mofcom.gov.cn/.

35.8 trillion RMB[3], playing a significant role in the country's economy's high-quality growth.

## 2.3 Influencing Factors of Digital Trade in China

China's digital trade is booming, but it faces many influencing factors, such as digital trade talents, international and multilateral rules, trade infrastructure construction, a digital regulatory system, and a legal environment for trade development.

### 2.3.1 Talent Factor

Talent is a fundamental resource that affects the development of all industries. Whether there are enough talents with rich practical skills will directly affect the development of trade.

### 2.3.2 Multilateral Rules

Developed nations or the first few sizable nations in the growth of digital trade have always controlled the rules of the game. The capacity to actively contribute to the creation of norms and to freely voice one's thoughts will have a direct impact on how digital trade develops.

### 2.3.3 Trade Infrastructure Construction

The level of infrastructural development in any given nation will, to some extent, directly influence the growth of digital trade. Building infrastructure is the cornerstone and prerequisite for the growth of digital trade. China's provinces and cities are aggressively pushing the development of infrastructure, such as comprehensive network coverage, to support the development of digital trade at the moment.

### 2.3.4 Legal Environment

Due to the virtual nature and globalization of digital trade, countries around the world will face different situations when legislating on digital trade and the increase of uncertainty. Therefore, only when countries around the world strengthen communication and exchange on digital trade legislation and improve the legal system of digital trade, violations can be avoided, thus promoting the healthy development of digital trade in the world.

## 3 The Double Cycle's Present Impact on China's Digital Commerce Development

Li Boning and Zhang Su [1] study China's digital trade development through literature collection and inductive methods and argue that China should break through the core

---

3 https://www.miit.gov.cn/.

technology challenges and participate in international rule-making, which in turn will help to improve China's digital trade development. However, digital trade development involves multiple aspects, so participation in international rule-making should be one of the conditions for digital trade development. Hong Jiang and John Peter Murman [2] compare China and the United States in terms of e-commerce and Internet-based services and argue that China should strengthen its digital technology business-to-business services. Zhang Tao, Wu Zaiqun and Zheng Xiaoyu [3] analyzed the development trends and achievements of the United States, the European Union and important international organizations in the field of digital economy and concluded that China should promote the development of digital economy in terms of talent training and other aspects. Hu, Yue, Zhou, Han Qian, Yan, Bin, Zou, Zhou and Li, Yu'an [4] demonstrates that the level of development of digital trade in China is positively influenced by factors such as Internet development, population income, industrial structure, ease of payment, investment in fixed assets, the scale of online transactions, and economic development, with ease of payment having the biggest influence.

Therefore, this paper will analyze China's digital trade development from the perspectives of cross-border e-commerce, digital service trade, and digital talents.

## 3.1 Cross-Border e-Commerce is Rapidly Developing

The e-commerce sector has expanded quickly in response to the spread of the Internet throughout the nation and the rising number of Internet users. Digital trade has emerged and flourished under the dual domestic and international cycle strategy, stimulating domestic demand and taking advantage of the large domestic market. From 2015 to 2020, China's digital trade volume continues to grow, from US$200 billion to US$294.76 billion, an increase of 47.4%. Digital trade is booming, and the cross-border e-commerce industry is gradually emerging.

**Table 1.** Statistics for cross-border e-commerce import and export in China, 2017–2021

| Year | Transaction volume (unit: trillion RMB) | Year-on-year growth |
|------|------------------------------------------|---------------------|
| 2017 | 0.09 | 44.4% |
| 2018 | 0.135 | 33.3% |
| 2019 | 0.186 | 27.4% |
| 2020 | 1.69 | 157% |
| 2021 | 1.98 | 15% |

Data source: Ministry of Commerce of China

**Table 2.** The ratio of cross-border e-commerce imports and exports to China's total import and export value, 2017–2021

| Year | Total value of imports and exports (unit: trillion RMB) | Transactions accounted for the proportion of total import and export value |
|------|------|------|
| 2017 | 27.79 | 0.32% |
| 2018 | 30.51 | 0.44% |
| 2019 | 31.54 | 0.59% |
| 2020 | 32.16 | 5.25% |
| 2021 | 39.1 | 5.06% |

Data source: General Administration of Customs of China

Table 1 shows that between 2017 and 2021, cross-border e-commerce in China would expand in value year over year from 0.09 trillion RMB to 1.98 trillion RMB. In the meantime, the value of cross-border e-commerce imports and exports rises yearly with an average growth rate of more than 30%, particularly in 2020 with a yearly growth rate of 157%. Data on cross-border e-commerce import and export volume from 2017 to 2021 show that China's sector is still developing and is at a crucial stage between early and mature. Meanwhile, Table 2 shows that between 2017 and 2021, the share of cross-border e-commerce transactions in China to the total value of imports and exports increased annually, with a growth rate ranging from 0.32% to 5.06%. The findings show that cross-border e-commerce is having an increasing impact on the total value of China's imports and exports and taking up more space in those transactions. Therefore, the growth of international e-commerce is crucial to China's economic development.

### 3.2 Digital Service Trade Industry Continues to Extend

The total trade in services in China declined by 15.7% in 2020 compared to the same period in 2019, according to data from the Ministry of Commerce Although the total trade in services is declining, the digital knowledge-intensive services trade is constant growth, which can demonstrate that digital service trade has obvious growth advantages, so it can be concluded that digital service trade can be beneficial. The digital knowledge-intensive services trade increased by 8.3% year-over-year, accounting for 44.5% of the total value of import and export of services trade, an increase of 9.9 percentage points.

Trade in services has a wide scope, covering 12 major fields such as communication, finance, commerce, tourism, sports, and health. To develop the digital service trade, all industry sectors have started to combine digital technology and digital technology continuously. For example, export collection time has been reduced from two to four days to only two hours. At the same time, customs clearance time has been reduced from 36 h to 1.8 h with the development of digital technology, and documents have likewise evolved with digital development to digital documents, thus allowing the tax refund cycle to be reduced from 60 days to 14 days. In addition, digital tourism is booming, consumers use various styles, types and different producers of electronic terminals and applications (for example Ctrip and Tongcheng Travel) for various scenic spots. Digital tourism improves the efficiency and convenience of trade-in services, but the same security presents a significant obstacle and issue. As a result, to strengthen the security of digital service trade, it is important to improve the development of the digital service system and speed up support for the growth of digital service trade businesses.

### 3.3 Companies are Competing in Digital Trade in a New Way

Enterprise competitiveness is being impacted by digital trade and is growing as a result of China's rising development of digital trade. If enterprises want to develop continuously in the industry, they have to improve their competitiveness, so they keep developing their competitiveness, and while the competitiveness is improving, the competition between enterprises is also changing. The way of competition between enterprises and the basis of competition has changed to different degrees.

First of all, traditional trade competition includes product competition, service competition, production factor competition, and price competition. Because of the prevalence of digital trade, costs for goods and materials typically go down, which lowers the expense of traditional trade routes and equalizes the playing field for both large and small businesses. Next, based on competition, traditional trade enterprises compete based on the use of various expenses, such as publicity costs and marketing costs. Therefore, in the context of digital trade, digital trade can reduce the financial pressure on enterprises in the process of marketing as well as product promotion.

## 4    China's Digital Trade Under the Double Cycle: Issues and Causes

### 4.1    China's Digital Trade Issues in the Context of the Double Cycle

#### 4.1.1    Insufficient Potential for the Development of Traditional Trade

Cross-border e-commerce has been acknowledged by the government for the first time in 2014 when Customs 56 and Customs 57 were introduced. As a result, China formally entered the cross-border e-commerce development phase. Cross-border e-commerce has been developing in China, especially in early 2020, and many countries have a series of rule restrictions as well as security precautions for international trade due to the epidemic. Traditional trade is restricted due to the epidemic and the anti-epidemic trade rules promulgated by various countries in response to the epidemic, making traditional trade unable to develop further in the current environment and lacking its further development potential. Contrarily, cross-border e-commerce actively encourages the growth of international trade in the current economic climate, and many domestic and international traders use cross-border e-commerce platforms to locate clients, discuss business, forge partnerships, and complete each import and export transactions. Additionally, countries around the world are currently dealing with varying degrees of epidemic issues and epidemic prevention challenges. As a result, cross-border e-commerce sees this as an opportunity for development and the nation vigorously develops cross-border e-commerce, replacing some traditional trade and completing business-related enterprises, minimizing the epidemic's impact on the sales of traditional trade enterprises, and assisting small and medium-sized enterprises.

### 4.1.2 Digital Service Trade Cannot Meet the Demand

In the background of the double cycle, under the big domestic cycle, to further stimulate domestic demand and promote demand-side reform, therefore, the state has introduced corresponding policies to stimulate consumer demand. While consumer demand is further stimulated, many consumer demands are stimulated in the field of digital service trade in services, and consumers want to consume trade through various types of digital service trade platforms, specifically for tourism as well as consulting services. Especially under the influence of the pandemic, many tourist attractions are banned from opening, so if consumers want to travel to the attractions, they must "cloud travel" to the tourist attractions of each country through the digital service trade platform. However, because the fact that China's digital services business is still developing in many ways, it is challenging to meet the demands of the majority of customers. Therefore, only by the ongoing enhancement of the digital service trade systems, thereby fostering the advanced digital service trade, can the digital service trade currently meet the needs of all consumers. Advanced digital service trade can more fully satisfy the needs of consumers of all service types, which is advantageous for the further development of service trade in China and can act as a catalyst.

### 4.1.3 Insufficient Digital Trade Talents Required by Enterprises

The sector of digital trade is flourishing, and there are an increasing number of mathematical trade enterprises as a result of the ongoing development of digital trade. This is especially true in light of the double cycles that are occurring both domestically and internationally. Because the fact that China's digital trade is a new industry, there is a shortage of talent supply. The rise in the number of businesses also means that there will be constant competition and friction between businesses in the same industry. However, the key component of the development of digital trade businesses is the element of talent. Therefore, if digital trade enterprises want to develop rapidly, break the competitive dilemma of the same industry, and become the leading enterprise in the industry, they must have a reserve of digital trade for talents, but for digital trade enterprises in most regions, the inability to find suitable digital trade talents is the most prominent problem faced by enterprises wanting to expand their development at present. In addition time, the number of digital trade talents provided by China's universities is low and does not match the standard required by enterprises, resulting in the need for digital trade enterprises to recruit employees facing a situation where no one can be recruited.

## 4.2 Reasons for the Existence of Digital Trade Problems in China Under the Double Cycle

### 4.2.1 Traditional Trade Under the Double Cycle is Subject to More Uncertainty Factors

China's imports and exports are heavily dependent on both trade in goods and trade in services. As a result, countries have created traditional trade in products and traditional trade in services from the beginning of global trade. And the development of international trade between countries, generally from a good relationship between the trading partners to trade. But traditional trade faces more uncertainties, especially in the context of double-cycle, such as interstate cooperation relations, unexpected events, etc. A good cooperative relationship between countries is the most important influencing factor for developing trade, and bilateral trade agreements as well as multilateral trade agreements between countries are signed to better promote trade between two countries and promote national economic development. Emergencies can also affect the development of international trade, especially under the new crown epidemic's influence in 2020, coupled with the double-cycle strategy, the development of international trade is facing huge challenges, the epidemic in some countries in the world, the local industrial chain will be interrupted, resulting in the normal completion of the production of some products, no products, there is no way to trade traditional goods between the two countries. In the same way, traditional services trade to tourism services trade, for example, under the epidemic, people dare not go out, but in the context of the double cycle, people's needs have been constantly stimulated, but people are facing the traditional services trade cannot solve the problem.

### 4.2.2  Digital Service Trade is Outstanding in Convenience and Timeliness

Compared with traditional service trade, the convenience as well as timeliness of digital service trade is incomparable. Traditional service trade takes a long time to complete each business on average, such as the use of cross-border bills. The work convenience of traditional service trade is poor. When enterprises face the demand of withdrawing and picking up goods, they hope to quickly change into payment by documents, to pick up goods by payment, but the use and transmission of some cross-border bills in the field of international settlement take a long time and face more handling procedures, resulting in the bills lacking their convenience. However, if an enterprise has an emergency, traditional service trade is unable to speed up the problem promptly, which will make the enterprise face the problem of untimely capital turnover, which is crucial for an enterprise, and if a company's capital turnover chain is stagnant, it may have a huge negative impact on the company and even face the danger of enterprise bankruptcy.

### 4.2.3  Insufficient Teaching Resources for Cross-Border e-Commerce in Universities

Colleges and universities have started offering cross-border e-commerce majors and courses in recent years to keep up with the growth of global trade and the current fashion. Most often, cross-border e-commerce textbooks and simulation exercises are used by universities to begin cross-border e-commerce courses. However, there are certain differences between genuine cross-border e-commerce and simulated cross-border e-commerce. At the same time, the university-required cross-border e-commerce textbooks are frequently updated slowly, and the books' release also takes a long time.

## 5   Measures to Support the Growth of China's Digital Trade

### 5.1   China's Cross-Border e-Commerce Import and Export Structure Modification

Products with relatively little added value and poor economic benefits make up the bulk of China's cross-border e-import commerce's and export structure. Therefore, in order for China's cross-border e-commerce to develop further, its import and export structure need to be further adjusted. At the same time, equivalent overseas warehouses need to be built by the location and environment of the target nations. Overseas warehouse for the import and export of low value-added products is conducive to reducing enterprise logistics costs and increasing the economic benefits of enterprises.

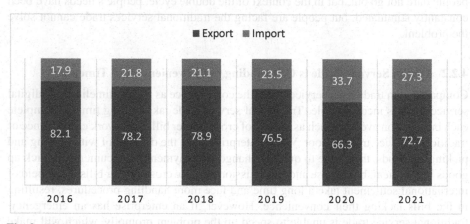

**Fig. 2.**   Share of import and export transactions of cross-border e-commerce in China, 2016–2021. (Data Source: General Administration of Customs of China)

Figure 2 depicts cross-border e-commerce import and export in China. It represents a large portion of export transactions. If the percentage of high value-added items in exports continues to climb, it will have the most immediate impact on highlighting the economic utility of businesses and encouraging their own growth. So attention must be paid to the production of high-value-added products as well as in the export. Although some nations have lax or nonexistent standards for cross-border e-commerce product restrictions, China's cross-border e-commerce is export-oriented, so manufacturers must be aware of product standards, support the systematization of digital trade rules, and work to avoid the restrictions of trade barriers imposed by other nations order to adapt to the development of the times as well as corporate profits. The development of China's import and export trade can be accelerated, and the high degree of development of digital trade is promoted, by adjusting the country's cross-border e-commerce import and export structure.

## 5.2  Lowering the Listing Conditions for Digital Service Enterprises

To seek company development, improve industry depth and expand enterprise scale, digital service trade enterprises often need a large amount of capital and multiple financing. The most convenient and quickest way for digital service trade enterprises to raise funds is to obtain equity financing by listing the company, but the conditions for listing enterprises in China are complicated and there are relatively more additional regulations, so it is difficult for digital service trade enterprises to meet the listing conditions. At the same time, most digital service enterprises are small and medium-sized enterprises, which have limited capital and poor risk resistance. Once new problems and challenges arise in the digital service trade, small and medium-sized digital service enterprises can hardly resist the impact and even face the possibility of bankruptcy and collapse. However, through the company's listing, more capital can be obtained, and through the continuous injection of capital, the company itself can further grow, and the product areas involved are more extensive, the company's foundation is more stable, and the anti-risk ability is continuously improved, which is conducive to the company's long-term development.

## 5.3  Intensify the Fusion of Business and Education in Universities and Colleges' Use of Digital Trade

The report of the Communist Party of China's 19th National Congress makes recommendations to further integrate business and education and to promote learning collaboration, which has set forth new criteria and new directions for the advancement of Chinese institutions. The development of a training program for digital trade abilities based on the fusion of business and education will aid in resolving the issue of "theory but not practice" for these skills, enhancing the instructive value of digital trade courses. In addition, under the integration of industry and education, the teaching of digital trade courses can be integrated with more teaching ideas and teaching cases, and the industrial orientation and talent training ideas will be clearer, which will eventually make the teaching of digital trade scientific, forward-looking and standardized, and promote the improvement of the teaching effect of digital trade.

# 6  Summary

Despite the COVID-19 pandemic's impact on the world economy, China's "dual domestic and international cycle" policy has boosted domestic consumer demand there. The volume of China's international trade will increase along with the country's domestic consumer demand. Under the "domestic and international double cycle" approach, digital trade in China is booming. The rapid growth of international e-commerce, the ongoing expansion of the digital services trade sector, and the recent emergence of enterprise digital trade rivalry are all notably mentioned in this study as the current conditions of China's development of digital trade. The export cross-border e-commerce has not yet established a stable development pattern, digital service trade cannot satisfy demand, and the digital trade abilities required by firms are insufficient, to name just a few challenges with China's existing digital trade. The low concentration of cross-border e-commerce sales models, challenges with direct financing for digital service trade businesses, and a lack of cross-border e-commerce teaching resources in universities are some of the specific causes for the problems' presence. Targeted countermeasures are suggested in response to the issues and root causes of China's digital trade, such as modifying the requirements for businesses to establish independent stations, easing the listing requirements for digital service businesses, and strengthening the connection between the digital trade sector and academic institutions. Implementing remedies will help China's level of digital trade development to continue to advance, which will help global commerce and the global economy to grow.

# References

1. Li, B., Zhang, S.: Research on the development path of China's digital trade under the background of the digital economy. J. Internet Digital Econ. (2022). Accepted 15 Jan 2022
2. Jiang, H., Murmann, J.P.: The rise of China's digital economy: an overview. Manag. Organ. Rev. **18**(4), 790–802 (2022)
3. Tao, Z., Zaiqun, W., Xiaoyu, Z.: Research on the international development trend of big data and digital economy and its reference to China. In: E3S Web of Conferences, vol. 233, p. 01171 (2021)
4. Hu, Y., Zhou, H.Q., Yan, B., Zou, Z., Li, Y.: An assessment of China's digital trade development and influencing factors. Front. Psychol. (2022). Accessed 26 Apr 2022

# A Systematic Mapping Study of Using the Cutting-Edge Technologies in Marketing: The State of the Art of Four Key New-Age Technologies

Kongratbay Sharipov [ID], Nigora Abdurashidova[✉] [ID], Aziza Valiyeva, Vasila Tuychieva, Mumtozbegim Kholmatova, and Murshida Minarova

Tashkent State University of Economics, Islam Karimov, 100066 Tashkent, Uzbekistan
n.abdurashidova@tsue.uz

**Abstract.** Fundamental shifts in marketing such as e-commerce and trading platforms make cutting-edge technologies a strategic priority for business and marketing leaders, although companies and firms found difficulty achieving their full potential, as a company culture-resistant marketing approach. The most important cutting-edge technologies (also known as key new-age technologies) as artificial intelligence, blockchain, the internet of things, and machine learning are expected to support many aspects of marketing such as meeting customer expectations and contact, recommendation of products, and identifying customer behavior and needs. However, the growing bodies of knowledge in cutting-edge technology research may disengage or disorient people who aim to integrate effectively those technologies in their business models based on their company strategy and needs because lack of systematization and categorization of massive information in the field may lead to irrelevant content retrieval, wasting time, and failure to identify the state of the art of those technologies. To address the systematic knowledge gaps in the field, this paper reports on a systematic mapping study that identified a recommended portfolio of 22 papers in the years 2017–2022, each proposing their own sets of applications and important research contributions in these four new-age technologies. The papers that were extracted from relevant and important databases through a systematic filtering process are the result of reviewing entirely, analyzing, and categorizing candidate studies to answer the research questions. This work also provides the current state of the art on using cutting-edge technologies in marketing illustrated by a taxonomy. The findings highlighted artificial intelligence technologies as the most common category of using cutting-edge technologies in marketing. Finally, the study also presents major implications for the marketing community and future research agenda in the field.

**Keywords:** cutting-edge · content taxonomy · marketing · classified portfolio · summary

## 1 Introduction

Digitalization and e-trading have made it easier for firms and customers to research, compare and order products or services, transforming their selling/buying processes

Y. Koucheryavy and A. Aziz (Eds.): NEW2AN 2022, LNCS 13772, pp. 381–389, 2023.
https://doi.org/10.1007/978-3-031-30258-9_33

and overall marketing strategies. In particular, artificial intelligence as the main indicator of digitalization has innovated much in how modern marketing works [1–4]. An interdisciplinary framework proposed by [1] is a business-to-business marketing framework for both academics and practitioners who aim to foster and increase AI-based innovation in their respective organizations. Additionally, other research studies [5, 6] emphasize the benefits of blockchain technologies in marketing, identifying the potential of cryptographic blockchain platforms and smart contracts to assist investors and industrial marketers with sales and promotional activities. [7, 8] have emphasized the need to develop quicken development of marketing strategies charting the complexities of cutting-edge technologies, especially blockchain. Rather than concentrating only on cutting-edge technologies, there is an opportunity for marketing researchers to explore different technologies such as virtual technologies [9, 10].

The marketing research community has contributed to advancing the literature on cutting-edge technology-enabled marketing, especially the work of [11, 13, 16]. While the volume of research resources on these topics is growing, the academic literature remains unclear and fragmented. Such difficulties and unknowns of knowledge representation bring limitations for realizing the cutting-edge technologies in marketing which afterward drive researchers and practitioners to develop new knowledge and methods. That is why there is a need for a more comprehensive and systematic framework regarding the use cases and significant research contributions of new-age technologies in marketing including artificial intelligence, blockchain, machine learning, and the internet of things.

Inspired by this need, we present a systematic mapping study (SMS) that provides a comprehensive overview of using state-of-the-art cutting-edge technologies in marketing. Similar studies were conducted by [11, 12] but they missed up-to-date summary knowledge and a systematic map which is a process of building a classification structure and categorizing key research studies. Unlikely those studies, the objective of this research paper is to identify, analyze, and characterize research bodies on the specific topic (cutting-edge technologies in marketing) to assist the marketing community to establish a foundation for using cutting key new-edge technologies and understand the state of the art on the target domain and recognize best practices.

The remainder of the paper is structured as follows. Section 2 represents mapping questions, research objectives, and methodology (such as search strategy and data analysis procedures). Section 3 highlights results from the data collection process and a summary of key studies. Finally, Sect. 4 provides implications for the study and outlines research limitations and future research agenda.

## 2   Methodology

The methodology that we used in this study is a systematic mapping study that is useful to identify, analyze and classify knowledge in the target research domain and present the state of the art. Based on the methodology that also conforms to systematic mapping methods of similar studies[14, 15], the whole research process includes the following steps: 1) defining mapping questions and study planning relevant to the specific topic, 2) conducting a search strategy for identifying candidate studies, 3) establishing inclusion &

exclusion criteria, 4) collecting and extracting data concerning pre-established criteria (research questions and selections criteria).

## 2.1 Systematic Mapping Questions

Following the first step of the research process, the following research questions are provided to identify the main aspects of the topic and describe the literature.

*Research question 1:* What are the publication trends in the studies of using the four cutting-edge technologies in marketing (artificial intelligence, blockchain, machine learning, internet of things)?

*Research question 2:* What are the common practices or methods of using those new-age technologies in marketing?

*Research question 3:* What mechanisms exist for managing cutting-edge technologies for the effective and constant implementation of marketing strategies?

*Research question 4:* What are the challenges of using key new-age technologies in marketing?

The first and second research questions aim to clarify scientific trends and practices of target research communities in artificial intelligence, blockchain, machine learning, and the internet of things. The third and fourth research questions are expected to map the mechanisms and challenges of using those technologies in different domains of marketing.

## 2.2 Planning the Study and Search Strategy

Based on our prior knowledge and related literature, we first planned to identify a search strategy and relevant databases. As the main purpose of the study is to explore and analyze the state of the art of using the four cutting-edge technologies in marketing, we also refer to the previously established mapping questions. In this regard, we generated a plan for the search string and selected academic databases.

The first aspect of the plan is to identify major terms and their more relevant synonyms. Those terms and their alternatives were aggregated concerning the research questions and the article title. Alternative phrases derived from the major terms help us to elaborate on the broader view of the topic. Table 1 below is an outline of the major and alternative terms that shaped our search string in combination or individually.

The second important aspect of the plan is to select academic databases to make inquiries and get insights about the general knowledge of using those technologies in marketing. In this sense, four academic databases relevant to cutting-edge technology applications in marketing are chosen as the main sources of information. The tabulated information below is the details of the selected databases in which inquiries are conducted including search areas (Table 2).

The selected databases are representative because they are useful in terms of the sources for study search in many related systematic mapping studies.

## 2.3 Selection Criteria

It is safe for us to establish inclusion & exclusion criteria so that we can select relevant studies and remove bias and noise of massive data generated in the previous search. To

**Table 1.** Outline of alternative terms and synonyms.

| Type of cutting-edge technology | Alternative terms for them |
|---|---|
| Artificial intelligence | Automated intelligence, automated feedback, imitating human behavior, automated routines |
| Blockchain | Decentralization, platforms, cryptography, contracts, negotiation |
| Machine learning | Data analysis, Supervised learning, unsupervised learning, reinforcement learning, machine learning algorithms, automated learning, self-learning algorithms |
| Internet of things | Sensors, regulators, computing systems, real-time data, connected devices |

**Table 2.** Outline of academic databases and search areas.

| Name of the database | Search area of the database |
|---|---|
| Science Direct | Title, keywords, and abstract |
| ACM digital libraries | Title, abstract, and key concepts |
| Research gate | Title and abstract |
| Springer Nature | Title, abstract, and indexing terms |

select candidate studies from the retrieved information from the database search, we used the following inclusion & exclusion criteria:

**Inclusion Criteria**

- Papers discuss directly at least one of four cutting-edge technologies in marketing
- Papers including the outline of the mechanisms for the management of using cutting-edge technologies in marketing
- Publications within the periods of 2017 – 2022 to keep the state-of-the-art quality
- Papers including broad approaches to systematizing methods or practices in using those technologies for marketing purposes

**Exclusion Criteria**

- Quality assessment studies over **technology-in-marketing** research since we aim to figure out best practices and the state of the art of using four cutting-edge technologies
- Duplicates of the same study
- Papers comprising self-reported outcomes instead of objective measures
- Articles are written by ineligible people showing inaccurate data, incompetent methods, and applying unscheduled appointments in the data collection process.

## 2.4  Data Collection and Extraction Methods

To identify candidate studies, the following activities were performed: manual analysis of articles conforming to key article components (title, keywords, abstract, and findings or conclusion) and consensus meetings of authors of this paper for the selection process of candidate studies. The researchers of the paper collectively determined the candidate studies according to inclusion & exclusion criteria and search string. They inquired about the preferred academic databases by using pre-established terms, research questions, and selection criteria. Then, they analyzed the candidate studies by reading the full contents of the papers and organized consensus meetings till reaching a consensus on acceptance of a candidate study.

Data analysis processes help us to reveal the forums of key publications that are of great benefit to present the state of the art of four key new-age technologies. The filtering process played a key role in this analysis, which relied upon search and selection strategies previously established. At the end of the data collection and extraction stages, a pool of relevant studies [1–13, 15–23] that was attached in the reference section of this paper was formed as a recommended portfolio of publication for those who want to establish a foundation for using new-age technologies in marketing. Figure 1 illustrates the data selection and extraction methods that were used in this systematic mapping study.

| Study planning | Search and selection strategies | Study execution & data extraction |
|---|---|---|
| **Defining systematic mapping questions** | **Creating search string** | **Manual analysis of candidate studies according to redefined criteria** |
| **Establishing research objectives** | **Selecting academic databases** | **Consensus meetings for acceptance of a candidate study** |
| **Identification of key terminologies** | **Establishing inclusion & exclusion criteria** | |
| | | **Forming a pool of recommended publications** |

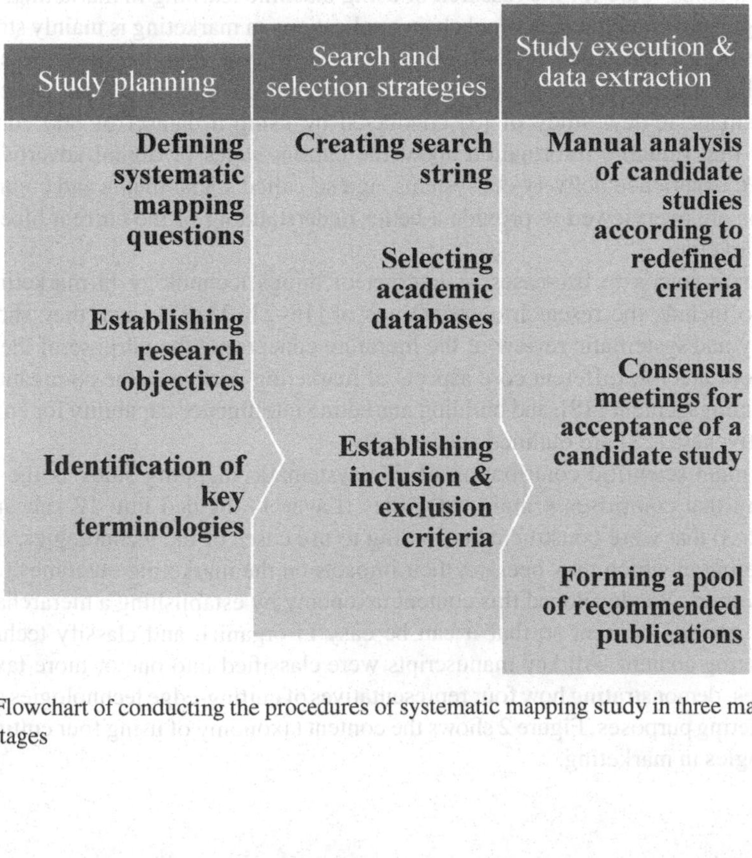

**Fig. 1.** Flowchart of conducting the procedures of systematic mapping study in three main stages and substages

This diagram explains how the study was conducted and the stages in which datasets were collected and analyzed.

## 3  Results

In this section, the results of the data extraction process such as a portfolio of key publications and taxonomy development were explained and the proposed research questions were answered.

The retail industry is one of the hot areas where technology is being actively integrated. As the main purpose of the manuscript is to structure the knowledge of four main categories of cutting-edge technology used in marketing (artificial intelligence, machine learning, internet of things, and blockchain), a summary of each of those technologies is needed.

Regarding the artificial intelligence and machine learning applications in marketing, it is noticed in [1–4] that automated analysis of customer behaviors is increasingly becoming a key for a successful marketing strategy to gain useful insight for boosting the sails and enhancing the rate of customer satisfaction. An interdisciplinary framework formulated by [1] is to assist AI-based innovation in business-to-business marketing with a recommended list of research questions for future research directions. Additionally, [22] provided an indirect framework for investigating machine learning techniques in detail that holds value for the research of using machine learning in marketing.

The general knowledge of blockchain applications in marketing is mainly structured by analyzing the discourse of [5–8] and their research contributions since these studies contain literature reviews and generalizations of blockchain applications. Specifically, the systematic review study of [5] conducted by using a dataset of 800 companies revealed that valuable information about the current states of digital advertising and content & experience delivery ecosystems, and so-called social media and e-commerce platforms are overviewed to provide a better understanding of the current blockchain-based marketing.

When it comes to use-cases of internet of things technology in marketing, it is agreed to include the research contributions of [16–21, 23–27] since they show high relevancy and systematic review of the literature concerning the purpose of the article. To be more precise, different core aspects of marketing such as value co-creation [17], customer engagement [18], and building marketing intelligence capability for enhancing competitiveness [23] are outlined successfully.

The main scientific contribution of this systematic mapping study is the content taxonomy that comprises 4 main categories (Layer 1) divided into 12 subcategories (Layer 2–3) that were constructed according to use cases of the technologies, domains of marketing in which they operate, their impacts on the marketing outcomes for firms and customers. We developed this content taxonomy by establishing a hierarchal structure and naming content so that it can be easy to organize and classify technology-in-marketing content. All key manuscripts were classified into one or more taxonomy categories, demonstrating how four representatives of cutting-edge technologies are used for marketing purposes. Figure 2 shows the content taxonomy of using four cutting-edge technologies in marketing.

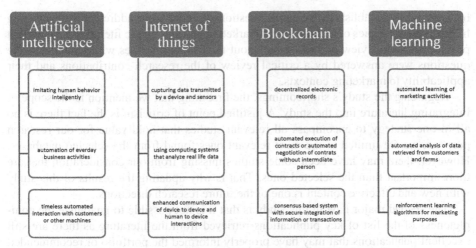

**Fig. 2.** Taxonomy of using cutting-edge technologies in marketing

The development of taxonomy is based on key words extraction and content categorization. By extracting keywords and concepts that define general characteristics of current state-of-the-art technologies used in marketing. We have also leveled the sub-categories in a top-down manner in terms of their importance and commonality of the use-case of each cutting-edge technology that the paper focuses on. Most importantly, this taxonomy was built by using the portfolio of key publications and summarizing the important aspects of topic-specific data so that the content can become manageable and discoverable.

## 4   Discussions and Conclusions

To grasp what has been accomplished in this comprehensive mapping project, we must reflect and conclude. This paper is expected to serve as a reference source for those who want to develop foundation knowledge about applying cutting-edge technologies to marketing domains.

The methodology that we used in this paper is a systematic mapping study that analyzes, classifies, and summarizes literature published in the years from 2017 to 2022. The taxonomy that users can use to identify and apply the state of the art of four cutting-edge technologies for controlling technology-based marketing activities in marketing is the main scientific contribution of this work.

Regarding the data collection and analysis process, we followed three general stages: study planning, search and selection strategies, and study execution & data extraction. Manual analysis of documents based on preestablished criteria (research questions and selection criteria) and content generalization methods are also used to structure information. A pool of key publications [1–13, 15–23] is achieved after deep analysis of selected candidate studies that were agreed on consensus discussion.

To obtain a categorization of use cases of cutting-edge technologies in marketing, we have also purposefully recognized the responses to our research questions that we had previously established. Research questions 1 and 2 were addressed by analyzing high-frequency topics of technology in marketing and systematic literature reviews that provide an overall view of knowledge about trends and practices while the rest of the questions were answered by a critical review of the research contributions and their applicability to marketing contexts.

Regarding the study's shortcomings, the first thing that we mention is the scope of integrating literature into the study. A justified point of criticism is the fact there is no all-in-one strategy to encompass all relevant studies that hold value for our research purpose, we are limited to the most relevant ones found from the selected databases. However, there may have been some studies missing from our consideration that are more important than the selected ones. That is why updating the results of this study with new and effective content is one of the future research directions.

The second major flaw in this study is that it is not possible to guarantee the completeness of the list of key publications retrieved from the literature as there are still excellent publications that may have properly informed the portfolio of recommended publications. Therefore, adding new valuable publications to this portfolio is another future research opportunity.

Finally, the results of this systematic mapping study are expected to serve as a comprehensive guide for supporting decision-making in applying cutting-edge technologies in marketing.

## References

1. Petrescu, M., Krishen, A.S., Kachen, S., Gironda, J.T.: AI-based innovation in B2B marketing: an interdisciplinary framework incorporating academic and practitioner perspectives. Ind. Mark. Manag. **103**, 61–72 (2022)
2. Kopalle, P.K., Gangwar, M., Kaplan, A., Ramachandran, D., Reinartz, W., Rindfleisch, A.: Examining artificial intelligence (AI) technologies in marketing via a global lens: current trends and future research opportunities. Int. J. Res. Mark. **39**(2), 522–540 (2022)
3. Haleem, A., Javaid, M., Qadri, M.A., Singh, R.P., Suman, R.: Artificial intelligence (AI) applications for marketing: a literature-based study. Int. J. Intell. Netw. (2022)
4. van Esch, P., Stewart Black, J.: Artificial intelligence (AI): revolutionizing digital marketing. Australas. Mark. J. **29**(3), 199–203 (2021)
5. Stallone, V., Wetzels, M., Klaas, M.: Applications of blockchain technology in marketing systematic review of marketing technology companies. Blockchain Res. Appl. 100023 (2021)
6. Lannquist, A.: Blockchain in an enterprise: How companies are using blockchain today. Blockchain at Berkeley (2018). https://blockchainatberkeley.blog/a-snapshot-ofblockchain-in-enterprise-d140a511e5fd
7. Lemos, C., Ramos, R.F., Moro, S., Oliveira, P.M.: Stick or twist—the rise of blockchain applications in marketing management. Sustainability **14**(7), 4172 (2022)
8. Antoniadis, I., Kontsas, S., Spinthiropoulos, K.: Blockchain applications in marketing. . In: Proceedings of the 7th ICCMI (2019)
9. Petit, O., Velasco, C., Spence, C.: Digital sensory marketing: integrating new technologies into the multisensory online experience. J. Interact. Mark. **45**, 42–61 (2019)
10. Marasco, A., Buonincontri, P., van Niekerk, M., Orlowski, M., Okumus, F.: Exploring the role of next-generation virtual technologies in destination marketing. J. Destin. Mark. Manag. **9**, 138–148 (2018)

11. Kumar, V., Ramachandran, D., Kumar, B.: Influence of new-age technologies on marketing: a research agenda. J. Bus. Res. **125**, 864–877 (2021)
12. Ma, L., Sun, B.: Machine learning and AI in marketing–Connecting computing power to human insights. Int. J. Res. Mark. **37**(3), 481–504 (2020)
13. Terho, H., Mero, J., Siutla, L., Jaakkola, E.: Digital content marketing in business markets: activities, consequences, and contingencies along the customer journey. Ind. Mark. Manag. **105**, 294–310 (2022)
14. Alarcón, C.N., Sepúlveda, A.U., Valenzuela-Fernández, L., Gil-Lafuente, J.: Systematic mapping on social media and its business relation. Eur. Res. Manag. Bus. Econ. **24**(2), 104–113 (2018)
15. Thaha, A.R., Maulina, E., Muftiadi, R.A., Alexandri, M.B.: Digital marketing and SMEs: a systematic mapping study. Libr. Philos. Pract. (e-journal), 5113 (2021)
16. Balaji, M.S., Roy, S.K.: Value co-creation with the Internet of things technology in the retail industry. J. Mark. Manag. **33**(1–2), 7–31 (2017)
17. Mehralian, M.M.: Effect of internet of things on marketing performance: the mediating role of entrepreneurship orientation. In: 25th Iranian Conference on Business Development and Digital Transformation (2022)
18. Ajayi, S., Loureiro, S.M.C., Langaro, D.: Internet of things and consumer engagement on retail: state-of-the-art and future directions. Eur. Med. J. Bus. (2022). (ahead-of-print)
19. Dlamini, N.N., Johnston, K.: The use, benefits, and challenges of using the Internet of Things (IoT) in retail businesses: a literature review. In: 2016 International Conference on Advances in Computing and Communication Engineering (ICACCE) (pp. 430–436). IEEE, November 2016
20. Nguyen, B., Simkin, L.: The Internet of Things (IoT) and marketing: the state of play, future trends and the implications for marketing. J. Mark. Manag. **33**(1–2), 1–6 (2017)
21. Malik, R.: Retail and internet of things: a digital transformation. In: Advancing Smarter and More Secure Industrial Applications Using AI, IoT, and Blockchain Technology, pp. 251–260. IGI Global (2022)
22. Eshbayev, O.A., Mirzaliev, S.M., Rozikov, R.U., Kuzikulova, D.M., Shakirova, G.A.: NLP and ML-based approach of increasing the efficiency of environmental management operations and engineering practices. In: IOP Conference Series: Earth and Environmental Science, vol. 1045, no. 1, p. 012058. IOP Publishing, June 2022
23. Abubakar, A., Abdullah, H.H.: Building marketing intelligence capability with the internet of things for competitiveness: empirical evidence of selected retail companies in Oman. J. Glob. Bus. Adv. **14**(6), 750–767 (2021)
24. Miskiewicz, R.: Internet of things in marketing: bibliometric analysis (2020)
25. Avezimbetovich Sharipov, K., Alisherovna Abdurashidova, N.: Benchmarking strategy for industrial enterprise development. In: Proceedings of the 5th International Conference on Future Networks & Distributed Systems, pp. 318–322, December 2021
26. Ikramov, M., Eshmatov, S., Samadov, A., Imomova, G., Boboerova, M.: Management marketing strategy for formation of local brand of milk and dairy products in the digital economy. Revista geintec-gestao inovacao e tecnologias **11**(2), 443–466 (2021)
27. Mirzaliev, S.M., Homidov, H.H., Sharipov, K.A., Kholikova, N.A.: Perspectives of use of agricultural drones in Uzbekistan. In: IOP Conference Series: Earth and Environmental Science, vol. 1045, no. 1, p. 012147. IOP Publishing, June 2022

# Social Media Marketing for Educational Purposes: Goals, Objectives and Content of the Training Course

Bahodir Zaripov[1]([⊠]) [iD], Feruza Zakirova[2] [iD], and Sanjar Mirzaliev[1] [iD]

[1] Tashkent State University of Economics, Tashkent, Uzbekistan
amirbahodir@gmail.com, s.mirzaliev@tsue.uz
[2] Tashkent University of Information Technologies, Tashkent, Uzbekistan
f.zakirova@tuit.uz

**Abstract.** In the context of the coronavirus pandemic, the professional activity of each educator has changed towards the use of Internet resources, namely social media. The article describes the goals, objectives and content of the training course for advanced training system for academic staff of Higher Educational of the Republic of Uzbekistan which revealed the specifics of using strategies and tools of Social Media Marketing (SMM) for educational purposes. Based on answers of the online survey of 105 academic staff who have completed advanced training in the use of SMM for educational purposes, the effectiveness of the "Educational SMM" training course was shown.

**Keywords:** Higher Education · Professional Development · Social Media Marketing · Curriculum Design

## 1 Introduction

Today, modern information and communication technologies offer innovative learning tools that serve not only to acquire new knowledge, but also to promote it in the educational services market. One such innovative tool is Social Media Marketing (hereinafter referred to as SMM).

SMM is commonly used in the economic field of human activity. In publications by D. Khalilov [1], J.H. Kietzmann [2], C. Ashley [3], A. Abdallah [4] were revealed ways to promote goods and services using social networks.

We propose to use strategies and tools of SMM for educational purposes in the system of professional development of academic staff. In 2021, a new training course was introduced into the curriculum of advanced training system for academic staff in the direction of "Information Systems and Technologies", which reveals the didactic possibilities of SMM and various ways of organizing the teaching process through portals of social media.

This article describes the goals, objectives and content of the training course on the "Educational SMM" in the system of professional development of the academic staff of higher educational institutions of the Republic of Uzbekistan.

Y. Koucheryavy and A. Aziz (Eds.): NEW2AN 2022, LNCS 13772, pp. 390–396, 2023.
https://doi.org/10.1007/978-3-031-30258-9_34

## 2 Literature Review

Sisira Neti [5] define social marketing as "a form of Internet marketing that utilizes social networking websites as a marketing tool. SMM is a strategic and methodical process to establish the company's influence, reputation and brand within communities of potential customers".

The goal of SMM is to produce content that users will share with their social network to help a company increase brand exposure and broaden customer reach. The value of social media in marketing and advertising campaigns is confirmed and highlighted by the fact that big brands and multinational companies are actively using social media to promote their companies and products. The most popular forms of social networking today include social networking sites (Facebook), websites, microblogging (Twitter), video sharing sites (YouTube), photo sharing sites and apps (Instagram), news and magazine sites, social networking sites, social bookmarking and voting sites, filesharing sites, gaming sites and forums, among others. Thus, the potential of social networks is huge.

As I. Taylor [6] notes, today's higher education institutions are striving to establish relationships with their target market and improve their communication strategies and marketing methods. At the same time, he notes that when used and developed effectively, social networks help to improve the brand of the university and increase its credibility.

As noted Salem Omar [7] Social media platforms are the most important channels to promote advertising campaigns and communicate with current and prospective students.

An analysis of [8] and [9] devoted to the use of social media platforms in education showed that they are used in two ways.

The first way of using platforms of social media is aimed at communication of educational institutions with the objects of the external environment, such as applicants, parents and other external parties. Mehmood [10] had investigated the use of SMM in the higher education sector in Pakistan and its perceived impact on admission of students. Mehmood also show that through SMM HEIs arable to better engage with their students, obtain necessary feedback, correct any misperceptions and help in career building. Publication [11] points to the effectiveness of using SMM in the higher education system in Malaysia.

The second way of using platforms of social media is aimed at organizing internal communication and interaction within an educational institution, such as students and educators.

We believe that social networks is so diverse that it can be used in any way best suits the interests and needs of education [12].

This article proposes another way to use SMM in education, which aims to improve the professional skills of academic staff in using platforms of social media to organize teaching based on strategies and methods of SMM.

## 3 Methodology

We studied the possibility of using strategies and tools of SMM for educational purposes on the example of advanced training courses for academic staff based on The

Branch Center for Retraining and Advanced Training of Pedagogical Staff of the Higher Education at Tashkent University of Information Technologies named after Muhammad al-Khwarizmi in the Republic of Uzbekistan.

Respondents were 105 academic personnel who, from January to June 2021, improved their qualifications in the direction of "Information Systems and Technologies".

The advanced training course on the "Educational SMM" was organized on mt.bimm.uz distance learning portal, where educators could find information on SMM (content was created in the state language) [13].

A telegram channel was also opened in the Telegram's open platform, where educators shared their opinions and work experience.

To identify the attitude of academic staff to the new training course on the "Educational SMM", an online survey was conducted.

The survey includes 10 questions and consists of three sections.

The first section is general information. This section covers 3 questions and asks the age of the respondents, their gender and favorite social media channel.

The second section includes 5 questions (3 "multiple choice" questions, 1 "yes/no" question and 1 "combo" question) to determine educators' preferences for using social media platforms in education.

The third section includes 2 open-ended questions. The first open-ended question determines the impact of SMM on the educational process. The second open-ended question identifies suggestions for further improvement of the content of the training course on the "Educational SMM".

## 4　Result and Discussion

The analysis of problems in the organization of education process in the context of the coronavirus pandemic revealed the need for academic staff to improve their professional skills and gain new knowledge in managing students' cognitive activities through using platforms of social media. Therefore, it was decided to create a new training course that increased educators' professional skills to use the possibilities of SMM for teaching.

To determine the goals and objectives of the new training course on the "Educational SMM", special literature on SMM, as well as the experience of using SMM for business purposes, was previously studied. In accordance with the goals and objectives of SMM, the goals and objectives of the training course on the "Educational SMM" were determined, which are reflected in Table 1.

To determine the content of the training course on the "Educational SMM", four main topics were selected:

- Basic terms, functions and principles of SMM. Didactic possibilities of social networks (theory – 2 h);
- Building SMM strategy – defining the goals and objectives of an educational channel in social networks, analyzing the educational services market, choosing social platforms, developing the content strategy, developing the visual style, media planning, performance evaluation (theory – 2 h, practice – 2 h, self study – 4 h);

**Table 1.** Table type styles

| Object | SMM | Educational SMM |
|---|---|---|
| Goal | Increase profits through the sale of products and services by converting visitors into buyers | Increasing the effectiveness of learning through the provision of educational products by turning student subscribers into active learners |
| Objectives | - Increasing brand awareness,<br>- Driving traffic<br>- Increasing coverage rates,<br>- Increasing income and reducing expenses | - Informing and providing feedback in training,<br>- Popularization of scientific views,<br>- Increasing the educational activity of students,<br>- Increasing the reputation of the teacher and his recognition on the Internet |

- Creation of the educational channel on various social platforms (YouTube or Telegram) and its maintenance (practice – 8 h, self study – 16 h);
- Determination of quality (practice – 2 h, self study – 4 h).

During the advanced training course, in addition to theoretical and practical classes, video lectures on SMM from various YouTube channels, webinars based on ZOOM and the specially created Telegram channel was used for communication and exchange of views. During the organization of the advanced training course, educators created their educational SMM projects mainly on YouTube and Telegram.

After completing the advanced training course on the "Educational SMM" module, an online survey was conducted.

An analysis of the responses to the first section provided the following data:

– average age of academic staff is 42.46;
– of the respondents 33.7% were females and 66.3% were male;
– 89.6% of respondents usually use Telegram most often.

The results of the survey for the second section are shown in Table 2.
An analysis of the responses to the second section provided the following data:

– 69.7% of educators have not previously used social media platforms for educational purposes;
– 80.3% of educators used social networks mainly to organize communication with students and transfer files;
– 69.9% of educators created an educational channel for the first time during the training course;
– 31.5% of educators decided to choose Telegram channel and 88.4% decided to choose YouTube;

**Table 2.** Survey result

| N | Question | Answer (%) |
|---|----------|-----------|
| 1 | What social media do you usually use in your daily life? | |
| | Telegram, | 89.7 |
| | YouTube, | 78.2 |
| | Facebook, | 45.2 |
| | Twitter, | 34.1 |
| | LinkedIn, | 6.9 |
| | Other | 1.2 |
| 2 | Did you use social media platforms in education before? | |
| | No, | 69.7 |
| | Yes used for: | 28.7 |
| | • Organization of communication, | 81.3 |
| | • File transfer, | 79.3 |
| | • Activation of students' activities, | 7.2 |
| | • Popularization of the subject, | 0 |
| | • Create feedback, | 0 |
| | • Improve your reputation as an educator, | 1.3 |
| | • Increase your awareness, | 1.1 |
| | • Other | 0.2 |
| 3 | Are you creating an educational channel for the first time? | |
| | o Yes, | 69.9 |
| | o No | 30.1 |
| 4 | Which social media platform did you decide to use to organize your training? | |
| | • Telegram, | 88.4 |
| | • YouTube, | 31.5 |
| | • Facebook, | 1.2 |
| | • Twitter, | 0 |
| | • Other | 0 |
| 5 | What purpose do you use social media platforms in education for? | |
| | • Give information, | 91.3 |
| | • Communication with students, | 98.3 |
| | • Communication with colleagues, | 4.3 |
| | • Activation of students' activities, | 82.3 |
| | • Popularization of the subject, | 10.5 |
| | • Create feedback, | 78.6 |
| | • Improving your reputation as an educator, | 9.3 |
| | • Increasing your awareness, | 8.1 |
| | • Other | |

– 82.3% of educators began to use social networks to enhance the educational activities of students; 78.6% – to create feedback and 17.4% to increase their reputation and recognition in the Internet world.

An analysis of the answer to the first open-ended question in the third section showed that teachers identified the following positive aspects in learning through social networks, namely, the study of the module helped to realize the originality of using social networks for educational purposes; social networks helped to connect theoretical knowledge with the interests of students; through educational social channels, it became possible to increase the practical orientation of training through the use of audio and video information; the use of an educational Telegram channel helps to provide feedback through various bots; special analytical software products help to easily organize the analysis, monitoring and forecasting of students' achievements.

An analysis of the answer to the second open-ended question in the third section showed that in the future, teachers want to increase the hours for the practical use of social networking platforms and consider methods for creating educational channels not only on YouTube and Telegram, but also on other social networking platforms.

## 5  Conclusions

The article reveals the goals, objectives, content of the training course on the "Educational SMM" in the curriculum of the advanced training system for academic staff. On the basis of an online survey of 105 educators was shown effectiveness of this training course. Currently, the presence of an educator on the Internet and constant communication with students is one of the main professional competencies. It is time for every educator to master social networks and organize the educational process with its help.

## References

1. Khalilov, D.: Marketing in social networks. Publishing House Mann, Ivanov and Ferber, Moscow, 376 p. (2013) (in Russian). https://brpo.by/wp-content/uploads/2021/11
2. Kietzmann, J.H., Hermkens, K., McCarthy, I.P., Silvestre, B.S.: Social media? Get serious! Understanding the functional building blocks of social media. Bus. Horiz. **54**(3), 241–251 (2011). https://doi.org/10.1016/j.bushor.2011.01.005
3. Ashley, C., Tuten, T.: Creative strategies in social media marketing: an exploratory study of branded social content and consumer engagement. Psychol. Market. **32**(1), 15–27 (2015)
4. Alalwan, A.A., Rana, N.P., Dwivedi, Y.K., Algharabat, R.: Social media in marketing: a review and analysis of the existing literature. Telemat. Inform. **34**(7), 1177–1190 (2017). https://doi.org/10.1016/j.tele.2017.05.008
5. Neti, S.: Social Media and its role in marketing. Int. J. Enterprise Comput. Bus. Syst. **1**(2), 2230–8849 (2011)
6. Taylor, I.: Why Social Media Should Be a Key Ingredient in Your Marketing Mix. Retrieved from Small Biz Trends: https://smallbiztrends.com/2008/05/social-media-key-to-marketing-mix.html
7. Omar, S.: Social Media Marketing in Higher Education Institutions. J. Sea Res. **8**, 191–196 (2020)
8. Richter, D., Schäfermeyer, M.: Social media marketing on multiple services – the case of the student run organisation AIESEC. In: ECIS 2011 Proceedings, 260. https://aisel.aisnet.org/ecis2011/260

9. Zehrer, A., Grabmüller, A.: Social media marketing in tourism education: insights into the development and value of a social network site for a higher education institution in tourism. J. Vacation Market. **18**(3), 221–228 (2012). https://doi.org/10.1177/1356766712449368

10. Muhammad, M.: Role of social media marketing (SMM) in HEI's admission. IBT J. Bus. Stud. **12**(2) (2016). https://doi.org/10.46745/ilma.jbs.2016.12.02.10

11. Aman, K., Hussin, N.: The effectiveness of social media marketing in higher education institution. Int. J. Acad. Res. Bus. Soc. Sci. **8**(9), 827–834 (2018). https://doi.org/10.6007/IJARBSS/v8-i9/4657

12. Mahaney, M. The Effectiveness of Social Media Marketing in Higher Education: State University of New York, the College at Brockport". Master's Theses and Honors Project (2012). https://digitalcommons.brockport.edu

13. Eminov, A., Saidova, F., Otamurodov, G., Zakirova, F.: EDUSMM as a training module in the curriculum of the advanced training course for academic staff. In: ACM International Conference Proceeding Series, pp. 46–50 (2021)

14. Zaripov, B., Mirzaliyev, S., Zohirov, K., Abdullayev, A.: Analysis and implementation of course quality optimization based on cloud computing. In: International Conference on Information Science and Communications Technologies: Applications, Trends and Opportnities, ICISCT 2021

# Digital Marketing and Smart Technology Marketing Systems as the Future of Metaverse

Abdulaziz Aliev[1]([envelope]) [iD] and Djavlonbek Kadirov[2] [iD]

[1] Department of Marketing, Tashkent University of Economics, Tashkent 100066, Uzbekistan
a.aliev@tsue.uz

[2] School of Marketing and International Business, Victoria University of Wellington,
Wellington 6140, New Zealand

**Abstract.** In this article the conventional view of the role of technology in digital marketing systems is scrutinized through the development of the smart-tech perspective of marketing systems. The current research outlines a) three processes of system matrix (tech-environmentalization, technological dissimulation, and tech-temporal distortion), b) four processes of system value utilization (co-construction of digital circuits and hyperreality journeys, switching between multiple realities and digital participation, alter-digitalization and digitally extended institutions, and tech-agentification), and c) four processes of system value generation (orchestrating value creation in response to the system-wide demand, systems parallelization, systeming transition via technology, and branding as the construction of virtual smart ecosystems) as some of the key trends that will shape marketing systems of future.

**Keywords:** digital marketing · marketing systems · technology · smart technologies · Marketing 5.0 · metaverse · business ecosystems

## 1 Introduction

The next generation of technological solutions is increasingly becoming the dominant element of marketing systems (Diamandis & Kotler, 2020; Grewal et al., 2020; Kotler et al., 2021). Labelled as "next tech", "smart technologies", "human-mimicking technologies", or "exponential technologies", these solutions are radically transforming the landscape of marketing systems as we know it. The concerted impact of metaverse technologies, artificial intelligence (AI), ambient intelligence (AmI), natural language processing (NLP), internet of things (IoT), virtual reality (VR), augmented reality (AR), extended reality (XR), sensor tech, robotics, blockchain, and nano/biotechnology is truly "magical" (Kravets, 2017; Terry & Keeney, 2022), although the macromarketing implications of these developments are not well understood. Specifically, how should our understanding of marketing systems be calibrated to be able to discern these profound changes? Following Layton's (2015) problematization of marketing systems, we reiterate the question of how marketing systems would form, grow, and change in future under the profound impact of smart-tech.

Y. Koucheryavy and A. Aziz (Eds.): NEW2AN 2022, LNCS 13772, pp. 397–410, 2023.
https://doi.org/10.1007/978-3-031-30258-9_35

As smart technologies saturate market systems and broader environments, the ways individual marketing system actors form their needs, perceptions, aspirations, motives, understandings, and practices will undergo significant changes (Arthur, 2017). The assumptions of free markets, rational economic exchanges, and voluntary participation by free willed agents may not hold in such circumstances as consumer preferences are now being shaped under the impact of at times invisible intelligent systems such as AI and ML solutions, search engines, personal digital assistants, preference predicting systems, recommendation systems, chatbots, AI content generation, ad allocation agents, and pricing/bidding algorithms (Arthur, 2017; Darmody & Zwick, 2020; Dholakia et al., 2021). The "second economy", digitalized business processes that are automatic, ubiquitous, and invisible, is becoming the new norm (Arthur, 2011). Similarly, marketing work is undergoing a revolution at an unprecedented scale (Kotler et al., 2021). Smart technologies are being embedded in most value creation processes reflected in the fast proliferation of marketing technology (MarTech) in areas such as advertising, digital marketing, content creation, analytics, and market research (Mela & Cooper, 2021; Seebacher, 2021). Such developments raise a plethora of ethical issues including loss of human agency, privacy trade-off, dehumanization, job loss, social deprivation, and disempowerment (Anderson et al., 2018; Arthur, 2017; Belk, 2021). Kravets (2017) calls macromarketers to "expand and deepen [our] discussion of technology and start by looking closely at the worldview that arguably defines technology today" (p. 331). A marketing system is generally characterized through the extent of its technological complexity, sophistication of its trade mechanisms, and development maturity seen in the examples of indigenous trade, the Makola marketplace, the Aalsmeer Flower Market, or convenience store chains in Japan (Layton, 2007). Layton (2009) indicates that the level of technology in marketing systems can range from low to high, while arguing that technological change is one of three fundamental factors (along with specialized roles and institutions) needed for growth in marketing systems.

This research submits that marketing systems of future will continue to be shaped by the following processes: systems matrix processes of tech-environmentalization, technological dissimulation, and tech-temporal distortion, value utilization processes of co-construction of digital circuits and hyperreality journeys, switching between multiple realities and digital participation, alter-digitalization and digitally extended institutions, and tech-agentification; and value generation processes of orchestrating value creation in response to the system-wide demand, systems parallelization, systeming transition via technology, and branding as the construction of virtual smart ecosystems.

## 2 Digital Marketing, Marketing Systems and Technology

### 2.1 Smart Technologies in Marketing

Reflecting Fisk's (1967) definition of marketing as a provisioning technology, the latest growth of smart technologies indeed is transforming marketing into the application of technology in a literal sense. According to Diamandis and Kotler (2015), once a technology becomes digitalized, it starts its journey as an exponential technology. The "the Six Ds of Exponentials" model predicts five more stages after digitalization: deception, disruption, demonetization, dematerialization, and democratization (Diamandis & Kotler,

2015). Deception refers to the period of uncertainty when early excitement is coupled with failures. Disruption occurs when the technology starts displacing some products and services from the market, while demonetization is associated with a significant decrease in production and use costs. Dematerialization involves tangible products transforming into software and digitalized services. Democratization is the stage when the use of technology becomes accessible to an increasing number of people. In their book titled The future is faster than you think: How converging technologies are transforming business, industries, and our lives, Diamandis and Kotler (2020) list key groups of exponential technologies including artificial intelligence, internet via satellite constellations, sensors, robotics, virtual reality, augmented reality, 3D printing, blockchain technology, nano- and bio-technology. The authors argue that the key aspect of technological evolution is democratized accessibility which means that exponential technologies will eventually become broadly available to be used by most of a country's population. The wider access to a new tool creates fairness and opportunities for a broad layers of market actors within a marketing system to significantly participate in value creation processes. In a sense, if the technology is democratized to the full extent, anyone can become a marketer. Moreover, Diamandis and Kotler argue that technological convergence is required to stimulate radical changes in established marketing systems. Specifically, the convergence between new communication technologies, alternative energy technologies, and innovative mobility technologies creates the right infrastructure to revolutionize existing industries. Kotler et al. (2021) define the future form of marketing as Marketing 5.0 which refers to "the application of human-mimicking technologies to create, communicate, deliver, and enhance value across the customer journey" (p. 6). Technological advances in the areas of artificial intelligence, natural language processing, sensors, robotics, augmented reality, virtual reality, internet of things, and blockchain are predicted to impact marketing work to the extent that the authors deem it warranted to pronounce the dawn of the new age of marketing (Kotler et al., 2021). In their view, new technologies mimic human capabilities: artificial intelligence mimics thinking, natural language processing mimics communication, sensor tech mimics perceiving, robotics mimic moving, augmented reality mimics imagining, and internet of things mimics connecting. From the macro perspective, the authors hope that these humanmimicking technologies will need to solve three macro-societal problems: generation gap, wealth gap, and the digital divide. In their review of Kotler et al.'s (2021) book, Khan and Kataria (2021) point out that the authors, while deeply subsumed into the potentialities of new marketing technology, chose to be silent about issues of consumer vulnerability and consumer ethics.

## 3 Toward the Vision of Smart-Tech Marketing Systems

We envision that a growing number of market exchanges in the near future will occur within the environments fully mediated through smart technologies. Smart-tech marketing systems will be based on technology-mediated radical transformation of human perception, aspirations, and needs which will in turn direct provisioning choices (Anderson et al., 2018; Darmody & Zwick, 2020; Dholakia et al., 2021). We identify three domains of processes pertaining to smart-tech marketing systems: system matrix, system value utilization, and system value generation. These three domains parallel the three mega-trends (mind versus machine, product versus platform, and core versus crowd) identified by McAfee and Brynjolfsson (2017) in their influential book titled Machine, platform, crowd: Harnessing our digital future.

System matrix refers to the locus of techno-cultural processes that comprises processes of radical transformation of a marketing system's environment (Layton, 2007; 2009). System matrix is the collection of techno-social-cultural spaces, and it extends the notion of "social matrix" proposed by Layton (2007; 2009; 2015). In addition to social and cultural forces which are described by Layton in detail, the system matrix is also characterized by the growing extent of technological ubiquity and technological mediation in business processes (McAfee & Brynjolfsson, 2017). We submit that the following unique processes distinguish the system matrix: tech-environmentalization, technological dissimulation, and tech-temporal distortion.

Next, the system value utilization domain comprises processes that radically transform the use of assortments created and made symbolically meaningful within the system matrix. Technologized environments will increasingly perpetuate unique processes underscored by co-construction of digital circuits and hyperreality journeys, switching between multiple realities and digital participation, alter-digitalization and digitally extended institutions, and tech-agentification. These processes will be discussed in the subsequent sub-section.

The next domain of system value generation comprises processes affecting the creation of assortments within technologized environments. These processes are orchestrating value creation in response to the system-wide demand, systems parallelization, systeming transition via technology, and branding as the construction of virtual smart ecosystems.

The ultimate vision of future marketing systems is the goal of implementing "the metaverse", an integrated space of 3D virtual worlds, that is poised to replace the current Internet (Ball, 2020; Dionisio et al., 2013). Still representing a science fiction at best, the metaverse is seen as a confluence of technologies (protocols, devices, services, gateways, software, hardware, communication) that would give rise to virtual worlds that are persistent, synchronous, interoperable, and scalable. These technologies, which do not currently exist but might gradually replace the Internet, will offer synchronous experiences spanning across interoperable systems where a person's virtual identity, property, tokens, and skills will seamlessly transfer from one virtual world to another. The metaverse will emerge as a getaway to realistic 3D digital experiences, while at the same time complementing, and perhaps mediating, human activity in the non-digital reality. Ball (2020) envisions the metaverse as the locus of a full-fledged economy incorporating virtual resources, virtual property, virtual labor, virtual companies, and virtual goods/services.

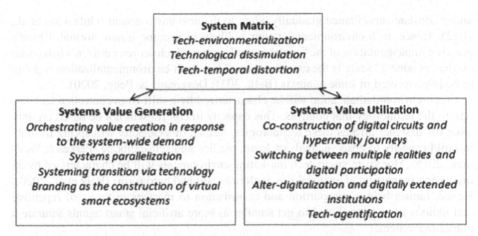

**Fig. 1.** System process changes within digital and smart-tech marketing environments

## 3.1 System Matrix

### 3.1.1 Tech-Environmentalization

Smart-tech marketing systems will increasingly exhibit greater levels of techno-environmentalization. Tech-environmentalization refers to the process of marketing systems' environments gradually transforming into technology mediated milieus which will not only contextually enable but also actively structure, shape, direct, and channel market action. Tech-environmentalization is not a case of few companies implementing focused technological breakthroughs. It involves a concerted cooperation of governments, corporations, law enforcement, medical and educational institutions, and socio-cultural communities to slowly build up the new environment. Technologies such as ambient intelligence (AmI), the internet of things (IoT), and smart environments (SmEs) are expected to usher the era of active technological environments (Aydin et al., 2019). These environments constitute devices, sensors, and process technologies (e.g., invisible computing, ubiquitous computing, affective computing) deeply integrated into material ecosystems. According to World Economic Foum's (2020) report titled State of the Connected World, a vast network of IoT devices predicted to reach 41.6 billion units by 2025 including consumer IoT, enterprise IoT, and public spaces IoT. These devices coupled with AI and AmI will shape smart environments which will actively sense, interact, and work with market actors as well as transforming the market actors' perception of the reality.

Tech-environmentalization might stimulate market activity through the suppression of anonymity while claiming human freedom and privacy as its victims. The fusion of technology and capitalism gave rise to surveillance capitalism (Belk, 2021; Zuboff, 2019). Implementing technological transformation throughout value chains and customer touchpoints, surveillance capitalists marketize human experience by transforming collected behavioural data into prediction products (Zuboff, 2019). Technological surveillance is becoming extensively ubiquitous requiring increased levels of freedom, dignity, and privacy trade-offs (Belk, 2021). Some experiments indicated that people under constant surveillance gradually adapt to the new environment (Oulasvirta et al., 2012). Hence, tech-environmentalization is likely to become a new normal. China's growing implementation of the "social credit" system which scores a citizen's behaviour on the "goodness" scale is the extreme case of how tech-environmentalization is going to be implemented in some contexts (Belk, 2021; Devereaux & Peng, 2020).

Tech-environmentalization will be characterized by a shift from controlled technology to the technology that controls. This capacity to control will not be based on only what the designer affords these technologies. Rather, this capacity will spring from its in-build capacity to observe, analyse, learn, predict, and self-calibrate (Parkes & Wellman, 2015). Moreover, smart-tech marketing environments will be characterised by an increasing proportion of artificial life, both in its soft and hard forms (Belk et al., 2020). Hence, human beings' proportion and contribution to markets in terms of repetitive and tedious labor is predicted to get smaller as more artificial smart agents saturate a marketing system.

Tech-environmentalization represents deep transformation of space. The environment will come "alive" in the shape pervasive intelligent spaces (Wang, 2010). Pervasive intelligent spaces will be designed to interact with the humans and other objects (Wang, 2010). These spaces can monitor internal and external surroundings, interact with agents and inhabitants within prescribed limits, perform modelling, make decisions, and adaptively learn. Human beings will then face the symbolic pressure of this kind of marketing systems (Kadirov & Varey, 2011), where meaningfulness will arise from the structure of technological environmentality. For instance, blockchain technology may completely transform societal institutions such as financial systems, investment practices, money creation, payment practices, and market transactions, while the meaning of ownership may become fully transformed due to the increased use of non-fungible tokens (NFT). These technologies are just the beginning. Clark (2003) argues that humanity is distinguished with the need for developing artificial environments - malls, offices, businesses, schools, public spaces - which in turn shape the ways the humans think, understand, act, and practice. Similarly, active technological environments will gradually solidify new institutions affecting people's provisioning logics and practices.

### 3.1.2 Technological Dissimulation

Techno-environmentalization will be accompanied by technological dissimulation. Technological dissimulation refers to a tendency of technology to stay concealed simply because it turns into a super-structure both supporting and dominating the market system environment within which market actors go about their micro actions. The paradoxical nature of tech-environmentalization is a strange possibility: the greater the extent of technologies infused into the environment, the greater the likelihood of this technology becoming less noticeable. In essence, technology fades away as it moves to the environment. The "absence presence" of technology in Ihde's (1990) terms signifies the current trends of smart technologies forming a broader environment within which market transactions occur. It must be noted that dissimulation has already occurred in the context of social media (e.g., Facebook, YouTube, Baidu, Telegram, WhatsApp) becoming an integral part of localized markets and peer-to-peer exchanges in both developed and developing countries. For example, in the Middle East and Central Asia the rise of Telegram as an alternative sales channel is currently helping many small entrepreneurs and micro service providers. It allows quickly building up customer groups and promote one-to-one products and services in small localities. The macro effect of such instrumentalization of market relationships is technological dissimulation where Telegram (or any other platform) is used as the synonym of a market.

Technological dissimulation creates "grey spaces" where intimate contexts are entangled with markets (King, 2020). King (2020) focuses on the military uses of drones and how these drones stay concealed while opening new spaces (e.g., peace zones) for war. In the similar vein, at a more general level, one can argue that smart technologies provide broad access for marketers to incorporate non-marketized spaces into the market where the technology poses as the environment. Technology turns various spaces into exchangeable loci, thus enabling quick transitions between the intimate and the market (King, 2020). This kind of transitions are documented by Makkar et al. (2020) in the context of Airbnb home sharing networks. The platform behaves as the marketing system within which the new intimacy-market fusion is normalized through a) making participants less sensitive to marketization; b) bundling rationality with intimate care; c) facilitating human bonding through market exchange; and d) resolving the problem of disreputable market action.

Technological dissimulation is the effect of immersive realism (Dionisio et al., 2013). The new metaverse technologies are built to create feelings of immersiveness (Riva et al., 2003). In this context, immersion refers to "the objective amount and quality of the perceptual input provided to the participant through technology" (Bombari et al., 2015, p. 3). Smart-tech technologies lead to high level of immersiveness within high-immersive virtual environments (HIVE) in contrast to low-immersive virtual environments (LIVE) represented by the current 2D virtual worlds such as Second Life and World of Warcraft (Innocenti, 2017). HIVEs offer a greater level of perceived realism (Schnack et al., 2019). The concept of "presence", the technological medium becoming increasingly transparent and invisible when one is immersed in a HIVE, has been widely studied in communication studies (Lee, 2004; Riva et al., 2003). Presence affects consumers response to marketing through evoking strong arousal (Grigorovici & Constantin, 2004; Lombard & Snyder-Duch, 2001). In summary, we note that smart-tech marketing systems will gradually attain a high level of operational seamlessness. Market actors will act naturally while engaging in exchanges mediated within HIVEs.

### 3.1.3 Tech-Temporal Distortion

Techno-environmentalization will lead to tech-temporal distortions. Tech-temporal distortion refers to transformations (e.g., time compression, acceleration, deceleration) in the flow of time within smart-tech marketing systems. Sociologists note that digital technologies lead to technological acceleration, i.e. the speeding-up distortion felt in the everyday life (Wajcman, 2008). Technological acceleration transforms chronological time into chronoscopic time, replaces the world of appearances with the world of disappearances, and leads to the "unprecedented temporal breakdown" in society (Virilio, 1997). The speeding up of time within virtual worlds makes the body and real places disappear in a sense that materiality is lost, and virtual objects come to dominate human perception. Rosa (2013) discusses social and technological acceleration in a high-speed society. Rosa discusses the paradox of technological acceleration leading to the greater pace of private life, instead of creating societal deceleration through the creation of free time. Time is increasingly being marketized and commodified employing time compression techniques (Wajcman, 2008).

Technology predetermines how time flows within the context of consumer-marketer interactions. In marketing systems, efficiency can be viewed as savings in time, acceleration, cycle compression, and quick reaction. The recent rise in agile marketing techniques capitalise on fast interactions with markets. The perception of time is a significant driver in marketing exchanges (Seow, 2008). The factors such as perceived duration (of service), user tolerance, response time, instantaneous responsiveness, progress indication, time anchors, and time violations determine how time is perceived by service users within the system (Seow, 2008).

Marketing systems, through the utilization of smart tech, will be able to better utilize time to the fraction of a second to accelerate value creation and market exchanges. Stock market algorithms that can perform millions of transactions within milliseconds have already become part of the financial system. Similarly, the revolution in the decentralised finance and blockchain technologies are leading to auto-staking systems where years are compressed into crypto epochs lasting from 15 to 30 min (e.g., Titano, Libero, Safuu). This means that market cycles within blockchain environments could occur in a compressed fashion. The cycles of inception, growth, maturity, decline, and crises could form within days or months rather than years and decades.

## 4  Systems Value Utilization

### 4.1  Co-construction of Digital Circuits and Hyperreality Journeys

Marketing system actors will operate within specific digital circuits (e.g., platforms, metaverse worlds, metaverse pods, software-as-a-service (SAAS) systems, interactive domains, gaming servers, Web3 projects, constricted spaces of smart ambiance). These digital circuits will be increasingly used as the building blocks of a marketing system. For example, personal metaverse pods would represent individual spaces/portals to which people could invite others, and within which they could exhibit their digital assets (Terry & Keeney, 2022). The granularity of these circuits will allow the deployment of different combinations of various blocks. For example, Wichmann et al. (2022) identify transaction blocks, community blocks, benchmarking blocks, guidance blocks, and inspiration blocks as parts of brand platforms. Specific digital circuits may be owned and orchestrated by individual actors in the form of broader business ecosystems (e.g., Facebook, Google, Amazon). However, a marketing system would cut across such ecosystems by including and excluding some aspects of these ecosystems. In the macromarketing literature, this view is echoed in the concept of hyperdigital marketspaces (Dholakia et al., 2021). Hyperdigital marketspaces represent "data- and information networked digital environments in which consumers are embedded and interlocked with other consumers, marketers, and Internet of Things" (Dholakia et al., 2021, p. 68). Taking the ecosystems perspective and extending Dholakia et al. 's view, we argue that both consumers and marketers, including other stakeholders, represent a specific kind of marketing system actors within the hyperreal circuits which are built and maintained through co-creative collaboration. Marketing system actors in their distinct but sometimes overlapping roles (e.g., individual, household, firm, organisation) are identical to each other by virtue of be-coming a resource integrator. Hence, there are no pure consumers nor pure producers (Ritzer, 2014).

### 4.2 Switching Between Multiple Realities and Digital Participation

To create value, marketing system actors will need to embark on hyperreality journeys which will intersect and interpenetrate with other marketing system actors' journeys of value creation and resource integration. The concept of exchange will be replaced by the concept of digital participation. The marketing systems will consist of digital participation occurrences. Digital participation refers one actor 's digital journey being included as a composite element within the other actors' value creation journey.

Digital participation is not a one-off process. In this, it is different from the concepts of exchange and transaction. Rather, it is a never-ending cycle of entrances and exits into/from hyperreality journeys. The marketing system actor will be constantly switching between different hyperrealities. In the perfect world, the marketing system actors will be seamlessly entering and exiting others' hyperreality journeys (including the journeys of firms, organizations, and institutions) through the participation and contribution of resources while receiving specific resources in return required for further cycles of resource integration. However, powerful actors will attempt to impose switching costs and lock-in through social engineering and the design of choices (Dholakia et al., 2021). These costs can be minimized if the marketing system actors develop openness in terms of digital participation in alternative journeys and systems.

### 4.3 Alter-Digitalization and Digitally Extended Institutions

Hyperreality journeys will be accompanied with the increasing levels of alter-digitalization of marketing system actors. Alter-digitalization refers to the tendency of marketing system actors gradually transforming into digitally extended entities. The concepts of the digitally extended self, data-doubles, and self-quantification underscore this tendency. Belk (2013) saw alter-digitalization as a natural process whereby consumers start seeing their online images and profiles as parts of themselves. The self is extended through not only the use of smartphones, tablets, and VR systems, but also avatars, online images, social media profiles, online relationships, and game "skins". Similarly, alter-digitalization is performed by data-driven marketers (i.e. market finders) who build consumers' "data doubles" through algorithm-driven monitoring, surveillance, identification, and profiling (Darmody & Zwick, 2020; Manzerolle & Smeltzer, 2011). Consumers perform self-surveillance through self-quantification that refers to the use of wearable devices and apps such as Fitbit, Apple Watch, and different apps (e.g. health) to digitally track, monitor, and share online one's different aspects of life (Belk, 2021; Lupton, 2016).

Within smart-tech marketing systems, marketing system actors are more than their real selves. They transform into hybrid digitally extended entities. This applies to not only individuals but also organizations and institutions. Specifically, societal institutions will also adapt to smart tech-environments, thus creating a renewed sociocultural matrix. The transformed culture, the social matrix (Layton, 2017), will require new moral standards to tackles new ethical challenges (Belk, 2021). Alter-digitalization and digitally extended institutions will lead to new ways of value creation. Such value creation within smart-tech marketing systems will be focused on benefiting these alter-digitalized entities. Instead of thinking of value only for human beings (e.g., customers), marketers will focus on generating value for alter-digitals, digitally extended institutions, cyborgs, robots, or purely digital systems (Belk et al., 2020).

### 4.4 Tech-Agentification

Tech-agentification refers to the ever-rising capability of smart technologies to exhibit agency or being perceived as an entity with legitimate agency (Novak & Hoffman, 2019). Smart objects such as Amazon Echo are considered to be "smart" because they can exercise agency in affecting others, authority in making decisions, and autonomy in acting independently (Novak & Hoffman, 2019). In business contexts, tech-agentification is reflected in AI systems being trained as rational agents. The rational agent dubbed as Machina Economicus is the ultimate goal of technology designers (Parkes & Wellman, 2015). The main idea that underscores the design of smart technologies is the creation of an "agent" that can perceive the world and act in it in a rational way (Parkes & Wellman, 2015). Specifically, AI systems should be able to recognize and reason about other AI systems. With the marketing ecosystem, multi-agent systems would operate where intelligent technologies interact with humans, other decision-making AI systems, and other smart systems (Parkes & Wellman, 2015).

AI systems are being trained so that Machina Economicus behaves rationally within specific constraints. Although these systems may not become perfectly rational, "reward shaping" techniques that is commonly used for animal learning tend to yield good outcomes. Rational machines optimize actions based on resource constrains, multiple goals, and the calculation of outcome probabilities. Since now AI systems are being treated as rational beings, it is maintained that social science theories of rationality might also apply to non-human agents (Parkes & Wellman, 2015). In evolving situations, advanced AI systems can interact with human beings based on a predictive modelling approach where the opponents and allies' moves are calculated in advance (Tambe, 2011). For example, AI security systems of large premises such as airports attempts to predict the adversaries moves and make decisions according to an evolving situation (Tambe, 2011). AI can model human behaviour and consider human deviation from theoretic rationality.

## 5  Systems Value Generation

### 5.1  Orchestrating Value Creation in Response to the System-Wide Demand

The institutional actors such as government, corporations, firms, organizations, communities, and other networks will need to adapt to the new demands of accelerating tech-environmentalization. For corporations, the focus will gradually shift from the customer demand to the composite demand imposed by the whole system, individual system actors, individual non-human smart agents, and the digital self The change in the nature of the demand will require innovative and dynamic business models offering new ways of value creation, value delivery, and value capture (Teece, 2018). Specific marketing system actors will need to respond not only to the needs of their customers, but also to the needs of the whole system for the purposes of maintaining, developing, and improving its overarching service parameters (Kadirov, 2018). For example, the response to hyper-digital environments is reflected in individual actors' adapting their choice and behaviour to the demands of engineered environments and agents in order to maximize relevance (Darmody & Zwick, 2020; Dholakia et al., 2021).

## 5.2 Systems Parallelization

The clear distinction between digital environments and real environments will gradually dissolve due to systems parallelization. Systems parallelization refers to the creation of mimicking virtual systems running in parallel to imitated real entities such as cities, enterprises, factories, transportation systems, and energy systems (Wang, 2010; Wang et al., 2022; Zhang et al., 2018). The recent developments in cyberphysical social systems technology (CPSS) would enable mapping existing organizations, communities, and cities in virtual cyberspace (Wang, 2010). CPSS integrates physical worlds, social-cultural worlds, and cyber worlds and it is being applied to the design of intelligent manufacturing, smart energy, power grids, smart vehicles, intelligent transportation, military operations, smart cities, and social computing. On a societal scale, CPSS will result in the integrated complex five grids: transportation grid, energy grid, information grid, IoT, and the Internet of Minds (IoM) (Zhang et al., 2018). The concept of "MetaEnterprise" is proposed to signify the creation of a parallelized organization (Wang et al., 2022). MetaEnterprise involves virtual depictions of real business structures, humans, processes, material and resource flows, and scenarios. It will comprise virtual humans, virtual objects, virtual organizations, and virtual scenarios.

## 5.3 Systeming Transition via Technology

The process we call "systeming transition" refers to some marketing system actors' attempts to shift from the foundational marketer-customer level to the meta-level of market building, market/transaction governance, and institutional regulation. Some marketing system actors may reach a certain degree of power that they can influence market governance to maximize positive outcomes for the self (Arthur, 1994; Kadirov et al., 2016). Within smart-tech marketing systems systeming transition will increasingly rely on technological innovations which will be used for the purposes of market shaping (Kaartemo & Nystrom, 2021).

Another manifestation of systeming transition via technology is the process of platformization or "the paradigm of the platform" (Casilli & Posada, 2019; Tauscher & Laudien, 2018; Wichmann et al., 2022). Platform-based business models represent the direct application of systeming transition whereby individual actors work to design marketplaces connecting the supply-side and the demand-side market actors (Tauscher & Laudien, 2018). Digital aggregators such as Amazon, Google Shopping, Alibaba, Shopify, Airbnb, and JD.com have become powerful market players because they operate based on the model of brand aggregation retail platform, i.e. a "mini marketing system" complete with technological infrastructure, governance, and social institutions, within which other markets actors can choose to operate (Wichmann et al., 2022). Brands are also attempting to construct what Wichmann et al. (2022) call brand-flagship platforms to counter the threat of systeming dominance of key brand aggregation platforms.

## 5.4 Branding as the Construction of Virtual Smart Ecosystems

In the era of tech-environmentalization of marketing systems, branding can increasingly become about the construction of virtual smart ecosystems rather than simply the generation of objects or symbols for consumption. A smart virtual object is essentially a software which is designed as a self-correcting ecosystem of digitalized objects, ideas, people, contexts, capital, materials, symbols, and narratives. Brands may transform into co-creational lived experience ecosystems (Ramaswamy & Ozcan, 2022). Such lived experience ecosystems represent both human and machine system-environment hybrids nested within each other. Brands constructed as a smart ecosystem will be designed to search and identify potential customers within virtual environments, attract their attention through creative visual performance and 3D graphical effects, and offer various means of engagement. Smart object as a sword that searches the potential customer (Diamandis & Kotler, 2020).

## References

Anderson, J., Rainie, L., Luchsinger, A.: Artificial intelligence and the future of humans. Pew Res. Cent. **10**, 12 (2018)

Arthur, W.B.: Increasing Returns and Path Dependence in the Economy. University of Michigan Press (1994)

Arthur, W.B.: The second economy. McKinsey Q. **4**, 90–99 (2011)

Arthur, W.B.: Where is technology taking the economy. McKinsey Q. **697** (2017)

Aydin, C., González Woge, M., Verbeek, P.-P.: Technological environmentality: conceptualizing technology as a mediating milieu. Philos. Technol. **32**(2), 321–338 (2019)

Ball, M.: The Metaverse: What It Is. Where to Find It, Who Will Build It, and Fortnite **13** (2020)

Belk, R.: Ethical issues in service robotics and artificial intelligence. Serv. Ind. J. **41**(13-14), 860–876 (2021)

Belk, R.W.: Extended self in a digital world. J. Consum. Res. **40**(3), 477–500 (2013)

Belk, R., Humayun, M., Gopaldas, A.: Artificial life. J. Macromark. **40**(2), 221–236 (2020)

Bombari, D., Schmid Mast, M., Canadas, E., Bachmann, M.: Studying social interactions through immersive virtual environment technology: virtues, pitfalls, and future challenges. Front. Psychol. **6**, 869 (2015)

Casilli, A., Posada, J.: The platformization of labor and society. Society and the internet: how networks of information and communication are changing our lives, pp. 293–306 (2019)

Clark, A.: Minds, Technologies, and the Future of Human Intelligence. Natural-Born Cyborgs (2003)

Darmody, A., Zwick, D.: Manipulate to empower: hyper-relevance and the contradictions of marketing in the age of surveillance capitalism. Big Data Soc. **7**(1), 2053951720904112 (2020)

Devereaux, A., Peng, L.: Give us a little social credit: to design or to discover personal ratings in the era of Big Data. J. Inst. Econ. **16**(3), 369–387 (2020)

Dholakia, N., Darmody, A., Zwick, D., Dholakia, R.R., Fırat, A.F.: Consumer choicemaking and choicelessness in hyperdigital marketspaces. J. Macromark. **41**(1), 65–74 (2021)

Diamandis, P.H., Kotler, S.: Bold: How to Go Big, Create Wealth and Impact the World. Simon and Schuster (2015)

Diamandis, P.H., Kotler, S.: The Future is Faster than You Think: How Converging Technologies are Transforming Business, Industries, and Our Lives. Simon & Schuster (2020)

Dionisio, J.D.N., Burns III, W.G.B., Gilbert, R.: 3D virtual worlds and the metaverse: current status and future possibilities. ACM Comput. Surv. (CSUR) **45**(3), 1–38 (2013)

Fisk, G.: Marketing Systems: An Introductory Analysis. Harper & Row (1967)

Grewal, D., Hulland, J., Kopalle, P.K., Karahanna, E.: The future of technology and marketing: a multidisciplinary perspective. J. Acad. Mark. Sci. **48**, 1–8 (2020)

Grigorovici, D.M., Constantin, C.D.: Experiencing interactive advertising beyond rich media: Impacts of ad type and presence on brand effectiveness in 3D gaming immersive virtual environments. J. Interact. Advert. **5**(1), 22–36 (2004)

Ihde, D.: Technology and the lifeworld: From garden to earth (1990)

Innocenti, A.: Virtual reality experiments in economics. J. Behav. Exp. Econ. **69**, 71–77 (2017)

Kaartemo, V., Nyström, A.-G.: Emerging technology as a platform for market shaping and innovation. J. Bus. Res. **124**, 458–468 (2021)

Kadirov, D.: Towards a theory of marketing systems as the public good. J. Macromark. **38**(3), 278–297 (2018)

Kadirov, D., Varey, R.J.: Symbolism in marketing systems. J. Macromark. **31**(2), 160–171 (2011). https://doi.org/10.1177/0276146710393519

Kadirov, D., Varey, R.J., Wolfenden, S.: Investigating chrematistics in marketing systems: a research framework. J. Macromark. **36**(1), 54–67 (2016). https://doi.org/10.1177/027614671 5608500

Khan, A.W., Kataria, N.: Book reviews: marketing 5.0: technology for humanity by Kotler, Philip, Hermawan Kartajaya, and Iwan Setiawan. J. Macromark. **41**(4), 699–701 (2021). https://doi. org/10.1177/02761467211044065

King, M.: DISSIMULATION: man, technology and modern conflict. Angelaki **25**(6), 108–121 (2020)

Kotler, P., Kartajaya, H., Setiawan, I.: Marketing 5.0: Technology for humanity. Wiley, Hoboken (2021)

Kravets, O.: On technology, magic and changing the world. J. Macromark. **37**(3), 331–333 (2017). https://doi.org/10.1177/0276146717715303

Layton, R.A.: Marketing systems - a core macromarketing concept. J. Macromark. **27**(3), 227–242 (2007)

Layton, R.A.: On economic growth, marketing systems, and the quality of life. J. Macromark. **29**(4), 349–362 (2009). https://doi.org/10.1177/0276146709345108

Layton, R.A.: Formation, growth, and adaptive change in marketing systems. J. Macromark. **35**(3), 302–319 (2015)

Lee, K.M.: Presence, explicated. Commun. Theory **14**(1), 27–50 (2004)

Lombard, M., Snyder-Duch, J.: Interactive advertising and presence: A framework. J. Interact. Advert. **1**(2), 56–65 (2001)

Lupton, D.: The Quantified Self. Wiley, Hoboken (2016)

Makkar, M., Yap, S.-F., Belk, R.: Stabilising collaborative consumer networks: how technological mediation shapes relational work. Eur. J. Mark. **55**, 1385–1410 (2020)

Manzerolle, V., Smeltzer, S.: consumer databases, neoliberalism, and the commercial mediation of identity: a medium theory analysis. Surveill. Soc. **8**(3), 323–337 (2011)

McAfee, A., Brynjolfsson, E.: Machine, Platform, Crowd: Harnessing Our Digital Future. WW Norton & Company (2017)

Mela, C., Cooper, B.: Don't buy the wrong marketing tech. Harv. Bus. Rev. 54–60 (2021)

Novak, T.P., Hoffman, D.L.: Relationship journeys in the internet of things: a new framework for understanding interactions between consumers and smart objects. J. Acad. Mark. Sci. **47**, 216–237 (2019)

Oulasvirta, A., et al.: Long-term effects of ubiquitous surveillance in the home. In: Proceedings of the 2012 ACM Conference on Ubiquitous Computing (2012)

Parkes, D.C., Wellman, M.P.: Economic reasoning and artificial intelligence. Science **349**(6245), 267–272 (2015). https://doi.org/10.1126/science.aaa8403

Ramaswamy, V., Ozcan, K.: Brands as co-creational lived experience ecosystems: an integrative theoretical framework of interactional creation. In: Research Handbook on Brand Co-Creation. Edward Elgar Publishing (2022)

Ritzer, G.: Prosumption: evolution, revolution, or eternal return of the same? J. Consum. Cult. **14**(1), 3–24 (2014)

Riva, G., Davide, F., Ijsselsteijn, W.: Persuasive effects of presence in immersive virtual environments (2003)

Rosa, H.: Social Acceleration. Columbia University Press, New York (2013)

Schnack, A., Wright, M.J., Holdershaw, J.L.: Immersive virtual reality technology in a three-dimensional virtual simulated store: Investigating telepresence and usability. Food Res. Int. **117**, 40–49 (2019)

Seebacher, Uwe G.: MarTech 8000: how to survive in jurassic park of dazzling marketing solutions. In: Seebacher, Uwe G. (ed.) B2B Marketing. MP, pp. 89–117. Springer, Cham (2021). https://doi.org/10.1007/978-3-030-54292-4_4

Seow, S.C.: Designing and Engineering Time: The Psychology of Time Perception in Software. Addison-Wesley Professional (2008)

Tambe, M.: Security and Game Theory: Algorithms, Deployed Systems, Lessons Learned. Cambridge University Press, Cambridge (2011)

Täuscher, K., Laudien, S.M.: Understanding platform business models: a mixed methods study of marketplaces. Eur. Manag. J. **36**(3), 319–329 (2018)

Teece, D.J.: Business models and dynamic capabilities. Long Range Plan. **51**(1), 40–49 (2018)

Terry, Q., Keeney, S.: The Metaverse Handbook: Innovating for the Internet's Next Tectonic Shift. Wiley, Hoboken (2022)

Virilio, P.: Open sky, trans. J. Rose. Verso, London/New York (1997)

Wajcman, J.: Life in the fast lane? Towards a sociology of technology and time. Br. J. Sociol. **59**(1), 59–77 (2008)

Wang, F.-Y.: The emergence of intelligent enterprises: from CPS to CPSS. IEEE Intell. Syst. **25**(4), 85–88 (2010)

Wang, F.-Y., Qin, R., Wang, X., Hu, B.: MetaSocieties in metaverse: MetaEconomics and Meta-Management for MetaEnterprises and MetaCities. IEEE Trans. Comput. Soc. Syst. **9**(1), 2–7 (2022)

Wichmann, J.R., Wiegand, N., Reinartz, W.J.: The platformization of brands. J. Mark. **86**(1), 109–131 (2022)

World Economic Forum: State of the Connected World, 2020 Edition, Issue (2020)

Zhang, J.J., et al.: Cyber-physical-social systems: the state of the art and perspectives. IEEE Trans. Comput. Soc. Syst. **5**(3), 829–840 (2018)

Zuboff, S.: The Age of Surveillance Capitalism: The Fight for a Human Future at the New Frontier of Power: Barack Obama's Books of 2019. Profile books (2019)

# The Impact of the Digital Economy
# on the Development of Higher Education

Marina Sagatovna Abdurashidova[1] (iD) and Muhammad Eid Balbaa[2](✉) (iD)

[1] Department of Finance and Business Analytics, Tashkent State University of Economics,
Tashkent, Uzbekistan
m.abdurashidova@tsue.uz
[2] Department of World Economy, Tashkent State University of Economics, Tashkent,
Uzbekistan
m.balbaa@tsue.uz

**Abstract.** Long time ago, education belonged to a conservative industry, changes in it took place slowly, without sharp jumps and bursts. But the development of science, engineering and technology in the 20th century, and especially at the beginning of the 21st century, has led to the fact that over the past decades, higher education in the service market has repeatedly undergone dramatic changes in generally accepted development trends. The competition in the education market is now very high, and with the expansion of international integration, it has become an obvious global competition. The structure of the service market is changing as a result of the introduction of digital technologies, and accordingly, the structure of the higher education market is also changing dramatically. The number of participants in the global higher education market, according to the results of the analysis of Transparency market Research [1] is growing steadily. At the moment, the composition of the participants consists of private institutions, government organizations, ministries of education, government bodies, educational organizations, consulting firms, rating agencies, etc. The integration of education into the international community has led to the fact that the coverage of countries, people and information becomes colossal. To simplify the work with such a database and the number of people, digital technologies came to the rescue. This, in turn, has changed the traditional model of higher education. As the era of digitalization begins, when there is no need for a real presence.

**Keywords:** digital economy · higher education · digital technologies · educational services market · competition · market structure

## 1 Introduction

The formation and development of the information society is a continuous process, it is constantly progressing. At present, in Uzbekistan, its development is clearly reflected in the digitalization of society and the economy as a whole. Due to large-scale digitalization, changes are taking place in all spheres of life, as digital realities require fundamental changes and a new understanding of everyday phenomena. In this regard, education is put forward in the first place as a factor that ensures the possibility of these changes. In particular, higher education plays a significant role.

In advanced economies, higher education and the research and development sector have formed the largest sector of the global service market. The results of research by analysts from the WTO showed that in 2019, trade in services on the international market amounted to 13.3 trillion USD [2] (Fig. 1).

However, only from 2005 to 2017, global trade in commercial services has grown significantly, broken down by sector [2]:

- Telecommunications, Computer and Audiovisual Services by 13.2%;
- Research and Development (R&D) by 1.4%;
- Educational Services by 0.8%.

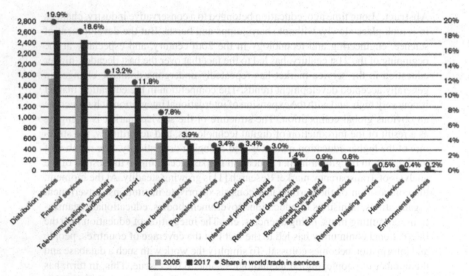

**Fig. 1.** Share of educational services among the world trade in services and its growth since 2005 to 2017. Source: WTO estimates 2019.

If we consider the period since 2012, then the education sector is the most growing (on average, the growth per year is about 23% annually), and the growth is observed precisely in the field of digital education. The most active growth began to be observed during the 2020 pandemic.

It should be noted that if in 2008 the market of higher education services accounted for 100 billion US dollars [3] of the total world market, then by 2030 analysts predict growth to 600–800 billion US dollars [4].

The leaders in the market of services in the field of education are the USA, Great Britain, Canada, Australia, as well as countries that have picked up the trend to develop higher education as an export industry.

## 2  Literature Review

Researchers all over the world are studying the impact of the digital economy on the development of higher education. Scientists such as: G.A. Krasnova "E-education in the era of digital transformation", Robert I.V. "Information Educational Space", Aidrus I.A., Filippov V.M. "The world market of educational services", Astratova G.V. "Modern trends in the development of the higher education services market", Sklyar M.A., Kudryavtseva K.V. "Digitalization: main directions, advantages and risks" - in Russia; Weimer Leasa "10 trends changing global higher education" - EAIE member, Kromydas T. "Rethinking higher education and its relationship with social inequalities: past knowledge, present state and future potential" in Scotland. This is small part of those who dedicated their time studying this question.

EAIE members have created a platform for learning, networking and knowledge sharing. Their activities are aimed at helping professionals achieve success; supplying academic and non-academic professionals with advanced skills and actionable solutions to the challenges of incorporation into the international community; providing a platform for the exchange of experience, strategic ideas and communications; promotion of international education not only in Europe but also beyond its borders. Holding conferences, seminars and gatherings, publishing collections and magazines with best practices, gathering world-famous specialists on their site - this is not a complete list of their activities.

Since 2010, priorities have changed in the educational services market. The emphasis has shifted towards global demography, expanding access to education for all segments of the population; a concept arose: a national strategy for the internationalization of education, multi-sectoral cooperation, new educational technologies, etc. All these issues are covered in the works of foreign and Russian scientists, such as: Brennan J., Brunsson N., Wedlin L., Krücken G., Kromydas T, Musselin Christine, Astratova G.V., Sklyar M.A., Kudryavtseva K.V., Larionova V.A., Tretyakov V.S. and so on.

In the Republic of Uzbekistan, scientists also conduct active scientific and analytical work. For example, employees of the Institute for Forecasting and Macroeconomic Research Ibragimova N.M. and Vakhabova D.Kh., an analysis of the effectiveness of creating an educational hub in the country was carried out. What he reflected in his article "Factors and conditions for the formation of an educational hub for the implementation of international educational programs in Uzbekistan." N.E. Chumachenko in the article "Information Economy and the New Economy: General and Special, Conceptual Apparatus and Content" makes an attempt to streamline and introduce the terms "information economy", "network economy" and "new economy" into a single concept. Assessing the fundamental changes in society and the economy caused by the widespread use of information technologies, Chumachenko comes to the conclusion that these "definitions divide the space of ongoing processes into meaningful, instrumental and productive". Improving the functioning of information systems is devoted to the work of domestic scientists - B.Yu., Musalieva A.A. and etc.

Domestic scientists S.S. Gulyamov, M.Kh Umarova, M.A. Makhkamova, A.F. Rasulov, A.M. Qoderov, in particular, analyzed the training of qualified personnel in this area.

Based on their developments, in our study, the emphasis is on considering the issues of the current situation both in the global context and in our country, with the identification of the specifics of solving this problem on the basis of the Presidential Decree "On approval of the concept of development of the higher education system of the Republic of Uzbekistan until 2030".

## 3 Research Methodology

This article is diagnostic and exploratory in nature. Research is based on general scientific methods, including system analysis, methods of factorial, logical and comparative analysis, the method of classification and analysis of data, selective assessment of phenomena in specific conditions based on the generalization of the experience of foreign and domestic research. The work contains an analysis of key indicators of socio-economic development of the Republic of Uzbekistan. They are collected from various national and international scientific articles, the official website of the State Committee of the Republic of Uzbekistan on Statistics, analytical data from the Institute of Forecasting and Macroeconomic Research of the city of Tashkent. Priority measures are determined to stimulate the processes of integration of international educational programs and the expansion of the international activities of the universities. The paper uses the methods of statistical and economic analysis, the method of expert evaluation and the method of calculating economic efficiency.

## 4 Analysis

For quite a long time, education belonged to a conservative industry, changes in it took place slowly, over a long period of time, without sharp jumps and splashes. But the development of science, engineering and technology in the 20th century, and especially in the early 21st century, has led to the fact that over the past decades higher education in the service market has repeatedly undergone dramatic changes in generally accepted development trends (Fig. 2).

For example, at the end of the 20th century, changes were noted:

- "in the growth of the educational services market;
- the ever-increasing mass market of educational services and ensuring the right to education for everyone (the opportunity and equal chances for each person to get an education in an educational institution of any type, regardless of nationality and race);
- diversification of the territorial structure of the educational services market and the emergence of new "players";
- globalization and internationalization of higher education, based on the comprehensive nature of knowledge and the mobilization of the collective efforts of the international educational and scientific community;
- universalization of the content of all types of education, which cannot be stopped in the era of the information revolution and the spread of the Internet;

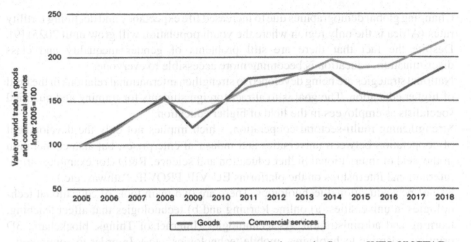

**Fig. 2.** Trade in services is growing faster than trade in goods. Source: WTO-UNCTAD

- democratization of the education system and the accessibility of education to the entire population of the country, the continuity of its stages and levels, the provision of autonomy and independence to educational institutions;
- an increase in the range of educational and organizational activities aimed at both satisfying the diverse interests and developing the abilities of students;
- the transformation of education into a priority object of financing in the developed countries of the world;
- Cross-cultural integration, tolerance for different cultures, traditions and customs; and etc." [5].

In Uzbekistan, reforms in the field of education that affect the market for higher education services are taking place in two main directions: improving the legislative framework and increasing competitiveness.

A Decree of the Cabinet of Ministers of the Republic of Uzbekistan "On improving the procedure for licensing activities in the provision of non-state educational services" was adopted in order to streamline the financing of the private sector in the field of higher education and provide them with legal support at this stage. The Resolution sets out the requirements for organizing the educational process in accordance with state educational standards (state requirements), and curricula [6].

Improving the competitiveness of higher education and its quality is ensured by the Decree of the Cabinet of Ministers of the Republic of Uzbekistan "On approval of the regulation on the organization of educational activities based on joint educational programs of higher educational institutions of the Republic of Uzbekistan and foreign partners" [7] and the Law of the Republic of Uzbekistan "On licensing, permitting and notification procedures" [8].

Since 2010, priorities in the higher education market have been changing and, according to analysts, the following manifestations have become the main trends:

- Changing global demographics due to increased life expectancy and declining fertility rates (Africa is the only region where the youth population will grow until 2025) [9].
- Despite the fact that there are still problems of gender inequality and class discrimination, education is becoming more accessible to everyone.
- National strategies are being developed to strengthen international relations in the field of higher education. The goal is to attract foreign students for training and qualified specialists as employees in the field of higher education.
- Strengthening multi-sectoral cooperation, which implies not only the development of cooperation between universities and industrial enterprises, but also cooperation in the field of international higher education and science, R&D (for example, virtual international internships on the platforms EU-VIP, PROVIP. Pathway, etc.);
- Use of new educational technologies. There are two main tools of educational technologies in universities: a) online learning and b) technologies that affect teaching, learning and administration. As technologies (Internet of Things, blockchain, 3D printing, adaptive technologies, mobile technologies, etc.). In order to continue the integration process into the real world, changing and transforming it, higher education must also change over time and integrate educational technologies that contribute to the development of international higher education;
- Growth in demand for specific competencies and skills, due to the fact that with the future automation of workplaces, a radical transformation of the labour market and the educational services market will also take place. Accordingly, universities will have to change educational programs in such a way as to guarantee relevant competencies and skills for graduates;
- Strengthening the influence of the English language, Although many consider English as a mean of business international communication, but English as a way to attract foreign students to receive international higher education is much more important, and this role is only growing every year; and etc." [10].

Starting from 2020, new directions have emerged in the education services market associated with increased competition in the global market; digitalization of higher education. The 2020 pandemic has accelerated the process of digitalization in education [11].

The competition in the education market is very high, and with the expansion of international integration, it has become an obvious global competition. The structure of the service market is changing as a result of the introduction of digital technologies, and accordingly, the structure of the higher education market is also changing dramatically.

The number of participants in the global higher education market, according to the results of the analysis of Transparency market Research [1] is growing steadily. At the moment, the composition of the participants consists of private institutions, government organizations, ministries of education, government bodies, educational organizations, consulting firms, rating agencies, etc. On the global market higher education leaders Speakers: Smart Technologies, Inc.; Xerox Corporation; Panasonic Corporation; Oracle Corporation; Edu Comp Solutions; Dell Inc.; Cisco Systems Inc.; Three River Systems; IBM; Blackboard Inc.; Adobe Corporation; and others, This is an indicator of the introduction of digital technologies in the field of education. It should be noted that digital technologies allow students and teachers to interact at a distance, makes it possible to use innovations in the learning process. The use of digital technologies expands the possibilities of education and blurs the boundaries between countries, and hence higher education institutions. This increases competition in the higher education market. To increase competitiveness and demand for their services, in order to attract as many clients (students) as possible, universities invite teachers from all over the world, attract business partners in the form of companies, research institutes and large corporations interested in qualified employees. Universities enter into agreements with associations and foundations both to finance their activities and for joint research and development. These actions form the international ranking of the university, and therefore increase the competitiveness of both public and private universities.

Currently, higher education institutions are experiencing competition not only from the side of the quality of education, but in the current economic situation, economic competition comes to the fore. All this leads to the fact that governments go by the wayside and universities must provide support for themselves. According to recent studies, the main struggle for a client is between universities in the USA, Germany, Great Britain, France, Japan, Australia, and Canada. More than 80% of all foreign students study within the walls of their universities [12].

Since the beginning of the 21st century, according to analysts in the field of higher education, the form, type and principles of competition have changed dramatically, but the main thing is that competition has become more ambitious and aggressive. This is due to the fact that universities have to fight not only for the number of students and the best teachers, but also for funding, as the system has switched to self-financing. Due to the fact that universities have integrated with scientific laboratories, innovation centers, design bureaus, etc., the form of competition has become multi-level. Competition in the field of education has acquired institutional and global features. This is also due to the fact that universities are now considered as full-fledged business competitors. Of course, the rating system that emerged in the second half of the 20th century is the defining criterion for business competition for universities. The rating survey is conducted regularly, the results are published annually. In particular, the lists THE, QS, ARWU, and a number of others are currently the most well-known. Top Ten Universities such as: Oxford University in the UK, Stanford University in the USA, Harvard University in the USA, etc., are the flagships in the field of education, and the rest of the universities are focused on their level and quality of service delivery.

International competition between universities is primarily a comparison of quality, where the main indicators are:

- availability of international relations and cooperation agreements
- form of education
- forms of financing and sources of investment
- number of scientific developments and achievements
- Scientific activity of university staff (citation index, degree of staff, etc.)

While talking about the international market of educational services, it is necessary to clarify that each state has its own culture, its own traditions and values, which means that each country has its own approach and requirements for higher education. Given the integration into the international community, universities around the world adhere to the mixed method, in which all known options are involved. At the same time, there are some universities that still retain the reputation and traditions of a certain model, and to some extent this tradition distinguishes them from all others [13].

Recently, competition for quality in higher education has transformed into competition for image (status, reputation). This is what has now begun to affect resources (budget, students and staff). [14] Universities are pursuing a policy of integration, tolerance for different rejuvenation of personnel" and preference is given to young masters, graduate students, and doctoral students. To increase the university ranking, preference is also given to specialists (non-residents of the country) from prestigious universities included in the TOP-100 or TOP-1000 [15]. Since universities have come to be seen as business competitors on which the country's economy directly depends, many countries, such as China, with rapidly developing economies, are investing multimillion-dollar funds in the development of higher education. Their competitive policy is aimed at creating a friendly environment for international professionals and students from all over the world. The integration of education into the international community has led to the fact that the coverage of countries, people and information becomes colossal. To simplify the work with such a database and the number of people, digital technologies came to the rescue. This, in turn, has changed the traditional model of higher education. The era of digitalization begins, when there is no need for a real presence [13].

## 5 Results

In Uzbekistan, the position of business competitors in the field of higher education affects the market. In the international context of the digitalization of higher education, Uzbekistan is also developing the market of higher education services not only in the traditional format of providing services, but also with the use of digital technologies, i.e. online education.

Recently, Uzbekistan has also begun to actively develop a policy of attracting foreign students and qualified specialists in the field of higher education. Since 2017, the number of foreign students studying in Uzbekistan has been steadily growing. The number of foreign students studying in higher educational institutions of the republic by years [16]:

- In the 2017/2018 academic year - 1.3 thousand students
- In the 2018/2019 academic year - 2.7 thousand students
- In the 2019/2020 academic year - 3.6 thousand students.

In the 2020/2021 academic year, the number of foreign students studying in higher educational institutions of the republic amounted to 4.2 thousand people, and in the 2021–2022 academic year, the number of students increased to 5140 people. In Uzbekistan, the share of higher education in 2020 was 54% (in 2017, the percentage was 47.4) of the total volume of educational services (Fig. 3).

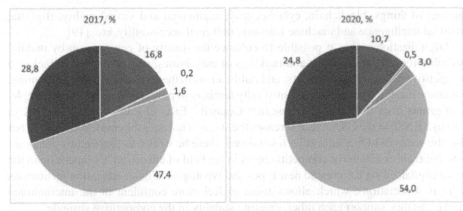

**Fig. 3.** Change in the structure of educational services in Uzbekistan in 2017–2020, %. Source: Data of the State Committee of the Republic of Uzbekistan on statistics

The ongoing policy of internationalization of higher education, increasing international competitiveness, focusing on the quality of services provided, allow us to say that that education services in the republic have a high potential for creating added value (for example, the value added of education services in the service sector reaches 15%, while the share of education in the total volume of services is only 5%) [17].

According to the Development strategy of the Higher Education System of the Republic of Uzbekistan until 2030, adopted in 2019, it is determined that the integration of domestic education into the international environment as a priority [18]. This allowed not only to increase the number of foreign students, but also led to a steady increase in the proportion of foreign teachers attracted to universities from 1% to 12%. Hubs are being created for the implementation of joint international educational programs. Joint programs are being opened (such as 2 + 2), branches of prestigious universities on the territory of Uzbekistan, where training is conducted in a native language. In the domestic market of educational services, competition is growing not only among national universities, but also among representatives of foreign universities. Universities of Russia, Belarus, Korea, Japan, Italy, Singapore, America, Austria, etc. are represented in a wide variety on the country's market. Despite the fact that China is the leading investor in the Uzbek market, the Chinese universities are not yet popular, may be because of the language barrier and the weak interest of the leading universities in China.

However, it should be noted that the government of Uzbekistan does not plan to act on the international market of educational services only as a consumer. Uzbekistan plans to study and adopt foreign experience in order to expand and accumulate its educational and scientific potential.

## 6  Conclusion

Competition among higher education institutions at the international level thanks to digital technologies has become much more organized and industrialized. Competition now uses impersonal quality assessment criteria using such digital technologies as: the

Internet of things, blockchain, cybersecurity, augmented and virtual reality, BigData, artificial intelligence and machine learning, universal accessibility, etc. [19].

Digitalization makes it possible to enhance the quality of competition by making available forms of inspections and rankings of universities, selection of personnel on a competitive basis, scientific papers, and publications in the format of remote accounting. We know that the participation of university teachers in prestigious grants (for example, with grants from the European Research Council - ERC in Europe, or TÜBİTAK in Turkey, or NSF in the USA, etc.) increases the status of not only the employee himself, but also the status of higher education institutions where he works, as prestigious grants are now the main criterion for competitiveness in the field of education. Competition in the era of digitalization has created new types and typologies. Higher education institutions unite in associations, which allows them to feel more confident in the international market, as they support each other, creating stability in the competitive struggle.

However, such competitive behavior also leads to more complex management of higher education institutions. The use of digital technologies to improve and take into account the ranking of the university also obliges them to be used to automate the process of collecting, processing, storing information, both external and internal, and of course, analytics. It is necessary to establish both internal communication (with staff, department staff) and external (with partners and universities, recipients, contractors and clients) in an online format.

The 2020 pandemic has accelerated the process of digitalization and transition to a distance format of higher education institutions. And at the same time, important issues of promoting modern educational technologies in universities were revealed. The pandemic forced a sharp transition to a distance learning format and, as practice has shown, the vast majority of universities were not ready for the widespread use of e-learning. First of all, this is due to the fact that universities are a conservative system, it cannot be mobile and sharply adapt to the spirit of the times. Established teaching methods and techniques cannot be canceled or radically changed overnight. As well as the time-tested organizational structure. The digitalization of the educational process is fundamentally changing everything: from the regulatory framework; organizational structures; interaction between management, teachers and students; the process of education itself; financing, etc. A separate issue arises when we talk about the psychological readiness of teachers. Many educators fear that e-learning will force them out of the job market; that their work in electronic format is not protected from copyright infringement. The problem is also the difficulty in adapting traditional teaching methods to distance requirements, etc. Students experience difficulties in doing work on their own, as they lack real interaction with the teacher. Digitalization depersonalizes the learning process and does not allow taking into account the preferences of certain students. Difficulties also arise in the objective assessment of the student's knowledge and the percentage of the course they have mastered, etc. The issue of financing occupies a special place. The introduction of digital technologies creates the need for additional funding for staff development, the purchase of equipment, software, maintenance of digital technologies, the creation of additional conditions for the development of e-education and service support teams, etc. This is not a complete list of problems that arise during the transition to e-education and the introduction of digital technologies in the education process.

However, despite everything, the introduction of digital technologies and the digitalization of the education process is necessary and justifies itself in modern realities.

# References

1. Higher Education Market – Global Industry Analysis, Size, Share, Trends, Analysis, Growth and Forecast 2016–2023. https://www.transparencymarketresearch.com/higher-education-market.html. Accessed 20 Aug 2022
2. World Trade Report 2019.The future of services trade. https://www.wto.org/english/res_e/booksp_e/00_wtr19_e.pdf. Accessed 20 Aug 2022
3. Aidrus, I.A., Filippov, V.M.: The world market of educational services: Textbook. - M.: RUDN, p. 194 (2008)
4. Universities 2030: Learning from the Past to Anticipate the Future. In: Nelson, A.R., Strohl, N.M. (University of Wisconsin-Madison) (2014). https://globalhighered.wordpress.com/2014/04/27/universities-2030-learning-from-the-past-to-anticipate-the-future/. Accessed 20 Aug 2022
5. Astratova, G.V.: Modern trends in the development of the market of higher education services. Science of Science. vol. 8, no. 4, pp. 22–23 (2016). – 27 s. http://naukovedenie.ru/PDF/95E VN416.pdf. Accessed 22 Aug 2022
6. Official website of the Republic of Uzbekistan "National database of the Republic of Uzbekistan" No. PKM-241 dated March 27, 2018. https://lex.uz/ru/docs/3601227. Accessed 20 Aug 2022
7. Official website of the Republic of Uzbekistan "National database of the Republic of Uzbekistan" No. PKM-421 dated July 6, 2021. https://www.lex.uz/docs/5500716. Accessed 20 Aug 2022
8. Official website of the Republic of Uzbekistan "National database of the Republic of Uzbekistan" No. ZRU-701 dated July 14, 2021. https://www.lex.uz/docs/5511900. Accessed 20 Aug 2022
9. Leasa, W.: 10 trends changing global higher education. Policy & Strategy (2017). https://www.eaie.org/blog/10-trends-changing-global-higher-education.html. Accessed 20 Aug 2022
10. Astratova, G.V.: Key trends in the development of the modern market for online services of higher education. World Sci. Pedagogy Psychol. 8(3), 17 (2020). https://mir-nauki.com/PDF/33PDMN320.pdf. Accessed: 20 Aug 2022
11. Aripova, E.A.: Transition to digitalization of education in Uzbekistan. Acad. Res. Educ. Sci. 2(11), 482–489 (2021). https://doi.org/10.24412/2181-1385-2021-11-482-489
12. Education at a Glance 2019. OECD indicators. OECD publishing. https://www.oecd-ilibrary.org/education/education-at-a-glance-2019_f8d7880d-en. Accessed 20 Aug 2022
13. Kromydas, T.: Rethinking higher education and its relationship with social inequalities: past knowledge, present state and future potential. Palgrave Commun. 3(1), 1–12 (2017). https://doi.org/10.1057/s41599-017-0001-8. Accessed 08 Aug 2022)
14. Brunsson, N., Wedlin, L.: Competition for status: the example of universities. In: Communication at the Competi-tion(s) Workshop at the Copenhagen Business School, for the 'Performances of Value: Competition and Competitions Inside and Outside Markets' project, supported by the Leverhulme Trust and led by David Stark (2016)
15. Balbaa, M., Ismailova, N., Kuldasheva, Z.: The impact of innovation and digitalization on service sector at post-pandemic era, pp. 334–342. Association for Computing Machinery, New York(2022). ISBN 9781450387347. https://doi.org/10.1145/3508072.3508127, ICFNDS 2021

16. Official site of the State Committee of the Republic of Uzbekistan on statistics. https://stat.
uz/ru/press-tsentr/novosti-goskomstata/17331-kakovo-kolichestvo-inostrannykh-studentov-
obuchayushchikhsya-v-vysshikh-uchebnykh-organizatsiyakh-nashej-respubliki.    Accessed
20 Aug 2022
17. Ibragimova, N.M., Vakhabova, D.: Factors and conditions for the formation of an educational
hub for the implementation of international educational programs in Uzbekistan. Higher Educ.
Russia **31**(3), 152–168 (2022). https://doi.org/10.31992/0869-3617-2022-31-3-152-168
18. National Database of Legislation of the Republic of Uzbekistan. Decree President of the
Republic of Uzbekistan On approval of the concept of development of the system of higher
education of the Republic of Uzbekistan until 2030. https://lex.uz/ru/docs/4545887. Accessed
20 Aug 2022
19. Sklyar, M.A., Kudryavtseva, K.V.: Digitalization: main directions, benefits and risks. Econ.
Revival Russia. **3**(61), 103–114 (2019)

# What is the State-Of-The-Art Contribution of the Higher Education System to the Digital Economy: A Systematic Mapping Study on Changes and Challenges

Ochilova Gulnoza Odilovna[✉], Musaxonova Gulnora Mavlyanovna,
Miraliyeva Dilafruz Toxirovna, Akbarova Sayyora Shuxratovna,
and Karimova Feruza Xamidullayevna

Tashkent State University of Economics, I. Karimov Str., 49, Tashkent 100066, Uzbekistan
gulnozaochilova5505@gmail.com

**Abstract.** The rise of the economy's productivity depends on the number of edu-cated employees since the efficiency of performing tasks is enhanced by skillful workers. This paper analyzes the relevance and state-of-the-art performance of educational services and programs for the higher education system's higher con-tribution to the digital economy. It reviews changes in three common aspects of education concerning digital economy challenges: funding mechanisms for edu-cation; changes in the duration of learning; changes in how and what we learn. The systematic mapping study aims to structure the most recent knowledge in higher education to contribute to the digital economy by identifying, classifying, and evaluating the current state of the art in the target research area. The research process followed common steps based on the guidelines of similar systematic mapping studies. A classified portfolio of key publications is recommended, each of which proposes its own sets of educational change solutions in reaction to digital economy challenges. The most commonly cited change in education rele-vant to the main challenge (integrated skills) in the digital economy is the STEAM movement, which is useful for educators and academic managers to know. Finally, we will show the future research agenda, weaknesses of the study, and observed trends.

**Keywords:** Digital Economy · Higher Education · Systematic Mapping Study · Trends · Contribution · Classified Portfolio

## 1 Introduction

Digital transformation is a key aspect of every leading country that tend to develop soci-ety and economy effectively. In this regard, the higher education system has become a catalyst as a knowledge-generating system responsible for training highly qualified cadres for the increasing demands of the digital economy. The first-class mindset per-sonnel is more likely to conduct high-quality research and innovative projects that boost economic development. Relationships between the digital economy and higher education have been explored by many studies [1–6]. The most stressed aspect of this research area is the adaptability and development of higher education in response to the challenges of the digital economy [2–4].

[1, 4] used content analysis and system analysis methods to explore different aspects of the higher education system related to digital economy challenges such as forming a holistic strategy to ensure the adaptability of higher education to modern challenges of the digital economy and identification of main trends in the progress of higher education under the conditions of the digital economy. [4] categorized the types of developmental problems of higher education under the challenges of the digital economy into contextual, legal, organizational, financial, logistical, and internationalization.

Based on SWOT analysis and interview results of HEIs, [6] identified contributions of HEIs to the digital economy such as student preparation to the labor market and contribution of HEIs to regional digital development. They also determined the challenges and motivations behind the adoption and implementation of digital transformation by higher education institutions. According to them, cultural and behavioral resistance, lack of change-oriented mindset, and lack of understanding of digital trends are the main challenges that HEIs face.

The academic contribution of [2] to the research of digital transformation of HEIs in response to digital economy challenges can be characterized by the proposal that non-violation of existing academic traditions and preventing commercial orientation of university management when adopting or implementing digital technologies.

The current challenges of higher education posed by the development of digital skills and performance indicators are outlined in [7]. Framing policies and significant initiatives are mentioned at the EU level concerning digital readiness. The remarkable work of [8–10] is also worthy to mention because of the research on the digital competence of educators, students' perceptions, and the digital economy.

The research area of exploring higher education and the digital economy is growing consistently and learning science and economics are being developed simultaneously. However, the growing bodies of scientific publications devoted to relationship studies of digital economy and education have remained unstructured and unclear. Thus, the purpose of the article is to structure the most recent knowledge of digital technology and education research studies related to the digital economy by seeking the state of the art to reduce the bias and increase the systematic view of a massive amount of data. Similar to our study, [1–4, 6, 7] analyzed the same aspects of higher education (adaptation of HEIs to digital economy challenges) but most of them are just reviews or logical generalizations. That is why the paper is expected to fill the gap of systematizing the knowledge in the target research area to provide a comprehensive overview of the target community of literature.

After this brief introduction, the rest of the article is as follows with a quick reference to higher education and digital economy concepts. In the second section, research questions, objectives, and methodology (such as search strategy and data analysis procedures) are clarified. The third section highlights results from the data collection process and analysis of surveys and literature. Finally, the fourth section presents the discussions and conclusions of the study, outlining research limitations and future research agenda.

## 2  Methodology

The main methodology that we employed in this study is the systematic mapping approach (SMS) that enables us to specify the research trends for the article topic, present the state of the art of higher education contribution to digital economy challenges and categorize the publications concerning predefined research questions. SMS process includes establishing research questions (relevant to research topic), research process (comprehensive search strategy, selection of studies using inclusion/exclusion criteria), and filtering process (extracting relevant and most valuable content from candidate studies and synthesizing the required data). Secondary methods that facilitated our research included logical generalization and content analysis, which allowed us to determine directions of interaction and analyze the essence of higher education and digital economy literature respectively.

### 2.1  Mapping Questions

Establishing research questions provides the vision for the study to explore the nature of the target research and describe the literature. It also guides the research process effectively through prescribed directions of focus.

Research question 1: How is higher education personnel (academic staff and students) being integrated into the digital transformation of the economy?

Research question 2: What are the publication trends in higher education and digital economy-focused research?

Research question 3: What kind of contributions of higher education has best facilitated digital economy development?

The goal of these general questions is to give a comprehensive overview of how higher education services can generally help sectors of the digital economy, being integrated into digital environments to provide quality research and a skillful workforce.

### 2.2  Search and Selection Strategy

To explore what has been published in the target literature, we established a search strategy that consisted of the search string and database selection. Conforming to the key terms of mapping research questions, the search strings were built and alternatives or synonyms of the terms are also considered relevant. As a result, the final search string can be expressed as follows.

("Higher education & Digital economy") AND ("Digital Transformation in education and economy") AND ("Higher education services & digital skills") AND ("digital literacy & digital economy challenges") AND ("educational process & digital markets") AND ("labor structure & digital technology & skilled talents") AND ("Publication trends & digital products") AND ("Human Resources & Digitalization").

By using those terms and relevant synonyms, the main subjects regarding the systematic mapping research questions, higher education, and digital economy were aggregated. Both alternative and key terms derived from research questions and topics shaped the search string. We also reviewed titles, abstracts, and keywords of publications.

To perform the search, we established a selection strategy for selecting academic databases. In this regard, academic databases for higher education and the digital economy were chosen as follows. Science direct preserves thousands of full-text articles with premium quality and original research in the domain of digital economy and higher education. More importantly, the academic database provided a specific aspect of relevant literature to get insight into what is happening in the area of the digital economy and higher education. Research gate is also another main source of information to enrich the content of the research, uniting many researchers all around the world. ACM digital library also provides valuable information in computing and information technology. Finally, google searches help us to overcome the scarcity of information researches relevant to the target research.

Meanwhile, it is safe for us to construct inclusion and exclusion criteria before conducting the initial search. This enabled us to extract relevant content and eliminate the massive weight of the papers generated from the initial search.

### 2.3 Inclusion and Exclusion Criteria

Below is the presentation of four inclusion criteria and four exclusion criteria created by using research needs and similar studies of systematic mapping:

Inclusion criteria.

- Published or reviewed works in conferences, journals, or workshops posed to expertise and original research (avoiding gray literature)
- Publications are written in English
- Open access papers available with full text
- Similar studies relevant to higher education and the digital economy

Exclusion criteria.

- Duplicates of the same studies
- Unpublished or shallowly reviewed publications
- Quality assessment studies since our aim are to review the state-of-the-art practices and contributions of higher education to the digital economy
- Studies unrelated to the research questions

### 2.4 Filtering Process

Data analysis procedures were implemented by referring to the aforementioned research questions, search strings, and inclusion/exclusion criteria to extract the relevant studies. Semi-structured interviews and surveys as supplementary data collection methods by the researchers of the articles contributed to the study because they provide authentic and practical insights about the target research area. After interviewing and surveying experts close to the target domain. Conducting the systematic analysis of the preferred academic databases, many candidate studies (approximately 2150 studies remaining) were collected for a secondary review. Manual annotation and review by the researchers of this systematic mapping study for the whole structure of the candidate studies (abstract, titles, keywords, etc.) are the secondary data analysis process to choose the best from the good candidate studies of the literature found in the initial search. Finally, a pool of key candidate studies [1–10, 13–19] was selected as the main base for addressing the research questions previously established. Meanwhile, there were many consensus discussions for accepting the key candidate studies organized by a research group of the systematic mapping study. Those discussions also contributed final decision on excluding or including collectively the candidate studies. Figure 1 below illustrates the whole research process ranging from data collection and analysis to information extraction.

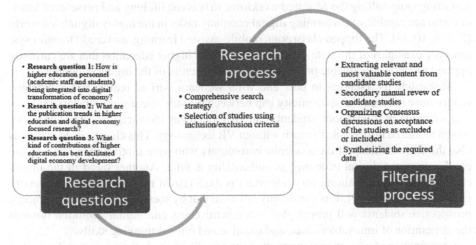

**Fig. 1.** The outline of research procedures of the systematic mapping study on higher education contributes to the digital economy development (Color figure online)

The highlighted keywords (in red) in visual representation of the systematic mapping study simplify the interpretation of the steps obtained by the researchers.

## 3   Results

This section highlights results from the data collection process and analysis of surveys/ interviews and literature review. The data analysis process in the systematic mapping study centered on three basic functions of educational services that closely affect the digital economy development: funding mechanisms for education; changes in the duration of learning; changes in how and what we learn. Regarding the first function of higher education, it is observed in the literature [7, 9, 10, 13, 15] that industrial collaboration and outreach activities of the academic staff have become a key indicator of academic performance, thereby emphasizing the role of academic knowledge in economic development. This is also ascertained by the experts who were interviewed/surveyed during the data collection process. This change in the academic performance of the university community can be explained by the rising challenge of the digital economy which is knowledge as a key production factor companies must consider becoming highly competitive in their target markets. Higher engineering education (software engineering, mechanical engineering, chemical engineering, and the like) is the second most important contribution direction of the higher education system to the digital economy since in the highly digitalized world, the value of engineering education is mostly being enhanced [11, 12] since digital economy tightly relies on engineering creativity and skills to build digital infrastructure.

The second important function of higher education is the duration of learning. Adapting to the challenges raised by the digital economy such as the digital transformation of the traditional job market, and corporate culture, higher education has been actively reskilling or upskilling the educated workforce to become lifelong and persevered learners who are capable of performing digital economy tasks in the highly digitalized world [2, 7, 8, 10, 13]. The flipped classroom, mobile-assisted learning, and credit transfer systems are examples of the state-of-the-art methods of higher education that are currently applied to cultivate valuable professionals for the sectors of the digital economy.

Regarding the changes in how and what we learn, virtual reality and augmented reality have reduced the authenticity gap between real-life situations and classrooms so that sitting in the classroom, students can visit a faraway industrial or economical site, which would be impossible to reach without VR technology. This change in education is also the craftsmanship of the academic community who were motivated by the real-life challenge of the digital economy as authenticity is vital. Another trend in the higher education system remaining very important is the STEAM movement in the university curriculum [14, 16–19]. It is commonly believed that by focusing on STEAM subjects, prospective students will propel global competitiveness and digital evolution through the generation of innovative ideas, and creative and critical thinking skills.

Automation of educational instructions and feedback is another main trend in higher education since managing a wide-scale classroom with different skills and interests is becoming more and more important than methodology change. Automation has become a key to handling that challenge since instant feedback and automated instruction (by natural language processing and artificial intelligence technologies) are capable of meeting the urgent needs of the students (such as instant feedback in student writing) [20].

Besides the above-mentioned trends/changes in higher education in response to the digital economy challenges, the summary of key studies in the form of a classified portfolio is another important finding of this systematic mapping study. The portfolio included 8 key publications [2–4, 10, 16, 17, 21] that are suggested for the academic community to review since they help to understand the state-of-the-art contribution of higher education to the digital economy development. Table 1 summarizes the contributions of the key publications classified concerning three different challenges of the digital economy.

## 4   Discussions and Conclusions

Education is a major field of the national economy that trains human capital and conducts quality research for industrial challenges. Combining higher education services with the challenges of the digital economy has become an increasing demand of any national economy. Scientific publications and expertise relevant to this area of research have been increasing at a higher speed and anyone new to the area may find difficulty quickly familiarizing themselves with the discourse and trends of the two directions.

**Table 1.** Classified portfolio of key publications with titles and research contributions in three challenges of the digital economy

| Challenges of Digital economy | Paper title and research contribution |
|---|---|
| The growing needs of upskilled workforce who are capable of fully functioning in the highly digitalized job markets | **Title:** Digital Development of Education and Universities: Global Challenges of the Digital Economy<br>**Contribution:** An assessment of the quality of education on the basis of system performance indicators, which makes it possible to evaluate education in the framework of management criteria<br><br>**Title:** The higher education adaptability to the digital economy<br>**Contribution:** the identification of promising vectors of higher education system development under the conditions of digitalization of national economy<br><br>**Title:** STEAM in practice and research: An integrative literature review.<br>**Contribution:** describing the overall purpose of STEAM education, creativity as a learning outcome<br><br>**Title:** Differences in creativity across Art and STEM students: We are more alike than unalike.<br>**Contribution:** investigating creativity differences, and the magnitude and nature of those differences, among university students. |
| Actively implementing information technologies in the sectors of digital economy | **Title:** Information and communication technologies as a tool of strategy for ensuring the higher education adaptability to the digital economy challenges.<br>**Contribution:** studying the role of information and communication technologies in the development of the higher education system and to ensure its adaptability to modern challenges of digital economy<br><br>**Title:** Educational technology conditions to support the development of digital age skills<br>**Contribution:** uncovering which technology-related elements are needed in schools for technology implementation to provide adequate opportunities for students to build digital age skills |
| Growing role of information and knowledge in the digital economy formation | **Title:** How Higher Education Institutions Are Driving to Digital Transformation: A Case Study<br>**Contribution:** identifying the influence that HEIs play in the digital development of regions<br><br>**Title:** Digital Economy and Demand Structure of Skilled Talents—Analysis based on the perspective of vertical technological innovation<br>**Contribution:** Regarding digital technology as a kind of technological innovation, and discussing the impact of digital economic development on labor structure on the basis of modeling analysis and empirical analysis. |

This study concentrated on systematic mapping of the literature and practices of the state-of-the-art contribution of higher education to the digital economy. Three mapping questions are investigated and analyzed based on the systematic mapping methodology. The search strategy and filtering process of the candidate studies were implemented according to those established research questions. Semi-structured interviews and surveys with experts are also employed as the second main source of data collection.

Research findings addressed the following research mapping questions.

*How are higher education personnel (academic staff and students) being integrated into the digital transformation of the economy?*

Active outreach activities and industrial collaboration of academic communities have become a hallmark of enhanced integration of higher education systems.

*What are the publication trends in higher education and digital economy-focused research?*

Automation of educational services, adoption of authentic content and environment in classrooms by VR technology, and STEAM education are captured as the trends in higher education and digital economy research.

*What kind of contributions of higher education has best facilitated digital economy development?*

Cultivating qualified and digitally-savvy cadres is the main contribution of higher education serves. Industry, entrepreneurship, and research are the indivisible aspects of highly effective education capable of boosting the digital economy.

This paper also proposes a classified portfolio to categorize key publications regarding three challenges of the digital economy. The portfolio outlines the titles and contributions of the studies that characterize how higher education contributes to digital economy development. Three basic functions of higher education (funding mechanisms for education; changes in the duration of learning; changes in how and what we learn) structure the organization of data analysis procedures. Higher engineering education, automated educational services, and VR technology-enhanced education are considered the main contributions to developing a digital economy with skillful graduates.

Conducting this research as a systematic mapping study is not free from risks and drawbacks and it has limitations. Because there is no all-in-one strategy for encompassing all aspects of the target research, this study also may neglect some relevant content that is of relevance and value, simply based on its search string and strategy.

Another main shortcoming of this study may be the inclusion of a higher proportion of local academic researchers and experts in the systematic study since local academic culture may fail to capture global trends of higher education contributions to the digital economy that international researchers are more likely to know.

Regarding future research directions, research opportunities lie in refreshing the content of this systematic mapping study with relevant content and studies. Another important direction of the research is the future consideration of novel functions of educational services (apart from the three functions mentioned in this study) such as the societal missions of universities in the digital era.

## References s

1. Akhmedov, B.A.: Use of information and communication technologies in higher education: trends in the digital economy. Ижтимоий фанларда инновация онлайн илмий журнали, 71–79 (2022)
2. Abduvakhidov, A.M., Mannapova, E.T., Akhmetshin, E.M.: Digital development of education and universities: global challenges of the digital economy. Int. J. Instr. **14**(1), 743–760 (2021)
3. Kholiavko, N., Popelo, O., Bazhenkov, I., Shaposhnykova, I., Sheremet, O.: Information and communication technologies as a tool of strategy for ensuring the higher education adaptability to the digital economy challenges. Int. J. Comput. Sci. Netw. Secur. **21**(8), 187–195 (2021)
4. Nataliia, K., Antonina, D., Maksym, D., Artur, Z., Ruslan, L.: The higher education adaptability to the digital economy. Научный журнал «Вестник НАН РК», (4), 294–306 (2020)
5. Schweighofer, P., Grünwald, S., Ebner, M.: Technology-enhanced learning and the digital economy: a literature review. Econ.: Concepts Methodologies Tools Appl., 20–33 (2015)
6. Teixeira, A.F., Gonçalves, M.J.A., Taylor, M.D.L.M.: How higher education institutions are driving to digital transformation: a case study. Educ. Sci. **11**(10), 636 (2021)
7. Fleaca, B., Fleaca, E., Maiduc, S.: Digital transformation and current challenges of higher education (2022)

8. Núñez-Canal, M., de Obesso, M.D.L.M., Pérez-Rivero, C.A.: New challenges in higher education: a study of the digital competence of educators in Covid times. Technol. Forecast. Soc. Chang. **174**, 121270 (2022)
9. Catal, C., Tekinerdogan, B.: Aligning education for the life sciences domain to support digitalization and industry 4.0. Procedia Comput. Sci. **158**, 99–106 (2019)
10. Huaping, G., Binhua, G.: Digital economy and demand structure of skilled talents—analysis based on the perspective of vertical technological innovation. Telematics Inform. Rep. **7**, 100010 (2022)
11. Broo, D.G., Kaynak, O., Sait, S.M.: Rethinking engineering education at the age of industry 50. J. Ind. Inf. Integr. **25**, 100311 (2022)
12. Cheah, C.G., Chia, W.Y., Lai, S.F., Chew, K.W., Chia, S.R., Show, P.L.: Innovation designs of industry 4.0 based solid waste management: machinery and digital circular economy. Environ. Res. **213**, 113619 (2022)
13. van Meeteren, M., Trincado-Munoz, F., Rubin, T.H., Vorley, T.: Rethinking the digital transformation in knowledge-intensive services: a technology space analysis. Technol. Forecast. Soc. Chang. **179**, 121631 (2022)
14. Malele, V., Ramaboka, M.E.: The design thinking approach to students' STEAM projects. Procedia CIRP **91**, 230–236 (2020)
15. Horng, J.S., Liu, C.H., Chou, S.F., Yu, T.Y., Fang, Y.P., Huang, Y.C.: Student's perceptions of sharing platforms and digital learning for sustainable behavior and value changes. J. Hosp. Leis. Sport Tour. Educ. **31**, 100380 (2022)
16. Perignat, E., Katz-Buonincontro, J.: STEAM in practice and research: an integrative literature review. Think. Skills Creativity **31**, 31–43 (2019)
17. van Broekhoven, K., Cropley, D., Seegers, P.: Differences in creativity across art and STEM students: we are more alike than unalike. Think. Skills Creativity **38**, 100707 (2020)
18. Khamhaengpol, A., Sriprom, M., Chuamchaitrakool, P.: Development of STEAM activity on nanotechnology to determine basic science process skills and engineering design process for high school students. Think. Skills Creativity **39**, 100796 (2021)
19. Zharylgassova, P., Assilbayeva, F., Saidakhmetova, L., Arenova, A.: Psychological and pedagogical foundations of practice-oriented learning of future STEAM teachers. Think. Skills Creativity **41**, 100886 (2021)
20. Eshbayev, O.A., Maxmudov, A.X., Rozikov, R.U.: An overview of a state of the art on developing soft computing-based language education and research systems: a survey of engineering English students in Uzbekistan. In: The 5th International Conference on Future Networks & Distributed Systems, pp. 447–452 (2021)
21. Olszewski, B., Crompton, H.: Educational technology conditions support the development of digital-age skills. Comput. Educ. **150**, 103849 (2020)

# Innovating Primary Education of Promoting Students' Language Competencies Through Mobile Assisted Language Learning Approach: Selection Framework of Innovative Digital Technologies

Yuldasheva Sharapat[1], Mirtursunova Yulduz[1], Miralieva Dilafruz[2(✉)], Bakieva Hilola[1], and Shodmonkulova Dilorom[1]

[1] Tashkent State Pedagogical University named after Nizami, Bunyodkor Street 27, Tashkent, Uzbekistan
[2] Tashkent State University of Economics, I. Karimov Street, 49, Tashkent 100066, Uzbekistan
Cool.miralieva@mail.ru

**Abstract.** The younger children are, the better they acquire language skills. That is why it is high time for parents who expect the best from their children and provide conditions for their personal development from their early childhood, including language acquisition. It is known that mobile phones as portable and accessible devices are being used for educational purposes, especially language education. The general aim of this study is to analyze innovative ways of promoting linguistic competencies of primary education school students through mobile-assisted language teaching and select appropriate technologies suitable to an ESL classroom of primary education in Uzbekistan. By using the analytical hierarchy process (AHP) approach and mobile application user survey, the study examines the prioritization of primary education teachers about using the selected technologies and shows students rating the usefulness and effectiveness of those technologies. The results show that the mobile applications used by students and the ranking status of those applications are the factors that contribute most to stimulating the academic achievement of language learning of primary education students.

**Keywords:** Mobile assisted language learning · Criteria · Analytical hierarchy process · Primary education · Mobile applications · Survey

## 1 Introduction

In the digital age, the young generation tends to spend a considerable amount of their time online [1–3]. Responding to this general habit of young students, educators have begun using mobile devices such as tablets or smartphones for pedagogical purposes. As a result, this turned the perspectives of teachers about mobile technologies into ones of considering them as learning tools [4–6].

Y. Koucheryavy and A. Aziz (Eds.): NEW2AN 2022, LNCS 13772, pp. 432–439, 2023.
https://doi.org/10.1007/978-3-031-30258-9_38

## 1.1 Literature Review

To build the theoretical background of this research, the study also conducted a systematic review of the literature on primary education and mobile-assisted language learning methodology. To begin with, studies on methodological and instructional practices of primary education [7–11] have been reviewed in general. Regarding that, the previous research conducted in Ethiopia on preschool participation and students' learning outcomes in primary school [7] was reviewed. Following that, a review of the instructional quality study in primary education [8] was also conducted, with the identification of patterns, predictors, and relations to student achievement and motivation. [9] examined social well-being in primary education students by using a mixed method approach that can be implemented in other contexts of primary education (especially language education) for maintaining student motivation and learning. Empirically, [10] analyzed students' responses based on item response theory to validate a computational thinking concepts test for primary education. The study of [11] contributed to promoting primary education students' social behavior.

Regarding the mobile-assisted language learning literature, mobile learning methodology based on games is proven to improve the students' linguistic competencies in an innovative manner [12–15]. Most importantly, this innovative way of mobile language learning is increasingly satisfying the basic needs of primary education students as they tend to provide an engaging learning environment where the students play games full of immersive, voluntary, and enjoyable activities. Language learning through gameplay not only provides a fun but also enables children to find their meanings by making sense of the language system, contradicting the traditional educational approaches that make the students stay passive and their instructor becomes the conductor of content and actions [12, 13]. Some games define learning outcomes designed to balance subject matter with gameplay [14, 15]. This kind of gameplay enables students to apply their conceptual knowledge.

Game-based learning tasks very often come up with the use of mobile devices in classrooms and teachers are faced with the design of game-based learning activities by integrating suitable mobile applications. In this regard, the selection of pedagogically relevant mobile applications becomes the primary objective of designing an appropriate lesson plan. For this reason, this paper aims to determine mobile applications and feedback of teachers who teach language to primary education students by using those applications, based on the literature analysis of selecting the mobile technology meeting the needs of the language classroom.

The prime contribution of the research paper is that it determines various significant evaluation criteria for effective mobile application selection in teaching language to primary education students. Similar studies have already explored the selection of mobile applications for mobile learning classrooms [16–20], but none of them has yet focused on mobile language learning of primary education students. Inspired by this need, this study intends to fill this research gap in mobile-assisted language learning literature and to provide an efficient framework for effective mobile application selection that can be used in the next levels of language education classrooms (such as higher education) as well.

The remainder of the paper is structured into the following sections: Sect. 2 outlines the methodology data collection procedures used in this study. Section 3 demonstrates the calculations performed and the results obtained in this research. Section 4 provides the study's pedagogical implications, conclusions, and some future research directions.

## 2 Methodology

Bates's actions model [21] has been used in this study, which serves us as the clearest multiple criteria to select the most important mobile application suitable to the conditions of primary language classrooms in Uzbekistan. According to the prioritization of teachers who attended the survey, Analytical Hierarchy Process (AHP) has been utilized to produce criteria weights, which were then applied in mobile application selection to assess the alternative technologies of teaching language. Before calculating criteria weights, the scale of the relative importance of each ACTIONS criterion (see Table 1) against another one is measured based on the data retrieved from a mobile application user survey in which teachers are asked to rate the importance of each ACTIONS criterion by considering the student needs and learning contexts. In this case, the scale of relative importance metrics is used to collect rating values of the teachers who participated in the survey about the mobile applications that they used (see Table 2). Based on the practices of primary education and mobile-assisted language teaching methodology [7–20], we identified four main mobile applications that suit with pedagogical and physiological needs of primary education students (aged from 12 to 16) because of their game and pedagogical features. They are Kahoot, toontastic, wooclap.com, and

**Table 1.** Bates's ACTIONS model for selecting digital technology

| Accessibility | Is the equipment your program requires available to the learners? Where will they be learning? At home? In the workplace? At a learning center? |
|---|---|
| Cost | Are the costs of production, delivery, and maintenance using this technology affordable? Are the costs appropriate to the number of learners who will be enrolled? |
| Teaching ability | Does the technology convey the level of facts, attitudes and skills your program requires? Is it suited to the kinds of learning required? |
| Interactivity and user-friendliness | Is the technology user-friendly? Can it convey adequate and timely feedback to the learner? |
| Organization | How open is your organization to change and the introduction of new media |
| Novelty | Is it important to your organization to be _leading edge'? Is this a technology that learners will want to try? |
| Speed | How fast can your program implement this technology? How much training do staff and students need in order to be able to use it? Will its use enable you to revise your materials as quickly as you need to? |

wordwall. From them, only toontastic 3D application is an offline mobile application that enables students to develop their digital storytelling and speaking skills.

**Table 2.** Saaty's scale of relative importance for numerical expressions of pair-wise comparisons

| | |
|---|---|
| 1 | Equal importance |
| 3 | Moderate importance |
| 5 | Strong importance |
| 7 | Very strong importance |
| 9 | Extreme importance |
| 2,4,6,8 | Intermediate importance |

The research procedures have been illustrated in Fig. 1. According to this proposed research teacher feedback is received about the score of each mobile application from the teachers using them for a long time. The Likert scale (from 1 to 5) is used to measure the score of teachers regarding mobile applications. In the case of statistical sampling, it is assumed that the scores (teachers) are collected purposefully to rank the alternative most suitable mobile applications based on the AHP technique after trying those applications in their classroom for a long time. This statistical purposive sampling strategy enables researchers to get data from teachers who are more likely to answer a mobile application user survey. The survey contains two sections that are ACTIONS criteria rating and the used mobile application scoring.

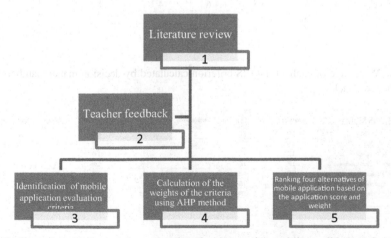

**Fig. 1.** Outline of research procedures for choosing innovative mobile applications for primary education students

# 3 Results

Individual calculation of each ACTIONS criterion is obtained in accordance with the rules of the AHP approach. The relative importance scale and weightage of each ACTIONS criteria are included in Table 3 and Table 4 respectively. Scaling of the relative importance of each criterion and scoring of each application by teachers have been used to calculate the total scores for each mobile application, which are presented in Table 5. Having merged the values given by decision-makers using data retrieved from a survey, the alternatives of mobile applications are sorted in descending order based on total scores.

**Table 3.** The values of relative importance given by the teacher for each ACTION criterion according to the needs of students and their learning contexts

| ACTIONS MODEL CRITERIA | Accessibility | Cost | Teaching ability | Interactivity and user-friendliness | Organization | Novelty | Speed |
|---|---|---|---|---|---|---|---|
| Accessibility | 1 | 7/5 | 6/8 | 2 | 8/5 | 6/4 | 3/5 |
| Cost | 5/7 | 1 | 4/7 | 6/5 | 7/6 | 8/5 | 2/3 |
| Teaching ability | 8/6 | 7/4 | 1 | 8/6 | 7/5 | 6/4 | 5/8 |
| Interactivity and user-friendliness | 2 | 5/6 | 6/8 | 1 | 2 | 3/4 | 4/5 |
| Organization | 5/8 | 6/7 | 5/7 | 2 | 1 | 6/8 | 6/7 |
| Novelty | 4/6 | 5/8 | 4/6 | 4/3 | 8/6 | 1 | 1/2 |
| Speed | 5/3 | 3/2 | 8/5 | 5/4 | 7/6 | 2 | 1 |

**Table 4.** Weightage of each ACTIONS criterion calculated by decision makers (authors) based on teacher feedback

| ACTIONS MODEL | Accessibility | Cost | Teaching ability | Interactivity and user-friendliness | Organization | Novelty | Speed | Totals | Weights |
|---|---|---|---|---|---|---|---|---|---|
| Accessibility | 1.00 | 1.40 | 0.75 | 2.00 | 1.60 | 1.50 | 0.60 | 8.85 | 0.15816 |
| Cost | 0.71 | 1.00 | 0.57 | 1.20 | 1.17 | 1.60 | 0.67 | 6.92 | 0.12365 |
| Teaching ability | 1.33 | 1.75 | 1.00 | 1.33 | 1.40 | 1.50 | 0.63 | 8.94 | 0.1598 |
| Interactivity and user-friendliness | 2.00 | 0.83 | 0.75 | 1.00 | 2.00 | 0.75 | 0.80 | 8.13 | 0.14535 |
| Organization | 0.63 | 0.86 | 0.71 | 2.00 | 1.00 | 0.75 | 0.86 | 6.80 | 0.12159 |
| Novelty | 0.67 | 0.63 | 0.67 | 1.33 | 1.33 | 1.00 | 0.50 | 6.13 | 0.10946 |
| Speed | 1.67 | 1.50 | 1.60 | 1.25 | 1.17 | 2.00 | 1.00 | 10.18 | 0.18199 |
| | | | | | | | | 55.96 | 1 |

According to the teacher who used the mobile application, the most critical criterion for selecting a suitable mobile application is speed, because the speed of learning how to the mobile application, integrating it with the language learning syllabus, and the materials retrieved from the application execution is typically the primary concern in the time bounded and simple language classroom of primary education. Teaching ability and

**Table 5.** Initial and total scores of each mobile application and weights of each criterion relevant to four mobile applications

| MOBILE APPLICATIONS | Kahoot | Toontastic | Wooclap.com | Wordwall |
|---|---|---|---|---|
| Accessibility | 1 | 4 | 1 | 2 |
| Accessibility weight | 0.15816 | 0.15816 | 0.15816 | 0.15816 |
| Accessibility score | 0.15816 | 0.63264 | 0.15816 | 0.31632 |
| Cost | 2.3 | 4 | 3.4 | 3.1 |
| Cost weight | 0.123652 | 0.123652 | 0.123652 | 0.123652 |
| cost score | 0.2843996 | 0.494608 | 0.4204168 | 0.3833212 |
| Teaching ability | 3.2 | 4.2 | 2.5 | 4.2 |
| Teaching ability weight | 0.159798 | 0.159798 | 0.159798 | 0.159798 |
| Teaching ability score | 0.5113536 | 0.6711516 | 0.399495 | 0.6711516 |
| Interactivity and user-friendliness | 5 | 4.3 | 2 | 3.1 |
| Interactivity and user-friendliness weight | 0.145352 | 0.145352 | 0.145352 | 0.145352 |
| Interactivity and user-friendliness score | 0.72676 | 0.6250136 | 0.290704 | 0.4505912 |
| Organization | 3 | 5 | 2 | 3.5 |
| Organization weight | 0.121588 | 0.121588 | 0.121588 | 0.121588 |
| Organization score | 0.364764 | 0.60794 | 0.243176 | 0.425558 |
| Novelty | 4.1 | 4.3 | 3.2 | 3.5 |
| Novelty weight | 0.109461 | 0.109461 | 0.109461 | 0.109461 |
| Novelty score | 0.4487901 | 0.4706823 | 0.3502752 | 0.3831135 |
| Speed | 4 | 3.5 | 3 | 3.1 |
| Speed weight | 0.181988 | 0.181988 | 0.181988 | 0.181988 |
| Speed score | 0.727952 | 0.636958 | 0.545964 | 0.5641628 |
| **Total score** | **3.2221793** | **4.1389935** | **2.408191** | **3.1942183** |

accessibility are the second and third most weighted criteria, as they are pedagogically relevant. This means that the pedagogical dimension is critical to achieving suitable mobile applications and should not be overlooked.

From Table 5, it appears that the total scores of Kahoot, Toontastic, and Wordwall - are the three most top mobile applications that are found to be useful and pedagogically relevant within the group of both teachers and students, whose ranks is 3.22, 4.13, and 3.19 respectively. This means they are increasingly important in terms of ranking. Specifically, toontastic 3D is found to be the most desirable and ranked mobile application.

## 4 Conclusions

This study presents Bates's actions evaluation criteria [21] for suitable mobile application selection based on teachers' opinions. Then, the research study measures the relative importance of those identified evaluation criteria by using the Analytical Hierarchy Process (AHP) method, which provides the statistical base for researchers working in the area of selecting the most useful mobile applications responding to the needs of students and their learning contexts.

Teachers who participated in this study are quite experienced in the mobile-assisted language learning methodology and provided their valuable feedback and ratings based on the present scenario of selecting appropriate mobile applications. Therefore, this research will support decision-makers in take proper and prudent mobile application selection decisions based on present situations.

The ranking of mobile applications shows the current state of the prominent local and global mobile applications in terms of usefulness and joyfulness, which is expected to support decision-makers for future decision-making.

The purpose of this study was to develop a selection framework for suitable mobile application selection in the language classroom of primary education which is one of

Uzbekistan's most important educational sectors. The Analytical Hierarchy Process's weighting of the mobile application evaluation criteria indicates that innovating language teaching in primary education is in the lead position. The highest priority is given to the Toontastic, followed by Kahoot and Wordwall.

Outcomes can be different for countries from different economic and social and pedagogical statuses, which is worth researching in the future. This study focuses only on the primary education sector. Other relevant sectors of language education such as higher education can be explored as well by utilizing the proposed mobile application selection framework.

# References

1. Camilleri, M.A., Camilleri, A.C.: The use of mobile learning technologies in primary education. In: Zheng, R.Z. (ed.) Cognitive and Affective Perspectives on Immersive Technology in Education, pp. 250–266. IGI Global (2020). https://doi.org/10.4018/978-1-7998-3250-8.ch013
2. Gunnars, F.: A large-scale systematic review relating behaviorism to the research of digital technology in primary education. Comput. Educ. Open **2**, 100058 (2021)
3. Crompton, H., Burke, D.: Mobile learning and pedagogical opportunities: a configurative systematic review of PreK-12 research using the SAMR framework. Comput. Educ. **156**, 103945 (2020)
4. Karakaya, K., Bozkurt, A.: Mobile-assisted language learning (MALL) research trends and patterns through bibliometric analysis: empowering language learners through ubiquitous educational technologies. System 102925 (2022)
5. Goksu, I.: Bibliometric mapping of mobile learning. Telemat. Inform. **56**, 101491 (2021)
6. Poláková, P.: Use of a mobile learning application in the process of foreign vocabulary learning. Procedia Comput. Sci. **207**, 64–70 (2022)
7. Kim, J.H.: Preschool participation and students' learning outcomes in primary school: evidence from national reform of pre-primary education in Ethiopia. Int. J. Educ. Dev. **94**, 102659 (2022)
8. Teig, N., Nilsen, T.: Profiles of instructional quality in primary and secondary education: patterns, predictors, and relations to student achievement and motivation in science. Stud. Educ. Eval. **74**, 101170 (2022)
9. Chiva-Bartoll, O., Moliner, M.L., Salvador-García, C.: Can service learning promote social well-being in primary education students? a mixed method approach. Child Youth Serv. Rev. **111**, 104841 (2020)
10. Kong, S.C., Lai, M.: Validating a computational thinking concepts test for primary education using item response theory: an analysis of students' responses. Comput. Educ, 104562 (2022)
11. Veldman, M.A., Hingstman, M., Doolaard, S., Snijders, T.A.B., Bosker, R.J.: Promoting students' social behavior in primary education through Success for All lessons. Stud. Educ. Eval. **67**, 100934 (2020)
12. Holden, C.L., Sykes, J.M.: Leveraging mobile games for place-based language learning. Int. J. Game-Based Learn. (IJGBL) **1**(2), 1–18 (2011)
13. Godwin-Jones, R.: Games in language learning: opportunities and challenges. Lang. Learn. Technol. **18**(2), 9–19 (2014)
14. Su, F., Zou, D., Xie, H., Wang, F.L.: A comparative review of mobile and non-mobile games for language learning. SAGE Open **11**(4), 21582440211067247 (2021)
15. Todd, R.W., Tepsuriwong, S.: Mobile mazes: Investigating a mobile phone game for language learning. CALL-EJ Online **10**(1), 10–11 (2008)

16. Hoi, V.N.: Understanding higher education learners' acceptance and use of mobile devices for language learning: a Rasch-based path modeling approach. Comput. Educ. **146**, 103761 (2020)
17. Azar, A.S., Nasiri, H.: Learners' attitudes toward the effectiveness of mobile assisted language learning (MALL) in L2 listening comprehension. Procedia Soc. Behav. Sci. **98**, 1836–1843 (2014)
18. Chen, Y., Mayall, H.J., York, C.S., Smith, T.J.: Parental perception and English learners' mobile-assisted language learning: an ethnographic case study from technology-based funds of knowledge approach. Learn. Cult. Soc. Interact. **22**, 100325 (2019)
19. Segaran, K., Ali, A.Z.M., Hoe, T.W.: Usability and user satisfaction of 3D talking-head mobile assisted language learning (MALL) app for non-native speakers. Procedia Soc. Behav. Sci. **131**, 4–10 (2014)
20. Alikovich Eshbayev, O., Xamidovich Maxmudov, A., Urokovich Rozikov, R.: An overview of a state of the art on developing soft computing-based language education and research systems: a survey of engineering English students in Uzbekistan. In: The 5th International Conference on Future Networks & Distributed Systems, pp. 447–452 (Dec 2021)
21. Hashim, E.W.A., Hashim, H.A.: Selection of appropriate media and technology for distance education. E-learning 1995 (2005.

# Econometric Assessment of the Dynamics of Development of the Export Potential of Small Businesses and Private Entrepreneurship Subjects in the Conditions of the Digital Economy

Jamshid Sharafetdinovich Tukhtabaev[1]([✉]), Gulnoza Toxirovna Samiyeva[2],
Abduxamit Norjigitovich Kushbakov[3], Aziza Abdusalomovna Goziyeva[4],
Barno Sayfiyevna Razakova[5], and Olimjon Abdugani Ugli Aktamov[3]

[1] Tashkent State University of Economics, Tashkent, Uzbekistan
jamshidtukhtabaev@gmail.com
[2] Karshi Engineering and Economic Institute, Karshi, Uzbekistan
[3] Samarkand Branch of Tashkent State University of Economics, Samarkand, Uzbekistan
[4] Termez Branch of Tashkent Medical Academy, Termez, Uzbekistan
[5] National University of Uzbekistan, Tashkent, Uzbekistan

**Abstract.** This article econometrically assesses the factors affecting the development of the export potential of small businesses and private entrepreneurship, and the levels of their impact in the context of the development of the digital economy. Within the framework of this topic, the scientific works of foreign and domestic scientists engaged in scientific research were studied. The factors influencing the increase in the export potential of small businesses and private entrepreneurship have been identified and analyzed. Based on the results of the analysis, the volumes of exports of goods and services produced by small businesses and private entrepreneurship operating in the Republic of Uzbekistan, and forecast indicators for 2022–2025, were determined. Econometric evaluation was developed using the Cobb-Douglas production function, Jacques-Bera, Student, Fisher and Darbin-Watson criteria.

**Keywords:** export potential · small business · foreign trade · regression · correlation · private entrepreneurship · export potential · goods and services · customs duty · tax benefits

## 1 Introduction

In the developed countries of the world, small business and private entrepreneurship activities are being rapidly developed as a strategic task of economic policy. "55–67% of the gross domestic product of the developed countries of the world is accounted for by small business and private entrepreneurship. This indicator is 52–55% in the USA,

52–57% in Japan, and 63–67% in the EU countries. 90.9% of the 17.1 million enterprises operating in the private sector in Western European countries are small business enterprises. They account for 50% of the total industrial volume, 67% of the service sector, and almost 90% of construction and trade. However, about 30–40% of the exports of developed countries in the world are accounted for by small businesses and private enterprises. This figure is 30% in the USA, 27% in the European Union countries, and 15% in Japan" [1]. In the developed countries of the world, small businesses and private business entities continue to increase their export potential as a priority.

Taking into account the socio-economic importance of small business and private entrepreneurship in the world, special attention is paid to scientific research in the direction of full and effective use of their economic potential. In particular, scientific research is being carried out in such priority areas as to identify additional internal opportunities for realizing the economic potential of small businesses and private entrepreneurship, to improve the mechanism for coordinating private interests and social responsibility in the process of managing the economy, and to improve the system for attracting the population to entrepreneurship, to provide state assistance to small businesses and private entrepreneurship affected by the global coronavirus pandemic, the implementation of a support project improving the financial support system for small business and private entrepreneurship, reducing poverty through the development of family entrepreneurship, and increasing the export potential of small business enterprises.

## 2 Literature Review

The development of small business and private entrepreneurship and increasing the export potential were researched by many scientists from foreign countries, including S. Badal, A.S. Kritikos, R. Nallari [2], O.J. Ademola [3], I. Hathaway, R.E. Litan, T. Mickiewicz, F.W. Nyakudya, N. Theodorakopoulos [4], F. Kellermanns, J. Walter, T.R. Crook, B. Kemmerer, V. Narayanan [5], V. Dobes, J. Friesner, C. Krenn, C. Rinaldi, S. Cortesi [6], H. Rawhouser, J. Villanueva [7], N. Boso, C. Danso, A. Leonidou, M. Uddin [8] and others.

The scientists of the CIS countries, F.F. Khamidullin, M.M. Khait, Ya. E. Ivanov, A.P. Jabin, E.V. Volkodavova, G.I. Yakovlev, Yu. O. Mashina, L.F. Gilemkhanova [9], Yu. A. Zapolskih, T.K. Guseynova [10], S.V. Trebova [11], P.S. Pleshakov, O.V. Artemova, N.M. Logacheva, I. Yu. Nesterenko [12], V.M. Baginova, V.G. Belomestnov [13], T. Saal, T. Savenkova [14], V.B. Dzobelova, A.V. Olisaeva [15], S. Yu. Tsyokhla, E.A. Polishchuk [16], and others focused on the research of issues of increasing the export potential of small businesses.

The economic content of small business and private entrepreneurship, the specific features of its development, and the issues of increasing the export potential have been studied by several scientists of our country, including U.V. Gafurov [17], N.K. Murodova [18], M.M. Baltabaeva [19], G.L. Yoziev [20], M.M. Ibragimova [21], M.A. Masharipova [22], M.S. Rustamov [23], A.G. Toychiev [24], J.S. Tukhtabaev [25], N.B. Fayzullaev [26], B.R. Tillaeva [27], D.T. Yuldashev [28], S.B. Goyipnazarov [29] and others. However, in the above studies, the issues of increasing the export potential of small businesses and private entrepreneurship have not been given due attention.

In the econometric study of the volume of exports of goods and services produced by small business entities in the Republic of Uzbekistan [30], it is necessary to first of all conduct an econometric study of the production processes of export-oriented products. Because the basis of export is the goods and services produced in the country.

## 3 Methodology

In the study of these processes, we use the rank multiplicative Cobb-Douglas production function. The use of this model requires the availability of three types of resources: the volume of products produced for export (billion Uzbek soums) (lnY), the value of the main production funds of exporting enterprises (billion UZS) (lnK), and the number of employees in exporting enterprises (persons) (lnL). (These resources contain data between 2000 and 2020).

Descriptive statistics are conducted on the variables and factors involved in constructing the Cobb-Douglas production function. Descriptive statistics results are presented in Table 1 below.

**Table 1.** Descriptive statistics by factors.

| Indicators | lnY | lnK | lnL |
|---|---|---|---|
| Mean (medium) | 9.667124 | 8.173181 | 8.977099 |
| Median (the median) | 9.831782 | 8.610920 | 9.064609 |
| Maximum (maximum) | 12.00827 | 10.87103 | 9.300017 |
| Minimum (minimum) | 6.633755 | 4.743191 | 8.404495 |
| Std. Dev. (standard deviation) | 1.664417 | 1.963154 | 0.288150 |
| Skewness (asymmetry) | −0.308819 | −0.282256 | −0.755592 |
| Kurtosis (kurtosis) | 1.920978 | 1.757554 | 2.215383 |
| Jarque-Bera | 1.352545 | 1.629553 | 2.536892 |
| Probability (probability) | 0.508509 | 0.442738 | 0.281268 |
| Sum (total) | 203.0096 | 171.6368 | 188.5191 |
| SumSq. Dev. (sum of standard deviations) | 55.40569 | 77.07948 | 1.660605 |
| Observations (observations) | 21 | 21 | 21 |

The average value (mean), median (median), maximum and minimum values (maximum, minimum) of each factor can be seen from the table data. In addition, the standard deviation of each factor (std. Giant (Standard Deviation) - the coefficient of standard deviation shows how much each variable deviates from the average value) values is given.

Skewness is a coefficient of asymmetry, and if it is equal to zero, it means that the distribution is normal and that the distribution is symmetrical. If this coefficient is significantly different from 0, then the distribution is asymmetric (that is, not symmetrical).

If the coefficient of asymmetry is greater than 0, that is, positive, then the normal distribution graph for the studied factor is shifted to the right. If it is less than 0, that is, it is negative, then the normal distribution graph for the studied factor is shifted to the left. It can be seen that the asymmetry coefficients of all factors for the processes we are studying are less than zero, and the graphs of the functions are shifted to the left (Fig. 1). These shifts mainly indicate changes in the dynamics of the studied factors. While some factors have had a sharp increase in some years, some of them did not change significantly. Graphs of normal distribution functions of all factors are presented in Fig. 1 below.

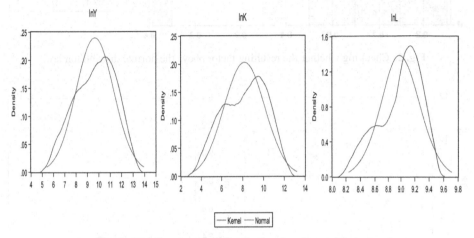

**Fig. 1.** Graphs of normal distribution functions of factors.

From Fig. 1, it can be seen that all factors obey the normal distribution law. Since the kurtosis coefficient of all factors is less than 3, it is flatter than the theoretical graph of normal distribution. The normal distribution graph of the outcome factor is shown in Fig. 2 below.

For this, the Jacques-Bera criterion is used. This criterion is a statistical criterion that tests the errors of observations to a normal distribution with moments of the third moment (asymmetry) and fourth moment (kurtosis) and $S = 0$ and $K = 3$.

From Fig. 2, it can be clearly seen that the resulting factor obeys normal distribution. This is confirmed by the calculated parameters and criteria, that is, the calculated Jacques-Bera coefficient is equal to 2.57 and its probability is less than 0.05 (prob = 0.006).

It can be seen that the connections between the resulting factor (lnY) and the influencing factors (lnK, lnL) are very tight (Fig. 3).

In order to analytically examine these close connections, we calculate the coefficients of specific and pairwise correlations between the resulting factor (lnY) and the influencing factors (lnK, lnL). The calculated correlation matrix values are listed in Table 2 below.

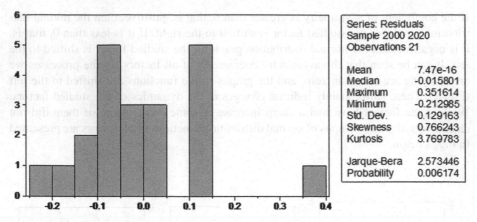

**Fig. 2.** Checking whether the resulting factor obeys the normal distribution law.

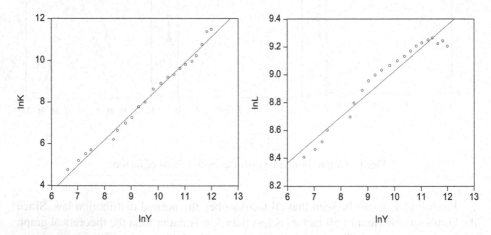

**Fig. 3.** Connection densities between the resulting factor and influencing factors.

## 4   Results

It can be seen from the data in Table 2 that there is a close connection between the resulting factor (lnY) and the factors influencing it (lnK, lnL). That is, the values of private correlation coefficients between factors are close to one. For example, private correlation coefficients between the volume of products produced for export in our republic, billion soums (lnY), and influencing factors - the value of the main production funds of exporting enterprises, billion soums (lnK), and the number of employees in exporting enterprises (lnL), respectively equal to $r_{lnYlnK} = 0.9969$, and $r_{lnYlnL} = 0.9698$. This shows that there are close connections between these factors.

In Table 2, the numbers under each correlation coefficient are Student's t-test values used to test the reliability of the correlation coefficient. If we pay attention to the data in Table 2, then the Student's t-test values under each correlation coefficient are large

**Table 2.** Matrix of individual and pair correlation coefficients between factors.

Covariance Analysis: Ordinary
    Date: 08/17/21 Time: 23:12
    Sample: 2000 2020
    Included observations: 21
    Correlation
    t-Statistic

| Probability | ln $Y$ | ln $K$ | ln $L$ |
|---|---|---|---|
| LNY | 1.000000 | | |
| LNK | 0.996939 | 1.000000 | |
| | 55.58163 | ----- | |
| | 0.0000 | ----- | |
| LNL | 0.951220 | 0.951196 | 1.000000 |
| | 13.43948 | 13.43590 | ----- |
| | 0.0000 | 0.0000 | ----- |

numbers (41.30973; 17.33151; 13.49136), which are greater than the Student's table value. This shows that the close connection between these factors is reliable.

Now we calculate the parameters of the production function. For this, we use the least squares method in EViews. The calculation results are presented in Table 3 below.

Using the data of Table 3, we present the analytical expression of the volume of products manufactured for export according to the Cobb-Douglas logarithmic production function:

$$\ln \hat{Y} = 1.3043 + 0.1849 \ln K + 0.8204 \ln L$$
$$(2.7996) \ (0.0555)(0.0502) \tag{1}$$

where the standard error values of each factor are in parentheses.

Let's put the calculated (1) Cobb-Douglas production function into multiplicative form. To do this, let's potentiate the function (1). As a result, the graded multiplicative Cobb-Douglas production function will have the following form:

$$Y = 3.6851 \cdot K^{0.1849} \cdot L^{0.8204} \tag{2}$$

(2) the multiplicative Cobb-Douglas production function shows that if the value of the main production funds (K) of exporting enterprises increases by 1%, then the volume of products produced for export increases by 0.1849% on average. If the number of employees in exporting enterprises increases by an average of 1%, the volume of products produced for export increases by an average of 0.8204%.

So, it can be concluded that it is necessary to attract the main production funds and technological lines based on more innovations in the production of products for export to foreign countries. That is, the capital capacity of products exported in the Republic

**Table 3.** Estimated production function parameters.

Dependent Variable: Y
  Method: Least Squares
  Date: 08/17/21   Time: 00:31
  Sample: 2000 2020
  Included observations: 21

| Variable | Coefficient | Std. Error | t-Statistic | Prob. |
|---|---|---|---|---|
| LNK | 0.184926 | 0.055548 | 3.329121 | 0.0093 |
| LNL | 0.820371 | 0.050254 | 16.32462 | 0.0000 |
| C | 1.304336 | 2.799609 | 0.465899 | 0.6469 |
| R-squared | 0.993978 | Mean dependent var | | 9.667124 |
| Adjusted R-squared | 0.993309 | S.D. dependent var | | 1.664417 |
| S.E. of regression | 0.136149 | Akaike info criterion | | -1.018563 |
| Sum squared resid | 0.333660 | Schwarz criterion | | -0.869345 |
| Log likelihood | 13.69491 | Hannan-Quinn criter. | | -0.986179 |
| F-statistic | 1485.487 | Durbin-Watson stat | | 1.827585 |
| Prob(F-statistic) | 0.000000 | | | |

of Uzbekistan should be high. On the one hand, this requires an increase in the number of innovative enterprises in our republic. On the other hand, products manufactured in innovative enterprises fully meet international ISO standards and can be exported to any country.

(2) from the multiplicative Cobb-Douglas production function, it can be said that the labor capacity of products produced for export is low. This shows that if we take into account that a 1% increase in the number of employees in exporting enterprises leads to an average increase in the volume of products produced for export by 0.8204%, it indicates the need to use managers with high professional qualifications, workers who perform specific operations in these enterprises.

In addition, it can be seen from function (2) that the scale effect of the use of resources used in the production of products by exporting enterprises in our republic is more than 1. That is, is equal to $\alpha + \beta = 0.1849 + 0.8204 = 1.0053$. This envisages more efficient use of the potential of exporting enterprises in the republic.

To check the quality of the constructed multiplicative Cobb-Douglas production function (2), we examine the coefficient of determination. The coefficient of determination shows how many percent of the resulting factor is made up of the factors included in the model. The calculated coefficient of determination ($R^2$ - R-squared) is equal to 0.9531. This shows that 95.31% of the volume of products produced for export in exporting enterprises in Uzbekistan depends on the value of the main production funds of exporting enterprises and the number of employees in these enterprises. The remaining 0.0061% is the influence of unaccounted factors.

The fact that the standard errors of the factors in the multiplicative Cobb-Douglas production function (2) also took small values indicates that the statistical significance of the model is high.

Fisher's F-criterion is used to check the statistical significance of the Cobb-Douglas production function (2) or its adequacy (suitability) to the studied process. Fisher's calculated F-criterion value is compared with its value in the table. If Fscore > Ftable, then the multifactor econometric model (2(2) is said to be statistically significant, and it can be used to forecast the final indicator - the volume of products produced for export in our republic (lnY) for future periods.

So, we find the table value of the F-criterion to check the statistical significance of model (2). We calculate the values according to degrees of freedom $k_1 = m$ and $k_2 = n - m - 1$ and (a) the level of significance. Based on the level of significance a = 0.05 and degrees of freedom $k_1 = 2$ and $k_2 = 21 - 2 - 1 = 18$ table value of the F-criterion is equal to Ftable = 3.55. The calculated value of the F-criterion is equal to Fscore = 1485.487 and since the condition of Fscore > Ftable is fulfilled, the multifactor econometric model (2)an be called statistically significant and it can be used to forecast the volume of products produced for export in our republic (lnY) for future periods.

Student's t-test is used to check the reliability of the calculated parameters (regression coefficients) of the calculated Cobb-Douglas production function (2). By comparing the calculated ($t_{score}$) and table ($t_{table}$) values of Student's t-test, we accept or reject the H0 hypothesis. To do this, we find the tabular value of the t-criterion based on the conditions of the selected reliability probability (a) and degree of freedom (d.f. = n - m - 1). Here n - the number of observations, m - the number of factors.

Probability of reliability a = 0.05 and degrees of freedom d.f. = 21 - 2 - 1 = 18 when t - the tabular value of the criterion $t_{table}$ = 2.1009 is equal to.

The table value of the t-criterion is equal to $t_{table}$ = 2.1009 when the reliability probability is a = 0.05 and degree of freedom is d.f. = 21 - 2 - 1 = 18.

## 5   Discussion

From the calculations, it can be seen that the calculated values of the t-criterion according to the free term a = 0.05 it can be seen that the accuracy is smaller than the table value (Table 1). An influencer in Cobb-Douglas production function (2) the value of the main production assets of exporting enterprises (lnK) and the number of employees in exporting enterprises (lnL) are reliable, and their values according to the calculated t-criterion are greater than the table value.

We use the Darbin-Watson (DW) test to test for autocorrelation in the resulting factor residuals of the estimated Cobb-Douglas production function (2).

The calculated DW value is compared with the DWL and DWU in the table. If DWscore < DWL, the residuals are said to have autocorrelation. If DWscore > DWU, the residuals are said to have no autocorrelation. The lower limit value of the Darbin-Watson criterion is DWL = 1.13 and the upper limit value is DWU = 1.54. DWscore =

1.8275. Therefore, since DWscore > DWU, there is no autocorrelation in the residuals of the resulting factor (the volume of products produced for export in our republic (lnY)).

The above analysis shows that (conclusions of the 2nd model), the economic growth in the enterprises producing export products in the republic has an extensive character and based on the 2nd model, $\alpha < \beta$ (0.1849 < 0.8204) represents equality. It can be seen that the innovation capacity of the products of enterprises that produce products intended for export is very low. This has a negative impact on the competitiveness of the products of national export enterprises in the world market. Also, the low technical level of product production in these enterprises leads to an increase in the cost of the products produced in these enterprises.

Taking into account the above circumstances, first of all, it is necessary to rapidly modernize these export-oriented enterprises and equip them with the latest production technologies.

Secondly, the commodity structure of the republic's export shows that the share of low-tech sectors in this structure is relatively high (light industry, food, raw materials, etc.). Based on this, it can be said that it is desirable to increase the share of export goods at the expense of high-tech industries (pharmaceutical, electrical engineering, mechatronics, robotics, etc.), and for this, it is necessary to create clusters in these industries.

The absence of autocorrelation in residuals of the resulting factor also indicates that the multiplicative Cobb-Douglas production function given above (2) can be used in forecasting.

(2) The actual (Actual), calculated (Fitted) values of the Cobb-Douglas production function and the differences between them (Residual) are presented in Fig. 2. 10 below.

It can be seen from Fig. 4 that (2) the graph of calculated values of the volume of products produced for export in the Republic of Uzbekistan according to the multiplicative Cobb-Douglas production function is very close to the graph of its actual values, the differences between them are not so great. This is one more proof that (2) the multiplicative Cobb-Douglas production function can be used to forecast the volume of products produced for export in the Republic of Uzbekistan for future periods.

From the calculated (2) Cobb-Douglas production function, it is necessary to calculate the coefficient of MAPE (Mean absolute percent error) when forecasting the result indicator for future periods.

If the calculated MAPE coefficient value is less than 15.0%, the model can be used to predict the resulting factor, otherwise it cannot be used. The MAPE coefficient is found using the following formula:

$$MAPE = \frac{1}{n} \sum_{i=1}^{n} \frac{|y_i - \hat{y}_i|}{y_i} \cdot 100\% \qquad (3)$$

Here $y_i$- actual values of the resulting factor, $\hat{y}_i$- calculated values of the resulting factor.

In the Republic of Uzbekistan, the value of the MAPE coefficient for the volume of products produced for export makes up 1.096% (Fig. 5).

This is less than 15.0% (MAPE = 1.096), that is, it is 1.096%. Therefore, (2) the Cobb-Douglas production function can be used to forecast the volume of products produced for export in our republic.

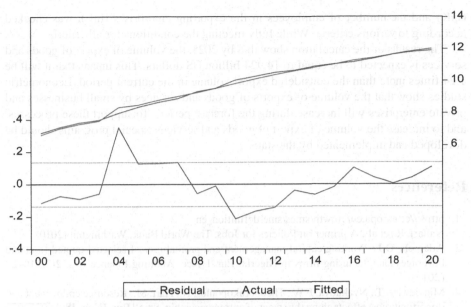

**Fig. 4.** Graph of the actual (Actual), calculated (Fitted) values of the volume of products (lnY) produced for export in the Republic of Uzbekistan and the differences between them (Residual).

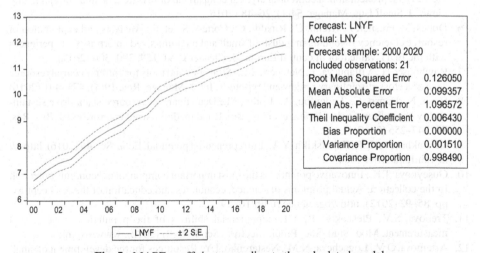

Forecast: LNYF
Actual: LNY
Forecast sample: 2000 2020
Included observations: 21

| | |
|---|---|
| Root Mean Squared Error | 0.126050 |
| Mean Absolute Error | 0.099357 |
| Mean Abs. Percent Error | 1.096572 |
| Theil Inequality Coefficient | 0.006430 |
| Bias Proportion | 0.000000 |
| Variance Proportion | 0.001510 |
| Covariance Proportion | 0.998490 |

**Fig. 5.** MAPE coefficient according to the calculated model.

## 6   Conclusions

To sum up, the multiplicative Cobb-Douglas production function, which is the factors affecting the change in the volume of products produced for export in the Republic of Uzbekistan (lnY) and the value of the main production funds of the exporting enterprises (lnK) and the number of employees in the exporting enterprises (lnL), was checked according to various criteria. While fully meeting the conditions for all criteria.

The results of the calculation show that by 2025, the volume of export of goods and services is expected to be equal to 14.924 billion US dollars. This means that it will be 1.24 times more than the considered export volume in the current period. Econometric studies show that the volume of exports of goods and services by small businesses and private enterprises will increase during the forecast period. To support these processes, and to increase the volume of export of goods and services, special programs should be developed and implemented by the state.

# References

1. https://ec.europa.eu/growth/smes/sme-definition_en
2. Nallari, R., et al.: A primer on Policies for Jobs. The World Bank, Washington (2010)
3. Ademola, O.J.: Working capital management and profitability of selected quoted food and beverages manufacturing firms in Nigeria. Eur. J. Acc. Auditing Finance Res. 2(3), 10–21 (2014)
4. Mickiewicz, T., Nyakudya, F.W., Theodorakopoulos, N., Hart, M.: Resource endowment and opportunity cost effects along the stages of entrepreneurship. Small Bus. Econ. 48(4), 953–976 (2016). https://doi.org/10.1007/s11187-016-9806-x
5. Kellermanns, F., Walter, J., Crook, R., Kemmerer, B., Narayanan, V.: The resource-based view in entrepreneurship: a content-analytical comparison of researchers' and entrepreneurs' views. J. Small Bus. Manage. 54(1), 26–48 (2016)
6. Dobes, V., Fresner, J., Krenn, C., Rinaldi, C., Cortesi, S., et al.: Analysis and exploitation of resource efficiency potentials in industrial small and medium-sized enterprises – experiences with the EDIT value tool in central Europe. J. Cleaner Prod. 159, 290–300 (2017)
7. Rawhouser, H., Villanueva, J., Newbert, S.L.: Strategies and tools for entrepreneurial resource access: a cross-disciplinary review and typology. Int. J. Manage. Rev. 19(4), 473–491 (2016)
8. Boso, N., Danso, C., Leonidou, A., Uddin, M.: Does financial resource slack drive sustainability expenditure in developing economy small and medium-sized enterprises? J. Bus. Res. 80, 247–256 (2017)
9. Gilemkhanova, L.F., Zapolskikh, Y.A.: Entrepreneurial potential. Econ. Sci. 46 (2016). https://novainfo.ru/article/6043
10. Guseynova, T.K.: Innovative potential is the most important component of economic potential. In the collection. Actual problems of science, economics and education of the XXI century, pp. 85–92 (2012). http://bgscience.ru/lib/10859
11. Trebova, S.V., Pleshakov, P.S.: Entrepreneurial abilities of the population: concept and measurement. Mod. Stud. Soc. Probl. Electron. Sci. J. 9(17) (2012). www.sisp.nkras.ru
12. Artemova, O.V., Logacheva, N.M., Nesterenko, I.Y.: Resources for the development of small and medium business in the region. Soc. Power 2(70), 48–55 (2018)
13. Baginova, V.M., Belomestnov, V.G.: Development potential of small industrial business in the region. In: Proceedings of the Irkutsk State Academy of Economics, vol. 6, pp. 999–1003 (2015)
14. Saal, T., Savenkova, T.: Economic and innovative potential of small business. In: Financial life. - M.: Academy of Management and Business Administration, pp. 22–31 (2014)
15. Dzobelova, V.B., Olisaeva, A.V.: Economic potential of small business in the north Caucasus federal district. Fundam. Res. 2–26, 5864–5868 (2015)

16. Tsyokhla, S.Y., Polishchuk, E.A.: The mechanism of formation and development of the potential of small business in the field of creating new jobs in the regional labour market. Russ. Entrepreneurship **18**(17), 2587–2598 (2017)
17. Gafurov, U.V.: Improving the economic mechanisms of state regulation of small business. Diss. (DSc). – T (2017)
18. Murodova, N.K.: Improving the theoretical foundations of state support for small businesses and private entrepreneurship. Diss. (DSc). – T (2016)
19. Baltabaeva, M.M.: Participation of women of the Republic of Uzbekistan in the development of small business and entrepreneurship (1991–2019) (2020). Diss. (PhD). – T
20. Yoziev, G.L.: The main directions of increasing the potential of small business and private entrepreneurship in the innovative development of the country (on the example of the experience of the countries of the Asia-Pacific region) (2019). Diss. (PhD). – T
21. Ibragimova, M.M.: Improving the efficiency of small businesses and private entrepreneurship based on structural changes (on the example of Namangan region) (2018). Diss. (PhD). – T
22. Masharipova, M.A.: Improvement of organizational and economic mechanisms for the development of small business in the service sector (2020). Diss. (PhD). – T
23. Rustamov, M.S.: Ways to improve the practice of lending to small businesses on the basis of advanced foreign experience (2019). Diss. (PhD). – T
24. Toychiev, A.G.: Improving the mechanism for financing the transfer of innovations to small businesses (2020). Diss. (PhD). – T
25. Tukhtabaev, J.S., et al.: The role of industrial enterprises in ensuring food security. In: IOP Conference Series: Earth and Environmental Science, vol. 1043, p. 012023 (2022). https://doi.org/10.1088/1755-1315/1043/1/012023. https://iopscience.iop.org/article/https://doi.org/10.1088/1755-1315/1043/1/012023
26. Fayzullaev, N.B.: Effective use of non-standard employment opportunities in the development of small business and private entrepreneurship (2018). Diss. (PhD). – T
27. Tillaeva, B.R., et al.: Ways of development of agriculture and processing industry enterprises manufacturing cooperation. In: IOP Conference Series: Earth and Environmental Science, vol. 1043, p. 012024 (2022).https://doi.org/10.1088/1755-1315/1043/1/012024. https://iopscience.iop.org/article/https://doi.org/10.1088/1755-1315/1043/1/012024
28. Yuldashev, D.T.: Improving the economic mechanism for the development of family business (2019). Diss. (PhD). – T
29. Goyipnazarov, S.B.: Improving the scientific foundations of labor protection in small business and private entrepreneurship (2018). Diss. (PhD). – T
30. Tukhtabaev, J.S.: Econometric evaluation of influential factors to increasing labor efficiency in textile enterprises. Webology, vol. 18, Special Issue on Information. Retrieval and Web Searchss (2021). https://www.webology.org/datacms/articles/20210129114502amWEB18024.pdf

# The Use of the Internet of Things to Ensure the Smooth Operation of Network Functions in Fintech

Olim Astanakulov[1] and Muhammad Eid Balbaa[2]

[1] International Islamic Academy of Uzbekistan, Tashkent, Uzbekistan
[2] Department of World Economy, Tashkent State University of Economics, Tashkent, Uzbekistan
m.balbaa@tsue.uz

**Abstract.** IoT (Internet of Things) covers network-connected devices that can improve various aspects of our lives. Every second in the world, 127 new devices join the internet. According to some estimates, by 2025, there will be 64 billion such "smart" devices. This is a significant jump when compared with 2018 when there were 10 billion of them. IoT gadgets are such touch points that collect information about the environment. They share data through the cloud, where they are analyzed to transform people's businesses and daily lives. In particular, technology has already penetrated deeply into the world of Finance. Today, there is no need to visit banks often. However, sometimes a visit is unavoidable. IoT is designed to help make it more convenient for customers. For example, queues are common for many financial institutions. IoT tools can quickly find the most suitable bank consultant. In this case, the customer enters their problem into the original equipment, then they are issued a ticket with information about the specialist, then the device notifies them when it is their turn. IoT allows bank managers to reduce the number of employees, and maintenance costs, and at the same time reduce the waiting time for the client. BMO Harris Bank has tested a "smart" branch, where instead of real employees – chatbots. In case of unexpected questions, chatbots contact a real consultant using video conferencing tools.

**Keywords:** IoT · Fintech · Finance · Technology

## 1 Introduction

Smart speakers allow you to use more convenient voice instructions. For example, in 2019, NatWest implemented a voice banking feature using Google Assistant. The feature was compatible with the Google Home smart speaker system and allowed customers to request account balances, recent transactions, and pending transactions [1].

In addition, the Internet of things can improve the ATM service experience. In some places, they are equipped with a live video streaming option, which allows customers to communicate with cashiers if they need additional help [2]. And Citibank has enabled a Bluetooth-based system with IoT beacons, which opens access to ATMs around the clock and seven days a week. IoT can also analyze how customers use ATMs in certain areas to reduce or increase their number [3].

Using internet-connected devices can change your financial habits [4]. The Interact IoT platform teaches you not to exceed the credit card limit. So, if the user ignores the warning and continues to spend more than the limit, the device can send a shock wave to the wrist. In addition, the technology will be useful for banks that lend to the agricultural sector. For example, with the help of the Internet of things, managers can estimate the yield of crops and offer the farmer appropriate financial conditions. Such information helps to build a strong relationship between the farmer and the bank [5].

Data collected by smart devices can also help the bank reduce the account balance or secure loan repayment. To do this, sensors are installed in borrowers' warehouses to track raw materials and inventory [6].

Amazon Go is one of the most popular examples of IoT use in fintech. The retailer implemented the concept of "shop without staff" thanks to this technology. Motion sensors, cameras, smart scales, as well as devices at the exit for scanning cards made it possible to fully automate the purchase process, in which there is no place for queues at the checkout [7].

However, IoT has long changed the way people make payments. Wearable devices – bracelets, watches, rings – have replaced smartphones and traditional bank cards and significantly accelerated transactions. Not surprisingly, payment systems are investing in IoT [8]. For example, with the help of an app developed by MasterCard, Samsung smart refrigerators not only control the temperature of food, but are also able to order food products. As you can see, IoT can transform many processes in business and everyday life. And given the dynamics of internet penetration and the increase in the number of smart devices, this is just the beginning.

## 2  Methodology

The banking services sector has undergone major changes. Online payments, mobile apps, and payments with electronic devices are becoming commonplace for bank users. Increased consumer demand for digital banking services has led to numerous technological advances in financial institutions.

Digital banking is the digitization of all levels of banking and customer service using digital technologies. Digital banking is carried out by both classic banks and digital banks. Digital banks rely on artificial intelligence to automate internal operations such as data processing, making the day-to-day work of employees much easier.

Digital banking will not only allow users to make remote transfers to their accounts, but also allow them to apply for loans faster and get access to personalized money management services.

Digital banking has emerged with increased consumer demands for more efficient ways to access bank records and perform financial transactions outside of the bank's branches. The transformation of digital banking services began with limited internet banking services before entering the digital-only market.

The main directions of digitalization of banking services are:

– digitalization of banking;

– predominance of contactless payments;
– the emergence of non-traditional payment gadgets and tools (using instant messengers as a payment method; tokenization of payments; payment using the NFC function, smartphone, smart watch, fitness bracelet, ring, etc.);
– emergence and development of FinTech projects;
– building financial ecosystems;
– integration of banking systems and creation of unified information platforms;
– Use of artificial intelligence (chatbots, robot administrators of the bank's operating room, etc.);
– Increased cybersecurity requirements.

## 3   Results

China and India are the leaders in terms of fintech service penetration, accounting for 87%. South Africa is slightly behind with an indicator of 82%. Among developed countries, the highest penetration rates are observed in the Netherlands (73%) and the United Kingdom (71%) [4].

The lowest penetration rates were found in the United States at 46%, Belgium and Luxembourg at 42%, and France at 35%. According to a report by McKinsey & Co, in May 2020 alone, the level of digital attraction in European countries increased to 20%, and the use of cash halved (Fig. 1).

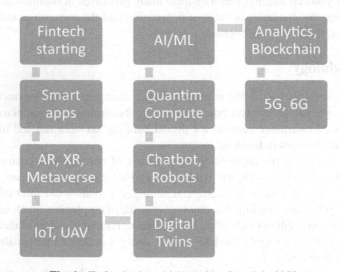

**Fig. 1.** Technologies which used by fintech in 2022

The fintech revolution is coming much faster than expected, and most of all it is changing the market landscape in developing countries, including Russia [5].

According to KPMG's Semi-Annual Report the Pulse of Fintech [3], it is worth noting the following global trends:

- fintech companies quickly adapt to the conditions of turbulence, understanding the needs of consumers, become more aggressive in expanding their basic product and service line, moving from mono-to multi-offers;
- banking-as-a-service platforms accelerate the movement of fintech towards opening bank accounts;
- some fintech companies, taking advantage of the liberalization of regulatory requirements, obtain banking licenses by creating their banks;
- Global regulators are reducing market entry barriers for fintech companies to weaken the level of monopoly of the traditional sector and increase market competition. The British regulator FCA, for example, was among the first to launch a pilot project to issue a limited "e-money license", which allowed fintech companies such as Revolut to introduce a payment transfer business through the so-called partner chartered bank, which reduced the time to enter the market for the company. Another example is that the Asian regulator the HKMA announced details on issuing a license to a virtual bank;
- traditional players are increasingly introducing digital products to the market, but they have a low level of interaction Experience (UX);
- there is a low level of global fintech access to public capital markets and IPOs;
- strengthening of global regulation in the field of crypto assets and digital currencies, which is associated with the dynamic development of the cross-border payment market involving virtual assets, as well as the growing interest of central banks in the development of the CBDC market;
- Providing fintech players with free access to digital platforms and products/services in the context of a global pandemic (starting in March 2020), which creates a new consumer experience and skills (Fig. 2).

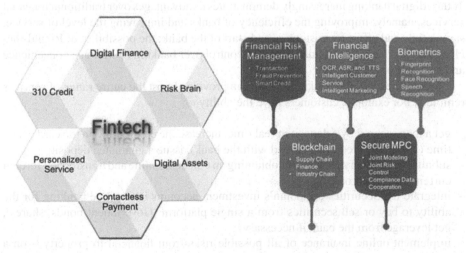

**Fig. 2.** Fintech technologies

Key trends of the fintech market in the global economy: mobile phone services, financial services and social networks, Alternative Payments, new business models, marketplaces, artificial intelligence, digital identification and biometrics, open application programming interfaces (APIs), InsureTech, neobanks, blockchain [1].

The Global fintech market, according to the catalog, has more than 100 fintech companies, the vast majority of which are payment service providers, and online lending and infrastructure solutions are also developed. Among large fintech companies, there is a fully mobile bank without any physical branches, and new players are emerging in this niche [2].

Summarizing the results of the presented research, it should be noted that one of the key factors in the development of the global financial market is the active introduction of fintechnologies in the service process. The analysis of the main trends of fintech made it possible to determine that the availability of smartphones and mobile internet, the growing dissatisfaction with traditional banking services and the loss of public distrust of the banking system are important drivers of its development. Also, the fintech market provides the necessary service and opportunities to earn money without leaving the office (home).

In modern banking, the most popular ones are mobile banking, internet banking, "zone 24", Electronic Balance, POS terminals, QR banking, smart gas station, Send money and photo booth.

Internet banking offers services that are provided on the bank's website. Subsequently, he inspired mobile banking, which allows you to perform various banking operations using a mobile application. Online banks that do not have physical branches, but exist only on the internet, have also begun to appear.

## 4 Discussions

Today, digital banking increasingly demonstrates its advantages over traditional financial services, namely: improving the efficiency of banks and improving the level of service, saving time and effort for customers and staff of the bank; the possibility of Round-the-clock service, including holidays; careful control over banking operations; convenience and speed of payments.

Today, due to digital banking, banks can provide almost the entire range of services remotely. For example, customers have the ability to:

– get a loan secured by a deposit in real time, increase the credit limit on the card at any time (within the credit line agreed with the bank), issue a guarantee deposit;
– submit the necessary package for obtaining an e-license online and transferring foreign currency funds abroad;
– integrate the Securities custodian's investment accounts into online banking for the ability to buy or sell securities from a single platform (Government bonds, shares), get leverage from the bank if necessary;
– implement online insurance of all possible risks-from financial to property – on a single internet platform;
– communicate in real-time with a personal banker or investment analyst (via both messages, calls, and video conferences);

– Get non-financial services, etc. [8].

Demand for digital banking has undoubtedly grown at an unbeatable pace as the IoT (Internet of Things) world empowers consumers and forces businesses to move towards digitalization to maintain competitiveness in financial services. Numerous industry verticals benefit from the monetary benefits generated by digital technologies, including retail, marketing, and education, although not as widely as the banking segment.

The development of digitalization of banking services is also supported at the state level. Thus, the strategy for the development of the financial sector of Europe until 2025 defines the strategic direction of "innovative development", the purpose of which is:

– development of an open architecture of the financial market and oversight;
– ensuring the development of the FinTech market, digital technologies, and regulatory platforms;
– Development of the digital economy [2].

So, digital banking is gaining more and more popularity every year. Each time there are new payment methods, such as Wireless Payment via smartphone using the NFC function. This will contribute to high competition in the banking services market and improve the quality of customer service in general.

Digitalization of the financial sector is an integral feature of the development of the modern world economy. For financial market participants to be successful and competitive, it is necessary to keep up with global trends in the introduction of advanced technologies and be "digital". The fulfillment of this task determines the transformation of traditional business models to meet the challenges of the modern world. Credit institutions, insurance companies, and other institutional investors are making significant changes in improving their operations under the influence of digital technologies.

Analyzing the digitalization of the financial sphere as an evolutionary stage in the development of modern society, it is necessary to consider the main stages of its formation. At the same time, it should be emphasized that the basis of this process is the active implementation of the achievements of the financial technology industry (hereinafter referred to as fintech) in financial relations [9].

Fintech is the dynamic development of a segment at the intersection of the financial services and technology sectors, in which technology startups and new market participants apply innovative approaches to products and services currently provided by the traditional financial services sector. Digitalization is rapidly developing, breaking the usual order of things in the traditional value chain [12] (Fig. 3).

Fintech companies using the latest technologies and new business lines are reshaping the picture of competition, blurring the established boundaries among players in the financial services sector.

The Fintech Ecosystem includes elements such as startups, technology companies, financial institutions, and infrastructure players [1].

The analysis of the subjects of the financial market of Europe showed: the largest volume of assets of banks (as reliable financial institutions with a wide range of financial services, professional intermediaries, dealers, etc.), low volume of assets had the organizers of financial trading, brokerage offices, depositories, asset management companies,

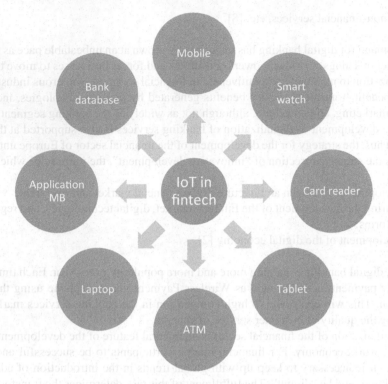

**Fig. 3.** IoT in fintech mobile banking

as institutions that provide services to participants in the stock market of a country that is not sufficiently developed and needs integration into the world space [2].

The largest volumes of banks' assets accounted for loans and Securities, and there were no insurance reserves, which is due to banking policy. Financial companies, in particular credit companies and investment funds, had no monetary gold assets, insurance reserves, and the largest volumes of shares and loans, which corresponded to the nomenclature of their main products. Insurance companies had the highest amounts of cash, deposits, and no monetary gold assets, or derivatives, which is due to their activities. Stock exchanges, brokerage offices, depositories, and asset management companies had the largest amounts of cash, deposits, and securities, there are no assets of monetary gold, insurance reserves, or loans, which revealed the concentration of their professional activities in the stock market [2].

The introduction of digital technologies requires a radical change in business strategies in all sectors of the economy. The high efficiency of applying innovative solutions forces the financial sector to transform both to strengthen its position in the market and to increase the level of interaction with customers and market participants.

The most noticeable trend is the digitalization of the European banking sector. Credit institutions seek to transform into high-tech financial corporations that meet the following requirements:

– providing customers with a comprehensive set of services within the ecosystem Fintech;
– increasing the transparency of information, which helps to eliminate mediation in the financial market;
– Continuous improvement of implemented digital solutions to ensure real-time operation and security, etc.

The change in the traditional business model is implemented through the transformation of a significant part of Information Technologies, which concentrate all areas of the bank's activities. This process includes:

1. Development of a digital strategy based on the business vision and its mission, taking into account the need for constant adjustments (high speed of digital innovations, changes in legislation, etc.).
2. Creating an IT system architecture or IT landscape. This stage involves the development of sets of software, computing and telecommunications tools built in a specific configuration and ensuring the operation of operational processes for business units;
3. Development of IT solutions and their commissioning.

A positive trend in recent years is the activation of domestic commercial banks and corporations in the innovation sector – in the form of support for incubation programs and accelerators, and investment in startups. According to a study by Mastercard, about 87% of representatives of the banking sector are ready to partner with fintech startups.

The creation of new acceleration programs in Europe will reduce the costs of fintech startups and encourage initial funding [12].

Future cooperation between domestic commercial banks and fintech companies can have various options for interaction-from simple use of fintech startup services to the full–fledged technological partnership, investment in the implementation of new systems, or purchase of already implemented projects [7]. At the same time, the partnership between commercial banks and fintech companies can successfully develop in the field of Payment Services, Big Data, Artificial Intelligence, Cybersecurity, Business Process Automation, P2P and P2B lending.

Commercial banks have recently shown a keen interest in the P2P and P2B lending market, where they can mutually cooperate with electronic credit platforms or create their similar platforms.

At the same time, for commercial banks that participate in the promotion of P2P and P2B platforms, there is no risk of liquidity and non-repayment of loans, and therefore there is no need to form reserves. In addition, thanks to cooperation with fintech companies commercial banks get access to an additional customer base and can provide them with additional and related banking services. Electronic credit platforms, for their part, gain access to a significant amount of banking resources. The participation of commercial banks in these credit projects increases confidence in them on the part of participants in the money credit market.

The development of P2P and P2B credit platforms operating with the participation of banks is constrained by the following factors: it does not fall under the law "on banks and banking activities" and is not regulated by the NBU; there is no legislative regulation of the liability of intermediaries, therefore, the rights of the person who is a leader in this scheme are not protected; deposits are also not guaranteed by the DGF, which increases the risk of loss of funds; P2P lending operations are not subject to reporting to central banks, and therefore the regulator cannot monitor, analyze and regulate these operations [5].

## 5   Conclusion

According to banking statistics, digital transformation measures have a positive impact on the financial situation of credit institutions, and significant investments are recouped by achieving a combination of goals. At the same time, we should mention the growing competition in the banking industry, where key players are actively developing new areas of digitalization. In these circumstances, credit institutions are required to allocate resources (financial, human, material) for the sustainable achievement of Strategic and tactical goals that arise under the influence of changing environmental factors.

Technology services are drivers and tools for changing your business strategy and achieving positive financial results. The activity of a credit institution in this direction will allow it to reach a qualitatively new level and become more attractive to the client, and inaction can lead to ousting the player from the market.

It should be noted that digital transformation carries not only potential opportunities and benefits, but also significant risks and threats. To eliminate them, it is necessary to harmonize the regulatory framework in the field of financial technology regulation, especially in terms of cybersecurity and data storage. It is important to emphasize that the sustainable development of the financial sector requires innovative drivers of economic growth as a whole.

## References

1. Alaraj, M., Abbod, M.F.: Classifiers consensus system approach for credit scoring. Knowl. Based Syst. **104**, 89–105 (2016)
2. Aydin, A.D., Cavdar, S.C.: Prediction of financial crisis with artificial neural network: an empirical analysis on Turkey. Int. J. Financ. Res. **6**(4), 36 (2015)
3. Cuipa, E., Ramani, S., Shetty, N., Smart, C.: Financing the Internet of Things: an earlyglimpse of the Potential M-RCBG Associate Working Paper Series, No. 85 (2018)
4. Dastkhan, H.: Network-based early warning system to predict financial crisis. Int. J. Financ. Econ. **26**(1), 594–616 (2021)
5. Dozat, T.: Incorporating Nesterov Momentum intoAdam ICLR Workshop, no. 1, 2013–2016 (2016)
6. Electron. J. (2017). Infosys Limited: IOT-Enabled Banking Services. https://doi.org/10.2139/ssrn.30717422.   https://www.infosys.com/industries/financial-services/white-papers/Documents/IoT-enabled-banking.pdf
7. Ma, F.X., Zhou, Y.Y., Mo, X.Y., Xia, Y.W.: The establishment of a financial crisis early warning system for domestic listed companies based on two neural network models in the context of COVID-19. Mathematical Problems in Engineering (2020)
8. Fernández-Arias, D., López-Martín, M., Montero-Romero, T., Martínez-Estudillo, F., Fernández-Navarro, F.: Financial soundness prediction using a multi-classification model: evidence from current financial crisis in OECD banks. Comput. Econ. **52**(1), 275–297 (2018)

9. Foes, O.R.: Fintech and banks, regulation, and the real sector. Eur. Econ. Banks Regul. Real Sect. **2**, 1–162 (2017). 8. S. in Join: 15 Top Fintech Companies in India 2018 (2018). https://www.whizsky.com/2018/04/20-top-fintech-companies-in-india-2018/

10. Hashim, F.A., Houssein, E.H., Mabrouk, M.S., Al-Atabany, W., Mirjalili, S.: Henry gas solubility optimization: a novel physics-based algorithm. Futur. Gener. Comput. Syst. **101**, 646–667 (2019)

11. Kuldasheva, Z., Ismailova, N., Balbaa, M.: Evaluating the Factors Affecting Consumer's Online Shopping Behavior: The Case of Uzbekistan, 2022. Association for Computing Machinery, New York, NY, USA, ICFNDS 2021, pp. 328–333 (2022). ISBN 9781450387347, https://doi.org/10.1145/3508072.3508126

12. Metawa, N., Pustokhina, I.V., Pustokhin, D.A., Shankar, K., Elhoseny, M.: computational intelligence-based financial crisis prediction model using feature subset selection with optimal deep belief network. Big Data **9**(2), 100–115 (2021)

13. Metawa, U.J.N., Shankar, K., Lakshmanaprabu, S.K.: Financial crisis prediction model using ant colony optimization. Int. J. Inf. Manag. **50**, 538–556 (2018)

14. Schubert, J.: 4 Top Challenges Facing the Banking Industry Right Now (2015). https://www.digitalistmag.com/industries/banking/2015/08/27/4-top-challenges-facing-banking-industry-right-now-03352186

15. Astanakulov, O.: National projects and government programmes: functional algorithm for evaluating and modelling using the data science methodology. Econ. Ann.-XXI **183**(5–6), 51–59 (2020). https://doi.org/10.21003/ea.V183-05

16. Schulte, P., Liu, G., Alerts, E., Journals, I.I.: FinTech is merging with IoT and AI to challengebanks: how entrenched interests can prepare. Inst. Investig. J. **20**(3), 41–57 (2018)

17. Story, C., Talk, I., Study, C.: Accelerating your journey to #truly digital banking (2017)

# Impact of E-government on Poverty Rate:
# A Cross-Country Empirical Assessment

Aziza Usmanova(✉)

Tashkent State University of Economics, Tashkent, Uzbekistan
a.usmanova@tsue.uz

**Abstract.** This paper assesses empirically the influence of e-government on poverty rate, using data of 54 countries over the timespan of 2008–2018. The results provide strong evidence for the claim that e-government is associated negatively with the poverty rate. It was revealed that, on average, a one-point increase in e-government is associated with the 7.1 percentage point reduction in poverty rate.

**Keywords:** Poverty · e-government · Panel data analysis

## 1 Introduction

Improvement of the digitalization processes in the economy of the country is one of the global aims. One of the directions of economic digitalization is e-government system. E-government is a use of information technologies for enhancing the delivery of public services online to benefit citizens, business entities and partners [1].

In accordance with the Goal 9 of the Sustainable Development Goals, set by the United Nations, inclusive industrialization, innovation and infrastructure provide a good environment in increasing wealth of the population [2]. That is the reason why more and more countries are focusing on the e-government development, as it provides the transparency of the government to the public [3]. Furthermore, e-government also creates additional benefits for the public via contributing to sustainable development [4–8], alleviating tax evasion [9], combating corruption [4, 10], and decreasing shadow economy [11].

While the e-government is associated with the progress, there is one major issue that slows it and this issue is called poverty [12–15]. Poverty is the statement "when one or more persons fall short of a level of economic welfare deemed to constitute a reasonable minimum, either in some absolute sense or by the standards of a specific society" [16].

Combating with the poverty is the Goal 1 of the Sustainable Development Goals as well as one of the important moments in implementing the governmental strategies. Countries are introducing different poverty alleviation strategies in order to increase the wealth of their citizens; thus, it is also interesting whether e-government can contribute to poverty reduction. Therefore, in this paper panel data analysis based on data of 54 countries is conducted in order to investigate the impact of e-government development on the poverty rate.

© The Author(s), under exclusive license to Springer Nature Switzerland AG 2023
Y. Koucheryavy and A. Aziz (Eds.): NEW2AN 2022, LNCS 13772, pp. 462–470, 2023.
https://doi.org/10.1007/978-3-031-30258-9_41

This paper has five sections. Section 2 is devoted to the previously conducted research on this topic. Section 3 describes data used in the paper and explains the methodology that was followed. Section 4 represents the outcome of the analysis, and the Sect. 5 includes the concluding remarks.

## 2 Literature Review

Due to the fact that e-government is a relatively new branch of the research, there is not a big number of investigations conducted on the influence of the e-government on poverty. In the conducted researches the influence of e-government on poverty reduction was analyzed together with the obstacles in implementation of e-government.

[17] analyzes both functional and dysfunctional e-government effects on the social life and investigates approaches in good e-governance creation. It was claimed that e-government can be a good tool in poverty eradication through creating equal opportunities in accessing resources Finally, authors proposed a "good e-governance" model.

In [18] challenges and barriers in e-government development are analyzed with the main focus on the situation in Botswana. Authors concluded that developing countries should direct e-government for diversifying the economy and delivering services.

[19, 20] discussed existing challenges and opportunities of e-government in South Africa. One of the challenges was poverty and the circumstances when poor people were not happy to seek services in Internet. It was mentioned that e-government should be infused in programmes of poverty reduction. Also, analysis of e-government projects was also conducted according to which some of them were effective in fighting against poverty via increasing living standards of the population.

In [21] were discussed also strategies and challenges of e-government implementation in Bangladesh in order to maintain sustainable development, and given recommendations on the its effective implementation.

Overall, it can be seen that although there were conducted investigations on the effect of the e-government on the poverty, they had more theoretical approach. However, to our knowledge, there is no calculations of the impact of e-government on poverty. This paper is aimed at filling this gap by providing empirical evidence of the e-government impact on poverty rate.

## 3 Data and Methodology

The aim of this paper is to analyze the impact of e-government development on poverty rate. For this purpose, the data of 54 countries was analyzed applying panel data analysis method. The timespan of the analysis is a decade from 2008 to 2018 with an interval in one year. There are two sources of used data: United Nation's E-Government Survey, which is conducted once in two years across 193 countries, and World Bank database [22].

All the indexes related to e-government progress are taken from E-Government Survey. The aim of these indexes is to analyze the level of e-government development in the country and to compare the progress with other countries. The main aggregated index of e-government development is EGDI. EGDI consists of three sub-indexes which serve as different dimensions of e-government: Human Capital Index (HCI), Online Service Index (OSI), and Telecommunication Infrastructure Index (TII). Furthermore, E-participation Index (EPI), which measures the level of e-interaction between government and individuals, is also used as an indicator of e-government development. Abovementioned indexes are ranged between zero and one, where the higher index implies the higher quality of e-government.

As the aim is to analyze the effect of e-government progress on poverty rate, the variable poverty rate is chosen as a dependent variable. Also, there are macroeconomic and demographic variables in the models which serve as control variables. As parameters of fiscal policy tax revenue as % of GDP, budget expenses as % of GDP and inflation rate are selected. To frame the economy of the countries, the following variables are chosen as control variables: GDP growth rate, agriculture (as % of GDP), industry (as % of GDP), unemployment rate (%), exports of goods and services (as % of GDP), imports of goods and services (as % of GDP), and Gini index. From demographic indicators the population growth rate (%) and the share of urban population (%) are used. These data are obtained from the World Bank's databank. Table 1 illustrates descriptive statistics about all used variables.

**Table 1.** Descriptive statistics

| Variable | Obs | Mean | Std. Dev. | Min | Max |
|---|---|---|---|---|---|
| Poverty rate | 278 | 20.151 | 11.008 | 1.3 | 76.4 |
| Expenses to GDP (%) | 235 | 31.428 | 10.15 | 8.56 | 62.369 |
| Taxes to GDP (%) | 240 | 18.732 | 6.119 | 8.107 | 46.046 |
| Agriculture (%) | 277 | 6.248 | 6.259 | .65 | 37.612 |
| Industry (%) | 277 | 27.089 | 8.54 | 9.985 | 65.519 |
| GDP (%) | 277 | 2.838 | 4.288 | −46.082 | 12.32 |
| Export to GDP (%) | 276 | 47.153 | 25.138 | 9.17 | 163.12 |
| Import to GDP (%) | 276 | 49.125 | 23.965 | 17.31 | 159.556 |
| Gini index | 251 | 35.57 | 7.668 | 24 | 63.4 |
| Inflation rate (%) | 276 | 5.943 | 23.703 | −1.8 | 379.848 |
| Unemployment rate (%) | 278 | 8.247 | 5.738 | .51 | 32.02 |
| Urban population (%) | 278 | 65.97 | 16.351 | 18.217 | 95.334 |
| Population growth rate (%) | 278 | .672 | .837 | −1.799 | 3.492 |
| EGDI | 278 | .623 | .154 | .142 | .916 |
| HCI | 278 | .831 | .122 | .221 | .993 |
| OSI | 278 | .573 | .21 | .008 | 1 |
| TII | 278 | .468 | .221 | .014 | .887 |
| EPI | 278 | .483 | .282 | 0 | 1 |

In order to investigate the relationship between variables, the correlation analysis was conducted (see Table 2 and Fig. 1), followed by panel data analysis. Five models were constructed in the panel data analysis. In the first model the impact of EGDI on poverty rate is shown whereas in the next three models the impact of EGDI's sub-indexes' impact is illustrated. And the last model represents the influence of EPI on the poverty rate. During the panel data analysis both Model of Fixed Effects and Model of Random Effects were created, among which the best model was selected using the Hausman test and shown in Table 3. These models are capable in controlling variations over time and among units and giving "more informative data, more variability, less collinearity among variables, more degrees of freedom and more efficiency" [23].

Model of Fixed Effects assumes the individual-specific coefficient β1i as time-invariant, and its formula is the following [24]:

$$Y_{it} = \beta_1 x_{it} + a_i + u_{it} \tag{1}$$

where:

$Y_{it}$ – dependent variable, where i = country and t = years;
$\beta_1$-independent variable's coefficient;
$x_{it}$ – independent variable;
$a_i$ (i = 1...54) is the unknown intercept for each country;
$u_{it}$ – error term

Model of Random Effects the heterogeneity over individuals considers as random component and its formula is [23]:

$$Y_{it} = \beta_1 x_{it} + a_i + (u_i + e_{it}) \tag{2}$$

where:

$Y_{it}$ – dependent variable, where i = country and t = years;
$\beta_1$-independent variable's coefficient;
$x_{it}$ – independent variable;
$a_i$ (i = 1...54) is the unknown intercept for each country;
$e_{it}$ – combined time-series and cross-section component of the error term
$u_{it}$ – cross-section or individual specific error component

In our analysis in all the created models except the fourth model, Model of Random Effects is chosen according to conducted Hausman test. In the fourth model according to Hausman test the best model is Model of Fixed Effects, which is chosen for the analysis.

## 4   Results and Discussion

This section is devoted to the analysis of obtained results and discussion. Outcomes of the correlation analysis are illustrated in Table 2. It can be seen that there is a medium and negative relationship between poverty rate and e-government (−0.5), which is statistically significant. Fiscal policy variables are correlated also negatively but weak with poverty rate. Among all variables poverty rate has the strongest relationship with Gini index (0.7), which is positive and statistically significant. As regards EGDI, it has the highest negative correlation with both agriculture and population growth rate at the point

0.7 and the highest positive association with the share of urban population. Results of correlation analysis imply that the improvement in e-government sphere might serve to the decrease of e-government. Furthermore, it also illustrates that the more urbanized countries have higher e-government level. The graphic form of the correlation results is shown in Fig. 1.

**Table 2.** Correlation matrix

| Variables | 1 | 2 | 3 | 4 | 5 | 6 | 7 | 8 | 9 | 10 | 11 | 12 | 13 | 14 |
|---|---|---|---|---|---|---|---|---|---|---|---|---|---|---|
| (1) EGDI | 1.0 | | | | | | | | | | | | | |
| (2) Poverty | −0.5 (0.0) | 1.0 | | | | | | | | | | | | |
| (3) Expenses | 0.5 (0.0) | −0.3 (0.0) | 1.0 | | | | | | | | | | | |
| (4) Taxes | 0.5 (0.0) | −0.2 (0.1) | 0.7 (0.0) | 1.0 | | | | | | | | | | |
| (5) Agriculture | −0.7 (0.0) | 0.3 (0.0) | −0.6 (0.0) | −0.4 (0.0) | 1.0 | | | | | | | | | |
| (6) Industry | −0.3 (0.0) | −0.0 (0.9) | −0.5 (0.0) | −0.5 (0.0) | 0.3 (0.0) | 1.0 | | | | | | | | |
| (7) GDP | −0.2 (0.0) | −0.0 (0.5) | −0.5 (0.0) | −0.3 (0.0) | 0.3 (0.0) | 0.1 (0.1) | 1.0 | | | | | | | |
| (8) Export | 0.2 (0.0) | −0.2 (0.0) | 0.1 (0.0) | 0.2 (0.0) | −0.2 (0.0) | −0.1 (0.1) | 0.1 (0.1) | 1.0 | | | | | | |
| (9) Import | 0.0 (0.9) | −0.1 (0.3) | 0.1 (0.1) | 0.2 (0.0) | 0.0 (0.7) | −0.3 (0.0) | 0.1 (0.0) | 0.9 (0.0) | 1.0 | | | | | |
| (10) Gini index | −0.5 (0.0) | 0.7 (0.0) | −0.5 (0.0) | −0.4 (0.0) | 0.2 (0.0) | 0.2 (0.0) | 0.3 (0.0) | −0.4 (0.0) | −0.3 (0.0) | 1.0 | | | | |
| (11) Inflation | −0.3 (0.0) | 0.3 (0.0) | −0.2 (0.0) | −0.1 (0.1) | 0.2 (0.0) | 0.3 (0.0) | −0.2 (0.0) | −0.1 (0.2) | −0.1 (0.5) | 0.1 (0.2) | 1.0 | | | |
| (12) Unemployment | 0.0 (0.5) | 0.2 (0.0) | 0.4 (0.0) | 0.3 (0.0) | −0.2 (0.0) | −0.4 (0.0) | −0.3 (0.0) | −0.1 (0.0) | −0.0 (0.7) | 0.1 (0.2) | 0.0 (0.8) | 1.0 | | |
| (13) Urban | 0.7 (0.0) | −0.3 (0.0) | 0.3 (0.0) | 0.4 (0.0) | −0.6 (0.0) | −0.2 (0.0) | −0.1 (0.3) | 0.0 (0.6) | −0.1 (0.0) | −0.1 (0.0) | −0.2 (0.0) | 0.0 (0.9) | 1.0 | |
| (14) Population | −0.7 (0.0) | 0.4 (0.0) | −0.4 (0.0) | −0.1 (0.1) | 0.4 (0.0) | 0.2 (0.0) | 0.1 (0.1) | 0.1 (0.4) | 0.0 (0.7) | 0.3 (0.0) | 0.1 (0.3) | −0.3 (0.0) | −0.1 (0.1) | 1.0 |

Table 3 represents economic results for poverty rate using the e-government development index and the additional controls. Apart from the fourth model, all other models provide the results from estimating Eq. (1), whilst the fourth model provides the results from estimating Eq. (2).

The obtained results are in line with considerations about positive effect of e-government on poverty reduction. The first model illustrates that a 1 unit increase in EGDI decreases poverty rate by about 7.14 percentage points. This coefficient is significant at a 5% level. Next following three models investigated the impact of sub-indexes of e-government on poverty rate. Interesting result was obtained in the second model where HII illustrated a positive influence on poverty rate at the significance level of 1%.

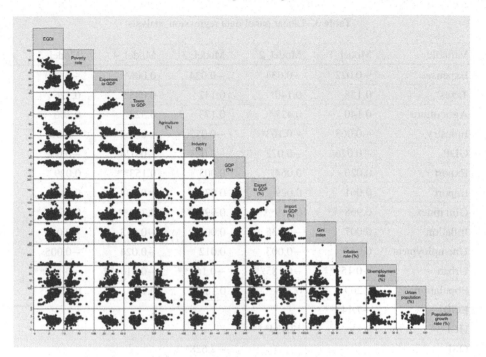

**Fig. 1.** Correlation relationship between variables

From the results it can be said that a 1 unit increase in HII also increases poverty rate by 17.43 percentage points. Negative impact of the remaining sub-indexes can be observed in the third and fourth models. So, if the coefficient of OSI was -2.63 with the 10% of significance level, the impact of TII was much higher in terms of both coefficient (-8.66) and significance rate (1%). The last model shows the effect of PII on poverty rate, which was also negative and statistically significant (1%), implying that an increase in PII by 1 unit decreases poverty rate by 2.63.

Regarding control variables, they remained relatively stable in all models. In general, it was revealed that the level of Gini index had a statistically significant (1%) and positive impact on poverty rate. Also, the proportion of urban population also had statistically significant but negative influence on poverty rate. Interestingly, the impact of exports to GDP became statistically significant (5%) when the influence of TII on poverty rate was analyzed. The remaining control variables had a statistically significant effect on poverty rate of the investigated countries.

**Table 3.** Linear panel data regression analysis

| Variable | Model_1 | Model_2 | Model_3 | Model_4 | Model_5 |
|---|---|---|---|---|---|
| Expenses | −0.022 | −0.034 | −0.024 | 0.006 | −0.023 |
| Taxes | 0.138 | 0.140* | 0.142 | 0.085 | 0.126 |
| Agriculture | 0.140 | 0.427* | 0.173 | 0.322 | 0.206 |
| Industry | −0.063 | −0.163* | −0.053 | −0.169 | −0.097 |
| GDP | −0.026 | −0.072 | −0.027 | −0.024 | −0.002 |
| Export | 0.020 | 0.064 | 0.003 | 0.153** | 0.029 |
| Import | 0.061 | 0.029 | 0.075 | −0.038 | 0.049 |
| Gini index | 0.968*** | 0.989*** | 0.995*** | 0.784*** | 0.964*** |
| Inflation | 0.007 | −0.035 | 0.005 | −0.013 | −0.015 |
| Unemployment | 0.017 | −0.003 | 0.012 | −0.024 | −0.005 |
| Urban | −0.157** | −0.185** | −0.160** | −0.510*** | −0.164** |
| Population | 0.209 | 0.368 | 0.188 | 0.189 | 0.252 |
| EGDI | −7.143** | | | | |
| HCI | | 17.434*** | | | |
| OSI | | | −2.628* | | |
| TII | | | | −8.662*** | |
| EPI | | | | | −2.633*** |
| _cons | −4.302 | −21.025** | −8.434 | 26.973 | −5.815 |

legend: * $p < .1$; ** $p < .05$; *** $p < .01$.

## 5 Conclusion

E-government has become one of the important parts of governance around the world. The investigations illustrate that the development of e-government impacts positively on the lives of people by maintaining economic growth, reducing corruption and providing sustainability.

This paper is aimed at analyzing how e-government influences on poverty rate. Thus, correlation analysis and the panel data analysis were conducted among fifty-four countries within a timeframe of a decade (2008–2018 years). It was revealed that the development of e-government index contributes to the reduction of the poverty rate significantly. Yet, there was an unexpected result with the impact of human capital index, which is the sub-index of e-government index, where the improvement of this index increased the poverty rate. As regards control variables, only urban population share and Gini index variables had a significant effect on poverty. Particularly, urban population share had a negative impact on poverty rate while Gini index's impact was positive.

It should be mentioned that poverty is a multidimensional phenomenon and poverty alleviation programmes should be complex and comprehensive. Our results illustrate that e-government improvement can serve as one of the tools of poverty reduction.

# References

1. Silcock, R.: What is e-government. Parliam. Aff. **54**(1), 88–101 (2001)
2. UN General Assembly (UNGA). A/RES/70/1Transforming our world: the 2030 agenda for sustainable development. Resolut **25**, 1–35 (2015)
3. United Nations E-Government Survey 2008, 2010, 2012, 1014, 2016, 2018
4. Elbahnasawy, N.G.: E-government, internet adoption, and corruption: an empirical investigation. World Dev. **57**, 114–126 (2014)
5. Niebel, T.: ICT and economic growth–comparing developing, emerging and developed countries. World Dev. **104**, 197–211 (2018)
6. Twizeyimana, J.D., Andersson, A.: The public value of E-government–a literature review. Gov. Inf. Q. **36**(2), 167–178 (2019)
7. Alisherovna Usmanova, A.: Whether a Higher E-Government Development Index Means a Higher GDP Growth Rate?. In: The 5th International Conference on Future Networks & Distributed Systems (2021)
8. Obydenkova, A.V., Salahodjaev, R.: Government size, intelligence and life satisfaction. Intelligence **61**, 85–91 (2017)
9. Uyar, A., Nimer, K., Kuzey, C., Shahbaz, M., Schneider, F.: Can e-government initiatives alleviate tax evasion? The moderation effect of ICT. Technol. Forecast. Soc. Change **166**, 120597 (2021)
10. Kim, S., Kim, H.J., Lee, H.: An institutional analysis of an e-government system for anti-corruption: the case of OPEN Government information quarterly. In: Proceedings of the IEEE 1st International Conference on Broadnets Networks (BroadNets'04), vol. 26, no. (1), pp. 42–50 networks. IEEE, Los Alamitos, CA, 210–217 ((2009))
11. Elbahnasawy, N.G.: Can e-government limit the scope of the informal economy? World Dev. **139**, 105341 (2021)
12. Usmanova, A., Aziz, A., Rakhmonov, D., Osamy, W.: Utilities of artificial intelligence in poverty prediction: a review. Sustainability **14**(21), 14238 (2022). https://doi.org/10.3390/su142114238
13. Aziz, A., Singh, K., Osamy, W., Khedr, A.M.: An efficient compressive sensing routing scheme for internet of things based wireless sensor networks. Wirel. Pers. Commun. **114**(3), 1905–1925 (2020). https://doi.org/10.1007/s11277-020-07454-4
14. Aziz, A., Salim, A., Osamy, W.: Adaptive and efficient compressive sensing based technique for routing in wireless sensor networks. In: Proceedings of INTHITEN (IoT and its Enablers) Conference (2013)
15. Aziz, A., Salim, A., Osamy, W.: Sparse signals reconstruction via adaptive iterative greedy algorithm. Int. J. Comput. Appl. **90**(17), 5–11 (2014)
16. Lipton, M., Ravallion, M.: Poverty and policy. Handb. Dev. Econ. **3**, 2551–2657 (1995)
17. Pourezzat, A.A., Nejati, M., Nejati, M.: E-government & public policy for poverty eradication and empowerment. In: Proceedings of 5th International Conference on E-Governance (ICEG2007), Computer Society of India-Special Interest Group on E-governance, India (2007)
18. Nkwe, N.: E-government: challenges and opportunities in Botswana. Int. J. Humanit. Soc. Sci. **2**(17), 39–48 (2012)

19. Mutula, S.M., Mostert, J.: Challenges and opportunities of e-government in South Africa. Electronic Library **28**(1), 38–53 (2010). https://doi.org/10.1108/02640471011023360
20. Mutula, S.M.: E-Government's role in poverty alleviation: case study of South Africa. In: Rahman, H. (ed.) Cases on Progressions and Challenges in ICT Utilization for Citizen-Centric Governance:, pp. 44–68. IGI Global (2013). https://doi.org/10.4018/978-1-4666-2071-1.ch003
21. Al Mamun, A., et al.: E-government services for sustainable development: the challenges and strategies of implementing e- government in Bangladesh. Int. J. Comput. Sci. Inf. Technol. Res. (2022)
22. World Bank. World Development Indicators (2018). https://datacatalog.worldbank.org/
23. Gujarati, D.N.: Econometrics by Example, vol. 1. Palgrave Macmillan, New York (2011)
24. Adkins, L.C.: Using Stata for Principles of Econometrics. Wiley Global Education (2011)

# An Empirical Investigation of the Relationship Between E-government Development and Multidimensional Poverty

Aziza Usmanova[✉]

Tashkent State University of Economics, Tashkent, Uzbekistan
a.usmanova@tsue.uz

**Abstract.** The aim of this paper is to analyze the impact of the e-government development on the multidimensional poverty. For this purpose, correlation analysis and panel data analysis were conducted using data of 43 countries over a decade period (2008–2018). To our knowledge, this is the first paper analyzing empirically the effects of e-government development on the global multidimensional poverty index. It was revealed that the e-government development index impacts negatively on the multidimensional poverty index, where, on average, a one-point increase in e-government is associated with the 0.302 points reduction in the global multidimensional poverty index.

**Keywords:** Multidimensional Poverty Index · E-government Development Index · Correlation Analysis · Panel Data Analysis

## 1 Introduction

Poverty is a phenomenon that affects adversely on the economy of the country as well as social well-being of the nation. Therefore, the aim of each government is to eliminate poverty. In order to achieve this goal, causes of the poverty should be analyzed as well as factors impacting on the poverty level.

As one of the factors affecting poverty is the government itself. Good governance leads to the reducing of poverty [1–3]. With the progress of information-communication technologies (ICT), governmental procedures have also been digitalizing, and the new term "e-government" has been introduced E-government means using ICT for improving access to public services as well as delivering public services to citizens and, business [4–7]. To evaluate the level of e-government introduction as well as compare the progress around the world, e-government development index (EGDI) was developed. To calculate this index, E-government Survey is conducted once in two years by the United Nations, which evaluates national websites and how essential services are delivered in accordance with e-government strategies and policies [8].

The aim of this paper is to analyze how e-government development influences on multidimensional poverty. Although there were conducted researches on the impact of e-government on poverty rate, in poverty measurement they applied monetary approach. To

Y. Koucheryavy and A. Aziz (Eds.): NEW2AN 2022, LNCS 13772, pp. 471–480, 2023.
https://doi.org/10.1007/978-3-031-30258-9_42

our knowledge, this is the first paper investigating the relationship between e-government and multidimensional poverty empirically. To conduct this analysis, data of 43 countries are used and two methods are applied: correlation analysis and panel data analysis.

This paper consists of five sections. Section 2 is focused on literature background of this topic. Section 3 provides information on used data applied methods. Section 4 illustrates outcomes and interpretations of the analysis. Section 5 gives concluding remarks.

## 2   Literature Review

Although poverty is one of the ancient issues of human society, still there is no consensus on the definition of poverty. During the evolution of economic theories and increasing data on economic and social indicators, different approaches to defining and measuring poverty have been developing. One of the eldest but still actual approaches to poverty is a monetary approach, which, in its turn, also can be income-based or consumption based [9, 10]. Another approach claims that not always poverty can be measured by money, that poverty is a multidimensional issue when a poor person is deprived from certain opportunities or conveniences [11–14].

Regarding these different approaches, investigations on the e-government impact on poverty also can be divided into three groups. First group of papers analyzes the effect of e-government on the poverty rate in the context of monetary approach [15, 16]. Second group of papers analyzes the influence of e-government on the multidimensional poverty [17, 18] and the last group considers poverty as a general term without detailing approach [19–21].

[15] and [16] analyzed empirically the impact of e-government and macroeconomic indicators on the poverty rate. As a poverty the income inequality index was used. Analysis showed that e-government development decreases poverty level.

[17] and [18] analyzed the influence of rural e-governance on poverty from different dimensions and concluded that e-governance can help to address poverty issues collectively not individually.

General effects of e-government on the poverty were discussed in [19], whereas in [20] and [21] challenges in e-government implementation and poverty reduction were investigated.

Overall, all authors made a conclusion that e-government can reduce the poverty. In order to test this conclusion on multidimensional poverty, this analysis is conducted.

## 3   Data and Methodology

This paper is focused on analyzing the impact of e-government on multidimensional poverty. Thus, data of 43 countries over the period between 2008–2018 is analyzed. As a poverty measurement global multidimensional poverty index (MPI) is used, together with two its two components: intensity of deprivation among the poor (average % of deprivations) and headcount ratio (% of population in multidimensional poverty) [22]. These three variables are used as dependent variables in our panel data analysis. MPI is a composite index which ranges between 0 and 1 (the higher is an index means the higher poverty rate) and consists of ten indicators which are combined into three dimensions: health, education and living standards [23]. Data on MPI is developed by Oxford Poverty & Human Development Initiative (OPHI) with the UN Development Programme (UNDP) [24].

As independent variables EGDI and its three sub-indexes are used: Human Capital Index (HCI), Online Service Index (OSI), and Telecommunication Infrastructure Index (TII). Also, E-participation Index (EPI) is also used in this analysis. These indexes also range between 0 and 1, and the higher index means higher quality of e-government. Data on these variables are used from the United Nation's E-Government Survey [25].

As control variables for the analysis were chosen 9 variables representing different aspects of the socio-economic state of the countries. So, as a representatives of fiscal policy elements are used budget expenses as % of GDP (Expenses), tax revenues as % of GDP (Taxes), and inflation rate. As a parameters of international trade imports of goods and services (as % of GDP) and exports of goods and services (as % of GDP) are chosen. The share of urban population (%) belongs to demographic indicator. To frame the economic growth the following variables are used: GDP growth rate (%), industry (as % of GDP) and agriculture (as % of GDP). All these variables are used from the World Bank's databank [26].

Descriptive Statistics of all used variables is illustrated in Table 1. It should be mentioned that owing to the absence of data of some variables for certain years, the dataset is unbalanced.

**Table 1.** Descriptive Statistics

| Variable | Obs | Mean | Std. Dev | Min | Max |
| --- | --- | --- | --- | --- | --- |
| MPI | 97 | .192 | .158 | 0 | .554 |
| EGDI | 97 | .346 | .143 | 0 | .646 |
| GDP | 97 | 4.505 | 3.312 | −1.617 | 19.675 |
| Inflation | 94 | 6.853 | 6.497 | −2.078 | 36.907 |
| Urban | 97 | 44.975 | 17.676 | 10.642 | 79.577 |
| Agriculture | 97 | 18.201 | 12.621 | 2.169 | 53.654 |
| Industry | 97 | 25.77 | 10.377 | 2.526 | 65.31 |
| Expenses | 56 | 20.683 | 8.835 | 9.477 | 42.695 |
| Taxes | 58 | 16.011 | 6.449 | 6.623 | 35.475 |
| Export | 94 | 29.172 | 12.633 | 6.653 | 62.603 |
| Import | 94 | 40.002 | 17.082 | 11.31 | 95.272 |

The research methodology consists of two parts. Initially, in order to see the association between variables, the correlation analysis is conducted [27]. Results of the correlation analysis are represented in Table 2 and Fig. 1. Next, panel data analysis is conducted. The strength of panel data analysis is that it can take into account explicitly the heterogeneity issue [28] and can control unobserved individual-specific characteristics [27].

In the paper for each created model three types of panel data analysis models were created (Fixed Effects Model, Random Effects Model and Pooled OLS Regression), and the best model was selected using Hausman Test and illustrated in the tables.

Fixed Effects Model (FEM) removes the effect of time-invariant attributes to evaluate the net effect of the predictors on the outcome variable [29]. The formula of Fixed Effects Model is the following [30]:

$$Y_{it} = \beta_1 x_{it} + a_i + u_{it} \tag{1}$$

where:

$Y_{it}$ – dependent variable, where i = country and t = years;

$\beta_1$-independent variable's coefficient;

$x_{it}$ – independent variable;

$a_i$ (i = 1...43) is the unknown intercept for each country;

$u_{it}$ – error term.

In the Random Effects Model (REM) the assumption is that although all individual differences are captured by the intercept parameters, the selection of the individuals of the sample was random, therefore individual differences should be treated as random rather than fixed [27]. The formula of Random Effects Model is the following [30]:

$$Y_{it} = \beta_1 x_{it} + a_i + (u_i + e_{it}) \tag{2}$$

where:

$Y_{it}$ – dependent variable, where i = country and t = years;

$\beta_1$-independent variable's coefficient;

$x_{it}$ – independent variable;

$a_i$ (i = 1...43) is the unknown intercept for each country;

$e_{it}$ – combined time-series and cross-section component of the error term.

$u_{it}$ – cross-section or individual specific error component.

In the Pooled Model (PM) different individuals' data are simply pooled together without taking into consideration individual differences. The formula of Random Effects Model is the following [28]:

$$Y_{it} = \beta_1 x_{it} + u_{it} \tag{3}$$

$Y_{it}$ – dependent variable, where i = country and t = years;

$\beta_1$-independent variable's coefficient;

$x_{it}$ – independent variable;

$u_{it}$ – error term.

As there are three dependent variables, three different analyses were conducted for them. For each dependent variable the impact of EGDI and its elements are analyzed via creating five models. For each model three types of panel data analysis are conducted and the best model is illustrated in the columns of the tables. All the illustrated models are statistically significant.

# 4   Results and Discussion

In this section the output of the analysis is described and discussed. Initially results of correlation analysis is discussed, followed by panel data models, analyzing the impact of EGDI and its components on MPI, headcount ratio and intensity.

From the results of Table 2, which shows the correlation between variables, it can be seen that there is very strong and negative association between MPI and EGDI with the coefficient of −0.832 (at the significance level of 1%). Also, there is strong and negative relationship at the 1% of significance level between MPI and the following variables: Urban (−0.588), Taxes (−0.507), Expenses (−0.697, and Industry (−0.433). There is strong and positive association (0.763) between MPI and agriculture with the 1% significance level. As regards EGDI, it is associated strongly and positively at the 1% significance level with Urban (0.607) and Expenses (0.563), and negatively with Agriculture (−0.654). The visualization of all these relationships is given in Fig. 1.

**Table 2.** Correlation matrix

| Variables | (1) | (2) | (3) | (4) | (5) | (6) | (7) | (8) | (9) | (10) | (11) |
|---|---|---|---|---|---|---|---|---|---|---|---|
| (1) MPI | 1.000 | | | | | | | | | | |
| (2) EGDI | −0.832 (0.000) | 1.000 | | | | | | | | | |
| (3) GDP | 0.269 (0.008) | −0.237 (0.020) | 1.000 | | | | | | | | |
| (4) Inflation | −0.007 (0.945) | −0.063 (0.547) | −0.108 (0.302) | 1.000 | | | | | | | |
| (5) Urban | −0.588 (0.000) | 0.607 (0.000) | −0.109 (0.290) | −0.060 (0.565) | 1.000 | | | | | | |
| (6) Agriculture | 0.763 (0.000) | −0.654 (0.000) | 0.167 (0.102) | 0.023 (0.825) | −0.592 (0.000) | 1.000 | | | | | |
| (7) Industry | −0.433 (0.000) | 0.337 (0.001) | 0.122 (0.236) | −0.191 (0.065) | 0.474 (0.000) | −0.617 (0.000) | 1.000 | | | | |
| (8) Expenses | −0.697 (0.000) | 0.563 (0.000) | −0.478 (0.000) | −0.027 (0.848) | 0.300 (0.025) | −0.621 (0.000) | 0.149 (0.274) | 1.000 | | | |
| (9) Taxes | −0.507 (0.000) | 0.313 (0.017) | −0.415 (0.001) | −0.113 (0.407) | 0.142 (0.287) | −0.514 (0.000) | −0.116 (0.387) | 0.800 (0.000) | 1.000 | | |
| (10) Export | −0.372 (0.000) | 0.235 (0.023) | 0.134 (0.200) | −0.152 (0.148) | 0.275 (0.007) | −0.373 (0.000) | 0.485 (0.000) | 0.243 (0.071) | 0.288 (0.029) | 1.000 | |
| (11) Import | −0.224 (0.030) | 0.013 (0.900) | 0.032 (0.757) | −0.141 (0.179) | −0.132 (0.204) | −0.174 (0.093) | 0.065 (0.532) | 0.374 (0.005) | 0.542 (0.000) | 0.646 (0.000) | 1.000 |

Table 3 illustrates the results of panel data analysis of the impact of EGDI and its elements on MPI. Model 1 shows that the impact if EGDI on MPI is negative and statistically significant at the 1%, which confirms the result of correlation analysis. From the Model 1 it can be said that a 1 unit increase of EGDI decreases MPI by 0.302 units. In the Model 2 it can be seen that the impact of HCI on MPI is statistically insignificant. Models 3 and 4 show the impact of the remaining sub-indexes of EGDI on MPI, which are also negative and statistically significant at 1%. So, if OCI and TII increase by 1 unit,

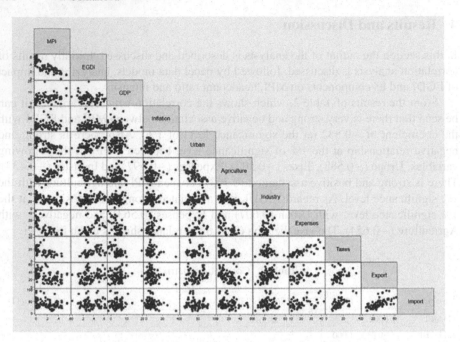

**Fig. 1.** Correlation relationship between variables

MPI will decrease by 0.111 and 0.137 units respectively. In the Model 5 the impact of EPI on MPI is given, which is also negative and statistically significant (1%), implying that a 1 unit increase in EPI will decrease MPI by 0.066 units. Regarding control variables, it can be seen that in all models they were almost stable with little variations. So, the influence of expenses, urban and import on MPI was negative and statistically significant.

Table 4 represents the impact of EGDI and its components on the headcount ratio. From the Model 1 it can be observed that EGDI affects adversely on the headcount ratio when a 1 unit increase in EGDI decreases headcount ratio by 51.404% point. As shown in Model 2, the impact of HCI on the headcount ratio is statistically insignificant. Impact of OSI on the headcount ratio is negative and statistically significant at 1% as is illustrated in Model 3. A 1 unit increase in OSI decreases the headcount ratio by 18.469% points. In the Model 4 and Model 5 are given the influence of TII and EPI on the headcount ratio, which are also negative and statistically significant at 5%. So, if TII increases by 1 unit, the headcount ratio will decrease by 22.574% points, whilst the increase of EPI by 1 unit will decrease the headcount ratio by 9.612% points. As in case of MPI, expenses, urban and import variables had a negative impact on the headcount ratio at the significance level of 1%.

Table 5 shows the results of panel data analysis on the impact of e-government on the intensity of MPI. It can be seen from the Model 1 that the impact of EGDI on the intensity is negative and significant statistically (1%), implying that a 1 unit increase of EGDI decreases intensity by 19.101% point. As in the previous analysis, the influence of HCI is insignificant statistically (Model 2). Negative impact of the remaining sub-indexes can be observed in Model 3 and Model 4. So, if the coefficient of OSI was −

**Table 3.** Linear panel data regression analysis on the impact of e-government and its components on MPI level

| Variable | Model_1 (REM) | Model_2 (REM) | Model_3 (REM) | Model_4 (PM) | Model_5 (REM) |
|---|---|---|---|---|---|
| GDP | −0.002 | −0.001 | −0.002 | −0.002 | −0.002 |
| Taxes | 0.003 | 0.004 | 0.005** | 0.002 | 0.004* |
| Expenses | −0.005*** | −0.006*** | −0.006*** | −0.004** | −0.005*** |
| Inflation | −0.002** | −0.002 | −0.002* | −0.002** | −0.002** |
| Urban | −0.002** | −0.003*** | −.003*** | −.003*** | −.003*** |
| Agriculture | 0.002 | 0.004* | 0.003* | 0.003 | 0.004* |
| Industry | 0.000 | 0.002 | 0.001 | 0.001 | 0.001 |
| Export | 0.002* | 0.002 | 0.002* | 0.002 | 0.002* |
| Import | −0.003*** | −0.003*** | −0.003*** | −0.003*** | −0.003*** |
| EGDI | −0.302*** | | | | |
| HCI | | 0.048 | | | |
| OSI | | | −0.111*** | | |
| TII | | | | −0.137*** | |
| EPI | | | | | −0.066*** |
| _cons | 0.470*** | 0.311** | 0.379*** | 0.372*** | 0.366*** |

legend: * $p < 0.1$; ** $p < 0.05$; *** $p < 0.01$

**Table 4.** Linear panel data regression analysis on the impact of e-government and its components on the headcount ratio

| Variable | Model_1 (REM) | Model_2 (REM) | Model_3 (REM) | Model_4 (REM) | Model_5 (REM) |
|---|---|---|---|---|---|
| GDP | −0.086 | 0.021 | −0.143 | −0.159 | −0.144 |
| Taxes | 0.632 | 0.757 | 0.964** | 0.483 | 0.710* |
| Expenses | −0.970*** | −1.191*** | −1.192*** | −0.965*** | −1.088*** |
| Inflation | −0.345* | −0.212 | −0.228 | −0.333 | −0.297 |
| Urban | −0.486*** | −0.655*** | −0.566*** | −0.574*** | −0.592*** |
| Agriculture | 0.321 | 0.614 | 0.532 | 0.474 | 0.571 |
| Industry | 0.109 | 0.296 | 0.233 | 0.165 | 0.224 |
| Export | 0.289 | 0.248 | 0.279 | 0.289 | 0.267 |
| Import | −0.523*** | −0.455*** | −0.555*** | −0.455*** | −0.494*** |

*(continued)*

**Table 4.** (*continued*)

| Variable | Model_1 (REM) | Model_2 (REM) | Model_3 (REM) | Model_4 (REM) | Model_5 (REM) |
|---|---|---|---|---|---|
| EGDI | −51.404*** | | | | |
| HCI | | 7.419 | | | |
| OSI | | | −18.469*** | | |
| TII | | | | −22.574** | |
| EPI | | | | | −9.612** |
| _cons | 91.038*** | 64.580*** | 75.511*** | 75.260*** | 72.860*** |

legend: * $p < 0.1$; ** $p < 0.05$; *** $p < 0.01$

5.104 with the 5% of significance level, the impact of TII was much higher in terms of both coefficient (−8.514) and significance rate (1%). The last model shows the effect of PII on the intensity, which was also negative and statistically significant (1%), implying that an increase in PII by 1 unit decreases intensity by 3.977 As regards control variables, expenses and import had negative and statistically significant effect on intensity, while the effect of export was positive and statistically significant.

**Table 5.** Linear panel data regression analysis on the impact of e-government and its components on the intensity

| Variable | Model_1 (PM) | Model_2 (PM) | Model_3 (PM) | Model_4 (REM) | Model_5 (REM) |
|---|---|---|---|---|---|
| GDP | −0.160 | −0.099 | −0.160 | −0.188* | −0.204* |
| Taxes | 0.199 | 0.252* | 0.327** | 0.161 | 0.276** |
| Expenses | −0.221** | −0.297*** | −0.312*** | −0.196* | −0.271*** |
| Inflation | −0.126** | −0.080 | −0.090 | −0.118** | −0.120** |
| Urban | −0.024 | −0.089 | −0.063 | −0.060 | −0.061 |
| Agriculture | 0.109 | 0.206* | 0.190* | 0.182 | 0.211* |
| Industry | −0.033 | 0.040 | 0.017 | 0.004 | 0.007 |
| Export | 0.137** | 0.126* | 0.144** | 0.148** | 0.152** |
| Import | −0.157*** | −0.126** | −0.158*** | −0.121** | −0.147*** |
| EGDI | −19.101*** | | | | |
| HCI | | 1.029 | | | |
| OSI | | | −5.104** | | |
| TII | | | | −8.514*** | |
| EPI | | | | | −3.977*** |
| _cons | 58.448*** | 49.108*** | 51.545*** | 50.499*** | 50.488*** |

legend: * $p < 0.1$; ** $p < 0.05$; *** $p < 0.01$

Overall, the obtained results are in line with the previous researches on the effectiveness of e-government in poverty reduction [15, 16, 19–21]. Also, the statistically stability and negative effect of expenses on MPI and its components in all models also proves the results of [21] and [31]. Our findings also confirm the negative relationship between urbanization and poverty rate [32].

## 5 Conclusion

Although poverty is a universal problem for each government, strategies combating with it differ from country to country. Nonetheless, this research attempted to reveal the impact of progress in e-government on multidimensional poverty on the global scale. To achieve this aim data of 43 countries over a ten-year period (2008–2018) was analyzed applying correlation analysis and panel data analysis methods. Findings of this analysis confirmed previous assumptions and results on the negative impact of e-government development on the poverty level. This means that e-government can serve as an effective tool in poverty reduction. Besides, it was also confirmed that urbanization process in the countries as well as budget expenses also can contribute to poverty reduction.

One of the limitations of this research is the unbalanced data owing to the insufficient information about MPI and some other macroeconomic indicators. Overall, it should be mentioned from the results that the governments should pay more attention on the e-government development, making it accessible to all the citizens, as when everyone can have access to public services and benefit from them, their living conditions can be improved which will decrease poverty level.

## References

1. Grindle, M.S.: Good enough governance: poverty reduction and reform in developing countries. Governance 17(4), 525–548 (2004)
2. Salahodjaev, R.: Tolerance, governance and happiness (in) equality: cross-country evidence. Int. J. Dev. Issues 20(2), 280–289 (2021)
3. Obydenkova, A.V., Salahodjaev, R.: Government size, intelligence and life satisfaction. Intelligence 61, 85–91 (2017)
4. Aziz, A., et al.: An efficient compressive sensing routing scheme for internet of things based wireless sensor networks. Wirel. Pers. Commun. 114(3), 1905–1925 (2020)
5. Silcock, R.: What is E-Government. Parliam. Aff. 54(1), 88–101 (2001)
6. Ahmed, A., et al.: Adaptive and efficient compressive sensing based technique for routing in wireless sensor networks. In: Proceedings of the INTHITEN (IoT and its Enablers) Conference (2013)
7. Aziz, A., Salim, A., Osamy, W.: Sparse signals reconstruction via adaptive iterative greedy algorithm. Int. J. Comput. Appl. 90(17), 5–11 (2014)
8. https://publicadministration.un.org/egovkb/en-us/About/Overview/-E-Government-Development-Index
9. Veit-Wilson, J.: Paradigms of poverty: a rehabilitation of B.S. Rowntree. J. Soc. Policy 15, 69–99 (1986). https://doi.org/10.1017/S0047279400023114
10. Usmanova, A., et al.: Utilities of artificial intelligence in poverty prediction: a review. Sustainability 14(21), 14238 (2022)

11. Sen, A.: Poverty: an ordinal approach to measurement. Econom. J. Econom. Soc. **44**, 219–231 (1976)
12. Noble, M., Wright, G., Smith, G., Dibben, C.: Measuring multiple deprivation at the small-area level. Environ. Plan. A **38**(1), 169–185 (2006)
13. Alkire, S., Foster, J.: Counting and multidimensional poverty measurement. J. Public Econ. **95**, 476–487 (2011)
14. Ahmed, A., et al.: Optimising compressive sensing matrix using chicken swarm optimisation algorithm. IET Wirel. Sens. Syst. **9**(5), 306–312 (2019)
15. Ullah, A., et al.: The role of E-Governance in combating COVID-19 and promoting sustainable development: a comparative study of China and Pakistan. Chin. Polit. Sci. Rev. **6**(1), 86–118 (2021)
16. Ullah, A., et al.: Sustainable utilization of financial and institutional resources in reducing income inequality and poverty. Sustainability **13**(3), 1038 (2021)
17. Misra, H.: Managing poverty fad towards sustainable development: will rural E-Governance help? In: 2020 Seventh International Conference on eDemocracy & eGovernment (ICEDEG). IEEE (2020)
18. Misra, D.C., Mittal, P.K.: E-Governance and digitalization of Indian rural development. In: Proceedings of the 12th International Conference on Theory and Practice of Electronic Governance (2019)
19. Pourezzat, A.A., Nejati, M., Nejati, M.: E-government & public policy for poverty eradication and empowerment. In: Proceedings of the 5th International Conference on E-Governance (ICEG2007), Computer Society of India-Special Interest Group on E-governance, India (2007)
20. Nkwe, N.: E-Government: challenges and opportunities in Botswana. Int. J. Humanit. Soc. Sci. **2**(17), 39–48 (2012)
21. Al Mamun, A., et al.: E-Government services for sustainable development: the challenges and strategies of implementing E- Government in Bangladesh. Int. J. Comput. Sci. Inf. Technol. Res. **9**(1), 65–74 (2021)
22. https://ophi.org.uk/multidimensional-poverty-index/data-tables-do-files/1
23. Alkire, S., Kanagaratnam, U., Suppa, N.: The global Multidimensional Poverty Index (MPI): 2020 revision, OPHI MPI Methodological Note 49, Oxford Poverty and Human Development Initiative, University of Oxford (2020)
24. https://ophi.org.uk/multidimensional-poverty-index/
25. United Nations E-Government Survey 2008, 2010, 2012, 1014, 2016, 2018
26. World Bank (2018). World Development Indicators. https://datacatalog.worldbank.org/
27. Hill, R.C., Griffiths, W.E., Lim, G.C.: Principles of Econometrics. John Wiley & Sons, Hoboken (2018)
28. Gujarati, D.M.: Basic Econometrics. McGraw-hill, New York (2022)
29. Stock, J.H., Watson, M.W.: Introduction to Econometrics, 2nd ed. Pearson Addison Wesley, Boston (2007)
30. Gujarati, D.N.: Econometrics by Example, vol. 1. Palgrave Macmillan, New York (2011)
31. Achdut, N., Achdut, L.: Joint income-wealth poverty in a cross-national perspective: the role of country-level indicators. Soc. Indic. Res. **164**(1), 499–541 (2022)
32. Alamanda, A.: The effect of government expenditure on income inequality and poverty in Indonesia. INFO ARTHA **4**, 1–11 (2020)

# On Digital Twin Software and Cyber Threats

Manfred Sneps-Sneppe[1]([⊠]) [iD] and Dmitry Namiot[2] [iD]

[1] Ventspils University of Applied Sciences, Ventspils International Radioastronomy Centre,
Ventspils, Latvia
manfreds.sneps@gmail.com
[2] Faculty of Computational Mathematics and Cybernetics, Lomonosov Moscow State
University, Moscow, Russia

**Abstract.** The purpose of this article is to show, using the examples from the
Defense department (available in open sources), that software products are becoming overly complex, practically exceeding the resources of mankind, especially
in the context of cyber warfare. For illustration, we use F-35 aircraft Autonomic Logistics Information System, a story about cyber threats of software-based
weapons systems, US Army Single Security Architecture as the failure in the fight
against cyber threats. Cyber-attack on the Colonial Pipeline is a case of cyber
war. In the context of an impending cyber war and given the failures to eliminate cyber threats in many projects, each comparable to the Manhattan nuclear
project it should be recognized that their implementation is currently beyond the
competence of individual companies and even governments and is becoming a
problem of international cooperation. Therefore, an international agreement on
cyber warfare is required, for example, like the Treaty on the Non-Proliferation
of Nuclear Weapons.

**Keywords:** digital twin · software cyber threats · cyber warfare · artificial
intelligence

## 1 Introduction

A digital twin is a real-time virtual representation of a real physical system or process
(the physical twin) that serves as a digital copy of it for practical purposes such as system
modeling, integration, testing, monitoring, and maintenance. The concept and model of
the digital twin in the modern sense were first publicly presented in 2002 [1].

Honesty speaking, some kind of digital twin one can find much earlier. In the late
1940s, Stanislaw Ulam invented the Markov Chain Monte Carlo method while he was
working on nuclear weapons projects (the Manhattan Project = the atomic bomb project).
Monte Carlo methods were central to simulating the distance neutrons would travel
through various materials (as a digital twin of atomic bomb explosion). The Manhattan
Project was very small at the beginning of 1939 but eventually grew to over 130,000
people and a total cost of over $20 billion at current prices [20].

Digital twins (DT) are typically complex software products. We do not pretend to be
a general analysis of the situation, since we are dealing with extremely complex issues,

© The Author(s), under exclusive license to Springer Nature Switzerland AG 2023
Y. Koucheryavy and A. Aziz (Eds.): NEW2AN 2022, LNCS 13772, pp. 481–493, 2023.
https://doi.org/10.1007/978-3-031-30258-9_43

to which an immense amount of work is devoted (the Google database on the *Digital Twin* topic gives 921,000 links, on the *Digital Twin software* topic - 249,000 links, on the *Software Cyber threats* topic - unimaginably a lot - 446 million links).

***Industry 4.0: The Case of the F-35.*** The Digital Twin is considered an important enabler for Industry 4.0 initiatives. Modern information and communication technologies, including data storage, data processing, and wireless data transmission, can be used to digitally reflect the life cycle of the corresponding physical product in increasing levels of detail. There are nearly two million references in the Google database on request *industry 4.0 software.* As part of the reference, we will indicate yet two reviews: [3] in English and [4] in Russian.

Let's call the manufacturing industry for F-35 as a case. The Lockheed Martin F-35 Lightning II is a family of amazing stealth combat aircraft of the future (under the Joint Strike Fighter program): single-seat, single-engine, all-weather, multi-role, designed for both air supremacy and strike. The aircraft has been developed by Lockheed Martin since 2001. The first F-35B entered service in 2015. It is assumed that the aircraft will be in service until 2070.

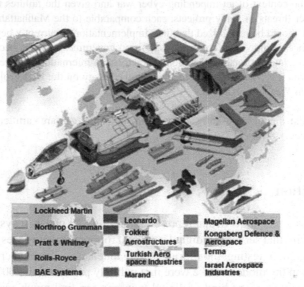

**Fig. 1.** Eight allied countries – the United Kingdom, Canada, Denmark, The Netherlands, Norway, Italy, Turkey, and Australia – are cost-sharing partners in the program with the United States in the F-35 program [7]

The F-35 approach enables Industry 4.0 in the defense domain but also draws from a much broader industrial transformation process as well. It is a whole new world for military aircraft production and sustainment [5]. The Lockheed Martin Aeronautics Common Analysis Toolset Data Manager (CATDM) is a tool that generates an aircraft's Structural Digital Twin [6]. It's a digital replica of manufacturing based on operational environments. CATDM is used to deliver F-35 structural engineering data and products in a connected, graphical fashion (Fig. 1).

Ubisense Smart Space program is a substantial part of CATDM (Fig. 2). Lockheed Martin Aeronautics has licensed Ubisense Smart Space for use in its F-35 program to improve manufacturing efficiency with a digital twin. Offering a new level of visibility and control, SmartSpace provides the foundation platform for manufacturers' Industry 4.0 strategy. By creating a real-time digital twin of the production environment, Ubisense technology links real-world activities with production control and planning systems [8].

**Fig. 2.** Ubisense SmartSpace: a digital twin of aerospace manufacturing facilities [8]

***MOSAIC Warfare as Digital Twin Case.*** Today, the best-known new technologies are artificial intelligence (AI) and autonomous systems, which are used by the Defense Department simply to speed up or automate operations already performed by humans. Instead, these technologies could form the basis of a decision-oriented approach to warfare.

The traditional basic concept of decision-oriented warfare is the so-called OODA loop = Observation-Orientation-Decision-Act loop. More recently, the U.S. military refined the idea of OODA decision cycle. The Mosaic Warfare concept has been developed within DARPA since 2017 [9]. Mosaic Warfare requires reliable and flexible communications links, as well as an extensive data sensor network. Rapid command decisions are also required. Taken together these are reasons why the OODA Loop approach is losing favour and in the modern sense of digital twin approach is replaced by the triad: sense – decide – act.

Artificial Intelligence (AI) and other algorithmic tools will be essential to achieving the MOSAIC vision. In the first drawing (Fig. 3a), a centralized commander can command and communicate with large, widely dispersed forces. It is so-called network-centric warfare. In the lower figure (Fig. 3b) – decision-centric warfare, communication is degraded and subordinate commanders must take command of the mission and perform tasks consistent with the forces they can communicate with, and their planning is facilitated by the machine-enabled control system.

The MOSAIC approach is an extremely complex design, including the latest advances: Machine learning and Deep Neural Network algorithms, which, accordingly, require the most complex software. The future will show the feasibility of such a complex approach. Will there be enough software developer resources?

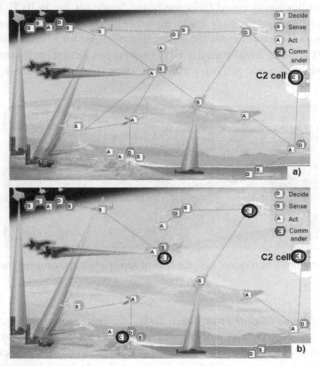

**Fig. 3.** Warfare concept evaluation (C2 = Command and Control): a) network-centric warfare -single commander, b) decision-centric warfare (MOSAIC approach) – four commanders (humans or machines) [12]

The purpose of this article is to show, using the examples from the Defense Department (available in open sources), that software products are becoming overly complex, practically exceeding the resources of mankind, especially in the context of cyber warfare. Section 2 talks about failure with ALIS – a digital twin for F-35. Section 3 is a story on cyber-threats, on the US Government Accounting Office sensational report (in 2018) that all software-based weapons systems that were tested between 2012 and 2017 have cyber vulnerabilities and can be hacked, that the F-35 aircraft remains, in all practical and legal senses, nothing more than a very expensive prototype. Section 4 explains US Army Single Security Architecture as the biggest failure in the fight against cyber threats. Section 4 explains in short that the cyber war has already begun (the Snowden revelation, cyber- attack on the Colonial Pipeline). In Conclusion (Sect. 6), we initiated an international agreement on cyber warfare is required, for example, like the Treaty on the Non-Proliferation of Nuclear Weapons.

## 2   A Tough Fight Against Cyber Threats

*AI and Trump.* Taking into an account the potential magnitude of Artificial Intelligence's impact on the whole of society, and the urgency of this emerging technology international race, President Trump signed the executive order "Maintaining American Leadership in Artificial Intelligence" on February 11, 2019 [10]. This is the so-called American AI Initiative, aimed at maintaining American leadership in competition (economic, geopolitical, etc.) with China. This was immediately followed by the release of DoD's first-ever AI strategy [11]. AI has recently become a focus of governments worldwide [12].

The Joint Artificial Intelligence Center (JAIC) is a focal point of the DoD AI Strategy. The goal is to produce prototypes of Predictive Maintenance solutions. These AI-based applications have the potential to predict more accurately maintenance needs on equipment, such as the E-3 Sentry (known as AWACS = Airborne Warning and Control System), multirole fighter aircrafts F-16 Fighting Falcon and F-35 Lightning II, as well as Bradley Fighting Vehicle.

**Fig. 4.** The F-35 testing by means of ALIS (Lockheed Martin)

*F-35 ALIS as Digital Twin.* Autonomic Logistics Information System (ALIS) is intended to provide the necessary logistics tools for the F-35 program (Fig. 4). ALIS consists of several software applications such as supply chain management, maintenance, scheduling, etc. During the flight, the aircraft transmits status data to the ALIS ground station. It could be, for example, planning the necessary technical repair upon arrival, ordering the necessary spare parts, and specialists.

In 2020, program leaders abandoned efforts to complete the $16.7 billion ALIS system, as the testing process found that there was not a single section of the F-35 program that was safe from cyberattacks. Pentagon officials have announced that ALIS will be replaced by a new cloud-based system called the Operational Data Integrated Network (ODIN) [13]. However, plans have changed. As [14] reported in April 2022, due to multiple factors that included budget cuts, lack of access to proprietary ALIS software code, and ongoing improvement to ALIS, the F-35 Joint Program Office decided to incrementally improve and modernize ALIS instead of replacing it with a new system. DOD officials renamed the system ODIN [15].

Already in 2012 [16], F-35 Program software contains 24 million lines of code. Nowadays the total amount of F-35 Program software is estimated above 80 million lines of code [34], summing up F-35 onboard software, Joint Simulation Environment, ALIS maintenance tools, and much more – Common Analysis Toolset Data Manager (CATDM) software platform for Industry 4.0 manufacturers.

***The US GAO Critics.*** In October 2018, the US Government Accounting Office (GAO) sensationally reported [17] that all software-based weapons systems that were tested between 2012 and 2017, including those created over the past ten years, have cyber vulnerabilities and can be hacked (Fig. 5). In response to the GAO rebuke, the Inspector General of the Department of Defense (DoD) in January 2019 submitted a report with disaster volumes, namely, 266 cyber vulnerabilities were discovered. Software updates and limited resources do not allow timely correction of deficiencies. For example, one test report states that only 1 out of 20 cyber vulnerabilities identified in a previous test were patched [18]. Is the situation hopeless?

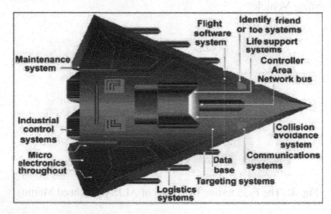

**Fig. 5.** Embedded software and information technology systems in weapon systems (represented via fictitious weapon system for classification reasons) [17]

***F-35 Combat Aircraft – How to Complete?*** Critics of the GAO [17] seem to have been referring to the Lockheed Martin F-35 Lightning II aircraft. The software, which is 8 million lines of software code built into the aircraft, controls most of its functions, including flight control, radar, communications, and weapon targeting. But a large amount of software inevitably has not only errors, but also unpatched vulnerabilities.

The vulnerabilities identified by GAO experts are perceived as a national disaster, because despite more than 20 years and approximately $62.5 billion spent on research and development alone, the F-35 aircraft remains, in all practical and legal senses, nothing more than a very expensive prototype [18]. This leads to the extremely important thought that the original concept of the Joint Strike Fighter was erroneous and went beyond practical technological reality. What to do? Starting over is unrealistic. But how to deal with cyber threats?

***On Single Security Architecture Failure.*** One of the key tasks of the U.S. Army Cyber Command is to create a Joint Information Environment (JIE) based on the Single Security Architecture (Fig. 6).

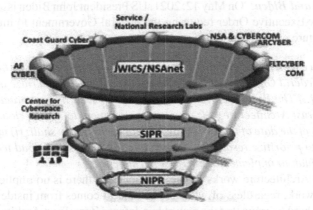

**Fig. 6.** Three layers of a unified security architecture – according to secrecy level [20] (Here: the top secrecy JWICS = Joint Worldwide Intelligence Communications System; NSAnet = National Security Agency net; SIPRNet = Secret Internet Protocol Router Network; NIPRNet = Non-classified Internet Protocol Router Network)

The main components of the JIE are the Joint Regional Security Stacks (JRSS). JRSS is an extremely sophisticated computing suite that performs the functions of a firewall, intrusion detection and prevention, enterprise management, virtual routing and forwarding, and many other network security requirements. A typical NIPR JRSS physical stack consists of 20 racks. The total scope of work includes the installation of 23 JRSS stacks on the NIPRNet service network and 25 JRSS stacks on the secret SIPRNet network (Fig. 7). By 2019, it was planned to transfer all cybersecurity programs to these stacks. But it did not work out.

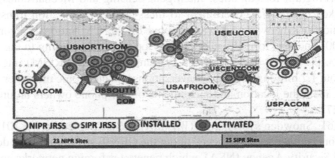

**Fig. 7.** 48 JRSS stacks in NATO forces (2019) [21]

In 2016, the GAO [22] demanded greater oversight of JRSS spending. At this time, discussions about the feasibility of the JRSS project as a whole began to appear in the press. Two years later (2018), the statement [23] that JRSS is too slow sounded like a verdict on the fate of the JRSS project. Five years later (in November 2021), the Pentagon suspended the $2 billion cybersecurity project [24]. What's next?

***Cybersecurity and Biden.*** On May 12, 2021, US President John Biden issued a National Cyber Security Executive Order requiring the Federal Government to implement Zero Trust Architecture everywhere [25]:

> *To keep pace with today's dynamic and increasingly sophisticated cyber threat environment, the Federal Government must take decisive steps to modernize its approach to cybersecurity [..] The Federal Government must adopt security best practices; advance toward Zero Trust Architecture [..]; accelerate movement to secure cloud services [..] Within 60 days of the date of this order, the head of each agency shall: (i) update existing agency plans to prioritize resources for the adoption and use of cloud technology [..]; (ii) develop a plan to implement Zero Trust Architecture.*

Zero Trust Architecture works on the principle that there is no implicit trust in any part of the network, regardless of whether the request comes from inside or outside its perimeter. It is hard to argue that the new cyber defense Zero Trust Architecture for Joint Information Environment will be any better than JRSS used. The JRSS project failed due to slow operation, which was contrary to the requirements of the network. In the Zero Trust model, the number of checks inevitably increases, and at first glance, it seems that the network will slow down even more. Will it be so?

## 3   The Cyber War has Already Begun

***The Snowden Revelation.*** Edward Snowden (born 1983) is a former CIA and US National Security Agency (NSA) employee. In June 2013, Snowden gave *The Guardian* and *The Washington Post* a large amount of classified information about the activities of the American intelligence services, including information about the PRISM project, as well as the X-Keyscore and Tempora projects [26].

PRISM (Program for Robotics, Intelligent Sensing and Mechatronics) is a set of measures taken by the US government to mass-collect information transmitted over telecommunications networks. It was adopted by the US National Security Agency (NSA) in 2007 and was formally classified as top secret. According to the *Washington Post* in 2013, the NSA's data collection systems (including PRISM) intercepted and recorded about 1.7 billion telephone conversations and electronic messages and about 5 billion facts about the location and movements of cell phone owners around the world every day [27].

Thanks to E. Snowden's revelations (*Washington Post*, September 30, 2013), the news came out about another secret project – about the GENIE spying program developed by the National Security Agency (NSA), which penetrates foreign networks and puts them under the control of the United States. By the end of 2013, at least 85 thousand strategic servers were infected. In 2014, the NSA introduced an even more powerful system, TURBINE, which manages spying implants to automatically collect intelligence and infected up to 100,000 servers.

***Cyber Attack on the Colonial Pipeline.*** This is a well-known example of a cyberattack on government infrastructure. The Colonial Pipeline is the largest pipeline system for petroleum products in the United States. The three-pipe pipeline is 8,850 km long and can transport 3 million barrels of fuel per day between Texas and New York (Fig. 8).

On May 7, 2021, the Colonial Pipeline suffered the largest cyber-attack on an oil infrastructure target in US history that affected the computerized equipment that manages the pipeline [28]. The Colonial Pipeline Company suspended all pipeline operations to contain the attack. The company paid the amount requested by the hacker group (75 bitcoins or $4.4 million) within several hours; after receiving the ransom, Colonial Pipeline Company was provided with an IT tool to restore the system. However, the tool had a very long processing time to help restore the system in time.

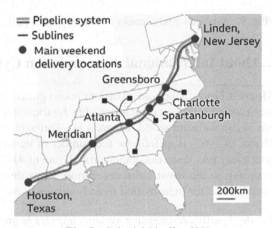

**Fig. 8.** Colonial Pipeline [28]

***Alarming Cyber Statistics for 2021.*** In 2021, the average number of cyberattacks and data breaches increased by 15.1% from the previous year [29]. In 93% of cases, an external attacker can breach an organization's network perimeter and gain access to local network resources. Cyber threats in the world are growing (Fig. 9).

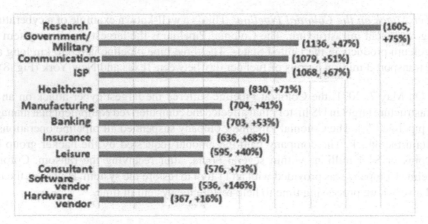

**Fig. 9.** Average weekly attacks by industry, 2021 [29]

## 4   Conclusion: About International Agreement on Cyber War

*Software Behind Moore's Law.*  In the context of continuous growth in the software volume, it is appropriate to compare the so-called Moor's law for the semiconductor industry and a similar pattern in the software world. Moore's law (referring to the observation made by Gordon Moore in 1965) is as follows: the number of transistors in integrated circuits doubles about every two years (an annual growth rate of 41%), or even faster – every 1.5 years, according to the latest estimates. Moore's law describes exponential productivity in the semiconductor industry and directly relates to the software world.

The amount of code in software-intensive systems appears is growing relentlessly. Hatton and co-authors [30] carried on the research of software world tendencies. They analyzed a reference base of over 404 million lines of open source and closed software systems to provide accurate bounds on source code growth rates. They find that software source code in systems doubles about every 42 months on average. Thus, the software industry is also growing exponentially, but somewhat more slowly [31], lagging behind Moore's Law, if you do not take into an account that integrated circuits are also a complex software product.

The demand for cloud services and innovative technologies such as blockchain, hybrid architecture, artificial intelligence, and machine learning is rising [32].

*Next Gen Aircraft – is it Possible?*  The Air Force's newly revealed fighter-jet prototype was designed with immersive simulations and other new digital tools that herald a new era for the creation and production of the U.S. military's weapons [33]. Having the 'eplane' will allow us to do much faster through design, much faster through assembly, get out to test faster These digital threads that are pulled through the life cycle of the program, appear to accelerate everything. For the NGAD, the Air Force used data from the F-35 Joint Strike Fighter to develop a virtual prototype, and then a physical, flying aircraft.

As depicted in Fig. 10, the source lines of code (SLOC) for each successive fighter aircraft have increased by an order of magnitude as ever more functionality is delivered via software [34]. The U.S. Air Force's F-35 fighter jet has more than 8 million SLOC and F-35 program in sum – 80 million SLOC. If the NGAD will require 50 to 100 million SLOC to operate basic aircraft systems, then the software to simulate every nut, bolt, actuator, and avionics box. That means 500 million to 1 billion SLOC. Assuming a linear relationship between time and code size, an 800 million SLOC project would take 2000 years to generate at the F-35 rate. Is it possible?

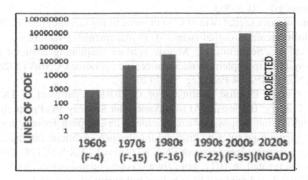

**Fig. 10.** Estimated SLOC in Various Aircraft [34]

It is quite possible that during the construction of NGAD it will be possible to avoid miscalculations with the F-35, but hardly ten times. And if today the F-35 is evaluated only as a prototype after 20 years of work, then what can be soothing about NGAD? An analysis of the F-35 experience suggests: has humanity reached the limits of the impossible? If we consider cyber threats, then the situation is extremely unfortunate – even in the whole world.

In summary, in the context of an impending cyber war and given the failures to eliminate cyber threats in such major projects as F-35 and Joint Regional Security Stacks, each comparable to the Manhattan nuclear project, as well as in many other projects in safety- and security-critical areas, it should be recognized that their implementation is currently beyond the competence of individual companies and even governments and is becoming a problem of international cooperation. Therefore, an international agreement on cyber warfare is required, for example, like the Treaty on the Non-Proliferation of Nuclear Weapons.

# References

1. Grieves, M.W.: Virtually intelligent product systems: digital and physical twins. In: Flumerfelt, S., Schwartz, K.G., Mavris, D., Briceno, S. (eds.) Complex Systems Engineering: Theory and Practice, pp. 175–200. American Institute of Aeronautics and Astronautics, Inc., Reston, VA (2019)
2. Johnston, L., Williamson, S.H.: What was the U.S. GDP then? In: MeasuringWorth (2022)

3. Semeraro, C., et al.: Digital twin paradigm: a systematic literature review. Comput. Ind. **130** 103469 (2021). https://doi.org/10.1016/j.compind.2021.103469

4. Kurganova, N., et al.: Digital twins' introduction as one of the major directions of industrial digitalization. Int. J. Open Inf. Technol. **7**(5), 105–115 (2019)

5. Laird, R.: Industry 4.0: the case of the F-35 (2018). https://sldinfo.com/2018/11/industry-4-0-the-case-of-the-f-35/

6. Delivering digitally for F-35 force management solutions (2021). https://www.lockheedm artin.com/f35/news-and-features/delivering-digitally-for-f35-force-management-solution. html

7. F-35 Joint Strike Fighter (JSF) program. Congressional research service (2022). https://crs reports.congress.gov. RL30563

8. IIoT platform creates a digital twin of F-35 manufacturing facilities (2017). https://www.sme. org/iiot-platform-creates-a-digital-twin-of-f-35-manufacturing-facilities

9. Clark, B., Patt, D., Schramm, H.: Mosaic warfare. Exploiting artificial intelligence and autonomous systems to implement decision-centric operations. CSBA (2020)

10. Exec. Order No. 13,859, 84 Fed. Reg. 3967 (2019)

11. U.S. Department of Defense. Summary of the 2018 Department of Defense. Artificial Intelligence Strategy: Harnessing AI to Advance Our Security and Prosperity (2019)

12. European Commission: proposal for a regulation of the European parliament and of the council laying down harmonised rules on artificial intelligence (Artificial Intelligence Act) (2021). https://eur-lex.europa.eu/legal-content/EN/TXT/?uri=CELEX:52021PC0206

13. F-35 program stagnated in 2021. https://www.pogo.org/analysis/2022/03/f-35-program-sta gnated-in-2021-but-dod-testing-office-hiding-full-extent-of-problem/

14. GAO-22–105995. F-35 sustainment DOD. Faces several uncertainties and has not met key objectives (2022)

15. Grazier, D.: F-35 Program stagnated in 2021 but DOD testing office hiding full extent of problem. In: Analysis (2022). https://www.pogo.org/analysis/2022/03/f-35-program-stagna ted-in-2021-but-dod-testing-office-hiding-full-extent-of-problem

16. Charette, R.N.: F-35 Program continues to struggle with software. IEEE Spectr. **19** (2012)

17. GAO-19-128. Weapon systems cybersecurity. DOD just beginning to grapple with scale of vulnerabilities, report to the committee on armed services, U.S. Senate, US GAO (2018)

18. Grazier, D.: What should we do about a generation of weapons vulnerable to cyberattacks? An obvious solution being ignored (2019). https://www.pogo.org/analysis/2019/01/what-sho uld-we-do-about-a%20generation-of-weapons-vulnerable-to-cyberattacks/

19. Thompson, M.: The U.S. Navy's Titanium "Tin Can", in Analysis (2019). https://www.pogo. org/analysis/2019/01/the-u-s-navys-titanium-tin-can

20. Cyber situational awareness - big data solution. https://docplayer.net/2357634-Cyber-situat ional-awareness-big-data-solution.html/

21. JRSS Deployments. https://c.ymcdn.com/sites/alamoace.siteym.com/resource/resmgr/ 2017_ace/2017_speakers/2017_AACE_Keynote_Presentations/doc_keynote_Yee.pdf/

22. GAO-16-593. Joint information environment: DOD needs to strengthen governance and management (2016)

23. Marks, J.: The pentagon has a big plan to solve identity verification in two years. In: Nextgov (2018). https://www.defenseone.com/technology/2018/05/pentagon-has-big-plan-solve-identity-verification-two-years/148280/

24. Pomerleau, M.: The pentagon is moving away from the joint regional security stacks (2021). https://www.c4isrnet.com/it-networks/2021/11/01/the-pentagon-is-moving-away-from-the-joint-regional-security-stacks/

25. Executive order on improving the nation's cybersecurity. https://www.whitehouse.gov/bri efing-room/presidential-actions/2021/05/12/executive-order-on-improving-the-nations-cyb ersecurity/

26. Edward snowden. https://en.wikipedia.org/wiki/Edward_Snowden#Revelations
27. Prism. https://en.wikipedia.org/wiki/PRISM#Responses_to_disclosures
28. Colonial pipeline ransomware attack. https://en.wikipedia.org/wiki/Colonial_Pipeline_ransomware_attack
29. Brooks, C.: Alarming cyber statistics for mid-year 2022, 3 Jun 2022. https://www.forbes.com/sites/chuckbrooks/2022/06/03/alarming-cyber-statistics-for-mid-year-2022-that-you-need-to-know/?sh=51f25a7b7864
30. Hatton, L., Spinellis, D., van Genuchten, M.: The long-term growth rate of evolving software: empirical results and implications. J. Software Evol. Process. **29**(5) (2017). https://doi.org/10.1002/smr.1847
31. Wester, R., Koster, J.: The software behind Moore's Law. IEEE Software, **32**(2) 37–40, (2015). https://doi.org/10.1109/MS.2015.53
32. Business software and services market size, share & trends analysis report, 2022–2030. https://www.grandviewresearch.com/industry-analysis/business-software-services-market
33. Tucker, P.: The virtual tools that built the air force's new fighter. In: Prototype (2020). https://www.defenseone.com/technology/2020/09/virtual-tools-built-air-forces-new-fighter-prototype/168505/
34. West, T.D., Blackburn, M.: Is digital thread/digital twin affordable? A systemic assessment of the cost of DoD's latest manhattan project. Procedia Comput. Sci. **114**, 47–56 (2017). https://doi.org/10.1016/j.procs.2017.09.003

# Local Services Based on Non-standard Wi-Fi Direct Usage Model

Dmitry Namiot[1]([✉]) [iD], Manfred Sneps-Sneppe[2] [iD], and Vladimir Sukhomlin[1] [iD]

[1] Faculty of Computational Mathematics and Cybernetics, Lomonosov Moscow State University, Moscow, Russia
dnamiot@cs.msu.ru

[2] Ventspils International Radioastronomy Centre, Ventspils University of Applied Sciences, Ventspils, Latvia

**Abstract.** This article discusses a new model for building applied mobile services that use location information and operate in a certain limited spatial area. As a basis for building such applications, a new interpretation of the standard features of Wi-Fi Direct is used. The Wi-Fi Direct specification, in addition to defining the form of device connection, also introduces the concept of a service, when one device offers some service functions to another within the framework of a Wi-Fi Direct connection. Each device can both represent several services and send out search requests for other services. Based on the network proximity architecture, where connections are not used, and wireless network advertising tools are used to convey user information, Wi-Fi Direct services can be considered as key-value databases that exist on mobile devices and can be searched by keys in some local areas. It is these storages that underlie the two models of application services presented in the article that use the spatial proximity of mobile devices: direct messaging between devices without centralized control and the hyper-local Internet model.

**Keywords:** location-based services · on-demand messaging · hyper-local Internet · Wi-Fi Direct

## 1 Introduction

In this article, we describe a new model for applied mobile services based on the non-standard use of Wi-Fi Direct capabilities [1]. In this case, we are talking about a different (not used by anyone before) model of use. The entire architecture is based on existing (standard) wireless network facilities, there are no protocol extensions (modifications) at all. We are talking about a pure software solution (application layer in terms of the OSI model).

We consider a class of services for mobile users using location information. This is perhaps one of the most widely used classes. This includes, of course, not only obtaining some information based on location (such as classical geo-information services), but also, for example, performing any actions upon entering a certain geographical area, upon leaving it (so-called geo-grids), allowing (prohibiting) any actions, changing the

Y. Koucheryavy and A. Aziz (Eds.): NEW2AN 2022, LNCS 13772, pp. 494–505, 2023.
https://doi.org/10.1007/978-3-031-30258-9_44

interface, etc. In fact, all mobile apps are (or at least should be) context-sensitive [2], and location is always part of the context [3]. In fact, this ensures the universality of services that use location information.

At the same time, it should be noted that mobile services that use location information are now rather components of other applications (in the end, all mobile applications). It all started with special mobile applications (for example, Foursquare), but in the future, the use of location information became an option in other systems. To a large extent, this was facilitated by the fact that location information on mobile devices began to be obtained simply from a technical and software point of view.

The history of mobile services using location information goes back just over 20 years. During this time, the ways of obtaining such information on mobile devices have also changed. Initially, such information could only be obtained from the telecommunications operator serving the mobile device. Further, independent databases appeared with geo-information about the connected structure of operators, and mashups became possible, which, based on data about the base stations used, could receive coordinates. Then smartphones spread rapidly, and the use of GPS became the main way to obtain coordinates.

At the programmatic level, the W3C standardized access to obtaining geo-coordinates from JavaScript, which contributed to the portability of web applications. The W3C Geolocation API looks simple [4]. At the web page load level, you can define your own callback for loading the page. For example,

```
<body onload="getLocation()">
```

And the getLocation function itself uses the navigator.geolocation object, which, in turn, is passed two callback functions that are called upon successful and unsuccessful determination of coordinates.

All this made the determination of coordinates simple and portable, which predetermined the wide distribution of such services. And the demand for them was determined by the fact that, as indicated above, location is always part of the context. Accordingly, for almost all mobile applications, their functionality (whatever that means) depends on the location. Note that the above programming model is a benchmark that alternative solutions for determining (or estimating) location can follow.

Despite the ease of use of GPS, the shortcomings of this approach are well known. These are, of course, poor indoor performance, high power consumption, cold start, and low accuracy in commercial applications. Of the latest problems, you can add more GPS spoofing [5]. The last problem, in fact, can completely eliminate the use of GPS in commercial services.

Classic services using location information almost always exclude dynamics and mobility. The lack of support for dynamic services (a service using a location that is provided over time or depending on some other external conditions) is associated with a rather old form of describing this very location in the form of a static geo-grid. This results in conditions being validated only at the application layer, not the data layer. The lack of mobility (the location to which the service moves) is associated, among other things, with the difficulties of using GPS - there are practical limitations on the frequency of obtaining such information.

All this leads to the fact that alternative methods of determining the location have always aroused interest. We can mention, for example, inertial navigation or assisted GPS technologies [6]. One of the approaches used in this paper is the network spatial proximity model [7]. Working with geo-coordinates is replaced here by calculating the spatial proximity of wireless network nodes. More specifically, we show how the standard features of Wi-Fi Direct can be used to develop new classes of mobile services that use the proximity of mobile devices.

The remainder of the article is structured as follows. In Sect. 2, we describe the model of spatial network proximity in the level of detail necessary for further consideration. Section 3 describes the characteristics of Wi-Fi Direct, also in such detail as is necessary for further consideration. Sections 4 and 5 are devoted to new service models. And Sect. 6 presents the conclusion.

## 2   On the Spatial Network Proximity Model

The network spatial proximity model used in this paper defines a new software architecture for services that use location information. In its classical form, services that use location information follow a typical client-server architecture: the client determines its own location and sends its coordinates to the server. It can be some application server or directly some kind of API for a geo-database (for example, a relational database with a geo-extension), the fundamental picture does not change. Having received such a request, the service provider selects the content for the client. This implicitly assumes that client-side content is associated with geo-coordinates. In its most general form, the content is tied to some geo-grid, the coordinates received from the client are used to calculate the hit in this geo-grid (calculate the distance to the boundaries of this geo-grid).

A typical model is shown in the figure below (Fig. 1).

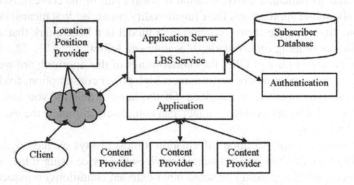

**Fig. 1.** Classic architecture of services using location information [8]

Such a scheme was inherited from geo-information systems and was not revised in any way. However, the disadvantages of this approach are obvious. Clients are mobile devices, and it will not work to describe a mobile service in this way - the coordinates of the geo-grid are static. This leads to the fact that in reality mobile (mobile) services are simply not considered when talking about services using location information. Location Position Provider in modern conditions is exclusively GPS, the problems of using which are known. As mentioned above, the main problems include poor indoor performance, high power consumption, slow speed (cold start), poor commercial accuracy, and GPS spoofing.

The idea of an alternative model of network spatial proximity is based on the fact that most of the services that use location information are, in fact, data on objects and operations in the vicinity of the requester. In this case, the coordinates transmitted by the client are used only to calculate the distance and compare it with some given limit. For example, for a formal description of a service in GeoSPARQL, it looks like this:

In the base data fetch statements

```
SELECT  ?what
WHERE {
?what geo:hasGeometry ?geom .

?geom geof:within (POINT | POLYGON | BOX | Literal)
}
```

The within primitive is actually the geof:within geof:nearby spatial proximity calculation function;

```
? x geo : nearby ? y :- x ? geom? g1
        y? geom? g2
        filter(distance(?g1, ?g2)<200)
```

in this case, data collection at a distance of up to 200 m.

For a geo-point (pair of coordinates), you can use the nearby function, for a polygon - a logical combination (AND OR) of the nearby functions.

Accordingly, the idea of an alternative approach is to completely abandon the work with coordinates and directly calculate the spatial proximity. This, of course, leads to the fact that the requested data must also be described in such a way that this spatial proximity can be calculated. The network spatial proximity model uses spatial proximity to a node or nodes of a wireless network(s). Accordingly, services (services) are provided through existing or specially created nodes of wireless networks. The area of availability (visibility) of the wireless network signal determines the spatial proximity [9]. And the intersection of the signal availability areas allows you to determine the geo-grid (Fig. 2).

Since geo-coordinates are not used, both existing wireless network nodes (all mobile devices, office buildings, cars, vehicles, vending machines, etc.) and especially (dynamically) created for fixing tasks can act as wireless network nodes proximity. For example, a Bluetooth point programmatically created on a mobile phone, the true coordinates of which are unknown. Accordingly, services can be provided in any place where at least one mobile device is present. Services thus defined will be both dynamic (the wireless

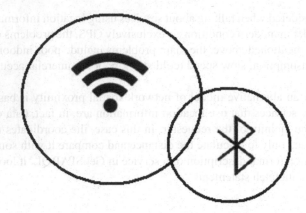

**Fig. 2.** Geo-grid as an intersection of signal availability areas.

node can turn on and off) and mobile (the defining wireless nodes themselves can move so that the service will be available close to their current location).

There are no connections between devices in this form, which is important for cyber-security. The client does not send its coordinates to the service provider, which means that the client cannot be tracked [10].

And the most important provision is that the availability of a wireless network signal is determined by software. That is, we get a classical cyber-physical system. From a programmatic point of view, determining the availability of a wireless network node is getting the identification information it distributes (it can be called differently, but is always present). This information can be customized and used to actually convey user-defined information. From a technical point of view, this would mean that wireless network vehicles would be used at the application layer.

The model of network spatial proximity has been developed in the works of the author since 2010 [11, 12]. It can be noted that all the put forward provisions underlying this model have been independently confirmed in the works of other companies. So in 2013, Apple practically confirmed the possibility of using a limited area of propagation of wireless network signals (BLE) to determine spatial proximity [13]. In 2017, the Bluetooth SIG released the Bluetooth Mesh specification, which described the transfer of data between Bluetooth nodes without establishing a connection, using special advertising packages. This practice has been recognized as a success, and in Bluetooth 5 the size of advertising packets will be increased in order to transmit multimedia data without establishing a connection [14]. And finally, the main confirmation came in April 2020, when Apple and Google released the Covid tracker specification [15]. Two mobile devices A and B exchange unique identifiers when they are up to 1.5 m apart. The presence of a device (in fact, the availability of a service for obtaining information about it) is implemented using the dynamic creation of a BLE wireless node.

The Wi-Fi Direct usage models described below are examples of how the network proximity model can be used. There is no work with geo-coordinates in any form, the location is estimated by the availability of wireless network signals, and advertising (representative) information of wireless nodes is customized and used to transmit user information. And there are no connections between client devices.

## 3  Wi-Fi Direct

Wi-Fi Direct is currently supported on all Android phones. On IoS, this is available under the name AirPlay or AirDrop. Many Smart TV devices support Wi-Fi Direct. At the same time, it should be noted that cyber security requirements and concerns have changed the attitude towards P2P connections. This, of course, does not only apply to Wi-Fi Direct. At the moment, there are probably no public services that are based on the direct connection of mobile devices. This is described in any cybersecurity guide as connecting to an unknown device and carries risks for both parties. P2P services, to date, have remained, perhaps, only as an internal component of other services. For example, as part of the implementation of Skype. Or, what, in our opinion, is the main application of P2P for the present and the near future - data offloading for telecom [16]. With regard to Wi-Fi Direct, reports of problems (possible problems) with security appeared simultaneously with the introduction of this technology [17]. This determines the fact that the technology, despite the available support in modern devices, is practically not used by end-users. It can also be noted that a similar, but slightly more recent Wi-Fi Aware technology [18] is already rather sparingly represented on mobile devices precisely because of low demand.

In the network spatial proximity architecture described above, connections between devices are not used (precisely because of cybersecurity problems) and, in such conditions, the use of Wi-Fi Direct in the models described in Sect. 2 is no different from the use of "big" Wi-Fi, for example. But the Wi-Fi Direct specification describes one interesting feature called services. Services in Wi-Fi Direct terminology are the capabilities of one device to provide some services to other devices (applications) after a connection has been made [19].

Service discovery, in the general sense, is a procedure that allows one device to determine (describe) the services it provides, and other devices to determine the presence of these services before making a connection. The last point is very important, because it is this fact that is used in this paper. Making a connection in the case of Wi-Fi Direct, in today's conditions, as indicated above, is a problem in terms of cybersecurity.

The service search procedure in this formulation is standard for wireless networks. If one of the devices is looking for another device that provides a specific service, then it sends a service request. Recipients of such a request send a return message with information about the service. The devices can then initiate a connection to use the service.

At the same time, it is obvious that the devices (search for the service and providing the service) must be located at a distance from each other, which is supported by the wireless network. In our case, this is Wi-Fi distance. That is, the search for a service (and the subsequent provision of a service) is a service that, by definition, operates in a limited spatial area, determined by the signal propagation area in a wireless network. Accordingly, both of these actions are a service using location information. Just like in the model of network spatial proximity presented above, the determining factor here is not the coordinates, but the current location of the device providing the service. You can find and receive a service only in the immediate spatial proximity of the device that provides it.

From this follows the basic idea of using Wi-Fi Direct services within the network spatial proximity model described above. It is necessary to break the service search chain - receiving a response (information) - connecting to the device and use only the service search and, accordingly, the information returned during the search.

The Service Discovery protocol in Wi-Fi Direct uses the Generic Advertisement Service (GAS) protocol/frame exchange. It is an IEEE 802.11u service that provides over-the-air transportation for frames of higher-layer advertisements between Wi-Fi stations. The idea behind 802.11u is to give the user more information about the services that will be available after the connection before connecting.

ANQP (Access Network Query Protocol) is used for queries. Technically, there are actually other features like Media Independent Handover (MIH) Information Service (802.21), MIH Command and Event Services Capability Discovery, and Emergency Alert System (EAS - supports emergency alerts from external networks), but they are not being used in this work.

Schematically, the advertising processing process is shown in the Fig. 3 below.

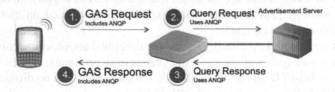

**Fig. 3.** Service advertising [20]

Having received a request, the station (the polled node) can either form a response directly or forward it to some external ad server. In our case, the response will be generated directly on the polled node. The GAS request and the GAS response consist of ANQP frames.

GAS protocol enables different higher layer service advertisement protocol types such as Bonjour (DNS SRV or RFC 2782 http://www.dns-sd.org/ServiceTypes.html), UPnP (Universal Plug and Play Forum http://www.upnp.org), and Web Services Dynamic Discovery (WS-Discovery) [21].

The provided (requested) services must be described in some way. The Wi-Fi Direct specification proposes to use an abstract representation in the form of a hash table (a database with a key-value model), where the keys are the names of characteristics (properties), and the values, respectively, are the values of these properties. Naturally, services can be created dynamically in this way. Key-value pairs appear in service lookup requests [22].

For the practical use of Wi-Fi Direct services, it was supposed to define specific profiles, where the keys would have specific values (for example, they would define print settings, etc.). For our consideration, it is the presence of an abstract representation that is interesting.

It turns out that in the absence of connections, grouping, and other networking capabilities, we can treat Wi-Fi Direct services simply as local databases with a key-value model on devices with a key lookup function defined for them. And the interpretation of keys (interpretation of their values) will determine the application service.

The second point that comes from the functionality of Wi-Fi Direct services is that we can use key lookup as a messaging mechanism. The initial (search) request is a broadcast message, and the response to it is a description of the appropriate service. And this last description can be dynamically updated on the mobile device that stores this description. Thus, the request-response search cycle will convey dynamic information that will be determined by mobile application users or even mobile applications themselves.

## 4   On Demand Messaging

The first service we want to introduce in this article is on-the-fly messaging.

The architecture of this service is as follows. Registering a messaging participant is registering the Wi-Fi Direct service directly on the participant's mobile phone. Such registration can be performed both in a mobile application through some user interface (UI), and programmatically.

The service information includes at least the following keys:

UserName - selected username

Topic – a topic for messages

Messages - list of sent messages

Authorization in the system is the announcement of the service. The service (in fact, a record about the user) becomes available for search.

Preparing a message is adding a message to the list of messages. All messages are stored directly on the author's mobile device. They become available to other members when those members find the author's service record. Thus, the author can edit his posts (for example, limit their lifetime, etc.).

Reception of messages is a search for services (in fact, it is a search for other participants) either by the name of the author (UserName key, which corresponds to one-to-one messaging) or by topic (Topic key, which corresponds to many-to-one exchange). This is illustrated in the Fig. 4.

Searching for a service by a key allows you to get the values of other keys of the found service record. User (device) A searches for a service by the name of user B and gets the opportunity to read the value of the Messages key from the found service (from user B, which is represented as a Wi-Fi Direct service). This is the main idea. There are no connections between devices or devices with a dedicated service (cloud application).

This specific open source implementation is described in the 2022 master's thesis by E. Stepanova (supervisor - Dmitry Namiot) - Messaging between mobile devices based on Wi-Fi Direct [22].

The form in the user interface is, in fact, a form for setting the keys (characteristics) of the Wi-Fi Direct service, which is created programmatically.

Previous attempts to implement this class of services were based on Bluetooth Low Energy, but it was Wi-Fi Direct services that turned out to be the most convenient

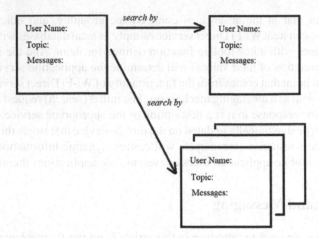

**Fig. 4.** Message exchange [23]

environment, providing a simple implementation of the above architecture. The source code for the implementation is available [24].

In this form, the messaging service does not require any server support, can work without telecommunications operators at all, does not require any centralized registration from participants, allows arbitrary entry and exit of participants, service records of exchange participants and their messages are stored on their own mobile devices.

If any enterprise application requires member restriction, then this can easily be added already at the application level, for example, considering only a limited set of device addresses.

Note that in the form described, a local (localized) messaging service can be easily added to arbitrary mobile applications. In our opinion, this is the most affordable way to organize an embedded messaging service. Note also that there is no location check in the spirit of the W3C code snippet described above. It is, in fact, a cyber-physical system. Outside a certain coverage area (Wi-Fi distance), the signal is physically unavailable. These are not any software checks, but the physical absence of a service.

## 5   On Hyper-local Internet

The next scheme for using Wi-Fi Direct services, which we present in this paper, is the organization of a hyperlocal Internet. The term hyper-local is commonly understood as a service that operates in a limited area. In this case, under the term hyper-local Internet, we mean a collection of web resources specially designated (dedicated) for access in the hyper-local area. In this case, access to this collection will be carried out using a web browser.

The specified web resources can be ordinary web links, for which some special significance is thus indicated in the local context. For example, these may be local shops or service centers. This works like markup for existing web resources [25].

An alternative solution is to directly present content that only exists locally. In this case, the Internet is really limited in space. One of the distinguishing features of such a solution is its security. Content is not really (physically) available outside some spatially limited area (Wi-Fi distance). In other words, in order to access the data, you must be physically present at the place where the data is provided.

The Wi-Fi Direct service on a specific device is just some web content. The service information includes at least the following keys: Name - the name of the resource, Content – the content of the resource.

For content that is directly presented on the device, the resource name is an analogue to DNS. In the local area, there is no need for hierarchical schemes, and resource names can directly correspond to search queries: cafe, taxi, etc. And for content creation, we suggested using HyperCat, an open source search engine for IoT [26]. In the HyperCat format, you can represent both a link to an existing web resource (URL) and the actual data in JSON format.

The search request (search by resource name) in this case is analogous to an HTTP GET request. In general, several nodes may return some resources in response to a search query. Their display is a complete analogue of the formation of a dynamic web page on the "classical" Internet.

And to display data on such a hyper-local Internet, you can use the so-called physical browser. This system was proposed precisely so that information about the network environment (the so-called network fingerprint) could be used on a web page.

Referring to the W3C example above, the physical browser implements an analogue of the *navigator.geolocation.getCurrentPosition()* function, which returns a visible list of wireless nodes instead of coordinates. The meaning of such an implementation is, for example, that using JavaScript code on the web page of the shopping center, you can determine where the mobile device on which this web page (website) is open is located: directly in the shopping center or somewhere outside its walls. According to the model of network spatial proximity presented above, the fact of location confirmation can be the visibility of local wireless networks (in the given example, the Wi-Fi network of a shopping complex, for example). The physical browser just allows you to access information about the network environment directly from JavaScript.

The browser is implemented as a webview-application on the Android platform. The browser as a mobile application has access to information about the network environment and can insert this data (as a JSON array) into the pages being viewed, emulating the W3C Location API above. It is this approach that can be used to receive content from Wi-Fi Direct nodes (in fact, receive data in the form of a response to a search query) and form a dynamic web page that users will view in a familiar web browser interface. There are several implementations of such a system [27, 28]. The last work presents the results of the master's thesis 2022 by A. Slabouzova (supervisor - Dmitry Namiot); the source code of the implementation is available [29].

## 6   Conclusion

The paper describes a new model for building applied mobile services that use location information, based on the non-standard use of the basic capabilities of the Wi-Fi Direct specification. Given the prevalence of this specification, we can say that such a model (mobile application architecture) is available on all modern Android devices. The model proposes to use the services defined in the Wi-Fi Direct specification as local databases with their own transport mechanism. Technically, this means using the transport mechanisms of a wireless network to develop applications (that is, as an application layer protocol). The main advantages of the proposed model include the use of only standard (existing) wireless network capabilities, the ability to work without the support of telecommunications operators, and the absence of connections between devices.

The paper considers two classes of possible applications - on-the-fly messaging and hyper-local Internet. A common feature of both classes of services is the ability to work without the support of telecommunications operators and without the presence of a server (cloud) infrastructure. Both service classes are both dynamic and mobile. In general, the proposed model is not limited to these applications. What more general applications can be called, for example, content-addressable networks (CAN), in-network computing, distributed computing, and edge models.

This research has been supported by the Interdisciplinary Scientific and Educational School of Moscow University «Brain, Cognitive Systems, Artificial Intelligence».

# References

1. Wi-Fi Direct. https://devopedia.org/wi-fi-direct. Accessed June 2022
2. Schilit, B., Adams, N., Want, R.: Context-aware computing applications. In: 1994 First Workshop on Mobile Computing Systems and Applications. IEEE (1994)
3. Hazas, M., Scott, J., Krumm, J.: Location-aware computing comes of age. Computer 37(2), 95–97 (2004)
4. Popescu, A.: Geolocation API specification. World Wide Web Consortium, Candidate Recommendation CR-geolocation-API-20100907 (2010)
5. Jafarnia-Jahromi, A., et al.: GPS vulnerability to spoofing threats and a review of antispoofing techniques. Int. J. Navig. Observ. 2012 (2012)
6. Zandbergen, P.A.: Accuracy of iPhone locations: a comparison of assisted GPS, WiFi and cellular positioning. Trans. GIS 13, 5–25 (2009)
7. Namiot, D., Sneps-Sneppe, M.: Geofence and network proximity. In: Balandin, S., Andreev, S., Koucheryavy, Y. (eds.) ruSMART NEW2AN 2013 2013. LNCS, vol. 8121, pp. 117–127. Springer, Heidelberg (2013). https://doi.org/10.1007/978-3-642-40316-3_11
8. Pontikakos, C., et al.: Location-based services: a framework for an architecture design. Neural Parallel Sci. Comput. 14(2/3), 273 (2006)
9. Namiot, D.: Network spatial proximity between mobile devices. Int. J. Open Inf. Technol. 9(1), 80–85 (2021). (in Russian)
10. Namiot, D., Sneps-Sneppe, M.: On the new architecture of location-based services. In: 2021 29th Conference of Open Innovations Association (FRUCT). IEEE (2021)
11. Namiot, D.: Geo messages. In: International Congress on Ultra Modern Telecommunications and Control Systems. IEEE (2010)
12. Namiot, D., Schneps-Schneppe, M.: About location-aware mobile messages: expert system based on wifi spots. In: 2011 Fifth International Conference on Next Generation Mobile Applications, Services and Technologies. IEEE (2011)
13. Gast, M.S.: Building Applications with IBeacon: Proximity and Location Services with Bluetooth Low Energy. O'Reilly Media, Inc. (2014)
14. Baert, M., et al.: The Bluetooth mesh standard: An overview and experimental evaluation. Sensors 18(8), 2409 (2018)

15. Gvili, Y.: Security analysis of the COVID-19 contact tracing specifications by Apple Inc. and Google Inc. Cryptology ePrint Archive (2020)
16. Rebecchi, F., et al.: Data offloading techniques in cellular networks: a survey. IEEE Commun. Surv. Tutor. **17**(2), 580–603 (2014)
17. Yoon, S., et al.: Security analysis of vulnerable Wi-Fi Direct. In: 2012 8th International Conference on Computing and Networking Technology (INC, ICCIS and ICMIC). IEEE (2012)
18. Wi-Fi aware. https://www.wi-fi.org/discover-wi-fi/wi-fi-aware. Accessed June 2022
19. Khan, M.A., et al.: Wi-Fi direct research-current status and future perspectives. J. Netw. Comput. Appl. **93**, 245–258 (2017)
20. How Interworking Works: A Detailed Look at 802.11u and Hotspot 2.0 Mechanisms. https://www.commscope.com/globalassets/digizuite/1528-1358-wp-how-interworking-works.pdf. Accessed June 2022
21. Roe, B., Weast, J., Yarmosh, Y.: Web services dynamic discovery (ws-discovery). Technical report, Microsoft (2005)
22. Use Wi-Fi Direct (P2P) for service discovery. https://developer.android.com/training/connect-devices-wirelessly/nsd-wifi-direct. Accessed June 2022
23. Stepanova, E.V.: Bluetooth Mesh in the IoT. Int. J. Open Inf. Technol. **10**(2), 36–41 (2022). (in Russian)
24. Wi-Fi Adviser. https://github.com/EvaStt/WifiAdviser. Accessed June 2022
25. Namiot, D., Sukhomlin, V.: Network proximity as a base for a new hyper-local Internet. Int. J. Open Inf. Technol. **10**(4), 99–103 (2022)
26. Namiot, D., Sneps-Sneppe, M.: On search services for internet of things. In: Vishnevskiy, V., Samouylov, K., Kozyrev, D. (eds.) DCCN 2017. CCIS, vol. 700, pp. 174–185. Springer, Cham (2017). https://doi.org/10.1007/978-3-319-66836-9_15
27. Namiot, D., Sneps-Sneppe, M.: On physical web browser. In: 2016 18th Conference of Open Innovations Association and Seminar on Information Security and Protection of Information Technology (FRUCT-ISPIT). IEEE (2016)
28. Slabouzova, A., Namiot, D.: Physical browser: concept and overview of existing API solutions. Int. J. Open Inf. Technol. **9**(11), 52–59 (2021). (in Russian)
29. Physical Browser. https://github.com/Anna-Sl/physical-browser-advanced.Accessed June 2022

# Compatibility Analysis Between 5G NR and Ultra-Wideband Devices in the 6425–7125 MHz Frequency Band

Alexander Pastukh[1]($\boxtimes$), Valeriy Tikhvinskiy[1,2], and Evgeniy Devyatkin[1]

[1] Radio Research and Development Institute, Moscow, Russia
apastukh@lenta.ru

[2] International Information Technologies University (IITU), Almaty, Kazakhstan

**Abstract.** This work presents studies of electromagnetic compatibility between fifth-generation new radio technologies (5G NR) and ultra-wide bandwidth technologies (UWB) operating in the frequency band 6425–7125 MHz. The study evaluates aggregate interference from UWB devices to 5G NR indoor small cells networks for the indoor-indoor scenario. Based on the simulation studies throughput loss of 5G NR downlink and uplink was calculated for different UWB activity factors and a different number of active UWB transmitters acting as interfering links in simulations.

**Keywords:** IMT-2020 · UWB · 5G NR · EMC · Spectrum management · Monte Carlo simulation · Electromagnetic compatibility · Sharing study

## 1 Introduction

Rolling out 5G NR networks expands innovation level of the world. To sustain that innovation growth, it is vitally important to have enough spectrum resources which are necessary to establish sufficient capacity levels for affordable connectivity. Lack of spectrum would require costly and sometimes economically non-viable network densification. The 6 GHz frequency range offers both capacity and coverage therefore, harmonization of the 6 GHz spectrum for IMT is imperative to sustain future capacity needs for affordable connectivity. Reserving the spectrum in the 6425–7125 MHz frequency range is essential to deliver the full potential of 5G-NR and its evolution in the future (i.e. 5G+ and 6G) [1]. The 6 GHz band is also used on a non-licensed basis by the low power ultra-wide bandwidth (UWB) devices. UWB technologies emerged at the beginning of the 2000s, yet at that time they were not that successful. However, 10 years later the sales of wireless consumer devices sky-rocketed, and today UWB has experienced a renaissance becoming very successful on the market, new use cases of UWB emerge including indoor navigation, smart home devices, social networks peer to peer location, retail, secure transactions, car access, location of valuables and many other use cases. According to UWB Alliance by 2022 more than 500 million UWB devices will be in circulation and by 2025 the rates will exceed 1 billion devices. UWB smartphone accessories will drive a 1:1 chip ratio with smartphones by the end of 2025 [2].

Y. Koucheryavy and A. Aziz (Eds.): NEW2AN 2022, LNCS 13772, pp. 506–516, 2023.
https://doi.org/10.1007/978-3-031-30258-9_45

The rapid increase of the number of UWB devices reveals the importance of electromagnetic compatibility with licensed services in the 6425–7125 MHz. To avoid congestion and interference, allowing regulators to license the spectrum is the answer. Regulating the spectrum is vital to the mobility and connectivity surging within today's data-heavy and tech-savvy generation. Therefore, compatibility between UWB and 5G NR in the 6425–7125 MHz frequency band is critically important for the proper functionality of 5G NR.

Taking into account that most of UWB application is indoor, it may lead to interference to 5G user equipment located indoor as well. Additionally, indoor small cells BS of 5G may also experience interference. Despite UWB devices output power is low, the interference for indoor-to-indoor scenario is a concern, since 5G devices and UWB devices will be located close to each other and there would be a very low propagation loss in the interference link. Figure 1 below shows a typical example of aggregate interference from UWB devices to 5G uplink and downlink.

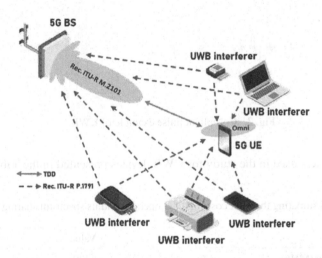

**Fig. 1.** Typical scenario of interference from UWB devices to 5G NR uplink and downlink.

Previously this issue hasn't been studied, the main reason for that is that ITU-R which considers the 6425–7125 MHz band for identification to IMT-2020 (5G NR) studies only compatibility of 5G NR with licensed services, whereas UWB operates on the unlicensed basis. At the same time many administrations which seek to use that band for 5G NR may not be aware of that issue since it has long-term impact. Thus, this paper gives raises that issue and provides some guidance based on the study results.

## 2  Simulation Parameters of UWB

The simulation is done in the area of 400 m$^2$ where UWB devices and 5G NR base station and user equipment are assumed to be located. The activity factors of UWB devices were considered 2% and 10% [3] and the number of interfering UWB devices for different scenarios was between 5–30 devices.

Figure 2 shows an example of UWB-compliant pulse p(t) along with the root raised consider reference pulse r(t) with $T_p = 2$ ns and the magnitude of the cross-correlation |φ (τ)|. The pulse p(t) is an 8th order Butterworth pulse with a 3 dB bandwidth of 500 MHz.

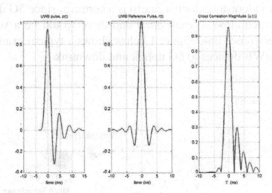

**Fig. 2.**  Compliant pulse example of UWB.

The parameters used in the study for UWB devices presented in the Table 1 [4, 5]:

**Table 1.**  Estimating the total costs of a 5G operator and its spectrum sharing costs.

| Parameter | Value |
| --- | --- |
| Centre frequency (MHz) | 6490 |
| Channel bandwidth (MHz) | 500 |
| Modulation | BPSK |
| Antenna gain (dBi) | 0 |
| Antenna pattern | Omni |
| Spectral power density (dBm/MHz) | -41.3 |

The transmitted spectrum shall be less than –10 dBr (relative to the maxmium spectral density of the signal for $0.65 * T_p < |f - f_c| < 0.8 * T_p$ and –18 dBr for $|f - f_c| > 0.8 * T_p$. Figure 3 shows transmit spectrum mask for channel 5.

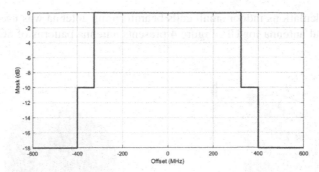

**Fig. 3.** Transmit spectrum mask for band 5 channel UWB

## 3 Simulation Parameters of 5G NR

At present, 5G NR characteristics are available in the WP 5D documents and 3GPP TR 38.803. These characteristics were adopted in WP 5D Chairman's Report Annex 4.4 «Characteristics of terrestrial component of IMT for sharing and compatibility studies in preparation for WRC-23». Since this study considers indoor scenario, 5G NR UEs as well as 5G NR BS for indoor small cells are considered as interference receptors.

Table 2 shows the characteristics of interference receptors, the characteristics are obtained from the document ITU-R 5D/422, as well as from 3GPP TR 38.803 [6].

**Table 2.** Estimating the total costs of a 5G operator and its spectrum sharing costs.

| Parameter | Base station (indoor small cell) | User equipment |
|---|---|---|
| Centre frequency (MHz) | 6490 | 6490 |
| Bandwidth (MHz) | 100 | 100 |
| Modulation | 256QAM, QPSK | 64QAM, QPSK |
| Output power (dBm) | 9 per element | 23 |
| Antenna gain (dBi) | 5.5 per element | −4 |
| Body loss | n/a | 4 |
| Antenna configuration | 4 × 4 | Omni |
| Antenna pattern | Recommendation ITU-R M.2101 | Omnidirectional |
| Noise floor (dB) | 14 | 13 |
| Antenna height above the floor (m) | 3 | 1.5 |
| Mechanical downtilt | Boresight is perpendicular to the ceiling | n/a |
| ACS (dB) | 42 | 32 |
| TDD factor | 75% | 25% |

For the calculations indoor small cells beamforming antenna was used for BS and omnidirectional antenna for UE. Figure 4 presents antenna patterns of 5G NR BS and UE.

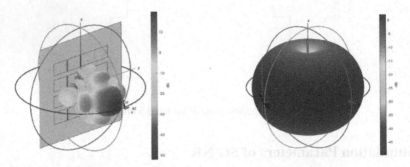

**Fig. 4.** Antenna pattern of BS and UE of 5G NR

Shopping malls, restaurants, public transportation, hotels, offices, industrial facilities, etc. are typical applications of indoor small cells.

## 4 Simulation Methodology

The simulation is done in the area of 400 m$^2$, where UWB devices and 5G NR base station and user equipment are assumed to be located. The activity factors of UWB devices were considered 2% and 10% and the number of interfering UWB devices for different scenarios was between 5–30 devices. It is worth noting that the choice of a square with an area of 400 m$^2$ is a very optimistic scenario, in comparison, the area of a metro car is about 30 m$^2$, which will lead to even greater interference impact on the 5G NR users. Many open space office spaces are also significantly smaller, resulting in interference to 5G NR small cell BSs.

For interference pathloss calculation Recommendation ITU-R P.1791 [7] was used and free space pathloss calculation for wanted link [8]. After that throughput loss was calculated and compared with the max throughput loss threshold. The max throughput threshold for 5G NR in the 6 GHz equals 1% according to 3GPP standards [5]. To calculate throughput loss of uplink and downlink of 5G NR, first, it is required to calculated signal-to-noise (SNR) ratio of 5G NR links and interference (I) from UWB transmitters. Then interference level from UWB should be added to the noise level of 5G NR victim receiver to calculate SINR.

The study uses Monte Carlo analysis, where 5G NR and UWB devices were randomly distributed within the simulated area with 1 000 000 simulation events, wanted link signal levels of 5G NR and interfering level of UWB transmit links were calculated at each step. Figure 5 presents the simulation example of interference from UWB devices to 5G NR uplink and downlink, where blue circles are UWB devices and red crosses are 5G NR user equipment devices:

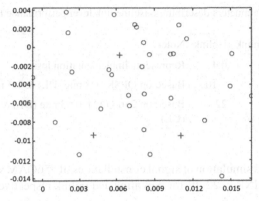

**Fig. 5.** Simulation of interference from UWB devices to IMT-2020 uplink and downlink

Simulation results for 5G NR as a victim shall be presented in terms of throughput reduction in percent relative to the reference throughput without external interference for all UE or BS. Based on the 3GPP TR 38.921 maximum throughput loss that is allowed for 5G NR in the 6425–7125 MHz is 1%.

The following equations approximate the throughput over a channel with a given SINR (dB), when using link adaptation:

$$Throughput(SINR), bps/Hz$$

$$= \begin{cases} 0 & for\ SINR < SINR_{MIN} \\ \alpha \cdot S(SINR) & for\ SINR_{MIN} \leq SINR < SINR_{MAX} \\ \alpha \cdot S(SINR_{MAX}) & for\ SINR \geq SINR_{MAX} \end{cases}$$

where:

$S(SINR)$    Shannon bound, $S(SINR) = \log_2(1 + 10^{SINR/10})$ (bps/Hz);
$SINR_{MIN}$    Minimum SINR of the code set, dB;
$\alpha$          Attenuation factor, representing implementation losses;
$SINR_{MAX}$    Maximum SINR of the code set, dB.

The parameters $\alpha$, $SINR_{MIN}$ and $SINR_{MAX}$ can be chosen to represent different modem implementations and link conditions. The parameters proposed in Table 3 represent a baseline case, which assumes:

– 1:1 antenna configurations;
– AWGN channel model;
– Link Adaptation (see Table 3 for details of the highest and lowest rate codes);
– No HARQ.

**Table 3.** Parameters describing baseline link level performance for 5G NR

| Parameter | Downlink | Uplink | Notes |
|-----------|----------|--------|-------|
| α | 0.6 | 0.4 | Represents implementation losses |
| $SINR_{MIN}$, dB | −10 | −10 | Based on QPSK, 1/8 rate (DL) & 1/5 rate (UL) |
| $SINR_{MAX}$, dB | 30 | 22 | Based on 256-QAM, 0.93 rate (DL) & 64-QAM, 0.93 rate (UL) |

Figure 6 presents simulation of signal constellations of 256QAM with SINR = 30 dB and 64QAM with SINR = 22 dB for downlink and uplink respectively.

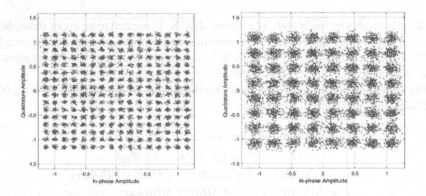

**Fig. 6.** Signal constellations of 256QAM for SINR = 30 dB and 64QAM for SINR = 22 dB

Based on the equations above, the bitrate mapping for downlink and uplink of 5G NR can be calculated. Figure 7 presents bitrate mapping of downlink and uplink of 5G NR in the 6 425–7 125 MHz frequency band.

To calculate throughput loss of uplink and downlink of 5G NR, it is primarily required to calculate signal-to-noise (SNR) ratio of 5G NR links and interference (I) from UWB transmitters. Then UWB interference level should be added to the noise level of 5G NR victim receiver to calculate SINR. The obtained SINR levels should be compared with the curves in Fig. 11 and throughput loss can be calculated using the expression below:

Overall channel throughput can be calculated using the following equation:

$$\text{Throughput } [Mbit/s] = \frac{N_{RB\_per\_UE}}{N_{total\_RBs}} \cdot S_{capacity}(SINR) \cdot B$$

where:

$BitRate$:        maximum bitrate in the channel, in bps;
$N_{RB\_per\_UE}$: number of research block per user;

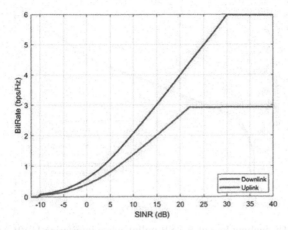

**Fig. 7.** Signal constellations of 256QAM for SINR = 30 dB and 64QAM for SINR = 22 dB

$N_{total\_RBs:}$     total number of resource blocks;
$B:$                channel bandwidth, in MHz;
$S_{capacity:}$     spectral efficiency depending on SINR, in bps/Hz.

## 5  Study Results

Following the calculations, throughput before the interference and after interference can be compared. It should be noted that according to 3GPP for the 6425–7125 MHz band acceptable throughput loss is 1% [6]. The curves below on Figs. 8 and 9 present the non-interfered bitrate and interfered bitrates depending on the number of transmitting UWB devices for activity factor 2%:

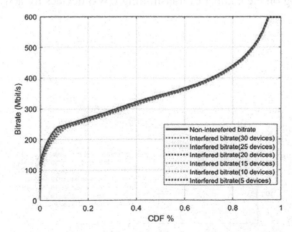

**Fig. 8.** Throughput loss of 5G NR downlink when interfering UWB AF is 2%

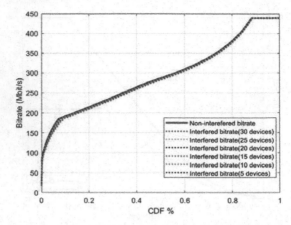

**Fig. 9.** Throughput loss of 5G NR uplink when interfering UWB AF is 2%

As can be noticed in the curves above, in many cases the throughput loss threshold is exceeded, Table 4 presents the level of throughput loss exceedance for 5G NR.

**Table 4.** Throughput loss of 5G NR when interfered by UWB with 2% AF

| Number of devices | 5 | 10 | 15 | 20 | 25 | 30 |
|---|---|---|---|---|---|---|
| downlink | 0.48% | 0.93% | 1.37% | 1.83% | 2.22% | 2.79% |
| Uplink | 0.26% | 0.55% | 0.82% | 1.12% | 1.36% | 1.68% |

The curves below on Figs. 9 and 10 present the non-interfered bitrate and interfered bitrates depending on the number of transmitting UWB devices for activity factor 10%:

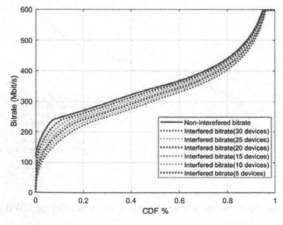

**Fig. 10.** Throughput loss of 5G NR downlink when interfering UWB AF is 10%

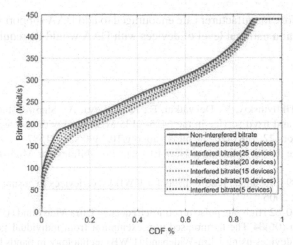

**Fig. 11.** Throughput loss of 5G NR uplink when interfering UWB AF is 10%

As can be noticed in the curves above, in many cases the throughput loss threshold is exceeded. Table 5 below presents throughput losses for uplink and downlink of 5G NR when impacted by a different number of UWB devices with 10% activity factor:

**Table 5.** Throughput loss of 5G NR when interfered by UWB with 2% AF

| Number of devices | 5 | 10 | 15 | 20 | 25 | 30 |
|---|---|---|---|---|---|---|
| downlink | 2.38% | 4.55% | 6.73% | 8.38% | 10.5% | 12.45% |
| Uplink | 1.38% | 2.75% | 4.09% | 5.32% | 6.64% | 7.62% |

## 6 Conclusion

The study results indicate that 5G NR and UWB devices are not compatible in an indoor environment. Given the rapid increase of UWB applications, the scenario where 5 or more UWB devices are located close to the 5G NR receiver will be very common in the 6 425–7 125 MHz band. The analysis showed that protection criterion of 5G NR is exceeded and that both downlink and uplink channels of 5G NR would be unacceptably impacted by UWB devices in the indoor environment. Thus, the achievement of compatibility between 5G NR and UWB devices in the frequency band 6 425–7 125 MHz may be very challenging in case the activity factor of UWB wouldn't be significantly reduced or UWB devices wouldn't use different channels. Given that today's UWB devices are consumer-like and it's hard to control their activity factor, the only solution for compatibility might be transferring UWB devices to the channels below or above the 6 425–7 125 MHz frequency band. Another way of avoiding the interference might be using detect and avoid (DAA) mechanisms [9], however not all UWB devices support

DAA [10], therefore manufacturers are encouraged to add DAA support in their devices, and certification at a national level of devices with DAA would be required.

# References

1. Pastukh, A., Tikhvinskiy, V., Devyatkin, E., Kulakayeva, A.: Sharing studies between 5G IoT networks and fixed service in the 6425–7125 MHz band with Monte Carlo simulation analysis. Sensors **22**, 1587 (2022). https://doi.org/10.3390/s22041587
2. UWB Alliance UWB – Enabling New Efficient Possibilities for Multi-Radio Consumer Devices, 2021
3. ECC Report 094 Technical requirements for UWB LDC devices to ensure the protection of FWA systems, 2006
4. ISO/IEC 24730-62 High rate pulse repetition frequency UltraWide Band (UWB) air interface
5. ECC Decision (06)04 The harmonised use, exemption from individual licensing and free circulation of devices using Ultra-Wideband (UWB) technology in bands below 10.6 GHz, 2011
6. 3GPP TR 38.921 (2021-03) Study on International Mobile Telecommunications (IMT) parameters for 6425-7025 GHz, 7025-7125 GHz and 10,0-10,5 GHz
7. Recommendation ITU-R P.1791 Propagation prediction methods for assessment of the impact of ultra-wideband devices
8. Recommendation ITU-R P.525 Calculation of free space attenuation
9. Ohno, K., Itami, M., Ikegami, T.: Detection and avoidance technique for UWB radio interfering to OFDM system using Guard Interval. In: 2009 IEEE 20th International Symposium on Personal, Indoor and Mobile Radio Communications, 2009, pp. 963–967 (2009). https://doi.org/10.1109/PIMRC.2009.5449818
10. ETSI TS 102 754 V1.1.1 Electromagnetic compatibility and Radio spectrum Matters (ERM); Short Range Devices (SRD); Technical characteristics of Detect-And-Avoid (DAA) mitigation techniques for SRD equipment using Ultra Wideband (UWB) technology, 2008

# 6 GHz Band Sharing Study for FWA Base Stations and GEO Satellite Receivers

Valery Tikhvinskiy[1,2]($\boxtimes$), Vitaly Urodlivchenko[3], Victor Koval[3], Alexander Frolov[3], Vladimir Ketat[3], and Vadim Belyavskiy[4]

[1] Radio Research and Development Institute, Moscow, Russia
[2] International Information Technologies University (IITU) Almaty, Almaty, Kazakhstan
[3] Geyser-Telecom Ltd, Moscow, Russia
[4] Spectre Ltd, Moscow, Russia

**Abstract.** One of the most demanded and promising application for unmanned aerial vehicles (UAVs) are video monitoring services of various remote objects. For this purpose, transmitting video information from UAV in real time has been implemented. For video signal transmission from UAV board, as well as for video camera control signals transmission from base stations (BS) of fixed wireless access (FWA), 5850–6425 MHz frequency band can be used on legal basis because this band is allocated by EU frequency allocation table for mobile and fixed services for FWA in Region 1 of RR and EU countries. This frequency band is also allocated to fixed-satellite service (Earth-to-space links). In case of large number BS utilization in interests of UAVs and FWA communications, harmful interferences from these BSs to satellite receivers in geostationary orbit (GEO) is possible.

The paper presented the results of 6 GHz band sharing study between BS transmitters support UAVs video services and GEO satellite receivers. Also presented the methodic for estimating influence of aggregated interferences from a totality of UAVs BS and FWA BS to GEO satellite receivers has been developed, which allowed determining value of aggregated (total) interferences at GEO satellite receivers input with a sufficiently high degree of accuracy without using of Electromagnetic compatibility (EMC) simulation methods like SEMCAT and other methods of EMC stochastic estimation.

**Keywords:** FWA · EMC · GEO · UAV · Harmful interference

## 1 Introduction

In the world video monitoring services market is expanding for oil and gas pipelines based on UAV utilization. UAV video monitoring services for various remote sites are among the promising UAV services that are already a significant part of total pipelines monitoring for oil and gas companies. Periodic checks of pipeline routes by UAVs using can significantly reduce costs of such companies on helicopter overflights numbers and reduce the risks of air accidents, as well as simplify pipelines control itself.

For video monitoring of remote objects using UAVs, it is necessary to solve a large number of problems associated not only with the use of airspace for UAV flights, but also with the use of the radio frequency spectrum for organizing communication lines and transmitting video information from the UAV board to the interacting base stations (named UAV BS) of FWA network.

The band 5850–6425 MHz in Region 1 of the Radio Regulations [1] and in EU countries [2] is allocated to Mobile service and Fixed-satellite service on the Earth-to-space link, as well as to Fixed service, which allows creation and deployment of FWA networks. These FWA networks, using part of BSs FWA, can transmit video camera control signals from FWA BS side and receive video signals from UAV board. Using a large number of BS transmitters can create harmful interferences from BS FWA transmitters to satellite receivers (GEO SR) of communication spacecraft in geostationary orbit.

The spectrum loading analysis in 6 GHz band in some of European regions of the Russian Federation showed that several thousand such FWA BSs can be deployed. As the video services market develops of UAV, the number BSs for UAV of utilizing FWA networks will continue to increase, which may result in high levels of unintentional interference affecting GEO SR in 6 GHz band. In addition, interference from on-board UAV transmitters to GEO Satellite RXs is also theoretically possible.

EMC evaluation between the above radio means and total interferences calculation from a large number of Tx BSs UAV and BSs FWA can be carried out using various software and hardware systems, for example, as Visualyse Professional V7 [3] or MATLAB [4], which allow taking into account when calculations a large number of statistical factors affecting of results accuracy. Authors proposed a simpler and more efficient method for estimating EMC, which can be an alternative to more complex simulation methods.

## 2   EMC Estimation Scenarios Between BS Transmitters of FWA Network and GEO Satellite Receivers

Spectrum sharing analysis in 6 GHz band by BS transmitters of FWA network and airborne transmitters UAV showed that there are two possible scenarios for harmful interferences impact from airborne transmitters UAV and BSs transmitters of FBA network on GEO satellite receivers:

Scenario 1. Impact of BSs transmitters of FWA network on GEO SRs.
Scenario 2. Impact of airborne transmitters UAV on GEO SRs.

Scenario 1 assumed that grouping of BSs for UAV and BSs of FWA network were located in a certain geographical area, and to simplify the EMC evaluation, an assumption was made about a uniform distribution of BSs FWA locations on the Earth's surface. Considering that airborne transmitters UAV have significantly lower EIRP compared to BS transmitters (by two orders of magnitude less), it was assumed that in Scenario 2, interference from airborne transmitters UAV to GEO SRs will not influence. This scenario was not considered further in the article. The BS FWA location model on the Earth's surface and GEO satellite used in EMC evaluation in Scenarios 1 and 2 is shown in Fig. 1.

Satellite visibility angles GEO ($\alpha$) for BS FWA placement points located at different latitudes on the Earth's surface, which will increase with decreasing BS placement latitude (from αmin to αmax). This, in turn, taking into account the antenna pattern (DNA) of BS FWA will cause EIRP of BS transmitter to decrease in the GEO satellite direction.

To calculate total harmful interferences from grouping of BSs of UAV and FWA BSs transmitters, the FWA BS location area is divided into n-«layers» of BS FWA which covered some number BSs from common grouping of BSs of UAV and FWA BSs transmitters. Further, for each « layer» of BSs FWA location area, the value of «equivalent» EIRP is calculated (the total value from all the FWA BS and FWA of each « layer»), which is taken into account in further EMC calculations.

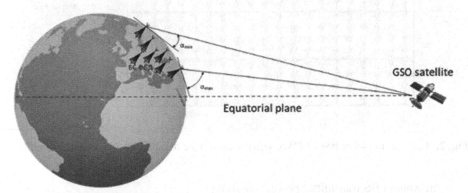

**Fig. 1.** Location model of BSs of FWA network on surface of the Earth and the GEO satellite

To EMC calculating is assumed that grouping of BSs UAV and BSs FWA are located with a uniform density in the region of 44°... 65° north latitude and 30° ... 55° east longitude.

To total interferences calculating in EMC evaluation UAV and FWA BSs grouping is divided into five geographically distributed subgroups («layers»), as shown in Fig. 2, located at north latitudes intervals: 45–50°, 50–55°, 55–60°, 60–65° and 65–70°.

1. When EMC evaluating and total interferences calculating from UAV BSs transmitters, the following characteristics of GEO satellite receivers were applied:

   - equivalent noise temperature - 900 K;
   - trunk bandwidth - 72 MHz;
   - satellite receiver antenna gain – 30 dBi.

2. The number of BS FWA (NBS) in frequency band 5850–6425 MHz, obtained based on the analysis of statistical data on deployed BSs [5], was about NBS = 6500.

3. The characteristics of BSs UAV and FWA transmitters that were used in EMC assessment were as follows:

   - maximum EIRP of BS transmitter – 23 dBW;

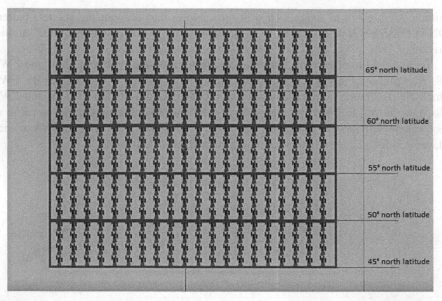

**Fig. 2.** Location model of BSs of FWA network on surface of the Earth and the GEO satellite

- maximum BS transmitter power – 0 dBW;
- width of antenna lobs of BS in vertical plane - 5 degrees;
- channel separation mode - TDD.

It was assumed that main beam of BS UAV or BS FWA antenna in the azimuthal plane was directed to GEO SR. In the elevation plane, BS antenna beam is directed parallel to the ground (elevation angle = 0 degrees). Antenna radiation pattern (ARP) model of BS transmitter, which was used in EMC evaluation, was selected in accordance with Rec. ITU-R F.1336-4 [6]. Dependence of gain factor (GA) of BS antenna on deviation from antenna electrical axis in vertical plane is shown in Fig. 3.

The angle of line of sight for GEO SR from BS location place is determined by the formula:

$$\varepsilon = \arcsin \frac{K \cos \varphi \cos \theta - 1}{\sqrt{K^2 + 1 - 2K\cos\varphi\cos\theta}}$$

where:

$\varphi$ – geographic latitude of BS FWA transmitter location;

$K = (R_{Earth} + h_{GEO})/R_{Earth} \approx 6{,}61$ (при $R_{Earth} = 6371$ km, $h_{GEO} = 35786$ km);

$\theta$ – difference between longitudes of BS transmitter location and sub-satellite point of GEO satellite in grad.

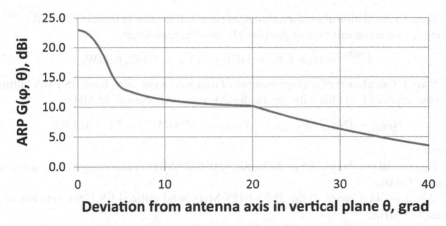

**Fig. 3.** Antenna radiation pattern of BS UAV or BS FWA transmitter in vertical plane

## 3 Methodic and Results Evaluation of Total Interference Impact from UAV and FWA BSS Transmitters Grouping on GEO SR

At present, 5G NR characteristics are available in the WP 5D documents and 3GPP TR 38.803. These characteristics were adopted in WP 5D Chairman's Report Annex 4.4 «Characteristics of terrestrial component of IMT for sharing and compatibility studies in preparation for WRC-23». Since this study considers indoor scenario, 5G NR UEs as well as 5G NR BS for indoor small cells are considered as interference receptors.

Proposed methodic for estimating EMC between BS FWA transmitters and GEO SR in 6 GHz band includes several steps for calculating GEO SR operation parameters and total interference from BS FWA transmitters at the GEO SR input.

When evaluating the possible impact of harmful interference from FGB BS transmitters on GEO SR, the criterion given in Recommendation ITU-R S.1432-1 [7] was adopted as a criterion for permissible levels of interference ensures EMC. In accordance with this criterion, the power of harmful interference at GEO SR input should is limited to 6% of the clear-sky system noise ($K_z = -12.2$ dB).

Let us consider sequences of necessary steps performed in EMC calculation and results obtained for these steps.

Step 1. Calculation of thermal noise power NUP normalized (recalculated) to GEO SR input:

$$N_{UP} = 10 \times \log(kT \, \Delta F_{beam}) = -120, 4 \, dBW, \tag{1}$$

where:

$\Delta F_{ствола}$ – equivalent receiver noise bandwidth equal to the bandwidth of GEO satellite channel (beam) in frequency band 5850–6425 MHz ($\Delta F_{beam} = 72$ MHz);

T – equivalent antenna noise temperature normalized to input of GEO satellite receiver (T = 900 K).

Step 2. Calculation of total interferences permissible value at input of GEO SR $I^{AVAL}$, taking into account criterion of permissible interferences level:

$$I^{AVAL} = N_{UP} + K_z = NUP - -12, 2 = -132, 6\,dBW,\qquad(2)$$

Step 3. Calculation of average number of transmitter emission band BS FWA falling into the beam of GEO SR with bandwidth $\Delta Fbeam$ ($\Delta Fbeam = 72$ MHz):

$$N_{FWA} = (N_{BS}/\Delta F_{band}) \times \Delta F_{beam} = (6500/575) \times 72 \approx 814\,BS,\qquad(3)$$

where:

$N_{BS}$ – total numbers FWA in the band 5850–6425 MHz in accordance EMC scenario ($N_{BS} = 6500$);

$\Delta F_{band}$ – total range of the 5850–6425 MHz band utilized BS FWA network and equal 575 MHz.

Step 4. Calculation of number of simultaneously operating BS FWA transmitters that use TDD mode:

$$N_{BS\,TDD} = N_{BS}/2 = 407\,BS,\qquad(4)$$

Considering that the total number of BS UAV and BS FWA is NBS = 407 due to TDD BS transmitters work in non-synchronic mode and the number of layers is 5, then in EMC evaluation, an assumption was made about the distribution of UAV and FWA base stations, in which each "layer" will contain about 80 BS UAV.

Step 5. Calculation of additional attenuation for GEO SR receiving antenna gain due to deviation from the main axis ($\Delta GADD$) was carried out in accordance with Appendix 30B of ITU Radio Regulations [8], the graph of which is shown in Fig. 4.

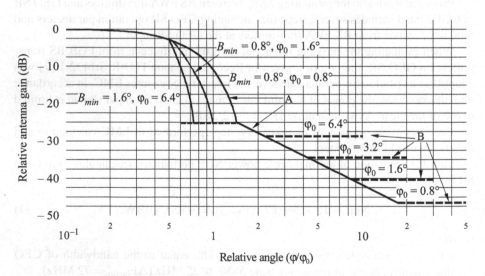

**Fig. 4.** Reference radiation patterns of satellite antennas [8]

Step 6. Calculation of total interferences from BS and BS FWA transmitters was carried out according to the following sequence.

Step 6a) Calculation of interference from each of the «layers» of BS UAVs and BS FWA transmitters. It was assumed that in each «layer» all BSs of UAV and FWA are artificially located at one point, while the antennas of BS transmitters are oriented in azimuth plane to GEO satellite.

Interference power from transmitter of one BS was determined as:

$$P_{oneBS\_int} = P_{BsTx} + G_{BS} + G_{SR} - \Delta G_{ADD} - L_{pol} - L_{LOS}, \tag{5}$$

где

$P_{BsTx}$ - BS transmitter power, dBW;

$G_{BS}$ - BS antenna gain, dBi;

$G_{SR}$ - antenna gain GEO SR, dBi;

$\Delta G_{ADD}$ - additional attenuation for GEO SR receiving antenna gain due to deviation from the main axis, dB;

$L_{pol}$ - polarization loss on propagation line, dB;

$L_{LOS}$ - free space transmission loss, dB.

Step 6б) Total interferences level $P^i_{int\_80BS}$ from 80 BS UAV transmitters and BS FWA transmitters from $i$-layer are equal:

$$P_{int\_80BS}(i) = P_{oneBS\_int} + 10Lg(80) = P_{oneBS\_int} + 19., \tag{6}$$

Calculation total interferences level from UAV and FWA BSs grouping:

$$P_{total} = \Sigma 10^{Piint\_80BS/10}(W), \text{ or}$$
$$P_{total} = 10 \times Lg(\Sigma 10^{Piint\_80BS/10})(dBW), \tag{7}$$

where: $i = 1...5$.

The final results of calculations of the total interferences from FWA BS transmitters for GEO SR with standing point of 36° E obtained using the technical data of Sect. 2 according to the analytical method (1)–(7) based on the sequential execution of 1–6 steps and are given in Table 1.

**Table 1.** Calculation total interferences results from FWA BSs transmitters to input of GEO satellite receiver with standing point of 36° E.

| Number of layers (i) | Northern latitudes | Elevation angle of BS | $G_{ДHA\_БД}$ dBi | $L_{LOS}$ dB | $\Delta G_{ADD}$ dB | $P_{oneBS\_int}$ dBW | $P_{iint\_80BS}$ dBW | $P_{total}$, dBW |
|---|---|---|---|---|---|---|---|---|
| 1 | 45°–50° | 39.2° | 3.7 | 200 | 1 | −170.3 | −151.3 | −141.5 |
| 2 | 50°–55° | 33.8° | 5.2 | 200 | 1.2 | −169.0 | −150.0 | |
| 3 | 55°–60° | 28.3° | 6.8 | 200 | 1.5 | −167.7 | −148.7 | |
| 4 | 60°–65° | 23.0° | 8.8 | 200 | 2 | −166.2 | −147.2 | |
| 5 | 65°–70° | 17.7° | 10.3 | 200 | 3 | −165.7 | −146.7 | |

Analysis of Table 1 shown that total interference power from UAV BSs and FWA BSs transmitters, reduced to the GEO SR input for different layers of the EMC assessment model, will have a value ranging from $-166.2$ to $-170.3$ dBW, and the total value of the total interference from all the considered transmitters of the BS BS and the FWA of the group - minus 141.5 dBW.

Comparing the obtained values of $P_{total}$ and permissible value of total interferences at input of GEO SR identified as $I^{AVAL}$, we can conclude that EMC between BSs transmitters support UAVs video services and GEO satellite receivers will be provided.

In order to compare the results of calculations obtained by the proposed analytical methodic (1)–(7), calculations were made of total interferences from UAV BSs and FWA BSs on the GEO SR using the software package Visualyse Professional V7 [3] and technical data of Sect. 2. The obtained simulation results of total interferences based on Visualyse Professional V7 showed that total interferences at the input of GEO satellite receiver is minus 142.8 dBW.

Comparison of modeling results for total interferences calculations from UAV BSs and FWA BSs transmitters for GEO satellite receivers showed that they differ by 1.3 dB or 0.9%, which meets the requirements for engineering accuracy of calculations and allows using a simpler calculation tool for EMC assessment than use of modeling complexes.

## 4   Conclusions

6 GHz band sharing for purposes of transmitting video services from UAV board using the FWA BSs network is not possible without solving EMC problem with GEO satellite receivers due to utilization of a common frequency band.

Methodic proposed by authors makes it possible to simplify the EMC calculations and does not require the involvement of the Visualyse Professional V7 software package or other modeling systems to evaluate EMC between UAV BSs and FWA BSs transmitters and GEO satellite receivers with engineering accuracy.

Value of total interferences from the UAV BSs and FWA BSs transmitters on GEO satellite receiver, calculated using developed methodic, differs from the value obtained using the Visualyse Professional V7 software modelling package by 1.3 dB or 0.9%.

## References

1. Radio Regulations, ITU, Geneve, 2020
2. ERC REPORT 25. The European table of frequency allocations and applications in the frequency range 8.3 kHz to 3000 GHz (ECA Table) Approved October 2018
3. Visualyse Professional V7, Transfinite Systems Ltd. https://download.transfinite.com/websit edownloads/AboutVisualyse7.pdf
4. MATLAB. https://www.mathworks.com/products/matlab.html
5. Report of Roskomnadzor RF, 2020. https://rkn.gov.ru/plan-and-reports/reports/
6. Recommendation ITU-R F.1336-5 (01/2019). Reference radiation patterns of omnidirectional, sectoral and other antennas for the fixed and mobile service for use in sharing studies in the frequency range from 400 MHz to about 70 GHz
7. Recommendation S.1432-1 Apportionment of the allowable error performance degradations to fixed-satellite service (FSS) hypothetical reference digital paths arising from time invariant interference for systems operating below 30 GHz
8. Appendix 30B of the Radio Regulations. The Allotment Plan for the fixed-satellite service using part of the 4/6 and 10 - 11/12 - 13 GHz frequency bands

# Federated Learning Strategies Over Wireless Channels

Amjad Ali[⊠]

Department of Electronic Engineering, MIEM HSE National Research University, Higher
School of Economics, Moscow, Russia
amjadali@hse.ru

**Abstract.** Machine learning over distributed data collected by many clients has
important applications in use cases where data privacy is a key concern or central
data storage is not an option. Federated learning has introduced solutions for
these scenarios, unlike the client-server approach, where all the training data is
centralized in the server side, the clients, in a federated learning approach, perform
machine learning updates locally over their data and the central server merely
aggregates the resulting models without accessing the client's local data. Article
reviews the characteristics and learning objectives of the federated learning setting
and gives an overview of the base algorithms that have been developed for FL,
compare between FEDAVG and Consensus algorithm and shows the drawbacks
and advantages of Consensus algorithm.

**Keywords:** Federated Learning · FEDAVG · Consensus · IID · Non-IID ·
Distributed strategies

## 1 Introduction

In 5G and 6G applications, a massive number of connected devices are expected to
produce huge data sets that are required to be trained and learned using complex models
to produce accurate estimations. Due to the limited power and bandwidth available at
the wireless agents, centralized solutions are becoming increasingly costly. In addition,
privacy preservation has become an important issue in new applications, which aim to
protect individual data's privacy to prevent the disclosure of sensitive information during
the learning process. Since the distributed machine learning (ML) scheme eliminates the
need to exchange local data between agents, preserves the agent's privacy, and uses the
communication resources more effectively, therefore distributed ML is becoming an
alternative to centralized ML.

Federated learning (FL) has been proposed as a privacy-preserving distributed ML
scheme. FL is a machine learning setting where many clients (e.g., mobile devices)
collaboratively train a model without exchanging the training data while keeping the
training data decentralized. FL allows to create a shared global model without saving
training data on a central server. FL aims to minimize the collected data and mitigate the
systemic privacy risks and costs resulting from traditional, centralized machine learning.

Y. Koucheryavy and A. Aziz (Eds.): NEW2AN 2022, LNCS 13772, pp. 525–533, 2023.
https://doi.org/10.1007/978-3-031-30258-9_47

This field of research has received significant interest, both from research and applied perspectives.

Many earlier works have been done to address the opportunities of federated learning and its challenges. For example, Stefano Savazzi explored emerging opportunities of FL for the next generation networked industrial systems [1]. Alharbi et al. [2] provided a study of FL with an emphasis on enabling software and hardware platforms, protocols, real-life applications, and use cases.

In this work, we review the concepts of federated learning and introduce simulation results of the comparison between the fully distributed strategies with FEDAVG algorithm. The next sections are formulated as follows: section II defines the learning goal of FL. Section III introduces the system model of FL and formulates the global cost function of the model. Section IV gives a review of algorithms that developed to increase the efficient of federated learning and strategies that can be employed to minimize FL global cost in a fully decentralized manner. Section V introduces simulation results of comparison between the FEDAVG and consensus strategy.

Notation. In the next sections, scalars are denoted normal font letters, column vectors are denoted boldface lowercase letters, and matrices are denoted boldface uppercase letters.

## 2 Motivation and Learning Objective

FL scheme considers a network consists of N agents that aim to estimate the same parameter vector, $\theta_0$. The vector is the minimizer of some global cost function, denoted by $J^{glob}(\theta)$, which the agents aim to optimize,

$$\theta_0 = \underset{\theta}{\arg\min} J^{glob} \tag{1}$$

Federated learning studies scenarios where the dataset is distributed over network nodes and each node has access just to its data. Since the local data on the node can't be too large, achievement of the global optimum using just its own data won't be achievable. So, if the node cooperates with the neighbors and the neighbors also cooperate with their neighbors, then these procedures will enable all the nodes in the network to converge towards the global optimum $\theta_0$.

The objective of decentralized processing is to allow spatially distributed agents to achieve a global objective by depending on local information and on in-network processing. Through a continuous process of cooperation and information sharing with neighbors, agents in a network can reach a global performance level.

In the next section we will describe the network model of FL and formulate the cost function (1).

## 3 Network Model

FL aims to estimate a $1 \times M$ unknown vector $\theta_0$ (1) from measurements collected at nodes distributed over a network. The network graph G consists of a set N denote the nodes, labeled k = 1...N, and a set E denote the edges in the graph. Figure 1 shows network consists of N = 10 distributed nodes and K = 15 edges. We call node $k$ a neighbor of node $l$ if nodes $k$ and $l$ can exchange information, that is $(k, l) \in E$. The vector signal of the nodes is defined by $x = [x_1, \ldots, x_N] \in R^N$, where the signal at node k is represented by $x_k$ and $x(i)$ represents the graph signal at time i. For each node k we define neighbor set $N_k$, which denotes the set of nodes connected to node k: $\{l : (l, k) \in N_k\}$. The weight of edge between node k and another node $l$ in $N_k$ is denoted by $c_{l,k}$. The weights $c_{l,k}$ are defined by matrix **S** of size N × N and their values satisfy [3] [8]:

$$c_{l,k} > 0, \sum_{l=1}^{N} c_{l,k} = 1, c_{l,k} = 0 \, if \, l \notin N_k \tag{2}$$

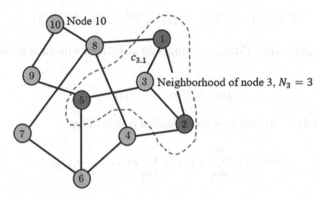

**Fig. 1.** Network graph consisting of 10 nodes and 15 edges.

Condition (2) shows that the neighbors of node k do not all have the same importance, and this makes sense since a heterogeneous network assumes the data on the nodes is non-IID. In the case of IID local datasets, the weights of the edges are identical and satisfy:

$$c_{l,k} \frac{1}{N} l, k \in N_k$$

The received signal at each node k is processed by linearly combining the samples $x_l$ from adjacent nodes:

$$x_k = \sum_{l \in N_k} c_{lk} x_l.$$

To define the output of the trained model, we consider linear filter $\boldsymbol{\theta}$ [4]:

$$\boldsymbol{\theta} \triangleq \sum_{m=0}^{M-1} \theta_m^o S^m \tag{3}$$

where $\theta_m$ denote the filter coefficients and M its order. The input vector $\mathbf{x}(i)$ is processed by (3) to get the output vector $\mathbf{y}(i)$ as follows:

$$y(i) = \sum_{m=0}^{M-1} \theta_m^o S^m x(i - m) + v(i) i > M - 1$$

where $v(i) = [v_1(i), v_2(i), \dots v_N(i)]$ represents an additive zero-mean white noise process and spatially independent.

We consider the mean-square-error criterion to estimate $\theta^o \triangleq col\{\theta_0^o, \dots, \theta_{M-1}^o\}$ [5],

$$J(\theta) = E|y(i) - X(i)\theta|^2 \tag{4}$$

where $X$ is an N × M matrix given by:

$$X(i) = \left[ x(i), Sx(i-1), \dots, S^{M-1}x(i - M + 1) \right]$$

The mean-square-error (MSE) cost function associated with each agent $k$ is defined by:

$$J_k(\theta) = E|y_k(i) - X_k(i)\theta|^2 \tag{5}$$

Using (4) and (5), we can express the global cost in (1) as:

$$J^{glob}(\theta) = \sum_{k=1}^{M} J_k(\theta) = \sum_{k=1}^{M} E|y_k(i) - X_k(i)\theta|^2 \tag{6}$$

In the next sections, we will introduce how we can employ distributed strategies to estimate the global cost formulated in (6).

The important question here is how we can employ the cooperation strategies to achieve better performance in comparison with the scenarios when each agent solves the optimization task individually. Next, we will show how we can employ decentralization strategies to answer these questions. First, we will give an overview of developed algorithms with the presence of a central server in the case of IID and non-IID datasets, then we will move to explain how decentralized strategies can solve the optimization problem in a fully decentralized manner in the absence of a central server.

## 4   Federated Learning Algorithms

### 4.1   FL Algorithms for IID Datasets

Independent and identically distributed (IID) data is a common assumption on the client data which is often used to simplify the mathematical relations and **to** simplify the theoretical convergence analysis of federated optimization algorithms. Having IID data at the client means that all the batches of the client's data used for the local update are statistically identical, and this applies to all local datasets at the clients. The IID assumption isn't practical since the clients independently collect their training data which vary in both size and distribution, and these data are not shared with other clients or the central node.

One of the most common approaches to optimize federated learning is the Federated Averaging algorithm. The FEDAVG algorithm consists of two rounds [6]. First, the nodes update the model locally (7). Second, the central server aggregates the client's models updates to update the general model (8). These two rounds are repeated until the general model reaches its convergence value. In each round, the server chooses a subset of clients S depending on the connectivity state of the nodes.

Each of these clients receives the last updated global model and applies **K** local updates using the form [7]:

$$y_i = y_i - \eta_l g_i(y_i) \qquad (7)$$

where $\eta_l$ is the local step-size. In the next round, the clients' updates are aggregated by the server to update the global model by the formula ($\eta_g$ is the global step-size):

$$x \leftarrow x + \frac{\eta_g}{|S|} \sum_{i \in S} (y_i - x) \qquad (8)$$

## 4.2 FL Algorithms for Non-IID Datasets

Federated learning uses local data generated at end-user devices, which have different behavior, so it's expected that the end users have varieties of non-IID data. Stochastic Controlled Averaging algorithm (SCAFFOLD) is exploited in [5] which overcome client-drift problem which appear in case of heterogeneous network. SCAFFOLD use correction parameter which is calculated at the server side in each communication round, then the server sends this parameter to the nodes. The nodes use this parameter to correct the local update. The authors show that this strategy successfully overcomes heterogeneity and converges in significantly fewer rounds of communication [8].

## 4.3 Distributed Strategies

In cooperative strategies, agents are connected over a graph has been described in section II and the global cost is defined as (6). Using (1) and (6), the global optimization problem can be defined as:

$$\theta = \arg \min_{\theta} J^{glob}(\theta) = \sum_{k=1}^{M} J_k(\theta) = \sum_{k=1}^{M} E|y_k(i) - X_k(i)\theta|^2 \qquad (9)$$

Distributed strategies enable the solution of (4) in a distributed and adaptive manner. There are several distributed strategies that we can consider to estimate the vector parameters $\theta$ in a distributed manner.

- Gossip algorithm which supposes at each communication round the node k chooses one neighbor edge to corporate with ($N_k = 1$), where the two nodes exchange the vector parameters $\theta$ to update the local model [9].

- Consensus strategy which supposes that the neighbor set $N_k$ satisfies $(1 < N_k < N)$ [10].

In this paper, we will employ the Consensus strategy, since Gossip is a special case of the Consensus strategy.

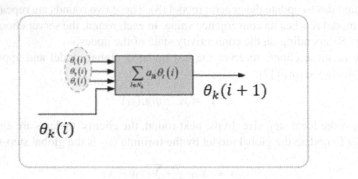

(a)    FEDAVG

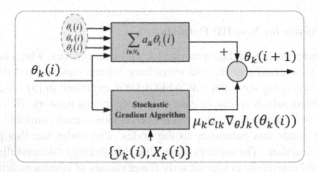

(b) Consensus strategy

**Fig. 2.** FEDAVG strategy vs consensus strategy (a) FEDAVG 9 (b) Consensus strategy

The consensus strategy extends the centralized Federated Averaging, in the consensus strategy, at each communication round $i$ each node k performs two steps:

(1)   Node k exchange weights it's updated model $\theta_k(i)$ with the neighbors $\theta_t(i)t \in N_k$.
(2)   The node updates its model $\theta_k(i)$ using the received weights to get the aggregated model:

$$\begin{cases} \varphi_k(i+1) = \sum_{l \in N_k} a_{lk}\theta_l(i) \\ \theta_k(i+1) = \varphi_k(i) - \mu_k c_{lk} \nabla_\theta J_k(\theta_k(i)) \end{cases} \tag{10}$$

where from (x) $J_k(\theta_k(i)) = E|y_k(i) - X_k(i)\theta|^2$ and the $c_{lk}, a_{lk}$ are nonnegative scalars satisfy (2).

The topology of FEEDAVG and consensus strategiess are shown in Fig. 2 [11].

## 5  Simulation Results

After we have introduced the federated averaging and the fully distributed strategies, in this section we simulate the performance of the Consensus strategy on a graph consisting of 50 nodes and compare the results with the performance of FEDAVG. The additional parameters of the simulation are listed in Table 1.

**Table 1.** The parameters of the simulation.

|           | Devices | Active devices | Samples | Batch size |
|-----------|---------|----------------|---------|------------|
| Consensus | 30      | 20             | 500     | 100        |
| FEDAVG    | 30      | 20             | 500     | 100        |

Experiments were executed on the EMNIST dataset. The task of the trained model is to classify handwritten digital image numbers into 10 classes. The implemented ML model takes as input images of size $28 \times 28$. The model comprises 2 convolution layers with a rectified linear unit (ReLu) as an activation function. Every layer employs an L2-norm regularization with weight decay of $10-7$. The output layer is a fully connected one of size $10$, followed by a normalization layer.

In this experiment, the consensus strategy performs model averaging from up to 3 neighbors, i.e. $|N_k| < 3$, varying on each round. We supposed that the network is heterogeneous, that's the signal vector x is non-IID. We simulated the performance for IID and non-IID local data, Fig. 3.

Simulation results show that for both types of data (IID and non-IID) the consensus strategy needs more communication rounds to convergence. This is expected since nodes in the consensus strategy exchange the model parameters with just the neighbors' nodes, on the other hand, all the nodes in FEDAVG send the model parameters to the central server at each communication round. The performance of consensus strategy is more stable in the case of network heterogeneity (non-IID) and this is the most advantage of consensus strategy compared to FEDAVG.

We can summarize the results of the experiments as follows: both strategies, consensus and FEDAVG have less stable convergence in the case of a heterogeneous network; consensus compensates for the absence of central server and has good performance but need more communications round for convergence in comparison with FEDAVG strategy.

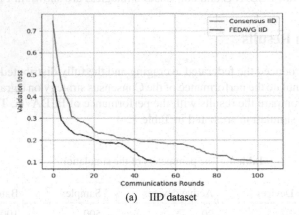

(a)    IID dataset

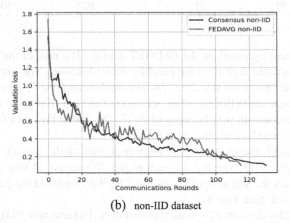

(b)    non-IID dataset

**Fig. 3.** Validation loss for Consensus Strategy vs FEDAVG in case of (a) IID and (b) non-IID dataset.

## 6  Conclusion

Federated learning gives the ability to move the training model to the distributed devices that make predictions, decoupling the ability to do machine learning from the need to store the data in the central server. Further federated Learning gives us new hope to work in a secure and smart way, since FL technology ensures that the communication between edge devices is encrypted and there is no loss of data or any privacy issue.

Motivated by the growing interest in federated learning research, this paper provided review of the last algorithms developed for this technology and simulations results of performance diffusion strategy-consensus in comparison with FEDAVG in case of IID and non-IID data.

# References

1. Savazzi, S., Nicoli, M., Bennis, M., Kianoush, S., Barbieri, L.: Opportunities of federated learning in connected, cooperative and automated industrial systems. IEEE Trans. Wireless Comm. **59**(29) (2021)
2. Aledhari, M., Razzak, R., Parizi, R.M., Saeed, F.: Federated learning: a survey on enabling technologies, protocols, and applications. IEEE Access **8**, 140699–140725 (2020)
3. Sery, T., Shlezinger, N., Cohen, K., Eldar, Y.C.: Over-the-air federated learning from heterogeneous data. IEEE Trans. Signal Process. **69** (2020)
4. Sayed, A.H.: Adaptation, learning, and optimization over networks. Found. Trends Mach. Learn. **7**, 311–801 (2014)
5. Doku, R., Rawat, D.B., Liu, C.: Towards federated learning approach to determine data relevance in big data. In: IEEE 20th International Conference on Information Reuse and Integration for Data Science (IRI), pp. 184–192, Los Angeles, USA (2019)
6. McMahan, H.B., Moore, E., Ramage, D., Hampson, S.: Communication-efficient learning of deep networks from decentralized data. arXiv preprint arXiv:1602.05629 (2016)
7. Liu, Y., et al.: FedCoin: a peer-to-peer payment system for federated learning. arXiv preprint arXiv:2002.11711 (2020)
8. Karimireddy, S.P., Kale, S., Mohri, M., Reddi, S., Stich, S., Suresh, A.T.: Scaffold: stochastic controlled averaging for federated learning. In: International Conference on Machine Learning, pp. 5132–5143. PMLR (2020)
9. Blot, M., Picard, D., Thome, N., Cord, M.: Distributed optimization for deep learning with gossip exchange. Neurocomputing **330**, 287–296 (2019). https://doi.org/10.1016/j.neucom.2018.11.002
10. Savazzi, S., Nicoli, M., Rampa, V.: Federated learning with cooperating devices: a consensus approach for massive IoT networks. IEEE Internet Things J. (2020). https://doi.org/10.1109/JIOT.2020.2964162
11. Sayed, A.H., Tu, S.Y., Chen, J., Zhao, X.: Diffusion strategies for adaptation and learning over networks: an examination of distributed strategies and network behavior. IEEE Signal Proces. Mag. **30**, 155–171 (2013)

# Data Routing in UAV Networks with Multiple Data Sources Using Steiner Tree

Sreejith Vidhyadharan[1]([✉])(iD), Paul Snyder[1](iD), Mayank Anchlia[2](iD),
and Pulkil Agrawal[2]

[1] Department of Aviation, University of North Dakota, Grand Forks, ND 58203, USA
{s.vidhyadharan,paul.snyder}@und.edu
[2] Department of CS&IS, BITS-Pilani KK Birla Goa Campus, Sancoale, India
{f20140053,f20140356}@goa.bits-pilani.ac.in

**Abstract.** Unmanned Aerial Vehicles (UAVs) have a plethora of applications in extreme time-sensitive use cases by forming an advantageous structure with low-power devices. In time-sensitive cases, effective communication plays an important role in low-power devices. It is challenging to design a communication protocol if the node poses mobility. In this paper, we propose an energy-efficient communication protocol for data transfer from multiple sources via mobile relay nodes. The paper proposes the use of *mobility vector* information, such as the location of the nodes, speed, and direction along with the communication range to route the data to the next hop. Once the gateway node detects the presence of multiple sources, a Steiner tree algorithm is used to calculate the best routing path connecting multiple sources to the gateway node via the mobile relay nodes. The proposed algorithm guarantees that the number of nodes participating in routing is minimal and is capable of dynamically selecting the neighboring nodes with respect to the varying topology. The simulation results show that the proposed approach is better in terms of packet delivery ratio and energy efficiency.

**Keywords:** Unmanned Aerial Vehicle · Mobile networks · Data Routing · Steiner Tree

## 1 Introduction

UAVs' mobility can be based on external stimuli like a dynamic environment or in a controlled manner. Energy-limited UAVs' have to be very efficient in making the decision for relocation for better communication. In controlled mobility, a node can easily relocate to improve network efficiency. But in the scenario where the UAVs which are enrolled in executing an ongoing application, the node would not have a say in the mobility like maneuvering in a small confined place. For example, a scenario where a swarm of UAVs performs a search operation while a

© The Author(s), under exclusive license to Springer Nature Switzerland AG 2023
Y. Koucheryavy and A. Aziz (Eds.): NEW2AN 2022, LNCS 13772, pp. 534–545, 2023.
https://doi.org/10.1007/978-3-031-30258-9_48

different UAV network can make use of the swarm nodes to relay the data from the source to a gateway node [10].

As an initial step in developing communication protocols with UAV based mobile relays in the networks, we considered a scenario of multi UAVs with the gateway node (ground station) being static while all other nodes (UAVs) are mobile. There are multiple sources present in the network and the mobility of the relay nodes is assumed to be random. The aim is to develop an energy-efficient routing protocol, by considering the multiple sources, so as to calculate the best routing path (with the minimum number of nodes participating in data communication). Since the network topology is dynamic, the probability that the same node participates in routing for a prolonged period of time will be less and hence the network lifetime is extended. The paper proposes to use a Steiner tree algorithm which guarantees that the number of nodes participating in the data communication is less when compared to each source communicating the data directly to the gateway node.

Section 2 brief the background of existing architecture and different routing protocol available. The proposed approach with algorithms is explained in Sect. 3. Implementation details with the results are given in Sect. 4 and Sect. 5 concludes the paper.

## 2   Background

Deploying a large number of UAVs includes challenges such as building efficient communication protocols and ensuring collision-free and seamless operations [9]. To achieve seamless cooperation and collaboration between UAVs, inter-UAV communication becomes necessary [8]. The most common single Pilot in Command (PIC) application includes a pilot operating a single UAV. Multi-path UAV systems may also include single PIC operations where multiple UAVs may link to each other in addition to the ground station. In Flying Ad-hoc Networks (FANET), the communication between UAVs is called UAV-to-UAV (U2U) link whereas the communication with UAV to the ground station is UAV-to-Infrastructure (U2I) U2G link respectively.

The dynamic topology of UAV networks makes it challenging to build a routing protocol. The uneven distribution of the node along with the mobility makes it more difficult to have a long-term multi-hop routing in FANET. Due to these factors, the communication protocols built for Mobile Ad hoc Networks (MANET) and Vehicle Ad hoc Networks (VANET) cannot be directly adapted. The design of the communication protocol has to be made based on the frequent topology changes owing to their high mobility [3].

Localization is one critical aspect in designing communication protocol. The network topology is determined by the accuracy of the UAV location in the system estimate. For example, if the node mobility is high and the GPS sampling time is less, then this may degrade the performance of the communication protocol in use. The use of advanced Kalman filter [12] with the help of GPS and Inertial measurement units can help in improving the localization accuracy. The presence of electromagnetic radiation and multipath reception can degrade the performance of location estimation [6].

Different routing protocols applicable to UAV networks were proposed in various literature. Arafat, M.Y. and Moh, S. [2] classified this into position-based, topology-based, cluster-based, deterministic, stochastic, and social-network-based touting protocols. The node mobility model plays a major role in designing an efficient routing protocol. The mobility model depends on the type of application the UAV is used for. In the scenario where the UAV paths are pre-defined, the mobility model is regular. UAV's such as Swarms or multi-UAV systems performing autonomous operations without a central control will come under the group mobility model. Random direction and Random way-point are the most commonly used, random mobility models. The efficiency of a wireless link depends on the mobility model. It is challenging to design a routing protocol with a random mobility model when compared with a deterministic mobility model. Routing protocol should be designed with the consideration of the mobility model to ensure end-to-end data delivery.

Few routing algorithms have been studied in the literature for this scenario, such as Greedy Perimeter Stateless Routing (GPSR) [5], and Receiver-based Opportunistic Forwarding Protocol (ROF) [7]. GPSR algorithm [5] consists of two methods to send a packet from the source to the destination. The first method, *greedy forwarding*, is when the node forwards it's a packet to its' geometrically closest neighbour node to the destination. When none of the node's neighbors are closer to the destination than the node itself, then the second method, *perimeter forwarding*, is used, where the packet is forwarded to a node on its perimeter. Even though this causes the packet to move farther in geometric distance from the destination temporarily, it improves reachability, as the perimeter node could forward the packet to the destination, and so there is a greater chance of the packet reaching the destination.

Mobility Management UAV-based Grouping routing protocol (MMUG) [1] creates an optimal path based on path length, bandwidth, distance, and broadcast message in three phases. The first phase ground station transmits the sensed data to the UAV. In the second phase, the UAVs vehicle groups the nodes based on the coverage range of the Group Head (GH). The group node which is close to the ground station collects the location of all nodes and if any UAV moves away within the range of GH or comes in the range of GH, the information of those nodes will be updated to the group node. The routing Metric is calculated for the selection of optimal paths based on minimum bandwidth, minimum delay, and minimum path length and selected by prioritizing length, bandwidth, and delay in an ordered manner which reduces the control overhead and routing overhead. In phase three, the GH communicates with the ground base station.

ROF protocol [7] uses a dual-channel based forwarding mechanism to send a packet from the source to the destination. The sender broadcasts the data packet to all its neighbors, and the neighbor nodes contend for forwarding rights with two steps. First, the neighbors which are farther away from the sender eliminate themselves. Then, the remaining nodes contend for the forwarding right according to a certain mechanism, and whichever node wins, starts to forward the data packet. Re-transmitting happens in overstep mode if there are no nodes attending the forwarding right contention.

The paper proposes a routing protocol for a scenario where multiple UAVs are used to sense the environmental data such as streaming a video of a specific incident or capturing an acoustic signal from a location and hence communicating to a common gateway node with the help of other UAVs present in the communication range.

# 3   Proposed Approach

*Problem Statement:* The network is composed of $K$ static nodes which are capable of capturing the environmental data, gateway nodes, and dense deployment of $N$ UAV nodes. All nodes have a communication coverage of radius $R_c$. The multiple sources in the network have data to transmit to the gateway. The aim is to relay the data from multiple sources o the gateway node via the UAV nodes available. This need to be done by selecting the best possible path for forwarding the packets and thereby enhancing network efficiency. Figure 1 shows the scenario of a UAV network with multiple data sources and UAV nodes deployed.

*Assumptions:* We assume that the nodes deployed in the network know their location using GPS or a similar localization technique. Also, the location of the gateway node is known to all the nodes in the network. The paper also assumes to use of a wireless communication protocol Zigbee which uses a cross-layered architecture is used to establish communication in the UAV network. Since the end-to-end connection establishment is not possible due to the dynamic topology, an approach very similar to a disruption tolerance network (DTN) is considered for data transferring. This means the intermediate nodes are capable of storing the data and the forward the data once the next hop neighbor is identified.

The proposed approach is presented below. The protocol has three phases: *i) Network Initialization, ii) Steiner Vertex calculation and iii) Data Communication.*

## 3.1   Phase $I$: Network Initialization

Network initialization is the first phase and is executed after the network deployment. The aim of the network initialization phase is to transfer the data from a source node and the gateway node. First, the node which has data broadcasts a discovery packet, $P_{disc}$ containing its location information to all its neighbors. A node which receives the $P_{disc}$ packet will reply with a $P_{rep}$ packet. This is done after a small time interval $\rho_t$, after receiving the $P_{disc}$ packet. The value of $\rho_t$ is different for different nodes even though $P_{disc}$ packet is received at the same time. The value of $\rho_t$ is calculated based on two factors which are i) the location of the gateway node and ii) contact time ($\hat{t}$). Contact time is the time of contact with respect to the communication range and with the mobility vector information. The value of $\rho_t$ is lesser for a UAV relay neighbor whose contact time, $\hat{t}$ is maximum and also which lies Euclidean distance close to the gateway node.

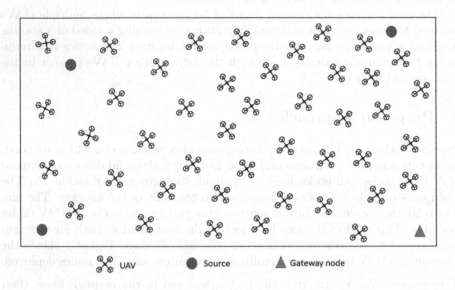

**Fig. 1.** Scenario: A multi UAV with multiple Sources

The calculation of $\hat{t}$ is given in Sect. 3.1. The varying $\rho_t$ is introduced in order to set high priority for a relay node which is in communication range of the sender for a longer time. The nodes whose location is between the source and the gateway nodes will have priority in communicating the data back to the gateway node.

$$\rho_t \propto \frac{d_{(i,bs)}}{\hat{t}}$$

where $d_{(i,bs)}$ is the Euclidean distance between a node $i$ and the gateway node. A node with a high value of $\hat{t}$ and with minimum Euclidean distance close to the gateway nodes will send $P_{rep}$ packet to the sender at the earliest. All neighbors that overhear the reply message refrain from sending a $P_{rep}$ message. The node from which the $P_{rep}$ is received first is treated as the immediate next hop for routing the data packet. The source continues to transmit the data for $\hat{t}$ units of time, which is the contact time for which the two nodes will remain within the transmission range of each other.

**Contact Time Calculation.** The contact time of the two mobile nodes $n_1$ and $n_2$ is the time for which the two nodes remain in transmission range $r$. Let $\overrightarrow{X_1(t)}$ is the position vector for node $n_1$. Similarly $\overrightarrow{X_2(t)}$ is the position vector of node $n_2$. The scenario is shown in Fig. 2.

Let $t_0$ be the instance from which the value $\hat{t}$ is to be calculated. Then,

$$|\overrightarrow{X_1}(t_0) - \overrightarrow{X_2}(t_0)|$$

is the distance between the nodes initially and this will be lesser than the transmission range $r$ of the nodes. Let $t'$ be the time when the nodes move beyond the communication range. That is

$$|\overrightarrow{X_1}(t') - \overrightarrow{X_2}(t')| \tag{1}$$

$$t' = \min t \quad | \quad |\overrightarrow{X_1}(t) - \overrightarrow{X_1}(t)| > r \tag{2}$$

Then, $t' - t_0$ is the contact time $\hat{t}$, for nodes $n_1$ and $n_2$.

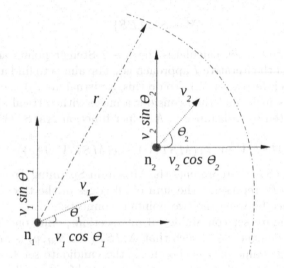

**Fig. 2.** Scenario of two mobile nodes moving with velocity $v_1$, $v_2$

Thus, relative velocity $v_r$ of the two nodes is $\overrightarrow{v_r} = \overrightarrow{v_1} - \overrightarrow{v_2}$
From [11] the contact time $\hat{t}$ can be obtained using the equation

$$\hat{t} = \left( \frac{r - \sqrt{(x_1 - x_2)^2 + (y_1 - y_2)^2}}{\sqrt{(v_1 \cos\theta_1 - v_2 \cos\theta_2)^2 + (v_1 \sin\theta_1 - v_2 \sin\theta_2)^2}} \right) \tag{3}$$

where $(x_1, y_1)$ and $(x_2, y_2)$ are the coordinate of $n_1$ and $n_2$ respectively. The relay nodes also forward it in the same way till the packet reaches the gateway node. When the gateway node receives the initial packets containing the locations from all of the source nodes, it moves to the next phase.

## 3.2   Phase $II$: Steiner Vertex Calculation

Phase II is initiated by the gateway node when it starts receiving data from the source node. When the gateway node receives data from more than one source node, it locally calculates the Steiner vertex set, $\mathbb{V}_{st}$. For Steiner set calculation, the location of the source node and the gateway node is used as input.

**Steiner Vertex Set Calculation.** The set of source nodes is defined as:

$$S = \{S_0, S_1, ..., S_{n-1}\} \tag{4}$$

Since there is only one gateway node ($BS$) to which the data finally needs to be transferred, the cumulative set of all vertices used for the Steiner point calculation is defined as $\mathbb{V}$, where $|\mathbb{V}| = n$.

$$\mathbb{V} = S \cup \{BS\} \tag{5}$$

The gateway node then calculates the $n - 2$ Steiner points according to a modified version of the iterative $I$ approach [4]. The aim is to find a near-optimal value of the Steiner vertex set $\mathbb{V}_{st}$. To do this, a virtual area $A$ is created, which contains all points in $\mathbb{V}$, and then consider a mesh with vertical and horizontal lines, each separated by a distance $\gamma$. A helper function $\Delta MST(V, v)$ is defined as:

$$\Delta MST(V, v) = c(MST(V)) - c(MST(V \cup \{v\})) \tag{6}$$

In the Eq. 6, $MST(V)$ represents the Minimum Spanning Tree for the set of vertices $V$, and $c(T)$ represents the sum of all edges of the tree $T$, where each edge is the distance between the two points it connects.

$\mathbb{C}$ is the candidate set containing all intersection points on the mesh. The aim is to find an element $v \in \mathbb{C}$ such that $\Delta MST(\mathbb{V} \cup \mathbb{V}_{st}, v)$ is maximized.

Initially, a large value of $\gamma$ is chosen for the candidate set $\mathbb{C}$, and once the element $v = (p, q)$ is identified, the process is repeated for a smaller value of $\gamma'$ for a smaller area $A'$. The area $A'$ is the area between the coordinates $(p - \gamma, q - \gamma)$ and $(p + \gamma, q + \gamma)$. Again, from the candidate set $C'$, a value $v'$ is chosen such that it maximizes Eq. 6. The Steiner vertex set is updated as $\mathbb{V}_{st} = \mathbb{V}_{st} \cup \{v\}$, and the entire procedure is repeated $n - 2$ times. The Steiner node calculation is shown in Algorithm 1.

**Algorithm 1.** Steiner Vertex Set calculation

1: **procedure** STEINER_VERTEX_SET($\mathbb{V}$)
2:    *Steiner_vertex_set* $\mathbb{V}_{st} \leftarrow \emptyset$
3:    **for** $n - 2$ times **do**
4:        Calculate *Candidate_set* $\mathbb{C}$ *with* $\gamma$
5:        $v \leftarrow \underset{x \in C}{max}\{\Delta MST(\mathbb{V} \cup \mathbb{V}_{st}, x)\}$
6:        Calculate *Candidate_set* $\mathbb{C}'$ *with* $\gamma' \ll \gamma$
7:        $v' \leftarrow \underset{x \in C'}{max}\{\Delta MST(\mathbb{V} \cup \mathbb{V}_{st}, x)\}$
8:        Update $\mathbb{V}_{st} \leftarrow \mathbb{V}_{st} \cup \{v'\}$
9:    **end for**
10:    **return** $\mathbb{V}_{st}$
11: **end procedure**

After calculating the Steiner vertex set, the gateway node creates a packet containing all the Steiner vertices and forwards it to all the source nodes. When a source node receives a list of the Steiner points from the gateway node, it selects the closest Steiner point to itself as the location to which all future packets from that source will be forwarded, and begins the third phase.

### 3.3 Phase $III$: Data Communication

In this phase, all source nodes send their packets to their closest Steiner point, which is a UAV node in the location identified. The UAV nodes forward the packet to the geographical area of the Steiner points.

At each Steiner point, a virtual area of radius $r_s$ is imagined. A UAV node present in this area is chosen as the Steiner node based on the amount of time the node will be present in the area. All packets destined for the geographic location of the Steiner point will be received by this Steiner node. When the Steiner node is about to leave the area, it designates another node in that area as the Steiner node. If the network supports a subset of UAV nodes that are in the controlled mobility category, a dedicated UAV (or a set of UAVs) can be assigned as a Steiner point to relay the data.

When a packet reaches the Steiner node $v$, the next closest Steiner point $v'$ to $v$ is calculated. The packet is forwarded to $v'$, if the gateway node is closer to $v'$ than to $v$. Otherwise, the packet is forwarded to the gateway node.

Thus, all communication is done as per the calculated Steiner tree of the network. Routing via Steiner nodes will guarantee that a minimum number of nodes will be participating in data communication connecting all the source nodes. A scenario of data communication using three sources is shown in Fig. 3.

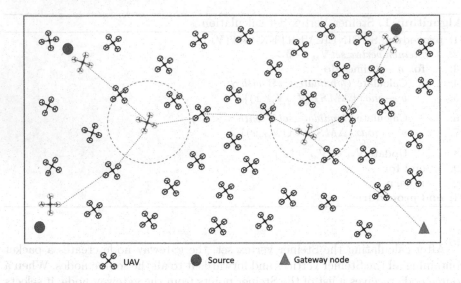

UAV          Source          Gateway node

**Fig. 3.** Scenario of three sources communicating with Gateway via a Steiner Node

## 4   Performance Evaluation

The proposed approach is simulated using Castalia, a network simulation framework in OMNET++. The performance evaluation is done by comparing the proposed approach with GPSR and ROF. The parameters chosen for the simulation are listed in Table 1. The simulation is done by varying the number of sources and packet rate. For simulation, the mobility model used is a random way-point model.

**Table 1.** Simulation Parameters

| Parameters | Values |
| --- | --- |
| Network Size | $100 \times 100$ m$^2$ |
| Number of Nodes | 50 nodes |
| Transmission Power | $-5$ db |
| Velocity | $0.5\,m/s$ to $10\,m/s$ |
| Number of Static Nodes | 1 (GateWay node) |
| Packet size | $128\,byte$ |
| Simulation Time | 500 s (Multiple Iterations) |
| Mobility Model | Random Way-point |

Multiple iterations of the simulation are done to compare the proposed approach with GPSR and ROF. Simulation is done by varying the velocity of the

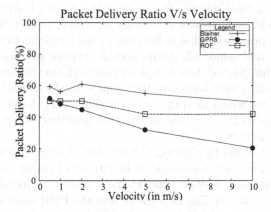

**Fig. 4.** PDR vs Velocity

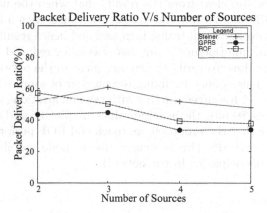

**Fig. 5.** PDR vs Number of Sources

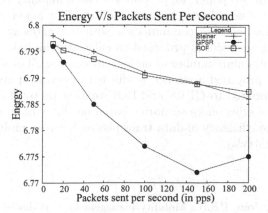

**Fig. 6.** Energy vs Packets per second

mobile nodes with four sources to compare the packet delivery ratio (PDR). From Fig. 4 it is clear that as the velocity increases, the PDR value decreases for all routing approaches. This is because of the dynamic topology, the nodes get disconnected and hence affect the overall network performance. It is clear from the graph that Steiner tree-based routing performs better than the GPRS and ROF. For Steiner tree-based routing approach, the overall hops connecting the nodes are fewer which in turn improves the packet delivery. The proposed approach performs better because of the best neighbor selection based on the contact time calculation.

Simulations are done by varying the number of sources with fixed velocity. The velocity, in that case, is assumed to be $10\,knots$ (5 m/s). Sources are placed randomly. Simulations are done with Multiple iterations to calculate the PDR rate with different sources. Figure 5 shows how the PDR value changes with the different numbers of sources. From Fig. 5, it is clear that the proposed approach performs better even though the initial case with two sources performs slightly below GPRS. It is also clear from the results that when the number of sources increases, the PDR values also reduce. This is because, with a higher number of sources in the network, overall traffic increases and hence results in the collision of packets. Network interference is another reason for reduced PDR.

Simulations are done to verify the energy spent in the network by increasing the sending rate. This is done by fixing the number of sources to four. Multiple iterations are done with sources starting with random locations for each iteration. Similar to the above results, the average values are plotted and are shown in Fig. 6. Results indicate that the proposed approach and ROF perform equally better when compared to GPSR. This is mainly due to node mobility and with less number of nodes participating in the network.

## 5   Conclusion

The paper proposes an energy-efficient routing protocol for UAV networks with multiple sources. In this paper, we propose the use of mobility vector information to calculate the best neighbor to transfer the data. The paper also considers the case where multiple sources communicate with the gateway node. A Steiner tree-based routing protocol is proposed to calculate the best path for routing the data with a minimum number of nodes participating. The simulation results indicate that the proposed approach is efficient in terms of energy and packet delivery ratio compared to GPRS and ROF routing protocol. Future Research would focus on covering more scenarios based on different dynamic topologies and improving the efficiency of data transmission between multiple mobile data sources and the gateway.

## References

1. Ananthi, J.V., Jose, P.S.H.: Mobility management UAV-based grouping routing protocol in flying ad hoc networks for biomedical applications. Int. J. Commun. Syst. **36**(1), e5362 (2022)

2. Arafat, M.Y., Moh, S.: Routing protocols for unmanned aerial vehicle networks: a survey. IEEE access **7**, 99694–99720 (2019)
3. Hong, J., Zhang, D.: TARCS: a topology change aware-based routing protocol choosing scheme of FANETs. Electronics **8**(3), 274 (2019)
4. Kahng, A.B., Robins, G.: A new class of iterative Steiner tree heuristics with good performance. IEEE Trans. Comput. Aided Des. Integr. Circuits Syst. **11**(7), 893–902 (1992)
5. Karp, B., Kung, H.T.: GPSR: greedy perimeter stateless routing for wireless networks. In: Proceedings of the 6th Annual International Conference on Mobile Computing and Networking, pp. 243–254. ACM (2000)
6. Kos, T., Markezic, I., Pokrajcic, J.: Effects of multipath reception on GPS positioning performance, pp. 399–402 (2010)
7. Li, L., Sun, L., Ma, J., Chen, C.: A receiver-based opportunistic forwarding protocol for mobile sensor networks. In: Distributed Computing Systems Workshops, 2008. ICDCS'08. 28th International Conference on, pp. 198–203. IEEE (2008)
8. Mishra, D., Trotta, A., Traversi, E., Di Felice, M., Natalizio, E.: Cooperative cellular UAV-to-everything (C-U2X) communication based on 5G sidelink for UAV swarms. Comput. Commun. **192**, 173–184 (2022)
9. Nemer, I.A., Sheltami, T.R., Belhaiza, S., Mahmoud, A.S.: Energy-efficient UAV movement control for fair communication coverage: a deep reinforcement learning approach. Sensors **22**(5), 1919 (2022)
10. Półka, M., Ptak, S., Kuziora, Ł: The use of UAV's for search and rescue operations. Procedia Eng. **192**, 748–752 (2017)
11. Sreejith, V., Surve, R., Vyas, N., Anupama, K.R., Gudino, L.J.: Area based routing protocol for mobile wireless sensor networks. In: 2018 International Conference on Information Networking (ICOIN), pp. 782–786 (2018). https://doi.org/10.1109/ICOIN.2018.8343224
12. Zhao, L., Ochieng, W.Y., Quddus, M.A., Noland, R.B.: An extended Kalman filter algorithm for integrating GPS and low cost dead reckoning system data for vehicle performance and emissions monitoring. J Navig. **56**(2), 257–275 (2003)

# Reduced Complexity Distributed Arithmetic Architecture for FIR Filters

Kirill Kozorez[✉] and Andrey Rashich[✉]

Peter the Great St.Petersburg Polytechnic University, St.Petersburg, Russia
kozorez.ks@edu.spbstu.ru, kkozorez00@gmail.com, rashich@cee.spbstu.ru

**Abstract.** Filters with a finite impulse response are important blocks in signal reception and processing applications. The relatively high complexity of FIR filters implementation in FPGA is due to the high number of multiply and accumulate (MAC) operations, and, consequently, the high number of on-chip multipliers used. Distributed arithmetic (DA) is an alternative approach of replacing on-chip multipliers with shift registers, look-up-tables (LUT) and adders. However, in DA approach the storage size grows rapidly as the filter order increases. Moreover the supported sampling frequency is inversely proportional to the input samples bit width in DA. This paper proposes a modified DA hardware architecture with reduced memory consumption and doubled maximum supported sampling frequency. The resources consumption of proposed architecture after its implementation in FPGA is lower compared to existing DA implementations.

**Keywords:** FIR Filter · Distributed Arithmetic · OBC · FPGA

## 1 Introduction

FIR filters are used in many digital signal processing systems to perform signal preprocessing, smoothing, bandwidth selection, decimation and interpolation, as well as to implement a low/high pass filtering (LPF/HPF) [1,2].

There are various hardware architectures of FIR filters. The chosen type of architecture is usually determined by the amount of operations and calculations required for a fixed number of clock cycles. Systolic and transposed architectures are the most common FIR filter hardware architectures. The advantages of systolic architecture include short critical path and high performance, the disadvantage of this architecture is relatively high delay. The transposed architecture provides a lower delay, but has low performance due to the high number of input signal branches (high fan-out) [3].

The main disadvantage of these architectures is the usage of on-chip multipliers. As the filter order increases, the number of MAC operations, which use on-chip multipliers, increases linearly. Consequently, implementation of FIR filters with high order becomes a difficult task, since multipliers are a limited FPGA resource.

© The Author(s), under exclusive license to Springer Nature Switzerland AG 2023
Y. Koucheryavy and A. Aziz (Eds.): NEW2AN 2022, LNCS 13772, pp. 546–556, 2023.
https://doi.org/10.1007/978-3-031-30258-9_49

One of various implementation techniques of FIR filters without on-chip multipliers was proposed in works of Peled and Liu [4] and Croisier [5]. Such an algorithm was based on the distributed arithmetic (DA). A DA based FIR filter is a way to implement a digital filter using sequential bit operations. The DA approach uses the decomposition of multiplication operation into shift registers, look-up-tables (LUT) and adders in such a way that multipliers are not required.

The DA architecture is used in the design of optical filters, adaptive filters [6,7] and special calculators, for example, based on the Fast Fourier Transform [8].

However, one of the important disadvantages of DA approach is high memory consumption and low maximum supported sampling frequency, which is inversely proportional to the bit width of the processed samples.

Various modifications of DA architecture are proposed. In [9], a method based on the offset binary coding (OBC) circuit is presented, which makes it possible to reduce memory size by half. The [10] proposes methods for partitioning a single memory block into several ones. The [11] presents architectures without LUT (LUT-less). These architectures are based on increasing the number of adders and adding 2:1 multiplexers.

This paper presents a modification of DA architecture based on the usage of dual-port memory with the adaptation of well-known methods OBC and BMP for memory consumption reduction [9,10]. The proposed architecture also increases the supported sampling frequency at least twice compared to traditional DA architectures.

The paper is organized as follows. Section 2 introduces the mathematical basics of DA approach and provides an overview of existing implementations of DA architecture. In Sect. 3 the proposed DA architecture for FIR filter is presented. Section 4 provides the implementation of the proposed architecture in FPGA with the estimates of hardware resources consumption and their comparison with other DA implementations. Final conclusions are drawn in Sect. 5.

## 2   Overview of DA

### 2.1   Classical DA Architecture

The main idea of the DA approach is to replace the multiplication block with sequential bit operations and look-up-tables (LUT). To do this, the input sample are presented in the two's complement form.

The output sample $y$ of the $N$-tap FIR filter is defined as:

$$y = \sum_{i=0}^{N-1} \omega_i x(N-i) \tag{1}$$

where $\omega_i$ is the weight coefficient of FIR filter and $x(N-i)$ is the input sample.

Let us write $x(N-i)$ as two's complement representation:

$$x(N-i) = -b_{i0} + \sum_{l=1}^{B-1} b_{il}2^{-l} \tag{2}$$

$$x(N-i) = b_{i0}, b_{i1}, \ldots, b_{i(B-1)}$$

Here $B$ is the bit width of the input sample, the bit $b_{i0}$ is its sign. Substituting $x(N-i)$ into (1) allows to get the result:

$$y = -\sum_{i=0}^{N-1} b_{i0}\omega_i + \sum_{l=1}^{B-1}(\sum_{i=0}^{N-1} b_{il}\omega_i)2^{-l} \tag{3}$$

Equation (3) is the basis for the classical DA architecture. Since each $b_{il}$ takes the value 0 or 1, the sum of the weight coefficients has $2^N$ possible linear combinations that can be calculated in advance and written to ROM.

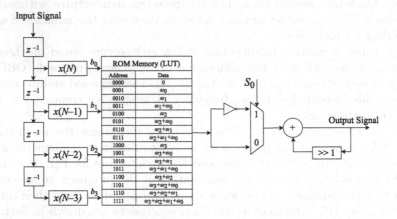

**Fig. 1.** Classical DA based FIR filter architecture, $N = 4$

The classical DA based FIR filter architecture is as shown on Fig. 1. This architecture consists of parallel shift register and accumulator, the central block is LUT (described as ROM memory), the elements of which store linear combinations of weight coefficients.

For classical DA architecture the necessary condition is the ratio of clock frequency to sampling frequency. The clock frequency must be more than $B$ times greater than the sampling frequency.

The new input sample enters the parallel shift register. Bit packets (the current $b_{il}$ bits of each input sample, $i = 0, \ldots, N-1$, $l = const$) are processed, starting from the lowest bit up to the sign bit. An address is generated from a bit packet, which enters the LUT. At a certain address, a linear combination of weight coefficients is selected from the LUT, which goes to the final adder. Also, this adder receives the result from the accumulator.

The result of the calculation goes to the output of filter and to the accumulator. The accumulator performs an arithmetic shift to the right of the previous result (partial sum). The partial sum obtained by analyzing the zero bits is added to the new linear combination at the next clock cycle, obtained at the address consisting of the first bits, etc. The control signal $S_0$ is targeted to process the sign bit packets ($S_0 = 1$ for $l = 0$, otherwise $S_0 = 0$).

The result of filtering (1) after $B$ clock cycles is output after analyzing the last bits (signed). After that the next input sample $x(N)$ arrives, pushing aside the previous one, which becomes $x(N - 1)$.

This architecture requires relatively smaller area compared to the MAC-based design used in transposed or systolic filter forms.

However, classical DA architecture has two main disadvantages: low supported sampling frequency and usage of high number of elements in the LUT. The maximum supported sampling frequency is $B$ times less than the clock frequency, because the $l$-th bit packet ($B$ is equal to the number of bit packets) is processed at each clock cycle. The high number of elements is determined by the filter order and the number of possible linear combinations of weight coefficients. The OBC scheme [9], the block memory partition algorithm [10] or both methods together allow to reduce the memory consumed.

## 2.2   OBC Circuit

The size of the LUT increases exponentially with increasing filter order, which reduces the performance. The OBC circuit [9] can be used to reduce the required LUT size in a DA architecture.

Let us write $x(N - i)$ as:

$$x(N - i) = 1/2(x(N - i) - (-x(N - i))) \tag{4}$$

The two's complement form of $-x(N - i)$ can be written as:

$$-x(N - i) = -\overline{b_{i0}} + \sum_{l=1}^{B-1} \overline{b_{il}} 2^{-l} + 2^{-(B-1)} \tag{5}$$

Substitute (2) and (5) in (4) and simplify, then:

$$x(N - i) = 1/2(-(b_{i0} - \overline{b_{i0}}) + \sum_{l=1}^{B-1} (b_{i0} - \overline{b_{i0}}) 2^{-l}) + 2^{-(B-1)}$$

For simple notation, let us assume:

$$s_{il} = \begin{cases} b_{i0} - \overline{b_{i0}} & l \neq 0 \\ -(b_{i0} - \overline{b_{i0}}) & l = 0 \end{cases}$$

$$x(N - i) = 1/2(\sum_{l=0}^{B-1} s_{il} 2^{-l}) + 2^{-(B-1)} \tag{6}$$

Substitute (6) in (1) and simplify, then:

$$y = \sum_{l=0}^{B-1}\left(\sum_{i=0}^{N-1}(s_{il}\frac{\omega_i}{2})2^{-l}\right) + 2^{-(B-1)}P_{init} \tag{7}$$

$$P_{init} = \sum_{i=0}^{N-1}\frac{\omega_i}{2}$$

The difference between result (7) and (3) is that the resulting linear combination of weight coefficients is represented by all non-zero coefficients. For example, we get a combination with all the "pluses". When calculating the remaining linear combinations of the weight coefficients, there will be a combination with all the "minuses".

In other words, the transformation allows to write the first combination into a LUT, and get the second one by inversion. This property allows to reduce the number of elements in the LUT from $2^N$ to $2^{N-1}$. Also $N-1$ bits are needed instead of $N$ to form an address.

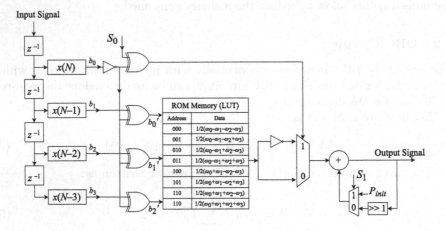

**Fig. 2.** DA based FIR filter architecture with OBC circuit, $N = 4$

An architecture of DA with OBC circuit is shown on Fig. 2. To add the $P_{init}$ term, the control signal $S_1$ is used, which takes the value 1 only on the first clock cycle.

## 2.3  Block Memory Partition

The algorithm based on block memory partition [10,11] consists in dividing a block of memory (with linear combinations of weight coefficients) into several sub-blocks. This representation of LUT allows to considerably reduce the number of linear combinations.

This is explained by a decrease in the bit width of the address. When dividing one memory block into $k$ sub-blocks, the address bit width decreases from $N$ to $N/k$ bits. Consequently, the number of elements in the LUT decreases.

Block memory partition algorithm works together with the OBC circuit (Fig. 3). Rearrange the summation operation to (7), then:

$$y = 1/2 \sum_{l=0}^{B-1} \left( \sum_{i=0}^{\frac{N}{k}-1} s_{il}\omega_i + \cdots + \sum_{i=(k-1)\frac{N}{k}}^{N-1} s_{il}\omega_i \right) 2^{-l} + 2^{-(B-1)} P_{init} \qquad (8)$$

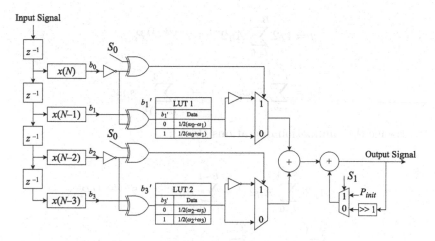

**Fig. 3.** DA based FIR filter architecture with OBC circuit and Block Memory Partition, $N = 4$, $k = 2$

With a linear increase in the number of sub-blocks $k$, the number of elements decreases from $2^{N-1}$ of OBC to $k \cdot 2^{N/k-1}$. Also the scheme has additional $k - 1$ adders and multiplexers.

## 3   Proposed Scheme

In this section we describe the proposed architecture for DA based FIR filter with algorithms for reducing memory consumption, given in Sect. 2.2 and Sect. 2.3.

All the architectures given in Sect. 2 have the ratio of clock frequency to sampling frequency $B$, where $B$ is the bit width of input sample. In this section, a method is proposed that allows to increase this ratio by at least twice.

The basis of the mathematical description of the proposed architecture is the architecture with block memory partition and OBC circuit. The output signal of the FIR filter with this architecture is presented in (8).

$$y = 1/2 \sum_{l=0}^{B-1} \left( \sum_{i=0}^{\frac{N}{k}-1} s_{il}\omega_i + \cdots + \sum_{i=(k-1)\frac{N}{k}}^{N-1} s_{il}\omega_i \right) 2^{-l} + 2^{-(B-1)} P_{init}$$

$$P_{init} = \sum_{i=0}^{N-1} \frac{\omega_i}{2}$$

When processing a one bit packet, one linear combination of weight coefficients can be calculated in one clock cycle.

Rewrite the (8) as:

$$y = 1/2 \sum_{l=0}^{B-1} A_{il} 2^{-l} + 2^{-(B-1)} P_{init}$$

$$A_{il} = \sum_{i=0}^{\frac{N}{k}-1} s_{il}\omega_i + \cdots + \sum_{i=(k-1)\frac{N}{k}}^{N-1} s_{il}\omega_i$$

Rearrange the summation operations (by 1):

$$y = 1/2 \left( \sum_{l=0}^{\frac{B}{2}-1} A_{il} 2^{-l} + \sum_{l=\frac{B}{2}}^{B-1} A_{il} 2^{-l} \right) + 2^{-(B-1)} P_{init}$$

$$y = 1/2 \left( \sum_{l=0}^{\frac{B}{2}-1} A_{il} 2^{-l} + \sum_{l=0}^{\frac{B}{2}-1} A_{il} 2^{-(l+\frac{B}{2})} \right) + 2^{-(B-1)} P_{init}$$

$$y = 1/2 \left( \sum_{l=0}^{\frac{B}{2}-1} A_{il} 2^{-l} + \sum_{l=0}^{\frac{B}{2}-1} A_{il} 2^{-l} 2^{-\frac{B}{2}} \right) + 2^{-(B-1)} P_{init} \tag{9}$$

The Eq. (9) shows that it is possible to process two bit packets together. The result of the second bit packet is arithmetically shifted to the right by $B/2$ bits. Also, this expression defines two groups for processing: the most $B/2$ and the least $B/2$ bits of a single input sample.

Now the ratio of clock frequency to sampling frequency has been changed. The clock frequency must be more than $B/2$ (instead of $B$ for classical DA architectures) times greater than the sampling frequency.

An example of modified DA architecture with proposed approach is shown on Fig. 4.

Consequently, the architecture with OBC circuit and block memory partition is corrected by introducing adder tree and shift registers.

The main disadvantage of the bitwise partition of the input sample is the increase of elements in the LUT. This is explained by the fact that two bit

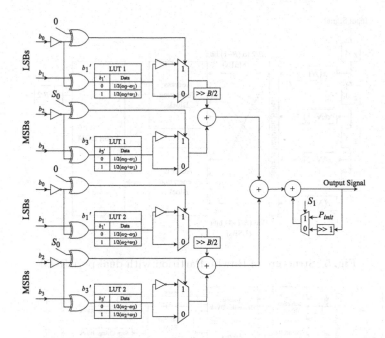

**Fig. 4.** DA based FIR filter architecture with proposed approach, $N = 4$, $k = 2$

packets use memory blocks with the same elements. These elements are presented as linear combinations of identical weight coefficients.

The solution to this problem is to use dual-port memory. Then the LUT block is represented by a dual-port ROM memory with two independent address inputs. An address is sent to each port, according to which the corresponding linear combination of weight coefficients is selected.

The structure using dual-port memory is shown on Fig. 5. The output of the Sample Partition Block obtains two groups of $B/2$ bits. By analogy with the classical DA architecture, bitwise processing is performed with a rate of two bit packets per a single clock cycle. The linear combination of weight coefficient after MSBs packet analysis is shifted by $B/2$ bits.

Increasing the ratio of clock frequency to sampling frequency by more than two times is possible. However, for this it is necessary to use more memory blocks that have the same composition of LUT elements, which significantly affects the amount of resources consumed. The additional memory blocks are required, because FPGA block memory can have maximum two data inputs/outputs (dual port mode).

Finally, combining the described modifications, the proposed DA architecture with increase maximum supported sampling frequency looks as on Fig. 6 ($N = 8$, $k = 2$).

At first, the input sample goes to *Parallel Register Bank*. The register size is determined by the filter order and the bit width of the input sample. The

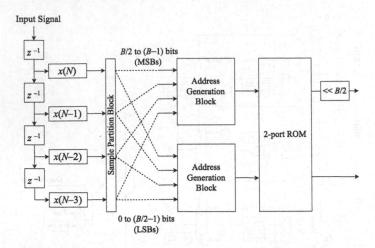

**Fig. 5.** Structure of Bitwise Partition with dual-port ROM

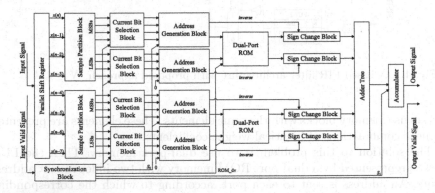

**Fig. 6.** Proposed DA based FIR filter hardware architecture, $N = 8$, $k = 2$

*Sample Partition Block* is a preprocessing block. In this block the input sample is divided into 2 groups of 8 bits each. The output of *Current Bit Selection Block* is the input sample (its half), coming out at a rate of 1 bit per 1 clock cycle. The OBC circuit is the basis of the *Address Generation Block.*

Secondly, according to the received address a linear combination of weight coefficients is selected from *2-port ROM*. The upper ROM contains linear combinations with weights from $\omega_0$ to $\omega_3$, the lower ROM contains linear combinations from $\omega_4$ to $\omega_7$. The *Sign Change Block* consists of a multiplexer and an inverter. It inverts the generated linear combination depending on the *inverse* signal. The resulting linear combinations arrive to *Adder Tree*, which consists of three adders and two shift by $B/2$ registers (see Fig. 4). The *Accumulator* accumulates partial sums to produce the filtering result. The *Synchronization Block* generates control signals from valid signal.

# 4   FPGA Implementation

The proposed FIR filter Da architecture was implemented and verified in Simulink bit-accurate model. This approach simplifies further FPGA implementation and helps to estimate resources usage. The main hardware resource for implementation are LUT-FPGA. LUT-FPGA is a simple resource of FPGA. The LUT (or LUT-DA) defined in previous sections is the block memory (ROM) with precomputed linear combinations of weight coefficients.

The target FPGA was xc7a35tcpg236-1 of the Xilinx Artix-7 family. All the analyzed DA architectures were implemented in the same FPGA to have the common basis for comparison. The synthesis strategy was the same for all implementations.

Table 1 and 2 shows the resources consumed by the LUT-FPGA in overall architecture and a memory block respectively for the proposed architecture and their comparison with classical [4], OBC circuit [9] and block memory partition (BMP) with $k = 2$ [10] DA architectures based FIR filter with filter order $N = 8$ and clock frequency $f_{clk} = 400$ MHz.

The FIR filter with proposed architecture increases the maximum supported sampling frequency relative to other DA architectures. Consequently, the complexity of these architectures was scaled up twice to make this sampling frequency the same for all of them.

**Table 1.** DA based FIR Filter Resources Estimates

| DA architecture | LUT-FPGA | Flip-Flop | Delay, clock cycles |
|---|---|---|---|
| Classical [4] | 502 | 854 | 22 |
| OBC circuit [9] | 434 | 782 | 23 |
| OBC + BMP [10] | 484 | 932 | 25 |
| Proposed | 362 | 797 | 20 |

**Table 2.** LUT-DA Recourses Estimates (for bit width of weight coefficients $C = 18$)

| DA architecture | LUT-FPGA | Flip-Flop | Number of elements | Bit width of elements |
|---|---|---|---|---|
| Classical [4] | 136 | 38 | 512 | 21 |
| OBC circuit [9] | 76 | 36 | 256 | 20 |
| OBC + BMP [10] | 56 | 40 | 32 | 20 |
| Proposed | 15 | 19 | 16 | 20 |

From the results, it can be concluded that there is a significant decrease LUT-FPGA recourses and number of elements for relatively the same values of flip-flops and delay.

## 5    Conclusion

This paper presents the modified DA architecture, based on OBC and BMP approaches and migration of LUT storage type from single-port to dual-port memory. The number of elements in the LUT has decreased from initial $2^N$ to $k \cdot 2^{N/k-1}$. The dual-port memory made it possible to double the maximum supported sampling frequency without memory consumption growth.

The example FPGA implementation shows the decrease of LUT-FPGA resources by more than three times in LUT-DA memory compared to the OBC + BMP DA architecture. Also implementation shows the 17% reduction of LUT-FPGA resources (from 434 to 362) in the overall architecture compared to the OBC DA architecture for $N = 8$, $k = 2$.

The proposed DA architecture has lower complexity compared to other known DA architectures.

## References

1. Rojo-Álvarez, J.L., Martínez-Ramón, M., Muñoz-Marí, J., Camps-Valls, G.: Introduction to Digital Signal Processing (2018)
2. Smith, S.W., et al.: The scientist and engineer's guide to digital signal processing (1997)
3. Hawkes, G.C.: Digital signal processing: designing for optimal results. high-performance DSP using virtex-4 FPGAs by xilinx, Edition 1.0 (2005)
4. Peled, A., Liu, B.: A new hardware realization of digital filters. IEEE Trans. Acoust. Speech Signal Process. **22**(6), 456–462 (1974)
5. Levilion, M.E., Rizo, V., Croisier, A., Esteban, D.J.: Digital filter for PCM encoded signals. U.S. Patent 00208345A (1973)
6. Allred, D.J., Yoo, H., Krishnan, V., Huang, W., Anderson, D.V.: LMS adaptive filters using distributed arithmetic for high throughput. IEEE Trans. Circ. Syst. I Regular Pap. **52**(7), 1327–1337 (2005)
7. Guo, R., DeBrunner, L.S.: A novel adaptive filter implementation scheme using distributed arithmetic. In: 2011 Conference Record of the Forty Fifth Asilomar Conference on Signals, Systems and Computers (ASILOMAR), pp. 160–164 (2011)
8. Rawski, M., Wojtynnski, M., Wojciechowski, T., Majkowski, P.: Distributed arithmetic based implementation of Fourier transform targeted at FPGA architectures. In: 2007 14th International Conference on Mixed Design of Integrated Circuits and Systems, pp. 152–156 (2007)
9. Hong, B., Yin, H., Wang, X., Xiao, Y.: Implementation of FIR filter on FPGA using DAOBC algorithm. In: The 2nd International Conference on Information Science and Engineering, pp. 3761–3764 (2010)
10. Schroder, H.: High word-rate digital filters with programmable table look-up. IEEE Trans. Circ. Syst. **24**(5), 277–279 (1977)
11. NagaJyothi, G., SriDevi, S.: Distributed arithmetic architectures for FIR filters-a comparative review. In: 2017 International Conference on Wireless Communications, Signal Processing and Networking (WiSPNET), pp. 2684–2690 (2017)

# Blockchain-Driven Hybrid Model for IoT Authentication

Truong Duy Dinh[1](✉) , Tran Duc Le[2] , Khanh Quoc Dang[2] ,
Vladimir Vishnevsky[3] , and Ruslan Kirichek[4]

[1] Posts and Telecommunications Institute of Technology, Hanoi, Vietnam
duydt@ptit.com.vn
[2] University of Science and Technology – The University of Danang, Danang,
Vietnam
letranduc@dut.udn.vn
[3] V. A. Trapeznikov Institute of Control Sciences of Russian Academy of Sciences,
Moscow, Russia
[4] The Bonch-Bruevich
Saint Petersburg State University of Telecommunications, Saint Petersburg, Russia
kirichek@sut.ru

**Abstract.** The Internet of Things has the potential to play a significant part in the ongoing Industrial Revolution. Machines, devices, and sensors are able to connect and communicate with each other via networks. These Internet of Things devices generate an enormous amount of data that is sensitive to privacy and security. For this reason, the security of these devices is of the utmost importance to guarantee the system's reliability and efficiency. It has been suggested that one efficient way to increase the safety of authentication for Internet of Things networks is to use blockchain technology for the purpose of authenticating users and devices on those networks. The purpose of this study is to conduct research and make a proposal for a blockchain-driven hybrid model for the Internet of Things authentication. This model is intended to be an improvement based on previously developed models and has shown promising results on the Ganache blockchain.

**Keywords:** Internet of Things · authentication model · Blockchain

## 1 Introduction

In recent years, the Internet of Things (IoT) has received much attention, and it is expanding quickly due to the spread of communication technology and the introduction of enough gadgets [1]. Based on the Ericsson Mobility Report[1], 550 million 5G subscriptions will be available in 2022, with 10% of all subscriptions located in Asia-Pacific. By 2022, over 29 billion connected devices are predicted, with approximately 18

---

[1] https://www.ericsson.com/en/about-us/company-facts/ericsson-worldwide/india/authored-articles/ushering-in-A-better-connected-future.

© The Author(s), under exclusive license to Springer Nature Switzerland AG 2023
Y. Koucheryavy and A. Aziz (Eds.): NEW2AN 2022, LNCS 13772, pp. 557–573, 2023.
https://doi.org/10.1007/978-3-031-30258-9_50

billion involved with IoT. According to the Internet of Things Team - IDC[2], there will be 41,6 billion connected IoT devices by 2025 in the world. These examples highlight the importance of IoT devices in today's digital society [2]. Additionally, IoT applications such as healthcare, smart home, and agricultural applications show that IoT has appeared everywhere and in all aspects of life.

Besides that, growth potential, IoT faces many challenges, such as interoperability, compatibility, limited bandwidth, data complexity, data volume, and especially security issues. The leading IoT security concerns are authentication, authorization, integrity, availability, and privacy [3–6]. In this research, we focus on the authentication issue in IoT networks because the authentication of users and devices in this network is still dependent on a third party.

Authentication determines whether a user or a device that wants to access the system is a valid user or device. Authentication is an essential requirement because it determines the security of the system. It allows valid users to operate and prevents system access and resource usage on the system from unauthorized users [7–9].

Recently, blockchain has emerged as a technology that can solve the authentication problem transparently and securely. In 2008, Satoshi Nakamoto proposed the blockchain [10]. All committed transactions are maintained in a sequence of blocks on a blockchain, which might be viewed as a public ledger. This chain expands continually as additional blocks are added. The essential properties of blockchain technology are decentralization, persistence, anonymity, and audibility. Integrating numerous essential technologies, including cryptographic hash, digital signature (based on asymmetric cryptography), and distributed consensus mechanism, enables blockchain to operate in a decentralized context. By using blockchain technology, a transaction may be conducted decentralized. Consequently, blockchain may significantly reduce costs and increase efficiency.

There are three main types of blockchain structures:

- **Public**: Public blockchains are decentralized and open to all participants. Public blockchains provide all blockchain nodes equal rights to access the blockchain, produce new data blocks, and validate data blocks. Cryptocurrencies such as Bitcoin, Ethereum, and Litecoin are exchanged and mined on public blockchains.
- **Private**: Private blockchains, also known as managed blockchains, are permissioned blockchains administered by a single entity. A central authority determines who can be a node in a private blockchain. In addition, the central authority does not always provide each node equal permissions to carry out functions. Private blockchains are only partially decentralized due to their restricted public accessibility. Ripple, a business-to-business virtual currency exchange network, and Hyperledger are private blockchains.
- **Consortium**: Consortium blockchains are permissioned blockchains administered by a group of organizations, as opposed to a single organization in the case of private blockchains. Therefore, consortium blockchains are more decentralized than private blockchains, resulting in greater security.

---

[2] https://www.businesswire.com/news/home/20190618005012/en/The-Growth-in-Connected-IoT-Devices-is-Expected-to-Generate-79.4ZB-of-Data-in-2025-According-to-A-New-IDC-Forecast.

To solve the authentication problem using blockchain, we also need Smart Contract [11]. Smart contracts are blockchain-based programs that execute when specific criteria are satisfied. Typically, they are used to automate the execution of an agreement so that all parties may know the outcome instantly, without the need for an intermediary or any time lost. In addition, they can automate a process by initiating the subsequent operation when certain circumstances are satisfied.

First, developers create snippet codes of Smart Contract and compile them into bytecodes. The bytecodes are deployed to the blockchain for future calls. Each time a user performs a transaction with Smart Contract, the EVM (Ethereum Virtual Machine) virtual machines will execute the Smart Contract command lines corresponding to the calls and update new states to the blockchain.

In the IoT authentication model, processing speed is also an essential factor. Recent studies indicate that fog computing can be a promising solution to this problem [12]. Fog computing is a distributed architecture that deploys storage and processing components to the cloud's edge. It is used to expand cloud computing. As a decentralized computing infrastructure, fog computing helps to bridge the gap between the cloud and where data is generated and operated. The objective is to serve new applications with lower latency needs while processing data more effectively to reduce network expenses. By bringing fog computing closer to IoT devices, instead of using cloud computing to perform real-time analytics and leverage computing power, the user experience can be significantly improved.

Based on the required authentication elements for IoT networks, we can divide authentication methods into user authentication, device authentication, and user and device authentication. Where authentication aims to answer the questions: Is it a valid user or not? Does the user own the data which he or she accesses? How to distinguish a malicious user from a legitimate user? Has the added device been used somewhere else by another user? Does one device have access to the other device's data? In recent studies, many authentication models for IoT networks based on blockchain have been proposed. However, most models only solve one of two problems: user authentication or device authentication. In our study, the authentication model will be used for both the authentication of users and devices in the network. The proposed model uses a Ganache[3] blockchain network with Smart Contract, fog computing simulated by NodeJS server, cloud, IoT devices and a web server. IoT devices are simulated with their MAC addresses and exchange information when requested. The simulation results show the usability of the proposed authentication model. This model can overcome some disadvantages of non-blockchain-based authentication and solve a few other problems in previous models.

The remainder of this study is organized as follows: Sect. 2 analyses the existing authentication methods based on blockchain for IoT networks. In Sect. 3, we propose an authentication model for both IoT devices and users. Section 4 shows the results of simulation and testing. Finally, Sect. 5 will provide the conclusions of this study.

---

[3] https://trufflesuite.com/ganache/.

## 2  Related Works

The essential qualities of blockchain are its distributed design, immutability, indestructibility, and fault tolerance. Due to these properties, blockchain-based authentication provides a novel and suitable method for authenticating IoT networks. Traditionally, IoT network authentication was conducted by a third-party intermediary who retained all information and fully controlled the user's authentication.

The existing IoT networks need authentication of both users and devices. User authentication aims to determine whether a valid user wants to access the resources within the scope of the authorized access to prevent the user from tampering with access to sensitive information. The primary purpose of device authentication is to determine which devices are genuine and which are malicious. In order to get information that compromises the security of user data, malicious devices may imitate regular devices by sending access requests to the whole network. Due to the limited processing power and storage capacity of IoT devices, a proper authentication mechanism may aid in securing devices from unauthorized access by attackers or malicious devices.

There has been some investigation into leveraging blockchain technology to provide transparent identity identification for IoT devices and users. The following are a few notable articles.

D. Li, W. Peng, W. Deng and F. Gai in [13] suggested using blockchain to construct a secure, tamper-proof ledger for IoT devices. Each device's unique ID was kept on the blockchain, enabling devices to validate each other without a central authority. New devices must register on the blockchain network to connect. Once authorized, the device may join the IoT network and share P2P data with other devices. It allows device-to-device communication and authentication. This might harm the IoT network and P2P devices if they cannot self-protect. This architecture authenticates network devices but not users utilizing devices.

An authentication model that utilizes fog nodes, which decrease network device processing power, was introduced in the paper [14]. As the number of devices increases, device authentication becomes more complicated, making network expansion harder. In addition, the smart contract offers mappings between devices and fog nodes and a list of user authentications. A device is only connected with a fog node under this approach, but a fog node may be connected to several devices. When a user needs to access a particular IoT device, it must send a request to the smart contract requesting authorization for this purpose. The user must make an access request to the fog node after gaining authorization to access the target device.

The study [15] presented a blockchain-based device and user authentication mechanism using gateways. In this study, a user requests a blockchain smart contract address from the gateway to access user and privacy policy information. If the request is accepted, the user will send another request to the gateway, which records user and device data on the blockchain. Besides user authentication, IoT devices must be authenticated by an administrator or another device manager. This model includes the IoT devices, users, and blockchain-connected gateway. Devices share information or resources with other users, devices under a device policy (smart contract). The blockchain-connected gateway will examine the user's eligibility (permissions and authentication) to access the device's information and resources. Once accepted, the user controls the device. The blockchain and deliver system data. The author assesses and implements the model on Ethereum's blockchain and analyzes its states and expenses.

R. Kabir, A. T. Hasan, M. R. Islam, and Y. Watanobe in [16] presented a system that allocated a unique identifier to each device. Data transaction records for each device using smart contracts were stored in a blockchain-based on the open-source project BigChainDB. This system consists of IoT devices, cloud servers and the blockchain network. IoT devices may be linked to one another, and smart contracts accompany them. The cloud stores and encrypts the data from these devices. Blockchain smart contracts will manage each access to a device by other IoT devices or users. In addition, this approach applies the Practical Byzantine Fault Tolerance (pBFT) consensus mechanism, which recognizes the aberrant synchronization of data in the blockchain ledger to improve the security and reliability of the system. However, the paper only proposed an authentication method for IoT devices and did not give the system's performance results.

The study in [17] suggested a blockchain-based authentication strategy for the IoT system, which comprises Device Manufacturer, IoT devices, data centre servers, and blockchain. In particular, the modular square root (MSR) approach is utilized to ensure the security and efficiency of the authentication process, and blockchain technology is employed to increase security and offer scalability for this system. By using a smart contract, the system can ensure that only the registered devices or users can get the service to which they have subscribed. The model has four phases: system initialization, registration, authentication, and update and revocation. In order to evaluate the feasibility of the system, the authors provided an implementation of an Ethereum test network, Remix. However, the paper does not consider the authentication mechanism for users, which substantially impacts the system's security.

Gong-Guo Z. and Wan Z. [18] presented an IoT-chain security authentication solution using the Hyperledger Fabric blockchain platform. Inside the system, there are three sorts of chain codes: access code, device code, and policy code. The access code is the primary software that implements the user safety authentication procedure. The device code provides a query technique for the URL of the resource data offered by the storage device, while the policy code indicates the administrator user's access control strategy. Experimentation demonstrates that IoT-chain can sustain high throughput and achieve consensus efficiently in a distributed system. The study proposed authentication mechanisms for both IoT devices and users. Using Hyperledger Fabric, a private blockchain makes this system difficult to ensure the same level of security and transparency as a public blockchain. In addition, the data access rate is not mentioned, and IoT-chain operation diagram is not apparent.

## 3   The Proposed Authentication Model for IoT Devices and Users

The proposed model uses a Ganache blockchain network with Smart Contract, fog computing simulated by *NodeJS* server, cloud, IoT devices and a web server. IoT devices are simulated with their MAC addresses and exchange information when requested. Figure 1 presents the proposed model.

In the proposed model, we assume they are local devices owned by the same user (green colour: device 1, device 2). They can easily exchange information and get each

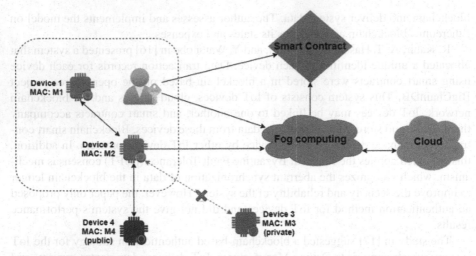

**Fig. 1.** The proposed authentication model for IoT network. (Color figure online)

other's data. There are other users' devices (red colour: device 3). These devices are private, and they do not share information. Another type of device is a public device (blue colour: device 4). Any user can access and get information from them.

### 3.1 Role of Smart Contract

A smart contract acts as an authentication centre storing information of users, devices, and relationships between users and devices. In this paper, Smart Contract is built using Solidity. The smart contract is compiled and migrated through Truffle. The compilation process will convert the Solidity code into bytecode and the Application Binary Interface (ABI). The bytecode will be used to deploy to the Ethereum network, while the ABI determines which function in the Smart Contract is called and returns the data in the expected format.

Migration is the process of converting compiled data onto the blockchain network. For Truffle, this process brings the compiled bytecode to a private blockchain network – specifically Ganache. Corresponding to each Smart Contract, an address will be used to identify it on the blockchain. This address is a long string of numbers and characters starting with 0x. Each address is associated with four different fields:

- Nonce: is an integer that is incremented every time the address sends any transaction.
- Balance: is the balance of the Smart Contract. If the user makes a transaction to this address, the balance will increase, and when the transaction is sent to another address, this balance will decrease.
- Code: source code of Smart Contract.
- Data: is where all the storage variables of a smart contract are stored. Memory variables cannot be stored in the blockchain.

## 3.2 Role of Fog Computing

We proposed to use fog computing as a bridge between users and devices. Fog computing will support storing data of devices and perform particular (pre-configured) calculation functions to reduce the computing pressure of the devices. Data such as MAC address is encrypted before being saved to the cloud. Every time a device or user wants to access another device, a request is sent to the Smart Contract to retrieve that device's information, and then compare it with the information submitted by the user/device to confirm the validation.

## 3.3 Simulation Model

The operating principle of the proposed model in Fig. 1 is shown through the simulation model. To build this model, we have some assumptions as follows:

- Cloud and fog computing will be simulated on the same server, which can receive and process user and device requests.
- The devices are simulated through the website service platform. They can receive and request data. The default settings are stored and exchanged with the server.
- The configuration of basic parameters on the device is saved as input values.

The operating principle of the proposed model is shown in Fig. 2.

We use *ReactJs* technology to support the user and device functions. There are some essential functions as follows:

- *getUsername, addInformation*: obtain and edit personal information including user-name and password;
- *addDevice, removeDevice*: add and remove devices;
- *getDeviceList*: get the entire list of devices owned by the current user;
- *switchDeviceStatus*: change the state of devices from private to public and vice versa;
- *getDeviceData*: retrieve data collected from other devices;
- *saveDataToCloud*: save collected information to the cloud.

The authentication model is based on asymmetric encryption using a public-private key pair generated and used as the user's wallet address. Users can log in via Metamask wallet in the simulation model. Users need to store the mnemonic phrase for future account recovery. The password is also used to authenticate the user who owns this wallet properly. For web browsers that have never used this wallet address, users need to enter the mnemonic phrase to log in to the wallet. Figures 3 and 4 depict registering

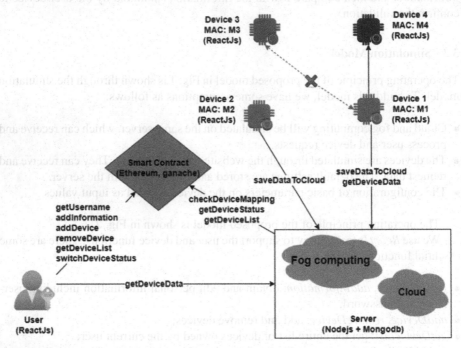

**Fig. 2.** Simulation model

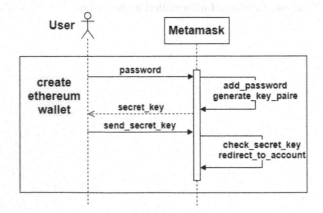

**Fig. 3.** Register a user account on the metamask e-wallet.

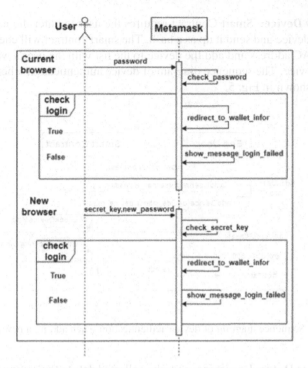

**Fig. 4.** Login to a metamask wallet on different web browsers.

a Metamask wallet and logging into it on one or more different browsers. There are some main functions: adding a new device, storing data, a user accesses the data of the device, a device gets data from other devices. In Figs. 5, 6, 7 and 8 below, the requests and responses in red are on-chain execution, and the requests and responses in black are off-chain execution.

**Adding a New Device:** Smart Contract requires the user to enter the name and MAC address of the device and send it up as a hash. The smart contract will check the uniqueness of this MAC address and add the device to the list with the user's wallet address if this is a new device. The sequence diagram of device authentication when a user adds a new device is shown in Fig. 5.

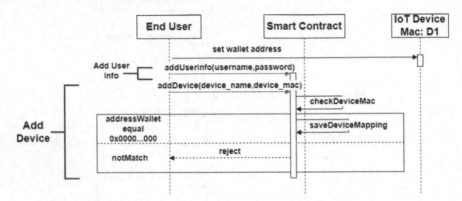

**Fig. 5.** Sequence diagram of device authentication when adding a new device.

**A Device Stores Data:** The device sends the collected data to fog computing along with its wallet address and MAC address. Fog computing will hash the device's MAC address and get the corresponding wallet address stored on the blockchain. Fog computing will check the match between the wallet address of the device owner and the wallet address stored on the blockchain. Fog computing saves the device's data to the cloud if they match. The sequence diagram for device authentication when a device stores data is shown in Fig. 6.

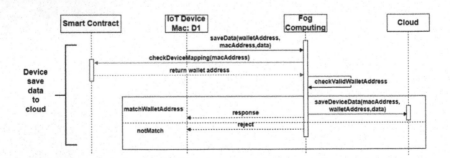

**Fig. 6.** Sequence diagram for device authentication when storing data.

**User Accesses the Device's Data:** The user must simultaneously send the device's wallet address and MAC address to fog computing to retrieve data from that device. Fog computing takes the list of MAC addresses corresponding to the wallet address and matches it. If the MAC address exists in the list, fog computing will take the data in the cloud and return it to the user. The sequence diagram of user and device authentication when a user accesses device data is shown in Fig. 7.

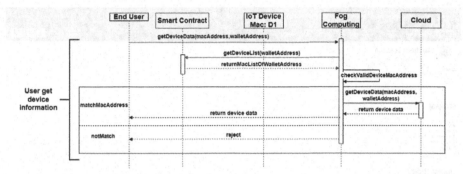

**Fig. 7.** Sequence diagram of user and device authentication when a user accesses device data.

**A Device Gets Data from Other Devices:** In this case, fog computing will check whether the data-retrieved device is a public device or has the same wallet address as the current device. If valid, it will return data from the cloud. If the data-retrieved device is private or another user owns it, the data cannot be obtained. The sequence diagram of device authentication when a device accesses data from another device is shown in Fig. 8.

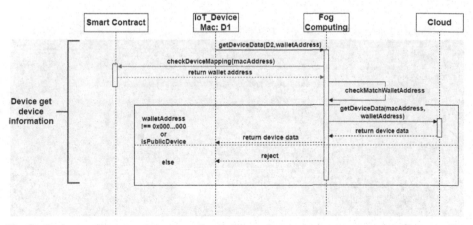

**Fig. 8.** Sequence diagram of device authentication when a device accesses data from another device.

## 4   Evaluation and Results

In this section, the testing result of the proposed model is presented. The Smart Contract is deployed with *Truffle* in Fig. 9. **CREATION TX** is the ID of a transaction. **STORAGE** is the memory of Smart Contract that stores value variables. **TRANSACTION** is the details of transactions performed with Smart Contract.

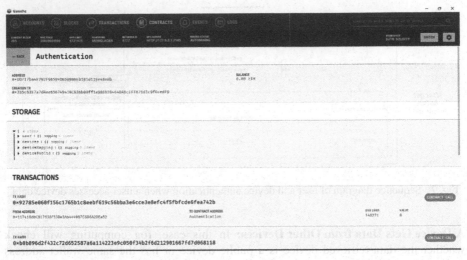

**Fig. 9.** Smart Contract on Ganache after deploying using Truffle.

In this scenario, we add a new device with a MAC address is 54:52:00:61:34:77 (Fig. 10). This transaction is confirmed in Fig. 11 and Fig. 12.

**Fig. 10.** Adding a new device.

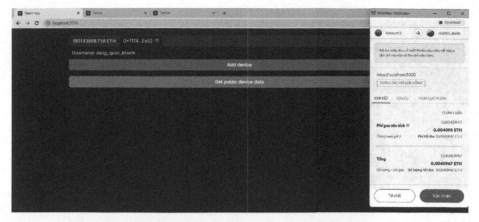

**Fig. 11.** Confirmation for the transaction of adding a new device.

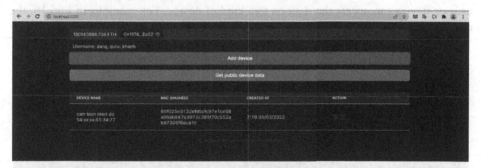

**Fig. 12.** Successfully adding device.

For simulation, we set the owner's wallet address (user dang_quoc_khanh) and manual data for the device to store in the cloud (Fig. 13).

Figure 14 shows the scenario when the user retrieves the stored data.

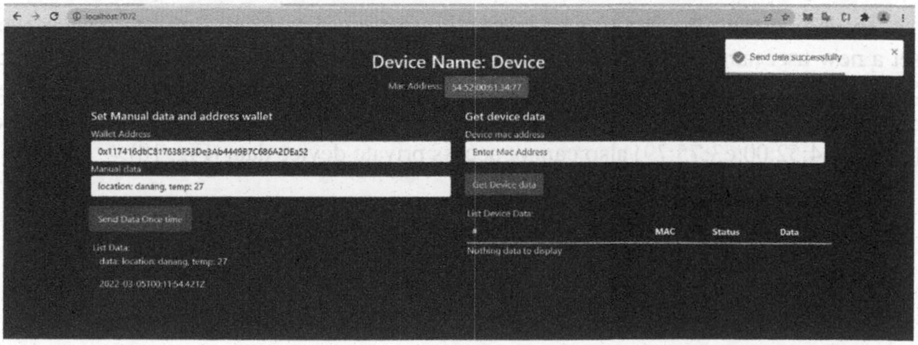

**Fig. 13.** The device enters the owner's wallet address and stores the data.

**Fig. 14.** The user retrieves the stored data.

We can set a device (MAC: 54:52:00:61:34:77) to public (Fig. 15). Then another user or device can access the data on this kind of device. For example, in Fig. 16, the device with MAC: 54:52:00:e3:75:79 can obtain data from this public device.

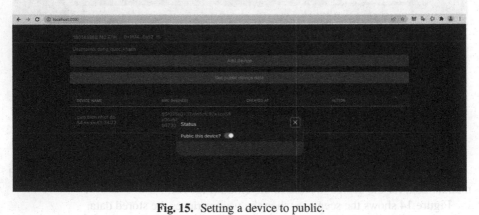

**Fig. 15.** Setting a device to public.

To demonstrate the function of preventing getting data from a private device, we set a new user named user_guest. This user can get the data of a public device (MAC: 54:52:00:61:34:77) (Fig. 16). However, user_guest cannot obtain the data of private data (MAC: 54:52:00:b1:c9:97) of the user dang_quoc_khanh (Fig. 17). Other devices (MAC: 54:52:00:e3:75:79) also cannot access private device data (Fig. 18).

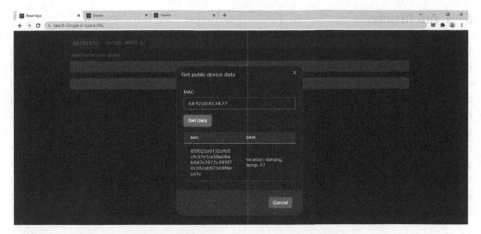

**Fig. 16.** Obtaining data from a public device.

**Fig. 17.** No data is returned if the device is private.

**Fig. 18.** Other devices also cannot access the data of a private device.

# 5 Conclusions

In this study, we proposed a blockchain-driven hybrid model for IoT authentication that is improved based on existing models. The model supports both user authentication and device authentication. It is simulated and tested by implementing a small system that applies a Ganache blockchain network with Smart Contract, fog computing simulated by NodeJS server, cloud, IoT devices and a web server. IoT devices are simulated with their MAC addresses and exchange information when requested.

We presented the authentication stages of IoT devices and users with sequence diagrams. Moreover, the validation process of the proposed model for each role and function was simulated. In addition, the transfer of a device owned by one user to another is taken into account and done easily. This leads to the conclusion that the system with device and user authentication outperforms a single user or device authentication.

**Acknowledgements.** The study was financially supported by the Russian Science Foundation within of scientific project No. 22-49-02023 "Development and study of methods for obtaining the reliability of tethered high-altitude unmanned telecommunication platforms of a new generation".

# References

1. Reyna, A., Martín, C., Chen, J., Soler, E., Díaz, M.: On blockchain and its integration with IoT. Challenges and opportunities. Future Gener. Comput. Syst. **88**, 173–190 (2018)
2. Janarthanan, T., Bagheri, M., Zargari, S.: IoT Forensics: an overview of the current issues and challenges. In: Montasari, R., Jahankhani, H., Hill, R., Parkinson, S. (eds.) Digital Forensic Investigation of Internet of Things (IoT) Devices. ASTSA, pp. 223–254. Springer, Cham (2021). https://doi.org/10.1007/978-3-030-60425-7_10
3. El-Hajj, M., Fadlallah, A., Chamoun, M., Serhrouchni, A.: A survey of internet of things (IoT) authentication schemes. Sensors **19**(5), 1141, 1–43 (2019)
4. Sazonov, D., Kirichek, R.: Digital object architecture as an approach to identifying Internet of Things devices. In: Vishnevskiy, V.M., Samouylov, K.E., Kozyrev, D.V. (eds.) DCCN 2019. CCIS, vol. 1141, pp. 597–611. Springer, Cham (2019). https://doi.org/10.1007/978-3-030-36625-4_48
5. Al-Bahri, M., Ruslan, K., Aleksey, B.: Integrating internet of things with the digital object architecture. In: Galinina, O., Andreev, S., Balandin, S., Koucheryavy, Y. (eds.) NEW2AN ruSMART 2019. LNCS, vol. 11660, pp. 540–547. Springer, Cham (2019). https://doi.org/10.1007/978-3-030-30859-9_47
6. Pomogalova, A., Sazonov, D., Donskov, E., Borodin, A., Kirichek, R.: Identification method for endpoint devices on low-power wide-area networks using digital object architecture with blockchain technology integration. In: Vishnevskiy, V.M., Samouylov, K.E., Kozyrev, D.V. (eds.) DCCN 2021. LNCS, vol. 13144, pp. 103–114. Springer, Cham (2021). https://doi.org/10.1007/978-3-030-92507-9_10
7. Vladimirov, S., Kirichek, R.: The IoT identification procedure based on the degraded flash memory sector. In: Galinina, O., Andreev, S., Balandin, S., Koucheryavy, Y. (eds.) ruSMART NsCC NEW2AN 2017. LNCS, vol. 10531, pp. 66–74. Springer, Cham (2017)
8. Vladimirov, S.S., Pirmagomedov, R., Kirichek, R., Koucheryavy, A.: Unique degradation of flash memory as an identifier of ICT device. IEEE Access **7**, 107626–107634 (2019)

9. Al-Bahri, M., Yankovsky, A., Borodin, A., Kirichek, R.: Testbed for identify IoT-devices based on digital object architecture. In: Galinina, O., Andreev, S., Balandin, S., Koucheryavy, Y. (eds.) NEW2AN ruSMART 2018. LNCS, vol. 11118, pp. 129–137. Springer, Cham (2018)

10. Nakamoto, S.: Bitcoin: a peer-to-peer electronic cash system. Decentralized Bus. Rev. 21260 (2008)

11. Mohanta, B.K., Panda, S.S., Jena, D.: An overview of smart contract and use cases in blockchain technology. In: 2018 9th International Conference on Computing, Communication and Networking Technologies (ICCCNT), pp. 1–4. IEEE (2018)

12. Amanlou, S., Hasan, M.K., Bakar, K.A.A.: Lightweight and secure authentication scheme for IoT network based on publish–subscribe fog computing model. Comput. Netw. **199**, 108465 (2021)

13. Li, D., Peng, W., Deng, W., Gai, F.: A blockchain-based authentication and security mechanism for IoT. In: 2018 27th International Conference on Computer Communication and Networks (ICCCN), pp. 1–6 (2018)

14. Almadhoun, R., Kadadha, M., Alhemeiri, M., Alshehhi, M., Salah, K.: A user authentication scheme of IoT devices using blockchain-enabled fog nodes. In: 2018 IEEE/ACS 15th International Conference on Computer Systems and Applications (AICCSA), pp. 1–8 (2018)

15. Yavari, M., Safkhani, M., Kumari, S., Kumar, S., Chen, C.M.: An improved blockchain-based authentication protocol for IoT network management. Secur. Commun. Netw. **2020**, 1–16 (2020)

16. Kabir, R., Hasan, A.T., Islam, M.R., Watanobe, Y.: A blockchain-based approach to secure cloud connected IoT devices. In: 2021 International Conference on Information and Communication Technology for Sustainable Development (ICICT4SD), pp. 366–370. IEEE (2021)

17. Yang, X., Yang, X., Yi, X., et al.: Blockchain-based secure and lightweight authentication for internet of things. IEEE Internet Things J. **9**(5), 3321–3332 (2021)

18. Gong-Guo Z., Wan Z.: Blockchain-based IoT security authentication system. In: 2021 International Conference on Computer, Blockchain and Financial Development (CBFD), pp. 415–418. IEEE (2021)

# An Heuristic Approach for Mapping of Service Function Chains in Softwarized 5G Networks

Jerzy Martyna[✉][iD]

Institute of Computer Science, Faculty of Mathematics and Computer Science, Jagiellonian University, ul. Prof. S. Lojasiewicza 6, 30-348 Cracow, Poland
jerzy.martyna@uj.edu.pl

**Abstract.** The Service Function Chain (SFC) defines an ordered or partially ordered set of abstract service functions (SFs) and ordering constraints that reduce the scale, capacity, and redundancy across the entire network. SFC mapping, by which network services are implemented in a virtualized network, is a key technique used in a software-defined network. Obtaining the efficiency of physical resources while ensuring high reliability, availability and minimal operating costs is the basic problem in this type of models. The paper presents an approximate solution to this problem using a heuristic algorithm. Conducted simulation studies confirmed the effectiveness of the proposed method.

**Keywords:** Service Function Chains · 5G cellular network · software defined network · radio resource allocation

## 1 Introduction

Currently, mobile networks are experiencing a steady increase in user-exchanged data traffic. The fifth generation of mobile networks (5G) provides strong support for all kinds of applications that require new services, such as URLLC and eMBB. The Ultra Reliable Low Latency Communications (URLLC) traffic type demands extremely reliable and low-latency radio transmission, i.e., one way radio transmission with a latency of 1 ms [1]. The massive Machine Type Communications (eMBB) traffic provides massive connectivity solutions for various implementations of the Internet of Things. To manage such a network, all possible network technologies must be mastered with diverse protocol stacks and various network applications.

Two new technologies meet these kinds of challenges. The first of them, known as Software-Defined Networking (SDN), can be successfully used for 5G networks [2]. The second of them, referred to as service function chains (SFC), allows the traditional hardware limitations of 5G networks to be overcome [3]. The SFC was introduced by Quinn [4] and Medhat [5]. It assumes that the functions providing a service (e.g., a firewall, load balancer, etc.) are inserted as

© The Author(s), under exclusive license to Springer Nature Switzerland AG 2023
Y. Koucheryavy and A. Aziz (Eds.): NEW2AN 2022, LNCS 13772, pp. 574–584, 2023.
https://doi.org/10.1007/978-3-031-30258-9_51

being arranged in a linear chain. Then, end-to-end services made available in a virtualized and layered network structure determine the processing properties of the entire system. The Service Function Chain thus consists of a set of virtual network functions (VNFs) connected by logical links. Multiple SFCs for different clients can share the same computing and network resources to improve resource utilization.

In order to minimize the cost of resource computation and transmission, an optimal arrangement of SFCs in software-defined networks is required. However, finding the optimal solution for SFC placement is an NP-hard problem. Obtaining an accurate solution requires a large amount of computational time, hence it is an impractical method for practical applications. A number of approaches have been used to find a solution to this problem. The most important of these are heuristic methods. Among others, a genetic-based algorithm as well as a bee colony-based algorithm to solve the SFC placement and routing problem to find a pareto optimal solution considering heterogenous physical nodes were proposed by Khoshkholghi et al. [6]. The optimization model was investigated by the authors using a pareto optimal solution so that it optimizes multiple objectives as much as possible. A heuristic algorithm to coordinate the composition of SFCs and their embedding into the substrate network was presented by Beck at al. [7].

In the paper by Rottenstreich et al. [8], the problem of minimizing delay in network function virtualization with shared pipelines was investigated. The concept of shared backup in which each backup server is a backup for multiple middleboxes was presented by Kanizo et al. [9]. In the paper by Sun et al. [10], a reliability-aware algorithm for reducing the cost of placement was introduced. On the other hand, the joint dynamic service placement and scheduling problem was studied using the mixed-integer programming (MILP) model with the aim of providing guaranteed quality of service (QoS) by Cao et al. [11].

The main contribution of this paper is a method of deploying SFCs in programmed 5G networks, which allows to take into account transmission reliability and availability. It can also be used to minimize system costs. Moreover, it provides a solution that is close to the optimal one. Simulation studies have confirmed the effectiveness of this method.

The paper is organized as follows. The model of the system is presented in the next section. Section 3 describes the placement of the SFC in the physical network taking into account reliability and cost. Section 4 introduces a heuristic algorithm for placing SFCs in the physical network. Test results confirming the effectiveness of the proposed algorithm are given in Sect. 5. The summary is included in the last section.

## 2  System Model

It is assumed that the system model includes a substrate network, defined as an undirected physical graph $G = (V, E)$, where $V$ is a set of $N$ edge (cloud) physical nodes expressed as $V = \{v_1, ..., v_N\}$, and $E$ is a set of $L$ physical links between nodes denoted by $E = \{e_1, ..., e_L\}$. It is assumed here that the physical node $v, v \in V$ is characterized by its processing power, memory size, etc. Let the set of service chains be given by $S$. A single service chain consists of a list of

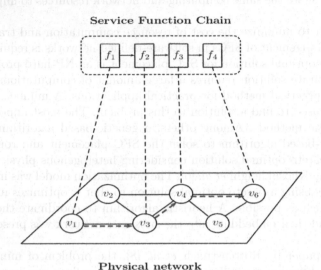

**Service Function Chain**

**Physical network**

**Fig. 1.** An example of service request.

VNFs and is represented by a directed graph $SF = (F, M)$, where $F$ is the set of virtual functions and $M$ is the set of virtual links, respectively. The set of virtual functions consists of requests for processing power, memory size, etc. In turn, each virtual link $m, m \in M$, consists of bandwidth requests, data rates, etc.

An ordered set of VNFs allows to construct an SFC that is connected by VNF links. An example of the constructed SFC is given in Fig. 1, which consists of four VNFs chained by VNF links.

The following mapping rule is adopted here. All requests from service chains $s$ must be allocated one or more VNFs $f$, provided that the following requirements are met. Each VNF $f$ can be placed on only one physical node $v$ which meets the defined constraints. Analogously, each $l$ can be mapped to only one physical path that satisfies the constraints. Moreover, due to the approach taken here, requests such as certain reliability and availability values must be taken into account.

Each type of request has service requirements which have an impact on the applications they use. Hence, there are different service requests, each of which may have different specific requirements in terms of high data rate, bandwidth demand, allowable delay, reliability, and availability. Each service request $s$ must be mapped onto a VNF to satisfy all its requirements. Moreover, it should also be considered whether VNF redundancy will be applied, which significantly affects the values of the mapped SFCs. Additionally, the virtual links in the SFC are mapped to the physical path of the NFV.

## 2.1 Network Reliability and Availability

Network reliability is defined as the probability that a system performs its intended functions successfully for a given period of time [12]. Otherwise, if the network operates successfully at time $t_0$, the network reliability yields the

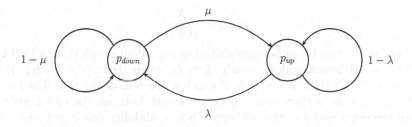

**Fig. 2.** A two-stage Markov model of the reliability of a link.

probability that in the interval 0 to $t_0$ there were no failures. It is assumed that the probability of successful communication between a source and a target node is $k$-terminal reliability, which is defined as the probability that a path exists and connects $k$ nodes in a network.

Hence, it can be assumed that the $k$-terminal reliability for the $k$ nodes $\{n_1, ..., n_k\}$ $V(G, p)$ for the graph $(G, p)$, where $p$ is the link failure probability, can be expressed as [13]:

$$R_C^{n_1,...,n_k}(G,p) = \sum_{i=w_{n_1},...,n_k}^{\omega} T_i^{n_1,...,n_k}(G)p^{\omega-i}(1-p)^i \tag{1}$$

where $\omega = |\, E(G)\, |$ is the size of the graph, $T_i^{n_1,...,n_k}(G)$ denotes the number of subgraphs connecting the nodes $n_1, ..., n_k$ with $i$-th edges. and $w_{n_1}, ..., w_{n_k}$ is the size of the minimum tieset connecting the nodes $n_1, ..., n_k$.

The $k$-terminal reliability defined above can also be represented as follows:

$$R_C^{n_1,...,n_k}(G,p) = 1 - \sum_{i=\beta(G)}^{\omega} C_i^{n_1,...,n_k}(G)p^i(1-p)^{\omega-1} \tag{2}$$

It is assumed that the network is in a steady-state ($t \to \infty$). Then the steady-state availability can be expressed as follows:

$$A = \frac{MTBF}{MTBF + MTTR} \tag{3}$$

where $MTBF$ is *Mean Time Between Failures* and $MTTR$ is *Mean Time To Repair*, respectively.

In turn, if the link in the network can be repaired after failure, then a two-stage Markov diagram can be used. Hence, one state represents the repaired link and the other state represents the broken link. Let the operational link failure $e_{ij}$ be an exponential distribution with a rate parameter $\mu$ (see Fig. 2).

For the link being up ($p_{up}$) or down ($p_{down}$), the state probabilities at the steady-state are as follows:

$$p_{up} = \frac{\mu}{\mu + \lambda} \tag{4}$$

$$p_{down} = \frac{\lambda}{\mu + \lambda} \tag{5}$$

Then, the network can be represented as a random graph $G$, in which there can be $k - 1$ different nodes, namely $d_i \in D$, where $D = \{d_1, \ldots, d_{k-1}\}$. It is also assumed that there is one node $r$ which is the root of the tree. The network is fully operational if there is an operational path between the root node $r$ and each of the other nodes in the network. Then availability can be expressed for $k$ nodes as $k$-terminal availability, namely:

$$A_C^{r,d_1,\ldots,d_{k-1}}(G, p_{down}) = 1 - \sum_{i=\beta(G)}^{\omega} C_i^{r,d_1,\ldots,d_{k-1}} p_{down}^i (1 - p_{down})^{\omega-i} \tag{6}$$

where $C_i^{r,d_1,\ldots,d_{k-1}}(G, p_{down})$ denotes the number of edge cutsets of cardinality $i$.

## 2.2 Processing Cost

It is assumed that the total cost of processing in a 5G system is composed of the resource cost $\theta(r)$, cost of physical nodes $\theta(w)$ and the cost of communication $\theta(c)$, which can be presented as follows:

$$\Theta(r, w, c) = \theta(r) + \theta(w) + \theta(c) \tag{7}$$

Since the physical nodes can be diverse, each VNF $f$ with respect to individual nodes can entail a different one:

$$\theta(r) = \sum_{s \in S} \sum_{v \in V} \sum_{w \in F} (cost_{sf}^{v_{CPU}} + cost_{sf}^{v_{mem}} + cost_{sf}^{v_{sto}}) X_{sf}^v \tag{8}$$

where $cost_{sf}^{v_{CPU}}$ is the CPU cost in physical node $v$ used by VNF $f$, $cost_{sf}$ is the memory cost of physical node v used by VNF $f$, $cost_{sf}^{v_{sto}}$ is the external memory cost of physical node $v$ used by VNF $f$. Binary variable $X_{sf}$ is equal to 1 if VNF $f$ from string $s$ is placed in physical node $v$. Otherwise, $X_{sf} = 0$.

The cost of physical nodes is related to the electricity cost used by those nodes. Its value is expressed as follow:

$$\theta(w) = \sum_{v \in V} (p_v^{max} + (p_v^{max} - p_v^{min}) \frac{1}{cap_{CPU}^v} \sum_{f \in F} d_{CPU,f}^v X_f^v) \cdot Z^v \qquad (9)$$

where $p_v^{min}, p_v^{max}$ are respectively the minimum and maximum value of the node energy consumption $v \in V$, $\cap_{CPU}^v$ is the average CPU processing speed of node $v$, $d_{CPU,f}^v$ is the CPU service time required in node $v$ belonging to VNF $f$. Binary variable $Z^v = 1$ if physical node $v$ is active, otherwise $Z^v = 0$.

Communication cost $\theta(c)$ is the sum of the bandwidth costs for physical paths across virtual links on which virtual links are deployed. It can be represented as

$$\theta(c) = \sum_{s \in S} \sum_{v \in V} \sum_{m \in M} (cost_{sm}^{eband} \cdot Q_{sm}^e) \qquad (10)$$

where $cost_{sm}^{eband}$ is the bandwidth cost of the physical path used by the $m$ virtual link. Binary variable $Q_{sm} = 1$ if the chain $s$ is distributed over the physical link $e \in E$. Otherwise, a variable this one is equal to 0.

## 3   Heuristic Algorithm for Mapping of Service Function Chains

Regardless of the physical topology of 5G network, the algorithm ensures that all elements of the network will be made available if sharing is requested. In addition, it takes into account redundancy of the individual elements of that network, including links and nodes. It also processes data service requests with data time constraints and requirements of data rate. The pseudocode for the above algorithm is shown in Fig. 3. Its purpose is to provide 5G in a given physical topology with the shortest paths between the existing root and tree leaves. Then, considering time constraints, some of them meet the requirements of reliability and processing costs. The availability of each VNF is randomly distributed in the range [0.9, 0.98]. For this purpose, the values of $k$-terminal reliability and processing costs are used. Where such a path is missing, the possibility of redundancy of individual elements is checked. Thanks to the redundancy of these elements, it is possible to find paths that meet the desired parameters. The paths found in this way are mapped to the SFC request data.

**Algorithm 1** Algorithm for SFC mapping

1: **procedure** RADIO RESOURCE ALOCATION
2: **Require:** $R_{con}, D_{con}, \Theta_{con}$;
3:     $[buffer] \leftarrow \varnothing$;
4:     **for** $\forall f \in VNF$ **do**
5:         sort $paths(f)$;
6:         put $bufor[sorted\ paths]$;
7:     **end for**
8:     **for** $\forall s \in S$ **do**
9:         **for** $\forall f \in VNF$ **do**
10:            compute $R_f$, $A_f$ and $\Theta(r, w, c)$ for $k$-terminal
11:            **while** $(R_f > R_{con} \land A_f > A_{con} \land \Theta(r, w, c) < \Theta_{con})$ **do**
12:                compute $end\ to\ end\ delay_f$
13:                **if** $end\ to\ end\ delay_f < D_{con}$ **then**
14:                    map $s$ in $buffer(sorted\ paths)$
15:                **else**
16:                    find redundant $path(s')$
17:                **end if**
18:                map s and $s'$ in buffer($sorted\ paths$)
19:            **end while**
20:        **end for**
21:    **end for**
22: **end procedure**

**Fig. 3.** Pseudo-code of algorithm for SVC mapping.

# 4   Simulation Results

It is assumed here that the physical 5G network has a two-tier architecture formed by three nodes. It is also assumed that each network node has its own data center with a capacity of 2000 units. There are two types of traffic in this network, namely URLLC and eMBB. The URLLC traffic requires reliable and low-delay radio transmission with an allowable delay of 1 ms. On the other hand, eMBB trafic provides very high transmission capabilities for the Internet of Things. It is assumed here that each data center provides six to eight virtual network functions. In such a model, the permissible packet error rate is equal to $10^{-3}$ [14].

The model thus described assumes that only 4 VNFs can process a service chain request in the network. Each of them requires two resources (power capacity memory size) and each virtual link has the required bandwidth of 200, 300, 400 Gb/s with equal probability. The following values are selected here for VNF processing delay: 60–120 $\mu s$ [15].

Using a specially written simulation program, the proposed algorithm was assessed in terms of performance. In the first scenario, the plausibility was tested of the proposed algorithm's capability of meeting the requirements for deploying requests from service chains. Then, the availability for both data streams was tested with the adopted allocation algorithm in place and its absence.

Figure 4 shows the reliability of the transmission service depending on the reception rate $\rho$. The admission rate used here was determined as the quotient of the number of accepted transmission requests with the required reliability to the number of all transmission requests. The graph shows that the algorithm used can significantly improve the reliability of transmission.

Figure 5 presents the dependence between the reliability of the transmission service found versus the probability of the link failure using a redundant path or no such path. It is evident that the use of a redundant path increases the reliability of the flow data for both flow classes.

Figure 6 shows availability depending on the average number of spare VNFs for both traffic types: URLLC and eMBB. It can be seen from the picture that the eMBB traffic requires more back-up VNFs than URLLC traffic for the same admission ratio $\rho = 0.95$.

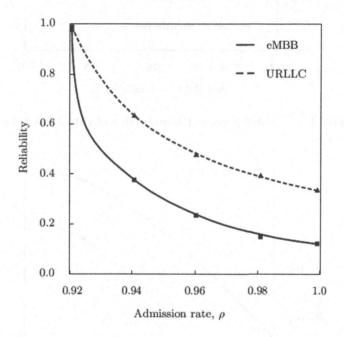

**Fig. 4.** The reliability of service versus the admission rate $\rho$.

Figure 7 shows the graph of processing costs depending on the average number of VNFs backups for the eMBB traffic at different values of the data rate. The graph demonstrates that the increasing number of VNFs backups increases the processing costs, which is especially evident at a high value of data rate.

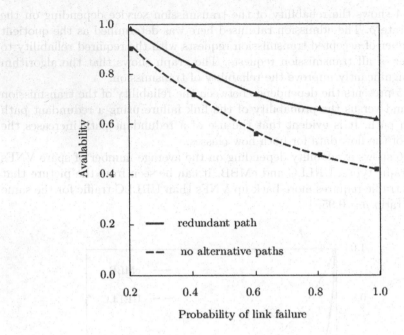

**Fig. 5.** The availability versus the probability of virtual link failure.

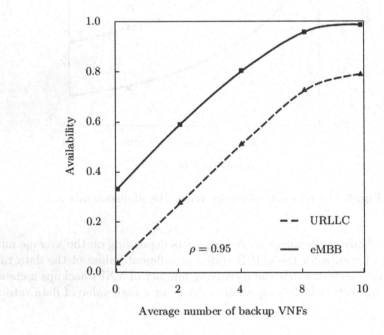

**Fig. 6.** The availability versus average number of backup VNFs.

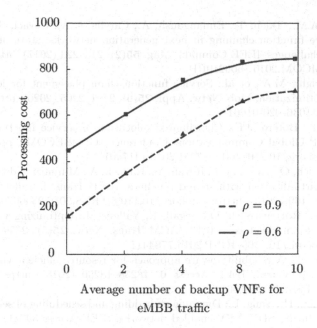

**Fig. 7.** The processing cost versus average number of backup VNFs.

## 5    Conclusion

The paper presents a heuristic algorithm for mapping SFCs chains in 5G software networks. It takes into account the reliability and availability of the network as well as the processing costs. The effectiveness of the introduced algorithm was tested using simulations. It was found, inter alia, that thanks to the inclusion of redundant VNFs a significant increase can be obtained in the eMBB flow rate. The use of this algorithm leads to better management of SFCs chains in virtualized 5G networks.

## References

1. Dahlman, E., et al.: 5G wireless access: requirements and realization. IEEE Commun. Mag. **52**(12), 42–47 (2014). https://doi.org/10.1109/MCOM.2014.6979985
2. Routray, S.K., Sharmila, K.P.: Software defined networking for 5G. In: 2017 4th International Conference on Advanced Computing and Communication Systems (ICACCS), pp. 1–5 (2017). https://doi.org/10.1109/ICACCS.2017.8014576
3. Yousaf, F.Z., Bredel, M., Schaller, S., Schneider, F.: NFV and SDN - key technology enablers for 5G networks. IEEE J. Sel. Areas Commun. **35**(11), 2468–2478 (2017). https://doi.org/10.1109/JSAC.2017.2760418
4. Quinn, P., Nadeau, T.: Problem Statement for Service Function Chaining, RFC 7498, Technical report 7498, April 2015. https://rfc-editor.org/rfc/rfc7498.txt

5. Medhat, A.M., Taleb, T., Elmangoush, A., Carella, G.A., Covaci, S., Magedanz, T.: Service function chaining in next generation networks: state of the art and research challenges. IEEE Commun. Mag. **55**(2), 216–223 (2017). https://doi.org/10.1109/MCOM.2016.1600219RP
6. Khoshkholghi, M.A., et al.: Service function chain placement for joint cost and latency optimization. Mob. Netw. Appl. **25**(6), 2191–2205 (2020). https://doi.org/10.1007/s11036-020-01661-w
7. Beck, M.T., Botero, J.F.: Coordinated allocation of service function chains. In: 2015 IEEE Global Communications Conference (GLOBECOM), pp. 1–6 (2015). https://doi.org/10.1109/GLOCOM.2015.7417401
8. Rottenstreich, O., Keslassy, I., Revah, Y., Kadosh, A.: Minimizing delay in network function virtualization with shared pipelines. IEEE Trans. Parallel Distrib. Syst. **28**(1), 156–169 (2016). https://doi.org/10.1109/TPDS.2016.2556670
9. Kanizo, Y., Rottenstreich, O., Segall, I., Yallouz, J.: Optimizing virtual backup allocation for middleboxes. IEEE/ACM Trans. Netw. **25**(5), 2759–2772 (2017). https://doi.org/10.1109/ICNP.2016.7784411
10. Sun, J., et al.: A reliability-aware approach for resource efficient virtual network function deployment. IEEE Access **6**, 18238–18250 (2018). https://doi.org/10.1109/ACCESS.2018.2815614
11. Cao, H., Zhu, H., Yang, L.: Dynamic embedding and scheduling of service function chains for future SDN/NFV-enabled networks. IEEE Access 39721–39730 (2019). https://doi.org/10.1109/ACCESS.2019.2906874
12. Sahner, K., Trivedi, K.S., Puliafito, A.: Performance and Reliability Analysis of Computer Systems: An Example-Based Approach Using the SHARPE Software Package. Kluwer Academic Publishers, Boston (1996). https://doi.org/10.1007/978-1-4615-2367-3
13. Egeland, G., Engelstad, P.E.: The reliability of wireless backhaul mesh networks. In: Proceedings of the 2008 IEEE International Symposium on Wireless Communication Systems, pp. 178–183 (2008). https://doi.org/10.1109/ISWCS.2008.4726042
14. Popovski, P., Trillingsgaard, K.F., Simeone, O.: 5G wireless network slicing for eMBB, URLLC, and mMTC: a communication-theoretic view. IEEE Access **6**, 55765–55779 (2018). https://doi.org/10.1109/ACCESS.2018.2872781
15. Basta, A., Kellerer, W., Hoffmann, M., Morper, H.J., Hoffmann, K.: Applying NFV and SDN to LTE mobile core gateways, the functions placement problem. In: Proceedings of the 4th Workshop on All Things Cellular: Operations, Applications, and Challenges, pp. 33–38. ACM (2014). https://doi.org/10.1145/2627585.2627592

# Multi-threshold Hysteresis-Based Congestion Control for UAV-Based Detection Sensor Network

Bashir Aliyu[1](✉)(iD), Evgeny Mokrov[1](✉)(iD), and Konstantin Samouylov[1,2](✉)(iD)

[1] Peoples' Friendship University of Russia (RUDN University),
6 Miklukho-Maklaya st., Moscow 117198, Russian Federation
bashaliyuu@gmail.com, mokrov-ev@rudn.ru
[2] Institute of Informatics Problems, Federal Research Center "Computer Science and Control" of Russian Academy of Sciences, 119333 Moscow, Russia
samouylov-ke@rudn.ru

**Abstract.** Nowadays, unmanned aerial vehicles (UAV) are considered for a variety of different applications. One of the important ones is automatic collection of sensory data. In this work, we study the use of UAV-based for secure remote monitoring network enabled via LoRaWAN lower-power wide area (LPWA) network. In the considered use-case the UAVs carry sensors collecting data and LoRa modules to transmit collected data to the stationary gateway. The work focuses on congestion control on the gateway. Specifically, we propose a multi-threshold hysteresis-based control mechanism to alleviate system overload by dropping some of the data send by the sensors. The considered system is modeled using the queuing system with multiple thresholds. The work studies time-dependent characteristics of the system: average time the system spends in overload and reduced load states. Our results demonstrate that using hysteresis control allows for the system to accept priority data traffic even under relatively high system load.

**Keywords:** UAV · WSN · queuing model · Markov process · hysteresis control · time-dependent characteristics

## 1 Introduction

With growing development of Internet of things (IoT) and machine-to-machine (M2M) communications wireless sensor networks (WSNs) gather a lot of attention due to their advantages in terms of cost and flexibility. Due to their popularity, new challenges in terms of networks capacity due to high amounts of data traffic generated by these devices arise [2,10]. This problem especially holds true for the problems of security remote monitoring in remote areas, since the amount of generated data is huge and the network may suffer from coverage problems and low infrastructure investments [9].

The research was supported by RSF (project No. 21-79-00157).

Unmanned aerial vehicles (UAV) are nowadays finding their applications in many applied areas including telecommunications. Specifically, they can be utilized as aerial base stations (BS) [8], part of integrated access and backhaul (IAB) infrastructure serving as relaying nodes [3,11]. In context of IoT systems, the use of UAV has been reported in context of relaying [6] and data collection and delivery [7].

The problem of insufficient infrastructure and coverage can be partially mitigated by implementing pre-programmed or remotely controlled unmanned aerial vehicles (UAVs). UAVs, thanks to their mobility and flexibility, can change their positions between gathering data and transmitting it to the gateway, thus gathering data in low coverage areas and transmitting it when they reach area with reliable coverage [7]. Another possible solution would be placing the gateway or re-transmitters on the mobile UAVs [5], thus creating temporary channels to low coverage areas and collecting data from sensors via predefined patrol route.

There are currently many studies on the UAVs with LoRa communication networks due to the affordability of this technology as well as its long transmission ranges of more then 15 km while. Real-time UAV-based LoRa network are usually classified into two types: UAV as a LoRa node or LoRa gateway [4]. UAV as a LoRa node carries sensors with a LoRa module to act as a mobile sensor, collect data and transmit it to the gateway after moving to its coverage area. A UAV-based LoRa gateway can be used as a temporary gateway in low coverage areas of the stationary network or collect data from the stationary sensors, deployed on its patrol route.

In our paper, we focus on the problem of congestion control in UAV-based WSN security remote monitoring system with LoraWAN technology. In the considered system sensors are placed on UAVs that collect video data on potential trespassing and send it to the gateway. Since Lora has high coverage rate, a single gateway can have coverage of more than 15 square kilometers. Assuming that this area contains large number of UAVs with sensors, the gateway may experience overloads. To this end we implement threshold-based hysteresis control mechanism in order to mitigate possible overloads experienced by the gateway in cases of high traffic activity from the sensors. In current work we study average time the system spends in states of reduced traffic load, when the algorithm drops some of the less relevant data messages and in state of overload, when relevant data may be lost.

The rest of the paper is organized as follows. In Sect. 2 we introduce our target scenario and system model. Then, we describe analytical model and metrics of interest. Numerical results are presented in Sect. 3. Finally, conclusions are drawn in Sect. 4.

## 2    System Model

### 2.1    Considered Scenario

We consider a farm trespassing scenario, on which a farm field deploys security system in order to set the alarm in case if a cattle herd trespasses. The security system consists of several video sensors deployed on the UAVs, patrolling around the fields on a set course. The surveyed area can be divided into two different areas: yellow and red. Yellow area is a warning area that shows if an entity is moving close to the field, but doesn't yet trespass. Red area shows actual trespassing to the fields. The first area is necessary in order to set a warning to the potential trespassers, while the second area is responsible for setting off the alarm due to the trespassing. The sensors are mounted on several UAVs, patrolling the set area of several farm fields as illustrated on Fig. 1. The gateway that receives the data from all the sensors can experience significant load in cases of mass trespassing due to the number of connected sensors. Thus we propose implementing hysteresis control mechanism on it to alleviate its load.

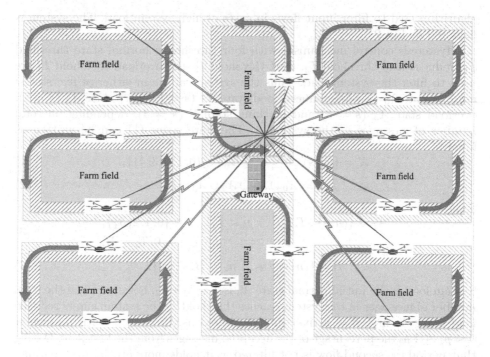

**Fig. 1.** Farm trespasser scenario (Color figure online)

## 2.2 Model Formalization

We consider a queuing model with a single server with exponential service rate $\mu$ and a buffer of size $B$. The messages occupy buffer from the moment they enter the system until the moment they leave it. The incoming flows from yellow and red areas are modeled as independent Poisson flows with parameters $\lambda_1(t)$ and $\lambda_2(t)$ correspondingly. The arrival rates are dependant on time due to hysteresis

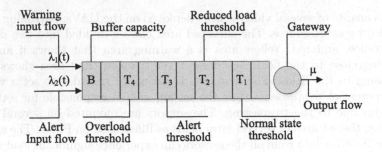

**Fig. 2.** WSN system model

algorithm used to filter input flows in cases of high system load. The system is depicted on Fig. 2.

Hysteresis control mechanism with four thresholds: normal state threshold $T_1$, reduced load threshold $T_2$, alert threshold $T_3$ and overload threshold $T_4$ are used to filter the system load. Thus the system can be in either of five states: normal state $\mathcal{X}_0$ ($s = 0$), reduced load state $\mathcal{X}_1$ ($s = 1$), alert state $\mathcal{X}_2$ ($s = 2$), overload state $\mathcal{X}_3$ ($s = 3$) and blocking state $\mathcal{B}$ ($s = 4$), depending on total number of messages in the system $n$. The state space (1) can be written as follows:

$$\mathcal{X} = \{(n, s) : 0 \leq n \leq B, s \in \{0, 1, 2, 3, 4\}\}, \tag{1}$$

$$\mathcal{X} = \mathcal{X}_0 \cup \mathcal{X}_1 \cup \mathcal{X}_2 \cup \mathcal{X}_3 \cup \mathcal{B}, \tag{2}$$

where

$$\mathcal{X}_i = \{(n, s) : T_{s-1} <= n < T_{s+1}, s \in \{0, 1, 2, 3\}\}, \tag{3}$$
$$T_{-1} = 0, T_5 = B,$$

$$\mathcal{B} = \{(n, s) : n_1 + n_2 = B, s = 4\}. \tag{4}$$

System load in the initial normal state $\mathcal{X}_0$ is $\lambda = \lambda_1 + \lambda_2$, however when the total number of messages in the system reaches threshold $T_2$ the system enters reduced load state $\mathcal{X}_1$ first flow arrival rate is filtered as $\lambda_1^* = p_1 \lambda_1$ with parameter $0 \leq p_1 \leq 1$ as the percentage of the accepted messages from the first flow. During that period the second flow is not filtered as it holds more crucial information.

After the system entered reduced load state $\mathcal{X}_1$ if the total number of messages in the system is reduced to threshold $T_1$, first flow arrival rate is returned to its initial value and the system returns to the normal state $\mathcal{X}_0$. However if instead the number of messages in the buffer keeps growing and passes threshold $T_3$, then the system stops accepting traffic of the first type and only accepts the second flow data entering the alert state $\mathcal{X}_2$.

In case the system is in alert state $\mathcal{X}_2$ and the number of messages in the system drops to $T_2$, the system returns to the reduced load state $\mathcal{X}_1$ and again starts accepting reduced flow $\lambda_1^*$ of the first type, while accepting the full flow of the second type. In case the number in the buffer still keeps increasing up to Level $T_4$, the second flow is reduced in the same way $\lambda_2^* = p_2 \lambda_2$ with parameter

$0 \leq p_2 \leq 1$ as the percentage of the accepted messages from the second flow. The first flow stays rejected in that case and the system enters overload state $\mathcal{X}_3$.

After the system entered the overload state $\mathcal{X}_3$, it may either return to the alert state $\mathcal{X}_2$ if the number of messages in the buffer reduces to $T_3$, or enter the blocking state $\mathcal{B}$ if the buffer becomes full. In the blocking state the system rejects any data arriving from the sensors as it does not have enough capacity to store it. As soon as a message is processed on the server and there appears an empty space in the buffer to accommodate new message, the system returns to the overload state $\mathcal{X}_2$.

The presented state space corresponds to Markov process $X(t) = \{(n(t), s(t))\}$, that describes the behavior of the system at time $t$. A state transition diagram of Markov process $\mathcal{X}(t)$ is shown in Fig. 3.

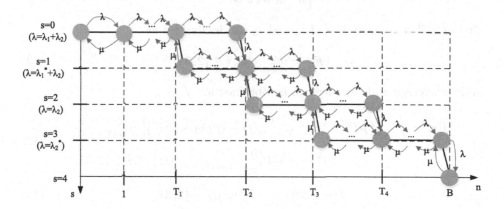

**Fig. 3.** State transition diagram for Markov process X(t)

### 2.3 Metrics of Interest

Here we consider time-dependent system characteristics, such as average and variance of system alert time $\tau_3$ when the system rejects second type of messages $\tau_2$ and average and variance of time system spends in overload state when the system drops a portion of high priority alert messages.

In order to acquire these characteristics we introduce reduced Markov processes $X^{(i)}(t), i \in \{2, 3\}$ with state spaces

$$\mathcal{X}^{(2)} = \mathcal{X}_2 \cup \mathcal{X}_3 \cup \{T_2, 1\} \cup \{B, 4\}, \tag{5}$$

$$\mathcal{X}^{(3)} = \mathcal{X}_3 \cup \{T_3, 2\} \cup \{B, 4\} \tag{6}$$

with time-dependent probabilities at time $t$ defined as

$$p_{(n,s)}^{(i)}(t) = P\{X^{(i)}(t) = (n, s), (n, s) \in \mathcal{X}^{(i)}\}, i \in \{2, 3\}, \tag{7}$$

$$\mathbf{p}^{(i)}(t) := (p_{(n,s)}^{(i)}(t))_{(n,s)\in\mathcal{X}^{(i)}}, i \in \{2,3\} \tag{8}$$

and probability transition matrix

$$(\mathbf{p}^{(i)})^T(t) = (\mathbf{p}^{(i)})^T(0)\mathbf{p}^{(i)}(t), i \in \{2,3\}. \tag{9}$$

The probability vector at time $t$ can be calculated as

$$\mathbf{P}^{(i)}(t) = (P_{(n,s),(m,r)}^{(i)}(t))_{(n,s),(m,r)\in X^{(i)}} = e^{A^{(i)}t}, i \in \{2,3\}. \tag{10}$$

Here $\mathbf{A}^{(i)}$ is a transition rate matrix for process $X^{(i)}$ derived similarly to [1]. and starting vectors are

$$\mathbf{P}^{(i)}(0) = \begin{cases} 1 & (n,s) \in (T_{i+1}, i) \\ 0 & otherwise \end{cases}, i \in \{2,3\} \tag{11}$$

Then CDF of average time of $\tau_2$ and $\tau_3$ can be derived as

$$F_{\tau_i} = p_{(T_2,1)}^{(i)}(t), i \in \{2,3\} \tag{12}$$

and its average and variance can be obtained as

$$E\tau_i = \int_0^\infty t \left( \mu P_{(T_{i+1}-1,i),(T_i,i-1)}^{(i)}(t) - (p_2\lambda_2 + \mu) P_{(T_{i+1},i),(T_i,i-1)}^{(i)} \right.$$
$$\left. (t) + p_2\lambda_2 P_{T_{i+1}+1,i),(T_i,i-1)}^{(i)}(t) \right) dt, i \in \{2,3\}, \tag{13}$$

$$D\tau_3 = E(\tau_i^2) - E^2(\tau_i), i \in \{2,3\}. \tag{14}$$

## 3   Numerical Analysis

In this section we present calculated results for the aforementioned metrics of interest. The default system parameters for the analysis are given in Table 1. Here system load in normal state is the total system load from both traffic types in worst case when none of the traffic type is reduced $\rho = \frac{\lambda_1+\lambda_1}{\mu}$. Also, from the presented data one can notice that the system goes to alert state only when half the buffer is occupied, since $T_3 = B/2$. First to second traffic type rate ratio shows how much more often the system receives first type of messages compared to the second type. First and second traffic type reduction parameters shows the percentage of the said traffic type accepted by the system under reduced load and overload states correspondingly.

**Table 1.** Default system parameters

| Parameter | Value | Description |
|-----------|-------|-------------|
| $B$ | 40 | Buffer size |
| $T_1$ | 10 | First threshold |
| $T_2$ | 15 | Reduced load threshold |
| $T_3$ | 20 | Third threshold |
| $T_4$ | 30 | Overload threshold |
| $\frac{\lambda_1}{\lambda_2}$ | $\frac{3}{2}$ | First to second traffic type rate ratio |
| $\mu$ | 1 | Service rate |
| $p_1$ | 0.5 | Warning traffic type reduction parameter |
| $p_2$ | 0.8 | Alert traffic type reduction parameter |
| $\rho$ | 0,...,3 | System load in normal state |

Figure 4 shows CDF of system alert $\tau_2$ and average time system spends in overload state $\tau_3$ under different load. One can be notice that under low load $\rho = 3$ both functions display ordinary behaviour. However under high system load of $\rho = 3$ overload CDF grows much faster than alert CDF. This is due to the fact that under this load system can still recover from the overload state since due to hysteresis control mechanism the system does not receive excess load as the accepted load is only $p_2\lambda_2 = 0.96 < 1$. While for the alert state the accepted load is $\lambda_2 = 1.2 > 1$ resulting in server not being able to serve the messages. However the load increased even more up to $\rho = 5$ to return to the reduced load state, as a result, the more time passes the less the probability the system can leave alert state resulting in heavily reduced CDF growth. Under even higher load the plots again behave similarly to the low load scenario with the exception that now they both are rising much slower due to low probability of leaving the corresponding state. Figure 4 illustrates average alert and overload system time. Figure 6 shows variance for these values. The logarithmic scale is to better showcase plots behaviour. Similarly to Fig. 4 the plots meet at $\rho = 2.2$ where the system experiences heavy load for the alert state, however in the Overload state the system still recieves relatively low load. At $\rho = 2.5$ the load in alert state reaches 1, while load in overload state stays at 0.8. After rising the load even more, the system in overload state also fails to handle the received load. The load in overload state reaches 1 under system load $\rho = 3.125$, however the system still leaves this state faster than the alert state until $\rho = 5$ when the corresponding plots meet for the second time (Fig. 5).

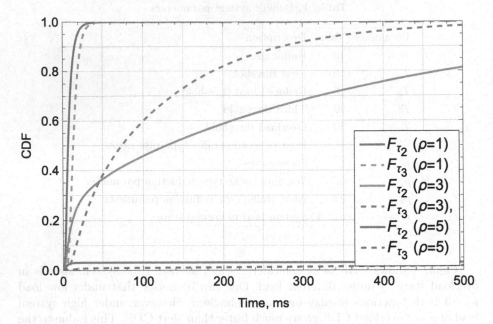

**Fig. 4.** CDF of time in alarm and overload states under different system load

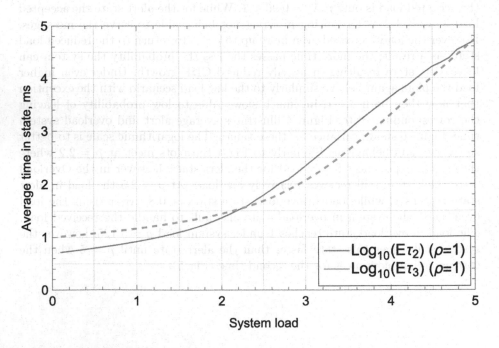

**Fig. 5.** Average time the system spends in corresponding states

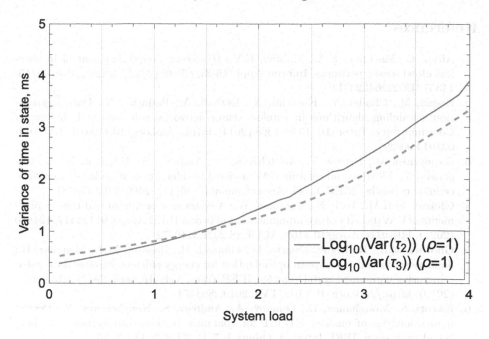

**Fig. 6.** Variance of time the system spends in corresponding states

## 4    Conclusions

In this work we studied UAV-based WSN network with two different traffic types and a single gateway under high load. We proposed a queuing theory mathematical model to study the considered system. In this model we utilised milti-threshold hysteresis mechanism to control gateway load. For the proposed model we introduced several reduced Markov pricesses in order to obtain time-dependent system characteristics.

The results for the average time the system spends in each of the studied states show similar behaviour in. Based on the acquired results an existing analytical model can be improved to consider time the system spends in each distinctive state from the state space, instead of union of several states. However in that case the reduced process would have two different absorbing states. In Future works we also plan to calculate the number of messages of each type in the system at a given time. In order to do this we plan to implement priority-based queue that puts alert messages at the start of the queue and additionally implement message TTL (time-to-live) to automatically drop outdated messages from the queue.

# References

1. Aliyu, B., Machnev, E.A., Mokrov, E.V.: Hysteretic congestion control in wireless cloud sensor networks. Inform. Appl. **16**(3), 83–89 (2022). https://doi.org/10.14357/19922264220311
2. Bagaa, M., Challal, Y., Ksentini, A., Derhab, A., Badache, N.: Data aggregation scheduling algorithms in wireless sensor networks: solutions and challenges. Commun. Surv. Tutor. **16**, 1339–1368 (2014). https://doi.org/10.1109/SURV.2014.031914.00029
3. Gapeyenko, M., Petrov, V., Moltchanov, D., Andreev, S., Himayat, N., Koucheryavy, Y.: Flexible and reliable UAV-assisted backhaul operation in 5G mmWave cellular networks. IEEE J. Sel. Areas Commun. **36**(11), 2486–2496 (2018)
4. Ghazali, M.H.M., Teoh, K., Rahiman, W.: A systematic review of real-time deployments of UAV-based LoRa communication network. IEEE Access **9**, 124817–124830 (2021). https://doi.org/10.1109/ACCESS.2021.3110872
5. Ghorbel, M.B., Rodríguez-Duarte, D., Ghazzai, H., Hossain, M.J., Menouar, H.: Joint position and travel path optimization for energy efficient wireless data gathering using unmanned aerial vehicles. IEEE Trans. Veh. Technol. **68**(3), 2165–2175 (2019). https://doi.org/10.1109/TVT.2019.2893374
6. Kavuri, S., Moltchanov, D., Ometov, A., Andreev, S., Koucheryavy, Y.: Performance analysis of onshore NB-IoT for container tracking during near-the-shore vessel navigation. IEEE Internet Things J. **7**(4), 2928–2943 (2020)
7. Komarov, M., Moltchanov, D.: System design and analysis of UAV-assisted BLE wireless sensor systems. In: Mamatas, L., Matta, I., Papadimitriou, P., Koucheryavy, Y. (eds.) WWIC 2016. LNCS, vol. 9674, pp. 284–296. Springer, Cham (2016). https://doi.org/10.1007/978-3-319-33936-8_22
8. Petrov, V., Gapeyenko, M., Moltchanov, D., Andreev, S., Heath, R.W.: Hover or perch: comparing capacity of airborne and landed millimeter-wave UAV cells. IEEE Wireless Commun. Lett. **9**(12), 2059–2063 (2020)
9. Polonelli, T., Qin, Y., Yeatman, E.M., Benini, L., Boyle, D.: A flexible, low-power platform for UAV-based data collection from remote sensors. IEEE Access **8**, 164775–164785 (2020). https://doi.org/10.1109/ACCESS.2020.3021370
10. Stusek, M., et al.: Optimizing NB-IoT communication patterns for permanently connected mMTC devices. In: 2022 IEEE Wireless Communications and Networking Conference (WCNC), pp. 1413–1418. IEEE (2022)
11. Tafintsev, N., et al.: Handling spontaneous traffic variations in 5G+ via offloading onto mmWave-capable UAV "bridges". IEEE Trans. Veh. Technol. **69**(9), 10070–10084 (2020)

# Analysis of the Capacity Gain of Probability Shaping QAM

Anton Sergeev and Rostislav Shaniiazov(✉)

National Research University Higher School of Economics (HSE), Moscow, Russia
slaros@vu.spb.ru

**Abstract.** In this work we analyze and compare channel capacity for transmission schemes (for Quadrature Amplitude Modulation, QAM) with and without probabilistic shaping (so called statistical modulation). Probabilistic shaping is a transmission method, which implies a delivery of nonuniform data source using a modulation (e.g. QAM) in which constellation points are selected according to the probability of input symbols. The aim is to use the unequal probability distribution of data symbols to get the resulting modulation signals with least average power that leads to better performance in terms of BER-SNR and energy efficiency. The key idea of this work is to estimate maximum achievable gain in Channel Capacity of the proposed Shaping QAM. Although the studies in combined precoding/shaping technique were started by Fischer et al. in the distant 1995 and Frank R. Kschischang et al. in 1993 the exact estimations for capacity gain are obtained for the first time. The analytical results show the upper bound for the achievable gains.

**Keywords:** Probabilistic Shaping · Statistical Modulation · Quadrature Amplitude Modulation · QAM · Channel Capacity

## 1 Introduction

In the classical mathematical model of a communication system, the source data symbols are mapped into a sequence of channel symbols. Then the channel produces the noisy output sequence, which is analyzed at the receiver attempting to reconstruct the initially transmitted symbols [1]. It is shown in Fig. 1.

There are several well-known theorems in the Information Theory which prove that to achieve the maximum entropy we need a uniform source and random mapping to the constellation points, which in its turn have equal transmission probabilities. However, it does not consider the energy cost of the different constellation points. The idea is to make the mapping of source-channel symbols so that symbols with small energy are chosen more often than points with large energy. Nonuniform signaling reduces the entropy of the transmitter output, and hence the average bit rate/capacity. But energy savings may compensate for this loss and even get some gain.

© The Author(s), under exclusive license to Springer Nature Switzerland AG 2023
Y. Koucheryavy and A. Aziz (Eds.): NEW2AN 2022, LNCS 13772, pp. 595–605, 2023.
https://doi.org/10.1007/978-3-031-30258-9_53

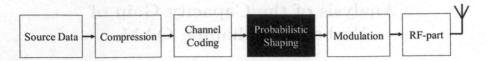

**Fig. 1.** A general scheme of communication system and place of probabilistic shaping stage

The concept of choosing constellation points with a nonuniform probability was independently suggested and discovered by different researchers and demonstrated in different publications during the last years.

Initially the fundamental article "Multidimensional Constellations" [2] by David Forney and Lee-Fang Wei had introduced this approach (alongside many others). The article is primarily devoted to the gain estimation for different coding and shaping schemes. Implicitly the authors assume throughout the paper that the probability distribution on a dimensional constellation is uniform. Most of the work they are assuming that a "probability distribution on the points in the constituent 2D constellation will be nonuniform in general". And then notice that the "frequency of occurrence of the outermost points in the constituent 2D constellation becomes small". David Forney and Lee-Fang Wei agrees that this fact may be used to improve the shaping gain in the future. Unfortunately, they never try to continue these research direction.

The next important step was done by Frank R. Kschischang and Subbarayan Pasupathy in [3]. Their paper answers the key research question: "When the criterion is one of minimizing the average transmitted energy for a given average bit rate what is the best possible source distribution with which to select constellation points?". It is theoretically demonstrated in their work that an optimal distribution, in this case, is a Maxwell-Boltzmann (MB) distribution. Like the predecessors in this field, the authors consider shaping gain as a part of the whole coded modulation system, in addition to coding gain. But such an approach made it difficult to the significance of shaping taken by itself.

From the principle of maximum entropy Maxwell-Boltzmann distribution maximizes bit rate for constellation points with fixed average energy. Constellation point $r$ and energy $|r|^2$ according to a Maxwell-Boltzmann distribution must be selected with probability $\frac{\exp(\lambda|r|^2)}{Z(\lambda)}$, where the parameter $\lambda$ regulates the tradeoff between bit rate and average energy. Maxwell-Boltzmann distribution for the source symbols (and therefore for channel QAM points after direct source-channel symbols' mapping) is used in our research too.

The next results for estimate capacity for Gaussian channels and shaping constellation was in the work of Fischer [4]. The authors estimate a gain in the general case for capacity and shaping. However, the authors pay attention it is not clear how to number of constellation's point (QAM) influence the shaping gain.

The next step linking the theory with practice was done in the research of A. Sergeev and A. Turlikov in [5,6]. They faced practical challenges of lossless video

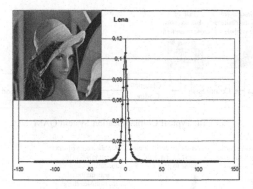

**Fig. 2.** Distribution of DIFF-frame points for Lena image. It was shown in [5] that PDF is close to geometric distribution. That in turn is very suitable for the practical usage of statistical modulation (probabilistic shaping)

transmission (as a set of the differential image frames) over the wireless channel under the severe power and computational constraints of the whole transmission system. It was decided to significantly reduce the required computational resources and energy consumption on the transmitter side by several interlinked decisions, including preprocessing of input symbols (instead of compression) and subsequent statistical modulation (SQAM, considering symbols probabilities):

- Differential frame (DIFF) is calculated pixel by pixel as the result of the JPEG-LS algorithm error prediction mechanism [5]. Point-estimate prediction $P_x$ of the image value $I_x$ at the pixel $x$ is determined by the values at the neighbouring positions a, b, and c specified in Fig. 3. Calculate error prediction at current as the difference between predicted and real value: DIFF $= I_x - P_x$; The scheme is quite simple from the computation efficiency point of view: several comparisons and subtractions are only needed per each pixel. As for a memory consumption it requires two rows of the original image only - current and previous ones. The distribution of the resulting differential values is close to geometrical distribution (Fig. 2).
- Differential data symbols obtained on a previous step are mapped to QAM modulation symbols in the way that the most frequent ones should be mapped into symbols with lowest energy level (see Fig. 3). It's clear that at decoder side the process is symmetrical.

It is shown in the paper that the proposed scheme has much less complexity costs and comparable QoS results than traditional video transmission pipeline with compression and error correction (with the same bit rate). This approach was later described in the patent (Intel Corp.) "Transmitting video between two stations in a wireless network" submitted by the same authors [6]. Now Statistical Shaping is appearing more and more frequently in practical tasks. For example in September 2016 Nokia Bell Labs and Technical University of Munich (TUM) presented the working prototype and showed that it is possible to increase the

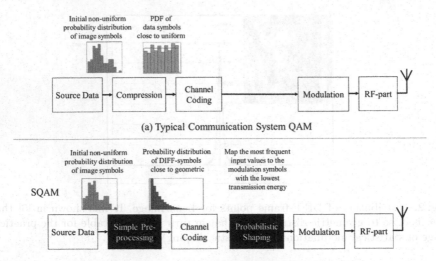

(a) Typical Communication System QAM

(b) Communication System with SQAM (Probabilistic Shaping)

**Fig. 3.** General schemes of communications systems: conventional (a) and with Statistical Modulation (SQAM or Probabilistic Shaping) based on work [5]

total throughput up to 30% in optical communication channels using probabilistic constellation shaping [7,8]. This work is based on three other papers. The first article explains the chief idea for constellation shaping and shows the optimal non-uniform distribution for Gaussian Channels [3]. The second paper describes the theoretical model for optical channel, approximates non-linear fiber propagation models and formalizes the so-called Gaussian-noise (GN) model [9]. The third article by G. Böcherer explains measuring achievable rate for bit-metric decoding [10]. In 2018 the Huawei team showed that it is possible to improve the Bit error rate (BER) performance up to 3 dB using shaping in an optical communication channels [11]. When the results of previous researchers are reviewed, it may be noted that the fair comparison of the conventional modulation scheme and statistical shaping considering the distribution of the source/channel symbols for the general case had not been implemented yet. It would appear logical to start with the estimating capacity gain for Quadrature Amplitude Modulation as one of the commonly used modulation schemes.

## 2   The Problem Statement

Estimate the maximum channel capacity gain for Statistical Shaping Modulation approach under the following conditions:

- Maxwell-Boltzmann [3] probability distribution of source symbols
- 1-to-1 mapping of source symbols to constellation points, 1 symbol per time unit

– Use of probabilistic shaping: minimizing the average transmitted energy by
  selection the channel symbols with smaller energy more frequently
– Modulation type: Quadrature amplitude modulation (QAM).

## 3  System Definition

Assume that a classical scheme is used of data transfer, which includes the source,
modulation algorithm and noisy communication channel. The source generates
symbols r with some probabilities p(r). Modulation algorithm is represented
by Quadrature Amplitude Modulation (QAM) and he generates some signal
X. Assume that the Additive White Gaussian noise with zero mean and some
variance $N_0$ is occurring in channel. The symbols after channels given by as

$$Y = X + N(0, N_0) \tag{1}$$

The scheme of data transfer is given in Fig. 4

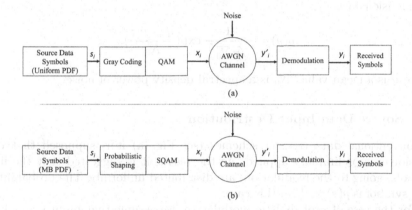

**Fig. 4.** Data transmitting model without (a) and with (b) probabilistic shaping stage

### 3.1  Quadrature Amplitude Modulation

QAM (quadrature amplitude modulation) is a method of combining two amplitude modulation (AM) signals into a single channel. It is used in our research
as a reference form of modulation because of its prevalence and high efficiency.
It is used in different communication from 3GPP to Wi-Fi. QAM-M (where M
is the number of different symbols which can be transmitted by one signal) is
found in most forms of high-speed data transmission. For more details one can
read [1].

One of the important parameter of communication scheme is the average
energy of constellation:

$$E_s = \sum_{M}^{i=1} p_i |s_i|^2, \tag{2}$$

where $p_i$ is a probability of symbol $s_i$. The maximum number of symbols is $M$. For typical transmission system it is proposed that all the pi are equal.

## 3.2    Channel Noise Model

Let the received symbol is defined as [1]:

$$y = k\sqrt{E_s}s + n, \tag{3}$$

where $k = 1/\sqrt{\frac{2}{3(M-1)}}$ is the normalizing factor. Value of $k$ can be used as $k = \frac{1}{\sqrt{10}}$ for $M = 16$, s is transmit symbol at the constellation and n is a noise. Assume that the additive noise $n \in N(\nu, N_0)$ follows from the Gaussian probability distribution function. For example, probability density function for N-dimensional case is:

$$p(y) = \frac{1}{\sqrt{\pi N_0}^N} \exp(\frac{|y - \nu|^2}{N_0}), \tag{4}$$

where $\nu$ is a mean value. $N_0$ is a spectral density power of noise.

## 3.3    Source Data Input Destribution

In conventional data transfer schemes (see Fig. 4a) it is supposed that compression was preliminary applied. As the result, it is suggested that the input symbols, going to the modulation, are distributed uniformly. The probability of each symbol is $p(s) = \frac{1}{N}$ in this case.

For the case of probabilistic modulation, we assume that input symbols are distributed according to Maxwell-Boltzmann PDF. As we mentioned before by the criterion is one of minimizing the average transmitted energy for a given average bit rate, the best possible distribution with selected constellation points is a Maxwell-Boltzmann [3].

Therefore, in that case the probability of input symbol $s$ is given by $p(s) = \frac{\exp(-\lambda|s|^2)}{Z(\lambda)}$ where $Z(\lambda) = \sum_s \exp(-\lambda|s|^2)$ is normalizing factor and $\lambda$ is the property of managing the bit-rate. It is clear that if $\lambda = 0$ then the uniform distribution takes place.

## 4    Constellation Shaping

As we defined before, the major idea of probability constellation shaping or SQAM for non-uniform distribution is to map the most frequent input symbols to the constellation QAM with the lowest transmission energy. As the result, the average energy of the transmission system is dramatically decreases because the low-energy modulation symbols are transmitted more often than the values with a higher energy level. This can, in turn, compensate the reduction of average signal power by increasing the distance between the constellation points [4,5]. And if so, the BER performance obviously increases too. We want to transmit signal with equal energy, thus let use the previous formula 2.

$$E_s = \frac{\sum_{i=1}^{M} |s|^2}{M} = \sum_{i=1}^{M} p_i |As|^2 = A^2 E_s', \tag{5}$$

where:

- $E_s$ is the energy of the signal in case of uniformly distributed data symbols,
- $E_s'$ is the energy in case of non-uniform (MB) of input symbols and
- $A$ is a coefficient of constellation points stretching.

The distance between points can be increased by $A$ coefficient using the formula:

$$A = \sqrt{E_s/E_s'}, \tag{6}$$

In Fig. 5 is shown an example of uniform and non-uniform distribution of a source after noisy Gaussian channel.

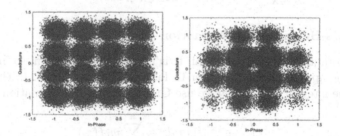

**Fig. 5.** Visualization of QAM-16 constellation points with uniform (left) and MB (right) distribution of input symbols (after AWGN channel).

## 5   Capacity Evaluation

Lets estimate the channel capacity gain for the both described approaches.

A theoretical equation for capacity C estimation is as following [1]:

$$C = \max_{p(x)} I(X;Y), \tag{7}$$

where $I(X;Y)$ is a mutual information for input symbols $X = \{s_1 \ldots s_M\}$ with probability $\{p(s_1) \ldots p(s_M)\}$ and $Y = \{-\infty, \infty\}$ for symbols after a channel.

For measuring the mutual information we will use the following formula:

$$I(X;Y) = H(X) - H(X|Y), \qquad (8)$$

where $H(X) = -\sum_{x \in X} p(x) \log p(x)$ is a Shannon's entropy, where $p(x)$ is a probability of input symbol $x$. $H(X|Y)$ is influence of noise(residual Entropy) for discrete input and continuous output of a channel $H(X|Y) = -\sum_{x \in X} \int p(x,y) \log p(x|y) dy$. Using the Bayes formula [1], we can obtain: $p(x|y) = \frac{p(y|x)p(x)}{p(y)}$. Where $p(y)$ is $p(y) = \sum_{x \in X} p(x)p(y|x)$

Assume we have additive white Gaussian noise in the channel, so, using the formula 4, the conditional probability for 2-dimensional constellation for a point is:

$$p(y|x) = \frac{1}{N_0 \pi} e^{-\frac{|x-y|^2}{N_0}} \qquad (9)$$

The final equation is:

$$C = \max_{p(x)} \sum_{x \in X} \int p(x)p(y|x) \log \frac{p(y|x)p(x)}{\sum_{x' \in X} p(x')p(y|x')} dy \\ - \sum_{x \in X} p(x) \log p(x) \qquad (10)$$

For uniform distribution the formula can be simplified:

$$C = \sum_{x \in X} \int \frac{1}{N} p(y|x) \log \frac{p(y|x)\frac{1}{N}}{\sum_{x' \in X} \frac{1}{N} p(y|x')} dy - \log N \qquad (11)$$

## 5.1　Gauss-Hermite Approximation

The final formula 11 has an integral. It is costly for calculation, so in this work we applying approximation in order to faster calculate results. In this work to go from the integral to the sum we use Gauss-Hermit approximation [12].

$$\int_{-\infty}^{\infty} e^{-x^2} f(x) \, dx \approx \sum_{i=1}^{n} w_i f(z_i) \qquad (12)$$

where $w_i$ and $z_i$ is pre-calculated constantants which were estimated for further calculations following the instruction given in [11].

Let use the following formula of condition entropy:

$$H(X|Y) = -\sum_{x \in X} \int p(x,y) \log p(x|y) dy = \\ -\sum_{x} p(x) \int p(y|x) \log p(x|y) dy = \\ \sum_{x \in X} p(x) H(X = x|Y) \qquad (13)$$

Applying for 2-dimention constellation we can obtain the formula for conditional entropy:

Let use: $t_1 = \frac{(y_1 - x_1)}{\sqrt{N_0}}$ and $t_2 = \frac{(y_2 - x_2)}{\sqrt{N_0}}$. Then equation is 11:

$$H(X = x|Y) = \\ -\int_{-\infty}^{\infty} \int_{-\infty}^{\infty} \frac{1}{\pi} \exp(-t_1^2 - t_2^2) \log \frac{\frac{1}{N_0 \pi} \exp(-t_1^2 - t_2^2)p(x)}{p(y)} dt_1 \, dt_2 \qquad (14)$$

Let rewrite the final gauss-Hermite formula:

$$H(X = x|Y) \approx - \sum_i \sum_j w_i w_j \frac{1}{\pi} \log \frac{\frac{1}{N_0 \pi} \exp\left(-z_i^2 - z_j^2\right) p(x)}{\sum_{x' \in X} p(x) p(y|x')} \approx$$

$$- \sum_i \sum_j w_i w_j \frac{1}{\pi} \log \frac{\frac{1}{N_0 \pi} \exp\left(-z_i^2 - z_j^2\right) p(x)}{\sum_{x' \in X} p(x) \exp\left(\frac{(z_i * \sqrt{N_0} + x_{real} - x'_{real})^2 * (..)^2}{N_0}\right)} \tag{15}$$

For uniform distribution (in case when every $p(x) = 1/M$):

$$H(X = x|Y) =$$
$$- \sum_i \sum_j w_i w_j \frac{1}{\pi}$$
$$\log \frac{\frac{1}{N_0 \pi} \exp\left(-z_i^2 - z_j^2\right) \frac{1}{M}}{\sum_{x' \in X} \frac{1}{M} \exp\left(\frac{(z_i * \sqrt{N_0} + x_{real} - x'_{real})^2 * (z_j * \sqrt{N_0} + x_{imag} - x'_{imag})^2}{N_0}\right)} \tag{16}$$

## 5.2   Calculation Optimization Using Gauss-Hermite Approximation

In this work we estimate a computing time with and without the Gauss-Hermite Approximation for $I(X;Y)$ from the formula 16. The calculation is done using PC with Core i7 7700/64 GByte RAM and Matlab 2020b. Table 1 with the values of calculation time shows Gauss-Hermite approach can improve the performance for calculating the capacity.

**Table 1.** A performance comparison of $C$ calculation time with an integral and Gauss-Hermite approximation

| QAM-M | QAM-4 | QAM-16 | QAM-64 | QAM-256 |
|---|---|---|---|---|
| Classical integral (seconds) | 0.22 | 0.1 | 0.2 | 1.6 |
| Gauss-Hermite approximation (seconds) | 0.011 | 0.018 | 0.083 | 0.69 |

## 6   Results

The calculation results (see Figs. 6, 7) show the channel capacity gain (QAM vs SQAM) up to 1.5 dB for the scenario with probabilistic shaping of MB-distributed symbols over the conventional transmission scheme. One can also see that the capacity gain grows with the constellation size. This is explained by the fact, that all the constellation points in case of statistical modulation have average energy gain convertible into larger distance between all of them. Therefore we get more efficient demodulation process when more noisy symbols are identified correctly. The considered scheme can work without preliminary compression while simple pre-processing is used instead. This also improves an overall benefit of the whole transmission system in terms of energy efficiency.

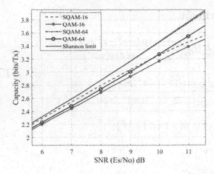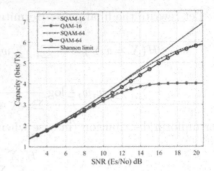

**Fig. 6.** Channel capacity: QAM-16 and QAM-64 for the conventional transmission scheme, SQAM-16 and SQAM-64 for the case with probabilistic shaping

Moreover we get latency savings because there are no time-wasting and energy-wasting compression stage with huge buffering of input symbols. This gain can be changed for better error correction or latency decreasing [13] on different OSI layers.

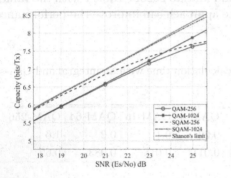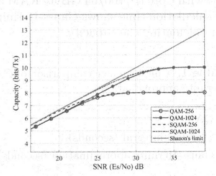

**Fig. 7.** Channel capacity: QAM-256 and QAM-1024 for the conventional transmission scheme, SQAM-64 and SQAM-256 for the case with probabilistic shaping

## 7   Conclusion

This is explained by the fact, that all the constellation points in case of statistical modulation have the average energy gain convertible into the *larger distance between all of them*. Therefore we get more efficient demodulation process when more noisy symbols are identified correctly at the receiver. One can see that the considered scheme has some great advantages. Firstly it can work without preliminary compression while simple pre-processing block instead. This also improves an overall benefit of the whole transmission system in terms of energy efficiency. Secondly we get latency savings because there are no time-wasting and energy wasting compression stage with huge buffering of input symbols. This gain can be changed for better error correction or latency decreasing [13] on different OSI layers.

# References

1. Burr, A.: Modulation and Coding for Wireless Communication. Prentice Hall, NJ (2001). ISBN: 10: 0201398575/ISBN 13: 9780201398571
2. Forney, G.D., Wei, L.-F.: Multidimensional constellations. IEEE J. Sel. Areas Commun. **7**(6), 877–892 (1989)
3. Kschischang, F.R., Pasupathy, S.: Optimal nonuniform signaling for Gaussian channels. IEEE Trans. Inf. Theory **39**(3), 913–929 (1993)
4. Fischer, R.F.: Precoding and Signal Shaping for Digital Transmission. Wiley, NY (2005)
5. Sergeev, A., Turlikov, A., Veselov, A.: Joint source coding and modulation for low-complexity video transmission. In: XII International Symposium on Problems of Redundancy in Information and Control Systems, pp. 313–322 (2009)
6. Sergeev, A., Turlikov, A.: Transmitting video between two stations in a wireless network. US Patent, S8437391B2, Current Assignee: Intel Corp. (2013)
7. Optical fiber transmits one terabit per second, press-release of Nokia Bell Labs, Deutsche Telekom T-Labs and the Technical 1/4 University of Munich (TUM) (2016). https://techxplore.com/pdf393493006.pdf
8. Fehenberger, T., Alvarado, A., Böcherer, G., Hanik, N.: On probabilistic shaping of quadrature amplitude modulation for the nonlinear fiber channel. J. Lightwave Technol. **34**(21), 5063–5073 (2016)
9. Poggiolini, P., Bosco, G., Carena, A., Curri, V., Jiang, Y., Forghieri, F.: The GN-model of fiber non-linear propagation and its applications. J. Lightwave Technol. **32**(4), 694–721 (2014)
10. Böcherer, G.: Achievable rates for shaped bit-metric decoding. arXiv preprint arXiv:1410.8075 (2014)
11. Böcherer, G.: On joint design of probabilistic shaping and forward error correction for optical systems. Opt. Fiber Commun. Conf. Exposition **2018**, 1–36 (2018)
12. Arasaratnam, I., Haykin, S., Elliott, R.J.: Discrete-time nonlinear filtering algorithms using Gauss-Hermite quadrature. Proc. IEEE **95**(5), 953–977 (2007)
13. Krouk, E., Sergeev, A., Afanasev, M.: A transport coding gain estimation in the conditions of time limitation for maximum acceptable message delay. In: Czarnowski, I., Howlett, R.J., Jain, L.C. (eds.) Intelligent Decision Technologies 2019. SIST, vol. 143, pp. 89–99. Springer, Singapore (2019). https://doi.org/10.1007/978-981-13-8303-8_8

# LoRa Mesh Network for Image Transmission: An Experimental Study

Van Dai Pham[1,2(✉)] ⓘ, Vladimir Vishnevsky[3], Dac Cu Nguyen[4],
and Ruslan Kirichek[1]

[1] Bonch-Bruevich Saint-Petersburg State University of Telecommunications,
193232 Saint Petersburg, Russia
fam.vd@spbgut.ru, kirichek@sut.ru
[2] Swinburne Vietnam, FPT University, Hanoi, Vietnam
[3] V. A. Trapeznikov Institute of Control Sciences of Russian Academy of Sciences,
117997 Moscow, Russia
[4] Faculty of Electrical and Electronic Engineering, Phenikaa University,
12116 Hanoi, Vietnam
cu.nguyendac@phenikaa-uni.edu.vn

**Abstract.** Nowadays, the Internet of Things (IoT) has been growing
continuously along with different networks providing connectivity methods for IoT devices. In this context, LoRa networks, or LoRa mesh networks, have been developed for long-range, low-power communication
for sensors. This paper studies an application of image transmission over
the LoRa mesh network by considering different images and energy consumption during a series of experiments. The experimental results show
a high packet delivery ratio via the network (over 90%). In addition, the
experiments also show the possibility of transferring 500 images taken
by battery-powered ESP32-CAM with a frame size of 480 × 320 and a
quality level of 30.

**Keywords:** IoT · mesh network · media transmission · energy
consumption · LoRa Mesh

## 1  Introduction

Nowadays, communication technologies are essential in connecting humans to
humans, machines to machines, and humans to machines. In the last decade, the
topic "Internet of Things (IoT)" has received much attention in both academic
and industrial fields [1,3,11]. Many IoT applications have been developed to
bring our lives more modern and convenient. In most IoT applications, there
are lots of sensor devices used to collect data that can be about the weather
as temperature, humidity, and pressure; or we can monitor how our health is
and how plants are growing by using sensors. The collected sensor data are
transmitted via networks to a remote server, where we can access the data via
the Internet [5,19].

The IoT paradigm has led to the emergence of other types of communication networks and communication technologies, which can be considered the connection infrastructure for "things" (devices). As one of the emerging technologies, the Long-Range (LoRa) network provides a connectivity solution for resource-constrained devices communicating over long distances [8,10]. In contrast to Zigbee, Bluetooth mesh, known as wireless sensor networks using ISM bands 2.4 GHz, LoRa networks use unlicensed bands such as 433, 868, and 915 MHz. Using Chirp Spread Spectrum modulation, LoRa-based devices can communicate in a long-range with low power consumption. The LoRa technology developed by Semtech Corporation is considered one of the promising technologies for building Low-Power Wide-Area Networks (LPWANs) in both urban and rural environments.

On the other hand, technologies such as IEEE 802.11, IEEE 802.15.4, or BLE (Bluetooth Low Energy) are also widely used in wireless sensor networks and IoT applications. However, these technologies ensure communication between devices in a short range. Therefore, [2,13] LoRaWAN, developed as a network protocol based on the LoRa technology, has been used in metering devices such as water and electric meters in Smart Cities.

In most of the solutions for organizing networks, we can see that the devices are connected in various topologies such as a star, mesh, multi-hop, or point-to-point. Depending on the requirements of the application, a topology can be chosen to build a network between devices. Initially, the networks based on the LoRa technology were proposed in work with the star topology, where many devices are connected to the external network via a base station or a gateway. Moreover, while considering networks such as ZigBee or Z-wave using mesh topology, the networks can be expanded easily. However, devices can communicate with others only at short distances in these networks. Thus, it becomes an idea to use a long-range mesh network as a LoRa network in star and mesh topology, which provides the devices far away from the gateway to transmit the data via the other devices.

Personal and energy-efficient long-range networks traditionally focus on transmitting data from IoT devices. The technologies included in these types of networks are used in devices for collecting telemetry data, ambient temperature, and other parameters. Sending data from devices is quite rare, and most of the time, the device is usually in "sleep" mode, due to which it is possible to save battery power for a long time. The main advantage of personal networks is self-organization through mesh topology and the ability to transmit data over long distances in LPWAN networks. Also, both types of networks are characterized by low power consumption. At the intersection of the advantages of the two types of networks, a new service was proposed that complements the functionality of these networks, namely the ability to transmit multimedia traffic (images and voice) through a fragment of an energy-efficient long-range mesh network. In [6,9], the authors performed studies to determine the possibility of transmitting multimedia data between two devices based on a fragment of the Zigbee and LoRa network over a transparent channel. It can be seen that LoRa-based applications are widespread in remote monitoring systems. The LoRa module can be installed on a UAV (Unmanned Aerial Vehicle), which collects data from sensor nodes in a remote area [12]. Considering the long-range communication (in line of sight conditions), we consider a LoRa mesh network to deliver the combined data to the public communication network with a low delay. For instance, some UAV-based applications require monitoring flying territory to assess the environments, such as disasters, fires, earthquakes, and equipment failures.

## 2   LoRa Mesh Network

As the physical layer of LoRa technology, the chirp spread spectrum (CSS) method is used, providing communication over long distances with low power consumption and bandwidth. LoRa networks operate in the unlicensed ISM frequency bands, which for Europe are the 867–869 MHz band with a center frequency of 868 MHz. The main parameters of this technology are bandwidth, spreading factor, and encoding rate. They can be configured for LoRa radios. LoRa uses 125, 250, and 500 kHz bandwidth to transmit signals, which makes LoRa immune to channel noise, long-term relative frequency, Doppler effects, and fading. Changing these parameters makes it possible to determine the optimal mode of operation for various data rate conditions between the transmitter and receiver [4,18].

Currently, mesh topology is actively used to organize networks in which devices can interact with each other to forward data to destination nodes outside the sender node's service radius. There are several advantages while using mesh topology, especially for organizing highly reliable ad-hoc networks due to duplication of transmission channels. In addition, the analysis of ongoing scientific research has shown that today exploratory research is underway on using mesh topology for LPWAN [14,15].

The LoRa mesh network provides a solution to increase communication range and packet delivery rate without installing additional LoRa gateways. In such a network, a node can relay the packet and communicate with other nodes to efficiently route the packet to the gateway. As shown in Fig. 1, nodes can act as relay nodes that receive and forward packets to the next node according to the routing rules. Mesh networks dynamically connect end nodes and self-organize routing [16,17]. The main advantage of this topology is that it has low transmit power and shorter communication channels, provides a reasonably long battery life and allows sending large amounts of data over the network. Moreover, the routing and configuration functions are designed for wireless mesh networks, and the load on mesh clients is significantly reduced. Thus, it makes the LoRa mesh network one of the promising ways to collect data from multiple sensors simultaneously.

# 3    Image Transmission

## 3.1    Image Transmission

In this paper, we study the application of the LoRa mesh network to transmit image data. Figure 1 presents a typical LoRa mesh network fragment to send images via intermediates nodes. A sending node equipped with a camera takes a photo after receiving a request from the server. Figure 2 shows an example of an image transmission session between the sender and the server. Thus, the user can send commands to the server to forward image requests to the camera node.

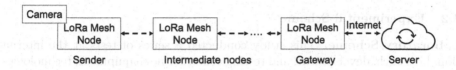

**Fig. 1.** A fragment of LoRa mesh network

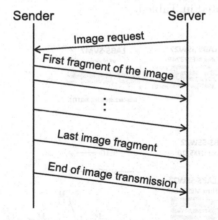

**Fig. 2.** Image transfer session between sender node and server

Since the size of the transmitted frame is limited to 255 bytes according to the LoRa specification, the image data can be split into several fragments and sequentially transmitted over the network. Figure 3 shows the packet format encapsulates the image fragments before sending them over the network. Each image has its identifier, and each fragment is assigned a fragmentation sequence number. This figure shows the packet encapsulating **N** payload bytes for transmitting an image fragment.

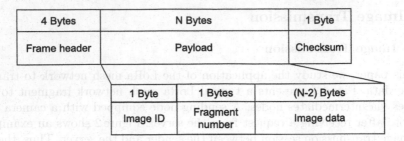

Fig. 3. Packet format for image transmission

## 3.2  Experimental Scheme

**Laboratory Scheme.** This study conducted a series of tests at the international research, development, and testing center for new equipment, technologies, and services supported by Rostelecom and the International Telecommunication Union (ITU-T) [7]. The scheme of the experimental zone is shown in Fig. 4, according to which image transmission traffic passes from node ESP32-CAM to the virtual server with MQTT broker, then from the server to laptop LABS-PC4 to evaluate the quality of the received images. The list of equipment used in the experiments is presented in Table 1.

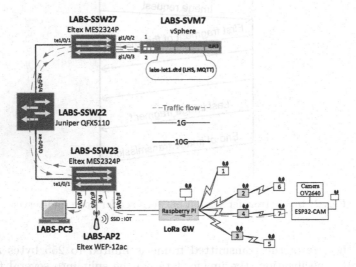

Fig. 4. Laboratory scheme in the experimental study

We used several YL-800N radio modules with the LoRa mesh support in this scheme. The development board ESP32-Camera equipped with an OV2640 camera was used to capture images and transmit them over the LoRa Mesh network to the remote server. The scheme of the experimental network with

**Table 1.** Laboratory equipment in the experiments

| Name | Usage |
| --- | --- |
| LABS-SVM7 | Virtual machine server |
| LABS-PC3 | Laptop for receiving images |
| LoRa Gateway | Routing data between LoRa and TCP/IP networks |
| ESP32-CAM | Capturing and transferring images |
| Relay nodes | Forwarding LoRa packets |

several intermediate nodes between the transmitter (ESP32-Camera) and the receiver (LoRa gateway to the server) is shown in Fig. 1. The ESP32-Camera board is connected to the YL-800N module via a serial port (UART - Universal Asynchronous Receiver-Transmitter) for data transmission. The ESP32-Camera board formulates a command and transmits it to the YL-800N module via the UART port via the application programming interface. The block diagram of the transmitter node is shown in Fig. 5. The device consists of the following components: development board ESP32-S, camera OV2640, LoRa module YL-800N, battery charging adapter, and battery.

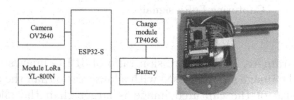

**Fig. 5.** The development board ESP32-Camera with the LoRa module

As a gateway, we developed a RaspberryPi-based LoRa gateway equipped with the module YL-800N to exchange traffic between LoRa and TCP/IP networks.

In addition, the power consumption of the sending node is also measured during the experiments with the support of Rohde & Schwarz equipment as listed in Table 2. The experiments follow the connection scheme of energy consumption measurement as shown in Fig. 6.

**Parameter Configuration.** According to the software application interface for the camera OV2640[1], we can set up different resolutions and quality levels for capturing JPEG images. The frame size can be with $240 \times 240$, $320 \times 240$, $480 \times 320$, $800 \times 600$. The quality levels (QL) can be configured from 0 to 63, where a lower number means higher quality for OV series camera sensors. We can

---

[1] https://github.com/espressif/esp32-camera.

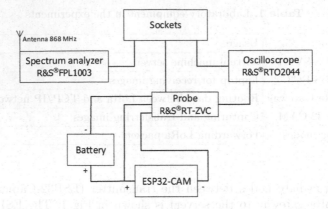

**Fig. 6.** Connection scheme of energy consumption measurement

**Table 2.** Energy measurement equipment

| Name | Usage |
| --- | --- |
| R&S RT-ZVC | Measurement of voltage and current at the same time |
| R&S RTO2044 | Oscilloscope for measuring, processing and recording results |
| R&S FPL1003 | Spectrum Analysis of LoRa Signals |
| Antenna | Capturing LoRa signals |

consider this parameter as a compression ratio of JPEG images. A low number indicates that the image is compressed with a lower ratio than the original image. However, the size of the captured image is larger than the allowable size of transmitted packets over the LoRa network. Therefore, the image is divided into fragments of 100 bytes each (packet structure according to Fig. 3).

The camera device transmits an image after receiving a request from the server (Fig. 2). The server sends a command to the node with the camera to request the transmission of an image. The ESP32-Camera board takes a photo after receiving the command and temporarily stores the photo as a byte array in memory. Then the board forms fragments of the image with a data size of 100 bytes. The images collected on the server are processed to recognize objects or text present in the images.

According to the specification of LoRa technology, network parameters can be varied. During this study, we used parameters presented in Table 3 to achieve the data rate of approximately 10.93 kbps. With the configured parameters, the LoRa node can have a reception sensitivity of up to −122 dBm. Moreover, we varied the OV2640 parameters (JPEG quality levels and resolution size) to receive different types of images.

**Table 3.** Parameter configuration in the experiments

| Parameter | Value |
| --- | --- |
| Frequency, MHz | 868 |
| Transmission power, dBm | 16 |
| Bandwidth, kHz | 250 |
| Spreading factor | 7 |
| Coding rate | 4/5 |
| OV2640 quality level (QL) | 10, 30, 60 |
| JPEG resolution size | 240x240, 320x240, 480x320 |

# 4  Experimental Results

## 4.1  Packet Delivery Ratio

As one of the primary metrics in network performance, we consider the packet delivery ratio (PDR) over the LoRa mesh network. Figure 7 shows the high PDR over 90% with each experiment. The high packet delivery ratio ensures that the transmitted JPEG images can be recovered on the receiving side with high probability.

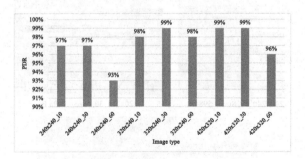

**Fig. 7.** Packet delivery ratio

## 4.2  Image Size and Required Number of Packets

According to the different camera configurations, the image size also changes. To determine the average size of images, we used a microSD card attached to ESP32-CAM to save the captured photos. Figure 8a shows the different sizes of the images depending on the frame size and quality level. Therefore, we can determine the number of packets required to transmit an image, as shown in Fig. 8b.

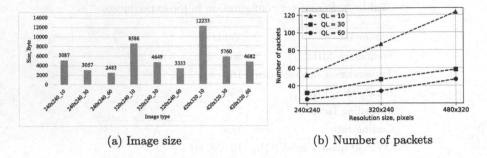

(a) Image size                              (b) Number of packets

**Fig. 8.** Image size and corresponding number of packets

As can be seen from the chart, the image size increases with increasing the frame size and decreasing the compression level. Moreover, the light level and color influence the size of images. Based on the experimental results, there is a big difference in image quality with the compression level of 10 and 60 by the camera OV2640. For instance, more than 40 packets (size = 100 Bytes) are required to transmit an image with a frame size of $240 \times 240$ and a quality level of 30. Examples of received images are shown in Fig. 9.

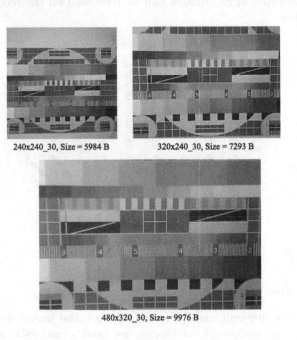

240x240_30, Size = 5984 B          320x240_30, Size = 7293 B

480x320_30, Size = 9976 B

**Fig. 9.** Comparison of received images

## 4.3    Energy Consumption

We performed energy measurements on the sending node ESP32-Camera during the experiments. We have received the average energy consumption in $\mu Ah$ with each image packet created and sent. The obtained results are shown in Fig. 10. According to the chart, the sending board required approximately the same power to send each packet in all cases (about 42–45 µAh. Therefore, we estimated how much energy was spent on transferring an image.

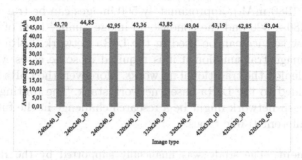

**Fig. 10.** Energy consumption per packet with size of 100 B

Obtaining the number of packets, we received the average power required to transfer different types of images. The average power consumption for transmitting a single image varies depending on the number of packets required to transmit that image. Figure 11 shows the average energy consumption corresponding to images with different frame sizes and quality levels. When using a 1200 mAh battery (theoretical capacity = 1080 mAh), the board can send approximately 500 images with a resolution of 480 × 320 and a quality level of 30.

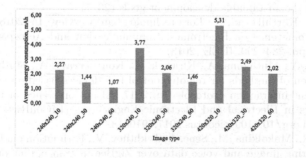

**Fig. 11.** Average energy consumption

## 5   Conclusion

In this paper, we have considered the LoRa Mesh Network provided to transmit small-resolution images. An experimental study was conducted to determine the acceptable image quality and the energy consumption required to send the images. When using the development board ESP32-CAM with settings such as a resolution size of $480 \times 320$ and an image quality level of 30, the quality of the resulting images is acceptable for recognition using optical character recognition packages. In addition, when using a 1200 mAh battery (theoretical capacity = $1200 \times 90\% = 1080$ mAh), approximately 500 images can be transmitted at the resolution of $480 \times 320$ and the conditional image quality level of 30.

Thus, a new service can be used in the LoRa network. LoRa-based devices can support image transmission if it is required in some cases when there are difficulties to deploy the traditional networks. Moreover, the LoRa mesh network also can be added to the LoRa-based network stack. The routing optimization in the LoRa mesh network might be a research challenge in the future to ensure transferring different traffic types.

**Acknowledgment.** The study was financially supported by the Russian Science Foundation within of scientific project No. 22-49-02023 "Development and study of methods for obtaining the reliability of tethered high-altitude unmanned telecommunication platforms of a new generation".

## References

1. Abbas, K., Tawalbeh, L.A., Rafiq, A., Muthanna, A., Elgendy, I.A., El-Latif, A.A.A.: Convergence of blockchain and IoT for secure transportation systems in smart cities. Secur. Commun. Netw. **2021**, 1–13 (2021). https://doi.org/10.1155/2021/5597679
2. Alliance, L.: LoRaWAN specification. LoRa Alliance, pp. 1–82 (2015)
3. Ben Dhaou, S., Lopes, N., Meyerhoff Nielsen, M.: Connecting cities and communities with the sustainable development goals (2017)
4. Devalal, S., Karthikeyan, A.: Lora technology-an overview. In: 2018 Second International Conference on Electronics, Communication and Aerospace Technology (ICECA), pp. 284–290. IEEE (2018)
5. Khakimov, A., Muthanna, A., Kirichek, R., Koucheryavy, A., Muthanna, M.S.A.: Investigation of methods for remote control IoT-devices based on cloud platforms and different interaction protocols. In: 2017 IEEE Conference of Russian Young Researchers in Electrical and Electronic Engineering (EIConRus). IEEE (2017). https://doi.org/10.1109/eiconrus.2017.7910518
6. Kirichek, R., Makolkina, M., Sene, J., Takhtuev, V.: Estimation quality parameters of transferring image and voice data over ZigBee in transparent mode. In: Vishnevsky, V., Kozyrev, D. (eds.) DCCN 2015. CCIS, vol. 601, pp. 260–267. Springer, Cham (2016). https://doi.org/10.1007/978-3-319-30843-2_27
7. Kirichek, R., Koucheryavy, A.: Internet of things laboratory test bed. In: Zeng, Q.-A. (ed.) Wireless Communications, Networking and Applications. LNEE, vol. 348, pp. 485–494. Springer, New Delhi (2016). https://doi.org/10.1007/978-81-322-2580-5_44

8. Kirichek, R., Kulik, V.: Long-range data transmission on flying ubiquitous sensor networks (FUSN) by using LPWAN protocols. In: Vishnevskiy, V.M., Samouylov, K.E., Kozyrev, D.V. (eds.) DCCN 2016. CCIS, vol. 678, pp. 442–453. Springer, Cham (2016). https://doi.org/10.1007/978-3-319-51917-3_39

9. Kirichek, R., Pham, V.-D., Kolechkin, A., Al-Bahri, M., Paramonov, A.: Transfer of multimedia data via LoRa. In: Galinina, O., Andreev, S., Balandin, S., Koucheryavy, Y. (eds.) NEW2AN/ruSMART/NsCC 2017. LNCS, vol. 10531, pp. 708–720. Springer, Cham (2017). https://doi.org/10.1007/978-3-319-67380-6_67

10. Koucheryavy, A., Vladyko, A., Kirichek, R.: State of the art and research challenges for public flying ubiquitous sensor networks. In: Balandin, S., Andreev, S., Koucheryavy, Y. (eds.) ruSMART 2015. LNCS, vol. 9247, pp. 299–308. Springer, Cham (2015). https://doi.org/10.1007/978-3-319-23126-6_27

11. Muthanna, A., Khakimov, A., Ateya, A.A., Paramonov, A., Koucheryavy, A.: Enabling M2M communication through MEC and SDN. In: Vishnevskiy, V.M., Kozyrev, D.V. (eds.) DCCN 2018. CCIS, vol. 919, pp. 95–105. Springer, Cham (2018). https://doi.org/10.1007/978-3-319-99447-5_9

12. Muthanna, M.S.A., Muthanna, M.M.A., Khakimov, A., Muthanna, A.: Development of intelligent street lighting services model based on LoRa technology. In: 2018 IEEE Conference of Russian Young Researchers in Electrical and Electronic Engineering (EIConRus). IEEE (2018). https://doi.org/10.1109/eiconrus.2018.8317037

13. Muthanna, M.S.A., Wang, P., Wei, M., Ateya, A.A., Muthanna, A.: Toward an ultra-low latency and energy efficient LoRaWAN. In: Galinina, O., Andreev, S., Balandin, S., Koucheryavy, Y. (eds.) NEW2AN/ruSMART 2019. LNCS, vol. 11660, pp. 233–242. Springer, Cham (2019). https://doi.org/10.1007/978-3-030-30859-9_20

14. Pham, V.D., Dinh, T.D., Kirichek, R.: Method for organizing mesh topology based on LoRa technology. In: 2018 10th International Congress on Ultra Modern Telecommunications and Control Systems and Workshops (ICUMT). IEEE (2018). https://doi.org/10.1109/icumt.2018.8631270

15. Pham, V.D., Le, D.T., Kirichek, R.: Evaluation of routing protocols for multi-hop communication in LPWAN. In: NEW2AN/ruSMART 2020. LNCS, vol. 12525, pp. 255–266. Springer, Cham (2020). https://doi.org/10.1007/978-3-030-65726-0_23

16. Pham, V.D., Le, D.T., Kirichek, R., Shestakov, A.: Research on using the AODV protocol for a LoRa mesh network. In: Vishnevskiy, V.M., Samouylov, K.E., Kozyrev, D.V. (eds.) DCCN 2020. LNCS, vol. 12563, pp. 149–160. Springer, Cham (2020). https://doi.org/10.1007/978-3-030-66471-8_13

17. Pham, V.D., Ovchinnikov, A., Zadorozhnaya, A., Kirichek, R., Myrova, L.: A hybrid wireless mesh network for sensor and actuator management in smart sustainable cities. In: The 4th International Conference on Future Networks and Distributed Systems (ICFNDS). ACM (2020). https://doi.org/10.1145/3440749.3442624

18. Semtech Corporation: Datasheet SX1276/77/78/79 LoRa Transciever (2019)

19. Yastrebova, A., Kirichek, R., Koucheryavy, Y., Borodin, A., Koucheryavy, A.: Future networks 2030: architecture & requirements. In: 2018 10th International Congress on Ultra Modern Telecommunications and Control Systems and Workshops (ICUMT). IEEE (2018). https://doi.org/10.1109/icumt.2018.8631208

# Blockchain Technology – Innovation for Better Collaboration and Increased Efficiency. The U.S. Logistics and Trucking Industry Case

Golib D. Tashmanov[1]([⊠]) and Alisher D. Toshmanov[2]

[1] Department of Accounting, Tashkent State University of Economics, Tashkent, Uzbekistan
g.tashmanov@tsue.uz

[2] Management Development Institute of Singapore in Tashkent, Tashkent, Uzbekistan

**Abstract.** The U.S. logistics and transportation industry have undergone substantial technological advancements over the last two decades. Simultaneously, customers' demand for same-day shipment has also increased dramatically, as has the amount of online transactions resulting in accelerated delivery. Latest technological changes have enabled commercial transportation businesses to efficiently service an all-time high demand while also adapting to shifting consumer tastes and expectations. According to American Trucking Associations (ATA), commercial trucks moved around 72.5% of the country's freight in 2020 which accounted for 732.3 billion USD in the same year. The industry employed 7.65 million people in total and nearly half of them were truck drivers. 1 Despite all these success and positive changes, the U.S. transportation industry has yet to overcome many core issues out of which most important one is the collaboration between parties within the industry. There is a huge gap in terms of communication between the shipper and the carrier because of the freight brokers' intervention. Moreover, there are other fundamental issues as well such as inefficiency, traceability of the loads, transparency of the transactions and overall reliability that the industry is in need for sole control tower which contains all the unbiased data. Blockchain technology has emerged as a potential solution to address these challenges and this new technology is spurring a great interest in the U.S. logistics sphere. However, the question still remains the same if the companies and their management are prepared and capable enough to deploy this new technology.

**Keywords:** Blockchain technology · American Trucking Associations (ATA) · U.S. logistics and trucking industry

## 1 Introduction

The trucking business is the practice of transporting products overland by road vehicles such as semi-trailers and light trucks. While it is most often used to move commodities from manufacturing facilities to retail distribution centers, it also has other typical functions in the construction sector, including as transportation of building supplies and materials.

Y. Koucheryavy and A. Aziz (Eds.): NEW2AN 2022, LNCS 13772, pp. 618–627, 2023.
https://doi.org/10.1007/978-3-031-30258-9_55

According to the American Trucking Association (ATA), the trucking business in the United States earned $732.3 billion in revenue in 2020, with 3.5 million drivers employed, accounting for 80.3 percent of the country's freight bill. 2 The trucking business is one of the leading indications for the direction of the global economy since it is such a large economic activity with significant linkages to all other industries.

Trucking companies are the backbone of the U.S. Logistics industry because trucks transport more than 70% of all freight volume and approximately 80% of freight expenditure in the United States (American Trucking Associations 2020). Trucking is a legacy sphere, diverse and competitive, with poor transparency, unstandardized procedures, and limited source of technology use (Smith 2018). There are around 1.5 million trucking businesses in the United States alone, employing roughly 3.5 million truck drivers. Around 90% of these businesses operate with little more than six vehicles (American Trucking Associations 2020) can be trusted yet it is sometimes difficult to track items across the whole supply chain. Furthermore, many logistical activities are still performed manually and on paper, which might result in lengthy processing delays.

## 2 Introduction to Blockchain Technology

Since Nakamoto (Nakamoto 2008) invented the blockchain and introduced Bitcoin in 2008, this decentralized and trustless peer-to-peer (P2P) technology has become one of the primary revolutionary forces in business, and is projected to be extensively used by a variety of industrial and service sectors (Iansiti 2017).

Blockchains are classified into two types: public and private. The only difference between them is who is permitted to join the network, execute the consensus process, and maintain the shared ledger. A public blockchain network is totally open, allowing anybody to join and participate, conducting transactions or validating the transactions of others (for example, bitcoin miners). One disadvantage of a public blockchain is the absence of transaction privacy, since transactions are broadcast to every participant (node), and each node therefore has an exhaustive record of the whole transaction history. On the other hand, a private blockchain is a programmable blockchain that is housed on private computer networks and utilizes an access control layer to regulate network access. To join the network, participants must get an invitation or authorization. In contrast to public blockchains, transactions are verified by a pre-selected group of participants who have been vetted by the network owner, and only the entities involved in the transaction will be aware of it; others will be unable to access it. One of the primary disadvantages of private blockchains is the inherent centralization they use to mitigate the scalability and privacy issues associated with public blockchains. By joining a private blockchain, you are implicitly putting your faith in a central source.

A blockchain is basically a distributed database of records, or a public ledger, of all transactions and digital events that have occurred and been shared across all network members. Each transaction is validated by most of the network's members prior to being recorded in the ledger using cryptographic processes (Alharby and Van Moorsel 2017). Once added into the public ledger, entries cannot be deleted or amended retrospectively without affecting all following blocks and the network functions' consensus. One of the most significant uses of blockchain technology is smart contracts. A smart contract is a piece of executable code that runs on the blockchain and is used to facilitate, execute, and enforce the terms of an agreement between untrustworthy parties, provided that certain predefined conditions are followed (Crosby 2016).

## 3  Blockchain Technology Benefits to Logistics and Transportation Industry

Blockchain technology offers great potential advantages in the logistics industry which enables the companies to achieve higher efficiency, better trackability and transparency. By producing an encrypted digital record that follows commodities at every level of the supply chain, the technology has the potential to address significant difficulties. It makes any abnormalities that might cause a shipment to be delayed or halted immediately evident, allowing firms to resolve issues as fast as possible. Furthermore, it has the potential to automate procedures while also making it simpler to authenticate goods–decreasing paperwork and facilitating end-to-end traceability in the process. Blockchain technology helps organizations to securely exchange data while also achieving their mutual objectives more effectively.

## 4  Research Objectives

Logistics is growing more complicated as more parties become engaged in supply chains, either directly or indirectly. This complexity creates communication and end-to-end visibility issues, rendering logistical procedures inefficient. In the meantime, all supply chain players' demands for openness, dependability, and service are also growing. Blockchain technology is emerging as an only answer for these challenges.

Despite optimistic expectations, there is presently limited knowledge on where and how blockchain technology may be efficiently applied and where it might deliver major economic benefits.

The connection between high expectations and a lack of competence is especially visible in the logistics industry, where many responsible managers appear to have zero or little awareness of blockchain and how blockchain-based applications may revolutionize or disrupt their company. Aside from a lack of understanding about the potential benefits of blockchain in this area, managers have even less information on where to begin in terms of implementation.

## 5  Methodology

The research project employs a design science research (DSR) methodology (Hevner 2007) to develop a blockchain-based model for increasing efficiency and cooperation in the transportation and logistics industries in the United States as a whole. DSR's principal purpose is to give knowledge that topic specialists may use to address their field's difficulties. Design sciences are concerned with determining what is practical and beneficial for the development of projected futures, rather than with what is now extant. This is akin to the aim of 'explanatory sciences,' such as natural sciences and sociology, which is to generate information for the purpose of describing, explaining, and predicting.

# 6 Literature Review

Collaboration in logistics occurs when two or more parties (shippers, clients, carriers, or thirdparty logistics providers) trade or share resources (tangible or intangible) such as trucks or demand information with the purpose of creating advantages that would not be possible separately. Audy et al. (2010) state that collaboration between partners may vary in intensity from information sharing to collaborative planning, joint execution, and strategic partnership.

In logistics, collaboration may take place on two levels: vertical and horizontal (Simaputang et al. 2002). Vertical collaboration occurs when partners at various stages of the supply chain (for example, a shipper and a carrier) pool or trade resources (Chopra et al. 2007). Horizontal cooperation occurs when rival firms operating at the same level of the supply chain (for example, two shippers or two carriers) form a partnership in order to maximize value and optimize resource use (Baratt 2004).

Vertical logistics collaboration studies have extensively been researched in the supply chain management literature (Soosay 2015; Stadtler 2009). Numerous studies have studied manufacturer-retailer vertical partnership concepts. Among the vertical cooperation models, Vendor-Managed Inventory (VMI) and Collaborative Planning, Forecasting, and Replenishment (CPFR) have garnered considerable attention from supply chain scholars and practitioners (Sari 2015).

In recent years, scholars have shown a growing interest in evaluating ideas, methodologies, and mathematical models relevant to horizontal cooperation in logistics and trucking sector. The emphasis of those works has been on the application of game theory to coalition building and gain sharing concerns, the mechanism of design for exchanging requests, and the development of optimization models for collaborative transportation planning. However, according to Pan (2019) and Nagarajan et al. (2008), despite the significance of real-time information interchange in horizontal cooperation, ICT concerns and potential have received less attention in the literature.

In today's trucking sector, where transactions are highly managed by freight brokers, both vertical and horizontal collaborative techniques are restricted. However, given the scale and fragmentation of the carrier market, horizontal coordination across carriers will be especially critical in tackling the trucking industry's sustainability concerns at the strategic level. Carriers may boost efficiency for key tasks (implementing collaborative route planning, eliminating empty hauling, raising load factors, reducing nights away from home, etc.) while lowering expenses for non-essential activities (vehicle purchasing, fuel, training, etc.). Furthermore, horizontal coordination allows small and medium-sized carriers to compete for bigger contracts with major shippers that they would be unable to complete alone owing to capacity restrictions. Scaled-up carriers may provide a higher level of service to their clients at a cheaper cost, for example, in terms of speed, frequency of deliveries, geographical coverage, and delivery time dependability.

Horizontal collaboration in the trucking industry is facilitated by information sharing among collaborating parties (for example, operational plans, existing orders, current and future capacity levels, and so on), alignment of individual and joint goals of collaborating parties, the existence of rapid dispute resolution mechanisms, and the availability of ICT infrastructure for faster and secure data exchanges among partners. On the other hand, horizontal collaboration in the trucking industry is hampered by difficulties in finding a trustworthy business partner, risks associated with malicious partners misusing sensitive information, challenges in sharing costs and gains fairly among partners, and a lack of ICT solutions (Basso et al. 2019, Cao et al. 2010 and Muir 2010).

It's worth noting that in the trucking sector, information exchange between companies is both a facilitator and a hindrance to horizontal collaboration's effectiveness. One of the most essential criteria in attaining carrier cooperation is a carrier's ability to acquire the confidence of its rivals. The issue is exacerbated by increased rivalry in the trucking industry, as well as a lack of efficient coordination among the main stakeholders. Islam et al. (2019) claim that transparently communicating company plans and other pertinent business information with partners helps to build confidence among partners and maintains the alignment of partners' individual and shared aims. However, a malevolent spouse's exploitation of such knowledge might have catastrophic ramifications for the other partner. Depending on the partners' initial strengths and limitations and how these strengths and weaknesses evolve over time, smaller firms in a partnership may lose customers or be forced out of the market entirely. Transportation control towers, sometimes known as trustee organizations, are relatively recent notions that have been considered in the logistics literature in order to remove trust difficulties among parties participating in horizontal cooperation in the trucking business. In essence, a trustee is an impartial, unbiased, and dependable third party who receives data from cooperating parties, maintains the data fully secret, and processes it with the purpose of maximizing profits for all partners (Cruijssen 2020).

In principle, the trustee concept—a central independent third party—seems promising; nevertheless, a method is still required to assure the trustee's impartiality and fairness while combining loads from various shippers, delegating the loads to carriers, and dividing the benefit to participants. Furthermore, the industry's single point of failure risk is borne by this tightly coupled business model with an independent trustworthy organization. Given the significant economic activity of the trucking sector, if the trustee loses its impartiality or is unable to operate for whatever reason, the financial effect on the connected shippers and carriers would be enormous. As a result, the trustee idea requires an innovative ICT solution that ensures the trustee's impartiality while also enabling shippers and carriers to authenticate the trustee's choices without jeopardizing the privacy of shared data. According to American Truckers Associations and the Truckers Report Magazine, blockchain technology has emerged to fill this gap and will be an ideal foundation of the transportation control tower.

Academic publications on blockchains in supply chain, logistics, and transportation journals are hard to come by. However, given the growing interest in the issue, we may expect a surge in the number of blockchain publications in the future years, with diverse uses of the technology for supply chains, logistics, and transportation.

Recent surveys of industry experts and supply chain and logistics managers indicate an interest in adopting blockchain technology, particularly in the context of supply chains (Pawczuk et al. 2018) and transportation and logistics (Carter and Koh 2018); however, we are still in the early stages of realizing the true potential of blockchain technology in global supply chains.

# 7  Methodology

The research study relies on design science research (DSR) framework (Hevner 2007) in order to create a blockchain-based model for improving efficiency and collaboration in the U.S. trucking and logistics industry overall. The primary objective of DSR is to provide information that experts.

# 8  Data

The research paper utilizes primary data collected directly from the industry participants as well as secondary data obtained from external resources such as journals and official web-sites. The paper discusses main differences and similarities between primary and secondary data.

Primary data refers to information that is gathered directly by the researcher in order to answer the research question. Primary data may be gathered using a variety of methods, including surveys, telephone or in-person interviews, focus groups, and a variety of other methods.

The interview technique of research will be used in this study since it adds more purpose to achieving the research's aim. The data collection process will be both objective and subjective. The objective technique is advantageous for eliciting responses based on facts and historical contexts, while the subjective approach directs the researcher to interpret the interviewee's ideas through the lens of his or her social context (Denzin 2001). (Heyl 2005).

Standardized and non-standardized interviews are both types of interviews. Standard and structured interviews are classified as structured interviews, whilst semi-structured and unstructured interviews are classified as non-structured interviews. Structured interviews are used to obtain measurable data via the use of a pre-defined set of questions, and the researcher must maintain the same tone throughout the interview to minimize bias. By contrast, semi-structured and in-depth interviews are used to do qualitative data analysis, such as a case study or grounded theory method. The researcher can place a greater emphasis on the 'why' rather than merely the 'what' and 'how' while using this technique.

During this specific study process, most of the primary data was collected through face-to-face interviews both physically and through an online platform Zoom. Some industry executives (freight brokers) preferred telephonic interviews and emails due to time difference and other constraints.

Compared to the face-to-face interviews, telephonic interviews and email communication methods were more inconvenient because it took more time and effort to get the answers accurately and promptly.

According to Vartanian (2011), the primary benefit of the secondary data is the fact that the researcher can save valuable resources while conducting the research such as time and money. Basically, there are two types of the secondary data, namely quantitative and qualitative. Obtaining data from primary sources may be a lengthy procedure; hence, secondary data sources are more beneficial and regarded a feasible choice for obtaining information that may also be sensitive in nature (Smith 2008). (Cowton 1998).

Secondary data may also be obtained through surveys and, when analyzed or reanalyzed, can provide significant new findings (Dale et al. 1988). Data derived from public sources demonstrates the validity of information and serves as a source of knowledge for everyone (Denscombe 2017).

## 9  Limitations

Gathering data from secondary sources is not always adequate to answer the research questions since the restrictions may be irrelevant and erroneous and may result in a failure to completely address the study topic or purpose. With the internet sources containing more and more misleading and irrelevant contents, it works as a barrier to study, making acquiring trustworthy information a time-consuming procedure.

Secondary data sources for this study will include reports directly from the U.S. Department of Transportation, companies' annual reports and statistical data from government-recognized regulatory agencies. Because Wernicke (2014) argues that national statistics data may be skewed, all the obtained secondary data in this study are then compared to the primary data obtained directly from the industry participants.

The U.S. logistics and transportation industry has many different parties operating in the same industry namely, shippers, freight brokers, insurance providers, carriers and finally the government. In order to gather sufficient data for the research process, the report will include several of each of the parties stated above. All the participants will be at managerial level or at higher decision-making capacity (president, partner and owner). As Becker (1998) claims higher level company executives will eliminate the chance of irrelevant information mislead the researcher and thus, will help achieve the research objectives.

## 10  Results

The suggested blockchain control tower will benefit all parties engaged in transportation operations in the U.S. logistics industry. Shippers may issue cargo tenders, search for credible carriers, write smart contracts outlining the conditions of the arrangement, and then execute the contract on the blockchain, all without relying on a trusted middleman or freight broker. Similarly, carriers may make themselves immediately visible to shippers through the blockchain network and establish a reputation for providing superior service to shippers. Additionally, utilizing data services, government and non-government organizations (NGOs) may monitor transportation activity on the blockchain network. For instance, the linked government body may examine the blockchain network's transactions to determine if the hours of service (HOS) law for shipments has been breached. Similarly, NGOs may conduct an analysis of vertical and horizontal cooperation prospects between shippers and carriers in order to minimize CO2 emissions and empty driving miles associated with trucking operations. Governments and non-governmental organizations (NGOs) may collaborate to promote sustainable transportation operations in the sector based on the blockchain transaction snapshot. Additionally, the system is accessible to other industry players. For instance, insurance information on carriers and shippers may be stored on the blockchain network, and insurance terms can be programmed into a smart contract that insurance firms can execute when the need arises. Finally, freight brokers might continue to operate as system users by offering technological consulting to their customers. For instance, they may handle transactions for client carriers that lack the requisite IT expertise to operate the system.

At least three critical application areas for the trucking sector are provided by the application layer: order management, horizontal cooperation, and sustainable trucking management.

Freight brokers have typically handled trucking orders in the contract (long-term) or spot (onetime) markets. This indirect interaction between shippers and carriers results in lengthy reconciliation procedures as well as restricts the extent to which shippers and carriers collaborate vertically. In a word, freight brokers arrange the capacity of reputable and available carriers on behalf of reputable shippers. Once a load is tendered to a carrier, the freight broker monitors the cargo's progress throughout the order's lifecycle and keeps the shipper informed of the cargo's condition. Additionally, the freight broker acts as an escrow agent for the shipper and carrier, keeping the invoiced amount on their behalf until both parties have fulfilled their shipping agreement duties. On the other hand, in our suggested system design, a privacy-preserving decision algorithm that is vetted and certified by blockchain miners takes the position of freight brokers as the matchmaker.

Along with enhancing the vertical interaction between shippers and carriers, the suggested architecture based on blockchain and smart contract technologies fosters horizontal cooperation within the trucking sector. For instance, the platform's decision system may connect numerous carriers with a strong reputation to complete a shipper's one heavy load order, which they cannot tender separately. This enables small carriers to expand their market share by conducting business with major shippers, while simultaneously assisting large shippers in reducing their reliance on large carriers by obtaining more competitive quotes for their load requests from smaller carriers. Additionally, the platform's smart contracts may be used to enable relay trucking models, in which two truck drivers exchange trailers at a meeting point and return to their home terminals with the new loads, bringing them closer to their ultimate destinations. Enabling truck drivers to spend more nights at home, relay trucking is often seen as a primary answer to the trucking industry's driver shortages/retention concerns and excessive empty mile.

## 11 Summary

The trucking industry, which employs millions of people and contributes a sizable amount of GDP to the United States, has a considerable influence on the three pillars of sustainability: the economy, society, and the environment. However, the worldwide trucking sector has long faced significant challenges, including poor working conditions for drivers, driver shortages and retention concerns, prolonged payment periods, and increasing expenses due to low load factors and a high number of empty miles. Any improvement in these areas would result in increased economic output and cheaper prices, better working conditions and decreased accident risks for society, and fewer carbon emissions and pollution for the environment. Having stated that, traditional business structures and conventional ICT solutions are ineffective in resolving these issues. The

EU, the World Economic Forum, and the OECD recognize the importance of collaboration between shippers and carriers in establishing a sustainable freight transportation system and call for more innovative technology solutions to foster collaboration in the trucking industry in their respective industry reports.

We discussed the trucking industry's general structure and major issues in this article, based on a literature analysis, industry reports, and interviews. After that, we explored the importance of horizontal cooperation in attaining sustainable transportation, as well as the challenges and facilitators to collaboration.

## 12 Recommendations

There are several study possibilities to investigate blockchain technology's possible application areas in the logistics business. To begin, additional research is necessary to ascertain the attitudes of large and medium carriers toward decentralized business models, as suggested in our design artifact, as well as to develop business models in which they can benefit as well by monetizing their excess resources or providing technology consulting to other carriers with less technological expertise. Additional research is required to analyze the benefits and disadvantages of current off chaining technologies for implementing our design artifact. Additionally, a prototype solution must be constructed to evaluate its performance and to get a better understanding of the trucking industry's technological adoption difficulties. Additionally, the suggested design artifact may be extended for use in other sectors where cooperation is critical. Finally, as with any other area of blockchain research, additional research is needed to address the barriers to wider adoption in the logistics industry, including regulatory clarity, high energy consumption, governance concerns, GDPR concerns, a lack of standardization, and a shortage of technical talent.

## References

Ani, W.U., Ugwunta, D.O., Okanya, O.: The effect of foreign exchange reforms on financial deepening: evidence from Nigeria. Int. J. Bus. Commer. **2**(3), 204–209 (2013)

Anyafo, A.M.O.: Nigerian Financial Market and Institutions. Banking and Finance Publications, Enugu (1999)

Baliamoune-Lutz, N.: Financial Reform and the Mobilization of Domestic Savings: The Experience of Morocco. Working Papers RP2006/100, World Institute for Development Economic Research (UNU-WIDER) (2006)

Bergen, J.V.: Factors that Influence Exchange Rates. Investopedia (2010). http://www.investopedia.com/articles/basics/04/050704.asp#axzz288SmcagR

Bundi, J.: The effects of financial liberalization on private domestic savings in Kenya (Thesis submitted to the School of Business). University of Nairobi (2013)

Clark, P., Tamirisa, N., Shang-Jin, W.: Exchange Rate Volatility and Trade Flows - Some New Evidence. International Monetary Fund (IMF) (2004)

Dornbusch, R., Fischer, S.: Exchange rates and the current account. Am. Econ. Rev. **70**(5), 960–971 (2003)

Egert, B., Helpern, L., MacDonald, R.: Equilibrium exchange rates in transition economies: taking stock of the issues. J. Econ. Surv. **20**, 257–324 (2006)

Engel, C.M., Flood, R.P.: The forward exchange market, speculation and exchange. Br. J. Mark. Stud. **4**(3), 1–11 (2016). Published by European Centre for Research Training and Development UK (www.eajournals.org) 11 ISSN 2055-0219(Print), ISSN 2055-0227(online) Market intervention. Q. J. Econ. **99**(1), 45–69 (1985)

Fisher, I.: The Theory of Interest. MacMillan, New York (2006)

Hill, C.W.L.: International Business Competing in the Global Market Place, 5th edn. McGraw-Hill College (2004)

Holub, T., Cihak, M.: Price Convergence: What Can the Balassa-Samuelson model Tell us? Working Paper Series. Czech National Bank (2003)

Hu, Y.: Renminbi real exchange rate and purchase power parity. Mod. Financ. Econ. **2** (2003)

Kanamori, T., Zhao, Z.: The Renminbi Exchange Rate Revaluation: Theory, Practice, and Lessons from Japan. ADBI Policy Papers, no. 9 (2006)

Karfakis, C., Kim, S.J.: Exchange rates and the current account news: some evidence from Australia. J. Int. Money Financ. **14**, 575–595 (1995)

Ling, T.H., Fayman, A., Michael, C.K.: Bank profitability: the impact of foreign currency fluctuations on in the USA. J. Appl. Bus. Econ. **16**(2) (2014)

Madura, J.: International Financial Management, 11th edn. South-Western College Publishing (2012)

Mbithi, A.M.: The effect of foreign exchange rates on the financial performance of firms listed at the Nairobi Securities Exchange (Master of Business Administration Thesis). University of Nairobi (2013)

Mohsen, B.-O., Abm, N.: Productivity bias hypothesis and the purchasing power parity: a review article. J. Econ. Surv. **19**, 671–696 (2015)

Mwega, F.M., Ngola, S.M., Mwangi, M.: Real Interest Rates and the Mobilization of Saving, A case study of Kenya. AERC Research Paper (1990)

Obidike, P.C., Ejeh, G.C., Ugwuegbe, S.: The impact of interest rate spread on the performance of Nigerian banking industry. J. Econ. Sustain. Dev. **6**(12), 131–140 (2015)

Obstfeld, M., Rogoff, K.: Exchange rate dynamics Redux. J. Polit. Econ. **103**(3), 624–660 (1995)

Owoeye, T., Ogunmakin, A.A.: Exchange rate volatility and bank performance in Nigeria. Asian Econ. Financ. Rev. **3**(2), 178–185 (2013)

Pugel, T.: International Economics, 13th edn. McGraw-Hill International Edition (2007)

Sadoulet, E., Janvry, A.D.: Quantitative Development Policy Analysis. The Johns Hopkins University Press, Baltimore and London (1995)

Solnik, B.: International Investments, 4th edn.. Addison-Wesley Copyright Addison Wesley Longman (2000)

Tica, J., Druzic, I.: The Harrod-Balassa-Samuelson Effect: A Survey of Empirical evidence. Working Paper Series No. 06–07. University of Zagreb, Zagreb – Croatia (2006)

# Econometric Study of the Impact of the Digital Economy on the Gross Product in Anti-monopoly Conditions

Bunyod Kuvondikovich Utanov[1], Akbar Jumayev[1], Dilobar Mavlyanova[2], Eldor Yuldashev[2(✉)], and Nihola Yuldasheva[2]

[1] Tashkent Institute of Finance, Tashkent, Uzbekistan
bunyod_utanov@tfi.uz
[2] Tashkent State University of Economics, Tashkent, Uzbekistan
e.yuldashev@tsue.uz

**Abstract.** The article conducts an econometric study of the impact of communication systems on the country's gross regional product, which are important in the formation of the digital economy, identifies the factors leading to the emergence of monopolies in the industry, and provides recommendations for their elimination.

**Keywords:** Monopoly · digital economy · gross regional product · Internet · competition · econometric models · optimal model

## 1 Introduction

The development of monopolies in individual branches and industries in the country cannot allow one to draw an optimistic conclusion when determining the long-term prospects for this industry and industry. Indeed, where there is a monopoly, self-employment is reduced, product quality deviates slightly from international standards and does not give consumers the opportunity to choose products. All countries are making great efforts to counteract the process of monopolization, which is of strategic importance or not included in the industry and industry, leading to the formation of the national image of the country. In this regard, significant work is being done in our country.

In particular, in accordance with the Resolution of the Cabinet of Ministers of the Republic of Uzbekistan dated March 2, 2021 "On measures to introduce a system of antitrust compliance" No.114 on antitrust enforcement in the country the implementation of the system "on the basis of the requirements set out in the road map" [1]. One of the most effective ways to combat monopolies in the context of developing information technology is to develop a digital economy in the country and thereby achieve economic growth. Today, the country pays more attention to the digital economy, which is regulated by the Decree of the President of the Republic of Uzbekistan dated July 13, 2021 PF-6261 "On approval of the Strategy" Digital Uzbekistan - 2030 "and measures for its effective implementation." [2]. The infrastructure of the Internet network in the country is an important factor in the development of the digital economy. If the Internet meets

Y. Koucheryavy and A. Aziz (Eds.): NEW2AN 2022, LNCS 13772, pp. 628–635, 2023.
https://doi.org/10.1007/978-3-031-30258-9_56

the requirements for the quality of communication at the international level and through which the country's socio-economic statistics are digitized, the data will be transparent and open to all consumers. As a result, entrepreneurs will have a competitive environment and opportunities to eliminate potentially monopolistic industries and sectors.

## 2  Literature Review

Chihiro Watanabe, Yuji Tou, and Pekka Neittaanmäki [5] proved in their research that changes in a country's gross domestic product statistics can also be achieved through the development of the digital economy. In this paper, a statistical assessment of the impact of the state's Internet structure, telecommunications system and Internet providers on the development of the digital economy. In the same study, the same authors drew attention to some inconsistencies in the indicators of the digital economy in the composition of gross domestic product [6].

The study, conducted by Rika Kurniaty, provides a comparative analysis of the characteristics and challenges of Indonesia's antitrust policy based on the Japanese experience. Recommendations have also been made to regulate the competitive environment [7]. In the research of Nicole Branger, René Marian Flacke, and Nikolai Gräbero, the impact of oil products on macroeconomic indicators was statistically assessed, and oil producers were economically evaluated from a monopoly point of view [1]. The research by Thee KianWie examines antitrust policy and digital economy processes in the Malaysian state. The study found that the digital economy is the most important tool for monopoly [2].

## 3  Method

We conduct econometric modeling based on the Panel model for a full and comprehensive study of the digital economy in the country.

The panel model is formed based on the panel data and is based on the data generated by the intersecting and time series.

In general, $x_{it}$ ($i$ and $t$) are used together in the equations of the Panel model. For example, when it is $x_{it}$, in the region $i$, t represents the time.

The panel model includes the following econometric models: Pooled OLS estimator(POLSE), First differences estimator(FDE), Fixed effects estimator(FEE), Random effects estimator(REE).

$POLS\ mode : y_{it} = \beta_0 + \beta_1 x_{1it} + \beta_2 x_{2it} + u_{it}$

$FDE\ model : \Delta\ y_{it} = \beta_0 + \beta_1\ \Delta\ x_{1it} + \beta_2\ \Delta\ x_{2it} + \Delta\ u_{it}$

$FEE\ model : y_{it} - \overline{y_i} = \beta_1(x_{1it} - \overline{x_{1i}}) + \beta_2(x_{2it} - \overline{x_{2i}}) + (u_{it} - \overline{u_i})$

$REE\ model : y_{it} - \overline{\theta y_i} = \beta_0 + \beta_1(x_{1it} - \overline{\theta x_{1i}}) + \beta_2(x_{2it} - \overline{\theta x_{2i}}) + (a_i - \overline{\theta a_i}) + (u_{it} - \overline{u_i})$

$$(1)$$

While the first model represents the same condition as the multivariate model constructed using the smallest squares, the second model takes into account the effect of the rate of change of the indicators in previous years. The reliability of the resulting models is tested by Hausman and Breusch Pagan tests.

## 4   Result

In order to achieve economic growth in the country, the main indicators of the degree of elimination of monopolies in the development of the digital economy were analyzed, and the data of the Panel, which influences the change of this indicator, were compiled [9].

As indicators of the impact on the digital economy, the regions of the country for the period from 2016 to 2021 were summarized on the basis of data from the State Statistics Committee and divided into two groups (Fig. 1).

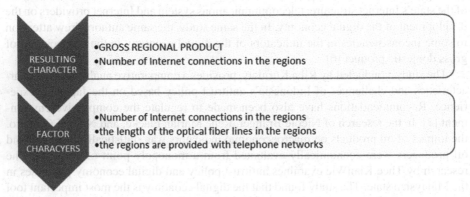

**Fig. 1.** A system of indicators affecting the digital economy

In order to determine the full correlation between the indicators we have chosen in the modeling of the digital economy, two models have been developed. In the first model, the result is a gross regional production, and in the second model, the number of internet subscribers [10]. According to the hypothesis, the length of optical fiber lines will increase the speed of the internet, and the speed of the internet will lead to the development of gross regional product, resulting in a strong system against the digital economy and monopolies (Fig. 2).

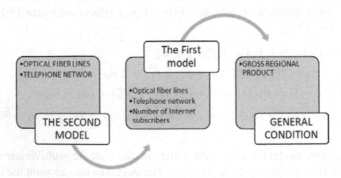

**Fig. 2.** Influence of indicators on gross income

In order to analyze the direction and density of the selected data link between regions, we construct a correlation of the indicators (Fig. 3).

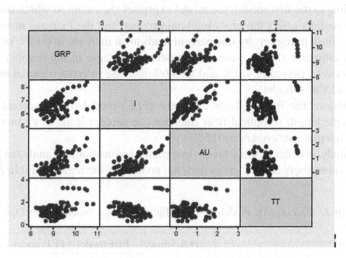

**Fig. 3.** Correlation

It was found that the correlation is closely and correctly connected to the gross regional product and Internet subscribers, and the number of Internet subscribers is similar to that of fiber-optic lines [11].

All indicators are converted to the logarithmic state, and based on their values we develop Panel models using the STATA program (Table 1).

**Table 1.** Economic modeling of lifestyle of the population on the basis of panel models

| | Indicators | POLSmodel | FDEmodel | FEEmodel | REEmodel |
|---|---|---|---|---|---|
| | 1-MODEL | | | | |
| 1 | The Number of Internet subscribers | −0,16 | 0.86 | 0.92!a | 0.59 |
| 2 | Length of optical fiber lines | 0,65 | −0.23 | −0.007 | 0.21 |
| 3 | Telephone network availability | 0,22 | −0.008 | −0.01 | 0.007 |
| 4 | Cons | 9.35 | | 3.05 | 5.06 |
| | 2-MODEL | | | | |
| 1 | Length of optical fiber lines | 0.83 | 0.38 | 0.56 | 0.64 |
| 2 | Telephone network availability | −0.009 | −0.38 | −0.75 | −0.39 |

When the reliability of our models developed using the Stata program was tested by Hausman and Breusch Pagan tests, it was found that all models were statistically significant [12].

Since the indicators are converted to a logarithm, in the interpretation of the model, each factor represents a percentage increase in the resulting sign regression coefficient as a result of a one percent increase in the sign.

According to the first model, the model expresses the extent to which the indicators in terms of regions affect the gross regional product, and the increase in the length of optical fiber lines in regions by one percent leads to an increase in 0.65% of GDP. First differences estimator (FDE) means a one-percent increase in the number of Internet subscribers over a period of years, and a 0.86% increase in gross regional product over the years under this model.

According to the Fixed effects estimator (FEE) model of the second model, an increase in the length of optical fiber lines by one percent leads to an increase in the number of Internet subscribers by 0.56%.

In our study, in order to study the co-integration connection, we analyzed the number of Internet subscribers and the gross regional product in the regions (Table 2).

**Table 2.** Econometric modeling of the digital economy based on panel models

| | Indicators | POLSmodel | FDEmodel | FEEmodel | REEmodel |
|---|---|---|---|---|---|
| | 1 Model | | | | |
| 1 | The Number of Internet subscribers | 0.33 | 0.83 | 0.92 | 0.88 |
| 2 | F test | 17.58 | 207.78 | 432.67 | 365.07 |
| 3 | R2 | 0.17 | 0.75 | 0.86 | 0.86 |
| 4 | Adj R$^2$ | 0.16 | 0.74 | | |
| | 2 Model | | | | |
| 1 | GRP | 0.52 | 0.89 | 0.93 | 0.92 |
| 2 | F test | 17.58 | 207.89 | 432.67 | 418.12 |
| 3 | R$^2$ | 0.17 | 0.75 | 0.86 | 0.86 |
| 4 | Adj R$^2$ | 0.16 | 0.74 | | |

When the reliability of these models was tested by Hausman and Breusch Pagan tests, the model parameters and the statistical significance of the models were determined.

Breusch and Pagan Lagrangian multiplier test for randomeffects.

I[id,t] = Xb + u[id] + e[id,t]

Estimated results:

Var sd = sqrt(Var)

I .4271971 .6536032

e .0198414 .1408596

u .342687 .5853948

Test: Var(u) = 0

chibar2(01) = 160.93

Prob > chibar2 = 0.0000

The results of our study confirm that the Breusch Pagan tests are statistically significant because the probability level is as small as 0.05.

Coefficients ----

(b)(B)(b − B) sqrt(diag(V_b − V_B))

fixed   random   Difference   S.E.

YaHM   .9342344   .9252081   .0090263

b = consistent under Ho and Ha; obtained from xtreg

B = inconsistent under Ha, efficient under Ho; obtained from xtreg

Test: Ho: difference in coefficients not systematic.

$chi2(1) = (b − B)'[(V_b − V_B)^{(−1)}](b-B) = −2.82$

chi2 < 0 == > model fitted on these data fails to meet the asymptotic assumptions of the Hausman test; see suest for a generalized test

The results of the Hausman test also confirm that all the parameters and statistical significance of the developed POLS, FDE, FEE, REE models are 95% reliable.

Based on these indicators, a cointegration linking algorithm for the development of the digital economy was developed (Fig. 4).

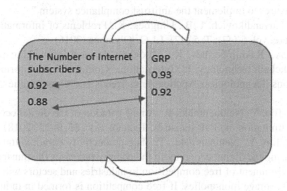

**Fig. 4.** Interconnection between the number of EHIM and Internet subscribers

The Fixed effects estimator (FEE) and Random effects estimator (REE) models are statistically significant in comparison to other models and have been proven to be reliable by both Breusch Pagan and Hausman tests.

According to co-integration, a one percent increase in the number of Internet subscribers will increase GDP by 0.93%, and a one percent increase in GDP will increase the number of Internet subscribers by 0.88%. Scientific research has shown that this is one of the main pillars of the digital economy and the fight against monopolies.

## 5   Conclusions

In general, the fight against monopolies in our country is developing rapidly. An appropriate regulatory framework has been created for the development of this situation, and we can see that systematic work is being done in this direction. The results of the analysis show that the role of the digital economy in the fight against monopolies is an important factor. Adequate Internet access in the development of the digital economy in the country increases the transparency of data. As a result, an environment of free competition in industries and sectors will be created, which will help to discourage monopolies. If free competition is formed in industries and sectors, it will lead to the growth of the country's regional products and, consequently, the growth of key macroeconomic indicators of the republic. In general, the widespread use of econometric analysis methods on such topics and the formation of conclusions through them are important dates.

# References

1. Decree of the President of the Republic of Uzbekistan PF-6019 of July 6, 2020 "On additional measures to further develop the competitive environment and reduce state participation in the economy."
2. Decree of the President of the Republic of Uzbekistan No. PF-6261 of July 13, 2021 "On approval of the Strategy" Digital Uzbekistan - 2030 "and measures for its effective implementation."
3. Resolution of the Cabinet of Ministers of the Republic of Uzbekistan No. 114 of March 2, 2021 "On measures to implement the antitrust compliance system."
4. Ibrokhim, K., Kuvandikovich, U.B., Ulugbek, K.: Problems of information security in the economic sphere, vol. 5 (47): T. 5 (47). LLC "Olympus (2016)
5. J. Arzieva, A.A., Rakhimberdiev, K.: Modeling the decision-making process of lenders based on blockchain technology. In: International Conference on Information Science and Communications Technologies: Applications, Trends and Opportunities, ICISCT, pp. 1–5 (2022)
6. Watanabe, C., Tou, Y., Neittaanmäki, P.: A new paradox of the digital economy - Structural sources of the limitation of GDP statistics. Technol. Soc. **55**, 9–23 (2018)
7. Watanabe, C., Tou, Y., Neittaanmäki., P.: The productivity paradox and the limitations of GDP in measuring the digital economy in the country increases the transparency of data. As a result, an environment of free competition in industries and sectors will be created, which will help to discourage monopolies. If free competition is formed in industries and sectors, it will lead to the growth of the country's regional products and, consequently, the growth of key macroeconomic indicators of the republic. In general, the widespread use of econometric analysis methods on such topics and the formation of conclusions through them are important dates
8. Juraev, G., Rakhimberdiev, K.: Mathematical modeling of credit scoring system based on the Monge-Kantorovich problem. In: 2022 IEEE International IOT, Electronics and Mechatronics Conference, IEMTRONICS 2022 Proceedings (2022)
9. Juraev, G., Rakhimberdiev, K.: Modeling the decision-making process of lenders based on blockchain technology. In: International Conference on Information Science and Communications Technologies: Applications, Trends and Opportunities, ICISCT, pp. 1–5 (2021)
10. Juraev, G., Rakhimberdiev, K.: Prospects of application of blockchain technology in the banking. In: International Conference on Information Science and Communications Technologies: Applications, Trends and Opportunities, ICISCT, pp. 1–5 (2022)
11. Karimov, M., Arzieva, J., Rakhimberdiev, K.: Development of approaches and schemes for proactive information protection in computer networks. In: International Conference on Information Science and Communications Technologies: Applications, Trends and Oppor-tunities, ICISCT, pp. 1–5 (2022)

12. Tashev, K., Arzieva, J., Arziev, A., Rakhimberdiev, K.: Method authentication of objects information communication systems. In: International Conference on Information Science and Communications Technologies: Applications, Trends and Opportunities, ICISCT, pp. 1–5 (2022)

# Predictive Models for Effective Management of E-commerce in New Uzbekistan

Islamov Bahtiyor Anvarovich[1] and Isokhujaeva Munira Yashnarovna[2($\boxtimes$)]

[1] Economics, Tashkent State University of Economics, Tashkent, Uzbekistan
[2] Economics, International Westminster University in Tashkent, Tashkent, Uzbekistan
misokhujaeva@wiut.uz

**Abstract.** According to the econometric analysis for effective management of e-commerce to improve the efficiency of such influencing factors, as regulatory and legal framework in the digital economy, regulatory quality, e-government development index, the global cybersecurity index is crucial. Judging from the model built and the initial forecast, by 2026 the e-commerce index of government efficiency in the Republic of Uzbekistan will grow insignificantly. Based on the study, the main goal of government policy in Uzbekistan for the future in the area of improving the efficiency of government should be the development of a state program to improve the quality of public administration, regulatory impact, providing a system of measures to facilitate business and innovation.

**Keywords:** Predictive models · management · E-commerce · Uzbekistan

## 1 Introduction

Digitalization is integral and important factor of the development of today's global economy. Digital technologies improve the quality of customer service, reduce risks and costs making trade more efficient, and combating fraud and money laundering. E-commerce is prioritizing a seamless customer experience, for which they are launching a new analytics platform that collects and processes customer data in real time to create relevant and timely personalized offers.

At the end of 2019, 14.1% of all global retail sales were e-commerce sales. Meanwhile, there are about 1.92 billion digital shoppers worldwide today. China has the largest e-commerce market at $740 billion. The world's largest online retailer, Alibaba, has $768 billion in gross merchandise value.

The current percentage of e-commerce retail sales is more than 15%, according to Statista, a German company that specializes in market and consumer data. That number is growing every year and Statista predicts that it will reach 22% in 2023. Given that a quarter of the world's population now shops online, these projections seem reasonable.

In Uzbekistan, largely due to the expansion of the Internet and electronic trading platforms in the country, the indicators for the development of e-commerce in 2019 increased by 6.7 times. The volume of trade through the Internet in 2019 amounted to 275.3 billion soums (growth rate - 6.7 times), which is 0.11% of the total volume of trade in the country (in 2018 - 0.02%). Since 2020, the volume of e-commerce has increased, taking into account the pandemic conditions.

For the purpose of analyzing the factors affecting the quality of state management of e-commerce in the transition to a digital economy in Uzbekistan, we will conduct an econometric analysis, where we will take Government Effectiveness as an outcome factor.

## 2 Literature Review

As part of the thematic focus of the study it is advisable to study in more detail the conceptual apparatus that is directly related to e-commerce and its importance in the digital economy.

One of the first scientists who defined the term "e-commerce" and made a tangible contribution to the theory of development of this concept is American economist David Cozier. According to his vision, the basis of e-commerce is the structure of traditional trade, and, in his opinion, the use of electronic networks makes it flexible.

Sokolova A.N. and Gerashchenko N.I. describe in their works the world experience of e-business, consider in detail the main components of e-business, describe the main directions of Internet commerce: selling books, music and video products, computers and software. In addition to traditional e-commerce, they analyze such areas of Internet business, as provision of tourist services, sale and delivery of flowers and gifts, information services.

Kobelev O.A. and Pirogov S.V. consider e-commerce to be the main and very important part of e-commerce, describing it as an entrepreneurial activity to carry out commercial transactions using electronic means of data exchange. They speak of e-commerce as a technology for conducting commercial transactions and managing production processes using electronic means of data exchange.

Western economists D. Amory and I. Goldovsky characterize e-commerce as the sale of goods, in which at least the organization of demand for goods is carried out through the Internet.

Bystrova N.V. and Maximova K.A. refer to the main criteria of e-commerce:

- the use of modern electronic payment systems as analogues of real money;
- transactions are carried out through the use of modern information technologies;
- uniformity of operations made by a user and the possibility to be measured and audited by a provider or a third-party organization;
- property rights and assets are in both traditional and digital electronic forms.

Uzbek authors in their works also consider the emergence and evolution of e-commerce in the world, as well as its development in Uzbekistan. They study and analyze the barriers that hinder the broader development of e-commerce and propose measures to overcome them.

The problems of modeling the activities of enterprises engaged in e-commerce are reflected in the works of a number of foreign and domestic authors. In particular, Vertakova Yu.V. and co-authors note that to predict the digital transformation of the economy the use of traditional forecasting methods is impossible, in connection with which they have constructed a composite leading index (TSLI), reflecting the level of development of the digital economy in the future, and the so-called "signal" indicators. The first of the indices is based on the indicators of the gross value added of the ICT sector, internal expenditures on research and development in ICT sector organizations, the share of households with access to the Internet, the share of households with a personal computer, etc.

Kiseleva I.A. and Iskajian S.O. when modeling the activities of companies engaged in e-commerce, highlight the factors that have a greater influence on the development of this market, taking into account the key factors of effective implementation of the selected association model and market trends - the availability of staff able to work in the Internet space, the relative share of the traditional market, the presence of a wide network of customers, etc.

Y.V. Melnikova built a mathematical model of the Russian e-commerce market, which allowed the author to build a forecast of the volume of its dynamics for the future. All kinds of mathematical models (linear, exponential, polynomial, power, logarithmic) were developed to build a forecast, of which the most qualitative model was selected on the basis of the coefficient of determination.

Practical examples of econometric analysis in the field of ICT and digital economy are studied and proposed in the works of Bobokhujaev Sh.I. and Otakuzieva Z.M. Legal factors influencing in digital economy are also studied by national researchers.

However, despite the existence of many works of domestic and foreign academic economists in this field, there are some gaps and the issues of improving the mechanisms of e-commerce management require further research.

## 3  Methods and Materials

To research this topic we use statistical materials from Stat.uz, Sciencedirect.com, Stata 14.0 and econometric methods and models, including the correlation matrix. The study is based on the dynamic series relating to the period from 2012 to 2021. A total of four sign factors are borrowed in the model, the total number of observations is 55. All indicators (both regressors and regressants) are presented as coefficients (indices).

Table 1 shows factors that we include in the model in the form of a time series. The factors are chosen based on the peculiarities of their impact on the efficiency of the government in the field of e-commerce.

Let us investigate the degree of stochastic dependence between the variables. For this purpose let us build a correlation matrix (see Table 2).

According to the calculations presented in the correlation matrix, we can see that there is a positive directional relationship between all the factors, with the closest - between the indicator of government effectiveness and the index of regulatory impact ($r = 0.87$), as well as the index of control over corruption ($r = 0.77$). This means that an increase in the above-mentioned indicators has the potential to significantly improve government efficiency.

**Table 1.** Description of variables.

| Designation | Variable |
| --- | --- |
| y | Government Efficiency |
| x1 | Efficiency of public administration |
| x2 | Regulatory impact |
| x3 | Control of corruption |
| x4 | Innovation Index |

**Table 2.** Correlation matrix.

|  | Y | X4 | X3 | X2 | X1 |
| --- | --- | --- | --- | --- | --- |
| Y | 1.00 | 0.43 | 0.77 | 0.87 | 0.57 |
| X4 | 0.43 | 1.00 | 0.49 | 0.50 | 0.63 |
| X3 | 0.77 | 0.49 | 1.00 | 0.95 | 0.71 |
| X2 | 0.87 | 0.50 | 0.95 | 1.00 | 0.73 |
| X1 | 0.57 | 0.63 | 0.71 | 0.73 | 1.00 |

## 4   Empirical Results and Analysis

Conducting descriptive statistics on the basis of the ADF test allowed us to conclude about the stationarity of series Y on the first difference, as with the probability $p = 0.002$ we have to reject the hypothesis about the presence of a unit root (see Table 3).

**Table 3.** Augmented Dickey-Fuller test.

| Variable | Coefficient | Std. Error | t-Statistic | Prob. |
| --- | --- | --- | --- | --- |
| D(Y(−1),2) | −2.785467 | 0.177830 | −15.66363 | 0.0006 |
| D(Y(−1),3) | 0.909747 | 0.104553 | 8.701332 | 0.0032 |
| C | −0.009733 | 0.004191 | −2.322224 | 0.1029 |
| @TREND("2011") | 0.002131 | 0.000574 | 3.709901 | 0.0340 |
| R-squared | 0.992208 | Mean dependent var | | −0.002857 |
| Adjusted R-squared | 0.984415 | S.D. dependent var | | 0.024300 |
| S.E. of regression | 0.003034 | Akaike info criterion | | −8.462601 |
| Sum squared resid | 2.76E−05 | Schwarz criterion | | −8.493510 |
| Log likelihood | 33.61910 | Hannan-Quinn criter | | −8.844624 |
| F-statistic | 127.3298 | Durbin-Watson stat | | 1.798630 |

Let's build a multifactor linear regression model in which the dependent variable Y is government performance (see Table 4).

**Table 4.** Augmented Dickey-Fuller test.

| Variable | Coefficient | Std. Error | t-Statistic | Prob. |
|---|---|---|---|---|
| X4 | 0.000797 | 0.002966 | 0.268641 | 0.7972 |
| X3 | −0.001997 | 0.002114 | −0.944731 | 0.3813 |
| X2 | 0.081461 | 0.032164 | 2.532659 | 0.0445 |
| X1 | −0.020128 | 0.035228 | −0.571360 | 0.5885 |
| C | 0.209284 | 0.090599 | | 2.310005 |
| R-squared | 0.804216 | Mean dependent var | | 0.237273 |
| Adjusted R-squared | 0.673694 | S.D. dependent var | | 0.017939 |
| S.E. of regression | 0.010248 | Akaike info criterion | | −6.020610 |
| Sum squared resid | 0.000630 | Schwarz criterion | | −5.839748 |
| Log likelihood | 38.11335 | Hannan-Quinn criter | | −6.134618 |
| F-statistic | 6.161509 | Durbin-Watson stat | | 1.928350 |
| Prob(F-statistic) | 0.025611 | | | |

The approximation error of the constructed model is within the normal range:

$$\overline{A} = \frac{1}{n} \cdot \sum_{i=1}^{n} \left| \frac{y - \hat{y}}{y} \right| \cdot 100\% = 2,81\% \tag{1}$$

Let us test the model for quality and adequacy. The coefficient of determination R-square $= 0.80$, which means that 80% of the variation of the dependent variable is explained by the four explanatory variables included in the model and only about 20% is due to the influence of unaccounted for in the model or random factors. According to the Fisher-Snedekor criterion, we can consider the model to be adequate. In our case F_observable $= 6,16$ and F_tabular $= 4,53$ with degrees of freedom $f_1 = m = 4, f_2 = n - m - 1 = 11 - 4 - 1 = 6$, which confirms the possibility of rejection of null hypothesis and, thus, reliability of regression model at 0.05 significance level. According to Fisher's criterion this model is adequate.

The table value of Student's t-test corresponding to a confidence probability $= 0.95$ and a given number of degrees of freedom $t_{critical} = t_{0,05;6} = 2,45$. Comparing the calculated t-statistics of the equation coefficients with the table value, we conclude that only the regression equation coefficient at x2 is statistically significant.

In order to make the most correct forecast, let us build another economic and mathematical model, explanatory and explanatory variables of which are presented in Table 5.

The use of correlation analysis techniques shows a close direct relationship between government performance and all explanatory variables, and based on the correlation

**Table 5.** Description of variables.

| Designation | Variable |
|---|---|
| y | Government Effectiveness |
| x1 | Regulatory and legislative framework in the digital economy |
| x2 | Regulatory quality |
| x3 | E-Government Development Index |
| x4 | Global Cybersecurity Index |

matrix we can make an assumption about the multicollinearity of the repressors (see Table 6).

**Table 6.** Correlation matrix.

| | Y | X4 | X3 | X2 | X1 |
|---|---|---|---|---|---|
| Y | 1.000000 | 0.808838 | 0.749727 | 0.910017 | 0.873102 |
| X4 | 0.808838 | 1.000000 | 0.939300 | 0.830962 | 0.943209 |
| X3 | 0.749727 | 0.939300 | 1.000000 | 0.813106 | 0.940481 |
| X2 | 0.910017 | 0.830962 | 0.813106 | 1.000000 | 0.856715 |
| X1 | 0.873102 | 0.943209 | 0.940481 | 0.856715 | 1.000000 |

Based on the data described in Table 5, let's build a multiple regression linear model (see Table 7) and check the regression coefficients for statistical significance.

Determination coefficient $R^2 = 0,91$ shows a close functional relationship between the factors. Fisher's criterion F_observ $= 15,41$, $[\![ F ]\!]$ _critical $= 4,53$. According to Fisher's criterion, this model is adequate. The probability of accepting the null hypothesis H_0 on the whole model is 0.003, which indicates the necessity of accepting the alternative hypothesis and the significance of the model as a whole.

Tabulated value of Student's t-test corresponding to confidence probability $\gamma = 0,95$ and number of degrees of freedom $v = n - m - 1 = 11 - 4 - 1 = 6$; $t_{critical} = t_{0,05;6} = 2,45$. Comparing the calculated t-statistics of the equation coefficients with the table value, we conclude that the most statistically significant are the coefficients at variables x1 and x2 of the regression equation. It should be added that probabilities of acceptance of the null hypothesis for the coefficients at the above variables take values below 0.05, which confirms their significance and correctness of the model built. The approximation error is an acceptable value (less than 15%):

$$\overline{A} = \frac{1}{n} \cdot \sum\nolimits_{i=1}^{n} \left| \frac{y - \hat{y}}{y} \right| \cdot 100\% = 1,25\% \tag{2}$$

Let's check the residuals for the presence of autocorrelation. For this purpose let's write down the value of Durbin-Watson's statistics from the Table 7: DW $= 2,30$. Using

**Table 7.** Multiple regression metrics (model 2).

| Variable | Coefficient | Std. Error | t-Statistic | Prob. |
|---|---|---|---|---|
| X4 | 0.004078 | 0.027109 | 0.150420 | 0.8854 |
| X3 | 0.146285 | 0.086035 | 1.700301 | 0.1400 |
| X2 | 0.050602 | 0.019337 | 2.616797 | 0.0398 |
| X1 | 0.051410 | 0.024820 | 2.071358 | 0.0837 |
| C | 0.370801 | 0.050516 | 7.340332 | |
| R-squared | 0.911283 | Mean dependent var | | 0.237273 |
| Adjusted R-squared | 0.852139 | S.D. dependent var | | 0.017939 |
| S.E. of regression | 0.006898 | Akaike info criterion | | −6.812171 |
| Sum squared resid | 0.000286 | Schwarz criterion | | −6.631310 |
| Log likelihood | 42.46694 | Hannan-Quinn criter | | −6.926179 |
| F-statistic | 15.40772 | Durbin-Watson stat | | 2.303285 |
| Prob (F-statistic) | 0.002607 | | | |

special tables, determine significant points dl and du for 5% significance level. For m = 4 and n = 11: dl = 0,444; du = 2,283. Since dl ≤ DW ≤ du, therefore, there is reason to believe that the test for autocorrelation does not provide a definite answer to the question.

Let's check the presence of autocorrelation using the Breusch-Godfrey test. It is based on the following idea: if there is a correlation between neighboring observations, it is natural to expect that in equation:

$$e_t = \rho \times e_{t-1}, \quad t = 1, \ldots, n \tag{3}$$

where $e_t$ is the regression residuals obtained by the ordinary least-squares method), the coefficient $\rho$ will turn out to be significantly different from zero.

The results of the Breusch-Godfrey test are presented in Table 8.

The results of the Breusch-Godfrey test indicate that the probability of accepting the null hypothesis of the absence of autocorrelation is Prob = 0.94 and, therefore, there is no autocorrelation in the model.

Let us establish the presence (absence) of heteroscedasticity of random deviations of the model, using Glaser test (see Table 9).

The Glaser test showed that since the probability of accepting the null hypothesis is higher than 5%, it indicates the absence of heteroscedasticity.

Let us test the model for residuals heteroscedasticity using the Breusch-Pagan test (see Table 10).

The Breusch-Pagan test showed that the probability of accepting the null hypothesis for the model as a whole is 33.1% and, therefore, we can accept the alternative hypothesis that there is no heteroscedasticity of the model residuals.

**Table 8.** Breusch-Godfrey Serial Correlation LM Test

| Variable | Coefficient | Std. Error | t-Statistic | Prob. |
|---|---|---|---|---|
| X4 | 0.009347 | 0.028417 | 0.328920 | 0.7555 |
| X3 | -0.000525 | 0.085520 | -0.006136 | 0.9953 |
| X2 | -0.005107 | 0.019843 | -0.257346 | 0.8072 |
| X1 | -0.007237 | 0.025641 | -0.282237 | 0.7891 |
| C | -0.008056 | 0.050811 | -0.158543 | 0.8802 |
| RESID(-1) | -0.583356 | 0.563226 | -1.035741 | 0.3478 |
| R-squared | 0.176651 | Mean dependent var | | -2.51E-17 |
| Adjusted R-squared | -0.646698 | S.D. dependent var | | 0.005343 |
| S.E. of regression | 0.006857 | Akaike info criterion | | -6.824728 |
| Sum squared resid | 0.000235 | Schwarz criterion | | -6.607695 |
| Log likelihood | 43.53601 | Hannan-Quinn criter | | -6.961538 |
| F-statistic | 0.214552 | Durbin-Watson stat | | 2.007988 |
| Prob (F-statistic) | 0.941760 | | | |

**Table 9.** Heteroskedasticity Test: Glejser.

| Variable | Coefficient | Std. Error | t-Statistic | Prob. |
|---|---|---|---|---|
| C | 0.012419 | 0.017901 | 0.693752 | 0.5138 |
| X4 | 0.005704 | 0.009606 | 0.593747 | 0.5744 |
| X3 | -0.005480 | 0.030487 | -0.179738 | 0.8633 |
| X2 | 0.004883 | 0.006852 | 0.712658 | 0.5028 |
| X1 | -0.000164 | 0.008795 | -0.018596 | 0.9858 |
| R-squared | 0.544393 | Mean dependent var | | 0.004336 |
| Adjusted R-squared | 0.240655 | S.D. dependent var | | 0.002805 |
| S.E. of regression | 0.002444 | Akaike info criterion | | -8.887055 |
| Sum squared resid | 3.59E-05 | Schwarz criterion | | -8.706193 |
| Log likelihood | 53.87880 | Hannan-Quinn criter | | -9.001062 |
| F-statistic | 1.792309 | Durbin-Watson stat | | 2.959294 |
| Prob(F-statistic) | 0.249030 | | | |

# 5  Discussion

The study showed that the model has no autocorrelation between the variables and the model is homoscedastic. Determination coefficient and Fisher's criterion also confirm high quality of the model, while approximation error of the second model is slightly lower

**Table 10.** Heteroskedasticity Test: Breusch-Pagan-Godfrey.

| Variable | Coefficient | Std. Error | t-Statistic | Prob. |
|---|---|---|---|---|
| C | 3.55E−05 | 0.000229 | 0.154717 | 0.8821 |
| X4 | 2.33E−05 | 0.000123 | 0.189181 | 0.8562 |
| X3 | 2.57E−05 | 0.000391 | 0.065762 | 0.9497 |
| X2 | 3.02E−05 | 8.78E−05 | 0.343553 | 0.7429 |
| X1 | 2.92E−05 | 0.000113 | 0.259258 | 0.8041 |
| R-squared | 0.487637 | Mean dependent var | | 2.60E−05 |
| Adjusted R-squared | 0.146061 | S.D. dependent var | | 3.39E−05 |
| S.E. of regression | 3.13E−05 | Akaike info criterion | | −17.60121 |
| Sum squared resid | 5.89E−09 | Schwarz criterion | | −17.42035 |
| Log likelihood | 101.8067 | Hannan-Quinn criter | | −17.71522 |
| F-statistic | 1.427611 | Durbin-Watson stat | | 3.120072 |
| Prob (F-statistic) | 0.331270 | | | |

than of the first model (see (1) and (2)), Akaike information criterion also confirms the necessity of choosing the second model:

$$AIC_1 = -6,02, \quad AIC_2 = -17,60 \tag{4}$$

In addition, based on the fact that in the first model built only one of the four coefficients on the variables is statistically significant, and in the second model two of the four are statistically significant, we conclude that it is necessary to build the forecast based on the second model[1].

As follows from the data obtained with the help of EViews least squares method (see Table 7), the resulting multifactor model will have the form:

$$Y = 0,371 + 0,051 \cdot x_1 + 0,051 \cdot x_2 + 0,015 \cdot x_3 + 0,004 \cdot x_4 \tag{5}$$
$$(t)\ (7,34)\ (2,07) \quad\quad (2,62) \quad\quad (1,70) \quad\quad (0,15)$$

Equation (5) expresses the dependence of the government performance indicator (Y) on the indicator of regulatory and legal framework in CE (x1), the indicator of regulatory quality (x2), e-government development index (x3) and the global cybersecurity index (x4). The coefficients of the equation show the quantitative impact of each factor on the outcome indicator, while the others remain unchanged. In our case, the government performance indicator:

– grows by 0.051 units with a 1 unit increase in the efficiency of the legal and regulatory framework in CE (assuming the other factors are unchanged);

---

[1] Source: Mkhitaryan, V.S., Arkhipova, M.Y., Balash, V.A., Balash, O.S., Dubrova, T.A., Sirotin, V.P.: Econometrics: A Textbook. Prospect, Moscow, p. 314 (2015).

– tends to grow by 0.051 units with the growth of the regulatory quality indicator by 1 unit (given that other factors remain unchanged);
– grows by 0.015 units with the growth of the e-Government development index by 1 unit (given that other factors remain unchanged);
– increases by 0.004 units with the growth of the global cybersecurity index by 1 unit (all other factors remaining unchanged).

Thus, the greatest increase in the index of government efficiency is given by the indicator of efficiency of regulatory and legal framework in the CE and the indicator of regulatory quality.

The study showed that model (5) can be used to make forecasts on its basis, having previously predicted the explanatory variables on the basis of trends (see Table 11).

**Table 11.** Characteristics of temporal models of explanatory variables.

| Variable | Type of model | Relationship equation | $R^2$ |
|---|---|---|---|
| x1 | Linear | $x_1 = 0,0912 \cdot t - 0,175$ | 0,8752 |
| x2 | Polynomial | $x_2 = -0,0011 \cdot t^3 + 0,0376 \cdot t^2 - 0,26773 \cdot t - 1,1073$ | 0,9592 |
| x3 | Linear | $x_3 = 0,0217 \cdot t + 0,43$ | 0,7313 |
| x4 | Linear | $x_4 = 0,0741 \cdot t - 0,0925$ | 0,7964 |

Based on the trends and model (5), let us construct the predicted values of the explanatory and explanatory variables (see Table 12).

**Table 12.** Forecast values of exogenous variables of the model until 2026.

| Years | Government efficiency | Regulatory and legal framework in CE | Regulatory quality | E-government development index | Global cybersecurity index |
|---|---|---|---|---|---|
| 2021 (fact) | 0,280 | 0,931 | −1,030 | 0,672 | 0,725 |
| 2022 | 0,280 | 0,919 | −0,801 | 0,690 | 0,797 |
| 2023 | 0,289 | 1,010 | −0,645 | 0,712 | 0,871 |
| 2024 | 0,299 | 1,101 | −0,498 | 0,734 | 0,945 |
| 2025 | 0,307 | 1,192 | −0,369 | 0,756 | 1,019 |
| 2026 | 0,314 | 1,283 | −0,264 | 0,777 | 1,093 |

Based on the obtained forecast, we can assume that over the next five years the efficiency index of the government of the Republic of Uzbekistan will grow, although insignificantly, but steadily.

Let's build several scenario forecasts - inertial (assuming that all processes will be carried out within the planned limits), pessimistic (assuming a 10% decrease in the growth rate of all explanatory variables) and optimistic (based on the assumption that the growth rate of all explanatory variables will increase by 10%). In the latter case, the government's efficiency would increase significantly (see Fig. 1).

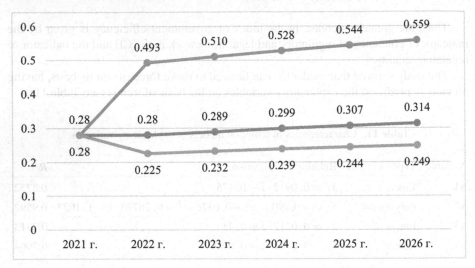

**Fig. 1.** Projected values of the efficiency index of the government of Uzbekistan in 2022–2026 (optimistic, inertial, and pessimistic)

## 6 Conclusion

Thus, according to the model built and the initial forecast, by 2026 the e-commerce index of government efficiency in the Republic of Uzbekistan will grow insignificantly, which may mean that effective measures to improve the efficiency of all influencing factors, including the regulatory and legal framework in the digital economy, regulatory quality, e-government development index, the global cybersecurity index.

Based on the study, the main goal of government policy in Uzbekistan for the future in the area of improving the efficiency of government should be the development of a state program to improve the quality of public administration, regulatory impact, providing a system of measures to facilitate business and innovation. The implementation of strategic goals in the area of improving the efficiency of government measures will lead to an increase in the democratization of society, increase the availability and quality of information resources, reduce corruption, and, ultimately, achieve the most important goals of sustainable development in Uzbekistan.

## 7 Declarations

Declaration of competing interest

The authors have no conflicts of interest relevant to this article
Suppliers
Stat.uz
Sciencedirect.com
Stata 14.0

**Acknowledgement.** The authors gratefully acknowledge the generous financial support of TSUE.

# References

1. Joint report of the digital development initiative program and the center for economic research: introduction of e-government and administrative reform in Uzbekistan - the relationship and mutual influence. DDI, CER, 54 p. (2018)
2. Kremer, N., Putko, B.A.: Econometrika. Unity-Dana, Moscow (2016)
3. Chepel, S.V., Shibarshova, L.I.: Macroeconomics and microeconomics. Collection of situational tasks and training examples. Practice of Uzbekistan. Textbook, 107 p. (2017)
4. Malysheva, M.A.: Theory and methods of modern public administration. Educational and methodical manual. Department of Operational Printing HSE, St. Petersburg, 280 p. (2011)
5. Efremov, A.A.: Assessment of the impact of legal regulation on the development of information technology: mechanisms and methodology. Law 3, 45–46 (2018)
6. Yuzhakov, V.N., Talapina, E.V., Klochkova, E.N., Efremov, A.A.: State management in the sphere of stimulating the development of information technologies: problems and directions of improvement. J. Leg. Res. 2(3), 89–100 (2017)
7. Isohujaeva, M.Y.: Topical issues of e-commerce management in the digitalization of the economy of Uzbekistan. Int. J. Econ. Central Asia 6(1) (2022). https://doi.org/10.18334/asia.6.1.114528
8. Islamov, B.A., Isokhujaeva, M.Y.: Needs for improvement of electronic commerce in Uzbekistan. Hokkaido University Collection of Scholary and Academic Papers. The Annals of Center for regional Economic and Business Networks (journal title). bulletin (article), vol. 10 (Needs for Improvement of Electronic Commerce in Uzbekistan: HUSCAP) (hokudai.ac.jp), pp. 93–107. http://hdl.handle.net/2115/80999
9. Turdiev, A.S., Isohuzhaeva, M.Y.: Methodology of economic efficiency evaluation of digital technologies in e-commerce. In: Section in the Collective Monograph of the Conference of the Belarusian National Technical University. Minsk, pp. 251–255 (2021). https://rep.bntu.by/handle/data/110793
10. Isohuzhaeva, M.Y.: Rakamli iktisodiyotga utish davrida tizhoratning rivozhlanishi. Arch. Sci. Res. 2(1) (2022). https://journal.tsue.uz
11. Isohujaeva, M.Y.: Main directions of improvement of innovative activity in the Republic of Uzbekistan. J. Sci. Res. Arch. 5(5) (2022). https://journal.tsue.uz
12. Isokhuzhaeva, M.Ya., Mirisev, A.A., Karimov, I.O., Ibragimov, S.O.: Legal factors effecting the efficiency of state management of the digital economy. J. Posit. School Psychol. 6(7), 5214–5220 (2022)
13. Anderson, R.J., Corydon, B., Staun, J., Bughin, J., Lunborg, J., Schröder, P.: A future that works: the impact of automation in Denmark. McKinsey and Company and the Tuborg Research Centre for Globalization and Firms at Aarhus University (2017)
14. Manyika, J., et al.: Harnessing automation for a future that works. McKinsey Global Institute (2017). www.mckinsey.com/featured-insights/digital-disruption/harnessing-automation-for-a-future-that-works

15. Grosz, B.J., et al.: Artificial intelligence and life in 2030 – one hundred year study of artificial intelligence. Stanford University (2016). https://ai100.stanford.edu/sites/default/files/ai_100_report_0831fnl.pdf. Accessed 28 Aug 2019
16. Bughin, J., et al.: Artificial intelligence – the next digital frontier? McKinsey and Company Global Institute (2017)
17. Corrales, M., Fenwick, M., Haapio, H.: Digital technologies, legal design and the future of the legal profession. In: Corrales, M., Fenwick, M., Haapio, H. (eds.) Legal Tech, Smart Contracts and Blockchain. PLBI, pp. 1–15. Springer, Singapore (2019). https://doi.org/10.1007/978-981-13-6086-2_1
18. Bobokhujaev, Sh.I., Otakuzieva, Z.M.: Evolution of electronic commerce and its development in Uzbekistan. Materials of the scientific-practical seminar held under the applied project BV-ATEX-2018-271. Role and problems of digital economy development in Uzbekistan. Tashkent, p. 205 (2019)
19. Bystrova, N.V., Maksimova, K.A.: E-commerce and prospects for its development. Innovative economy: prospects for development and improvement **7**(33) (2018). https://cyberleninka.ru/
20. Vertakova, Y.V., Klevtsova, M.G., Polozhentseva, Y.S.: Forecasting the digital transformation of the economy on the basis of leading and signal indicators. Econ. Manag. **11**(157) (2018). https://cyberleninka.ru/
21. Galochkin, V.T.: Econometrics: Textbook and Practical Work For Universities, p. 293. Publishing House Yurait, Moscow (2022). https://urait.ru/bcode/490094
22. Kiseleva, I.A., Iskajyan, S.O.: Modeling the activity of an Internet company. ITportal **3**(15) (2017). https://cyberleninka.ru/
23. Kobelev, O.A.: Electronic commerce. Textbook. 5th edn., Stereotyped, p. 685. Dashkov and K., Moscow
24. Mardas, A.N.: Econometrics: Textbook and Practical Work for Universities, p. 180. Publishing House Bright, Moscow (2022). https://urait.ru/bcode/490427
25. Melnikova, U.V.: Mathematical modeling of the economic conjuncture of the Russian market of Internet commerce. Izv. of Sarat. un-tat Nov. ser. Ser. of Economics. Management. Law. 2 (2020). https://cyberleninka.ru/
26. Mkhitaryan, V.S., Arkhipova, M., Balash, V.A., Balash, O.S., Dubrova, T.A., Sirotin, V.P.: Econometrics: A Textbook, p. 314. Prospect, Moscow (2015)
27. Okrepilov, V.V.: Modeling of socio-economic systems using the tools of economics of quality. Econ. Manag. 11(145) (2017). https://cyberleninka.ru/
28. Sokolova, A.N., Gerashchenko, N.I.: E-commerce: World and Russian Experience. Open Systems, Moscow, p. 145 (2000)
29. Timakov, A.A., Plyusnina, L.K.: The use of e-commerce in the development of the brand. Forum Young Sci. **11**(51), 291–295 (2020). https://www.elibrary.ru/item.asp?id=44418955

# The Role of IT on Transportation, Logistics and the Economic Growth Among Central Asian Countries

Saidjon Khayitov(✉) (iD) and Komilov Ulugbek

Tashkent State University of Economics, Tashkent, Uzbekistan
ulugbek.komilovich77@gmail.com

**Abstract.** This study examines the role of information technology on transportation, logistics and the economic growth among Central Asian countries. Central Asian countries have rich natural resources and convenient location among Eastern and Western countries, however, their economic growth is lower than other countries. There 3 low-income countries which are Afghanistan, Kyrgyz Republic and Tajikistan. In addition, Uzbekistan is single country which should cross 2 countries to use sea ports directly. But it cannot be cause to development for Central Asian countries. Rising the role of information technology on logistics, transportation and integration among these countries can help to achieve economic growth.

**Keywords:** Logistics · Transportation and integration · Economic growth · Asian economy · Transportation infrastructure · FDI · Information technology

## 1 Introduction

Time is the most precious resource in human's life. People want to spare their time in modern society, and they are preferring to hire products and services online. IT and new technologies are playing an important role in the development of countries economy. Technology are saving the time, and it takes to produce a good or deliver a service. Covid-19 pandemic influenced the role of technologies and caused to use widely them. During pandemic, logistics companies more hired new technologies such as drones and artificial intelligence (AI technologies) technologies to deliver goods and products to their clients. AI technologies has high potential to deliver products very fast and safe to customers. K. Ganesh, S.C. Lenny Koh, A. Saxena and R. Rajesh investigated that the logistic management is critical activities of businesses and it forms the crux of entire dealing. Zang said that the better logistics leads better development, better development leads better life. Marusin A.V, Ablyazov T.H said that development of logistics is linked with the development of new technologies. Alvin Tofler reported that many companies started using advanced information technologies and high-speed transportation to deliver products to their customers during the 1990s, and this process was started to use worldwide. Goose wrote that U.S Internet sales had grown to nearly $7 billion in the late 1999. These results are showing that internet and modern technologies are getting common and we should more focus on them.

Y. Koucheryavy and A. Aziz (Eds.): NEW2AN 2022, LNCS 13772, pp. 649–655, 2023.
https://doi.org/10.1007/978-3-031-30258-9_58

## 2  Literature Review

Researchers always compete about different drivers of economic growth in the developing countries. They consist of innovations, new technologies, energy consumption, FDI, international trade, logistics, transportation (e.g. K. Ganesh, S.C. Lenny Koh, A. Saxena, R. Rajesh; Mohammad Mafizur Rahman; Monika Klein). Modern economists are consisting of transportation and logistics as one of main factors to achieve economic growth. Transportation includes roads, sea ports, railways, runways and airports. Furthermore, transportation and logistics will create new job places and will attract FDI flows to developing counties. Logistics and transportation fill each other, and society we cannot select each other in our modern society.

Transportation. Mohammad Ali Mosaberpanah and Sina Darban Khales (2013) examined that transportation infrastructure is an important component to the economic growth and it requires responsibilities. When transportation is more efficiently, it creates social and economic opportunities. As well, this influences better to other parts of society and economy such as markets, employment and investment. In addition, other authors reported that efficient transport system cause to decrease transportation and product costs, while inefficient transport system causes to increase them. Marek Ogryzek, Daria Adamska-Kmiec and Anna Klimach studied modern transportation system in the modern society. They wrote that sustainable transportation system more focuses on planning, politics and high technologies. Sustainable transportation reduces the price of goods and services. Many economists mention that high-quality transportation system also creates opportunities to businesses and enterprises. Corinne Blanquart and Martin Koning gave an opinion about the benefits of transportation infrastructure to the economy of country. They said that building and reconstructing roads, railways, airport or seaports create more job places to unemployment people. For example, the High-Speed 2 train which was projected to connect London and North England, created 22,000 new jobs directly or indirectly. Orkibi H has taken advantage of this difficult time in the pandemic to conduct research aimed at creating resilient and flexible economic models based on innovation and new technologies, which can be seen as a weapon to fight COVID-19. Umar M, Ji X, Kirikkaleli D, Xu Q said that the main aim of transportation logistics companies is to store and distribute goods efficiently through flexible supply chains in the country. Dovbischuk I. wrote that innovation is more effective way to recieve to fight with different problems and had focused their interest and research potential on it.

Logistics. Logistics is getting essential element in developing countries' economy. The globalization and the development of the economy logistics is an essential tool in the creation of single market. Well-organized logistics in markets has high advantages over other economies. Improving logistics infrastructure may cause competitiveness of companies and it also effects to rising market share. Jacyna-Gołda et al., Kush et al., Semenov and Filina-Dawidowicz, Yang et al., Zimon et al. examined that the efficient operation of supply chains is complex problem that takes account material, financial resources, as well as economic, environmental, technological, structural and other types of drivers. Li, Liu mentioned that logistics and distribution centers regularly improve their facilities and apply modern technological solutions in order to adapt to the global or regional market needs. Furuya et al. focused on to the improvement of storage location recommendation technology which able to sequential formulation of recommendations for storage location of incoming pallet load units to be stored. K. Ganesh, S.C. Lenny Koh, A. Saxena and R. Rajesh mentioned that logistics means the management of material, service, information and capital flows. It includes the increasingly complex information, communication and control systems required in modern's business environment. Economists continued their opinion with that logistics is the future of modern society. In fact, during the Pandemic logistics and transportation have not been stopped, but ethics of attitude changed. George Thiers and Leon McGinnis studied modern logistic system and found that every small improvement in Global supply chains and logistics have large effects to society. This helps to explain the sustaining strong interest in logistics systems modeling and analysis. If companies want to enhance their opportunities, firstly they should improve their logistic system. Logistics is useful for improving quality, competitiveness and capacity.

# 3 Methodology

We identified and selected 5 countries which are Afghanistan, Kazakhstan, Kyrgyz Republic, Tajikistan and Uzbekistan. All countries which we selected are located in Central Asia, however, Turkmenistan was not mentioned because of no enough data. We used two data sources which are World Bank and World Investment Record. We took time between 2002 and 2019. We used panel data to identify our econometric results and we strongly balanced panel data. We used FE panel models to calculate our results. Fixed effect model explores the connection between predictor and out-come variables within an entity. Fixed effect regression removes the impact of time-invariant characteristics. Another essential assumption of the fixed effect regression is that time-invariant characteristic is unique to the individuals and it should not be cor-related with other individual characteristics.

The equation for the fixed effects model becomes:

$$Y_{i,t} = \beta_1 X_{i,t} + \alpha_i + u_{i,t}$$

where,

$\alpha_i$ (i = 1....n) is the unknown intercept for each entity, n is entity-specific intercepts;
$Y_{i,t}$ is the dependent variable, where i = entity and t = time;
$X_{i,t}$ is one independent variable;
$\beta_1$ is the coefficient for independent variable;
$U_{i,t}$ is the error term;

In addition, we used Hausman test to check our model. We used $H_0$ is hypothesis which reject our model, however, if our hypothesis will not available for first hypothesis, we use $H_1$ hypothesis which means we use this model in our research. In $H_0$ we mentioned that if prob > $chi^2$ is bigger than 0.05, our $H_0$ hypothesis will be available. If it will be less than 0.05, we will use $H_1$ hypothesis. Our results showed that our $H_1$ hypothesis is available and we used Fixed effect model in our research (Table 1).

General production function is modelled that

$$Y = (GDP\ pc;\ T;\ LG;\ U;\ IT)$$

**Table 1.** Description and measurement of variables.

| Variable | Description | Measurement |
|---|---|---|
| Y | Gross Domestic Product | (Current US$) |
| GDP pc | Gross Domestic Product per capita | (Current US$) |
| IT | Information technologies | Number of individuals using internet (% of population) |
| T | Transportation | Kilometers of road |
| LG | Logistics | Logistics performance index: Overall |
| U | Urbanization | % of total population |

where Gross Domestic Product Y is related with information technologies (IT), transportation (T), Gross Domestic Product per person (GDPpc), logistics (LG), and urbanization (U).

We used log-transformation of variables, as follows:

$$\ln Y_{t,i} = \beta_0 + \beta_1 \ln GDPpc_{t,i} + \beta_2 \ln IT_{t,i} + \beta_3 \ln T_{t,i} + \beta_4 \ln LG_{t,i} + \beta_5 U_{t,i} + \varepsilon_{t,i}$$

where Y is natural-log of GDP, lnGDP pc is natural-log of Gross Domestic Product per person, lnIT shows natural-log of transportation, lnLG indicates natural-log of logistics, and lnU shows natural-log of urbanization, lnIT is IT technologies. The subscript $t = 1$, 2, …., 10 denotes time period. $\beta$ indicates coefficients and $\varepsilon$ represents standard error of econometric modelling. i presents country of in our modelling.

In making our model, we entered and calculated other factors. However, the influence role of Gross Domestic Product per person, transportation, logistics, IT technologies and urbanization are higher for achieving economic growth than other factors in Central Asian countries.

## 4 Results and Discussion

Table 2 shows the correlation results among variables. There is positive correlation between GDP and all other variables. IT has the lowest correlation result with GDP, but GDP pc has the highest correlation with GDP. Transportation has the highest correlation between GDP per capita and transportation. IT also has also positive correlation with GDP per capita. Transportation has the highest correlation with IT technologies. However, logistics has the lowest correlation with new IT technologies. Urbanization has the biggest correlation with transportation.

Table 3 presents the effect of independent variables to the dependent variables. In the 1st column, we examined the impact of independent variables to the GDP. GDP per capita, urbanization and IT has positive significant effect on GDP. It means that GDP will increase .9592%, 1.57% and .0671% respectively, when GDP per capita, urbanization and IT increase 1%. In the 2nd column, we mentioned GDP per capita as the dependent variable. GDP has positive significant effect on the GDP per capita. When

**Table 2.** Correlation results

|  | GDP | GDP pc | IT | Transportation | Logistics | Urbanization |
|---|---|---|---|---|---|---|
| GDP | 1 | | | | | |
| GDP pc | 0.8546 | 1 | | | | |
| IT | 0.4611 | 0.6229 | 1 | | | |
| Transportation | 0.7054 | 0.7988 | 0.3215 | 1 | | |
| logistics | 0.4633 | 0.6224 | 0.6469 | 0.4989 | 1 | |
| urbanization | 0.7003 | 0.7631 | 0.3401 | 0.9465 | 0.4798 | 1 |

**Table 3.** FE regression results

| Variables | GDP | GDP pc | Transportation | Logistics |
|---|---|---|---|---|
| GDP | 1 | $1.01^{***}$ (0.000) | −.0018 (0.981) | .4475 (0.393) |
| GDP pc | $.9592^{***}$ (0.000) | 1 | −.0281 (0.707) | −.4735 (0.352) |
| Transportation | −.0045 (0.981) | −.0721 (0.707) | 1 | −.6241 (0.404) |
| Logistics | .0233 (0.393) | −.0261 (0.351) | −.0134 (0.404) | 1 |
| Urbanization | $1.57^{***}$ (0.000) | $-1.60^{***}$ (0.000) | $-.3922+$ (0.069) | −.3353 (0.822) |
| IT | $.0671^{***}$ (0.000) | $-.0556^{***}$ (0.000) | $.0396^{***}$ (0.000) | .1026 (0.103) |
| N | 80 | 80 | 80 | 80 |
| $R^2$ | 0.7183 | 0.3773 | 0.8818 | 0.2280 |

Note: values are estimated with significant levels, $^{***}$, $^{**}$, $^{*}$, and + at 1%, 5%, 10% and more 10%

GDP increases 1%, it causes increasing 1.01% to GDP. However, urbanization and IT have negative significant impact on the dependent variable. It means that if urbanization and IT decrease 1%, GDP per capita will increase 1.60% and -.0556% respectively. Other variables have not impact on the dependent variable in the 2nd column. In 3rd column, we calculated the effect of other independent variables on the transportation. Only IT has positive significant effect on the dependent variable. If IT rises 1%, it impacts .0396% rising of transportation. But urbanization has negative significant effect on the transportation. When urbanization increases 1%, the value of transportation decreases -.3929%. Other variables have not impact on the dependent variable. In the 4th column, we calculated logistics as the dependent variables. Interestingly, there is not the impact of independent variables on the dependent variable. However, IT has some effect on logistics in comparison with other independent variables.

## 5 Conclusion

This study has investigated the relationship among economics growth, IT, logistics and transportation in Central Asia between 2002 and 2019 (20 years). We did a panel data for Central Asian countries. Our results show that GDP per capita, urbanization and IT have the most effective impact on the economic growth for Central Asian countries. Essentially, IT technologies has significant effect on the dependent variables in the first 3 columns. It means that IT technologies is very important variables in the Central Asian countries' economy.

Transportation infrastructure is one of the main problems in Central Asian countries. Countries are not available using sea or ocean ports rightly and it will impact negatively transport cost. Using new technologies to construct transportation system is one of essential thing in the economy of countries. Using internet and modern technologies will help us to increase the productivity of transport system. We can also mention this opinion with logistics.

Furthermore, the level of human capital, technology and political risks also plays main role in improving transportation and logistics. There should be well-educated staffs and high-quality technologies, it will rise the quality of working. As well, political and social stability is being essential part of developing transportation and logistics. For example, un-stability situation in Afghanistan is affecting negatively to other countries. Because, Afghanistan is the biggest corridor for Central Asian countries.

## References

1. Moyano, A., Coronado, J.M., Garmendia, M.: How to choose the most efficient transport mode for weekend tourism journeys: an HSR and private vehicle comparison. The Open Transp. J. 10(1), 84–96 (2016)
2. Blanquart, C., Koning, M.: The local economic impacts of high-speed railways: theories and facts. Eur. Transp. Re. Rev. 9(2), 1–14 (2017)
3. Blanquart, C., Koning, M.: The local economic impacts of high-speed railways: theories and facts. Eur. Transp. Res. Rev. 9(2), 12 (2017)
4. Donaldson, D., Hornbeck, R.: Railroads and American economic growth: a "Market access" approach. Working Paper 19213. http://www.nber.org/papers/w19213. (2013)
5. Dovbischuk, I.: Innovation-oriented dynamic capabilities of logistics service providers, dynamic resilience and firm performance during the COVID-19 pandemic. The Int. J. Logistics Manag. 33(2), 499–519 (2022)
6. Kulipanova, E.: International Transport in Central Asia: Understanding the Patterns of (Non-) Cooperation. Working paper. No. 2 (2012)
7. Esfahani, H.S., Ramirez, M.T.: Institutions, infrastructure, and economic growth. J. Dev. Econ, 70(2), 443–477 (2003)
8. Thiers, G., McGinnis, L.: Logistics systems modelling and simulation. https://www.researchgate.net/publication/254050194 (2011)
9. Godinot, S.: From Crisis to Opportunity: Five Steps to Sustainable European Economies, p. 4. WWF-World Wide Fund for Nature: Brussels, Belgium (2015)

10. Azmi, I., Abdul Hamid, N., Nasarudin, M., Hussin, M., Ibrahim, N.I.: Logistics and supply chain management: the importance of integration for business processes. J. Emerg. Econ. Islamic Res. **5**(4), 73 (2017)
11. Button, K.: Transportation economics: some developments over the past 30 years. J. Transport. Res. Forum **45**(2), 7–30 (2015)
12. Sharipbekova, K., Raimbekov, Z.: Influence of logistics efficiency on economic growth of the CIS countries. Eur. Res. Stud. J. **XXI**(Issue 2), 678–690 (2018). https://doi.org/10.35808/ersj/1032
13. Ganesh, K., Lenny Koh, S.C., Saxena, A., Rajesh, R.: Logistics design and modelling – a simulation perspective. Logistics Supply Chain Manag. (LSCM) Res. Group (2011)
14. Khadaroo, A. J., Seetanah, B. (2008).-"Transport infrastructure and foreign direct investment."- Journal of International Development. 22, 103–123
15. Kumo, W.L.: Infrastructure investment and economic growth in South Africa: A Granger causality analysis. In: (Working paper No. 160) African Development Bank (2012)
16. Ogryzek, M., Adamska-Kmieć, D., Klimach, A.: Sustainable transport: an efficient transportation network—case study. Sustainability **12**(19), 8274 (2020)
17. Mosaberpanah, M.A., Darban Khales, S.: The Role of Transportation in Sustainable Development, pp. 441–448. Conference Paper. https://www.researchgate.net/publication/255991703 (2013)
18. Rahman, M.M.: The dynamic nexus of energy consumption, international trade and economic growth in BRICS and ASEAN countries: a panel causality test. Energy **229**, 120679 (2021)
19. Kherbacha, O., Mocana, M.L.: The importance of logistics and supply chain management in the enhancement of Romanian SMEs. Procedia – Soc. Behav. Sci. **221**, 405–413 (2015)
20. Orkibi, H.: Creative adaptability: conceptual framework, measurement, and outcomes in times of crisis. Front. Psychol. **11**, 588172 (2021)
21. Prajogo, D., Olhager, J.: Supply chain integration and performance: the effects of long-term relationships, information technology and sharing, and logistics integration. Int. J. Prod. Econ. **135**(1), 514–522 (2012)
22. Ballou, R.H.: The evolution and future of logistics and supply chain management. Eur. Bus. Rev. **19**(4), 332–348 (2007)
23. Ballou, R.H.: Business logistics: importance and some research opportunities. Gest. Prod. **4**(2), 117–129 (1997)
24. Regional Economic Impact Analysis of High-Speed Rail in China. Main Report. World Bank (2014)
25. Kim, S.T., Lee, H.-H., Hwang, T.: Logistics integration in the supply chain: a resource dependence theory perspective. Int. J. Qual. Innov. **6**(1), 1–14 (2020). https://doi.org/10.1186/s40887-020-00039-w
26. Szostak, R.: The Role of Transportation in the Industrial Revolution: A Comparison of Eighteenth Century England and France, p. 337. McGill–Queens University Press, Montreal (1991)
27. Umar, M., Ji, X., Kirikkaleli, D., Xu, Q.: COP21 roadmap: do innovation, financial development, and transportation infrastructure matter for environmental sustainability in China? J. Env. Manag. **271**, 111026 (2020)
28. Anca, V.: Logistics and supply chain management: an overview. Stud. Bus. Econ. **14**(2), 209–215 (2019)
29. Williamson, J.: Practitioners of development. In the Washington Consensus as Policy Prescription for Development. World Bank (2004)
30. Wolfensohn Center for Development at the Brookings Institution and the Carnegie Endowment for International Peace, in partnership with the Asian Development Bank and the Central Asia Regional Economic Cooperation Program: Integrating Central Asia into the World Economy: The Role of Energy and Transport Infrastructure (2007)

# Author Index

Y. Koucheryavy and A. Aziz (Eds.): NEW2AN 2022, LNCS 13772, pp. 657–659, 2023.
https://doi.org/10.1007/978-3-031-30258-9

Printed in the United States
by Baker & Taylor Publisher Services

Printed in the United States
by Baker & Taylor Publisher Services